D1605990

The Writings of

# Henry D. Thoreau

*The Correspondence*

Volume 1: 1834-1848

*Textual Center*

*The Writings of Henry D. Thoreau*

*The University of California, Santa Barbara*

# The Correspondence of Henry D. Thoreau

## VOLUME 1: 1834-1848

EDITED BY

ROBERT N. HUDSPETH

PRINCETON, NEW JERSEY

PRINCETON UNIVERSITY PRESS

MMXIII

*The editorial preparation of this volume was supported by grants from the National Endowment for the Humanities, an independent federal agency.*

*Copyright © 2013 by Princeton University Press*
*Published by Princeton University Press, 41 William Street, Princeton, New Jersey 08540*
*In the United Kingdom: Princeton University Press, 6 Oxford Street, Woodstock, Oxfordshire OX20 1TW*

*pup.princeton.edu*

*Jacket illustration: Collage by Frank Mahood. Thoreau's desk and pen from the collection of the Concord Museum, Concord, MA; photographs by David Bohl*

*Library of Congress Cataloging-in-Publication Data*

*Thoreau, Henry David, 1817-1862.*
*[Correspondence]*
*The correspondence of Henry D. Thoreau / edited by Robert N. Hudspeth.*
*volumes cm. — (The writings of Henry D. Thoreau)*
*Includes bibliographical references and indexes.*
*ISBN 978-0-691-15892-1 (v. 1)*
*1. Thoreau, Henry David, 1817-1862—Correspondence. 2. Authors, American—19th century—Correspondence. 3. Intellectuals—United States—Correspondence. 4. Naturalists—United States—Correspondence. I. Hudspeth, Robert N. II. Title.*
*PS3053.A3 2013      818.'309—dc23*
*[B]     2012043255*

*Printed on acid-free paper ∞*

*Printed in the United States of America*

*10   9   8   7   6   5   4   3   2   1*

# Contents

Letters 1834-1848                                    1

EDITORIAL APPENDIX

Notes on Illustrations                             395
Acknowledgments                                    398
Editorial Contributions                            401
General Introduction                               402
Historical Introduction                            438
Textual Introduction                               460
Library Symbols                                    476
Short Titles                                       479
Bibliography                                       485
Index                                              495

# The Correspondence

1834-1848

## To Oliver Sparhawk
*1834*

Mr Sparhawk
Sir
   The occupants of Hollis 32¹ would like to have that room painted and whitewashed, also if possible to have a new hearth put in

yours respectfully<br>Thoreau & Richardson

*Correspondent:* Oliver Sparhawk (1805-1835), son of Samuel and Elizabeth McKinstry Sparhawk of Portsmouth, New Hampshire, attended Norwich Academy in Norwich, Vermont. He graduated from the school in 1823 and became a businessman in Conway, New Hampshire. Sparhawk later moved to Cambridge, where he kept books for Harvard's treasurer before being appointed steward of the college in 1831, a position he held until his death in June 1835. Sparhawk married Sarah B. Coffin (1809?-1861), daughter of Charles and Dorcas Parker Coffin, in 1834.

  ¹ T and James Richardson Jr. (1817-1863), one of T's college friends who corresponded with him, were roommates in Harvard's Hollis Hall during the 1834 academic year.

*Copy-text:* ALS (MaLiTIW, Walden Woods Project)

*Published:* "Earliest Thoreau Letter Purchased," *Notes from Walden Woods* (Lincoln, Mass.: The Walden Woods Project, 2008): 5

*Editor's Notes*
   This letter is addressed "Mr O Sparhawk".
   PE supplies the year "1834" based on the fact that T and James Richardson Jr. roomed together only during that year.

## From Augustus Goddard Peabody
*May 30, 1836*

Cambridge May 30. 1836.

Dear Thoreau,
   After nine days of constant rain, we have some prospect of pleasant weather. I cannot describe my feelings of joy, rapture, and astonishment, but you may have some idea

of the effect produced on me, from the fact that to this circumstance alone, you owe the present letter.[1]

I have somewhere seen an essay, to prove that a man's temper depends greatly on the weather; I will not however give the arguments brought forward to prove this important fact for two reasons. Firstly because it appears to me self evident; and secondly because I do'nt intend to write a theme, but a letter.

Strange that any person in his sober senses, should put two such sentences as the above in a letter, but howesomedever, "what's done cant be helped".[2]

Everything goes on here as regular as clock work, and it is as dull as one of Dr Ware's sermons.[3] (a very forcible comparison that, you must allow).

The Davy Club[4] got into a little trouble the week before last, from the following momentous circumstance.

Hen. Williams[5] gave a lecture on Pyrotechny, and illustrated it with a parcel of fire works he had prepared in the vacation. The report spread through college, that there was to be a "display of fire works," and on the night of their meeting, the Davy room was crowded, and those unfortunate youths who could not get in, stood in the yard round the windows. As you may imagine, there was some slight noise on the occasion. In fact the noise was so slight, that Bowen[6] heard it at his room in Holworthy.[7]

This worthy, boldly determined to march forth and disperse the "rioters." Accordingly in the midst of a grand display of rockets, et cetera, he step't into the room, and having gazed round him in silent astonishment for the space of two minutes, and hearing various cries of,–Intrusion–Throw him over–Saw his leg off–Pull his wool &c &c he made two or three dignified motions with his hand to gain attention, and then kindly advised us to "retire to our respective rooms." Strange to say he found no one inclined to follow this good advice, and he accordingly thought fit to withdraw.

There is (as perhaps you know) a law against keeping powder in the college buildings.

The effect of "Tutor Bowens" intrusion was evident on the next Monday night, when Williams and Bigelow[8] were invited to call and see President Quincy,[9] and owing to the tough reasoning of Bowen, who boldly asserted that "powder was powder", they were each presented with a public admonition.

We had a miniature volcanoe at Websters[10] lecture the other morning, and the odours therefrom, surpassed all ever produced by Araby the blest.[11]

Imagine to yourself, all the windows and shutters of the above named lecture room closed, and then if possible stretch your fancy a little farther, and conceive the delightful scent produced by the burning of nearly a bushel of Sulphur, Phospuretted Hydrogen, and other still more pleasant ingredients.

As soon as the burning commenced there was a general rush to the door, and a crowd collected there, running out every half minute to get a breath of fresh air, and then coming in to see the volcanoe.

"No noise nor nothing."[12]

Bigelow and Dr Bacon[13] manufactured some "laughing gas," and administered it on the Delta.[14] It was much better than that made by Webster.

Jack Weise[15] took some as usual. King,[16] Freshman, took a bag, and produced surprising effects, merely by running into all the unhappy individuals he met, who seemed by[a] no means desirous of his company. Wheeler, Joe Allen, and Hildreth,[17] each received a dose. Wheeler proceeded to dance for the amusement of the company, Joe signalized himself by jumping over the Delta fence, and Sam raved about Milton Shakespeare Byron &c. Sam took two doses. It produced great effect on him. He seemed to be as happy as a mortal could desire, talked with Shakespeare, Milton & co, and seemed to be quite at home with them.

It was amusing to trace the connexion of his ideas, and on the whole he afforded greater entertainment than any other person there, it affected him however very strongly, and he did not get over it till he was led off the Delta and carried into Wheelers room; he was well enough however next day.

This letter containeth a strange mixture.

All possible allowance must be made for want of time, not being accustomed to letter writing &c &c.

Hope you are all well, at home.

Yours truly
A. G. Peabody.

*Correspondent:* Augustus Goddard Peabody (1818-1877), son of Augustus and Miranda Goddard Peabody, graduated from the Harvard Medical School in 1844 and became a doctor in Machias, Maine. In 1856 he married Elizabeth S. Holway (1820-1895), daughter of John and Leonice Crocker Holway.

[1] Illness forced T to withdraw from Harvard on May 21, 1836; thus he missed the rest of the school year.

[2] A proverbial expression that occurs in many forms dating to classical antiquity.

[3] Peabody refers either to Henry Ware Sr. (1764-1845), Hollis Professor of Divinity at Harvard, or to his son Henry Ware Jr. (1794-1843), Professor of Pulpit Eloquence and the Pastoral Care at the Harvard Divinity School. The appointment of the elder Ware provoked a split between liberals and conservatives at Harvard that led to the establishment of the Divinity School. The younger Ware had been minister at Boston's Second Church, where his assistant was Ralph Waldo Emerson (1803-1882). Peabody's invocation of dullness suggests the elder Ware, whose style was not engaging.

[4] The Harvard chemistry club, which first met on December 28, 1815, was named for Sir Humphry Davy (1778-1829), who first discovered the exhilarating effects of inhaled nitrous oxide.

[5] Henry Williams Jr. (1816-1901) was the class of 1837 secretary.

[6] Francis Bowen (1811-1890), an 1833 Harvard graduate, taught philosophy at his alma mater from 1835 to 1839. He later edited the *North American Review.* In 1853 he was appointed the Alford Professor of Philosophy at Harvard. With the publication of his highly negative essay-review of Emerson's *Nature* in the January 1837

issue of the *Christian Examiner and General Review* (pp. 371-385), Bowen became a prominent leader of the conservative wing of the American Unitarians.

[7] A Harvard dormitory.

[8] T's classmate Henry Jacob Bigelow (1818-1890) was the son of Dr. Jacob Bigelow and Mary Scollay Bigelow. In addition to the "public admonition" Peabody describes in the letter, Bigelow was dismissed from Harvard from April 24, 1837, to "the Saturday before commencement" that year because "three guns and a quantity of powder, shot, and bullets were found" in his room, and "one of the posts in the room was found perforated with musket bullets" (MH-Ar Faculty Records UAIII 5.5.2.IX, 311). Bigelow later became a doctor, and in 1846 he joined the Massachusetts General Hospital, where he taught and practiced. In October of that year he arranged a demonstration of an operation performed on a patient who had inhaled ether to put him into a deep sleep. The event's success contributed to the acceptance of the administration of ether as an effective and safe method of anesthesia. Bigelow published a number of papers on the subject. In 1848 he married Susan Sturgis (1825-1853), daughter of William and Elizabeth Davis Sturgis of Boston.

[9] Josiah Quincy (1772-1864) served as Harvard's president from 1829 to 1845. Quincy instituted the unpopular numerical grading system and treated student rebellions harshly, but he succeeded in attracting distinguished men to the faculty and established the Harvard Law School.

[10] John White Webster (1793-1850), son of Redford and Hannah White Webster, graduated from Harvard in 1811 and became a doctor and a professor of chemistry. In 1827 he was named Erving Professor of Chemistry and Mineralogy at Harvard. He was hanged in August 1850 for the murder of Dr. George Parkman, a wealthy Boston physician and speculator. Webster had borrowed money from Parkman and killed him in a dispute over a loan.

[11] "Araby the blest" is Milton's translation of *Arabia felix*, the Latin name used to describe the southern, fertile part of the Arabian Peninsula. Milton compares the fragrant breezes of Eden to those met by sailors who have rounded the Cape of Good Hope and traveled north of Mozambique, where "off at sea north-east winds blow / Sabean odours from the spicy shore / Of Araby the blest" (vol. 2, *Paradise Lost*, 4.161-163).

[12] An allusion to Francis Beaumont and John Fletcher's *The Elder Brother*, 2.4.58-59: "Let me have no Noise, nor nothing to disturb me, I am to find a Secret" (*The Works of Mr. Francis Beaumont, and Mr. John Fletcher*, 2:125).

[13] John Bacon (1817-1881), class of 1837, was the son of John and Ann Hart Bacon. He received his medical degree in 1840 but never practiced. From 1857 to 1871 Bacon served on the Harvard Medical School faculty.

[14] A college playing field between Hollis Hall and the Cambridge Common.

[15] John Weiss (1818-1879), class of 1837, was the son of John and Mary Galloupe Weiss of Boston. He later became a Unitarian minister. The high-spirited Weiss had difficulty keeping a pulpit but achieved some success in his literary pursuits. His most important work was *Life and Correspondence of Theodore Parker* (London: Longman, Roberts, and Green, 1863). In 1844 he married Sarah Fiske Jennison (1818-1909), daughter of Samuel and Mary Ellery Jennison of Worcester, Massachusetts.

[16] Two members of the class of 1840 had the surname King: John King (1816-1890), born in Randolph, Massachusetts, became a lawyer, fought in the Civil War, and then settled in Boone, Iowa; Jacob Gore King (1819-1867) became a judge in New York City.

[17] Charles Stearns Wheeler (1816-1843), son of Charles and Julia Stearns Wheeler, was T's closest friend in the class of 1837 and one of its most promising members. He later became a tutor in Greek at Harvard. Joseph Henry Allen (1820-1898) was the son of Joseph and Lucy Ware Allen (his mother was the daughter of Henry Ware Sr.). He graduated from Harvard in 1840 and from the Harvard Divinity School in 1843. Like his father, Allen became a Unitarian clergyman. In 1845 he married Anna Minot Weld (1820-1907), daughter of William Gordon and Hannah Minot Weld. Allen later taught school, wrote a series of Latin manuals, and helped to edit the *Christian Examiner and General Review*, a distinguished, conservative Unitarian magazine. He lectured on ecclesiastical history at the Harvard Divinity School from 1878 to 1882. Samuel Tenney Hildreth (1817-1839), son of Rev. Hosea Hildreth and Sarah McLeod Hildreth, was the 1837 class poet.

*Copy-text:* ALS (NNPM, MA 920)

*Published: HDT* 1882, 55-56; *Cor* 1958, 4-6

*Editor's Note*
This letter is addressed "David H. Thoreau. / Concord. / Mass.", postmarked "CAMBR{*illegible*}GE Ms. MAY 31", and endorsed "A. G. Peabody".

*Author's Alteration*
by] no

*To Henry Vose*
*July 5, 1836*

Concord, July 5.<sup>th</sup> 1836.

Dear Vose.

You will probably recognise in the following dialogue a part which you yourself acted.

Act 1<sup>st</sup>.

Scene 1<sup>st</sup>.

T. Come, Vose, let's hear from a fellow now and then.

V. We—ll, I certainly will, but you must write first.

T. No, confound you, I shall have my hands full, and moreover shall have nothing to say, while you will have<sup>e</sup> bon-fires, gunpowder plots, and deviltry enough to back you.[1]

V. Well, I'll write first, and in the course of our correspondence we can settle a certain other matter.—

Now 'tis to this "certain other matter" alone that you are indebted for this epistle. The length and breadth, the height and depth, the sum & substance, of what I have to say, is this. Your humble servant will endeavor to enter the Senior Class of Harvard University next term, and if you intend taking a room in College, and it should be consistent with your pleasure, will joyfully sign himself your lawful and proper "Chum".

Should the case be otherwise, you will oblige him much if you will request that sage doughface[2] of a Wheeler to secure me one of the following rooms. Agreeably to his polite offer.

H. 23

St. do

H 27

St. do

St 28<sup>a</sup>

H. do[3]

Look well to the order.

I shall expect to hear from you forthwith. I leave it to you to obtain a room, should it be necessary.

Yrs

Matter-of-factly

D H Thoreau

*Correspondent:* Henry Vose (1817-1869), son of Elijah and Rebecca Bartlett Vose, was born in Charlestown, Massachusetts, but lived for several years in Concord, where he attended the Concord Academy. After graduating from Harvard, Vose studied law in Greenfield with George T. Davis and became a lawyer in Springfield. In 1842 he married Martha Barrett Ripley (1817-1870), daughter of Franklin and Charlotte Barrett Ripley of Greenfield. He was elected to the Massachusetts legislature and in 1859 was named a justice of the Massachusetts Superior Court.

[1] T may refer to the custom among Harvard students of lighting bonfires with wood secretly loaded with gunpowder to annoy the authorities.

[2] "A mask made of dough" or "one who allows himself to be moulded or worked upon" (*OED*).

[3] "H" and "St" refer to Hollis and Stoughton, Harvard dormitories.

*Copy-text:* ALS (CSmH, HM 7002)

*Published: Fifth Year Book* (Bibliophile Society, 1906), 55-56; *Life of HDT* 1917, 56-57; *Cor* 1958, 6-7

*Editor's Notes*

This letter is addressed "Henry Vose. / Cambridge / Mass.", postmarked "Concord Ms July 5", and endorsed "Thoreau." and "Letter from / D. H. Thoreau. / 1836."

have] *PE*; h{*MS torn*}e

*Author's Alteration*

8] 4

## From Charles Wyatt Rice
*July 31, 1836*

                                        Brookfield, July 31, 1836

Friend David,

Pardon, pardon for not better fulfilling my promise. The term has past and gone, and the end of nearly two weeks of vacation finds me at home, passing the week days in the hay-field and the sabbath in attendance upon church. I came home sick, went immediately to haying, and now do not know that I was ever better in my life than I am at this moment. The hay-field is a capital place for a sick man. The scent of the hay is good and healthy, and the work among it truly invigorating. Part of the time I have been hoeing potatoes and corn. This is being right in the dirt, and you know that there is nothing more healthy. I am not sure that it would work well with you, but I would advise you, if you have an opportunity, to try the experiment of working among the hay and dirt. For myself, I believe that if I had not tried this, I should have been upon my bed at this moment. I hope that I shall see you back at Cambridge in the commencement of next term in fine health and spirits.

As for news from Cambridge, I am ignorant of the greatest–those of exhibition and class day,[1] except from report. Being unwell I chose to go home the saturday before these eventful days. I have learnt however that the chapel was crowded on both days. Hale's oration is said to have been very excellent. Phillip's oration good, but not well adapted to the occasion; Prince's poem–poor.[2] But all this you have probably heard before.

As for your own occupation, I conclude that you are digging for indian remains. What success? Do you find any thing as curious as the head, that was dug up 'all along shore', and exposed to sale before the Antiquarian[a] Bookstore, Boston?[3] If you will come to Brookfield, I will show you ponds where the Indians used to fish, and passages

into and through rocks, which the imagination easily con-
verts into caves formerly inhabited by the Indians. There
is one place in Brookfield called Cranberry hill that contains several of these.[4] Before I became a collegian and
since, I have[a] occupied considerable time in examining
these, and think it very probable, that they were once
dwelling places of the Indians. They are at least objects of
curiosity, well worth visiting and examining

Vose has been with me this vacation. He was intending to visit Northampton, and we made our arrangements
so that he went with Russell[5] and staid till teusday of the
week after the close of the term. Then on returning from
a jaunt in the northen part of the county, I took him in at
Princeton, and brought him home with me, and the next
day he started for Northampton. He had had a very severe attack of the asthma at Princeton and was very unwell when I saw him, teusday. The next day, however, he
appeared to be much better.

Do you read any french, now? Chateaubriand's Travels[6]–have you finished them? You may well suppose that
my farming occupations allow me little time for reading.
This will my excuse for not reading more than I shall, this
vacation. Concord is said to be one of the most beautiful
towns in New England. It must contain many pleasant retreats for[a] one of your musing temperament. Write to me
some of the results of your musings. I am not to be disappointed of a letter, as I perhaps have disappointed you,
and therefore I allow you one week only from the *date* of
this letter, to write me one in return. Do not disappoint
me. Friend and Classmate–good night.

Yr's &c.

Charles Wyatt Rice

*Correspondent:* Charles Wyatt Rice (1817-1844), son of Parker and
Alona Boyden Rice of Brookfield, Massachusetts, moved to the
South after graduation. He taught school in South Carolina and
later became a lawyer and commission agent in Griffin, Georgia.
He married Mary A. Chambers of Fayetteville, Georgia, in 1841.

[1] T's class of 1837 had its exhibition on Monday, July 18, 1836. The following day, the class of 1836 had its "Valedictory Exercises of the Senior Class."

[2] T and Rice's classmate Horatio Emmons Hale (1817-1896), son of David and Sarah Buell Hale, gave the English Oration, "The American Literary Character." Upon graduation, Hale joined the Wilkes naval exploring expedition (1838-1842) as an ethnologist and philologist and studied the languages of Polynesia and the American Northwest. He later worked among several Indian tribes. In 1854 he married Margaret Pugh (1834-1910), daughter of William and Eliza Cristy Pugh. Grenville T. Phillips (1816-1863) and Frederick O. Prince (1818-1899) of the class of 1836 both became lawyers. Phillips, son of John and Sally Walley Phillips, spent much of his life in Europe. His father was Boston's first mayor, and his brother Wendell was a prominent abolitionist. Prince became active in Massachusetts politics and was elected mayor of Boston for four terms. In 1848 he married Helen Susan Henry (1822-1885), daughter of Bernard Henry of Philadelphia.

[3] The Antiquarian Bookstore was established on Boston's Cornhill Street in 1830 by Samuel Gardner Drake (1798-1875), a prominent antiquarian and historian and the author of *Indian Biography* (Boston: J. Drake, 1832).

[4] The specific location of Cranberry Hill is unclear, but early maps show an "Ancient Indian Town" just to the southeast of Quaboag Pond (Louis Roy, *History of East Brookfield, Massachusetts* [1970], p. 132); a similar site lay on "Indian hill," north of Great Pond in Brimfield (J. H. Temple, *History of North Brookfield, Massachusetts* [1887], p. 30).

[5] Charles Theodore Russell (1815-1896), son of Charles and Persis Hastings Russell of Princeton, Massachusetts, entered the bar in 1839 and practiced for a time with Henry Holton Fuller, Margaret Fuller's uncle. He later joined the Harvard Law School faculty, was elected to the state legislature, and served two terms as mayor of Cambridge. In 1849 he married Sarah Elizabeth Ballister (1817-1897), daughter of Joseph and Sarah Yendell Ballister of Boston.

[6] In April and May 1836, T checked out *Voyages en Amérique et en Italie*, volumes 6 and 7 of François-René Chateaubriand's *Œuvres Complètes*.

*Copy-text:* ALS (MCo-SC, Henry David Thoreau Papers, 1836-[1862], Series IV, Box 2, Folder 7)

*Editor's Note*
This letter is addressed "Mr. David H. Thoreau / Concord Mass.",

postmarked "BROOKFIELD MAS AUG 1", and endorsed "Charles Rice".

## To Charles Wyatt Rice
*August 5, 1836*

                         Concord, Aug. 5ᵗʰ, 1836.

Friend Rice,

   You say you are in the hay-field: how I envy you! Methinks I see thee stretched at thy ease by the side of a fragrant rick, with a mighty flagon in one hand, a cold cold slice in the other, and a most ravenous appetite to boot. So much for haying. Now as I cannot hay nor scratch dirt, I manage to keep soul and body together another way. I have been manufacturing a kind of vessel in miniature, not a "εὔσσελμον νγα"¹ as Homer has it, but a kind of oblong bread-troughᵉ.

> In days of yore, 'tis said, the swimming alder²
> Fashioned rude, with branches lopt, and stripped of its
>     smooth coat,
> Where fallen tree was none, and rippling streams vast
>     breadth
> Forbade adventurous leap, the brawny swain did
>     bear
> Secure to farthest shore.
> The book has passed away, and with the book the layᵉ
> Which in my youthful days I loved to ponder.
> Of curious things it told, how wise men 3 of Gotham
> In a bowl did venture out to sea,
> And darkly hints their awful fate.³
> If men have dared the main to tempt in such frail
>     barks,
> Why may not wash tub round, or bread-troughsᵉ
>     square oblong

Suffice to cross the purling wave and gain the destin'd
port.[4]

What, think you, do these capitals mean? When I begin
to feel bluey I just step into my hog-trough, leave care behind, and drift along our sluggish stream at the mercy of
the winds and waves. The following is an extract from the
log-book of the Red Jacket, Captain Thoreau.

Set sail from the Island[5]–the Island! how expressive!–
reached Thayer's after a tedious voyage, having encountered a head wind during the whole passage–waves
running mountain-high, with breakers to the leeward–
however, arrived safe, and after a thorough refit, being
provided with extra cables & a first-rate birch[a] main-mast,
weighed anchor at 3 o'clock P. M. Aug. 1st, 1836, N. S. wind
blowing N. N. E. The breeze having increased to a gale,
tack'd ship–stationed myself at the helm and prepared for
emergencies. Just as the ship was rounding point Dennis[6] a squall struck her, under a cloud of canvas, which
swept the deck. The aforesaid mast went by the board,
carrying with it our only mainsail. The vessel being left at
the mercy of the waves, was cast ashore on Nawshawtuck
beach.–[7]  Natives a harmless inoffensive race, principally
devoted to agricultural pursuits–appeared somewhat astonished that a stranger should land so unceremoniously
on their coast.[8] Got her off at 20 minutes of 4, and after a
short and pleasant passage of 10 minutes arrived safely in
port with a valueable cargo.–

"Epistolary matter", says Lamb, "usually comprises
3 topics, news, sentiment and puns."[9] Now as to news I
don't know the coin–the newspapers take care of that.
Puns I abhor and more especially deliberate ones. Sentiment alone is immortal, the rest are short-lived–evanes-
cent. Now this is neither matter-of-fact, nor *pun*gent, nor
yet sentimental–it is neither one thing nor the other, but
a kind of hodgepodge, put together in much the same
style that mince pies are fabled to have[a] been made, ie,
by opening the oven door, and from the further end of the

room, casting in the various ingredients–a little lard here, a little flour there–now a round of beef and then a cargo of spices–helter skelter.

I should like to crawl into those holes you describe–what a crowd of associations 'twould give rise to! "One to once, gentlemen."

As to Indian remains the season for grubbing is past with me, the Doctor having expressly forbidden both digging and chopping. My health is so much improved that I shall return to C. next term if they will receive me. French I have certainly neglected, Dan[10] Homer is all the rage at present.

This from your friend and classmate,<br>D. H. Thoreau.

P. S.  It would afford me much pleasure if you would visit our good old town this vacation, *in other words*, *myself*. Dont fail to answer this forthwith; tis a good thing to persevere in well doing.[11] How true it is that the postscript contains the most important matter invariably.

*Correspondent:*  See p. 10.

[1] Sometimes translated as "well-benched ship," a recurring epithet in *The Iliad* and *The Odyssey*.

[2] Probably an echo of Virgil's *Georgics*, 1.136-137, "Then first did rivers feel upon their backs boats of hollowed alder"; and *Georgics*, 2.450-451, "So, too, the light alder, launched upon the Po, swims the raging stream" (Loeb).

[3] T quoted the passage "how ... fate" in an essay about the love of stories that he wrote for Edward Tyrell Channing a few weeks later; see *Early Essays* 1975, p. 46.

[4] Sanborn's version of this poem in *Life of HDT* 1917 differs slightly; see *Collected Poems* 1964, p. 246.

[5] The island in Fair Haven Bay.

[6] A promontory on the Sudbury River, south of the railroad bridge, near the residence of Samuel Dennis.

[7] At the bottom of a hill just west of the junction of the Assabet and Sudbury rivers.

[8] Probably an allusion to Ulysses's arrival in the country of the Phaeacians in book six of *The Odyssey*.

⁹ Charles Lamb, "Distant Correspondents," in *Elia: Essays Which Have Appeared under That Signature in the London Magazine*, p. 206.

¹⁰ Master, an honorific once commonly used with the names of old poets.

¹¹ Gal. 6:9: "And let us not be weary in well doing: for in due season we shall reap, if we faint not."

*Copy-text:*  MSC in an unknown hand (IU, Samuel A. Jones Papers, Folder 23)

*Published:  Two Thoreau Letters* (Mesa, Ariz.: Edwin B. Hill, 1916); *Life of HDT* 1917, 59-60, 62-63; *Cor* 1958, 8-9; *Companion* 1964, 7, 10, 12; *TSB* 145 (fall 1978): 5-6

*Editor's Notes*

The text of the letter is followed by a note written by Samuel Arthur Jones:

> This copy was procured for me by L. P. Gould, of Owosso, Mich. (now deceased) from some relative of Mr. Rice–the holograph being treasured as a precious memento. For an account of Thoreau's class-mate, Charles Wyatt Rice, see "Memorials of the Class of 1837 [H. U.]" p. 25.
>
> Sam'l A. Jones.

This note suggests that the recipient's copy was still extant in the late nineteenth century, although it has not surfaced.

Edwin B. Hill almost certainly based his text of the letter on a copy provided by Jones; see *Toward the Making of Thoreau's Modern Reputation* (Urbana: University of Illinois Press, 1979), ed. Fritz Oehlschlaeger and George Hendrick, p. 88n1. In *Life of HDT* 1917, Sanborn notes that the letter "was in the collection of Alfred Hosmer at Concord" (p. 61); however, no copy of the letter exists in the Hosmer material now at the Concord Free Public Library. It is likely that Sanborn based his edition of the letter on Hill's printing.

bread-trough] *PE*; bread- / trough *in MS*

Fashioned ... lay] *At the ends of the lines* Fashioned ... coat, Forbade ... bear, *and* The book ... lay, *the copyist positioned the last few words to indicate that the lines ran on in the original:* of its smooth coat, did bear, *and* the lay *are interlined with carets and preceded by open brackets. PE places the endings as indicated, omitting the open brackets.*

bread-troughs] *PE*; bread- / troughs *in MS*

*Alterations*

Changes appearing in the manuscript copy are reported below;

they could be either faithful representations of the original manuscript or errors made and corrected by the copyist.

   birch] *interlined with a caret*
   have] *interlined with a caret*


## From James Richardson Jr.

*September 7, 1837*

                    Dedham, September 7th, 1837.

Friend Thoreau,

   After you had finished your part in the Performances of Commencement,[1] (the tone and sentiment of which by the way I liked much, as being of a sound philosophy,) I hardly saw you again at all. Neither at Mr Quincy's levee, neither at any of our Classmates' evening entertainments[a], did I find you, though for the purpose of taking a farewell, and leaving you some memento of an old chum, as well as on matters of business, I much wished to see your face once more. Of course you must be present at our October meeting,[2]–notice of the time and place for which will be given in the Newspapers. I hear that you are comfortably located, in your native town, as the guardian of its children, in the immediate vicinity, I suppose, of one of our most distinguished Apostles of the Future–[a]R. W. Emerson,[3] and situated under the ministry of our old friend Rev[a] Barzillai Frost,[4] to whom please make my remembrances. I heard from you, also, that Concord Academy, lately under the care of Mr Phineas Allen[5] of Northfield, is now vacant of a preceptor; should Mr Hoar[6] find it difficult to get a scholar–[a]college-distinguished, perhaps he would take up with one, who, though in many respects a critical thinker, and a careful philosopher of language among other things, has never distinguished himself in his class as a regular attendant on college studies and rules. If so, could you do me the kindness to mention my name to him, as of one intending to make teaching his profession, at least for a part of his life. If recommendations are necessary, President Quincy has offered me one, and I can easily get others. My old instructor Mr Kimball[7] gave, and gives me credit for having quite a genius for Mathematics, though I studied them so little in College, and I think that Dr Beck[8] will approve me as something of a Latinist.– I did intend going to a distance, but my father's[9] and other friends' wishes, beside my own desire of a proximity to Harvard and her Library, has constrained me. I have had the offer and opportunity of several places, but the distance or smallness of salary were objections,[a] I should like to hear about Concord Academy from you, if it is not engaged. Hoping that your situation affords you every advantage for continuing your mental education and developement I am

with esteem & respect<br>Yr classmate & friend<br>James Richardson jr

P. S.  I hope you will tell me something about your situation, state of mind, course of reading, &c; and any advice you have to offer will be gratefully accepted. Should the place, alluded to above, be filled, any place, that you may hear spoken of, with a reasonable salary, would perhaps answer for your humble serv't

–JR–

*Correspondent:* James Richardson Jr. (1817-1863), son of James and Sarah Richards Richardson of Dedham, Massachusetts, was an indifferent student, though he was thought to have literary talent. He taught for a time and graduated from the Harvard Divinity School in 1845. After serving several churches, he left the ministry and became a farmer in Connecticut. In 1856 he married Henrietta Harris (b. 1828?) of Brooklyn. Richardson joined the army as a private in 1862, but he served as an aide, rather than as a combat soldier.

[1] At the 1837 Harvard commencement, T, Charles Rice, and Henry Vose were to be in a conference together, each reading a lecture on the theme of "The Commercial Spirit of Modern Times, considered in its Influence on the Political, Moral, and Literary Character of a Nation." Rice, who was absent, was to speak first about the influ-

ence of the commercial spirit on the political character of a nation; T spoke about its influence "on the Moral Character of a Nation," and Vose closed the conference with a lecture about its influence on literary character (Bradley P. Dean and Ronald Wesley Hoag, "Thoreau's Lectures before *Walden*: An Annotated Calendar," *SAR* 1995, pp. 133-134).

² The class had its first post-graduation meeting at Fenno's in Boston on October 2, 1837.

³ Soon after his graduation in 1837, T took a job teaching at the Center School in Concord, where he had formerly been a student. He resigned at the end of his second week–after he had been ordered by Nehemiah Ball, a member of the school committee, to inflict corporal punishment on the students. T was living with his family in the Parkman House in Concord, near the intersection of Main Street and Sudbury Road; Ralph Waldo Emerson and his second wife Lydia (Lidian) Jackson (1802-1892) had recently moved into the Coolidge House on the Cambridge Turnpike outside of Concord's center. Emerson had just the week before delivered "The American Scholar" to the Phi Beta Kappa Society at Harvard.

⁴ Barzillai Frost (1804-1858) graduated from Harvard University in 1830 and from the Harvard Divinity School in 1835. He was ordained as the junior minister at Concord's First Parish on February 1, 1837, and succeeded Rev. Ezra Ripley in 1841. On June 1, 1837, he married Elmira Stone (1810-1891), daughter of Daniel and Sarah Buckminster Stone. Frost was an ardent abolitionist but at best a mediocre thinker. Although he never exerted intellectual leadership, he was active in Concord public life as a member of the school committee and as a proprietor of the library.

⁵ Phineas Allen (1801-1885), son of Phineas and Ruth Smith Allen, graduated from Harvard in 1825. In 1828 he married Clarissa Fiske (1801-1887), daughter of Jonathan and Sally Flagg Fiske. He taught in Concord from 1827 to 1836 and then moved to Northfield, Massachusetts, and again to West Newton, where he lived from 1860 until his death. T, once a student of Allen's, later had this to say about him: "I was fitted, or rather made unfit for college, at Concord Academy and elsewhere, mainly by myself, with the countenance of Phineas Allen, Preceptor" ("Elizabeth Hoar of Concord and Thoreau," *TSB* 106 [winter 1969]: 2).

⁶ Samuel Hoar (1778-1856), an 1802 Harvard graduate and Concord's most prominent citizen, began his law practice in Concord in 1805. In 1812 he married Sarah Sherman (1783-1866), daughter of Roger and Rebekah Prescott Sherman. An active antislavery advocate, Hoar served in the U.S. Congress from 1835 to 1837, helped

found the Free-Soil Party in 1848, and was one of the organizers of the Massachusetts Republican Party in 1855. In Concord he often served on the school committee.

[7] Rev. Daniel Kimball (1778-1862) graduated from Harvard in 1800 and was the Latin tutor there from 1803 to 1805. He was ordained as an evangelist at large on December 17, 1817, but continued to teach school.

[8] Charles Beck (1798-1866) earned his doctorate at Tübingen University in 1823. Political oppression in Germany drove him to the United States in 1824. He taught at the Round Hill School in Northampton, Massachusetts, and then in Philipstown, New York, before joining the Harvard faculty in 1832 as a professor of Latin.

[9] James Richardson Sr. (1771-1858) graduated from Harvard in 1797 and practiced law in Dedham, Massachusetts. In 1813 he married Sarah Elizabeth Richards (1789-1820), daughter of Samuel and Mary White Richards.

*Copy-text:* ALS (NN-BGC, Henry David Thoreau Collection, 1837-1917, Series IV)

*Published:* *FL* 1894, 10n; *FL* 1906, 10n-11n; *Life of HDT* 1917, 188; *ESQ* 5 (1956): 3; *ESQ* 7 (1957): 3; *Cor* 1958, 11-12; *ATQ* 2 (1969): 86; *ARLR* 1989, 225

*Editor's Note*

This letter is addressed "Henry D. Thoreau / Concord / Mass", postmarked "DEDHAM Ms. SEP 8", and endorsed "James. Richardson".

*Author's Alterations*

    entertainments] entertains
    Future-] future,
    Rev] *inserted*
    scholar-] ~.
    objections,] ~;


*To Henry Vose*

*October 13, 1837*

Concord Oct 13th –37

Friend Vose

You don't know how much I envy you your comfortable settlement–almost sine-cure–in the region of Butternuts.[1] How art thou pleased with the lay of the land and the look of the people? Do the rills tinkle and fume, and bubble and purl, and trickle and meander as thou expected'st, or are the natives less absorbed in the pursuit of gain than the good clever homespun and respectable people of New England?

I presume that by this time you have commenced pedagogueizing in good earnest. Methinks I see thee, perched on learning's little stool, thy jet black boots luxuriating upon a well-polished fender, while round thee are ranged some half dozen small specimens of humanity, thirsting for an idea:

> Pens to mend, and hands to guide.

> O,[a] who would a schoolmaster be?

Why I to be sure. The fact is, here I have been vegetating for the last three months. "The clock sends to bed at ten, and calls me again at eight." Indeed[e],[a] I deem "conformity one of the best arts of life".[2] Now should you hear of any situation in your neighborhood, or indeed any other, which you think would suit me, such as your own, for instance, you will much oblige me[a] by dropping a line on the subject, or, I should rather say, by making mention of it in your answer to this.

I received a catalogue from Harvard, the other day, and therein found Classmate Hildreth set down as assistant instructor in Elocution, CHas Dall divinity student– Clarke and Dana law do, and C. S. W. resident graduate.[3] How we apples swim![4] Can you realize that we too can now moralize about College pranks, and reflect upon the pleasures of a College life, as among the things that are past? May'st thou ever remember as a fellow soldier of[e] the campaign of –37[5]

Yr friend and classmate<br>Thoreau.

Ps I have no time for apologies.

*Correspondent:* See p. 8.

[1] The details of Vose's teaching position are unknown. Butter-

nuts, now called Gilbertsville, was a village in Otsego County, New York.

[2] T alludes to Elizabeth Montagu's letter of April 8, 1741, to the Duchess of Portland: The clock "sends me to bed at ten, and makes me rise, oh barbarous! at eight. I go to bed, awake, and arise asleep; but I have ever held conformity one of the best arts of life, and though I might choose my own hours, I think it proper to follow theirs" (*The Letters of Mrs. Elizabeth Montagu*, 1:88). T wrote an essay on this passage at Harvard on May 19; see *Early Essays* 1975, pp. 105-106.

[3] Charles Henry Appleton Dall (1816-1886), son of James and Henrietta Dall, graduated from the Harvard Divinity School in 1840. In 1844 he married Caroline Healey (1822-1912), daughter of Mark and Caroline Foster Healey; his wife later became an accomplished writer and social activist. A minister at large, Dall founded a mission school in St. Louis and continued his work among the poor at another mission school in Baltimore. He later preached in Toronto and in Needham, Massachusetts. Despite poor health, Dall heeded a call to become a Unitarian missionary in India, where he spent the last thirty-one years of his life. Manlius Stimson Clarke (1816-1853), son of Rev. Pitt Clarke and Mary Jones Clarke of Norton, Massachusetts, was admitted to the bar in 1840 and became a successful Boston lawyer. He married Frances Lemist (b. 1817) in 1841. Richard Henry Dana (1815-1882), son of Richard Henry and Ruth Charlotte Smith Dana of Cambridge, Massachusetts, had interrupted his college studies because of poor health. He sailed to California in 1834 as a common seaman and published an account of his experience in *Two Years before the Mast* (New York: Harper and Brothers, 1840). In 1841 he married Sarah Watson (1814-1907), daughter of William and Mary Marsh Watson of Hartford, Connecticut. Dana became a lawyer and an antislavery activist. In 1851 he defended the men who freed Shadrach, the first runaway to become a victim of the Fugitive Slave Law; in 1854 he tried to free Anthony Burns, who was convicted under the same law and was the subject of a well-publicized court trial. Dana was part of the prosecution team that charged Jefferson Davis with treason after the Civil War. "C. S. W." is Charles Stearns Wheeler. The abbreviation "do" stands for "ditto," i.e., law students.

[4] The proverb "see how we apples swim, quoth the horse turd" dates from 1616.

[5] In May of its freshman year, T's class precipitated a student rebellion after one of its members refused to recite for Christopher Dunkin, the instructor in Greek. The student body disrupted the college for several days, despite a threat from President Quincy

that he would bring civil charges against the students. Not only were several members of T's class dismissed, but the entire class of 1836 was suspended for a term for their part in the disruption.

*Copy-text:* ALS (NN-BGC, Henry David Thoreau Collection, 1837-1917, Series III)

*Published:* *NEQ* 13 (1940): 28-29; *ESQ* 5 (1956): 4; *ESQ* 7 (1957): 4; *Cor* 1958, 12-13; *ATQ* 2 (1969): 87

*Editor's Notes*
    This letter is addressed "Mr Henry Vose / Butternuts / N. York", postmarked "CONCORD MAS. 13", and endorsed "Letter / from / D. H. Thoreau. / 1837".
    Indeed] *PE*; Inded *in MS*
    of] *PE*; o{*MS torn*}

*Author's Alterations*
    O,] Oh
    Indeed,] ~.
    me] your


## From Henry Vose
*October 22, 1837*

Butternuts. Oct. 22.<sup>nd</sup> 1837.

Friend Thoreau
    I received by yesterday's mail your favor of the 13.<sup>th</sup> with great pleasure, and proceed at once to indite you a line of condolence on your having nothing to do. I suspect you wrote that letter during a fit of ennui or the blues. You begin at once by expressing your envy of my happy situation, and mourn over your fate, which condemns you to loiter about Concord, and grub among clamshells.[1] If this were your only source of enjoyment while in C. you would truly be a pitiable object. But I know that it is not. I well remember that "antique and fishlike office of *Major* Nelson,[2] [to whom and Mr Dennis and Bemis, and J Thoreau I wish to be remembered];[3] and still<sup>a</sup> more vividly do I remember the fairer portion of the community in C. If from<sup>a</sup> these two grand fountain heads of amusement in

that ancient town, united with its delightful walks and your own internal resources, you cannot find an[a] ample fund of enjoyment, while waiting for a situation, you deserve to be haunted by blue devils[4] for the rest of your days.

I am surprised that, in writing a letter of two pages and a half to a friend and "fellow soldier of the –37th" at a distance of 300 miles, you should have forgotten to say a single word of the news of C. In lamenting your own fate you have omitted to even hint at[a] any of the events that have occurred since I left. However this must be fully rectified in your next. Say something of the *Yeoman's Gazette*[5] and of the politics of the town and county, of the events, that are daily transpiring there, &c.

I am sorry I know of no[a] situation whatever at present for you. I, in this little, secluded town of B. am the last person in the world to hear of one. But If I do, you may be assured that I will inform you of it at once, and do all in my power to obtain it for you.

With my own situation I am highly pleased. My duties afford me quite as much labor[a] as I wish for, and are interesting and useful to me. Out of school hours I find a great plenty to do, and time passes rapidly and pleasantly.

Please request friend W. Allen[6] to drop me a line and to inform of his success with his school. You will please excuse the brevity of this: but as it is getting late, and every body has been long in bed but myself, and I am deuced sleepy I must close. Write soon and long, and I shall try to do better in my next.

Yours truly
Henry Vose.

*Correspondent:* See p. 8.

*Correspondent:* See p. 8.

[1] Possibly a reference to Samuel Dennis's farm on the Sudbury River, which had a large quantity of clamshells and also some Indian artifacts, the remnants of Indian feasts held on the site. Samuel Dennis (1784-1864), son of Adonijah and Eunice Sibley

Dennis, married Cynthia Barrett (1791-1857), daughter of Benjamin and Sarah Chamberlin Barrett, in 1811. They were the parents of T's friend Hiram Barrett Dennis.

[2] Albert Hobart Nelson (1812-1858), son of Dr. John Nelson and Lucinda Parkhurst Nelson of Carlisle, Massachusetts, attended the Concord Academy and then Harvard, where he graduated in 1832. He graduated from the Harvard Law School in 1837 and formed a law partnership with John Keyes in Concord. Unsuccessful in Concord, Nelson moved to Woburn, where he became the district attorney. Later he was elected to the Massachusetts legislature and served as chief justice of the Superior Court for Suffolk County. He married Elizabeth B. Phinney (1815-1907), daughter of Elias and Elizabeth Cole Phinney, in 1840. Apparently Nelson was T's fishing companion, as Vose plays on Trinculo's sneer at Caliban, whom Trinculo accuses of having "a very ancient and fish-like smell" (Shakespeare, vol. 1, *The Tempest*, 2.2.26-27). The military title Vose refers to (actually colonel, not major) came from Nelson's militia appointment.

[3] Hiram Barrett Dennis (1816-1846), son of Samuel and Cynthia Barrett Dennis of Concord, graduated from Harvard in 1835 and became a drama critic in New York City. He later taught in Nantucket, became editor and proprietor of the *Inquirer*, and was elected to the state legislature. Bemis is either George Bemis (1816-1878) or Charles Vose Bemis (1816-1906). George Bemis, another member of the class of 1835, was the son of Seth and Sarah Wheeler Bemis of Waltham, Massachusetts. He graduated from the Harvard Law School in 1839, practiced in Boston, and became a prominent penal reformer. He was an associate counsel for the prosecution of Dr. John Webster in 1850. Charles Vose Bemis, son of Charles and Anna Vose Bemis of Boston, graduated from Harvard University in 1835 and from the Harvard Medical School in 1839. He married Elizabeth Fanny Henry (1821-1888), daughter of William and Fanny Goodhue Henry, in 1841. He was for many years director of the Massachusetts General Hospital. T's brother John (1814-1842) was in Concord at this time; in November he began his second session as a teacher in the Hopewell district of Taunton.

[4] "Despondency, depression of spirits, hypochondriac melancholy" (*OED*).

[5] *Yeoman's Gazette*, the weekly Concord Whig newspaper, ran from March 4, 1826, to July 18, 1840. At the time of this letter it was published by Elbridge G. Jefts and George F. Bemis. Jefts (1812-1856) of Billerica later became a forty-niner and fought in the Civil War. Bemis (1809-1890) of Lincoln became a prosperous printer and real estate investor.

6 William Allen (1815-1895), son of Barzillai and Lucy Baldwin Allen of East Bridgewater, Massachusetts, graduated from Harvard and taught school, first in Concord, then in Maine, and finally for fourteen years in East Bridgewater. Allen was elected to the Massachusetts legislature and served first as inspector, then as clerk, of the Boston Custom House. In 1845 he married Amanda Cole (1823-1904), daughter of David and Pamela McArthur Cole of Maine.

*Copy-text:* ALS (NNPM, MA 920)

*Published:* FL 1894, 19; *T: Home* 1902, 79; *FL* 1906, 18; *ESQ* 5 (1956): 5; *Cor* 1958, 14-15; *ATQ* 2 (1969): 88

*Editor's Note*
This letter is addressed "Mr. D. H. Thoreau. / Concord. / Mass. tts.", postmarked "Butternuts Ny Oct 23", and endorsed "H. Vose".

*Author's Alterations*
still] *preceded by cancelled* more
from] *interlined with a caret*
an] *interlined with a caret*
at] *interlined with a caret*
no] *interlined with a caret*
labor] *interlined with a caret*


## To Helen Louisa Thoreau
*October 27, 1837*

Concord Oct 27 1837

Dear H.

Please you, let the defendant say a few words in defence of his long silence.¹ You know we have hardly done our own deeds, thought our own thoughts, or lived our own lives, hitherto. For a man to act himself, he must be perfectly free; otherwise, he is in danger of losing all sense of responsibility or of self-respect. Now when such a state of things exists, that the sacred opinions one advances in argument are apologised for by his friends, before his face, lest his hearers receive a wrong impression of the man,–when such gross injustice is of frequent occurrence, where shall we look, & not look in vain, for men, deeds, thoughts? As well apologize for the grape that it is sour,–or the thunder that it is noisy, or the lightning that it tarries not. Farther, letterwriting too often degenerates into a communing of facts, & not of truths; of other men's deeds, & not our thoughts. What are the convulsions of a planet compared with the emotions of the soul? or the rising of a thousand suns, if that is not enlightened by a ray?

Your[a] affectionate brother,

Henry

*Correspondent:* Helen Louisa Thoreau (1812-1849), the oldest of the Thoreau children, was a schoolteacher. Her poor health limited her opportunities to teach, but she was an active abolitionist and a member of the Concord Women's Anti-Slavery Society.

[1] As was her brother John, Helen was teaching in Taunton, Massachusetts, where her maternal relatives lived.

*Copy-text:* MSC by Ralph Waldo Emerson (NN-BGC, Henry David Thoreau Collection, 1837-1917, Series III)

*Published: Boston Advertiser* (August 3, 1882); *Boston Traveller* (August 3, 1882); *Springfield Daily Republican* (August 7, 1882), 2-3; "Thoreau's Manuscripts" 1883, 125; *FL* 1894, 12-13; *FL* 1906, 12-13; *Life of HDT* 1917, 191-192; *ESQ* 5 (1956): 5; *Cor* 1958, 15; *ATQ* 2 (1969): 88; *Concord Harvest* 1970, 67; *Response to Transcendental Concord* 1974, 234, 236; *ARLR* 1988, 54, 55

*Editor's Note*

Sanborn was responsible for all of the nineteenth- and early-twentieth-century publications of this letter, and in every instance he refers to his source as a copy in Emerson's hand.

*Alteration*

A change appearing in the manuscript copy is reported below; it could be either a faithful representation of the original manuscript or an error made and corrected by the copyist.

Your] Yours

*To John Thoreau Jr.*
*November 11 and 14, 1837*

Musketaquid[1] two hundred and two Summers–two moons–eleven suns since the coming of the Pale Faces.[2]

Tahatawan–Sachimaupan–to his brother sachem–Hopeful–of Hopewell–hoping that he is well.[3]

Brother, it is many suns that I have not seen the print of thy moccasins by our council fire, the Great Spirit has blown more leaves from the trees and many clouds from the land of snows have visited our lodge–the earth has become hard like a frozen buffaloe skin, so that the trampling of many herds is like the Great Spirit's thunder–the grass on the great fields is like the old man of eighty winters–and the small song-sparrow prepares for his flight to the land whence the summer comes.

Brother–I write thee these things because I know that thou lovest the Great Spirit's creatures, and wast wont to sit at thy lodge door–when the maize was green–to hear the blue-bird's[e] song. So shalt thou in the land of spirits, not only find good hunting grounds and sharp arrowheads–but much music of birds.

Brother. I have been thinking how the Pale-Faces have taken away our lands[4]–and was a woman. You are fortunate to have pitched your wigwam nearer to the great salt lake, where the Pale-Face[a] can never plant corn.

Brother–I need not tell thee how we hunted on the lands of the Dundees–a great war-chief never forgets the bitter taunts of his enemies. Our young men called for strong-water–they painted their faces and dug up the hatchet. But their enemies the Dundees were women[a]–they hastened to cover their hatchets with wampum. Our braves are not many–our enemies took a few strings from the heap their fathers left them, and our hatchets were buried.–  But not Tahatawan's–his heart is of rock when the Dundees sing–his hatchet cuts deep into the Dundee braves.

Brother–there is dust on my moccasins– I have journeyed to the White[a] lake in the country of the Ninares.[5] The Long-knife[a] has been there–like a woman I paddled his war-canoe. But the spirits of my fathers were angered.– the waters were ruffled and the Bad Spirit troubled the air.

The hearts of the *Lee*-vites are gladdened–the young Peacock has returned to his lodge by Nawshawtuck.[6] He is the medicine of his tribe, but his heart is like the dry leaves when the whirlwind breathes. He has come to help choose new chiefs for the tribe in the great council house when two suns are past.–[7] There is no seat for Tahatawan in the council-house. He lets the squaws talk–his voice is heard above the warwhoop of his tribe, piercing the hearts of his foes–his legs are stiff, he cannot sit.

Brother, art thou waiting for spring that the *geese* may fly low over thy wigwam? Thy arrows are sharp, thy bow is strong. Has Anawan killed all the eagles? The crows fear not the winter. Tahatawans eyes are sharp–he can track a snake in the grass, he knows a friend from a foe–he welcomes a friend to his lodge though the ravens croak.

Brother hast thou studied much in the medicine books of the Pale-Faces? Dost thou understand the long talk of the great medicine whose words are like the music of the mockingbird[e]. But our chiefs have not ears to hear him–they listen like squaws to council of old men–they understand not his words. But Brother, he never danced the war-dance, nor heard the warwhoop of his enemies. He was a squaw–he staid by the wigwam when the braves were out, and tended the tame buffaloes.

Fear not, the Dundees have faint hearts, and much wampum. When the grass is green on the great fields, and the small titmouse returns again we will hunt the buffaloe to gether.

Our old men say they will send the young chief of the Karlisles[8] who lives in the green wigwam and is a great medicine, that his words may be heard in the long talk which the wise men are going to hold at Shawmut[9] by the salt-lake. He is a great talk–and will not forget the enemies of his tribe.

————

14th sun.

The fire has gone out in the council house. The words of our old men have been like the haunts of the Dundees. The Eagle-beak[10] was moved to talk like a silly Pale-Face, and not as becomes a great warchief in a council of braves. The Young Peacock is a woman among braves–he heard not the words of the old men–like a squaw, he looked at his medicine-paper. The young chief of the green wig-wam has hung up his moccasins, he will not leave his tribe till after the buffaloe have come down onto the plains.

Brother this is a long talk–but there is much meaning to my words–they are not like the thunder of canes when the lightening smites them.

Brother I have just heard *thy talk* and am well pleased–thou are getting to be a great medicine.

| The Great Spirit confound the enemies of thy tribe. | Tahatawan his mark  |

*Correspondent:* T's older brother John Thoreau (1814-1842) was the second child of John and Cynthia Dunbar Thoreau. Henry and John enjoyed a close relationship: from 1839 to 1841 they ran the Concord Academy together, and between the school's summer and fall sessions in 1839 they took a two-week boat trip on the Concord and Merrimack rivers, a trip that Henry memorialized in his first book. John died from lockjaw on January 11, 1842.

[1] The Indian name for Concord and for the Concord River.

[2] T dates the first part of this letter from the coming of the English to Concord in September 1635, i.e., November 11, 1837.

[3] Tahattawan was an Indian sachem living in what is now Concord before the arrival of the English. "Sachimaupan" means "he that was prince here" (Roger Williams, "A Key into the Language of America," in *Collections of the Massachusetts Historical Society,* 1st ser., vol. 3 [1794; repr. 1810], p. 237). Hopewell was the district in Taunton where John was teaching.

⁴ T refers to the land that English settlers bought from the local Indian tribes to establish Concord.

⁵ White Pond in Nine-Acre Corner.

⁶ Nawshawtuck Hill was also known as Lee's Hill; many generations of the Lee family lived there.

⁷ Massachusetts elected its representatives to the state legislature (the "great council house") on November 16.

⁸ Probably Albert H. Nelson, born in Carlisle, Massachusetts. Nelson, a Whig, lost to Stedman Buttrick, the Democrat incumbent, who polled 170 votes to 134 for Nelson.

⁹ The Indian name for Boston.

¹⁰ Probably Samuel Hoar.

*Copy-text:* ALS (NN-BGC, Henry David Thoreau Collection, 1837-1917, Series III)

*Published:* FL 1894, 14-18; FL 1906, 13-17; ESQ 5 (1956): 7; Cor 1958, 16-18; ATQ 2 (1969): 90

*Editor's Notes*
This letter is addressed "Sachem Hopeful. / of Hopewell."
blue-bird's] *PE*; blue- / bird's *in MS*
mockingbird] *PE*; mocking- / bird *in MS*

*Author's Alterations*
Pale-Face] pale-face
women] woman
White] white
Long-knife] long-knife

## To Orestes Augustus Brownson
*December 30, 1837*

Concord Dec 30ᵗʰ 1837

Dear Sir

I have never ceased to look back with interest, not to say satisfaction, upon the short six weeks which I passed with you. They were an era in my life–the morning of a new *Lebenstag.*¹ They are to me as a dream that is dreamt, but which returns from time to time in all its original freshness. Such a one as I would dream a second and a third time, and then tell before breakfast.

I passed a few hours in the city, about a month ago,

with the intention of calling on you, but not being able
to ascertain, from the directory or other sources, where
you had settled, was fain to give up the search and return
home.

My apology for this letter is to ask your assistance in
obtaining employment.[2] For, say what you will, this frost-
bitten 'forked carrot' of a body must be fed and clothed
after all. It is ungrateful, to say the least, to suffer this
much abused case to fall into so dilapidated a condition
that every northwester may luxuriate through its chinks
and crevices, blasting the kindly affections it should shelter, when a few clouts would save it. Thank heaven, the
toothache occurs often enough to remind me that I must
be out patching the roof occasionally, and not be always
keeping up a blaze upon the hearth within, with my German and metaphysical cat-sticks.[3]

But my subject is not postponed *sine die*.[4] I seek a situation as teacher of a small school, or assistant in a large
one, or, what is more desirable, as private tutor in a gentleman's family.

Perhaps I should give some account of myself. I would
make education a pleasant thing both to the teacher and
the scholar. This discipline, which we allow to be the end
of life, should not be one thing in the schoolroom, and
another in the street. We should seek to be fellow students with the pupil, and we should learn of, as well as
with him, if we would be most helpful to him. But I am
not blind to the difficulties of the case; it supposes a degree of freedom which rarely exists. It hath not entered
into the heart of man[5] to conceive the full import of that
word–Freedom–not a paltry Republican freedom, with a
*posse comitatus*[6] at his heels to adminster it in doses as to
a sick child–but a freedom proportionate to the dignity of
his nature–a freedom that shall make him feel that he is
a man among men, and responsible only to that Reason
of which he is a particle, for his thoughts and his actions.

I have ever been disposed to regard the cowhide as a

nonconductor. Methinks that, unlike the electric wire, not a single spark of truth is ever transmitted through its agency to the slumbering intellect it would address. I mistake, it may teach a truth in physics, but never a truth in morals.

I shall be exceedingly grateful, if you will take the trouble to inform me of any situation of the kind described that you may hear of. As referees I could mention Mr^e Emerson–Mr Hoar–and Dr Ripley.[7]

I have perused with pleasure the first number of the 'Boston Review'. I like the spirit of independence which distinguishes it. It is high time that we knew where to look for the expression of *American* thought. It is vexatious not to know beforehand whether we shall find our account in the perusal of an article. But the doubt speedily vanishes, when we can depend upon having the genuine conclusions of a single reflecting man.[8]

Excuse this cold business letter. Please remember me to Mrs Brownson, and dont forget to make mention to the children[9] of the stern pedagogue that was–

> Sincerely and truly yours,
> Henry D. Thoreau.^e

Ps.  I add this postscript merely to ask if I wrote this formal epistle. It absolutely freezes my fingers.

*Correspondent:* Orestes Augustus Brownson (1803-1876), a self-educated Vermont native, married Sally Healy (1804-1872), daughter of John and Polly Rudes Healy of Elbridge, New York, in 1827. Originally a Presbyterian, Brownson became a Universalist minister in 1826; then he left the Universalists and served as an unaffiliated minister. In 1832 he became a Unitarian, serving first as the minister at Walpole, New Hampshire, and then at Canton, Massachusetts. T had taught school in Canton during the winter quarter of 1835-1836 and spent six weeks in Brownson's home. The two apparently studied German together. In 1836 Brownson left the Unitarians to form a Society for Christian Union and Progress; he converted to Catholicism in October 1844. In the 1830s and early 1840s Brownson was noted for the radical secular and theological politics he espoused in the journals he founded and edited, first in the *Boston Quarterly Review* and then in *Brownson's Quarterly Review*.

¹ "Day of one's life" (*Heath's New German Dictionary*, ed. Elizabeth Weir [Boston: D. C. Heath, 1888]).

² T had resigned his teaching job in Concord in September of that year, after only two weeks at the school. Nehemiah Ball, a member of the school committee, urged him to use corporal punishment to keep order in the school; after his conversation with Ball, T returned to the schoolroom and immediately feruled several students for minor infractions. He resigned that evening.

³ T may mean either a bat used in a boy's game or a short piece of kindling.

⁴ Indefinitely.

⁵ 1 Cor. 2:9: "Eye hath not seen, nor ear heard, neither have entered into the heart of man, the things which God hath prepared for them that love him."

⁶ A body of men "whom the sheriff may summon or 'raise' to repress a riot or for other purposes; also, a body of men actually so raised and commanded by the sheriff" (*OED*).

⁷ Rev. Ezra Ripley (1751-1841), minister at Concord's First Parish since November 7, 1778, was Emerson's stepgrandfather and a powerful presence in the town.

⁸ Brownson dated the first number of his *Boston Quarterly Review* January 1838 and continued its publication until October 1842, when he merged it with the *United States Magazine, and Democratic Review*. In his introduction to the first number of the *Boston Quarterly Review*, Brownson wrote, "I want it for a medium through which I may say to those who may choose to listen to my voice, just what I wish to say" (p. 4). He wrote everything in that number; it included essays on Christianity, the nature of democracy, and Locke and the Transcendentalists, as well as reviews of Emerson's Phi Beta Kappa address and of a volume of John Greenleaf Whittier's poems. Later numbers included pieces by Margaret Fuller, George Bancroft, George Ripley, and Elizabeth Peabody.

⁹ Orestes A. Brownson Jr. (1828-1892), John Healy (1829-1857), William Ignatius (1834-1864), and Henry Francis (1835-1913).

*Copy-text:* PE lines 30.28-32.20 (Concord ... was–), AL (InNd, BRO); PE lines 32.21-22 (Sincerely ... Thoreau.), *Orestes A. Brownson's Early Life* 1898, 206; PE lines 32.23-24 (Ps.... fingers.), AL (InNd, BRO)

*Published: Orestes A. Brownson's Early Life* 1898, 204-206; *Cor*

1958, 19-20; *Transcendentalists and Minerva* 1958, 1:247-248; *ESQ* 51 (1968): 53

*Editor's Notes*

This letter is addressed "Rev. O. A. Brownson. / Chelsea, / Mass." and postmarked "CONC{*illegible*} 31".

The copy-text is a composite of a manuscript source at InNd and a published source, *Orestes A. Brownson's Early Life* 1898. The closing and signature were cut from the manuscript; PE prints them as they appear in *Brownson's Early Life*.

Mr] *PE*; M{*MS torn*}
Sincerely ... Thoreau.] *MS cut*

## To David Greene Haskins

*February 9, 1838*

Concord. Feb. 9th 1838.

Dear Classmate,

I wrote to Mr Hawkins on Monday last, but not knowing the gentleman's terms, was unable to say whether I would accept or not. But since I have heard from friend Hayward[1] that you have given up all thoughts of going south, and are moreover empowered to procure a subsitute, I have thought it would be better to ascertain those terms from you, so that I might close with that gentleman at once. I do not quite understand Hayward's letter, that part at least relating to a larger school in the "building." Will you take the trouble to write me immediately, as definitely[a] as possible on this point, so that one more letter to Mr Hawkins may suffice?

Please inform me what are the expenses of the journey, and also what prospect there is of obtaining scholars.

Should you meet H–, please *thank* him for me[a] for his kind letters, and friendly exertions in my behalf, not forgetting to appropriate a share to yourself.

That you are located, in all respects, to your mind, is the wish of

your friend and classmate
Thoreau.

*Correspondent:* David Greene Haskins (1818-1896), a cousin of Emerson's, was the son of Ralph and Rebecca Greene Haskins. In 1842 he married Mary Cogswell Daveis (1820-1909), daughter of Charles S. and Elizabeth Gilman Daveis of Portland, Maine. Haskins was ordained in the Episcopal Church in 1847, following a decade of teaching. He established several parishes in the Boston area and was later dean of the Theological School at the University of the South.

[1] Charles Hayward (1817-1838), son of Charles and Ellinor Dorr Hayward, was the class orator. He studied law for a year before entering the Harvard Divinity School in 1838. He died of typhoid fever on November 5 of that year.

*Copy-text:* ALS (NjP, Robert H. Taylor Collection of English and American Literature, 1280s-1950, Series III, Box 19, Folder 32)

*Editor's Note*
This letter is addressed "Mr D. G. Haskins. / at Mr Greene's Academy, / Jamaica Plains, / Roxbury, / Mass.", postmarked "CONCORD MAS. FEB 9", and endorsed "D. H. Thoreau. / Feb 9. 1838."

*Author's Alterations*
definitely] definite
for me] *followed by cancelled* for me

## To John Thoreau Jr.
*February 10, 1838*

Dear John,

Dost expect to elicit a spark from so dull a steel as myself, by that flinty subject of thine? Surely one of your copper percussion caps would have fitted this nail head better. Unfortunately the Americana[1] has hardly two words on the subject. The process is very simple. The stone is struck with a mallet so as to produce pieces, sharp at one end, and blunt {*MS torn*} the other. These are laid upon a steel line (probably a chisel's edge) and[e] again struck with the mallet, and[e] flints of the required size are broken off. A skilful work-man[a] may make a thousand in a day. So much for the Americana. Dr. Jacob Bigelow in his Technology, says,–"Gun-flints are formed by a skilful work-man[e], who breaks them out with a hammer, a roller,

and steel chisel, with small repeated strokes."[2] Your ornithological commission shall be executed. When are you
coming home?

from aff. brother–
Henry D Thoreau

*Correspondent:* See p. 29.

[1] *Encyclopaedia Americana.*

[2] Jacob Bigelow, *Elements of Technology*, p. 12, reads, "Gun-flints
are formed by practised workmen, who break them out with a
hammer, a roller, and steel chisel, with small repeated blows." Bigelow (1786-1879) graduated from Harvard in 1806 and received
his medical degree from the University of Pennsylvania in 1810. He
practiced in Boston and taught at the Harvard Medical School. He
was also the most important botanist of his day, the first to study
Massachusetts plants systematically. His books about botany were
very influential, as were many of his lectures.

*Copy-text:* Facsimile of ALS (location of MS unknown)

*Published: FL* 1894, 20-21; *FL* 1906, 18-19; *Cor* 1958, 23

*Editor's Notes*
PE supplies the date "February 10, 1838" following *FL* 1894, p. 20;
Sanborn gives no rationale for assigning this date.
  and] *PE*; a{*MS torn*}
  and] *PE*; an{*MS torn*}
  work-man] *PE*; work- / man *in MS*

*Author's Alteration*
  work-man] work- *interlined with a caret*

## To John Thoreau Jr.
*March 17, 1838*

Concord, March 17th 1838

Dear John,

Your box of relics[1] came safe to hand, but was speedily deposited on the carpet I assure you. What could it
be? Some declared it must be Taunton herrings Just
nose it sir. So down we went onto our knees and commenced smelling in good earnest, now horizontally from

this corner to that, now perpendicularly from the carpet up, now diagonally, and finally with a sweeping movement describing the entire circumference. But it availed not. Taunton herring would not be smelled. So we e'en proceded to open it *vi et chi*sel.[2] What an array of nails! Four nails make a quarter four quarters a yard,–i faith this is'nt cloth measure. Blow away old boy, clap in another wedge, there!–there!  softly she begins to gape–  Just give that old stickler with a black hat on a hoist  Aye! he'll pare his nails for him. Well done old fellow there's a breathing hole for you  "Drive it in," cries one, "rip it off," cries another. Be easy I say. What's done, may be undone[3]  Your richest veins don't lie nearest the surface. Suppose we sit down and enjoy the prospect, for who knows but we may be disappointed? When they opened Pandora's box, all the contents escaped except hope,[4] but in this case hope is uppermost and will be the first to escape[a] when the box is opened. However the general voice was for kicking the cover-lid off.

The relics have been arranged numerically on a table. When shall we set up housekeeping[e]? Miss Ward[5] thanks you for her share of the spoils, also acept many[e] thanks from your humble servant "*for yourself*".

I have a proposal to make. Suppose by the time you are released, we should start in company for the West and there either establish a school jointly, or procure ourselves separate situations. Suppose moreover you should get reddy to start previous to leaving Taunton, to save time. Go *I* must at all events. Dr Jarvis[6] enumerated nearly a dozen schools which I could have–all such as would suit you equally well.[7] I wish you would write soon about this. It is high season to start. The Canals are now open, and travelling comparatively cheap. I think I can borrow the cash in this town. There's nothing like trying

Brigham[8] wrote you a few words on the eigth. which father[9] took the liberty to read, with the advice and consent of the family. He wishes you to send him those of the library of health[10] received since –38, if you are in Concord[a], otherwise[e], he says, you need not trouble yourself[e] about it at present. {*MS torn*} is in {*MS torn*} and enjoying better health than usual. But one number, and that you have, has been received.

The blue-birds made their appearance the 14th day of March–robins and pigeons have also been seen. Mr. E– has put up the blue-bird box in due form.[11]

All send their love. From[a]

Y'r Aff. brother

H. D. Thoreau[e]

*Correspondent:* See p. 29.

[1] T records the following in an undated entry in his Journal that covers the years from 1842 to 1844: "I have the following account of some relics in my possession which were brought from Taunton in Bristol County. Many a field which had been planted with corn for many years The sod being broken the wind began to blow away the soil and then the sand–for several years until at length it was blown away to the depth of several feet–where it ceased–  And the ground appeared strewed with the remains of an Indian village–with regular circles of stones which formed the foundation of their wigwams–and numerous implements beside" (*Journal 2: 1842-1848*, ed. Robert Sattelmeyer [Princeton, N.J.: Princeton University Press, 1984], p. 60).

[2] By underlining only the first three letters of "chisel," T possibly plays on the Greek letter "chi" and its rhyme with "vi" or, more likely, on the Latin phrase "vi et armis" ("by main force"), which has the connotation of forcibly interfering with another's goods.

[3] T plays on a proverb that can be found in a number of sources, including Shakespeare, vol. 1, *Macbeth*, 5.1.70: "What's done, cannot be undone".

[4] In Greek mythology, Pandora, the first woman, was made of clay by Vulcan and given to Prometheus to be his wife. Prometheus declined the marriage, fearing a trick by the gods, but his brother Epimetheus married her. When Epimetheus opened the box that Jupiter had given Pandora, "there issued from it a multitude of evils and distempers.... Hope was the only one who remained at the bottom of the box" (*Classical Dictionary* 1806).

[5] Prudence Ward (1795-1874) was the daughter of Joseph (1737-

1812) and Prudence Bird Ward (1765-1844). Joseph Ward, a school-teacher, had fought at Lexington in the American Revolutionary War and had been captured by the British troops. He later became a Boston businessman. Prudence and her mother were active abolitionists and helped to found the Women's Anti-Slavery Society in Concord. In 1837 they became permanent boarders at the Thoreaus.

[6] Edward Jarvis (1803-1884), a Concord native, graduated from Harvard University in 1826 and from the Harvard Medical School in 1830. He married his childhood sweetheart Almira Hunt (1804-1884) in 1834. Jarvis practiced in Louisville from 1837 to 1843, specializing in the treatment of mental illness. Long interested in vital statistics, he became a nationally known expert and was consulted on federal census enumerations.

[7] John agreed to Henry's proposal, came back to Concord, and prepared to leave for Kentucky. Henry, however, applied for a teaching position in Alexandria, Virginia, that President Quincy had described to him. John then took a job in Roxbury, Massachusetts.

[8] Brigham is probably Charles Henry Brigham (1820-1879), an 1839 Harvard graduate. He graduated from the Harvard Divinity School in 1843 and became a Unitarian minister and a scholar. Brigham published extensively on public health, among other subjects. There is, however, no known connection between him and the Thoreaus.

[9] John Thoreau Sr. (1787-1859), a pencil maker, married Cynthia Dunbar (1787-1872) in 1812.

[10] Probably the *Library of Health, and Teacher on the Human Constitution*, a Boston periodical edited by William Andrus Alcott (1798-1859), Amos Bronson Alcott's cousin, and published monthly from 1837 through 1842.

[11] In his Journal entry for April 26, T wrote a poem titled "The Bluebirds"; the first two lines read: "In the midst of the poplar that stands by our door, / We planted a bluebird box" (*Journal 1* 1981, p. 42). John had put up a bluebird nesting box for Emerson, who recalled it on January 17, 1862, in the dark early days of the Civil War: "Long ago I wrote of 'Gifts,' & neglected a capital example. John Thoreau, Jr. one day put up a bluebird's box on my barn fifteen years ago, it must be,–and there it is still with every summer a melodious family in it, adorning the place, & singing his praises. There's a gift for you which cost the giver no money, but nothing he could have bought would be so good" (*JMN*, 15:165).

*Copy-text:* ALS (CSmH, HM 7003)

*Published:*  FL 1894, 21-23; *FL* 1906, 19-22; *Life of HDT* 1917, 200; *Cor*
1958, 24-25

*Editor's Notes*

This letter is addressed "Mr. John Thoreau. / Taunton. / Mass."
and postmarked "CONCORD MAS. Mar 17".

housekeeping] *PE*; house- / keeping *in MS*

many] *PE*; may *in MS*

otherwise] *PE*; othe{*MS torn*}ise

yourself] *PE*; you{*MS torn*}lf

H. D. Thoreau] *followed in MS by postscript by Helen Thoreau to
John Thoreau Jr.:*

Dear John,

Will you have the kindness to inquire at Mr Marstons[1]
for an old singing book I left there, the Handel & Hayden
Collection[2] without a cover– Have you ever got those red
Hdks. Much love to the Marstons, Crockers[3] & Muen-
schers.[4] Mr Josiah Davis[5] has failed. Mr & Mrs Howe[6] have
both written again, urging my going to Roxbury, which
I suppose I shall do– What day of the month shall you
return?

Helen

[1] John Marston (1756-1846), son of John and Elizabeth Green-
wood Marston, was a wealthy Boston merchant and served in
the Revolutionary Army. He married Anna Randall (d. 1804) of
London in 1784. He lived in Taunton, Massachusetts, probably
with his daughter Louisa (1792-1874).

[2] Lowell Mason, *The Boston Handel and Haydn Society Collection of Church Music* (Boston: Richardson and Lord, 1822).
Which of the many editions of this book Helen owned is not
known.

[3] Three Crocker brothers lived with their families in Taunton
at this time, and it is not clear which Crocker family Helen was
referring to. William Allen Crocker (1801-1871), son of William
Augustus and Sally Ingell Crocker, graduated from Brown University in 1822 and, with his brothers, established the Taunton
Copper Manufacturing Company. In 1824 he married Frances Church Thomas (1800-1868), daughter of Isaiah and Mary
Fowle Thomas of Worcester. William's brothers were Samuel L.
Crocker (1804-1883) and George Augustus Crocker (1805-1864).
Samuel married William's sister-in-law Hannah Weld Thomas
(1803-1827) in 1825 and, following her death, married her sister

Caroline (1802-1875). George married Helen Gilchrist Gordon (1811-1897), daughter of William and Helen Gilchrist Gordon, in 1833.

⁴ William Muenscher (1796-1871) was a cashier at the Bristol County Bank. In 1820 he married Lydia Brown Monro (1802-1858), daughter of George and Elizabeth Borden Monro of Bristol, Rhode Island.

⁵ Josiah Davis (1773-1847), son of Josiah and Abigail Hubbard Davis of Concord, married Betsey Gardner Waters (1784-1847), daughter of Rev. Cornelius Waters and Sibyl Waters, in 1803. Davis began his merchant career in 1805 with his brother, Jonathan, whom he bought out in 1812. One of the donors who erected the Concord Academy building in 1822, Davis was said to have been the wealthiest man in Concord before his business failed. He moved to Boston in 1839 and kept a boarding house there.

⁶ Probably Rev. Mark Antony DeWolf Howe (1809-1895), rector of the new St. James parish in Roxbury, Massachusetts, and his wife Julia Bowen Amory Howe (1804-1841), daughter of Thomas and Elizabeth Bowen Amory. Howe taught in Boston after graduation from Brown University in 1828. He was ordained in 1832. He married in 1833, moved to St. Luke's parish in Philadelphia in 1846, and became the first bishop of the diocese of Central Pennsylvania in 1871.

*Author's Alterations*
escape] escaped
Concord] concord
From] from

## From Josiah Quincy
*April 12, 1838*

Sir.

The school is at Alexandria the students are said to be *young men* well advanced in yᵉ knowledge of yᵉ Latin & Greek Classics–the requisitions are qualification & *a person who has had experience in school keeping*–

Salary $600 a year besides washing & Boardᵃ duties to be entered on yᵉ 5ᵗʰ or 7ᵗʰ· of May.

If you choose to apply I will write as soon as I am

informed of it–[1] State to me your experience in school keeping

Ys

Josiah Quincy

Cambridge

12. April 1838.

*Correspondent:* Josiah Quincy (1772-1864), son of Josiah and Abigail Phillips Quincy, graduated from Harvard in 1790 and served as the university's president from 1829 to 1845. He had previously been a member of the U.S. Congress and the mayor of Boston. In 1797 he married Eliza Susan Morton (1773?-1850), daughter of John and Maria Kemper Morton of New Jersey.

[1] Quincy had written a generic letter of recommendation for T on March 26 (MaLiTIW, Thoreau Society Archives, Raymond Adams Collection):

*Harvard University.*

Cambridge 26. March. 1838

To whom it may concern.

I certify that Henry D. Thoreau, of Concord, in this state of Massachusetts, graduated, at this Seminary in August. 1837. that his rank was high as a scholar, in all the branches, and his morals & general conduct unexceptionable & exemplary. He is recommended as well qualified, as an instructer, for employment in any public or private school, or private family.

Josiah Quincy.

President of

Harvard University

How this letter came to T is not known: T may have picked it up from Quincy; Quincy may have mailed it to T, separately or enclosed with the April 12 letter; or Quincy may have sent it to T in Concord with someone who was traveling there. There is no address, but T endorsed the letter "Josiah Quincy".

*Copy-text:* ALS (MaLiTIW, Thoreau Society Archives, Raymond Adams Collection)

*Published:* *HDT* 1882, 61-62; *Cor* 1958, 25-26

*Editor's Note*

This letter is addressed "M[r] Henry D. Thoreau / <u>Concord</u> / Massachusetts", postmarked "CAMBRIDGE MS. APR 12", and endorsed "Josiah Quincy".

*Author's Alteration*
   & Board] of clothing

*To Henry Vose*
*May 28, 1838*

                    Concord May 28<sup>th</sup>–1838.

Dear Vose,

Concluding that you still live in, or upon, Butternuts,
I venture to direct to you, accordingly, a purely business
letter, which, you must know, is the only species of letter
writing I have at all affected for<sup>a</sup> the past winter. I have just
returned from a tour to the eastward–Old Town–Bangor,
etc. etc.–whither I had gone in search of the whereabouts
to establish myself as a furtherer of the liberal arts and
sciences,–but unfortunately discovered too late that I was
just one month behindhand<sup>a</sup>, or three months too early.[1]
If I remember aright you are to commence your studies
in the fall,[2] and will accordingly then vacate the situation
you at present occupy. If this be the case, and the gentleman you are with, wishes to employ a private tutor another year, will you<sup>a</sup> be so kind as to mention my name to
him, and as soon as may be, inform me of his intentions?
   I have passed my winter and spring very agreeably in
old Concord, devoting myself, for the most part, to the
cultivation of general literature. Hoping that you have
been and are still<sup>a</sup> situated to your mind, I remain

                    Your friend and classmate
                    Henry D. Thoreau.

Ps. The Whigs have not succeeded in electing A. H. Nelson, county treasurer, this Season,[3] though they probably
will another. Please inform me just how you are situated–
in an official and Social respect.

*Correspondent:* See p. 8.

   [1] Because he had not gotten the position in Alexandria, Virginia,
and because John was still teaching in Roxbury, Massachusetts, T

set out for Maine on May 2 on a two-week job-hunting tour. Ezra Ripley gave T a letter of recommendation and a list of clergy to visit.

[2] Vose was to study law with George T. Davis in Greenfield, Massachusetts.

[3] Albert H. Nelson's 3,498 votes fell short of the 4,433 that reelected Stedman Buttrick.

*Copy-text:* ALS (ViU, Clifton Waller Barrett Library, Henry David Thoreau Collection [#6345])

*Published: Over Thoreau's Desk: New Correspondence, 1838-1861,* ed. Kenneth Walter Cameron (Hartford, Conn.: Transcendental Books, 1965), 6

*Editor's Note*
This letter is addressed "Henry Vose, / Butternuts. / Chenango County, N. York.", postmarked "CONCORD MAS. MAY 28", and endorsed "Henry David Thoreau. / 1838."

*Author's Alterations*
for] *added in margin*
behindhand] too
you] *interlined with a caret*
are still] *interlined with a caret*

## To John Thoreau Jr.
*July 8, 1838*

Concord July 8th 38–

Dear John,

We heard from Helen today and she informs us that you are coming home by the first of August, now I wish you to write, and let me know exactly when your vacation takes place, that I may take one at the same time.[1] I am in school from 8 to 12 in the morning, and form 2 to 4 in the afternoon; after that I read a little Greek or English, or for variety, take a stroll in the fields. We have not had such a year for berries this long time–the earth is actually blue with them. High bluberries, three kinds of low–thimble and rasp-berries constitute my diet at present. (Take notice–I only diet between meals.) Among my deeds of charity I may reckon the picking of a cherry tree for two helpless single ladies who live under the hills–but i'faith it was robbing Peter to pay Paul–for while I was *exalted* in charity towards them, I had no mercy on my own stomack. Be advised, my love for currants continues. The only addition that I have made of late to my stock of Ornithological information–is in the shape, not of a Fring. Melod.[2] but surely a melodious Fringilla–the F. Juncorum,[3] or rush sparrow. I had long know him by his note but never by name. Report says that Elijah Stearns[4] is going to take the town School. I have four scholars, and one more engaged. Mr. Farrar left town yesterday. Among occurrences of ill omen, may be mentioned the falling out and cracking of the inscription stone of Concord monument. Mrs Lowell and children are at Aunt's.[5]

Peabody walked up last Wednesday–spent the night, and took a stroll in the woods. Sophia[6] says I must[e] leave off and pen a few lines for her to Helen. S Good bye. Love from all and among them yr

aff brother<br>HDT

*Correspondent:* See p. 29.

[1] John and Helen were teaching in Roxbury, Massachusetts; Henry had opened a private school in the family home.

[2] Song sparrow.

[3] Field sparrow.

[4] Elijah Wyman Stearns (1813-1896), son of Elijah and Elizabeth Stearns of Bedford, Massachusetts, graduated from Harvard in 1838, taught for several years, and then became a druggist in Bedford.

[5] T's aunt Nancy Thoreau (1789-1815) married Caleb Callender Billings (1788-1833) of Bangor, Maine, in 1810. Their first child, Mary Ann Thoreau Billings (1810-1888), married Charles Lowell (1807-1895), a Bangor merchant, in 1834. The Lowell children were Elizabeth Lowell (1835-1909) and Caleb Callender Lowell (1836-1902). The Lowells were probably staying at the home (and boarding house) of Elizabeth Thoreau (1784-1839), the oldest of T's paternal aunts.

[6] Sophia Elizabeth Thoreau (1819-1876) was the fourth child of John and Cynthia Dunbar Thoreau.

*Copy-text:* ALS (RPB, Albert Edgar Lownes Collection on Henry David Thoreau, 1837-1965, Ms. 80.1, Series 1, Box 1, Folder 1)

*Published:* FL 1894, 25-26; *T: Home* 1902, 80-81; *FL* 1906, 23-24; *Life of HDT* 1917, 203; *Cor* 1958, 27

*Editor's Notes*
    This letter is addressed "John Thoreau / West Roxbury / Mass." and postmarked "CONCORD MASS JUL 16".
    must] *PE*; mu{*MS torn*}


## To Andrew Bigelow
*October 6, 1838*

Concord Oct. 6th -38

Sir,

    I learn from my brother and sister, who were recently employed as teachers in your vicinity, that you are at present in quest of some one to fill the vacancy in your high school, occasioned by Mr. Bellows'[a] withdrawal.[1] As my present school, which consists of a small number of well advanced pupils, is not sufficiently lucrative, I am advised to make application for the situation now vacant. I was graduated at Cambridge in -37, and have since had my share of experience in schoolkeeping[e].

    I can refer you to the–President and Faculty of Harvard College–to Rev. Dr. Ripley, or Rev. R. W. Emerson–of this town, or to the parents of my present pupils, among whom I would mention–

    Hon. Samuel Hoar–Hon. John Keyes[2]–& Hon. Nathan Brooks.[3] Written recommendations by these gentlemen[e] will be procured if desired.

    If you will trouble yourself to answer this letter immediately, you will much oblige your

humble Servant,
Henry D. Thoreau

*Correspondent:* Andrew Bigelow (1795-1877), son of Timothy and Lucy Prescott Bigelow of Groton, Massachusetts, graduated from

Harvard University in 1814 and from the Harvard Divinity School in 1817. He was ordained in Cambridge in 1820 and served as minister at Taunton from 1833 to 1842. He married Amelia Sargent Stanwood (1806-1893), daughter of Theodore and Sarah Rogers Stanwood, in 1824.

[1] John Nelson Bellows (1805-1857), son of John and Betsey Eames Bellows of Boston, had served two terms as preceptor at the Bristol Academy in Taunton, Massachusetts. Bellows studied at Harvard but did not graduate. In 1833 he married Mary Nichols (1810-1887), daughter of William and Catharine Wood Nichols. He became a Unitarian minister in 1840.

[2] John Keyes (1787-1844), son of Joseph and Sarah Boyden Keyes, graduated from Dartmouth College in 1809 and became a lawyer in Concord in 1812. In 1816 he married Ann Stow Shepard (1792-1881), daughter of Timothy and Mary Stow Shepard of Boston. Keyes was the longtime county treasurer, and he served in both houses of the Massachusetts legislature.

[3] Nathan Brooks (1785-1863), son of Joshua and Martha Brooks and a prominent citizen in Concord, was born in Lincoln, Massachusetts. He graduated from Harvard in 1809, went on to study law, and in 1813 began practicing in Concord, where he lived for the rest of his life. In 1823 he married Mary Merrick (1801-1868), daughter of Tilly and Sally Merrick of Concord. Brooks was at various times a member of the Massachusetts legislature and of the Governor's Council.

*Copy-text:* Facsimile of ALS (location of MS unknown)

*Published: Cor* 1958, 656; *ARLR* 1990, 298

*Editor's Notes*
    This letter is addressed "Rev. Andrew Bigelow. / Taunton / Mass." and postmarked "CONCORD MAS. OCT 6".
    schoolkeeping] *PE*; school- / keeping *in MS*
    gentlemen] *PE*; gentle- / men *in MS*

*Author's Alteration*
    Bellows'] Biglows'

*To Helen Louisa Thoreau*
*October 6, 1838*

Concord Oct. 6<sup>th</sup> –38.

Dear Helen,

I dropped Sophia's letter into the box immediately on taking yours out, else the tone of the former had been changed.

I have no acquaintance with "Cleavelands First Lessons," though I have peeped into his abridged Grammar,[1] which I should think very well calculated for beginners, at least, for such as would be likely to wear out one book, before they would be prepared for the abstruser parts of Grammar. Ahem! As no one can tell what was the Roman pronunciation, each nation makes the Latin conform, for the most part, to the rules of its own language; so that with us, of the vowels, only å has a peculiar sound.

In the end of a word of more than one syllable, it is sounded like ah–as pennah, Lydiah Hannah, &c. without regard to case.–but da is never sounded dah because it is a monosyllable.

All terminations in es and plural cases in os, as you know, are pronounced[e] long–as homines (hominēse) dominos (dominōse) or in English Johnny Voss. For information see Adam's Latin Grammar–before the Rudiments[2] This is all law and gospel in the eyes of the world–but remember I am speaking as it were, in the third person, and should sing quite a different tune, if it were I that made the quire. However one must occasionally hang his harp on the willows, and play on the Jew's harp, in such a strange country as this.[3]

One of your young ladies wishes to study Mental Philosophy–hey?  well tell her that she has the very best text book that I know of already in her possession. If she do not believe it, then she should have bespoken a better in another world, and not have expected to find one at "Little and Wilkins."[4] But if she wishes to know how poor

an apology for a Mental Philosophy men have tacked together, synthetically or analytically, in these latter days-
how they have squeezed the infinite mind into a compass
that would not nonpluss a surveyor of Eastern Lands-
making Imagination and Memory to lie still in their respective apartments, like ink-stand and wafers in a lady's[e]
escritoire-why let her read Locke-or Stewart, or Brown.[5]
The fact is, Mental Philosophy is very like poverty-which,
you know, begins at home;[6] and, indeed, when it goes
abroad, it is poverty itself.

Chorus. I should think an abridgment of one of the
above authors, or of Abercrombie,[7] would answer her
purpose. It may set her a-thinking.

Probably there are many systems in the market of which
I am ignorant. AS for themes-say first "Miscellaneous
Thoughts"-set one up to a window to note[a] what passes
in the street, and make her comments thereon; or let her
gaze in the fire, or into a corner where there is a spider's
web, and philosophize[a]-moralize-theorize, or what not.

What their hands find to putter about, or[a] their Minds
to think about,-that let them write about.-  To say nothing of Advantages or disadvantages-of this, that, or the
other. Let them set down their ideas at any given Season-
preserving the chain of thought[e] as complete as may be[e].

This is the style pedagogical. I am much obliged to you
for your peice of[a] information. Knowing your dislike to a
sentimental letter I remain

Yr affectionate brother.<br>HDT

*Correspondent:* See p. 26.

[1] Charles Dexter Cleveland, *First Lessons in Latin*. By "his
abridged Grammar" T probably means *Adam's Latin Grammar:
With Numerous Additions and Improvements*, an expanded edition
of Alexander Adam's grammar book that Cleveland edited.

[2] At Harvard T used *Adam's Latin Grammar, with Some Improvements*. In this volume, "The Pronunciation of Latin" (pp. 9-10),

which gives rules for the placement of accents and the pronunciation of vowels, immediately precedes "The Rudiments of Latin Grammar." T draws his discussion of the "Roman pronunciation" from these two pages, particularly from the section called "Rules for the Sound of the Vowel," where two of T's examples, "penna" and "homĭnes," appear.

³ See Ps. 137:2-4: "We hanged our harps upon the willows in the midst thereof. For there they that carried us away captive required of us a song; and they that wasted us *required of us* mirth, *saying,* Sing us *one* of the songs of Zion. How shall we sing the Lord's song in a strange land?"

⁴ Charles Coffin Little (1799-1869) and John Hubbard Wilkins (1794-1861) joined the Boston bookstore of Carter, Hilliard and Company in 1821 and 1822, respectively. In 1827 the company became Hilliard, Gray and Company. Wilkins left to form his own paper-selling business in 1833; Little remained and became senior partner. He renamed the firm Charles C. Little and Company (later Little and Brown) and made it the country's leading publisher of legal works. Little was the son of David and Sarah Chase Little of Kennebunk, Maine, and in 1829 he married Sarah Ann Hilliard (1808-1848), daughter of William (Little's partner) and Sarah Lovering Hilliard. In 1854 Little married Abby Wheaton (1820-1875), daughter of Henry and Catharine Wheaton of Providence, Rhode Island. Wilkins, son of Samuel and Dorcas Towne Wilkins of Amherst, New Hampshire, graduated from Harvard in 1818. In 1826 he married Thomasine Bond Minot (1778?-1864), daughter of William and Hannah Cranch Bond. Wilkins studied for a time at the Harvard Divinity School, became a Swedenborgian, and wrote a well-regarded textbook on astronomy.

⁵ T owned a copy of John Locke's *Essay concerning Human Understanding,* which he had read at Harvard. Dugald Stewart (1753-1828) and Thomas Brown (1778-1820) were prominent Scottish Realists. T owned copies of Stewart's *Elements of the Philosophy of the Human Mind* and Brown's *Lectures on the Philosophy of the Human Mind.*

⁶ T plays on the proverb "Charity begins at home," which was current by the fourteenth century.

⁷ John Abercrombie (1780-1844) was another of the Scottish Realists. T owned a copy of his *Inquiries concerning the Intellectual Powers, and the Investigation of Truth.*

*Copy-text:* ALS (NN-BGC, Henry David Thoreau Collection, 1837-1917, Series III)

*Published:* FL 1894, 27-30; FL 1906, 25-27; Cor 1958, 28-29

*Editor's Notes*

This letter is addressed "Miss. Helen L. Thoreau, / Roxbury. / Mass." and postmarked "CONCORD MAS. OCT 6".

pronounced] *PE*; pronoun{*MS blotted*}
lady's] *PE*; lady{*MS torn*}
thought] *PE*; tho{*text obscured by sealing wax*}ht
may be] *PE*; ma{*text obscured by sealing wax*}e

*Author's Alterations*

to note] win
philosophize] philosophise
or] *preceded by erased* that
peice of] *interlined with a caret*

## *To Charles Stearns Wheeler*

*November 28, 1838*

Concord Nov. 28th 1838.

Friend Wheeler,

Does it jump with your inclinations and arrangements to read a lecture before our Lyceum on the second or third week of December?[1] Mr. Frost informs me that to such date we are supplied, and no further– So, concluding that you are[a] not lacking in bowels of compassion[2] I have ventured to indite this epistle. We must trouble you to say definitely on which, of in either of the above evenings or on any other, you will do us this favor.

If[e] you chance meet any one in the course of the winter, who is desirous to express his thoughts publicly, will you please suggest our town?

From yr. Classmate
Henry D. Thoreau
(one of the Curators)

*Correspondent:* Charles Stearns Wheeler (1816-1843), son of Charles and Julia Stearns Wheeler of Lincoln, Massachusetts, was a member of the Harvard class of 1837. He became a tutor in Greek at Harvard, published a two-volume edition of *Herodotus, from the*

*Text of Schweighaeuser with English Notes* (Boston: James Munroe, 1842), and assisted Emerson with his American edition of Carlyle's *Critical and Miscellaneous Essays*, 4 vols. (Boston: James Munroe, 1838-1839). In 1842 Wheeler went to Germany to study; he died there on June 13, 1843.

[1] On October 18, T was elected the Concord Lyceum's secretary and on November 8 he was elected curator, both for the 1839-1840 lecture season. Wheeler did not appear before the Concord Lyceum until January 23, 1839; his subject was "The Early History of the Quakers."

[2] 1 John 3:17: "But whoso hath this world's good, and seeth his brother have need, and shutteth up his bowels of *compassion* from him, how dwelleth the love of God in him?"

*Copy-text:*  Facsimile of ALS (location of MS unknown)

*Published:*  *ESQ* 48 (1967): 74; *ARLR* 1990, 12

*Editor's Notes*
This letter was offered for sale in *The Flying Quill* (Boston: Goodspeed's, 1967, item 11). The description in the sale catalog includes the following:

> A.L.S., Concord, November 28, 1838, one quarto page, with integral postmark address leaf.

If] *PE*; I *in MS*

*Author's Alteration*
are] were

## From Ralph Waldo Emerson
*February 15, 1839*

Friday, 15 Feb.

My dear Sir

The dull weather & some inflammation still hold me in the house, and so may cost you some trouble. I wrote to Miss Fuller at Groton a week ago that as soon as Saturday (tomorrow) I would endeavor to send her more accurate answers to her request for information in respect to houses likely to be let in Concord.[1] As I know that[a] she & her family must be anxious to learn the facts, as soon as may be, I beg you to help me in procuring the information today, if your engagements will leave you space for this charity.

My questions are 1. Is Dr Gallup's[2] house to be vacant shortly, &, if so, what is the rent? It belongs, I believe, to Col. Shattuck.[3] 2. What does Mrs Goodwin[4] determine in regard to the house now occupied by Mr Gourgas?[5] since, if she do not wish to apply for that house, I think that will suit Mrs F. If it is to be had, what is the rent? Col. Shattuck is also the lessor of this house. 3. What is the rent of your Aunt's house, & when will it be rentable? 4 Pray ask your father if he knows of any other houses in the village that may want tenants in the spring.

If sometime this evening you can without much inconvenience give me an answer to these queries,[6] you will greatly oblige your imprisoned friend

R. W. Emerson.

*Correspondent:* Ralph Waldo Emerson (1803-1882), son of William and Ruth Haskins Emerson of Boston, graduated from Harvard University in 1821 and taught school for several years. After study at the Harvard Divinity School, he became the minister of Boston's Second Church. He resigned that position in 1832 and moved to Concord with his second wife, Lydia (Lidian) Jackson (1802-1892). By 1839 he had established himself as a writer and lecturer and had become the central figure in the Transcendentalist movement, which came to include both T and Margaret Fuller.

[1] Sarah Margaret Fuller (1810-1850) was living with her family in Groton, Massachusetts. The Fullers had sold their farm and were looking for a new residence. The possibility of living close to Emerson was undoubtedly attractive to Fuller, but the family eventually moved to Jamaica Plain in the spring of 1840. In his February 7 letter to Fuller, Emerson said that Francis Gourgas might vacate the house he was then renting from Nathan Brooks and Daniel Shattuck, and he suggested the boarding house (originally bought by T's grandfather) that Elizabeth Thoreau ran but reported that Mrs. Thoreau called it "a damp house." Emerson also mentioned that Dr. William Gallup might leave town in the spring and thus vacate the house he was renting (*Letters of RWE* 1939, 2:181).

[2] William Gallup (1805-1883) studied medicine at Dartmouth

College and became a homeopathic doctor; he practiced for four years in Concord before moving permanently to Bangor, Maine.

[3] Daniel Shattuck (1790-1867), son of John and Betsey Miles Shattuck and a prosperous Concord grocery and dry goods store owner, branched out into banking, insurance, and real estate. In 1816 he married Sarah Edwards (1794-1859), daughter of Abraham and Rebecca Edwards. A hard-drinking, convivial man, Shattuck collected antiques and took a part in many Concord projects, including selecting inscriptions for the Battleground Monument.

[4] Amelia Mackay Goodwin (1806?-1846) married Rev. Hersey Bradford Goodwin (1805-1836), son of William and Lydia Sampson Goodwin, in 1834. Rev. Goodwin was Rev. Ezra Ripley's assistant, and Amelia was his second wife.

[5] Francis Richard Gourgas (1811-1853), son of John Mark and Peggy Sampson Gourgas, was admitted to Harvard in 1830, but he was suspended for a year for vandalizing a faculty member's room and did not graduate. He came to Concord in 1835 to edit the *Concord Freeman* and became a power in Democratic politics following his appointment in 1839 as the Concord postmaster. Gourgas served in both houses of the Massachusetts legislature. In 1836 he married Abigail P. Hastings (1817-1896), daughter of Francis and Abigail Peirce Hastings of Weston, Massachusetts. A spirited, outspoken man, Gourgas built the first indoor bathroom in Concord, loved good books and paintings, and dressed well.

[6] Apparently T got the information Emerson wanted and gave it to him, for later that same day Emerson wrote Fuller to say that Dr. Gallup was not to leave Concord, that Mrs. Goodwin had not yet decided to take the house occupied by Gourgas, that the Thoreau house, though "not very eligible," would be available April 1 for eighty dollars, and that the only other house coming on the rental market was a second one joined to the one occupied by Gourgas, which would rent for one hundred dollars (*Letters of RWE* 1939, 2:183).

*Copy-text:* ALS (MCo-SC)

*Published:* "Emerson-Thoreau Correspondence," *AM* 69 (June 1892): 751n; *Cor* 1958, 32; *Letters of RWE* 1990-1995, 7:331-332

*Editor's Notes*
   This letter is addressed "Mr Henry D. Thoreau."
   The copy-text is tipped into volume 1 of Alfred W. Hosmer's grangerized copy of Henry S. Salt's *Life of Henry David Thoreau*, 2nd ed. (London: Walter Scott, 1896), at page 42.

PE supplies the year "1839" from the contents of Emerson's February 15, 1839, letter to Fuller about available houses in Concord (*Letters of RWE* 1939, 2:183-184). In the manuscript "1840" was added in a hand other than Emerson's, possibly that of Sanborn, who misdated the letter in "Emerson-Thoreau Correspondence."

*Author's Alteration*
    that] *interlined with a caret*


## To Charles Stearns Wheeler
*January 3, 1840*

                                    Concord Jan. 3ᵈ 1840.
Friend Wheeler–

Can you by hook or by crook come and lecture for us next Wednesday evening?ᵃ⁻¹ Weᵃ begin absolutely to doubt the march of intellect, such a dearth is there in this neighborhood.

Ifᵉ you cannot come, will you disclose this *rare opportunity* of making one's début in literature to any *clever* person of your acquaintance?ᵃ–say Dana–or Clarke–or Morison²–Whomᵃ I know to be such–or any new lights that may have arisen.

We only pay one's expenses. i.e. $4.00?ᵃ Greenough is to come week after next,³ and Dr. Follen, will commence his course on Switzerland after him.⁴ Now I think of it–Wish you happy new year! You will oblige us by answering this as soon as convenient.

                                                    Yrs
                                        &c Henry D. Thoreau

*Correspondent:* See pp. 51-52.

¹ Thomas Dawes, not Wheeler, lectured at the Concord Lyceum on January 8 (see p. 57, note 1).

² Horace Morison was a member of the class of 1837, as were Richard Henry Dana and Manlius Stimson Clarke. Morison (1810-1870), son of Nathaniel and Mary Ann Hopkins Morison of Peterborough, New Hampshire, married Mary Elizabeth Lord (b. 1817), daughter of Samuel and Nancy McClary Lord, in 1841. He taught

at the University of Maryland, then a mediocre school perpetually in turmoil, and served as dean of the undergraduate college from 1841 until his resignation in 1854. He was an unpopular dean and was forced from the position after being accused of using college property for his own gain.

[3] William Whitwell Greenough (1818-1899), son of William and Sarah Gardner Greenough of Boston, was another classmate of T's. He gave up plans to be a teacher of languages in order to enter his father's hardware business. In 1841 he married Catherine Scollay Curtis (1820-1899), daughter of Charles Pelham and Anna Scollay Curtis of Boston. Greenough later took charge of the Boston Gaslight Company. He belonged to the American Oriental Society of Boston, the Société Orientale of Paris, and the Massachusetts Historical Society, and he served as a trustee and, for twenty-two years, president of the Boston Public Library. The lecture he gave on January 15 was "The Life and Writings of Sir Philip Sidney."

[4] A German refugee and an ardent abolitionist, Dr. Charles Follen (1796-1840) taught German at Harvard from 1825 to 1835. In 1828 he married Eliza Lee Cabot (1787-1860), a writer and reformer. Follen's lecture series was scheduled to begin on January 22, but, returning home on January 13 after lecturing in New York City, he was killed when the steamboat *Lexington* caught fire and burned (see p. 61, note 5).

*Copy-text:* ALS (NjP, Robert H. Taylor Collection of English and American Literature, 1280s-1950, Series III, Box 19, Folder 34)

*Published:* *ESQ* 48 (1967): 75; *ARLR* 1990, 13

*Editor's Notes*
    This letter is addressed "Mr. Charles S. Wheeler / Cambridge / Mass." and postmarked "CONCORD MA{*illegible*} JAN 3".
    If] *PE*; I *in MS*

*Author's Alterations*
    evening?] ? *inserted*
    We] we
    acquaintance?] ? *inserted*
    Whom] whom
    $4.00?] ? *inserted*

*From Charles Stearns Wheeler*
*January 6, 1840*

Cambridge, Jan. 6th, 1840.

Dear Thoreau,

I have the pleasure of informing you that in my inability to come up to Concord next Wednesday evening, I have secured a lecture to you from Dawes,[1] of the Divinity School, who has had some experience in that line, and who I make no doubt will please your good people. My engagements for that evg. are such that I cannot be with you, nor if they were otherwise[a] have I[a] a lecture prepared, or time to write one. Clarke and Dall are also unable[e] to write a lecture in so short a time. Dawes has one which he will give, and so my commission is happily discharged. I should be happy to come to Concord to lecture, and will hope to be able to come at some future time.

Wishing you many happy new Years and happy retrospects of old ones, and desiring to be remembered to my Concord friends,

I am truly your friend and Classmate,

C. S. Wheeler.

*Correspondent:* See pp. 51-52.

[1] Thomas Dawes (1818-1904), son of Thomas and Eliza Cunningham Dawes of Baltimore, graduated from Harvard University in 1839 and from the Harvard Divinity School in 1842. He was ordained at Fairhaven, Massachusetts, in 1844. In 1845 he married Lydia Ames Sawin (1823-1892), daughter of Ezekiel and Martha Dunn Sawin of Fairhaven. Dawes's topic on January 8 was "Elocution."

*Copy-text:* ALS (Sewall)

*Editor's Notes*

This letter is addressed "Mr. H. D. Thoreau, / Concord / Mass.", postmarked "CAMBRIDGE Ms. JAN 7", and endorsed "C. S. Wheeler."

unable] *PE*; {*text obscured by sealing wax*}nable

*Author's Alterations*
  otherwise] at
  I] *inserted*

*To Helen Louisa Thoreau and Sophia Elizabeth Thoreau*
*January 23, 1840*

Concordiae, Dec. Kal. Feb. Æ. MDCCCXL.[1]

Care Soror,

Est magnus acervus nivis ad limina, et frigus intolera-
bile intus. Coelum ipsum ruit, credo, et terram operit.
Sero stratum linquo et maturè repeto; in fenestris multa
pruina prospectum absumit, et hîc miser scribo, non
currente calamo, nam digiti mentesque torpescunt. Ca-
nerem cum Horatio, si vox non faucibus haeserit–

"Vides, ut altâ stet nive candidum
*Nawshawtuct*, nec jam sustineant onus
  Silvae laborantes, geluque
    Flumina constiterint acuto?
Dissolve frigus, ligna super foco
Large reponens; etc."[2]

Sed olim, Musâ mutatâ, et laetiore plectro,

–"neque jam stabulis gaudet pecus, aut arator igni,
  Nec prata canis albicant pruinis,
  Jam Cytherea choros ducit Venus, imminente lunâ;"[3]

Quum turdus ferrugineus ver reduxerit, tu, spero,
linques curas scholasticas, et negotio religato, desiperc
in loco audebis, aut mecum inter inter sylvas, aut super
scopulos Pulchri-Portus, aut in cymba super lacum
Waldensem, mulcens fluctus manu, aut speciem miratus
sub undas.

Bulwerius[4] est mihi nomen incognitum, unus ex ig-
nobili vulgo, nec refutandus nec laudandus. Certe alicui
nonnullam honorem habeo qui insanabile Cacoêthe[a]
scribendi teneatur.

Species flagrantis Lexingtonis non somnia detur-
bat?[5] At non Vulcanum Neptunumque culpemus cum

superstitioso grege. Natura curat animalculis aequê ac hominibus; cum serena, tum procellosa amica est.

Si amas historiam et fortia facta heroûm non depone Rollin,[6] precor, ne Clio[7] offendas nunc, nec illa det veniam olim.

Quos libros Latinos legis? legis, inquam, non studis. Beatus qui potest suos libellos tractare et saepe perlegere sine metu domini urgentis!  ab otio injurioso procul est; suos amicos et vocare et dimittere quandocunque velit potest. Bonus liber opus est nobilissimum hominis![8] Hinc ratio non modo cur legeres sed cur tu quoque scriberes. Nec lectores carent; ego sum. Si non librum meditaris, libellum certê. Nihil posteris proderit te spirâsse et vitam nunc lenîter nunc asperê egisse, sed cogitâsse praecipue et scripsisse.

Vereor ne tibi pertaesum hujus epistolae sit; necnon alma lux caret,

"Majoresque cadunt altis de montibus umbrae."[9]

Quamobrem vale, imô valete, et requiescatis placidê Sorores.[10]

H. D. Thoreaus.

Memento Scribere.[e]


Concord, January 23, 1840[1]

Dear Sister,

There is a huge snowdrift at the doorstep, and the cold inside is intolerable. The sky itself is falling down, I think, and covers up the earth. I get out of bed late and return early; the thick frost on the windows covers up the view, and I write here in pain, with a pen that doesn't work, since both my fingers and my mind are numb. I would sing like Horace, if my voice did not stick in my throat–

"Do you see how *Nawshawtuct*,
Deep in snow, stand shining,
And the laboring woods,
Scarce bear their burden,

And the streams lie frozen, with
Sharp cold? Dissolve the cold,
Putting firewood freely on the hearth, etc."[2]

But soon, with a change of Muse, and in a happier vein
–"no longer does the flock rejoice in
Its stall, or the ploughman by his fire,
No more are the meadows white with hoary frost
For Cytherean Venus leads her chorus,
Under the hanging moon."[3]

When Robin Redbreast brings back the Spring, you, I hope, will lay aside your academic cares, and having settled all your business, will dare to play the fool when the occasion warrants, either with me in the woods, or upon the Fairhaven crags, or in my boat on Walden pond, caressing the flowing waters with your hand, or wondering at the spectacle below the waves.

Bulwer[4] is to me a name unknown, one of the ignoble crowd, neither to be reproved nor praised. To be sure, I have not a little honor for anyone who is held by the incurable passion for writing.

Doesn't the sight of the Lexington fire trouble your dreams?[5] But we may not blame Vulcan and Neptune like the superstitious herd. Nature cares as much for animals as for men; she is both a fair weather and a stormy friend.

If you like history and the brave deeds of heroes, do not put aside Rollin,[6] I beg of you, lest you offend Clio[7] now, and she not forgive you sometime in the future. What Latin books do you read? "Do you read," I say, not "Do you study." Happy the man who can take down his books and read them often, without the fear of an overbearing master! He is far from harmful idleness. He can call and dismiss his friends whenever he wishes. A good book is the noblest work of man.[8] Hence there is a reason not only why you should read, but also why you should write as well. Readers aren't lacking: I am one. If you cannot prepare a book, then surely a tract. It will of no profit to posterity that you have taken breath and passed life, now smoothly, now roughly, but to have thought and written outstandingly.

I fear lest you may become weary of this letter; moreover sweet light is lacking:

"And longer shadows fall beneath the tall hills."[9]

So farewell, indeed to both of you, and rest peacefully, my sisters.[10]

H. D. Thoreau

Remember to write.

(Translation by K. P. Van Anglen, with Robert Morstein-Marx)

*Correspondent:* See pp. 26 and 172.

[1] "Dec. Kal." means ten days from the first day of the next month, in this case February. The phrase can be construed in two different ways. The tenth day counting backwards starting on February 1 gives January 23; if T meant that there are ten days between the present day and February 1, then the letter would be dated January 21. PE follows *FL* 1894, p. 30, in choosing the first alternative.

[2] Horace, vol. 1, *Odes*, 1.9.1-6.

[3] Horace, vol. 1, *Odes*, 1.4.3-5.

[4] Edward George Bulwer-Lytton (1803-1873), a popular novelist, had by this time published a dozen novels, many of them based on historical themes.

[5] The steamboat *Lexington*, bound from New York for Stonington, Connecticut, caught fire on Long Island Sound on the evening of January 13, 1840. The wooden vessel burned, and it sank around 3:00 the following morning. T might have seen a version of Nathaniel Currier's "Awful Conflagration of the Steam Boat *Lexington*," originally published in the *New York Sun* on January 16, headed "The Extra Sun." Many copies of the extra were printed, and copies were shipped to other cities.

[6] At Harvard, T had checked out all eight volumes of Charles Rollin's *The Ancient History of the Egyptians, Carthaginians, Assyrians, Babylonians, Medes and Persians, Macedonians, and Grecians*. He later owned a copy of a four-volume edition of this work published in New York in 1837.

[7] Clio, the muse of history, whose office was "faithfully to record the actions of brave and illustrious heroes" (*Classical Dictionary* 1806).

[8] T plays on a line in Pope's *Essay on Man*, 4.248 (*Poetical Works*, vol. 1, p. 69): "An honest man's the noblest work of God."

[9] Virgil, *Eclogues*, 1.82-83.

[10] Helen and Sophia were living and teaching in Roxbury.

*Copy-text:* ALS (NNPM, MA 920)

*Published: Boston Advertiser* (August 3, 1882); *Boston Traveller* (August 3, 1882); *Boston Evening Transcript* (August 4, 1882); "Thoreau's Manuscripts" 1883, 125; *FL* 1894, 30-35; *T: Home* 1902, 46-47; *FL* 1906, 27-31; *Cor* 1958, 35-38; *Concord Harvest* 1970, 67; *Response to Transcendental Concord* 1974, 234, 236, 237-238; *ARLR* 1988, 54, 55, 56

*Editor's Notes*

This letter is addressed "Ad Helenam L. Thoreau / Roxbury / Mass." and postmarked "CONCORD {*illegible*}S JAN {*illegible*}."

Four lines of pencilled text, written in an unknown hand, appear vertically in the left margin of page 3 of the letter:

It is by stealth th[a]t I write a word for Th[o' not willing] {*MS torn*} [  h          ] was giving yo{*MS torn*} [  ]eal [          ] I expect it [wi]ll {*MS torn*} [                    ] to find [   ] {*MS torn*} [central], and that it is not {*MS torn*} [                    ] Do let me h{*MS torn*} from you immediately

Scribere.] *followed in MS by a horizontal line and a postscript by Cynthia Dunbar Thoreau to Sophia Thoreau, in T's hand (MS is torn; missing portions, enclosed in brackets, are taken from FL 1894, pp. 32-33):*

Care Sophia,

Samuel Niger[1] crebris aegrotationibus, quae agilitatem et aequum animum abstulere, obnoxious est; iis temporibus ad cellam descendit et [multas horas (ibi) manet.

Flores, ah crudelis pruina! parvo leti discrimine sunt. Cactus frigore ustus est, gerania vero adhuc vigent.

Conventus sociabiles hac hieme reinstituti fuere. Conveniunt (?) ad meum domum mense quarto vel quinto, ut tu hic esse possis. Matertera Sophia[2] cum nobis remanet; quando urbem revertet non scio. Gravedine etiamnum, sed non tam aegre, laboramus.]

Adolescentula E. White apud pagum paulisper moratur. Memento scribere intra duas hebdomedas.

Te valere desiderium est
Tui Matris C. Thoreaus.[3]

Amanuense, H. D. T.

[P. S. Epistolam die solis proxima expectamus.]

Dear Sophia,

Sam Black[1] is liable to frequent illnesses, which take away his agility and good nature. At such times he goes down to the cellar and [stays there for many hours.

The flowers–oh the cruel frost!–are little more than dead. The cactus has been burnt by cold but the geraniums still flourish.

Social circles have started up again this winter. They meet (?) at my house in April or May, so you may be able to be here. Aunt Sophia[2] stays with us; when she will return to the city I don't know. We still suffer from head colds, but not so badly as before].

Young Miss E. White remains in the country a bit longer. Remember to write within two weeks.

> That you may be well is the desire
> Of your mother, C. Thoreau.[3]

By the hand of H. D. T.

[P. S. We expect a letter next Sunday.]

(Translation by K. P. Van Anglen)

[1] The Thoreaus' cat.

[2] Sophia Dunbar (1781-1868), daughter of Asa and Mary Jones Dunbar, married Luther Lapham in 1805.

[3] Cynthia Dunbar (1787-1872), daughter of Asa and Mary Jones Dunbar, married John Thoreau Sr. (1787-1859), son of John and Jane Burns Thoreau of Boston, in 1812.

*Author's Alteration*

Cacoêthe] Cacoëthe

## To Charles Stearns Wheeler
*March 2, 1840*

Concord March 2nd 1840.

Friend Wheeler,

As Mr. Emerson will probably go to Providence after returning from New York, at least one week more than was expected will intervene before he will lecture here[1]– nevertheless we venture to propose to you the eleventh inst.[2]–which may not after all be earlier than you had expected–and if that evening suits will not expect any answer.

I shall be happy to see you, and any of your friends, should they accompany you, at our house.

Yrs. &c<br>Henry D. Thoreau

*Correspondent:* See pp. 51-52.

[1] T was trying to solidify his roster for the lecture season. Emerson was deep into his new lecture series "The Present Age," which he first read in Boston between December 4, 1839, and February 12, 1840. Emerson then delivered an introduction to the course at Concord on March 4. He went to New York City on March 8 and read three lectures there between March 10 and March 17 before going to Providence, Rhode Island, where he read six lectures at the Franklin Lyceum between March 20 and April 1. Emerson returned home to close the Concord season with eight lectures delivered between April 8 and May 6.

[2] Wheeler lectured on March 18, rather than on March 11, on "The Mythology of the Greeks."

*Copy-text:* Facsimile of ALS (location of MS unknown)

*Published: ESQ* 48 (1967): 75; *ARLR* 1990, 14

*Editor's Note*
This letter is addressed "Mr. Charles S. Wheeler / Cambridge / Mass." and postmarked "CONCORD MAS. MAR 2".

## From Charles Stearns Wheeler

*March 4, 1840*

Wed. Evg.

Dear Thoreau,

On looking over the list of my duties for the next three weeks I find it[a] will suit me about fifty per cent better to come to Concord[a] on the 18th than on the 11th of March. Unless then I hear to the contrary, I will ride up and preach you a sermon on the 18th inst.

Yours, truly, and in haste,<br>C. S. Wheeler.

*Correspondent:* See pp. 51-52.

*Copy-text:* ALS (Sewall)

*Editor's Notes*
This letter is addressed "Mr. David Henry Thoreau, / Concord, / Mass.", postmarked "CAMBRIDGE Ms MAR 5", and endorsed "C. S. Wheeler".

PE supplies the date "March 4, 1840" assuming that Wheeler answered T on the Wednesday following T's Monday, March 2, 1840, letter to him.

*Author's Alterations*
it] I
to Concord] *interlined with a caret*

## To David Greene Haskins
*April 6, 1840*

Concord Ap. 6th 1840

Dear Haskins,

I improve this the first opportunity of sending your cloak by the Accommodation Stage.[1]

I hope that the next time you visit Concord Nature will postpone her snow-storms, and, if you have a lecture in your pocket, the Lyceum be in a situation to pay somewhat in proportion to the value received.

Yrs &c.
Henry D. Thoreau

*Correspondent:* See p. 35.

[1] The Concord Accommodation Stage made the seven-hour trip between Concord and 11 Elm Street, Boston, each day.

*Copy-text:* Facsimile of ALS (location of MS unknown)

*Editor's Notes*
This letter is addressed "Mr. D. G. Haskins".

The letter was offered for sale in *Paul C. Richards Autographs Catalogue 141* (Templeton, Mass.: Paul C. Richards, n.d., item 79); the description in the sale catalog includes the following:

Autograph Letter Signed. 1p., 4to. Concord, April 6, 1840. Addressed on the verso to Mr. D. G. Haskins.

*To Helen Louisa Thoreau*
*June 13, 1840*

Concord June 13.<sup>th</sup> 1840,

Dear Helen,

That letter to John, for which you had an opportunity doubtless to substitute a more perfect communication, fell, as was natural, into the hands of his "transcendental brother", who is his proxy in such cases, having been commissioned to acknowledge and receipt all bills that may be presented {*MS torn*} But what's in a name?[1] Perhaps it does not matter whether it be John or Henry. Nor will those same six months have to be altered, I fear, to suit his case as well:–but methink they have not passed entirely without intercourse, provided we have been sincere though humble worshippers of the same Virtue in the meantime. Certainly it is better that we should make ourselves quite sure of such a communion as this, by the only course which is completely free from suspicion–the coincidence of two earnest and aspiring lives–than run the risk of a disapointment by relying wholly or chiefly on so meagre and uncertain a means as speech–whether written or spoken affords. How often when we have been nearest each other bodily, have we really been farthest[a] off. Our tongues were the withy[2] foils with which we fenced each other off. Not that we have not met heartily and with profit as members of one family–but it was a small one surely–and not that other human family. We have met frankly and without concealment ever, as befits those who have an instinctive trust in one another–and the Scenery of whose outward lives has been the same, but never as prompted by an earnest and affectionate desire to probe deeper our mutual natures. Such intercourse, at least, if it has ever been, has not condescended to the vulgarities of oral communication, for the ears are provided with no lid, as the eye is, and would not have been deaf to it in sleep. And now glad am I if I am not

mistaken in imagining that some such transcendental in-
quisitiveness has travelled post *thither*–for as I observed
before, where the bolt hits, thither was it aimed–any[a] ar-
bitrary direction notwithstanding.

Thus much at least our *kindred* temperament of mind
and body–and long *family*-arity–have done for us, that
we already find ourselves standing on a solid and natural
footing with respect to one another, and shall not have to
waste time in the so often unavailing endeavor to arrive
fairly at this simple ground. Let us leave trifles then to accident, and politics, and finance, and such gossip, to the
moments when diet and exercise are cared for, and speak
to each other deliberately as out of one infinity into another–you there in time and space, and I here. For beside
this relation all books and doctrines are no better than
gossip, or the turning of a spit.

Equally to you and Sophia–from

Yr aff. brother H. D. Thoreau

*Correspondent:* See p. 26.

[1] T quotes Shakespeare, vol. 2, *Romeo and Juliet*, 2.2.42-43.
[2] "Flexible and tough" (*Webster*).

*Copy-text:* ALS (ViU, Clifton Waller Barrett Library, Henry David
Thoreau Collection [#6345])

*Published: LVP* 1865, 1-3; *FL* 1894, 37-39; *FL* 1906, 32-34; *Cor* 1958,
39-40

*Editor's Note*
This letter is addressed "Miss. Helen L. Thoreau / Roxbury /
Mass." and postmarked "Concord MS June 13".

*Author's Alterations*
farthest] furthest
any] and

*To Unknown Recipient*
*June 20, 1840*

Concord June 20th 1840.

Dear Sir,

I have made inquiry of sundry songlovers and song-wrights in the neighborhood, with a view to your pro-posals, with what result, favorable or unfavorable, will appear. Mr Wood[1] pronounces in his cool–experienced way that the scholars will not be forthcoming–for why? The town or parish contemplate a school the next winter which shall be public, and open equally to old and young–learned and unlearned. The people, he says, have been accustomed to look to the parish for these[a] things,[2] and to them a dollar ever[e] has lost some of its weight when it has passed once through the assessor's hands.

Mr Whiting,[3] the Superintendent of the sabbath school, affirms that there are whole platoons of children, whom the parish would be glad to have in a condition to do sing-ing, but have never yet accomplished the thing by voting it, or once correctly pitching the tune. So he stands ready to render smooth official assistance by public notice to the school–and the like.

But of what avail all this ballancing of reasons–depend upon it nothing good was ever done in accordance with, but rather in direct opposition to–advice. Have you not the sympathy of parish votes–that it will have singing? Or rather have you you not the assurance of your own reso-lution that you will give it them at any rate?

Mr. Wood then, who more than any man has gaged all throats–Juvenile and senile–in the vicinity–raises the cold water bucket.

Mr. Whiting–and Nelson[4]–and others rely mainly on the incalculable force there is in a man–who was[e] sternly resolved to do what is in him to do,–the phial of laud-num–and nodding poppy–and Concord river running nine times round[5]–to the contrary notwithstanding.

At present I read in the faces of the children[e] neither encouragement nor discouragement they having had no hint of the future.

Yrs to command

Henry D. Thoreau

[1] Elijah Wood (1790-1861), son of Daniel and Hannah Barrett Wood of Concord, was a farmer and a shoemaker. Wood had two marriages, first to Elizabeth Farmer (1795-1843) in 1815 and then to Lucy Barrett (1792-1869), daughter of Benjamin and Sarah Chamberlin Barrett of Carlisle, Massachusetts, in 1844. Concord's singing master, he frequently conducted singing schools in town and was in charge of singing at the First Parish from 1808 to 1851. Wood was elected deacon of the parish on April 29, 1841, a post he held until his death.

[2] The Concord First Parish supported public singing of sacred music through a singing fund that originated in a bequest from Abigail Dudley in 1814. The town had long supported singing schools, which were created every two or three years. The groups, made up of both men and women, young and old, met at the schoolhouse throughout the winter. On November 3, 1840, the Concord selectmen voted to appropriate one hundred dollars for a singing school for that season and appointed Wood and two others to create the group.

[3] William Whiting (1788-1862), son of William and Rebecca Brown Whiting of Sterling, Massachusetts, moved to Concord as a youth and became a prosperous carriage maker. In 1811 Whiting married Hannah Conant (1788-1859), daughter of Lot and Hannah Johnson Conant. He was one of the original proprietors of the Concord Academy and a consistent supporter of the Concord Lyceum. A temperance advocate and a Garrisonian abolitionist, Whiting held office in both the Middlesex and Massachusetts antislavery societies.

[4] Albert H. Nelson.

[5] T had associated the slowness of the Concord River with the dullness of the townspeople at least since 1837, when he wrote in his Journal that one could not tell "how much of the proverbial moderation of the inhabitants was caught from its dull circulation" (*Journal 1* 1981, p. 12). A version of this Journal passage appears in the opening chapter of *A Week on the Concord and Merrimack Rivers*, where T writes, "It has been proposed, that the town should adopt for its coat of arms a field verdant, with the Concord circling

nine times round" (*A Week* 1980, p. 9). In this letter T alludes to the river Styx, which is said to flow nine times around hell and whose waters, when drunk (as punishment) by gods who perjured themselves, "lulled them for one whole year into a senseless stupidity" (*Classical Dictionary* 1806).

*Copy-text:*  ALS (MHi, Grenville H. Norcross Autograph Collection)

*Published:*  *Cor* 1958, 40-41

*Editor's Notes*
    ever] *PE*; *possibly* even *in MS*
    was] *PE*; *possibly* has *in MS*
    children] *PE*; childr{*MS torn*}

*Author's Alteration*
    these] this


## From Margaret Fuller
*December 1, 1840*

1ˢᵗ Decʳ.

I am to blame for so long detaining your manuscript.[1] But my thoughts have been so engaged that I have not found a suitable hour to reread it as I wished till last night. This second reading only confirms my impression from the first. The essay is rich in thoughts, and I should be *pained* not to meet it again. But then[a] the thoughts seem to me so out of their natural order, that I cannot read it through without *pain*. I never once feel myself in a stream of thought, but seem to hear the grating of tools on the mosaic. It is true as Mr E. says, that essays not to be compared with this have found their way into the Dial. But then those are more unassuming in their tone, and have an air of quiet good-breeding which induces us to permit their presence. Yours is so rugged that it ought to be commanding. Yet I hope you will give it me again, and if you see no force in my objections disregard them.

S. M. Fuller.

*Correspondent:* Sarah Margaret Fuller (1810-1850), daughter of Timothy and Margarett Crane Fuller, served as the first editor of the *Dial* during 1840-1842. A literary critic and translator of Johann Eckermann's *Conversations with Goethe* (Boston: Hilliard, Gray, and Company, 1839), Fuller later wrote the influential *Woman in the Nineteenth Century* (New York: Greeley and McElrath, 1845). In 1844, Fuller moved to New York City to be the review editor for Horace Greeley's *New-York Daily Tribune*. She left the city in 1846 and traveled in Europe. In Rome she met and married Giovanni Angelo Ossoli (1821-1850), son of a noble family in the papal service. The Ossolis took part in the Italian Revolution of 1848-1849, joining the ranks of the Roman revolutionaries in 1849 when the French attacked the city. After the defeat of the Roman Republic, they fled to Florence and then sailed to the United States, where Fuller planned to resume her writing career. Fuller may have been the model for the woman T describes in *A Week on the Concord and Merrimack Rivers*, "who possesses a restless and intelligent mind, interested in her own culture, and earnest to enjoy the highest possible advantages" (*A Week* 1980, p. 279).

[1] Though Fuller had published T's "Aulus Persius Flaccus" in the first number of the *Dial* (July 1840, pp. 117-121), she rejected "The Service," which was not published during T's lifetime (see *Early Essays* 1975, pp. 122-127, and *Reform Papers* 1973, pp. 3-17). Fuller did publish a total of four of T's poems: "Sympathy" in *Dial* 1 (July 1840): 71-72; "Stanzas" in *Dial* 1 (January 1841): 314; "Sic Vita" in *Dial* 2 (July 1841): 81-82; and "Friendship" in *Dial* 2 (October 1841): 204-205. See *Collected Poems* 1964, pp. 64-66 ("Lately, alas, I knew a gentle boy"), p. 70 ("Nature doth have her dawn each day"), pp. 81-82 ("I am a parcel of vain strivings tied"), and pp. 71-73 ("Let such pure hate still underprop").

*Copy-text:* ALS (NNPM, MA 607)

*Published:* *HDT* 1882, 172-173; *Life of HDT* 1917, 279-280; Elizabeth Derring Hanscom, *The Friendly Craft* (New York: Macmillan, 1908), 196; *Cor* 1958, 41-42; *Transcendentalists and Minerva* 1958, 3:957-958; *Letters of Margaret Fuller*, 2:185; *"My Heart Is a Large Kingdom": Selected Letters of Margaret Fuller*, ed. Robert N. Hudspeth (Ithaca, N.Y.: Cornell University Press, 2001), 133

*Editor's Notes*
This letter is addressed "H. D. Thoreau." and endorsed "S. M. Fuller."
PE supplies the year "1840" from the contents of the letter.

*Author's Alteration*
then] *interlined with a caret*

*To Cyrus Stow*
*January 6, 1841*

Concord Jan 6th 1841

Mr Clerk
Sir

I do not wish to be considered a member of the First Parish in this town.[1]

Henry. D. Thoreau.

*Correspondent:* Cyrus Stow (1787-1876), son of Nathan and Abigail Merriam Stow of Concord, was elected town clerk on March 2, 1840, and served until 1848. A leading Concord Democrat, he had already served as a selectman and an assessor, and he had represented the town in the state legislature from 1835 to 1836. In 1843 he married Matilda Wyman (1803?-1878), daughter of John and Elizabeth Miles Wyman. With his brother Nathan, Cyrus owned a butcher shop and a candle factory. In the early 1820s he had gone into business with T's uncle, Charles Dunbar, to develop a plumbago mine. They were, however, unable to take ownership of a profitable mine they discovered because they failed to secure the title.

[1] By resigning from the First Parish, T freed himself of the obligation to support it financially. The church had added his name to the tax roll in 1840.

*Copy-text:* ALS (MCo-SC, First Parish in Concord Records, 1695-1994, Series V, Box 8, Folder 1)

*Published:* TSB 120 (summer 1972): 7

*Editor's Note*
This letter is endorsed "Certificate / H. D. Thoreau / Jany–6 1841."


*To Samuel Gridley Howe*
*March 9, 1841*

Concord March 9th 1841.

Sir,

I observed in your paper of March 5th an advertisement for an Asssistant Teacher in a Public Institution &c"– As I expect to be released from my engagements here in a fortnight, I should be glad to hear further of the above–if the vacancy is not already filled.[1]

I was graduated at Cambridge in '37, previous to which date I had had some experience in school-keeping–and have since been constantly engaged as an instructor–for the first year, as principal of the Academy[a] here, and for the last two, as superintendant of the classical department alone.

I refer you to Samuel Hoar esq., Rev. R. W. Emerson, or Dr. Josiah Bartlett,[2] of this town, or to Pre[st] Quincy of Harvard University.

Yrs. respectfully<br>Henry D. Thoreau

*Correspondent:* Samuel Gridley Howe (1801-1876) graduated from Brown University in 1821 and received his medical degree from Harvard in 1824. He then went to Greece and joined the Greek independence movement as a soldier and doctor. He returned to Boston after six years in Greece and in 1831 opened the Perkins School for the Blind, which he directed for the next forty years. In 1843 Howe married the New York poet Julia Ward (1819-1910), daughter of Samuel and Julie Rush Ward, who later became known as the author of the lyrics to the "Battle Hymn of the Republic." Always active in social movements, Howe joined forces with Dorothea Dix in fighting for humanitarian care of the mentally ill and with Horace Mann for school improvement. He was a prominent supporter of John Brown and a member of the "secret six," a group of men who funded the ill-fated raid on Harpers Ferry in 1859.

[1] The Thoreau brothers closed their school on April 1. Both were in frail health, although Henry soon recovered. John left for a trip to New Hampshire, and Henry, failing to gain a place with Howe, made plans to buy a farm on the Sudbury River. The purchase fell through when the owner backed out, claiming that his wife had changed her mind.

[2] Josiah Bartlett (1797-1878), son of Dr. Josiah Bartlett and Elizabeth Call Bartlett of Charlestown, Massachusetts, graduated from Harvard University in 1816 and from the Harvard Medical School in 1819. He moved to Concord in 1820 and married Martha Tilden Bradford (1799-1860), daughter of Gamaliel and Elizabeth Hickling Bradford, the following year. An outspoken man of strong beliefs, Dr. Bartlett was an active member of the Underground Railroad and a temperance advocate. He also took part in many town affairs and was an accomplished historian.

*Copy-text:* ALS (MWatP, Letters 1840 to 1841, p. 189)

*Published: The Lantern* (Watertown, Mass.: Perkins School for the Blind) 29 (March 15, 1960): 2

*Editor's Note*
The copy-text is bound in a volume of Perkins School correspondence.

*Author's Alteration*
Academy] academy

## From Ralph Waldo Emerson

*June 3, 1841*

My dear Henry

We have here G. P. Bradford, R Bartlett, Lippitt C S Wheeler & Mr Alcott.[1] Will you not come down & spend an hour?–

Yours<br>R. W. E.

Thursday. P. M.

*Correspondent:* See p. 53.

[1] George Partridge Bradford (1807-1890), son of Gamaliel and Elizabeth Hickling Bradford, was a descendant of Gov. William Bradford and of John Alden. Bradford graduated from Harvard University in 1825 and from the Harvard Divinity School in 1828. He became a schoolteacher and an accomplished naturalist. He and Emerson, already friends, became even closer during their Divinity School days. Bradford introduced Emerson to Bronson Alcott in 1835. On May 31, 1841, Bradford joined the Brook Farm reform community, where he taught the older children and became friends with Hawthorne. Robert Bartlett (1817-1843), son of Isaac and Rebecca Bartlett of Plymouth, Massachusetts, graduated from Harvard in 1836 and was currently working there as a tutor. George Warren Lippitt (1816-1891), son of Warren and Eliza Seamans Lippitt of Providence, Rhode Island, graduated from Harvard University in 1838 and from the Harvard Divinity School in 1841. He was ordained at South Boston in May 1844 but abandoned his vocation because of the conflict between Theodore Parker and the Unitarian leadership (see pp. 128-129, note 23). From 1853 to 1856 Lippitt was the United States Consul at Vienna. He married Matilda Florianna von Miller in 1855. Amos Bronson Alcott (1799-1888) and his wife Abigail (1800-1877), daughter of Joseph and Dorothy Sewall

May, had moved to Concord in March 1840 after Alcott closed his Temple School in Boston. The improvident Alcott had been so deeply in debt that, in December 1840, Emerson offered to have the family move into his home for a year. Alcott declined and the family remained in their small rented Concord house.

*Copy-text:* ALS (NN-BGC, Henry David Thoreau Collection, 1837-1917, Series IV)

*Published:* "Emerson-Thoreau Correspondence," *AM* 69 (May 1892): 577n; *Cor* 1958, 44; *Letters of RWE* 1990-1995, 7:454

*Editor's Notes*
This letter is addressed "H. D. Thoreau"; the copy-text and the address are both in pencil.
PE supplies the date "June 3, 1841" following Tilton, who assigns the date based on Emerson's remark in a June 4, 1841, letter to Caroline Sturgis: "Mary Russell is here & Henry Thoreau, not to mention occasional flights of fanatical birds–of croaking or prophesying song" (*Letters of RWE* 1990-1995, 7:455).

## *From Ralph Waldo Emerson*
*June 7, 1841*

My dear Sir,
Will you not come up to the Cliff[1] this P. M. at any hour convenient[e] to you where our ladies will be greatly gratified to see you & the more they say if you will bring your flute for the echo's sake; though now the wind blows.

R. W. E.

Monday
1 o'clock P. M.

*Correspondent:* See p. 53.

[1] The southern side of Fair Haven Hill, a favorite haunt of T's.

*Copy-text:* ALS (NN-BGC, Henry David Thoreau Collection, 1837-1917, Series IV)

*Published:* *HDT* 1882, 155; *Cor* 1958, 30; *Letters of RWE* 1990-1995, 7:455-456

*Editor's Notes*
This letter is addressed "Mr Henry D. Thoreau".
PE supplies the date "June 7, 1841." Rusk conjectures November

12, 1838, as the date of the letter (*Letters of RWE* 1939, 2:174); Tilton, with a more elaborate and convincing argument, conjectures June 7, 1841 (*Letters of RWE* 1990-1995, 7:455-456). PE adopts the latter date on the grounds that such an outing would more likely have occurred in June than in November.

convenient] *PE*; con / venient *in MS*


## To Lucy Jackson Brown
*July 21, 1841*

Concord, July 21, 1841.

Dear Friend:–

Don't think I need any prompting to write to you; but what tough earthenware shall I put into my packet to travel over so many hills, and thrid so many woods, as lie between Concord and Plymouth? Thank fortune it is all the way down hill, so they will get safely carried; and yet it seems as if it were writing against time and the sun, to send a letter east, for no natural force forwards it. You should go dwell in the west, and then I would deluge you with letters, as boys throw feathers into the air to see the wind take them. I should rather fancy you at evening dwelling far away behind the serene curtain of the west,– the home of fair weather,–than over by the chilly sources of the east wind.

What quiet thoughts have you now-a-days which will float on that east wind to west, for so we may make our worst servants our carriers,–what progress made from *can't* to *can*, in practice and theory? Under this category, you remember, we used to place all our philosophy. Do you have any still, startling, well moments, in which you think grandly, and speak with emphasis? Don't take this for sarcasm, for not in a year of the gods, I fear, will such a golden approach to plain speaking revolve again. But away with such fears; by a few miles of travel, we have not distanced each other's sincerity.

I grow savager and savager every day, as if fed on raw meat, and my tameness is only the repose of untamableness. I dream of looking abroad summer and winter, with free gaze, from some mountain-side, while my eyes revolve in an Egyptian slime of health,[1]–I to be nature looking into nature, with such easy sympathy as the blue-eyed[e] grass in the meadow looks in the face of the sky. From some such recess I would put forth sublime thoughts daily, as the plant puts forth leaves. Now-a-nights I go on to the hill to see the sun set, as one would go home at evening,–the bustle of the village has run on all day, and left me quite in the rear; but I see the sunset, and find that it can wait for my slow virtue.

But I forget that you think more of this human nature than of this nature I praise. Why won't you believe that mine is more human than any single man or woman can be? that in it,–in the sunset there, are all the qualities that can adorn a household,–and that sometimes in a fluttering leaf, one may hear all your Christianity preached.

You see how unskilful a letter-writer I am, thus to have come to the end of my sheet, when hardly arrived at the beginning of my story. I was going to be soberer, I assure you, but now have only room to add,–that if the fates allot you a serene hour, don't fail to communicate some of its serenity to your friend,

                    Henry D. Thoreau.

No, no. Improve so rare a gift for yourself, and send me of your leisure.

*Correspondent:* Lucy Cotton Jackson (1798-1868), daughter of Charles and Lucy Cotton Jackson of Plymouth, Massachusetts, and sister-in-law of Emerson, married Charles Brown in 1820. Charles abandoned the family in 1835 when his commission business failed; he fled to Europe and died in 1870 in Dublin. Lucy had boarded with the Thoreaus when T was at Harvard, and she often visited the Emerson home. Emerson built her a house near his in 1845.

[1] "Egyptian slime" is associated with the fertility of the Nile, whose mud "serves to fertilize the overflowed lands" (*Encyclopaedia Americana*, 9:292).

*Copy-text:* LVP 1865, 3-5

*Published:* *LVP* 1865, 3-5; *FL* 1894, 40-43; *FL* 1906, 35-37; *Cor* 1958, 44-45

*Editor's Note*
  blue-eyed] *PE*; blue- / eyed *in copy-text*


## To Ralph Waldo Emerson
*July 1841*

I send you my "story without an end"–which is our only news from the country–with some lines which you have heard before, that you may know how it had a beginning.[1] Great news, you know, is no news but only confirmation– and nature herself is not so novel as fresh.

I cant learn that any are ailing here more than usual– indeed we are all well–both fair and *fowl*, and above all

Y'r Friend<br>H. D Thoreau.

*Correspondent:* See p. 53.

[1] Emerson was at Nantasket, Massachusetts, from July 8 to July 20, writing and resting. On July 18 Lidian sent him a packet of letters that probably included this letter and the material T mentions: "Henry sends you some verses which you will doubtless greet with pleasure" (*Letters of Lidian Jackson Emerson* 1987, p. 96). On July 27 Emerson wrote Fuller that he had from T "a sort of ode to the Mountains" (*Letters of RWE* 1939, 2:435), probably the poem "With frontier strength ye stand your ground" (see *Collected Poems* 1964, pp. 47-50). Later that autumn, T revised the poem and submitted it to Fuller for the *Dial*, but she declined to publish it. The poem was later included in "A Walk to Wachusett" in the January 1843 *Boston Miscellany of Literature and Fashion* (see *Excursions* 2007, pp. 29-31) and subsequently included with a redaction of that essay in *A Week on the Concord and Merrimack Rivers* (see *A Week* 1980, pp. 163-165). T's phrase "story without an end" alludes to *Das Märchen ohne Ende*, written by Friedrich Wilhelm Carové (1789-1852), a German philosopher. Sarah Austin translated the title as *Story without an End*; the 1836 Boston edition of the translation, which T probably knew of, had a preface and "key to the emblems" by Bronson Alcott.

*Copy-text:*  Facsimile of ALS (location of MS unknown)

*Editor's Note*

This letter is addressed "R. W. Emerson." and endorsed "H. D. Thoreau / July 1841". PE supplies the date "July 1841" following the endorsement.

## To Lucy Jackson Brown
*September 8, 1841*

Concord Wedn's[y] eve. Sep. 8th

Dear Friend

Your note came wafted to my hand, like the first leaf of the Fall on the September wind, and I put only another interpretation upon its lines, than upon the veins of those which are soon to be strewed around me. It is nothing but Indian summer here at present–I mean that any weather seems reserved expressly for our late purposes, whenever we happen to be fulfilling them. I do not know what right I have to so much happiness, but rather hold it in reserve[e] till the time of my desert. What with the crickets, and the lowing of kine, and the crowing of cocks, our Concord life is sonorous enough.[1] Sometimes I hear the cock bestir himself on his perch under my feet, and crow shrilly long before dawn, and I think I might have been born any year for all the phenomena I know.

We count about sixteen eggs daily now, when arithmetic will only fetch the hens up to thirteen,–but the world is young, and we wait to see this eccentricity[a] complete its period.

My verses on Friendship are already printed in the Dial,[2] not expanded but reduced to completeness, by leaving out the long lines, which always have, or should have, a longer[a] or at least another, sense, than short ones.

Just now I am in the mid-sea of verses, and they actually rustle round me, as the leaves would[a] round the head of Autummus himself, should he thrust it up through some vales which I know.,[3]–but alas! many of them are but crisped and yellow leaves like his, I fear, and will deserve no better fate than to make mould for new harvests.

I see the stanzas rise around me, verse upon verse, far and near, like the mountains from Agiocochook,[4] not all having a terrestrial existence as yet, even as some of *them* may be clouds, but I fancy I see the gleam of some Sebago lakes and Silver Cascades,[5] at whose well I may drink one day. I am as unfit for any practical purpose, I mean for the further-ance of the world's ends, as gossamer for ship tim- ber–  And I who am going to be a pencil-maker to-mor- row, can sympathise with god Apollo, who served king Admetus for awhile on earth–[6]  But I believe he found it for his advantage at last–as I am sure I shall–though I shall hold the nobler part at least[e] out of the service.

Dont attach any undue seriousness {*text obscured by sealing wax*} this threnody–for I love my fate to the very core and rind, and could swallow it without paring I think

You ask if I have written any more poems–excepting those[e] which Vulcan is now forging,[7] I have only dis- charged a few more[a] bolts into the horizon, in all three hundred verses, and sent them as I may say over the mountains to Miss Fuller,[8] who may have occasion to re- member the old rhyme

"Three scipen gode
Comen mid than flode,
Three hundred cnihten–"[9] but these are far more Vandalic than they.

In this narrow sheet there is not room even for one thought to root itself, but you must consider this an odd leaf of a volume, and that volume

Your Friend
Henry D. Thoreau

*Correspondent:* See p. 77.

[1] On August 20, 1841, T wrote in his Journal:

It seems as if no cock lived so far in the horizon but a faint vibration reached me here–spread the wider over earth–as the more distant.

In the morning the crickets snore–in the afternoon they chirp–at midnight they dream. (*Journal 1* 1981, p. 323)

² Emerson gave a copy of "Friendship" to Fuller in 1840 and asked for its return in July 1841; Fuller included it in the *Dial* for October of that year (pp. 204-205). See *Collected Poems* 1964, pp. 71-73 ("Let such pure hate still underprop").

³ In the fall of 1841 T was at work on a group of interrelated poems in which he explored the character of the poet, the experience of inspiration, and the influence of the natural phenomena of Concord on both. The extant fair-copy versions of these poems occupy fourteen leaves; a surviving draft that represents T's intention to link these poems constitutes sixteen leaves. One can easily imagine T surrounded by these rustling leaves of paper as he composed and revised. See Elizabeth Hall Witherell, "Thoreau's Watershed Season as a Poet: The Hidden Fruits of the Summer and Fall of 1841," *SAR* 1990, pp. 49-106.

⁴ The Indian name for Mount Washington in New Hampshire.

⁵ Sebago Lake is in south-central Maine; Silver Cascade is in Crawford Notch, New Hampshire.

⁶ In one of T's favorite myths, Apollo, enraged that Jupiter had killed his son Æsculapius, in turn killed the Cyclops who had made the deadly thunderbolts. Jupiter then banished Apollo from heaven. In exile Apollo served King Admetus of Thessaly as a shepherd for nine years.

⁷ On a leaf (now at MaLiTIW, Thoreau Society Archives, Raymond Adams Collection) containing a draft of the first paragraph of this letter, T pencilled several stanzas that were included in a version of "Inspiration" he was working on at this time. See Witherell, "Thoreau's Watershed Season as a Poet," *SAR* 1990, pp. 94-95.

⁸ Fuller had at this time at least a draft of "With frontier strength," which she returned to T on October 18. She rejected it for the *Dial*, saying that she did not find it "improved by mere compression, though it might be by fusion and glow" (p. 81).

⁹ In a footnote in *The History of the Anglo-Saxons*, 1:90n6, Sharon Turner quotes Lazamon [Layamon]: "Threo scipen gode comen mid than flode, threo hundred cnihten" (Three good ships came on that tide, three hundred knights). T had copied these lines into his Journal for December 27, 1837: "The most important is apt to be some silent and unobtrusive fact in history. In 449 three Saxon cyules arrived on the British coast– 'Three scipen gode comen mid than flode, three hundred cnihten'–" (*Journal 1* 1981, p. 23).

*Copy-text:* ALS (ViU, Clifton Waller Barrett Library, Henry David Thoreau Collection [#6345])

*Published:* LVP 1865, 5-8; *Life* 1890, 37; *FL* 1894, 43-45; *T: Home* 1902, 235; *FL* 1906, 37-39; *Cor* 1958, 46-47

*Editor's Notes*

This letter is addressed "Mrs. L. C. Brown / Plymouth / Mass." and postmarked "CONCORD MAS. SEP 9".

PE supplies the year "1841" on the basis that it is the only year during the publication of the *Dial* in which September 8 fell on a Wednesday.

reserve] *PE*; resere *in MS*
least] *PE*; lea{*text obscured by sealing wax*}t
those] *PE*; *possibly* these *in MS*

*Author's Alterations*

eccentricity] excentricity
a longer] *interlined with a caret*
would] *followed by cancelled* do
more] *followed by cancelled* thunder


## From Isaiah Thornton Williams

*September 24, 1841*

Buffalo N.Y. Sept. 24, 1841–

Mr. D. H. Thoreau
My dear Sir,

Your kind offer to receive and answer any communication from me, is not forgotten– I owe myself an apology for so long neglecting to avail myself of so generous an offer. Since I left Concord I have hardly found rest for the sole of my foot.[1] I have followed the star of my destiny till it has, at length, come and stood over this place.[2] Here I remain engaged in the study of Law– Part of the time I have spent in New-Hampshire part in Ohio & part in New-York–and so precarious was[a] my residence in either place that I have scarcely known whither you might direct a letter with any certainty of its reaching me.

When I left Concord I felt a strong desire to continue the conversation I had so fortunately commenced with some of those whom the Public call Trancendentalists. Their sentiments seemed to me to possess a peculiar fitness. Though full of doubt I felt I was fed & refreshed by those interviews. The doctrines I there heard have[a] ever since, been uppermost in my mind–and like balmy sleep over the weary limbs, have they stolen over me quite un-awares. I have not embraced them–but they have em-braced me– I am led, their willing captive. Yet I feel I have but yet taken the first step. I would know more of this matter. I would be taken by the hand and led up from this darkness and torpidity where I have so long grov-eled like an earth-worm[e]. I know what it is to be a slave to what I thought a Christian faith–and with what rapture do greet the hand that breaks my chains–& the voice that bids me–live–

Most of the books you recommended to me I was not able to obtain–"Nature"[3] I found–and language can[a] not express my admiration of it. When gloom like a thick cloud comes over me in that I find an Amulet that dis-sipates the darkness and kindles anew my highest hopes. Few copies of Mr Emerson's Essays[4] have found their way to this place– I have read part of them and am very much delighted with them. Mr Parker's Sermon[5] I have also found–and as much as I should have[a] shrunk from such sentiments a year ago–half, do I already receive them. I have also obtained "Hero[a] Worship[a]"[6]–which of course I read with great interest–and as I read I blush for my former bigotry and wonder that I had[a] not known it all before wonder what there is in chains that I should have loved them so much– Mr. E's oration[7] before the Theo-logical class at Cambridge I very much want. If–you have it in your possession, allow me to beg you to forward it to me & I will return it by mail after perusing it. Also Mr. Al-cott's "Human Culture"–[8] I will offer no apology for ask-ing this favor–for I know you will not require it.

I find I am not alone here, your principals are working their[a] way even in Buffalo–this emporium of wickedness and sensuality. We look to the east for our guiding star for there our sun did rise. Our motto is[a] that of the Grecian Hero–"Give but to see–and Ajax asks no more"–[9]

For myself my attention is much engrossed in my studies– Entering upon them as I do without a Public Education–I feel that nothing but the most undivided attention[a]
and entire devotion to them will ensure me even an ordinary standing in the profession. There is something false–
in such devotion– I already feel its chilling effects I
fear I shall fall into the wake of the profession which is in
this section proverbially bestial– Law is a noble profession it calls loudly for men of genius and integrity to fill
its ranks. I donot aspire to be a great Lawyer–I know I cannot be, but it is the sincere desire of my heart that I may
be a true one

You are ready to ask–how I like the West– I must answer–not very well– I love New England so much that the
West is comparatively[a] odious to me– The part of Ohio
that I visited was on dead Level–often did I–strain my
eyes to catch a glimpse[a] of some distant mountain–that
should transport me in imagination to the wild country
of my birth, but the eternal level spread itself on & on & I
almost felt myself launched forever. Aloud did I exclaim–
"My own blue hills–[10] O, Where are they"!– I did not
know how much I was indebted to them for the happy
hours I'd passed at[a] home– I knew I loved them–and my
noble river too–along whose banks–I'd roamed half uncertain if in earth or Heaven– I never shall–I never can
forget them all–though I drive away the remembrance of–
them which ever in the unguarded moment[a] throngs me
laden with ten thousands incidents before forgotten & so
talismanic its power–that I wake from the enchantment
as from a dream. If I were in New-England again I would
never leave her. but–now I am away–I fear forever–I must
eat of the Lotus–and forget her.[a] Tis true we have a noble
Lake–whose pure waters kiss the foot of our city–and
whose[a] bossom bears the burdens of our commerce–her[a]
beacon light now looks in upon me through my window
as if to watch, lest I should say untruth of that which is[a]
her nightly charge But hills or mountains we have none.

My sheet is nearly full & I must draw to a close– I fear I have already wearied your patience. Please remember me to those of your friends whose acquaintance I had pleasure to form while in Concord– I engaged to write your brother– Mr Alcott also gave me the the same privelege–which I hope soon to avail myself of. I hope sometime to visit your town again which I remember with so much satisfaction–yet with so much regret–regret that I did not earlier avail myself of the acquaintances, it was my high privelege to make while there[a] and that the lucubrations of earlier years did not better fit me to appreciate & enjoy– I cheer myself with fanning the fading embers of a hope that I shall yet retrieve my fault. that such an opportunity will again be extended to me–and that I may once more look upon that man whose name I never speak without reverence–whom of all–I most admire–almost adore–Mr Emerson– I shall wait with impatience to hear from you– Believe me

ever yours–<br>Isaiah T. Williams.

*Correspondent:* Isaiah Thornton Williams (1819-1886), son of Isaiah and Martha Tenney Williams, was educated at the Exeter Academy in New Hampshire and studied law in Buffalo in the office of Millard Fillmore. In 1849 he married Ellen E. White (1826-1877), daughter of Ferdinand and Dorothy Gardner White of Boston. After practicing law in Buffalo, Williams moved to New York City in 1854, where he often defended Horace Greeley in libel suits brought against the aggressive editor. He left his law practice in 1867 to become registrar of bankruptcy for New York County.

[1] Gen. 8:9: "But the dove found no rest for the sole of her foot".

[2] Matt. 2:9: "and, lo, the star, which they saw in the east, went before them, till it came and stood over where the young child was."

[3] Emerson's first book was published in September 1836. T probably read it the following April.

[4] Emerson's first volume of *Essays* was published on March 19, 1841, by James Munroe and Company.

[5] Theodore Parker, *A Discourse on the Transient and Permanent in Christianity.*

[6] Thomas Carlyle, *On Heroes, Hero-Worship, and the Heroic in History*. Carlyle sent Lidian Emerson proof sheets for the book in February 1841, and T lists the sheets with other titles in an April 15 entry in a reading list he kept from December 5, 1840, through June 3, 1841.

[7] Emerson gave his Divinity School Address on July 15, 1838. Munroe published a thousand copies, which were all sold by July 1, 1839.

[8] Bronson Alcott's *The Doctrine and Discipline of Human Culture* was published in 1836 both as a pamphlet and as an introduction to his *Conversations with Children on the Gospels*; see also p. 142, note 2.

[9] *The Iliad of Homer*, vol. 1, 17.730: "Give me to see and Ajax asks no more".

[10] Williams may have in mind Felicia Hemans's poem "The Cambrian in America," in which the speaker yearns for the landscape of home. The poem, included in *The Poetical Works of Mrs. Felicia Hemans*, contains the lines "But happier, could the weary-hearted / Look on his own blue hills, and die!" (p. 477).

*Copy-text:* ALS (NN-BGC, Henry David Thoreau Collection, 1837-1917, Series V)

*Published:* *Cor* 1958, 47-50

*Editor's Notes*
    This letter is addressed "Mr. D. H. Thoreau, / Concord / Mass–", postmarked "BUFFALO N.Y. SEP 25", and endorsed "I. T. Williams".
    earth-worm] *PE*; earth- / worm *in MS*

*Author's Alterations*
    was] *interlined above cancelled* has been
    have] *interlined with a caret*
    can] *interlined above cancelled* will
    have] *interlined with a caret*
    Hero] hero
    Worship] worship
    had] *interlined above cancelled* did
    their] they
    is] *interlined with a caret*
    attention] *followed by cancelled* will
    comparatively] *interlined with a caret*
    a glimpse] *interlined with a caret*
    at] in
    moment] moments
    her.] *followed by cancelled* forever–

whose] *interlined above cancelled* its
her] *interlined above cancelled* its
is] *interlined above cancelled* was
while there] *interlined with a caret*


## To Lucy Jackson Brown
*October 5, 1841*

Concord, October 5, 1841.

Dear Friend:–

I send you Williams's letter as the last remembrancer to one of those "whose acquaintance he had the pleasure to form while in Concord." It came quite unexpectedly to me, but I was very glad to receive it, though I hardly know whether my utmost sincerity and interest can inspire a sufficient answer to it. I should like to have you send it back by some convenient opportunity.

Pray let me know what you are thinking about any day,– what most nearly concerns you. Last winter, you know, you did more than your share of the talking, and I did not complain for want of an opportunity. Imagine your stove-door out of order, at least, and then while I am fixing it, you will think of enough things to say.

What makes the value of your life at present? what dreams have you? and what realizations? You know there is a high table-land[1] which not even the east wind reaches. Now can't we walk and chat upon its plane still, as if there were no lower latitudes? Surely our two destinies are topics interesting and grand enough for any occasion.

I hope you have many gleams of serenity and health, or, if your body will grant you no positive respite,–that you may, at any rate, enjoy your sickness occasionally, as much as I used to tell of. But here is the bundle going to be done up, so accept a "good-night" from

Henry D. Thoreau.

*Correspondent:* See p. 77.

[1] T also uses this image in his August 6, 1841, Journal entry (*Journal 1* 1981, p. 316). It is probably drawn from the description of the elevated country of southern India in Hugh Murray et al., *Historical and Descriptive Account of British India*, 1:34.

*Copy-text:* LVP 1865, 8-9

*Published:* LVP 1865, 8-9; FL 1894, 45-46; FL 1906, 40; Cor 1958, 50-51

## To Isaiah Thornton Williams
*October 8, 1841*

Concord Sept. 8th 1841.

Dear Friend,

I am pleased to hear from you out of the west, as if I heard the note of some singing bird from the midst of its forests which travellers report so grim and solitary–   It is like the breaking up of Winter and the coming in of Spring, when the twigs glitter and tinkle, and the first sparrow twitters in the horizon. I doubt if I can make a good echo[a]–  Yet it seems that if a man ever had the satisfaction to say once entirely and irrevocably what he believed to be true, he would never leave off to cultivate that skill.

I suppose if you see any light in the east it must be in the eastern state of your own soul and not by any means in these New England states. Our eyes perhaps do not rest so long on any as on the few who especially love their own lives–who dwell apart at more generous intervals, and cherish a single purpose behind the formalities of society with such steadiness that of all men only their two eyes seem to meet in one focus. They can be eloquent when they speak–they can be graceful and noble when they act.

For my part if I have any creed it is so to live as to preserve and increase the susceptibleness of my nature to noble impulses–first to observe if any light shine on me and then faithfully to follow it. The Hindoo scripture says "Single is each man born; single he dies; single he receives the reward of his good, and single the punishment

of his evil, deeds."[1] Let us trust that we have a good conscience. The steady light whose ray every man knows will
be enough for all weathers. If any soul look abroad even
today it will not find any word which does it more justice
than the New Testament, yet if it be faithful enough it will
have experience of a revelation fresher and directer than
that, which will make that to be only the best tradition.
The strains of a more heroic faith vibrate through the
week days and the fields than through the sabbath and
the church. To shut the ears to the immediate voice of
God, and prefer to know him by report will be the only
sin.

Any respect we may yield to the paltry expedients of
other men like ourselves–to the Church–the State–or the
School–seems purely gratuitous, for in our most private
experience we are never driven to expediency. Our religion is where our love is. How vain for men to go musing
one way and worshipping another! Let us not fear to worship the muse. Those stern old worthies–Job, and David,
and the rest, had no sabbath day worship–but sang and
revelled in their faith, and I have no doubt that what true
faith and love of God there is in this age will appear to
posterity in the happy rythm of some creedless[e] poet.

I think I can sympathise with your sense of greater
freedom–  The return to truth is so simple that not even
the nurses can tell when we began to breathe health-
ily, but recovery took place long before the machinery
of life began to play freely again,[e] when on our pillow at
midnoon or midnight some natural sound fell naturally
on the ear. As for creeds and doctrines we are suddenly
grown rustic–and from walking in streets and squares–
walk broadly in the fields–as if a man were wise enough
not to sit in a draft, and get an ague–but moved boyantly
in the breeze.

It is curious that while you are sighing for New England the scene of our fairest dreams should lie in the

west–it confirms me in the opinion that places are well nigh indifferent. Perhaps you have experienced that in proportion as our love of nature is deep and pure we are independent upon her. I suspect that erelong when some hours of faithful and earnest life have imported serenity into your Buffalo day the sunset on Lake[a] Erie will make you forget New England. It was the Greeks made the Greek isles and sky, and men are beginning to find many an Archipelago elsewhere as good. But let us not cease to regret the fair and good, for perhaps it is fairer and better than to possess[e] them. I am living with Mr. Emerson in very dangerous prosperity.[2] He gave me three pamphlets for you to keep, which I sent last Saturday.[3] The "Explanatory Preface" is by Elizabeth Peabody who was Mr. Alcotts assistant; and now keeps a bookstore and library in Boston.[4] Pray let me know with what hopes and resolutions you enter upon the study of law–how you are to make it a solid part of your life. After a few words interchanged we shall learn to speak pertinently and not to the air. My brother and Mr. Alcott express pleasure in the anticipation of hearing from you–And I am sure that the communication of what most nearly concerns you will always be welcome to

Yrs sincerely

H. D. T.

*Correspondent:* See p. 85.

[1] T quotes Manu, *Institutes of Hindu Law; or, The Ordinances of Menu*, which is translated by Sir William Jones. T may have also used the 1799 edition of *The Works of Sir William Jones*, which includes *Institutes of Hindu Law* in volume 3. T began to mention and quote Manu in his Journal as early as August 1840. He had copied this passage into a commonplace book and included it in a selection of sayings he published in the January 1843 issue of the *Dial* (pp. 331-340; see *Early Essays* 1975, p. 135).

[2] T had moved into the Emerson home on April 26, where he was gardener, handyman, and close family friend.

[3] In his reply of November 27, Williams mentions two of these

pamphlets: Emerson's *The Method of Nature: An Oration* and Alcott's *The Doctrine and Discipline of Human Culture.* The third item is Elizabeth Peabody's forty-three-page *Method of Spiritual Culture: Being an Explanatory Preface to the Second Edition of "Record of a School,"* which T mentions next.

⁴ Elizabeth Palmer Peabody (1804-1894) was Alcott's assistant at the Temple School from 1834 to 1836. She opened a bookstore in Boston in 1840.

*Copy-text:* ALS (NNPM, MA 2711)

*Published: Cor* 1958, 51-53

*Editor's Notes*
This letter is addressed "Isaiah T. Williams / Buffalo / N.Y.", postmarked "CONCORD MAS OCT 8", and endorsed "Buffalo N.Y. / H. D. Thoreau / Concord Mass. / Oct 8 1841–".

PE supplies the month "October" from the contents of the letter and the postmark; T apparently wrote "Sept." by mistake.
creedless] *PE*; creedles{*text obscured by sealing wax*}
again,] *PE*; *possibly* ~. *in MS*
possess] *PE*; {*text obscured by sealing wax*}ossess

*Author's Alterations*
echo] *followed by cancelled* to them
Lake] lake


## To Rufus Wilmot Griswold
*October 9, 1841*

Concord Oct. 9ᵗʰ 1841.

Dear Sir,

I am sorry that I can only place at your disposal three small poems printed in the "Dial"–that called "Sympathy" in no. 1.–"Sic Vita" in no. 5–and "Friendship" in no. 6. If you see fit to reprint these will you please to correct the following errors?[1]

In the second stanza of "Sympathy"[a]

|     |     |     |     |     |     |
| --- | --- | --- | --- | --- | --- |
|     |     |     | for posts read ports. |     |     |
| " | " | 5ᵗʰ | " | " breeze | " haze. |
| "ₑ | " |     | " | *the* eyes | " *our* eyes |

| "e | " | " | worked " works. |
| " | 13th | " " | dearest " truest. |
| " | 4th | " " | "Friendship" |
| | | | for our read one. |
| " | 10th | " | " warden " warder. |

I was born in Concord, Massachusetts, in 1817, and was graduated at Harvard University, in 1837.

> Yrs respectfully
> Henry D. Thoreau.

*Correspondent:* Rufus Wilmot Griswold (1815-1857), a journalist, editor, and writer, was planning an anthology of American writing that he would publish as *The Poets and Poetry of America* (Philadelphia: Carey and Hart, 1842). Griswold worked for Horace Greeley before becoming the assistant editor of *Graham's Magazine.*

[1] Griswold solicited poems from Emerson for his anthology, but Emerson prompted T to submit some of his own work instead. Although Emerson wrote Griswold recommending T, none of the poems mentioned in the letter were included in his anthology. All three appeared in the *Dial*: "Sympathy" in *Dial* 1 (July 1840): 71-72; "Sic Vita" in *Dial* 2 (July 1841): 81-82; and "Friendship" in *Dial* 2 (October 1841): 204-205. See *Collected Poems* 1964, pp. 64-66 ("Lately, alas, I knew a gentle boy"), pp. 81-82 ("I am a parcel of vain strivings tied"), and pp. 71-73 ("Let such pure hate still underprop").

*Copy-text:* ALS (NN-BGC, Henry David Thoreau Collection, 1837-1917, Series III)

*Published: Cor* 1958, 54-55

*Editor's Note*
This letter is addressed "Rufus W. Griswold, / Care of Mr. Fields, / at Ticknor's bookstore, / Boston / Mass." and postmarked "CONCORD MAS. OCT 9".
    "] *repositioned in PE*
    "] *added in PE*

*Author's Alteration*
    "Sympathy"] *preceded by cancelled* the

*From Margaret Fuller*
*October 18, 1841*

18th Oct[r] 1841.

I do not find the poem on the mountains[1] improved by mere compression, though it might be by fusion and glow.

Its merits to me are a noble recognition of nature, two or three manly thoughts, and, in one place, a plaintive music. The image of the ships[2] does not please me originally. It illustrates the greater by the less and affects me as when Byron compares the light on Jura to that of the dark eye of woman.[3] I cannot define my position here, and a large class of readers would differ from me. As the poet goes on to

Unhewn, primeval timber
For knees so stiff, for masts so limber"[4]

he seems to chase an image, already rather forced, into conceits.

Yet now that I have some knowledge of the man, it seems there is no objection I could make to his lines, (with the exception of such offences against taste as the lines about the humors of the eye &c[5,a] as[a] to which we are already agreed) which I could not make to himself. He is healthful, sane, of open eye, ready hand, and noble scope. He sets no limits to his life, nor to the invasions of nature; he is not wilfully pragmatical, cautious, ascetic or fantastical. But he is as yet a somewhat bare hill which the warm gales of spring have not visited. Thought lies too detached,[a] truth is seen too much in detail, we can number and mark the substances embedded in the rock. Thus his verses are startling, as much as stern; the thought does not excuse its conscious existence by letting us see its relation with life; there is a want of fluent music.

Yet what could a companion do at present unless to tame the guardian of the Alps too early? Leave him at peace amid his native snows. He is friendly; he will find the generous office that shall educate him. It is not a soil for the citron and the rose, but for the whortleberry, the pine or the heather. The unfolding of affections, a wider and deeper human experience, the harmonizing influences of other natures, will mould the man, and melt his verse. He will seek thought less and find knowledge the more. I can have no advice or criticism for a person so sincere, but if I give my impression of him I will say He says too constantly of nature She is mine; She is not yours till you have been more hers. Seek the lotus, and take a draught of rapture. Say not so confidently All places, all occasions are alike. This will never come true till you have found it false.

I do not know that I have more to say now, perhaps these words will say nothing to you; If intercourse should continue, perhaps a bridge may be made between the minds so widely apart, for I apprehended you in spirit, and you did not seem to mistake me as widely as most of your kind do. If you should find yourself inclined to write to me, as you thought you might, I dare say many thoughts would be suggested to me; many have already by seeing you day by day. Will you finish the poem in your own way and send it[a] for the Dial. Leave out "And seems to *milk* the sky"[6,a] The image is too low. Mr Emerson thought so too. Farewell. May Truth be irradiated by Beauty!– Let me know whether you go to the lonely hut, and write to me about Shakspeare, if you read him there.[7] I have many thoughts about him which I have never yet been led to express.

                                              Margaret F.

The pencilled paper Mr E. put into my hands. I have taken the liberty to copy it  You expressed one day my own opinion that the moment such a crisis is passed we may speak of it. There is no need of artificial delicacy, of secrecy, it keeps its own secret; it cannot be made false.

Thus you will not be sorry that I have seen the paper.[8] Will you not send me some other records of the *good week*.[9]

*Correspondent:* See pp. 70-71.

[1] Fuller refers to T's poem "With frontier strength ye stand your ground"; see p. 78, note 1. The version T sent to Fuller has not survived. T incorporated some of Fuller's suggestions into a manuscript version that exists among Emerson's papers; this indicates that T acted on Fuller's request that he "finish the poem in [his] own way and send it for the Dial."

[2] In the manuscript version he gave Emerson, T describes the mountains as follows (*Henry David Thoreau: Collected Essays and Poems* [New York: Library of America, 2001], p. 546):

> Ships of the line each one
> That westward run,
> Always before the gale,
> Under a press of sail,
> Convoying clouds
> Which cluster in your shrouds–
> With your slant masts 'tis sixes and sevens
> But that ye rake the heavens,
> So near the edge ye go,
> Under the roof so low;
> With weight of metal all untold,
> I seem to feel ye in my firm seat here,
> Immeasurable depth of hold,
> And breadth of beam, and length of running gear.
> The vessels on the sea
> Are relative to ye,
> Sailing by sympathy.

[3] Fuller refers to the following lines by Byron (*Childe Harold's Pilgrimage*, 3.92.1-9):

> The sky is changed!–and such a change! Oh night,
> And storm, and darkness, ye are wondrous strong,
> Yet lovely in your strength, as is the light
> Of a dark eye in woman! Far along,
> From peak to peak, the rattling crags among
> Leaps the live thunder! Not from one lone cloud,
> But every mountain now hath found a tongue,
> And Jura answers, through her misty shroud,
> Back to the joyous Alps, who call to her aloud!

[4] T retained these lines in the published versions; see "A Walk to Wachusett," in *Excursions* 2007, p. 30, and *A Week* 1980, p. 164.

[5] Fuller may refer to the following lines, which are omitted from the published versions and are quoted here from the version found in Emerson's papers (*Henry David Thoreau: Collected Essays and Poems* [New York: Library of America, 2001], p. 545):

> The iris of the sky,
> Ye run
> Round the horizon of its eye
> Whose pupil is the sun.

[6] T omitted this line from the published versions.

[7] On December 24 of the same year, T wrote in his Journal, "I want to go soon and live away by the pond where I shall hear only the wind whispering among the reeds– It will be success if I shall have left myself behind, But my friends ask what I will do when I get there? Will it not be employment enough to watch the progress of the seasons?" (*Journal 1* 1981, p. 347). Flint's Pond (also known as Sandy Pond), rather than Walden, may have been the pond that first attracted T.

[8] The "pencilled paper" is not extant. The "crisis" Fuller refers to may have been described in some autobiographical sketch that T apparently had written at this time; or she may refer to some early, preliminary material for an essay or lecture based on T and John's 1839 trip to the White Mountains in New Hampshire. No other material describing this crisis survives.

[9] This phrase, much commented upon, may refer to the days Fuller had spent visiting Emerson in the first week of October, when T was also living in Emerson's house. It could not refer specifically to *A Week on the Concord and Merrimack Rivers*, for T did not conceive of that book until after John's death in 1842.

*Copy-text:* ALS (TxAuHRH, Ms Thoreau, H. D. Recip.)

*Published:* *HDT* 1882, 169-172; *Life* 1890, 50, 80; *Life* 1896, 47, 63; *T: Home* 1902, 246; *Friendly Craft* 1908, 194-195; *Cor* 1958, 56-57; *Letters of Margaret Fuller*, 2:242-243

*Editor's Note*
This letter is addressed "Henry Thoreau."

*Author's Alterations*
&c] *followed by cancelled* with regard
as] *interlined with a caret*
detached,] *interlined above cancelled* obvious

it] *followed by cancelled* me
sky"] *interlined below*


## From Isaiah Thornton Williams
*November 27, 1841*

Buffalo N.Y. Nov 27 1841–
My dear Friend

I feel rebuked as I draw your most interesting letter from my file and sit down to answer it–that I have so
long delayed so grateful a task–  For–though I rarely get
away from the world & Law long enough to retire within
myself and inquire how I am–how I feel and what sentiments and what responses[a] my heart gives out in answer
to your voice whose notes of sweetest music comes from
that "Land–of every land the pride Beloved of Heaven o'er
all the World beside" "That spot of earth divinely blest–
That dearer sweeter spot than all the rest"[1] Yet–when
weary and heart sick–when disgusted with the present–
and memory, as if to give relief, retires to wander in the
'Graveyard of the past'–she passes not unmindful nor
lingers briefly around that spot where more than in any
other I feel I first tasted of that bread I hope will yet nour-
ish my youth strengthen my manhood–cheer and solace
"when the daughters of music are brought low".[2]

Time's devastating hand is begining already to obliter-
ate the traces of my youthful feelings–and I am becoming
more & more contented with my present situation and
feel less and less a desire inexorable to return and be a
child once more–

This I suppose to be the natural[a] tendency of the circumstances in which I am placed. Man's ends are shaped
for him[3] and he must abide his destiny. This seems a little
like fatality–yet, how can we avoid the conclusion that the
Soul is shaped by circumstances and many of those circumstances beyond man's control[a]? I think that could I

always be "true to the dream of Childhood" I should be always be happy– I can imagine circumstances in which I think I might be so–but they are not my present circumstances–these are my fate– I would not complain of them did they not war against what I feel to be my highest interest and indeed I will not as it is–for I know not what is my highest good– I know not the good whither I am bound, and as I donot know but all is well as far as the external is concerned I will trust to the author of my being–the author and creator of those beautiful fields and woods I so much enjoy in my morning and evening walks–the author of the glorious Lake sunsets–that all is well. I have already half answered your interrogatory in relation to my hopes and feelings as I enter upon the study of Law– With so little knowledge–so a–stranger in its walks–with my face only set toward the temple just spying its tapering finger pointing to the heaven[a] as the throne of its justice–its golden dome glittering as though it were the light of that city which "has no need of a candle neither the light of the Sun"[4]–not yet passed under its gateway–or wandered among the trees and flowers of its paradisean garden–viewed the stones of its foundation or laid hold of its mossy pillars–I barely know what to hope or how to feel atall– I must say, if I would speak truly,[a] that I donot "burn with high hopes"[5] Tis not that "the way seems steep and difficult"[6] but that "the event is feared";[7] tis the prospect of a a life[a] in[a] "daily contact with the things I loath"–[8] I love the profession It[a] presents a boundless field–a shoreless ocean where my bark may drift–and bound & leap from wave to wave in wild but splendid rage–without the fear of rock or strand. Yet[a] I chose it not so much for the love I bore it–for I knew that in it my intercourse must be with the worst specimens of humanity–as knowing that by it I might get more knowledge, dicipline and intellectual culture than in any other which I could choose simply as a means of livelihood–have more time to devote to literature and philosophy–and, as I have said, be better prepared intellectually for progress in these pursuits than in any other branch of business followed simply to provide for the bodily wants– So–you see–this profession I chose simply as a means to enable me to pursue what I most delight in–and for that end I think it the wisest selection I could make  I know this motive will not lead me to any eminence in the profession–yet I donot know as I wish to be great in that respect even if I could– My books tell me that on entering the profession I must bid adieu to literature–every-thing[a] and[a] give up myself wholy to Law– I thought I would do so for a time[a]–and I sat down to Blackstone[9] with a heavy heart– Adieu ye Classic halls–My Muse adieu! I wept–as I took perhaps[a] my last look of her–her form lessening in the distance–she cast her eye over her shoulder to to rest once more on me– O, it was all pity, love and tenderness– I called aloud for her–but She hastened on–grieved, She heeded not my call– It was too much– What ever might by standing as a Lawyer–I would not turn my back to literature–philosophy theology or poetry– Would give them their place & Law its place– A thousand thanks for the pamphlets you forwarded me. I have read them with great pleasure–and shall read them many times more– The Oration at Waterville I very much admire–it is circulating among Mr. E.s admirers in this place who all express great admiration of it– Human Culture I admire more and more as I read it over.[10] I loaned it to a young man who told me on returning it that he had almost committed it to memory–and wished the loan of it again as soon as the other friends had read it  I have read some of your poetry in the Dial– I want to see more of it–it transports me to my Childhood and makes and makes every thing look as playful as when first I looked upon them in my earliest morning– I only wish it were more liquid–smooth  I should admire Pope's Homer if it were for nothing but that it flows so smoothly.[11]

Remember me affectionately to the friends in Concord and believe me

ever yours
I. T. Williams

*Correspondent:* See p. 85.

*Correspondent:* See p. 85.

[1] See James Montgomery, "The West Indies," 3.1-2, 3.65-66, 3.15-16, and 3.67-68, in *The West Indies, and Other Poems*.

[2] See Eccl. 12:4: "And the doors shall be shut in the streets, when the sound of the grinding is low, and he shall rise up at the voice of the bird, and all the daughters of musick shall be brought low".

[3] Probably a reference to Hamlet's well-known assertion: "There's a divinity that shapes our ends, / Rough-hew them how we will" (Shakespeare, vol. 2, *Hamlet*, 5.2.10-11).

[4] Rev. 22:5: "And there shall be no night there; and they need no candle, neither light of the sun; for the Lord God giveth them light: and they shall reign for ever and ever."

[5] See Byron's description of the soldiers soon to die in Belgium (*Childe Harold's Pilgrimage*, 3.27.5-9):

> Ere evening to be trodden like the grass
> Which now beneath them, but above shall grow
> In its next verdure, when this fiery mass
> Of living valour, rolling on the foe
> And burning with high hope, shall moulder cold and low

[6] See Milton, vol. 2, *Paradise Lost*, 2.70-72: "But perhaps / The way seems difficult and steep to scale / With upright wing against a higher foe."

[7] See Milton, vol. 2, *Paradise Lost*, 2.81-82: "The ascent is easy then; / The event is fear'd".

[8] See George Croly, *Catiline: A Dramatic Poem*, 3.2.83-85: "Banish'd from Rome! What's banish'd, but set free / From daily contact of the things I loathe? / 'Tried and convicted traitor!' Who says this?" (*The Poetical Works of the Rev. George Croly*, 2:103).

[9] Probably William Blackstone's *Commentaries on the Laws of England*.

[10] Emerson's *The Method of Nature: An Oration* and Alcott's *The Doctrine and Discipline of Human Culture* are two of three pamphlets T sent Williams on October 2 at Emerson's behest. See pp. 90-91, note 3.

[11] Alexander Pope translated *The Iliad* into heroic couplets in a six-volume edition published 1715-1720. He also translated *The Od-*

*yssey* in five volumes, published 1725-1726. T owned a nineteenth-century edition of each translation.

*Copy-text:* ALS (NN-BGC, Henry David Thoreau Collection, 1837-1917, Series V)

*Published: Cor* 1958, 58-60

*Editor's Note*
    This letter is addressed "H. D. Thoreau / Concord / Mass.", postmarked "BUFFALO N.Y. NOV 29", and endorsed "I. T. Williams".

*Author's Alterations*
    responses] *followed by cancelled* I
    natural] *followed by cancelled* result of
    control] controls
    heaven] *followed by cancelled* of its
    truly,] *followed by cancelled* that
    a life] *preceded by cancelled* daily
    in] *interlined above cancelled* of
    It] it
    Yet] –
    every-thing] *followed by cancelled* but
    and] any
    for a time] *interlined with a caret*
    perhaps] *interlined with a caret*

## To Lucy Jackson Brown
*March 2, 1842*

Concord March 2<sup>nd</sup> 1842.

Dear Friend,
    I believe I have nothing new to tell you, for what was news you have learned from other sources. I am much the same person that I was, who should be so much better; yet when I realize what has transpired, and the greatness of the part I am unconsciously acting, I am thrilled, and it seems as if there were none in history to match it.
    Soon after John's death[1] I listened to a music-box, and, if, at any time, that event had seemed inconsistent with the beauty and harmony of the universe, it was then

gently constrained into the placid course of nature by those steady notes, in mild and unoffended tone echoing far and wide under the heavens. But I find these things more strange than sad to me. What right have I to grieve, who have not ceased to wonder?

We feel at first as if some opportunities of kindness and sympathy were lost, but learn afterward that any *pure grief* is ample recompense for all. That is, if we are faithful;–for a just grief is but sympathy with the soul that disposes events, and is as natural as the resin on[a] Arabian trees.– Only nature has a right to grieve perpetually, for she only is innocent. Soon the ice will melt, and the blackbirds sing along the river which he frequented, as pleasantly as ever. The same everlasting serenity will appear in this face of God, and we will not be sorrowful, if he is not.

We are made happy when reason can discover no occasion for it. The memory of some past moments is more persuasive than the experience of present ones– There have been visions of such breadth and brightness that these motes were invisible in their light.

I do not wish to see John ever again–I mean him who is dead–but that other whom only he would have wished to see, or to be, of whom he was the imperfect representative. For we are not what we are, nor do we treat or esteem each other for such, but for what we are capable of being.[2]

As for Waldo, he died as the mist rises from the brook, which the sun will soon dart his rays through.[3] Do not the flowers die every autumn? He had not even taken root here. I was not startled to hear that he was dead;–[e]it seemed the most natural event that could happen. His fine organisation demanded it, and nature gently yielded its request. It would have been strange if he had lived.

Neither will nature manifest any sorrow at his death, but soon the note of the lark will be heard down in the meadow, and fresh dandelions will spring from the old stocks where he plucked them last summer.

I have been living ill of late, but am now doing better.[4] How do you live in that Plymouth world, now-a-days?– Please remember me to Mary Russell.–[5] You must not blame me if I do *talk to the clouds*, for I remain

Your Friend,

Henry D. Thoreau.

*Correspondent:* See p. 77.

[1] T's brother cut his finger on January 1, contracted lockjaw by January 8, and died on January 11.

[2] An earlier version of this sentence occurs in a Journal entry written just before March 2 (*Journal 1* 1981, p. 367).

[3] Emerson's son Waldo (1836-1842) died of scarlet fever on January 27.

[4] T, who nursed John during his ordeal, showed symptoms of the same disease from January 22 through January 24; he was bedridden for a month and debilitated for the remainder of that spring.

[5] Mary Howland Russell (1820-1906), daughter of Thomas and Mary Goodwin Russell of Plymouth, Massachusetts, had lived with the Emersons in the summer of 1841, when T was also living with the family. A close friend of Lidian's from childhood, Russell tutored young Waldo and was, as were all of the Emersons' friends, stricken at the boy's death. John Shepard Keyes (1821-1910), of Concord, was attracted to Russell but thought that she was partial to the Thoreau brothers, both of whom were interested in her for some time. In 1846 Russell married Benjamin Marston Watson (1820-1896), son of Benjamin M. and Lucretia Burr Sturges Watson of Plymouth. T and the Watsons were good friends until T's death.

*Copy-text:* ALS (MH-H, MS Am 1280.226 [4114])

*Published:* LVP 1865, 9-11; *Life* 1890, 54; *FL* 1894, 47-49; *T: Home* 1902, 95; *FL* 1906, 41-43; *T as Remembered* 1917, 130-131; *Cor* 1958, 62-63; *Letters of Lidian Jackson Emerson* 1987, 108

*Editor's Notes*
  This letter is addressed "Mrs. L. C. Brown / Plymouth".
  dead;–] *PE; semicolon written over dash in MS*

*Author's Alteration*
  on] of

*To Ralph Waldo Emerson*
*March 11, 1842*

Concord March 11th 1842

Dear Friend,

I see so many "carvells ticht, fast tending throw the sea" to your El Dorado, that I am in haste to plant my flag in season on that distant beach, in the name of God and king Henry.[1] There seems to be no occasion why I who have so little to say to you here at home should take pains to send you any of my silence in a letter–[2] Yet since no correspondence can hope to rise above the level of those homely[a] speechless hours, as no spring ever bursts above the level of the still mountain tarn whence it issued–I will not delay to send a venture. As if I were to send you a piece of the house-sill–or a loose casement rather. Do not neighbors sometimes halloo with good will across a field, who yet never chat over a fence?

The sun has just burst through the fog, and I hear blue-birds,[a] song-sparrows, larks, and robins, down in the meadow. The other day I walked in the woods, but found myself rather denaturalized by late habits.[3] Yet it is the same nature that Burns and Wordsworth loved–the same life that Shakspeare and Milton lived. The wind still roars in the wood, as if nothing had happened out of the course of nature. The sound of the waterfall is not interrupted more than if a feather had fallen.

Nature is not ruffled by the rudest blast– The hurricane only snaps a few twigs in some nook of the forest. The snow attains its average depth each winter, and the chic-a-dee lisps the same notes. The old laws prevail in spite of pestilence and famine. No genius or virtue so rare & revolutionary appears in town or village, that the pine ceases to exude resin in the wood, or beast or bird lays aside its habits.

How plain that death is only the phenomenon of the individual or class– Nature does not recognise it, She finds her own again under new forms without loss. Yet death is beautiful when seen to be a law, and not an accident– It is as common as life. Men die in Tartary–in Ethiopia–in England–in Wisconsin. And after all what portion of this so serene and living nature can be said to be alive? Do this year's grasses and foliage outnumber all the past. Every blade in the field–every leaf in the forest–lays down its life in its season as beautifully as it was taken up. It is the pastime of a full quarter of the year. Dead trees–sere leaves– dried grass and herbs–are not these a good part of our life? And what is that pride of our autumnal scenery but the hectic flush–the sallow and cadaverous countenance of vegetation–its painted throes–with the November air for canvass–

When we look over the fields we are not saddened because these particular flowers or grasses will wither–for the law of their death is the law of new life. Will not the land be in good heart *because* the crops die down from year to year? The herbage cheerfully consents to bloom, and wither, and give place to a new.

So is it with the human plant. We are partial and selfish when we lament the death of the individual, unless our plaint be a paean to the departed soul, and we sigh as the wind sighs over the fields, which no shrub interprets into its private grief.

One might as well go into mourning for every sere leaf–but the more innocent and wiser soul will snuff a fragrance in the gales of autumn, and congratulate nature upon her health.

After I have imagined thus much will not the Gods feel under obligations to make me realize something as good?

I have just read some good verse by the old Scotch poet John Bellenden–

"The fynest gold or silver that we se,
May nocht be wrocht to our utilitie,
Bot flammis kein & bitter violence;

The more distress, the more intelligence.
Quhay sailis lang in hie prosperitie,
Ar sone owreset be stormis without defence."[4]

From your friend
Henry D. Thoreau

*Correspondent:* See p. 53.

[1] T quotes John Bellenden, "Allegorie of Vertue and Delyte," in *Chronicle of Scottish Poetry*, 2:56. T borrowed volume 2 from the Harvard College Library in 1837, and he borrowed all four volumes of the collection in 1841. By using Bellenden's ship and El Dorado images, T implies that many letters sail from New England to New York City, Emerson's El Dorado, the place where he made money as a lecturer.

[2] Emerson arrived in New York City on February 25, delivered his six-lecture series "The Times" between March 3 and March 14, and returned to Concord on March 18.

[3] See p. 103, note 4.

[4] John Bellenden, "Allegorie of Vertue and Delyte," 2:55.

*Copy-text:* ALS (NN-BGC, Henry David Thoreau Collection, 1837-1917, Series III)

*Published:* *Scribner's Magazine* 17 (1895): 352-353; *Cor* 1958, 63-65

*Editor's Note*
This letter is addressed "R. W. Emerson / New York." and endorsed "H. D. Thoreau / March 1842".

*Author's Alterations*
homely] *followed by cancelled* but
blue-birds,] *followed by cancelled* and

## To Isaiah Thornton Williams
*March 14, 1842*

Concord March 14th 1842

Dear Williams,

I meant to write to you before but John's death and my own sickness, with other circumstances, prevented. John died of the lock-jaw, as you know, Jan. 11th  I have been

confined to my chamber for a month with a prolonged
shock of the same disorder–from close attention to, and
sympathy with him, which I learn is not without prece-
dent. Mr. Emerson too has lost his oldest child, Waldo, by
scarlet fever, a boy of rare promise, who in the expectation of many was to be one of the lights of his generation.

John was sick but three days from the slightest apparent
cause–an insignificant cut on his finger, which gave him
no pain, and was more than a week old–but nature does
not ask for such causes as man expects–when she is ready
there will be cause enough. I mean simply that perhaps
we never assign the sufficient cause for anything–though
it undoubtedly exists. He was perfectly calm, ever pleasant while reason lasted, and gleams of the same serenity and playfulness shone through his delirium to the
last. But I will not disturb his memory. If you knew him, I
could not add to your knowledge, and if you did not know
him, as I think you could not, it is now too late, and no
eulogy of mine would suffice–  For my own part I feel that
I could not have done without this experience.

What you express with regard to the effect of time on
our youthful feelings–which indeed is the theme of universal elegy–reminds me of some verses of Byron–quite
rare to find in him, and of his best I think. Probably you
remember them.

> "No more, no more,! Oh never more on me
>     The freshness of the heart can fall like dew
> Which out of all the lovely things we see,
>     Extracts emotions beautiful and new,
> Hived in our bosoms like the bag o' the bee,
>     Think'st thou the honey with these objects grew
> Alas! 'Twas not in them, but in thy power,
>     To double even the sweetness of a flower.
>
> No more, no more! Oh, never more, my heart!
>     Canst thou be my sole world, my universe

Once all in all, but now a thing apart,
   Thou canst not be my blessing, or my curse;
The illusion's gone forever–"[1,e]

———

It would be well if we could add new years to our lives
as innocently as the fish adds new layers to its shell–no
less beautiful than the old. And I believe we may if we will
replace the vigor and elasticity of youth with faithfulness
in later years.

When I consider the universe I am still the youngest
born. We do not *grow* old we *rust* old. Let us not consent
to be old, but to die (live?) rather. Is Truth old? or Virtue–
or Faith? If we possess them they will be our *elixir vitæ*
and fount of youth. It is at least good to remember our innocence; what we regret is not quite lost–   Earth sends no
sweeter strain to Heaven than this plaint. Could we not
grieve perpetually, and by our grief discourage time's en-
croachments? All our sin too shall be welcome for such is
the material of Wisdom, and through her is our redemp-
tion to come.

'Tis true, as you say, "Man's ends are shaped for him",[2]
but who ever dared confess the extent of his free agency?
Though I am weak, I am strong too. If God shapes my
ends–he shapes me also–and his means are always equal
to his ends. His work does not lack this completeness,
that the creature consents. *I* am my destiny. Was I ever in
that straight that it was not sweet to do right? And then for
this free agency I would not be free of God certainly–   I
would only have freedom to defer to him   He has not
made us solitary agents. He has not made us to do without him   Though we must "abide our destiny", will not he
abide it with us? So do the stars and the flowers. My destiny is now arrived–is now arriving. I believe that what I
call my circumstances will be a very true history of myself–for God's works are complete both within and without–and shall I not be content with his success? I welcome
my fate for it is not trivial nor whimsical[e]. Is there not a

soul in circumstances?–and the disposition of the soul to circumstances–is not that the crowning circumstance of all? But after all it is *intra*-stances, or how it stands within me that I am concerned about. Moreover circumstances are past, but I am to come, that is to say, they are results of me–but I have not yet arrived at my result.

All impulse, too, is primarily from within The soul which does shape the world is within and central.

I must confess I am apt to consider the trades and professions so many traps which the Devil sets to catch men in–and good luck he has too, if one may judge. But did it ever occur that a man came to want, or the almshouse from consulting his higher instincts? All great good is very present and urgent, and need not be postponed. What did Homer–and Socrates–and Christ and Shakspeare & Fox?[3] Did they have to compound for their leisure, or steal their hours? What a curse would civilization be if it thus ate into the substance of the soul– Who would choose rather the simple grandeur of savage life for the solid leisure it affords? But need we sell our birthright for a mess of pottage?[4] Let us trust that we shall be fed as the sparrows are.[5]

"Grass and Earth to sit on, water to wash the feet, and fourthly, affectionate speech are at no time deficient in the mansions of the good"[6]

You may be interested to learn that Mr. Alcott is going to England in April.[7]

That you may find in Law the profession you love, and the means of spiritual culture, is the wish of your friend

Isaiah T. Williams                    Henry D. Thoreau.
Buffalo, N.Y.

*Correspondent:* See p. 85.

[1] Byron, *Don Juan*, 1.214.1-8; 1.215.1-5.

[2] See p. 100, note 3.

[3] George Fox (1624-1691) founded the Society of Friends.

[4] An allusion to Gen. 25:29-34.

[5] Matt. 6:26: "Behold the fowls of the air: for they sow not, neither do they reap, nor gather into barns; yet your heavenly Father feedeth them. Are ye not much better than they?" See also Luke 12:24.

[6] Manu, *Institutes of Hindu Law; or, The Ordinances of Menu*. T had copied this passage into a commonplace book and included it in a selection of sayings he published in the January 1843 issue of the *Dial* (pp. 331-340; see *Early Essays* 1975, p. 133). See also p. 90, note 1.

[7] Alcott left Concord on May 6, sailed from Boston on the *Rosalind* on May 8, and arrived in England on May 31. He stayed until September 28 and returned to Concord on October 21.

*Copy-text:* MSC by Elizabeth Hoar (NN-BGC, Henry David Thoreau Collection, 1837-1917, Series III)

*Published:* *Cor* 1958, 66-68

*Editor's Notes*

"No more ... gone forever–"] *Hoar placed open double quotation marks in the left margin of each line of the poetry. This use of marginal quotation marks is seen in many handwritten documents of the eighteenth and nineteenth centuries.*

whimsical] *PE*; whim / sical *in MS*


## To Charles Stearns Wheeler

*June 15, 1842*

Concord June 15th 1842

Dear Sir,

Shall I trouble you to return *these* books to the Library viz. The Bruce–Lodge & Chalkhill–and Ralegh–five vols.[1] They are all I have.

Yrs. &c

Henry D. Thoreau

I hope you will smuggle some poetical treasures into the country on your return.

*Correspondent:* See pp. 51-52.

[1] Wheeler, a tutor at Harvard, sometimes checked out books for T at his request. On January 10, 1842, Wheeler checked out John Barbour, *The Bruce; or, The History of Robert I. King of Scotland*;

Thomas Lodge, *Glaucus and Silla, with Other Lyrical and Pastoral Poems*; and John Chalkhill, *Thealma and Clearchus: A Pastoral Romance* (Harvard's copies of the latter two works were bound in one volume). T had borrowed volume 8 of *The Works of Sir Walter Ralegh, Kt* on December 10, 1841; this was probably the volume he was asking Wheeler to return.

*Copy-text:* ALS (Children of Dr. John William Lowder)

*Published: ESQ* 48 (1967): 75; *CS* 6 (June 1971): 4, 5; *ARLR* 1990, 16

*Editor's Notes*
   This letter is addressed "C. S. Wheeler".
   The copy-text is mounted under glass. The present editor was able to inspect only page 1; the address is taken from a photocopy made before the letter was mounted.


## From Isaiah Thornton Williams
*June 23, 1842*

                                        Buffalo June. 23. 1842–
Dear Thoreau
   I have not written you for a long time–but I am not going to apologize for of course you only wish to heer when & what I wish to write  The poor thoughts that have occupied my busy little mind since I last wrote you have been many & often   had I seen you should I have inflicted upon your ear the sad narration of them, or at least some of them–& I donot know why I should withhold any of them   they were sent by a power above me, at the beck & bidding of another did they come & go–  I know that men have but little to do with the affairs of this world–still I feel a responsibility to myself for all things that befall me in life–though to no other. To live this life well I feel a strong desire. I also feel a presentiment that I shall fail in part–if not totally fail to do so. I donot know what it is to live well–or how to do it if I did–between idea & idea I swing[a] like a pendulum–  I know 'tis weakness, yet such I am–  But I must not disgust you by talking too much of myself–& I know it is not well to afflict myself with my own image.

Still it is pretty much all I know–the source of most I have
ever learned. Perhaps this has been my fault–I have often
repented & as often sinned again–  What a succession of
falls is life! I wonder if that is the object of it–& this that we
may know how to stand when it is past–  I donot suppose
it is of any use to speculate about life–we know but little of
it & if it were well for us to know it would be taught us–&
I am coming more & more every day to the settled prac-
ticable bilief that the true mode of life is to live & do from
moment to moment the duty or labor before us with no
questions about its fitness or end and no thought for the
Morrow. I sometimes think further–that it is also best to
be of men & like them while with them–to love what they
love be interested in what they are interested–share their
hopes & joys their dejection & sorrows–seek the ends &
have the objects of pursuit that they have take their for-
tunes in life as I must in death & when the curtain shall
have fallen–have to think my fortune & fate–is & has ever
been that of my race–  I fear it will be a hard one if it is, but
"such is the sovreign doom & such the will of Jove"[1]  Of
one thing I am certain. My race have an indisputable
claim upon my best–all the services I am able to render
while I live–I will not withhold from them the pittance
due from me–  With this thought before me I have en-
deavoured to join in the reforms of the day–  I make Temperance speeches, such as they are–at any rate the best I
can–I go to Sabbath School & talk to & endeavour to instruct the children what I can–& where-ever I see an opportunity to do any thing for others I have a kind of general design to lend my aid–though not to interfere with
my duties to myself. Whether I am taking the best course[a]
to benefit myself & others–that is the question–  Yet if I
do as well I know–& know as well as I can I shall never
accuse myself–  After all I am not wholly satisfied with
myself or with this view of things I fear there is something
beyond & higher I ought to know & seek–  Is it given to
man in this state of existence to be satisfied? Is not this

very dissatisfaction but the breathing of an imortal nature that whispers of eternal progress? Shall not hope change this very dissatisfaction into the highest fruition? Say to me in reply what these desultory thoughts suggest to your mind–& as my sheet is nearly full I will say a few words more & fold[a] & forward it for your perusal.

Your letter of March 14 gave me much pleasure though I need not say that I sympathize with you most deeply in the loss you sustain by the death of your brother– I knew him but little–yet I thought I had never met with a more flowing generous spirit– It was not fitted for a cold & hard-hearted world like this–in such a nature do I see a strong assurance of a better existence when this is over. Ever will his name float down my memory untainted by those folies & crimes I am forced to associate with those of so many of my race. And Mr Emerson–how did he endure the loss of his child? It was a cruel stroke–did his philosophy come to his aid as does the Christian Faith to administer consolation to the bereaved? I wish to know what were his feelings. for the consolations that a christian faith affords[e] the bereaved & afflicted is one of its strongest holds upon my credulity. If there is consolation from his philosophy in trials like those–it will do much toward settling my belief– I wish to know minutely on this point– I think much on Death & sometimes doubt if my early impressions upon that subject are ever effaced– The fear of it occasions a thousand folies– I feel it is unmanly–but yet "that undiscovered country"[2] Who shall tell us whether to fear–or disire it? As to myself–I am less homesick than at first though I am not satisfied with the west–nor quite with my profession– Perhaps I ought to be I often think my feelings feelish. Do you think engaged in the practice of Law[a] the best way of spending ones life? Let me hear from you soon– I will not be so remiss in my future correspondence–

Yours &c–
I. T. Williams

*Correspondent:* See p. 85.

[1] *The Iliad of Homer*, vol. 1, 1.7-8: "Since great Achilles and Atrides strove, / Such was the sovereign doom, and such the will of Jove!"

[2] From Shakespeare, vol. 2, *Hamlet*, 3.1.78-80: "But that the dread of something after death,– / The undiscover'd country, from whose bourn / No traveller returns".

*Copy-text:* ALS (NN-BGC, Henry David Thoreau Collection, 1837-1917, Series V)

*Published:* *Cor* 1958, 69-71

*Editor's Notes*
This letter is addressed "H. D. Thoreau / Concord / Mass– / Mr. Brown" and endorsed "I. T. Williams".
affords] *PE*; offerds *in MS*

*Author's Alterations*
swing] *preceded by cancelled* but
course] *followed by cancelled* for
fold] *followed by cancelled* it
of Law] *interlined with a caret*

## To Isaiah Thornton Williams
*October 10, 1842*

Concord Oct. 10th 1842.
Dear Williams,

That your letter seems[a] fresh is[e,a] apology enough for my not having made haste[a] to answer it–but as you say, I will send you a letter now, and not an apology for none. I must confess your's sounds a little sad, but that too is one strain of the harp. You say that you have a presentiment that you may fail to live this life well–but *so* perhaps even our own failure does not concern us. Something will succeed–  Let us sympathise then with success–not with failure. Give me but the sight to see success, and no matter into what sloughs my feet lead. With what significance an old poet sang–

"How blind, that cannot see serenitie!"[1]

Thank[a] fortune, life is no such idle ease as youth paints it.[a] Perhaps the youth did not dream of an Elysium so worthy his manhood as the stern but kind fates provide. Our life needs the raciness which these sour reverses supply. Is not adversity always respectable? It should be a field worthy of us.–[a]

*Correspondent:* See p. 85.

[1] T quotes Thomas Storer's *The Life and Death of Thomas Wolsey, Cardinall*:

> How are they blinded then, that dare conspire
> > The least offence against great soveraigntie:
> Or, with Prometheus, touch one sparke of fire
> > Kindled within the breast of majestie,
> > How blind, that cannot see serenitie.

This poem, first published in 1599, is included in *Heliconia: Comprising a Selection of English Poetry of the Elizabethan Age*, 2:60. T had checked out *Heliconia* from the Harvard College Library on December 7, 1841; he probably read Storer's poem there.

*Copy-text:* AL draft (CSmH, HM 926)

*Editor's Notes*
  The document also contains other material in T's hand.
  is] *PE*; is be *in MS*

*Author's Alterations*
  seems] *interlined in pencil above* is still *cancelled in pencil*
  is] *interlined in pencil above cancelled (in pencil)* in my mind will *and uncancelled* be
  haste] *preceded by* greater *cancelled in pencil*
  Thank] *preceded by* Let us succeed with God, and not fail with any less. *cancelled in pencil*
  it.] *followed by* The failures and reverses which await men, and one after another sadden the brow of youth, add a dignity to the prospect which would be wanting to an Arcadian happiness. *cancelled in pencil*
  us.–] *followed by* True it does not become us to boast, unless we borrow of that confidence which the gods supply, nor should we esteem much a *cancelled in pencil*

## From Orestes Augustus Brownson
*November 29, 1842*

Boston, Nov. 29, 1842

My Dear Sir,

I regret that it is not in my power to lecture for you on the evening you name, as I am enjoined for that evening to lecture in the city of New-York. If some evening, say the last Wednesday, in December[e], will answer your purpose, I shall be happy[e] to lecture before your Lyceum.[1]

Yours very truly

O. A. Brownson.

H. D. Thoreau.

*Correspondent:* See pp. 32-33.

[1] Brownson lectured on "Government" on December 28.

*Copy-text:* ALS (NNPM, MA 2101)

*Editor's Notes*
This letter is addressed "Henry D. Thoreau / Concord / Mass", postmarked "BOSTON Mass NOV 29", and endorsed "Brownson".
   December] *PE*; Decem / ber *in MS*
   happy] *PE*; hap / py *in MS*

## From James Richardson Jr.
*December 9, 1842*

Friend Thoreau

I have been desirous of sending to some of my mystic brothren–some selections from certain writings of mine, that wrote themselves, when "I was in the spirit on the Lord's Day".[1] Some of these are so utterly and entirely out of all my rational faculties, that I can't put *any* meaning in them; others I read over, and learn a great deal from. This, I send you, seems to be a sort of Allegory–[2] When you return it, will you be so kind as to tell me all that it means, as there are some parts of it I do not fully understand my-self– I have a grateful remembrance of the moments I saw you in. Mr Emerson too I have less awe of, and more love for,[a] than formerly  His presence has always to me something infinite as well as divine about it. Mrs Emerson I am very desirous of knowing.

Your family give my love to–

James Richardson jr

December 9

D[y] College Cam.[3]

*Correspondent:* See p. 17.

[1] Rev. 1:10-11: "I was in the Spirit on the Lord's day, and heard behind me a great voice, as of a trumpet, Saying, I am Alpha and Omega, the first and the last: and, What thou seest, write in a book".

[2] Richardson's enclosure is not extant.

[3] Harvard Divinity School.

*Copy-text:* ALS (NNPM, MA 920)

*Published:* *Cor* 1958, 71; *ARLR* 1989, 225; *ARLR* 1990, 17

*Editor's Notes*

This letter is addressed "D. Henry Thoreau. / Concord / Care of R. Waldo Emerson" and endorsed "J. Richardson".

PE supplies the year "1842," the only year in which Richardson was in Harvard Divinity School and T was living with the Emerson family. In addition, Richardson refers in the letter to visiting in Concord: he lectured at the Concord Lyceum on December 7, 1842.

*Author's Alteration*

for,] *inserted*

## To Richard Frederick Fuller

*January 16, 1843*

Concord Jan 16th 1843.

Dear Richard,

I need not thank you for your present for I hear its music,[1] which seems to be playing just for us two pilgrims marching over hill and dale of a summer afternoon–up those long Bolton hills and by those bright Harvard lakes,[2] such as I see in the placid Lucerne on the lid–and whenever I hear I hear it[e] it will recall happy hours passed with its donor.

When did mankind make that foray into nature and bring off this booty-? For[a] certainly it is but history that some rare virtue in remote times plundered these strains from above, and communicated them to men. Whatever we may think of it, it is a part of the harmony of the spheres[3] you have sent me, which has condescended to serve us Admetuses, and I hope I may so behave that this may always be the tenor of your thought for me.

If you have any strains, the conquest of your own spear or quill to accompany these, let the winds waft them also to me.

I write this with one of the "primaries" of my osprey's wings, which I have preserved over my glass for some state occasion–and now it offers.

Mrs. Emerson sends her love–

Yr friend,
Henry D. Thoreau

*Correspondent:* Richard Frederick Fuller (1824-1869), Margaret's brother and the seventh child of Timothy and Margarett Crane Fuller, came to Concord in the fall of 1841 to prepare to enter Harvard with advanced standing. He became T's friend and sometime walking companion. Fuller later became a lawyer. In 1849 he married Sarah K. Batchelder (1829-1856), daughter of Francis and Sarah Kollock Batchelder.

[1] T refers to a music box that Fuller sent him from Cambridge after entering Harvard as a member of the class of 1844.

[2] In July 1841, T and Fuller walked from Concord to Mount Wachusett, spent the night in Sterling, Massachusetts, and returned by way of the town of Harvard, where they spent a second night. In his essay based on that excursion, "A Walk to Wachusett," T describes the hill west of the village of Bolton as follows: "It was such a place as one feels to be on the outside of the earth, for from it we could, in some measure, see the form and structure of the globe" (*Excursions* 2007, p. 33). He does not mention a specific body of water near Harvard, but the largest is Bare Hill Pond, to the southwest.

[3] In his Journal entry for August 5, 1838, T describes the music of the spheres as "pure, unmixed music–in which no wail mingles" (*Journal* 1 1981, p. 50).

*Copy-text:* ALS (NNPM, MA 2107)

*Published: LVP* 1865, 11-12; *FL* 1894, 52-53; *FL* 1906, 45-46; *Cor* 1958, 74

*Editor's Notes*
    This letter is addressed "Richard F Fuller / Cambridge / Mass." and postmarked "CONCORD MAS. JAN 16".
    I hear I hear it] *The first* I hear *is cancelled in pencil; after* it *a comma is inserted in pencil. These revisions were probably made for LVP 1865, which incorporates them.*

*Author's Alteration*
    For] for


## To Lucy Jackson Brown
*January 24, 1843*

Concord Jan 24ᵗʰ 1843

Dear Friend,
    The other day I wrote you a letter to go in Mrs Emerson's bundle[1] but as it seemed unworthy I did not send it,[2] and now to atone for that I am agoing to send this whether it be worthy or not–  I will not venture upon news for as all the household are gone to bed,–I cannot learn what has been told you. Do you read any noble verses now a days– or do not verses still seem noble?–  For my own part they have been the only things I remembered–or that which occasioned them–when all things else were blurred and defaced. All things have put on mourning but they–for the elegy itself is some victorious melody and joy escaping from the wreck.[3]
    It is a relief to read some true book wherein all are equally dead–equally alive. I think the best parts of Shakspeare would only be enhanced by the most thrilling and affecting events. I have found it so. And[a] so much the more, as they are not intended for consolation.
    Do you think of coming to Concord again?–  I shall be glad to see you–  I should be glad to know that I could see you when I would.

We always seem to be living just on the brink of a pure and lofty intercourse, which would make the ills and trivialness of life ridiculous. After each little interval, though it be but for the night, we are prepared to meet each other as gods and goddesses.– I seem[a] to have lodged all my days with one or two persons, and lived upon expectation–as if the bud would surely blossom–and so I am content to live.

What means the fact–which is so common–so universal–that some soul that has lost all hope for itself can inspire in another listening soul an infinite confidence in[a] it, even while it is expressing its despair–?

I am very happy in my present environment–though actually mean enough myself and so of course all around me–yet I am sure we for the most part are transfigured to one another–and are that to the other which we aspire to be ourselves. The longest course of mean and trivial intercourse may not prevent my practising this divine courtesy to my companion. Notwithstanding all I hear about brooms and scouring and taxes and house keeping,–I am constrained to live a strangely mixed life–as if even Valhalla[4] might have its kitchen. We are all of[a] us Apollo's serving some Admetus.

I think I must have some muses in my pay that I know not of–for certain musical wishes of mine are answered as soon as[a] entertained– Last summer I went to Hawthorne's suddenly for the express purpose of borrowing his[a] music box, and almost immediately Mrs. H proposed to lend it to me.[5] The other day I said I must go to Mrs Barrett's[6] to hear hers–and lo straightway Richard Fuller sent me one for a present from Cambridge. It is a very good one. I should like to have you hear it. I shall not have to employ you to borrow for me now. Good night.

from your affectionate friend<br>H. D. T.

*Correspondent:* See p. 77.

[1] Lidian's bundle included issues of Horace Greeley's *New-York Daily Tribune* and also the *National Anti-Slavery Standard*, a weekly paper published from 1840 to 1870 and edited at this time by Lydia Francis Child.

[2] T almost certainly refers to the following letter, which was mistakenly dated "Friday Evening, January 25, 1843." in the version published in *LVP* 1865 (pp. 15-18). January 25 was not a Friday but a Wednesday. The manuscript for this letter is not extant.

Concord, Friday Evening,<br>January 25, 1843.

Dear Friend:–

Mrs. E– asks me to write you a letter, which she will put into her bundle to-morrow along with the Tribunes and Standards, and miscellanies, and what not, to make an assortment. But what shall I write. You live a good way off, and I don't know that I have anything which will bear sending so far. But I am mistaken, or rather impatient when I say this,–for we all have a gift to send, not only when the year begins, but as long as interest and memory last. I don't know whether you have got the many I have sent you, or rather whether you were quite sure where they came from. I mean the letters I have sometimes launched off eastward in my thought; but if you have been happier at one time than another, think that then you received them. But this that I now send you is of another sort. It will go slowly, drawn by horses over muddy roads, and lose much of its little value by the way. You may have to pay for it, and it may not make you happy after all. But what shall be my new-year's gift, then? Why, I will send you my still fresh remembrance of the hours I have passed with you here, for I find in the remembrance of them the best gift you have left to me. We are poor and sick creatures at best; but we can have well memories, and sound and healthy thoughts of one another still, and an intercourse may be remembered which was without blur, and above us both.

Perhaps you may like to know of my estate nowadays. As usual, I find it harder to account for the happiness I enjoy, than for the sadness which instructs me occasionally. If the little of this last which visits me would only be sadder, it would be happier. One while I am vexed by a sense of meanness; one while I simply wonder at the mystery of life; and at another, and at another, seem to rest on my oars, as if propelled by propitious breezes from I know not what quarter. But for the most part, I am an idle, inefficient, lingering (one term will do as well as another, where all are true and none true enough) member of the great commonwealth, who have most need of my own charity,–if I could not be charitable and indulgent to myself, perhaps as good a subject for my own satire as any. You see how, when I come to talk of myself, I soon run dry, for I would fain make that a subject which can be no subject for me, at least not till I have the grace to rule myself.

I do not venture to say anything about your griefs, for it would be unnatural for me to speak as if I grieved with you, when I think I do not. If I were to see you, it might be other-wise. But I know you will pardon the trivialness of this letter; and I only hope–as I know that you have reason to be so–that you are still happier than you are sad, and that you remember that the smallest seed of faith is of more worth than the largest fruit of happiness. I have no doubt that out of S–'s death you sometimes draw sweet consolation, not only for that, but for long-standing griefs, and may find some things made smooth by it, which before were rough.

I wish you would communicate with me, and not think me unworthy to know any of your thoughts. Don't think me un-kind because I have not written to you. I confess it was for so poor a reason as that you almost made a principle of not an-swering. I could not speak truly with this ugly fact in the way; and perhaps I wished to be assured, by such evidence as you could not voluntarily give, that it was a kindness. For every glance at the moon, does she not send me an answering ray? Noah would hardly have done himself the pleasure to release his dove, if she had not been about to come back to him with tidings of green islands amid the waste.

But these are far-fetched reasons. I am not speaking directly enough to yourself now, so let me say *directly* from

Your friend,
Henry D. Thoreau

[3] T may be alluding to the death of Lucy Brown's daughter, So-phia (1821?-1842), on December 19.

[4] "In Old Northern mythology, the hall assigned to those who have died in battle, in which they feast with Odin" (*OED*).

[5] Nathaniel Hawthorne (1804-1864) and Sophia Peabody (1809-1871), both of Salem, Massachusetts, married on July 9, 1842, and took up residence at the Old Manse in Concord later that day. Haw-thorne and T became friends.

  [6] Either Susan Hudson Barrett (1783-1855) or Mary Fuller Barrett (1805-1853). Susan was the daughter of William and Lucy Kingman Hudson and widow of Samuel Barrett, who owned a grist mill. Mary, daughter of Lemuel and Mary Fuller and wife of Nathan Barrett Jr., was described by John Shepard Keyes as a "bright, lively, handsome" woman, whose home was the scene of "frolics" (*Memoirs of the Social Circle* 1888, p. 267).

*Copy-text:* ALS (DFo, MS Y.c.6262)

*Published:* *LVP* 1865, 13-15; *Life* 1890, 68-69; *FL* 1894, 49-52; *FL* 1906, 43-45; *Cor* 1958, 75-76

*Editor's Note*
  This letter is addressed "Mrs. Lucy C. Brown / Plymouth / Mass."

*Author's Alterations*
  And] *followed by cancelled* they
  seem] seemed
  in] *followed by cancelled* that
  of] us
  as] *followed by cancelled* as a
  his] *inserted*


## To Ralph Waldo Emerson

*January 24, 1843*

Concord Jan 24<sup>th</sup> 1843

Dear Friend,

  The best way to correct a mistake is to make it right. I had not spoken of writing to you,[1] but as you say you are about to write to me when you get my letter, I make haste on my part in order to get yours the sooner. I dont well know what to say to earn the forthcoming epistle–unless that Edith[2] takes rapid strides in the arts and sciences–as music and natural history–as well as over the carpet–that she says "papa" less and less abstractedly every day, looking in my face–which may sound like a Ranz-des Vaches[3] to yourself–and Ellen[4] declares every morning that "Papa *may* come home to-night"–and by and by it will have changed to such positive street news as that "Papa came home *lakst* night." Elizabeth Hoar[5] still flits about these clearings, and I meet her here and there, and in all houses but her own, but as if I were not the less of her family for all that, I have made slight acquaintance also with one Mrs Lidian Emerson, who almost persuades me to be a Christian,[6] but I fear I as often relapse into Heathenism.

Mr O'Sullivan[7] was here three days. I met him at the Atheneum, and went to Hawthornes to tea with him   He expressed a great deal of interest in your poems, and wished me to give him a list of them, which I did; he saying he did not know but he should notice them.[8] He is a rather puny looking man, and did not strike me. We had nothing to say to one another, and therefore we said a great deal. He however made a point of asking me to write for his Review, which I shall be glad to do.[9] He is at any rate one of the not-bad-but does not by any means take you by storm-no-nor by calm-which is the best way. He expects to see you in N.Y. After tea I carried him and H. to the Lyceum.

Mr Alcott has not altered much since you left-I think you will find him much the same sort of person. With Mr Lane[10] I have had one regular chat-à la George Minot[11]- which of course was greatly to our mutual grati- and edification-but as two or three as regular conversations have taken place since, I fear there may have been a precession of the equinoxes.[12] Mr Wright[13] according to the last accounts is in Lynn with uncertain aims and prospects-maturing slowly perhaps.-as indeed are all of us.

I suppose they have told you how near Mr A- went to the jail[14]-but I can add a good anecdote to the rest. When Staples[15] came to collect Mrs Ward's taxes, My sister Helen asked him what he thought Mr A. meant-what his idea was[16]-and he answered "I vum-I believe it was nothing but principle-for I never heard a man talk honester."- There was a lecture on Peace[a] by a Mr Spear[17] (ought he not to be beaten into a ploughshare[18]) the same evening,[a] and as the gentlemen (L & A)[a] dined at our house while the matter was in suspense–that is while the constable was waiting for his receipt from the jailer–we there settled it that we–that is Lane and myself perhaps, should agitate the state while Winkelried[19] lay in durance. But when over the audience I saw our hero's head moving in the free air of the Universalist Church, my fire all went out–and the state was safe as far as I was concerned, but Lane it seems, had cogitated and even written on the matter[20] in the afternoon–and so, out of courtesy taking his point of departure from the Spear-man's lecture, he drove gracefully in medias res–and gave the affair a very good setting out–but to spoil all, our martyr very characteristically, but as artists would say in bad taste, brought up the rear with a "My Prisons" which made us forget Silvio Pellico himself.–[21] The 50 dollars have been rec[d].[22] Mr Lane wishes me to ask you to see if there is anything for him in the N.Y. office, and pay the charges– Will you tell me what to do with Mr Parker who was to lecture Feb. 15th?[23] Mrs E. says that my letter is instead of one from her.

At the end of this strange letter I will not write what alone I had to say to thank you and Mrs Emerson for your long kindness to me– It would be more ungrateful than my constant thought I have been your pensioner for nearly two years and still left free as under the sky– It has been as free a gift as the sun or the summer–though I have sometimes molested you with my mean acceptance of it–I who have failed to render even those slight services of the *hand* which would have been for a sign at least, and by the fault of my nature have failed of many better and higher services. But I will not trouble you with this–but for once thank you as well as Heaven

Yr friend<br>H. D. T.

*Correspondent:* See p. 53.

[1] Emerson was in Philadelphia lecturing on "New England."

2 Edith (1841-1929) was Emerson's second daughter.

3 A type of irregular melody "peculiar to Swiss herdsmen, usually played on an Alpine horn" (*OED*).

4 Ellen Tucker Emerson (1839-1909), Emerson's oldest daughter, was named for his first wife.

5 Elizabeth Sherman Hoar (1814-1878) and T had known each other since childhood, when they were fellow students at the Concord Academy and neighbors on Main Street.

6 Acts 26:28: "Then Agrippa said unto Paul, Almost thou persuadest me to be a Christian." Lidian, in her January 15 letter to Emerson, reported that T had uncharacteristically gone to church: "I had a conversation with him a few days since on his heresies–but had no expectation of so speedy a result" (*Letters of Lidian Jackson Emerson* 1987, p. 118).

7 John Louis O'Sullivan (1813-1895) and S. D. Langtree founded the *United States Magazine, and Democratic Review* in 1837. The magazine published the work of Edgar Allan Poe, William Cullen Bryant, and Hawthorne, as well as political commentary devoted to the Democratic Party. O'Sullivan's support of Hawthorne was crucial to the writer, and the two came to be good friends. Emerson apparently first met O'Sullivan on February 12, 1843, and was less than impressed with a man who "is politico-literary and has too close an eye to immediate objects" (*Letters of RWE* 1939, 3:146-147).

8 O'Sullivan did not review Emerson's poems.

9 T ventured outside the *Dial* with "The Landlord," published in the October 1843 issue of the *United States Magazine, and Democratic Review* (pp. 427-430) and then, in the November issue, with "Paradise (To Be) Regained" (pp. 451-463), a review of J. A. Etzler's book *The Paradise within the Reach of All Men*. See *Excursions* 2007, pp. 47-54, and *Reform Papers* 1973, pp. 19-47.

10 Charles Lane (1800-1870), an English journalist and reformer, began a correspondence with Alcott in 1839. The two met in London in May 1842, and Lane and his son accompanied Alcott when he returned to the United States on October 21. Lane stayed with Emerson for a couple of days and grew to know his friends, including Fuller and T. In May 1843, with the help of Alcott's brother-in-law Samuel May, Lane bought a farm near the town of Harvard, Massachusetts, and began the Fruitlands experiment.

11 George Minott (1783-1861), son of Ephraim and Abigail Minott, was a Concord farmer whom T admired: "Minot is perhaps the most poetical farmer–who most realizes to me the poetry of the farmer's life–that I know. He does nothing (with haste and drudgery–) but as if he loved it. He makes the most of his labor and takes

infinite satisfaction in every part of it" (*Journal 4: 1851-1852*, ed. Leonard N. Neufeldt and Nancy Craig Simmons [Princeton, N.J.: Princeton University Press, 1992], p. 116). In his Journal, T reports a number of conversations with Minott, most of which concerned Minott's observations of natural phenomena.

[12] The precession of the equinox, the slow, continuous change in the direction of the earth's spin axis, makes a conical motion with a period of twenty-six thousand years.

[13] Henry Gardiner Wright (1814-1846), a disciple of the English reformer James Pierrepont Greaves's, met Alcott in June 1842 during the latter's visit to England. Alcott wrote his impressions of Wright in a letter to Mrs. Alcott: "I had not dreamed even of finding this oneness in all things–particularly with Mr Wright. He is a younger disciple of the same Eternal Verity which I have loved and served so long" (*The Letters of A. Bronson Alcott*, ed. Richard L. Herrnstadt [Ames: Iowa State University Press, 1969], p. 69). Wright accompanied Lane and Alcott to Boston, lived unhappily with the Alcotts for a time in Concord, and grew restive under the strict diet he found there. He left Concord on January 3, 1843. For several months he lived in Lynn with Mary Gove, a reformer who was separated from her husband and who nursed Wright through a cancer operation. Wright returned to his wife in England in the summer of 1843.

[14] Alcott, who apparently had paid no taxes since moving to Concord in 1840, was arrested for failure to pay his 1842 poll tax of $1.50. He had joined the Garrisonian Non-Resistance Society, whose aim was to withdraw from all cooperation with the state. As he recalled in later years, Alcott spent only a few hours at the jail, for his taxes were immediately paid by Samuel Hoar. The exact date of his arrest is uncertain, but Abigail Alcott and Charles M. Spear, who lectured that evening, both record it as January 17 in their journals.

[15] Samuel Staples (1813-1895), son of Alpheus and Polly Torrey Staples, was at various times a carpenter, hostler, bartender, auctioneer, tax collector, jailer, and representative to the Massachusetts legislature. A character in a town of characters, Staples lived on Lexington Road, near Alcott and Emerson. In 1839 he married Lucinda Wesson (1818-1881), daughter of Thomas and Lucinda Rogers Wesson; Emerson performed the marriage ceremony. Staples was appointed tax collector in 1842 and served for four years; in July of 1846 he arrested T for refusing to pay his poll tax.

[16] Alcott spoke at the conclusion of Spear's lecture.

[17] Charles M. Spear (1801-1863), a Universalist minister and reformer, opposed capital punishment and lectured on prison reform. Of the evening's events, Spear wrote in his journal, "Mr. Lane

and Alcott spoke. The latter had refused to pay his taxes. I could hardly go with him. The Saviour's example seems to be in favour of taxes" (Barry Kritzberg, "The Mr. Spear Who Ought to Have Been Beaten into a Ploughshare," *TSB* 183 [spring 1988]: 4-5).

[18] Isa. 2:4: "And he shall judge among the nations, and shall rebuke many people: and they shall beat their swords into plowshares, and their spears into pruninghooks: nation shall not lift up sword against nation, neither shall they learn war any more."

[19] Arnold von Winkelried, a Swiss hero, was said to have caused the defeat of the Austrians in 1386 by plunging himself into the enemy ranks and gathering the spears in reach, thus creating a breach in their lines.

[20] Lane's "State Slavery–Imprisonment of A. Bronson Alcott–Dawn of Liberty" appeared in the *Liberator* on January 27, 1843. He wrote: "no one has yet, it seems, ventured to act upon the conviction, and passively endure the consequences, whatever they might be, of a faithful adherence to principle. It is often said, that in a condition of society where one is obliged to let pass so much that is immoral, it is not worth while to undergo so much inconvenience as close imprisonment on account of State prosecution. Very different to this, however, has been the feeling of A. Bronson Alcott of Concord."

[21] Silvio Pellico (1789-1854), an Italian patriot imprisoned for ten years by the Austrians, detailed his experience in *My Prisons*. In "Resistance to Civil Government," T again mentions *My Prisons* in his account of his own arrest and night in jail; see *Reform Papers* 1973, p. 84.

[22] Emerson had sent Lidian an order for this amount in his letter of January 14. She apparently neglected to acknowledge it, for he mentioned it again on January 20.

[23] Theodore Parker (1810-1860) had graduated from the Harvard Divinity School in 1836 and was the Unitarian minister at Roxbury. The learned, combative Parker often offended his conservative brethren. For example, in his essay "Hollis Street Council," published in the October 1842 issue of the *Dial* (pp. 201-221), he castigated the Unitarians who had attempted to force Rev. John Pierpont from his pulpit for intemperate preaching. On January 23, the day before T's letter, the Boston Association of Congregational Ministers, a group of twenty-nine Unitarian clergymen, met with Parker to censure him not only for the *Dial* article but for his "deistical" writings and skepticism about miracles. Although Parker never left the church, his breach with his fellow Unitarian ministers became irreparable after this action. Probably because of this

controversy, in addition to poor health and fatigue stemming from overwork, Parker delayed his Concord lecture until March 22. On February 15, "Mr. Knapp of Lexington" lectured in his stead. Kenneth Walter Cameron speculates that the lecturer is either Francis Bellows Knapp (1820-1896) or his brother Frederick Newman Knapp (1821-1889), both then seniors at Harvard ("Thoreau and the Concord Lyceum–A Strategy for Enlarging Our Knowledge," *ARLR* 1990, p. 20). Neither had a connection with Lexington.

*Copy-text:* ALS (InU-Li, American Literature Manuscripts)

*Published: Life* 1890, 69-70; "Emerson-Thoreau Correspondence," *AM* 69 (May 1892): 578-579; *Alcott* 1893, 348-350; *FL* 1894, 58-62; *Life* 1896, 58; *T: Home* 1902, 94; *FL* 1906, 50-53; *Recollections* 1909, 447; *Magazine of History* 1915, 117; *Cor* 1958, 76-78

*Editor's Note*
This letter is addressed "Ralph Waldo Emerson / Philadelphia / PA", postmarked "CONCORD MAS. JAN 24", and endorsed "H. D Thoreau / Jany: 1843".

*Author's Alterations*
Peace] peace
evening,] ~.
(L & A)] *interlined with a caret*

## From Ralph Waldo Emerson
*February 9?, 10, and 11, 1843*

Carlton House:
New York Feb 1843

My dear Henry,

I have yet seen no new men in N.Y. (excepting young Tappan)[1] but only seen again some of my old friends of last year. Mr Brisbane[2] has just given me a faithful hour & a half of what he calls his principles, and he shames truer men by his fidelity & zeal, and already begins to hear the reverberations of his single voice from most of the states of the Union. He thinks himself sure of W. H. Channing here, as a good Fourierist.[3] I laugh incredulous whilst he recites (for it seems always as if he was repeating paragraphs out of his master's book) descriptions of the self augmenting potency of the solar system which is destined to contain 132 bodies I believe and his urgent inculcation of our *stellar duties*.[4] But it has its kernel of sound truth and its insanity is so wide of New York insanities that it is virtue & honor.

10. I beg you my dear friend to say to those faithful lovers of me who have just sent me letters which any man should be happy & proud to receive–I mean my mother & my wife that I am grieved that they should have found my silence so vexatious, & think that some letter must have failed for I cannot have let ten days go by without writing home[5]  I have kept no account but am confident that that cannot be. Mr Mackay[6] has just brought me his good package & I will not at this hour commence a new letter but you shall tell Mrs E. that my first steps in N.Y in this visit seem not to have been prudent & so I lose several precious days. 11 Feb.[a] A Society invited me to read my Course before them in the Bowery[7] on certain terms one of which was that they guaranteed me a thousand auditors. I referred them to my brother William[8] who covenanted with them. It turned out that their Church was in a dark inaccessible place a terror to the honest & fair citizens of N.Y. & our first lecture had a handful of persons & they all personal friends of mine from a distant part of the city.

But the Bereans felt so sadly about the disappointment that it seemed at last on much colloquy not quite good-natured[e] & affectionate to abandon them at once but to read also a second lecture & then part. The second was read with faint success & then we parted. I begin this evening anew in the Society Library[9] where I was last year. This takes more time than I could wish, a great deal–& I grieve that I cannot come home. I see W. H Channing & Mr James at leisure & have had what the Quakers call "a solid season", once or twice.[10] With Tappan a very happy

pair of hours & him I must see again. I am enriched greatly
by your letter & now by the dear letters which Mr Mackay
has bro't me from Lidian Emerson & Elizabeth Hoar and
for speed in part &[a] partly because I like to write so I make
you the organ of communication[e] to the whole household
& must still owe you a special letter. I dare not say when
I will come home as the time so fast approaches when I
should speak to the Mercantile Lib.[y].[11] Yesterday eve. I was
at Staten Island where William had promised me as a lecturer & made a speech at Tompkinsville. Dear love to My
Mother  I shall try within 24 hours to write to my Wife.
Thanks thanks for your love to Edie.[12] Farewell!

R Waldo E

*Correspondent:* See p. 53.

[1] William Aspinwall Tappan (1819-1905), son of Lewis and Susanna Aspinwall Tappan, was one of a number of young men Emerson befriended and championed. At their first meeting, the two
talked "two or three hours" until Emerson "forgot everything but
Montaigne & Michel Angelo." Tappan later married Caroline Sturgis (1819-1888), another Emerson protégée and the daughter of William and Elizabeth Davis Sturgis (*Letters of RWE* 1939, 3:143).

[2] Albert Brisbane (1809-1890), a New York journalist and intellectual, had studied in Europe, first with Victor Cousin and François
Pierre Guillaume Guizot, then with Hegel, and finally with François Marie Charles Fourier (1772-1837). On his return to the United
States in 1834, Brisbane became Fourier's chief American propo-
nent. Emerson first met Brisbane in February 1842 in the company
of Horace Greeley. Brisbane immediately tried to recruit Emerson
to the Fourierist cause, and Emerson as quickly saw that he could
not "content" his two new friends: "They are bent on popular action: I am in all my theory, ethics, & politics a poet and of no more
use in their New York than a rainbow or a firefly" (*Letters of RWE*
1939, 3:18). Emerson did publish one essay by Brisbane, "Means of
Effecting a Final Reconciliation between Religion and Science," in
the July 1842 number of the *Dial* (pp. 90-96).

[3] William Henry Channing (1810-1884), son of Francis Dana and
Susan Higginson Channing, graduated from Harvard University
in 1829 and from the Harvard Divinity School in 1833. He married
Julia Allen (1813-1889), daughter of William and Maria Verplanck

Allen, in 1836. Channing followed an eclectic career as minister, writer, and reformer. He took a Unitarian pulpit in Cincinnati in 1838, helped James Clarke edit the *Western Messenger*, and went to New York City in 1842. Channing had known Fuller and Clarke from the late 1820s and Hedge from at least 1833. Emerson first mentions Channing in his journal for November 8, 1837, where he speaks of him as an acquaintance of some time. T and Channing may have met in September 1838, when the latter visited Emerson in Concord. By 1843 Channing had become deeply interested in the work of Fourier.

⁴ Fourier developed a theory of societies divided into "phalansteries," each a self-sustaining social and economic unit. He derived his social system from his understanding of the cosmos, according to which "[p]lanets can copulate: 1st with themselves by means of the north and south poles, like plants; 2nd with another planet by means of emissions from opposite poles; 3rd with an intermediary: the Tuberose is engendered from three aromas: Earth-South, Herschel-North and Sun-South" (Charles Fourier, *The Theory of the Four Movements*, ed. Gareth Stedman Jones and Ian Patterson, trans. Ian Patterson [Cambridge: Cambridge University Press, 1996], p. 45n). Fourier estimated that there are 32 bodies in our solar system (p. 311), rather than 132, as Emerson reports here. Years later, Emerson evaluated the Fourierists in his "Historic Notes on Life and Letters in New England," *AM* 52 (October 1883): 529-543.

⁵ Emerson had written Lidian on February 1 and February 7.

⁶ Tristram Barnard MacKay (1802-1884), son of William and Amelia Hussey MacKay, had been an auctioneer and commission merchant in Boston. After retiring from his business, he divided his time between Boston and Concord, sometimes staying in the village the entire year.

⁷ Emerson began his lecture series for the Berean Society with "The Origins of New England Character" on February 7 and "Trade" on February 9. The Berean Society, which met at a Universalist church near the Bowery, was founded in June 1841. Its members were American followers of Rev. John Barclay (1734-1798), a Scottish minister who founded the Berean Assembly in Edinburgh in 1773.

⁸ William Emerson (1801-1868), son of William and Ruth Haskins Emerson, graduated from Harvard in 1818, studied in Germany, and became a lawyer in New York City. In 1833 he married Susan Haven (1807-1868), daughter of John and Ann Woodward Haven. The couple lived on Staten Island, where T tutored their son William (1835-1864) in 1843.

⁹ Emerson gave the whole New England series at the New York Society Library: "Genius of the Anglo-Saxon Race" on February 11, "Trade" on February 15, "Manners and Customs of New England" on February 17, "Recent Literature and Spiritual Influences" on February 20, and "Results and Tendencies" on February 22. The New York Society Library was formed in 1754 by a group of prominent citizens; users, most of whom were well-to-do, paid a fee to subscribe. Its collection, which grew from two collections given to the city in 1700 and 1729 for a public library, was housed first in City Hall, later at its own building on Nassau Street, and then, in 1840, at Broadway and Leonard Street.

¹⁰ Henry James Sr. (1811-1882), a member of Albert Brisbane's intellectual circle, was, like many of Emerson's New York friends, very interested in Fourier. When he first met James in March 1842, Emerson called him "a very manlike thorough seeing person" (*Letters of RWE* 1939, 3:23). That meeting developed into a lasting, if edgy, friendship. When Emerson arrived in 1843 to lecture, James himself was giving his first lectures, a three-evening series on the "Inward Reason of Christianity," on February 2, February 9, and February 16. Emerson's success in that same period contrasted sharply with James's failure to move or retain his audience.

¹¹ After completing his course at the New York Society Library, Emerson moved to the Broadway Tabernacle, a spacious hall engaged by his sponsor, the Mercantile Library Association. He gave two lectures there: "Domestic Life" on February 28 and "Politics" on March 7. The Mercantile Library Association, a subscription library like the New York Society Library, was founded in 1820 by merchant clerks. It opened in February 1821 in rented rooms on Fulton Street; in 1830, as the Clinton Hall Association, the library moved to another set of rented rooms at the corner of Nassau and Beekman streets.

¹² In a letter dated February 1 and February 3, Lidian told Emerson that Edith was listening to T's music box.

*Copy-text:* ALS (NN-BGC, Henry David Thoreau Collection, 1837-1917, Series IV)

*Published: HDT* 1882, 133-134; "E-T" May 1892, 581-582; *Alcott* 1893, 522; *Cor* 1958, 81-82; *Letters of RWE* 1990-1995, 7:525-526

*Editor's Notes*
This letter is addressed "Henry D. Thoreau. / Concord. / Mass." and postmarked "NEW-YORK FEB 11".
The first date for this letter could be either February 8 or 9. PE supplies "9?" following Rusk's conjecture. On February 7 Emerson

wrote Lidian that he had met Tappan the evening before and that his letter to T was "yet to be written" (*Letters of RWE* 1939, 3:143).

good-natured] *PE*; good- / natured *in MS*
communication] *PE*; communi / cation *in MS*

*Author's Alterations*
11 Feb.] *interlined above*
&] I

## To Ralph Waldo Emerson
*February 10, 1843*

Concord Feb. 10th 1843.

Dear Friend,

I have stolen one of your own sheets to write you a letter upon, and I hope with two layers of ink to turn it into a comforter.

If you like to receive a letter from me too, I am glad, for it gives me pleasure to write. But[a] dont let it come amiss–it must fall as harmlessly as leaves settle on the landscape. I will tell you what we are doing here now.

Supper is done and Edith the dessert perhaps more than the desert–is brought in–or even comes in per se–and round she goes now to this altar and then to that with her monosyllabic invocation of "oc" oc"– It makes me think of "Langue d'oc"  she must belong to that province.[1] And like the gipsies she talks a language of her own while she understands ours. While she jabbers Sanscrit-Parsee-Pelvhi[2]– Say Edith go bah![3] and bah it is– No intelligence passes between us–she knows. It is a capital joke–that is the reason she smiles so. How well the secret is kept!  she never descends to explanation–  It is not buried like a common secret bolstered up on two sides, but by an eternal silence on the one side at least–  It has been long kept and comes in from the unexplored horizon like a blue mountain range to end abruptly at our door one day (dont stumble at this steep simile)[a].–  And now she studies the heights and depths of nature on shoulders whirled in some eccentric orbit fast by old Pestum's temples[4] and, the perch where Time doth plume his wings.– And how she runs the race over the carpet while all Olympia applauds Mamma Grandma and Uncle Good Grecians all– and that dark-hued Barbarian–Partheania Parker whose shafts go through and through not backward.

Grandmama smiles over all–and Mamma is wondering what Papa would say–should she descend on Carlton House some day– "Lask's Night"s abed dreaming of "pleased faces" far away. But now the trumpet sounds– the games are oer–  Some Hebe comes and Edith is translated–I don't know where, it must be to some cloud for I never was there.

Query–What becomes of the answers Edith thinks but can not express? She really gives you glances which are before the world was. You cant feel any difference of age– except that you have longer legs and arms.

Mrs Emerson said I must tell you about domestic affairs–when I mentioned that I was going to write–perhaps it will inform you of the state of all–if I only say that I am well and happy in your house here–in Concord–

Your Friend Henry.

Dont forget to tell us what to do with Mr. Parker when you write next. I lectured this week–[5]  It was as bright a night as you could wish–  I hope there were no stars thrown away on the occasion.

*Correspondent:* See p. 53.

*Correspondent:* See p. 53.

[1] The language spoken in medieval France in the southern province of Languedoc; "oc" was the word for "yes" in that language (*OED*).

[2] Pahlavi, or Pehlvi, was the "name given by the followers of Zoroaster to the character in which are written the ancient translations of their sacred books and some other works of the same age" (*OED*).

[3] Probably a play on "Erin go bragh!" (Ireland forever!), a refrain in Thomas Campbell's "Exile of Erin" (*The Poetical Works of Thomas Campbell*, pp. 116-117).

⁴ Paestum, a coastal town in southern Italy founded ca. 600 BCE, is known as the site of several ancient walls and temples.

⁵ T's February 8 lecture before the Concord Lyceum was titled "The Life and Character of Sir Walter Raleigh" (see *Early Essays* 1975, pp. 178-218). He did not publish the lecture during his lifetime but included a small part of it in *A Week on the Concord and Merrimack Rivers*.

*Copy-text:* Facsimile of ALS (location of MS unknown)

*Published:* "Emerson-Thoreau Correspondence," *AM* 69 (May 1892): 579-580; *FL* 1894, 62-64; *FL* 1906, 54-55; *Magazine of History* 21 (July-December 1915): 117; *Cor* 1958, 83-84

*Editor's Notes*
This letter is addressed "Ralph Waldo Emerson / New-York / NY" and endorsed "H. D. Thoreau– / 1843".

Harding and Bode note in *Cor* 1958, p. 84, that T did not mail this letter immediately but enclosed it with his February 12 letter to Emerson.

*Author's Alterations*
But] *followed by cancelled* it must
(dont ... simile)] *interlined with a caret*


*To Ralph Waldo Emerson*
*February 12, 1843*

February 12, 1843.
Dear Friend,–As the packet still tarries,¹ I will send you some thoughts, which I have lately relearned, as the latest public and private news.

How mean are our relations to one another! Let us pause till they are nobler. A little silence, a little rest, is good. It would be sufficient employment only to cultivate true ones.

The richest gifts we can bestow are the least marketable. We hate the kindness which we understand. A noble person confers no such gift as his whole confidence: none so exalts the giver and the receiver; it produces the truest gratitude. Perhaps it is only essential to friendship that some vital trust should have been reposed by the one in the other. I feel addressed and probed even to the remote parts of my being when one nobly shows, even in trivial things, an implicit faith in me. When such divine commodities are so near and cheap, how strange that it should have to be each day's discovery! A threat or a curse may be forgotten, but this mild trust translates me. I am no more of this earth; it acts dynamically; it changes my very substance. I cannot do what before I did. I cannot be what before I was. Other chains may be broken, but in the darkest night, in the remotest place, I trail this thread. Then things cannot *happen*. What if God were to confide in us for a moment! Should we not then be gods?

How subtle a thing is this confidence! Nothing sensible passes between; never any consequences are to be apprehended should it be misplaced. Yet something has transpired. A new behavior springs; the ship carries new ballast in her hold. A sufficiently great and generous trust could never be abused. It should be cause to lay down one's life,–which would not be to lose it. Can there be any mistake up there? Don't the gods know where to invest their wealth? Such confidence, too, would be reciprocal. When one confides greatly in you, he will feel the roots of an equal trust fastening themselves in him. When such trust has been received or reposed, we dare not speak, hardly to see each other; our voices sound harsh and untrustworthy. We are as instruments which the Powers have dealt with. Through what straits would we not carry this little burden of a magnanimous trust! Yet no harm could possibly come, but simply faithlessness. Not a feather, not a straw, is entrusted; that packet is empty. It is only *committed* to us, and, as it were, all things are committed to us.

The kindness I have longest remembered has been of this sort,–the sort unsaid; so far behind the speaker's lips that almost it already lay in my heart. It did not have far to go to be communicated. The gods cannot misunderstand, man cannot explain. We communicate like the burrows of foxes, in silence and darkness, under ground. We are undermined by faith and love. How much more full is Nature where we think the empty space is than where we place the solids!–full of fluid influences. Should we ever communicate but by these? The spirit abhors a vacuum more than Nature. There is a tide which pierces the pores of the air. These aerial rivers, let us not pollute their currents. What meadows do they course through? How many fine mails there are which traverse their routes! He is privileged who gets his letter franked by them.

I believe these things.

Henry D. Thoreau.

*Correspondent:*  See p. 53.

[1] The "packet" for Emerson apparently included two letters from T, this one and another dated February 10, along with one from Lidian dated February 12.

*Copy-text:* "Emerson-Thoreau  Correspondence," *AM*  69  (May 1892): 580-581

*Published:* "Emerson-Thoreau  Correspondence," *AM*  69  (May 1892): 580-581; *FL* 1894, 65-67; *FL* 1906, 56-58; *Magazine of History* 21 (July-December 1915): 117; *Cor* 1958, 86-87

## From Ralph Waldo Emerson
*February 12, 1843*

New York 12 Feb[y]

My dear Henry,

I am sorry I have no paper but this unsightly sheet this Sunday eve. to write you a message which I see must not wait– The Dial for April– –[1]  What elements shall compose it? What have you for me? What has Mr Lane? Have you any Greek translations in your mind? Have you given shape to the comment on Etzler?[2] (It was about some sentences on this matter that I made some day a most rude

& snappish speech, I remember, but you will not,–& must give the sentences as you first wrote them.) You must go to Mr Lane with my affectionate respects & tell him that I depend on his important aid for the new number, and wish him to give us the most recent & stirring matter that he has. If (as he is a ready man) he offers us anything at once, I beg you to read it, & if you see & say decidedly that it is good for us you need not send it to me: but if it is of such quality that you can less surely pronounce, You must send it to me by Harnden.[3] Have we no more news from Wheeler? Has Bartlett none?[4]

I find Edw. Palmer here studying medicine & attending medical lectures.[5] He is acquainted with Mr Porter whom Lane & Wright[6] know & values him highly. I am to see Porter. Perhaps I shall have no more time to fill this sheet. if so, farewell

Yours<br>R. Waldo E.

*Correspondent:* See p. 53.

[1] Emerson had agreed to become the editor of the *Dial* in March 1842 when Margaret Fuller resigned from the position. With this letter (and one to Fuller dated the same day), Emerson began collecting material for the April *Dial*, his fourth issue. He solicited and received work from Fuller, James Clarke, and Lydia Child. T assisted Emerson in editing this number: he reviewed Charles Lane's substantial contributions, offered his own translations of eleven poems of Anacreon with commentary, selected Confucius's sayings for the "Ethnical Scriptures" section, and provided four of his own poems.

[2] T published "Paradise (To Be) Regained," a review of J. A. Etzler's *The Paradise within the Reach of All Men*, in the November 1843 issue of O'Sullivan's *United States Magazine, and Democratic Review* (pp. 451-463), not in the *Dial*. See *Reform Papers* 1973, pp. 19-47.

[3] The Harnden Express Company was founded by William Frederick Harnden (1812-1845) in 1839. The company made regular deliveries of small packages and letters between Boston and New York, Philadelphia, and Albany.

⁴ Charles Stearns Wheeler was studying in Germany at this time, and Emerson had asked him for literary news for the *Dial*'s "Literary Intelligence" column. Robert Bartlett, Emerson's friend and a tutor at Harvard, often corresponded with Wheeler and thus would have been a source of information.

⁵ Edward Palmer (1802-1886) of Maine left the medical profession to become an itinerant reformer. He opposed the use of money. Emerson had failed to interest Fuller in one of Palmer's essays for the *Dial*, but George Ripley had reviewed Palmer's book *A Letter to Those Who Think* (Worcester: n.p., 1840) in the October 1840 number. Palmer had visited Emerson in Concord at least twice. In March 1842, Emerson wrote in his journal: "Here was Edward Palmer, with somewhat ridiculous yet much nobility, always combined in his person & conversation" (*JMN*, 8:216).

⁶ Henry Gardiner Wright.

*Copy-text:* ALS (MCo-SC)

*Published:* "E-T" May 1892, 582; *FL* 1894, 68; *FL* 1906, 58; *Cor* 1958, 85; *Letters of RWE* 1990-1995, 7:527-528

*Editor's Notes*
This letter is addressed "Henry D. Thoreau. / Concord / Mass." and postmarked "{*illegible*} MS. FEB 14".

The copy-text is tipped into volume 1 of Alfred W. Hosmer's grangerized copy of Henry S. Salt's *Life of Henry David Thoreau*, 2nd ed. (London: Walter Scott, 1896), at page 55.

PE supplies the year "1843" from the contents of the letter.

## To Ralph Waldo Emerson
*February 15, 1843*

Concord Feb. 15ᵗʰ 1843

My dear Friend,

I got your letters–one yesterday and the other to-day–and they have made me quite happy.

As a packet is to go in the morning I will give you a hasty account of the Dial. I called on Mr Lane this afternoon–and brought away–together with an abundance of good-willᵉ–1ˢᵗ a bulky catalogue of books without commentary–some 800 I think he told me–with an introduction filling one sheet–Ten or a dozen pagesˡ–say–though I have only glanced at them. 2[nly] A Review–25 or 30 printed pages–of Conversations on the Gospels–Record of a School–and Spiritual Culture. with rather copious extracts–[2] However it is a good subject and Lane says it gives him satisfaction. I will give it a faithful reading directly.

And now I come to the little end of the horn–for myself I have brought along the Minor Greek Poets and will mine there for a scrap or two–at least.[3] As for Etzler–I dont remember any[a] rude and snappish speech that you made–and if you did it must have been longer than anything I had written–  However here is the book still and I will try. Perhaps I have some few scraps in my Journal which you may choose to print. The translation of AEschylus I should like very well to continue anon[4]–if it should be worth the while.–  As for poetry I have not remembered to write any for sometime–it has quite slipped my mind–but sometimes I think I hear the muttering of the thunder. Dont you remember that last summer we heard a low tremulous sound in the woods and over the hills–and thought it was partridges or rocks–  And it proved to be thunder gone down the river–  But[a] sometimes it was over Wayland way and at last burst over our heads–  So we'll not despair by reason of the drought.

You see it takes a good many words to supply the place of one deed.–a hundred lines to a cob-web–and but one cable to a man-of war.

The Dial cover needs to be reformed in many particulars–  There is no news from Wheeler–none from Bartlett.

They all look well and happy in this house–where it gives me much pleasure to dwell–

Yrs in haste

Henry

*Correspondent:* See p. 53.

[1] When Charles Lane came to the United States with Alcott in October 1842, he brought with him from England a fine library that

included almost a thousand volumes given to him by James Pierrepont Greaves, an English educational reformer. Lane's "Catalogue
of Books," a condensed version of the "bulky" list, closed the April
1843 *Dial* (pp. 545-548).

[2] Lane's review article "A. Bronson Alcott's Works" was the lead
essay for the April 1843 *Dial* (pp. 417-454). A considerable portion
of the essay was devoted to extracts from three books: Alcott's
*Conversations with Children on the Gospels*, Elizabeth Palmer Peabody's *Record of a School: Exemplifying the General Principles of
Spiritual Culture*, and James Pierrepont Greaves's *Spiritual Culture; or, Thoughts for the Consideration of Parents and Teachers*, in
which an edition of Alcott's *The Doctrine and Discipline of Human
Culture*, titled *Doctrine of Spiritual Culture*, follows Greaves's work
(pp. 79-108).

[3] T had translated three of Anacreon's poems in his Journal in
December 1838, but he included only one of them, "Anacreon," in
the group of eleven published in the April 1843 *Dial* (pp. 484-490).
His source was a copy of the 1598 Commelin edition of *Carminum
poetarum novem*, a collection of a number of Greek poets including Anacreon, which is bound with a copy of the 1598 Commelin
edition of Pindar's odes. This edition was included in Lane's "Catalogue of Books" as "Pindari. Alcœi, Sapphus, Stesichori, Anacreon-
tis, Simonidis, Alemonis, &c. Greece et Latine. Heidelberge, 1597"
(*Dial* 3 [April 1843]: 548). See *Translations* 1986, pp. 55-62, 164-168.

[4] T had translated *The Prometheus Bound* for the January 1843
*Dial* (pp. 363-386; see *Translations* 1986, pp. 3-53, 160-164). He
translated *The Seven against Thebes* in the summer of 1843, but
he did not publish the translation in his lifetime (see *Translations*
1986, pp. 63-110, 168-170). His source for both works was probably
Aeschylus, *Tragoediae: Ad exemplar glasguense accurate expressae.*

*Copy-text:* ALS (NNC-RB, Manuscript Collections)

*Published:* "Emerson-Thoreau Correspondence," *AM* 69 (May
1892): 583; *FL* 1894, 69-71; *FL* 1906, 59-61; *Magazine of History* 21
(July-December 1915): 117-118; *Cor* 1958, 87-88

*Editor's Notes*
    This letter is addressed "R. Waldo Emerson / New-York / N.Y."
and endorsed "H D Thoreau".
    good-will] *PE*; good- / will *in MS*

*Author's Alterations*
    any] *followed by cancelled* words
    But] but

## To Ralph Waldo Emerson
*February 20, 1843*

Concord, February 20, 1843.

My Dear Friend,–I have read Mr. Lane's review,[1] and *can* say, speaking for this world and for fallen man, that "it is good for us." As they say in geology, time never fails, there is always enough of it,[2] so I may say, criticism never fails; but if I go and read elsewhere, I say it is good,–far better than any notice Mr. Alcott has received, or is likely to receive from another quarter. It is at any rate "the other side," which Boston needs to hear. I do not send it to you, because time is precious, and because I think you would accept it, after all. After speaking briefly of the fate of Goethe and Carlyle in their own countries, he says, "To Emerson in his own circle is but slowly accorded a worthy response; and Alcott, almost utterly neglected," etc. I will strike out what relates to yourself, and, correcting some verbal faults, send the rest to the printer with Lane's initials.[3]

The catalogue needs amendment, I think.[4] It wants completeness now. It should consist of such books only as they would tell Mr. Hedge[5,e] and Parker[e] they had got; omitting the Bible, the classics, and much besides,–for there the incompleteness begins. But you will be here in season for this.

It is frequently easy to make Mr. Lane more universal and attractive; to write, for instance, "universal ends" instead of "the universal end," just as we pull open the petals of a flower with our fingers where they are confined by its own sweets. Also he had better not say "books designed for the nucleus of a *Home* University," until he makes that word "home" ring solid and universal too. This is that abominable dialect. He has[v] just given me a notice of George Bradford's Fénelon for the Record of the Months,[6] and speaks of extras of the Review and Catalogue, if they are printed,–even a hundred, or thereabouts. How shall this be arranged? Also he wishes to use some manuscripts of his which are in your possession, if you do not. Can I get them?

I think of no news to tell you. It is a serene summer day here, all above the snow. The hens steal their nests, and I steal their eggs still, as formerly. This is what I do with the hands. Ah, labor,–it is a divine institution, and conversation with many men and hens.

Do not think that my letters require as many special answers. I get one as often as you write to Concord. Concord inquires for you daily, as do all the members of this house. You must make haste home before we have settled all the great questions, for they are fast being disposed of. But I must leave room for Mrs. Emerson.

Yours,<br>Henry.ᵉ

*Correspondent:* See p. 53.

¹ Charles Lane's "A. Bronson Alcott's Works" appeared in the April 1843 *Dial* (pp. 417-454).

² T probably refers to a passage from Aristotle's *Meteorologica*, which he read in Charles Lyell's *Principles of Geology*, 1:22. He copied the passage into his Journal entry for October 11, 1840: "As time never fails, and the universe is eternal, neither the Tanais, nor the Nile, can have flowed forever" (*Journal 1* 1981, p. 187).

³ The published version of the quoted passage, edited by T, reads: "And, not to mention others, Alcott, almost utterly neglected by contemporaries, must seek his truer appreciation beyond the great waters" ("A. Bronson Alcott's Works," *Dial* 3 [April 1843]: 420).

⁴ T edited Lane's full catalog of nearly a thousand titles down to fewer than four printed pages for the April *Dial* (pp. 545-548); see pp. 141-142, note 1.

⁵ Frederic Henry Hedge (1805-1890), son of Levi and Mary Kneeland Hedge, graduated from Harvard University in 1825 and from the Harvard Divinity School in 1828. He first became a pastor at West Cambridge, Massachusetts; from 1835 to 1850 he was the Unitarian minister at Bangor, Maine. Hedge later joined the Harvard faculty and served as president of the American Unitarian Association. He had studied in Germany, and his knowledge of German philosophy helped shape the Transcendental movement.

⁶ Lane's review of George Bradford's *Thoughts on Spiritual Sub-jects, Translated from the Writings of Fenelon* (Boston: Samuel G. Simpkins, 1843) never appeared in the *Dial*. It was not in the April issue, and Emerson reported that it was "crowded out" of the July issue "by the unexpected length of [the] printed articles" in that number (*Dial* 4 [July 1843]: 133).

*Copy-text:* "Emerson-Thoreau Correspondence," *AM* 69 (May 1892): 584

*Published:* "Emerson-Thoreau Correspondence," *AM* 69 (May 1892): 584; *FL* 1894, 73-75; *FL* 1906, 62-64; *Cor* 1958, 90-91

*Editor's Notes*

Hedge] *PE;* [F. H.] Hedge *in copy-text, FL 1894, and FL 1906*
Parker] *PE;* [Theodore] Parker *in copy-text, FL 1894, and FL 1906*
Henry.] *followed in copy-text by postscript by Lidian Emerson to Ralph Waldo Emerson:*

My dear Husband,–

Thinking that Henry had decided to send Mr. Lane's manu-script to you by Harnden¹ to-morrow, I wrote you a sheet of gossip which you will not ultimately escape. Now I will use up Henry's vacant spaces with a story or two. G. P. Bradford has sent you a copy of his Fénelon, with a freezing note to me, which made me declare I would never speak to him again; but Mother says, "Never till next time!" William B. Greene has sent me a volume of tales translated by his father.² Ought there to be any note of acknowledgment? I wish you may find time to fill all your paper when you write; you must have millions of things to say that we would all be glad to read.

Last evening we had the "Conversation," though, owing to the bad weather, but few attended. The subjects were: What is Prophecy? Who is a Prophet? and The Love of Nature. Mr. Lane decided, as for all time and the race, that this same love of na-ture–of which Henry was the champion, and Elizabeth Hoar and Lidian (though L. disclaimed possessing it herself) his faithful squiresses–that this love was the most subtle and dan-gerous of sins; a refined idolatry, much more to be dreaded than gross wickednesses, because the gross sinner would be alarmed by the depth of his degradation, and come up from it in terror, but the unhappy idolaters of Nature were deceived by the refined quality of their sin, and would be the last to enter the kingdom.³ Henry frankly affirmed to both the wise men that they were wholly deficient in the faculty in question, and therefore could not judge of it. And Mr. Alcott as frankly answered that it was because they went beyond the mere material objects, and were filled with spiritual love and perception (as Mr. T. was not), that they seemed to Mr. Thoreau not to appreciate outward nature. I am very heavy, and have spoiled a most excellent story. I have given you no idea of the scene, which was ineffably comic, though it made no laugh at the time; I scarcely laughed at it myself,–too deeply amused to give the usual sign. Henry was brave and noble; well as I have always liked him, he still grows upon me. Elizabeth sends her love, and says she shall not go to Boston till your return, and you must make the 8th of March come quickly.

[1] The Harnden Express Company; see p. 139, note 3.

[2] William Batchelder Greene (1819-1878) was the son of Nathaniel and Susan Batchelder Greene. A former army officer, Greene graduated from the Harvard Divinity School in 1845 but left the ministry to become a writer. He published an essay, "First Principles," in the January 1842 issue of the *Dial* (pp. 273-285). The volume of tales translated by Nathaniel Greene is *Tales and Sketches: Translated from the Italian, French and German* (Boston: C. C. Little and J. Brown, 1843).

[3] For examples of the common locution in the Christian scriptures, see Matt. 18:3: "Except ye be converted and become as little children, ye shall not enter into the kingdom of heaven", and Matt. 19:23: "Verily I say unto you, That a rich man shall hardly enter into the kingdom of heaven."

*Substantive Variant*

The text of this letter is based on a published source, "Emerson-Thoreau Correspondence"; a potentially authoritative substantive reading in *FL* 1894 and *FL* 1906 is reported below.

has] *in copy-text;* had *in FL 1894 and FL 1906*

## From Elizabeth Palmer Peabody
*February 26, 1843*

Feb. 26th 1843

My dear Sir

I understand you have begun to print the Dial and I am very glad of it on one account–viz–that if it gets out early enough to go to England by the steamer of the 1st of the month–it does not have to wait *another month*–as was the case with the last number–[1]

But I meant to have had as a first article a letter to the "Friends of the Dial" somewhat like the rough draft I enclose[2]–And[a] was waiting Mr[a] Emerson's arrival to consult him about the manner of it. I have now written him at New York on the subject & told him my *whys* & *wherefores*. The regular[e] income of the Dial does not pay *the cost* of its printing & paper–& there are readers enough of it to support it if they would only subscribe & they will[a] subscribe if they are convinced[e] that only by doing so can they secure its continuance– He will probably write you on the subject–

I want to ask a favour of you– It is to procure me a small phial of that black lead *dust* which is to be found as Dr C. T. Jackson[3] tells me at a certain lead pencil manufactory[e] in Concord[4]–& send it to me by the first opportunity.– I want lead in this *fine dust* to use in a chemical Experiment–

Respectfully yrs<br>E P Peabody

P.S.–I hope you have got your money from Bradbury & Soden.–[5] I have done all I could about it–

Will you drop the enclosed letter for Mrs. Hawthorne into the Post Office–[6]

---

*Correspondent:* Elizabeth Palmer Peabody (1804-1894), daughter of Nathaniel and Elizabeth Palmer Peabody and a longtime teacher, was a friend of Dr. William Ellery Channing, Hawthorne, and Emerson. She taught at Alcott's Temple School in the mid-1830s, opened a bookstore in Boston in 1840, and was for a brief time the *Dial*'s publisher. She wrote three essays that appeared in the *Dial*, "A Glimpse of Christ's Idea of Society" in October 1841, pp. 214-228; "Plan of the West Roxbury Community" in January 1842, pp. 361-372; and "Fourierism" in April 1844, pp. 473-483. In 1849 she published T's "Resistance to Civil Government" in her short-lived journal *Aesthetic Papers* (see *Reform Papers* 1973, pp. 63-90). She was later prominent in the kindergarten movement.

[1] Peabody had trouble with details such as getting the magazine to the English market.

[2] The draft is not extant.

[3] Charles Thomas Jackson (1805-1880), Emerson's brother-in-law, graduated from the Harvard Medical School in 1829. After a brief career as a doctor, he became a chemist and mineralogist and led geological surveys of Massachusetts, Maine, Rhode Island, and New Hampshire. Jackson's life was marked by bitter controversies about his claims to have invented the telegraph and to have discovered ether as an effective anesthetic.

[4] T had designed a grinder for his father's pencil factory that produced an uncommonly fine powdered graphite.

[5] Waymond Bradbury and Samuel S. Soden published the *Boston Miscellany of Literature and Fashion* from January 1842 to February 1843. They published T's essay "A Walk to Wachusett" in the January 1843 number (pp. 31-36; see *Excursions* 2007, pp. 29-46) but did not pay him for it. Bradbury (1811-1875) was the son of Edward and Abigail Hill Bradbury of Framingham, Massachusetts; Soden (1819-1844) was the son of Thomas and Mary G. Soden of Watertown. In 1841 Soden married Ferona A. Johnson of Framingham.

[6] The enclosure is not extant.

*Copy-text:*  ALS (ViU, Clifton Waller Barrett Library, Elizabeth Peabody Collection [#6952-A])

*Published: Critic* 48 (1906): 346; *Recollections* 1909, 560-561; *Cor* 1958, 92-93; *Transcendental Epilogue: Primary Materials for Research in Emerson, Thoreau, Literary New England, the Influence of German Theology, and Higher Biblical Criticism*, ed. Kenneth Walter Cameron (Hartford, Conn.: Transcendental Books, 1965), 3:41; *Letters of Elizabeth Palmer Peabody*, ed. Bruce A. Ronda (Middletown, Conn.: Wesleyan University Press, 1984), 260-262

*Editor's Notes*
    This letter is addressed "Mr. Henry D. Thoreau / Concord–" and endorsed "E. P. Peabody".
    regular] *PE*; regu / lar *in MS*
    convinced] *PE*; convined *in MS*
    manufactory] *PE*; manu / factory *in MS*

*Author's Alterations*
    And] but
    Mr] any
    will] *followed by cancelled* only

*To Ralph Waldo Emerson*
*March 1, 1843*

Wednesday Evening

Dear Friend

I have time to write a few words about the Dial[a]. I have just received the first 3 signatures–which do not yet complete Lane's piece[1]  He will place five hundred copies for sale at Monroe's bookstore–[2]  Wheeler has sent you two full sheets–more about the German universities–and proper names which will have to be printed[a] in alphabetical order for convenience,–what this one has done that one is doing–and the other intends to do–Hammer Purgstall (von Hammer)[3] may be one for ought I know. However there are two or three things in it as well as names–  One of the books of Herodotus[4] is discovered to be out of place. He says something about having sent to Lowell by the last steamer a budget of Literary news which he will have communicated to you ere this.[5]

Mr Alcott has a leter from Heraud and a book written by him–The Life of Savonarola–which he wishes to have republished here–  Mr Lane will write a notice of it.[6] The latter says that what is in the N.Y. post office *may* be directed to Mr. Alcott.

Miss Peabody has sent a "Notice[a] to the readers of the Dial"[7]–which is not good.

Mr Chapin lectured this evening–but so rhetorically–that I forgot my duty and heard very little.[8]

I find myself better than I have been–and am meditating some other method of paying debts than by lectures and writing which will only do to talk about–  If any thing of that "other" sort should come to your ears in N.Y. will you remember it for me?[9]

Excuse this scrawl which I am writing over the embers in the dining room. I hope that you live on good terms with yourself and the gods–

Yrs in haste
Henry.

*Correspondent:* See p. 53.

[1] Charles Lane, "A. Bronson Alcott's Works," *Dial* 3 (April 1843): 417-454.

[2] James Munroe (1808-1861) founded his Boston and Cambridge firm in the early 1830s. In 1843 he and his partner, William H. Dennett, were located at 134 Washington Street in Boston and in the Lyceum Building, Harvard Square, Cambridge.

[3] Joseph Freiherr von Hammer-Purgstall (1774-1856) was an Austrian orientalist. Emerson owned a copy of his *Geschichte der Schönen Redekünste Persiens* (Wien: Heubner und Volke, 1818). Wheeler did not mention him in his "Literary Intelligence" column for the April number.

[4] T apparently omitted the information about Herodotus, for it does not appear among the discussions of German writers and books in "Literary Intelligence" in the April 1843 *Dial* (pp. 541-544).

[5] Both Emerson and James Russell Lowell had asked Wheeler for literary news from Germany, Emerson for the *Dial* and Lowell for his new magazine the *Pioneer*. Despite an understanding that Emerson had the right to Wheeler's letters, Robert Carter, acting as Lowell's editor, published in the March 1843 *Pioneer* some material ("Letters from Germany," pp. 143-144) from Wheeler's correspondence that had appeared in "Literary Intelligence" in the January 1843 *Dial* (pp. 387-397).

[6] John Abraham Heraud (1799-1887), whom Alcott met in England, was a poet, dramatist, and editor. He was a friend of the Carlyles' and had recently edited the *Monthly Magazine*. In his review for the April 1843 *Dial*, Charles Lane wrote of Heraud's *The Life and Times of Girolamo Savonarola* (London: Whittaker, 1843): "The present volume, though in its pains-taking erudition it grows occasionally discursive, and in needless efforts to prove that the Roman Catholic Church is really the protestant establishment, becomes somewhat controversial, is yet a valuable addition to our standard literature" (p. 540).

[7] Peabody's notice did not appear in the April *Dial*.

[8] Edwin Hubbell Chapin (1814-1880), a Universalist minister, lectured before the Concord Lyceum on March 1. Chapin held pulpits in Virginia and Massachusetts before moving to New York City. He was known as an accomplished speaker.

[9] Emerson arranged for T to move to Staten Island to live with William Emerson and work as a tutor for his son William.

*Copy-text:* ALS (NN-BGC, Henry David Thoreau Collection, 1837-1917, Series III)

*Published:* "Emerson-Thoreau Correspondence," *AM* 69 (May 1892): 583-584; *FL* 1894, 71-72; *FL* 1906, 61-62; *Magazine of History* 21 (July-December 1915): 118; *Cor* 1958, 89

*Editor's Note*
  PE supplies the date "March 1, 1843" based on T's reference to Chapin's lecture.

*Author's Alterations*
  Dial] dial
  printed] *followed by cancelled* for
  Notice] notice


## To Richard Frederick Fuller
*April 2, 1843*

Concord April 2<sup>nd</sup> 1843

Dear Richard,

  I was glad to receive a letter from you, so bright and cheery. You speak of not having made any conquests with your own spear or quill as yet, but if you are tempering your spear-head<sup>e</sup> during these days, and fitting a straight and tough shaft thereto, will not that suffice? We are more pleased to consider the hero in the forest cutting cornel or ash for his spear, than marching in triumph with his trophies. The present hour is always wealthiest when it is poorer than the future ones, as that is the pleasantest site which affords the pleasantest prospects.

  What you say about your studies furnishing you with a "mimic idiom" only, reminds me that we shall all do well if we learn so much as to talk–to speak truth. The only fruit which even much living yields seems to be often only some trivial success–the ability to do some slight thing better. We make conquest only of husks and shells for the most part–at least apparently–but sometimes these are cinnamon and spice, you know. Even the grown hunter you speak of slays a thousand buffaloes and brings off only their hides and tongues. What immense sacrifices– what hecatombs and holocausts the gods exact for very slight favors! How much sincere life before we can even utter one sincere word–

What I was learning in College was chiefly, I think, to express myself, and I see now that as the old orator prescribed 1$^{st}$ action, 2$^{nd}$ action, 3$^{d}$ action,[1] my teachers should have prescribed to me 1$^{st}$ sincerity 2$^{nd}$ sincerity, 3$^{d}$ sincerity. The old mythology is incomplete without a god or goddess of sincerity, on whose altars we might offer up all the products of our farms, our workshops[e], and our studies. It should be our Lar[2] when we sit on the hearth, and our Tutelar Genius when we walk abroad. This is the only panacea. I mean sincerity in our dealings with ourselves mainly–any other is comparitively easy–but I will stop before I get to 17$^{thly}$– I believe I have but one text and one sermon.

Your rural adventures beyond the W. Cambridge hills, have probably lost nothing by distances of time or space– I used to hear only the sough of the wind in the woods of Concord, when I was striving to give my attention to a page of Calculus– But depend upon it you will love your native hills the better for being separated from them.

I expect to leave Concord, which is my Rome–and its people, who are my Romans, in May, and go to N. york to be a tutor in Mr William Emerson's family–[3] So I will bid you good bye till I see you or hear from you again.

Yr friend

H. D. Thoreau

PS. Will you take the trouble to carry the inclosed letter to Richardson[4] for me–and the vol. which Bartlett (Robert) took from the library for me–either to Samuel Longfellow,[5] who I believe attends to his concerns, or to the librarian?

*Correspondent:* See p. 118.

[1] T may refer to an anecdote he had read in Francis Bacon's essay "Of Boldnesse": "Question was asked of Demosthenes, what was

the chief part of an orator? he answered, action: what next? action: what next again? action" (*Essays Moral, Economical, and Political*, p. 49).

[2] A "household or ancestral deity" (*OED*).

[3] Emerson negotiated the terms with his brother William: T was to tutor young William Emerson for "board, lodging (washing?) a room by himself to study in, . . . and a hundred dollars a year." T also asked for clerical work in Emerson's law firm and for an advance of twenty dollars (*Letters of RWE* 1939, 3:158-159). Waldo Emerson wrote Charles Stearns Wheeler that T's term was to be "a year, or more" (*Letters of RWE* 1990-1995, 7:536). T, however, stayed only from May 7 to mid-December.

[4] James Richardson Jr. was studying at the Harvard Divinity School.

[5] Samuel Longfellow (1819-1892), son of Stephen and Zilpah Wadsworth Longfellow and brother of Henry Wadsworth Longfellow, graduated from Harvard University in 1839 and from the Harvard Divinity School in 1846. One of a group of young radicals who were deeply affected by Emerson and Parker, Longfellow was active in the abolition movement, but it was as a writer of hymns that he made his lasting mark.

*Copy-text:*  ALS (Morrier/Hobby)

*Published:  LVP* 1865, 18-20; *FL* 1894, 77-79; *FL* 1906, 66-68; *Cor* 1958, 93-94

*Editor's Notes*
    This letter is addressed "Richard F. Fuller / Cambridge / Mass."
    spear-head] *PE*; spear- / head *in MS*
    workshops] *PE*; work- / shops *in MS*


## From Ellery Channing
*April 6, 1843*

My dear Thoreau

I leave with you, a schedule of repairs & improvements, to be made on the Red Lodge[1] before I move into it, & upon the place generally.

*Cellar*, sand put in enough to make it dry–underpinned with stone, pointed inside & out. New cellar stairs to be put.

*Bank* to be made round the house, round well, & in woodshed. (This is to sodded after planting.)

*House interior*. Kitchen-floor painted, & the woodwork of the kitchen. All the plastering white-washed. Lock to be put on front-door. Glass reset where broken. New sill put to front-door & back-door, & steps if necessary. Leaky-place about chimney, caused by pinning up the house, to be made tight.– A new entry laid at front-door.

*Washroom*–to be white-washed–& a spout made from sink, long enough to carry off dirty water, so as to keep it from[a] running[a] into[a] well.

*Well*. To be cleaned out, inner stones reset (as I understand the Captain told you originally)–an outside wall to be built up, high enough to keep out all wash; this outside wall to be filled round. A new pump to be put in, & to pump up good, clean, fresh water.

*The Acre*, to be measured, & fenced around with a *new* four rail fence. The acre[a] to be less wide than long.

*Privy*.–To be moved from where it is now, behind the end of the barn,[a] the filth carried off; & hole filled in. The privy to be whitewashed, & have a new door, & the floor either renewed or cleaned up.–

*Barn*. (Not done at once as I understood). New sill, & pinned up, so as to make it dry.

*Correspondent:* William Ellery Channing the Younger (1817-1901), known by his contemporaries as Ellery, was the son of Dr. Walter Channing and Barbara Perkins Channing of Boston. He entered Harvard in September 1834 and left four months later. In the fall of 1839 he took up farming in McHenry County, Illinois, but he sold his land there in October 1840 and returned to Massachusetts. In December of that year, Channing met Emerson through their mutual friends Samuel Ward and Caroline Sturgis. In spring 1841, he moved to Cincinnati to work for his uncle, James Perkins, who introduced him to Ellen Fuller (1820-1856), daughter of Timothy and Margarett Crane Fuller and sister of Margaret. Channing and Fuller married in September 1841, while he was editor of the *Cincinnati Gazette*; the couple returned to Massachusetts in September 1843. After spending the winter in Cambridge, they moved to Concord, where they rented a house next to Emerson's. Later they moved to a house near the Thoreau residence. Channing became T's closest friend and first biographer. A moody, unpredictable, sometimes irascible man, he often offended his friends, including Emerson, Alcott, and Margaret Fuller. Convinced that he was a poet, Channing devoted his life to his writing, but with modest success.

¹ The Red Lodge was a small red farmhouse located on the Cambridge Turnpike adjoining Emerson's land; T had arranged for Channing to rent this house from Sheriff Abel Moore (1777-1848) for fifty-six dollars a year. A land trader and an accomplished agriculturalist, Moore was known as a practical joker and a hard drinker; his temperament would have suited Channing.

*Copy-text:* AL (VtMiM, Channing W E/1)

*Published: Cor* 1958, 96; "Letters of William Ellery Channing the Younger" 1989, 186-188

*Editor's Notes*
   This letter is endorsed "W. E. Channing".
   PE supplies the date "April 6, 1843" from the contents of Channing's letter to Emerson, sent from Cambridge and dated "Fast-Day April 6th 1843". In that letter, Channing describes the Red Lodge as needing repairs and indicates that he would "put down" in "the Postscript" a list of "these affairs" for T to attend to. The postscript, written on either an attached or enclosed sheet, apparently refers to the letter printed here ("Letters of William Ellery Channing the Younger" 1989, pp. 185, 188n2).

*Author's Alterations*
   from] *followed by cancelled* it *and cancelled* into *interlined with a caret*
   running] *followed by cancelled* garden.
   into] *interlined with a caret*
   The acre] *preceded by cancelled* The fence
   of the barn,] *interlined with a caret*


*To Henry Vose*
*April 11, 1843*

Concord April 11ᵗʰ 1843

Friend Vose,
   Vague rumors of your success as a lawyer in Springfield have reached our ears in Concord from time to time, and lately I have heard other news of interest regarding you

from our mutual acquaintance Mrs. Jackson[1] of Boston–
All which concern an old school–and class-mate. Davis[2]
too is with you seeking his fortune also–  Please give my
respects to him

The last time you wrote to me in days gone by, I think
you asked me to write you some political news, to enliven
your residence in that drear Chenango Country–but alas
I could hardly be sure who was President already–still
less who was about to be–  And now I have to trouble you
with matters of far different tenor.–  To be short–My Sisters–whom perhaps you remember–who for the last three
of four years have been teaching a Young-ladies school
in Roxbury–with some *eclat* and Satisfaction, and latterly
have passed a long vacation here, are desirous to establish themselves in one of those pleasant Connecticut-
river towns–if possible, in Springfield. They would like,
either to take charge of some young-ladies school already
established, or else, commencing with the few scholars
that might be secured, to build up such an institution by
their own efforts–Teaching, besides the common English
branches, French; Music, Drawing, and Painting.

And now I wish to ask if you will take the trouble to ascertain if there is any opening of the kind in your town, or
if a few scholars can be had which will warrant making a[a]
beginning.

Perhaps Davis' profession acquaints him with this portion of the statistics of Springfield–and he will assist us
with his advice.

Mr Hoar,[3] Mr Emerson, and other good men will stand
as referees.

I hear of no news of importance to write you–unless
it may be news to you that the Boston and Fitchburg
railroad[e] passing through this town, is to be contracted
for directly–[4]  I am going to reside on Staten-Island this
summer. If you will answer this as soon as convenient you
will oblige

Your Classmate and Well-wisher<br>
Henry D. Thoreau.

*Correspondent:* See p. 8.

[1] Mrs. Jackson may be Susan Bridge Jackson (1816-1899), daughter of Nathan and Elizabeth Bartlett Bridge of Charlestown, Massachusetts. In 1834 she married Charles Thomas Jackson, Lidian Emerson's brother, but her connection to T and Vose is not clear.

[2] William Davis (1818-1853), son of Nathaniel and Harriet Mitchell Davis, was a member of the class of 1837. He studied law at Harvard and practiced in Plymouth, Massachusetts, where he married Helen Russell (1825-1900), daughter of John and Deborah Spooner Russell, in 1850.

[3] Samuel Hoar.

[4] Alvah Crocker, a Fitchburg railroad builder, began construction of the Boston-Fitchburg rail line on May 15, 1843. It reached Concord on June 17, 1844. Concord had enthusiastically supported the railroad and contributed significantly to its capital funding.

*Copy-text:* ALS (RPB, Albert Edgar Lownes Collection on Henry David Thoreau, 1837-1965, Ms. 80.1, Series 1, Box 1, Folder 2)

*Published:* *Cor* 1958, 95

*Editor's Notes*
This letter is addressed "Henry Vose Esq. / Springfield / Mass.", postmarked "CONCORD MA{*illegible*} 11", and endorsed "D. H. Thoreau. / 15. Ap. 1843".
railroad] *PE*; rail- / road *in MS*

*Author's Alteration*
a] *preceded by cancelled* the


## From Ellery Channing
*May 1, 1843*

See them, O beloved Thoreau, how greatly convenient a house of one's own will be! {*text lacking*} that will keep him Greek reading a half a year. {*text lacking*} So many have been your benevolences that my wish is too shallow to know how to bring you into my debt. Only so much, as offering you a shelter under my roof, when I may have one, can show effect.

*Correspondent:* See pp. 154-155.

*Copy-text: The Stephen H. Wakeman Collection of Books of Nine-*

*teenth Century American Writers* (New York: American Art Association, 1924), item 997

*Editor's Notes*

PE supplies the date "May 1, 1843" based on information in the Wakeman sale catalog.

In the Wakeman sale this letter was offered with Channing's annotated copy of *A Week on the Concord and Merrimack Rivers*, inscribed to him by T. The description in the sale catalog includes the following:

> Autograph Letter Signed from W. E. Channing to Henry D. Thoreau, with the addressed portion on the last page reading "Henry D. Thoreau, care Ralph Waldo Emerson, Concord, Massachusetts." 3pp. 4to, May 1 Cambridge '43. A very interesting letter in which he addresses Thoreau in one of the sentences as "O my beloved Thoreau." In this letter Channing requests Thoreau to have the banks around his, Channing's, house sodded and thereby keep the sand from blowing into the rooms. Channing apparently had a house built and forgot to have this part of the work attended to for he writes "See them, O beloved Thoreau, how greatly convenient a house of one's own will be!" He also writes that he is sending Thoreau a Greek book "that will keep him Greek reading a half a year." In his last sentence he writes "So many have been your benevolences that my wish is too shallow to know how to bring you into my debt. Only so much, as offering you a shelter under my roof, when I may have one, can show effect."

PE uses "{*text lacking*}" to represent the text omitted from the Wakeman sale catalog.

## From Elizabeth Sherman Hoar

*May 2, 1843*

Dear Henry,–The rain prevented me from seeing you the night before I came away, to leave with you a parting assurance of good will and good hope. We have become better acquainted within the two past years than in our whole life as schoolmates and neighbors before; and I am unwilling to let you go away without telling you that I, among your other friends, shall miss you much, and follow you with remembrance and all best wishes and confidence. Will you take this little inkstand and try if it will carry ink safely from Concord to Staten Island? and the pen, which, if you can write with steel, may be made sometimes the interpreter of friendly thoughts to those whom you leave beyond the reach of your voice,–or record the inspirations of Nature, who, I doubt not, will be as faithful to you who trust her in the sea-girt Staten Island as in Concord woods and meadows. Good-by, and εὖ πράττειν,[1] which, a wise man says, is the only salutation fit for the wise.

Truly your friend,<br>E. Hoar.

*Correspondent:* Elizabeth Sherman Hoar (1814-1878), daughter of Samuel and Sarah Sherman Hoar, had been engaged to Emerson's brother Charles, who died of tuberculosis in 1836. Waldo Emerson for the rest of his life called Elizabeth "sister." She and T had known each other since childhood.

[1] Fare well, or live well.

*Copy-text:* "Emerson-Thoreau Correspondence," *AM* 69 (May 1892): 595n

*Published:* "Emerson-Thoreau Correspondence," *AM* 69 (May 1892): 595n; *FL* 1894, 138n-139n; *FL* 1906, 116n; *Cor* 1958, 98

*Editor's Note*
PE supplies the date "May 2, 1843" based on information in "Emerson-Thoreau Correspondence," which gives the location as "Boston".

## To Cynthia Dunbar Thoreau
*May 11, 1843*

Castleton, Staten-Island,<br>May 11th 1843.

Dear Mother and Friends at home,

We arrived here safely at 10 o'clock on Sunday morning, having had as good a passage as usual, though we ran aground and were detained a couple of hours in the

Thames river,[1] till the tide came to our relief. At length we curts'eyed up to a wharf just the other side of their castle Garden,[2] very incurious about them and their city. I believe my vacant looks absolutely inaccessible to questions did at length satisfy an army of starving cab-men–that I did not want a hack, cab, or any thing of that sort as yet. It was the only demand the city made on us; as if a wheeled vehicle of some sort were the sum and summit of a reasonable man's wants. "Having tried the water," they seemed to say, "will you not return to the pleasant securities of land carriage? Else, why was your boat's prow turned toward the shore at last?"

They are a sad looking set of fellows–not permitted to come on board–and I pity them. They had been expecting me it would seem, and did really wish that I should take a cab, though they did not seem rich enough to supply me with one–  It was a confused jumble of heads, and soiled coats dangling from flesh-colored faces, all swaying to and fro, as by a sort of undertow, while each whip-stick, true as the needle to the pole, still preserved that level and direction in which its proprietor had dismissed his forlorn interrogatory. They took sight over them, the lash being wound up thereon, to prevent your attention from wandering, or to make it concentre upon its object by the spiral line. They began at first, perhaps, with the modest but rather confident inquiry–"Want a cab sir"? but as their despair increased, it took the affirmative tone, as the disheartened and irresolute are apt to do–"you want a cab sir"; or even, "You want a nice cab sir, to take you to Fourth[a] street." The question which one had bravely and hopefully began to put, another had the tact to take up and conclude with fresh emphasis, twirling it from his particular whip stick as if it had emanated from his lips–as the sentiment did from his heart–  Each one could truly say "Them's my sentiments."[3] But it was a sad sight.

I am 7 1/2 miles from New-York,[4] and as it would take half a day at least have not been there yet. I have already

run over no small part of the island, to the highest hill and
some way along the shore. From the hill directly behind
the house, I can see New-York–Brooklyn &[a] Long-Island–
the Narrows,[5] through which vessels bound to and from
all ports[e] of the world chiefly pass–Sandy Hook[6] and the
Highlands of Neversink[7] (part of the coast of New Jersey)–
and by going still farther up the hill, the Kill van Kull,[8] and
Newark Bay. From the pinnacle of one Madame Grimes'
house,[9] the other night at sunset, I could see almost round
the island. Far in the horizon there was a fleet of sloops
bound up the Hudson[a], which seemed to be going over
the edge of the earth–and in view of these trading ships
commerce seemed quite imposing.

But it is rather derogatory that your dwelling place
should be only a neighborhood to a great city[a] To[a] live
on an inclined plane. I do not like their cities and forts
with their morning and evening gun, and sails flapping
in ones eye. I want a whole continent to breathe in.–and
a good deal of solitude and silence, such as all Wall street
cannot buy–Nor[a] Broadway with its wooden pavement. I
must live along the beach on the southern shore which
looks directly out to sea–and see what that great parade
of water means that dashes and roars and has not yet
wet me as long as I have lived. I must not know any thing
about my condition and relations here till what is not permanent is worn off. I have not yet subsided. Give me time
enough and I may like it. All my inner man heretofore has
been a Concord impression, and here come these Sandy
Hook and Coney Island breakers to meet and modify the
former, but it will be long before I can make nature look as
innocently grand and inspiring as in Concord.

> Yr affectionate son
> Henry D Thoreau

*Correspondent:* Cynthia Dunbar (1787-1872) was the daughter of
Asa and Mary Jones Dunbar. In 1812 she married John Thoreau Sr.
(1787-1859), son of John and Jane Burns Thoreau of Boston. Cynthia
was lively and outspoken, and she was a firm abolitionist.

[1] T left Concord for Staten Island on May 6, accompanying Susan Haven Emerson back to her home. They were detained at New London, Connecticut.

[2] At the Battery in New York City.

[3] The repeated ejaculation of the narrator's rogue companion in Washington Irving's "The Poor Devil Author" (*Tales of a Traveller*, 2:33-68). T included this line in "The Landlord" (see *Excursions* 2007, p. 53).

[4] The Emersons lived on Richmond Road, Castleton, Staten Island.

[5] The wide channel that separates Staten Island and Brooklyn and forms the entrance to Upper New York Bay.

[6] A spit of land that stretches north from New Jersey into Lower New York Bay, directly south of Brooklyn. A lighthouse was built on it in 1764.

[7] In 1828 the federal government built twin lighthouses on the Highlands of Navesink (pronounced "neversink") in New Jersey, in what is now the town of Highlands.

[8] The narrow channel separating Staten Island and Bayonne, New Jersey.

[9] Cayetana Susana Bosque y Fangui (1796-1881) was the daughter of Bartolome and Felicidad Fangui Bosque. Her father was a wealthy New Orleans merchant. She married twice, first to W. C. C. Claiborne (1775-1817), governor of Louisiana, and then to John Randolph Grymes (1786-1854), a Virginian who became prominent in New Orleans. After she separated from him, Madame Grymes built a mansion, which she named Capo di Monte, on Signal Hill north of William Emerson's home. Grymes became a noted society hostess.

*Copy-text:* ALS (ViU, Clifton Waller Barrett Library, Henry David Thoreau Collection [#6345])

*Published:* FL 1894, 80-83; *FL* 1906, 68-71; *Cor* 1958, 98-100; *Over Thoreau's Desk: New Correspondence, 1838-1861*, ed. Kenneth Walter Cameron (Hartford, Conn.: Transcendental Books, 1965), 11-12

*Editor's Notes*
This letter is addressed "Mrs. Cynthia Thoreau / Concord / Mass." and postmarked "NEW-YORK MAY 12".
ports] *PE*; *possibly* parts *in MS*

*Author's Alterations*
Fourth] fourth
&] *added in margin*

Hudson] hudson
a great city] *interlined above cancelled* something / else
To] to
Nor] nor


## From Henry James Sr.

*May 12, 1843*

New York May 12 1843
21 Washington Place

My dear Sir–

I feel indebted to Mr Emerson for the introduction he has given me to you.[1] I hope you will call at my house when you next come to the city and give me some of the good tidings wherewith you are fraught from Concord. I am in at at all hours & shall be glad to see you at any. I am liable I believe to be called to albany[e] any day between now and next Thursday–though when I do go I shall stay but a day. Remember when you come over I am at 21 Wash. *Place*, a little street running from the Washington Square to Broadway, flanked on one corner[a] by the University, and on the opposite by a church. You will easily find it. Meanwhile I remain

Yours truly
H. James

Mr H D Thoreau

*Correspondent:* Henry James Sr. (1811-1882), father of the philosopher William James and the novelist Henry James Jr., was wealthy enough to indulge his interest in religion and philosophy untrammeled by the cares of a profession. Raised in Presbyterian orthodoxy, James developed his own perspective on religious topics with the help of the writings of Emanuel Swedenborg. He published several volumes, among them *Moralism and Christianity* (New York: J. H. Redfield, 1850).

[1] Emerson wrote James on May 6: "Thoreau is a profound mind and a person of true magnanimity, and if it should happen that there is some village pedantry & tediousness of facts, it will easily be forgotten when you come at what is better." Emerson asked

James to mention T to Parke Godwin, William Cullen Bryant's son-in-law, who was active in New York literary circles and who might thus help T further his writing career (*Letters of RWE* 1990-1995, 7:542-543).

*Copy-text:* ALS (NNPM, MA 920)

*Published: Cor* 1958, 101

*Editor's Notes*
   This letter is addressed "Mr H. D Thoreau / Care of W. Emerson Esq / 64 Wall St." and endorsed "Henry James".
   albany] *PE*; *possibly* Albany *in MS*

*Author's Alteration*
   corner] side

## From Ralph Waldo Emerson
*May 21, 1843*

Concord Sunday Eve. 21 May, 1843

My dear friend,

Our Dial is already printing & you must, if you can, send me something good by the 10th June certainly, if not before.[1] If William E. can send by a private opportunity, you shall address it to Care of Miss Peabody 13 West Street, or, to be left at Concord Stage Office. Otherwise, send by Harnden, W. E. paying to Boston & charging to me. Let the pacquet bring letters also from you & from Waldo[2] & Tappan,[a] I entreat. You will not doubt that you are well remembered here, by young, older, & old people and your letter to your mother was borrowed & read with great interest pending the arrival of direct accounts & of later experiences especially in the City. I am secure that you are under[a] sacred protection, if I should not hear from you for years. Yet I shall wish to know what befals you on your way.

Ellery Channing is well settled in his house & works very steadily thus far & our intercourse[e] is very agreeable to me. Young Ball[3] has been to see me & is a prodigious reader & a youth of great promise,–born too in the good

town. Mr Hawthorn is well; and Mr Alcott & Mr L. are re-
volving a purchase in Harvard of 90 acres.[4]

Yours affectionately,

R. W. Emerson.

My wife will reopen my sealed letter, but a remembrance
from her shall be inserted.

*Correspondent:* See p. 53.

[1] T sent Emerson on May 23 "some verses from [his] journal" (p.
174) and on June 8 his essay "A Winter Walk," which he describes
as "very hastily written out" (p. 182). Emerson received the essay
on June 15; by that time the July number of the *Dial* had been filled.
He told T that he would publish it in the October number unless T
found a better place for it (p. 193). The essay appeared in the October *Dial* (pp. 211-226; see *Excursions* 2007, pp. 55-77).

[2] Giles Waldo (1814-1849) was working as a clerk for Lewis Tap-
pan in New York City. Emerson, who had been impressed with
Waldo when he met the young man earlier that year, had written
Waldo about T's planned trip to Staten Island.

[3] Benjamin West Ball (1823-1896), son of Benjamin and Mary
Rogers Ball of Concord, graduated from Dartmouth in 1842 and
led a career as a lawyer, a journalist, and a poet. In 1853 Ball married Dora S. Hurd (1827-1902), daughter of Joseph D. and Sarah
Folsom Hurd of New Hampshire. Emerson met Ball on May 18 and
described the visit in his journal as follows: "[Ball] towered away
in such declamatory talk that at first I thought it rhodomontade &
we should soon have done with each other. But he turned out to be
a prodigious reader, and writer too.... With a little more repose of
thought, he would be a great companion" (*JMN*, 8:399).

[4] On May 25, 1843, Charles Lane bought from Maverick Wyman
a farm in Harvard, Massachusetts, that became the Fruitlands reform community. He paid eighteen hundred dollars for the land
and was allowed to use the house rent-free for a year. Lane per-
suaded Samuel May, Abigail Alcott's brother, to become trustee for
the deed and to sign a note for three hundred dollars. After he paid
Alcott's creditors, Lane, his son, and the Alcott family moved to the
farm on June 1.

*Copy-text:* ALS (NNPM, MA 920)

*Published: HDT* 1882, 135; "Emerson-Thoreau Correspondence,"
*AM* 69 (May 1892): 585-586; *Cor* 1958, 102; *Letters of RWE* 1990-1995,
7:544-545

*Editor's Notes*
　This letter is addressed "Henry D. Thoreau– / Care of W. Emerson, Esq. / 64 Wall Street / New York".
　intercourse] *PE*; inter / course *in MS*

*Author's Alterations*
　Tappan,] ~.
　under] in


## To Lidian Jackson Emerson
*May 22, 1843*

　　　　　　　　　Castleton, Staten Island, May 22ᵈ

My Dear Friend,
　I believe a good many conversations with you were left in an unfinished state, and now indeed I dont know where to take them up. But I will resume some of the unfinished silence. I shall not hesitate to know you. I think of you as some elder sister of mine, whom I could not have avoided–a sort of lunar influence–only of such age as the moon, whose time is measured by her light. You must know that you represent to me womanᵉ–for I have not travelled very far or wide–and what if I had? I like to deal with you, for I believe you do not lie or steal, and these are very rare virtues. I thank you for your influence for two years– I was fortunate to be subjected to it, and am now to remember it. It is the noblest gift we can make– What signify all others that can be bestowed? You have helped to keep my life "on loft," as Chaucer says of Griseldaᵃ, and in a better sense.[1] You always seemed to look down at me as from some elevation, some of your high humilities,[2] and I was the better for having to look up. I felt taxed not to disappoint your expectation–for could there be any accident so sad as to be respected for something better than we are? It was a pleasure even to go away from you, as it is not to meet some, as it apprised me of my high relations, and such a departure is a sort of further introduction and meeting. Nothing makes the earth seem so spacious as to

have friends at a distance. They make the latitudes and longitudes.

You must not think that fate is so dark there, for even here I can see a faint reflected light over Concord, and I think that at this distance I can better weigh the value of a doubt there. Your moonlight–as I have told you, though it is a reflection of the sun, allows of bats and owls and other twilight birds to flit therein. But I am very glad that you can elevate your life with a doubt–for I am sure that it is nothing but an insatiable faith after all that deepens and darkens its current–  And your doubt and my confidence are only a difference of expression.

I have hardly begun to live on Staten Island yet, but like the man who, when forbidden to tread on English ground, carried Scottish ground in his boots,[3] I carry Concord ground in my boots and in my hat–and am I not made of Concord dust? I cannot realize that it is the roar of the sea I hear now, and not the wind in Walden woods. I find more of Concord after all in the prospect of the sea, beyond Sandy-Hook than in the fields and woods.

If you were to have this Hugh the gardener[4] for your man you would think a new dispensation had commenced. He might put a fairer aspect on the natural world for you, or at any rate[e] a screen between you and the alms house. There is a beautiful red honeysuckle now in blossom in the woods here, which should be transplanted to Concord, and if what they tell me about the tulip tree be true, you should have that also. I have not seen Mrs Black[5] yet, but I intend to call on her soon. Have you established those simpler modes of living yet?– "In the full tide of successful operation?"–[6]

Tell Mrs. Brown that I hope she is anchored in a secure haven, and derives much pleasure still from reading the poets–And that her constellation is not quite set from my sight, though it is sunk so low in that northern horizon. Tell Elizabeth Hoar that her bright present *did* "carry ink safely to Staten Island", and was a conspicuous object in Master Haven's inventory of my[a] effects.–[7] Give my respect to M[me] Emerson,[8] whose Concord face I should be glad to see here this summer; and remember me to the rest of the household who have had vision of me. Has Edith degenerated or Ellen regenerated yet;[a] for I fear and hope that so it will be?

Shake a day-day to Edith, and say "Good[a] night" to Ellen for me.

Farewell–Henry D. Thoreau

*Correspondent:* Lydia Jackson (1802-1892), daughter of Charles and Lucy Cotton Jackson of Plymouth, Massachusetts, married Emerson in 1835; he changed her name to Lidian, "anticipating that New Englanders might call her *Lydiar Emerson* because of their tendency to connect two vowels with an *r*" (*Letters of Lidian Jackson Emerson* 1987, p. xiii). She brought to Concord "a love of gardens and gardening, a carpenter's eye, a talent for drawing, a poetic gift for rhyming, and an unparalleled love of society, coupled with a love for argument, an amusement that excelled any other in her judgment" (*Letters of Lidian Jackson Emerson* 1987, p. xiii).

[1] See Chaucer's "Clerkes Tale": "And ay she kept hire fadres lif on loft / With every obeisance and diligence, / That child may don to fadres reverence" (Alexander Chalmers, ed., *The Works of the English Poets, from Chaucer to Cowper*, 1:63).

[2] The phrase "high humilities" occurs in William Cecil, Baron Burghley, *Certaine Preceptes, or Directions, for the Well Ordering and Carriage of a Mans Life*, pp. 14-15. T's source is unknown.

[3] T's source for this anecdote is not known, but it is probably the life of St. Colum Cille (St. Columba, 521-597), an Irish priest who left Ireland in 565, either voluntarily or as an exile, and became a missionary to the Picts in modern-day Scotland. Colum Cille's presence at a gathering at Drum Ceat in Ireland in 575, which seems to contradict accounts that he had been banished, has been explained in various ways in the several surviving lives of the saint. Manus O'Donnell writes that Colum Cille, upon leaving in 565, had taken a vow not to "set foot on Irish soil ever again nor look upon her men or women nor consume her food or drink" and that he "had a sod of Scottish soil under his feet all the time he was in Ireland" (*The Life of Colum Cille*, ed. Brian Lacey [Dublin: Four Courts Press, 1998], p. 174). This story, which exists in various versions, is

probably what T had in mind, even though he substitutes English for Irish ground. Manus O'Donnell's life, completed in 1532, was not published until 1918, so it could not have been T's direct source. Manuscript copies of O'Donnell's life, however, did circulate and the story exists in several variants beginning with the *Amra Choluim Chille* (Eulogy of Colum Cille) written by Dallán Forgaill soon after Columba's death in 597.

⁴ Hugh Whelan was Emerson's gardener and handyman. Emerson later recorded the following in his journal: "Henry described Hugh as saving every slip & stone & seed, & planting it. He picks up a peach stone & puts it in his pocket to plant. That is his vocation in the world, to be a planter of plants" (*JMN*, 9:121).

⁵ Probably Rebecca Gray Black (1805-1853?), daughter of Rebecca Ashton Gray. In 1825 Rebecca Gray and John Black (d. 1847) were married in a Presbyterian church in New York City. Rebecca Black had become a Swedenborgian by the 1840s. Following her husband's death she worked as a seamstress in Brooklyn.

⁶ Possibly an allusion to a phrase in Thomas Jefferson's first inaugural address: "In the full tide of successful experiment."

⁷ John Haven Emerson (1840-1913) was William Emerson's second son; he later became a doctor. For more information about Elizabeth Hoar's present to T, see pp. 158-159.

⁸ Emerson's mother, Ruth Haskins Emerson (1768-1853), lived with the Emerson family. Daughter of John and Hannah Upham Haskins, she married William Emerson (1769-1811) in 1796.

*Copy-text:* ALS (MBU, Richards Collection)

*Published: LVP* 1865, 20-23; *Life* 1890, 73; *FL* 1894, 89-92; *T: Home* 1902, 232; *FL* 1906, 76-78; *Friendly Craft* 1908, 224-226; *Recollections* 1909, 483; *Magazine of History* 1915, 118; *Cor* 1958, 103-104

*Editor's Notes*
This letter is addressed "Mrs. Lidian Emerson / Concord / Mass".
PE supplies the year "1843" from the contents of the letter.
woman] *PE*; *possibly* Woman *in MS*
rate] *PE*; ra{*MS torn*}

*Author's Alterations*
of Griselda] *interlined with a caret*
my] *followed by cancelled* good
yet;] ~?
Good] good

*To Sophia Elizabeth Thoreau*
*May 22, 1843*

Castleton, Staten Island, May 22nd

−43

Dear Sophia,

I have had a severe cold ever since I came here, and have been confined to the house for the last week with bronchitis, though I am now getting out, so I have not seen much in the botanical way. The cedar seems to be one of the most common trees here, and the fields are very fragrant with it. There are also the gum and tulip trees. The latter is not very common, but is very large and beautiful, bearing flowers as large as tulips and as handsome. It is not time for it yet. The woods are now full of a large honeysuckle in full bloom, which differs from ours in being red instead of white, so that at first I did not know its genus. The painted cup is very common in the meadows here. Peaches, and especially cherries, seem to grow by all the fences.

Things are very forward here compared with Concord[a]. The apricots growing out of doors are already as large as plums. The apple, pear, peach, cherry, and plum trees, have shed their blossoms.

The whole Island is like a garden, and affords very fine scenery. In front of the house is a very extensive wood beyond which is the sea, whose roar I can hear all night long, when there is no wind, if easterly winds have prevailed on the Atlantic. There are always some vessels in sight–ten, twenty, or thirty miles off–and Sunday before last there were hundreds in long procession, stretching from New York to Sanday Hook, and far beyond, for Sunday is a lucky day.

I went to New York Saturday before last. A walk of half an hour, by half a dozen houses, along the Richmond road, ie. the road that leads to R–on which we live–brings me to the village of Stapleton,[a] in Southfield[a], where is the lower dock; but if I prefer I can walk along the shore three quarters of a mile further toward New York, to Quarantine,[1] a[a] village of Castleton, to the upper dock, which the boat leaves five or six times every day, a quarter of an hour later than the former place. Further on is the village of New-Brighton–and further still Port Richmond, which villages another steam-boat[e] visits.

In New York I saw Geo. Ward,[2] and also Giles Waldo[3] and William Tappan, whom I can describe better when I have seen them more– They are young friends of Mr Emerson. Waldo came down to the Island to see me the next day. I also saw the Great Western, the Croton Water works, and the picture gallery of the National Academy of Design.[4] But I have not had time to see or do much in N.Y. yet.

Tell Miss Ward I shall try to put my[a] microscope[5] to a good use, and if I find any new and pressible flower, will throw it into my common place book. Garlic, the original of the common onion, grows like grass here all over the fields, and during its season spoils the cream and butter for the market, as the cows like it very much. Tell Helen there are two schools just established in this neighborhood, with large prospects, or rather designs, one for boys, and another for girls. The latter by a Miss Errington[6]–and though it is very small as yet–I will keep my ears open for her in such directions– The encouragement is very slight.

I hope you will not be washed away by the Irish sea.[7] Tell Mother I think my cold was not wholly owing to imprudence   Perhaps I was being acclimated.

Tell Father[a] that Mr Tappan whose son I know–and whose clerks young Tappan and Waldo are–has invented and established a new and very important business[8]– which Waldo thinks would allow them to burn 99 out of 100 of the stores in NY, which now only offset and cancel one another. It is a kind of intelligence office for the whole

country–with branches in the principal cities, giving information with regard to the credit and affairs of every
man of business in the country. Of course it is not popular
at the south and west. It is an extensive business and will
employ a great many clerks.

Love to all–not forgetting aunt and aunts[9]–and Miss
and Mrs Ward.

Y[rs] Affectionate Brother
Henry D. Thoreau.

*Correspondent:* Sophia Elizabeth Thoreau (1819-1876), T's younger
sister and the fourth child of John and Cynthia Dunbar Thoreau,
studied at the Concord Academy and became a schoolteacher. A
capable and active woman, she sang, played the piano, painted,
helped T manage the family business after the death of their father, and ran the business herself after T's death. A devoted sister,
Sophia carried food to T when he stayed at Walden Pond, kept a
scrapbook that contained reviews of his work, nursed him on his
deathbed, and edited his unpublished manuscripts after his death.

[1] In 1799 New York established a lazaretto at Tompkinsville on
Staten Island, where passengers with contagious diseases were
taken from their ships to be quarantined. The thirty-acre facility
had a health officer, a doctor, and an aide.

[2] George Washington Ward (1802-1855), Prudence Ward's
brother, lived in New York City.

[3] In a letter to Emerson on May 14, Waldo wrote, "My interview
with Thoreau has shown me how desperately ignorant I have been
content to remain of books." On scholarly subjects, Waldo observed, "there could be but little sympathy between us,–at least
that he had nothing to learn of me, while I must owe everything
to him" (Harmon Smith, "Henry Thoreau and Emerson's 'Noble
Youths,'" *CS* 17 [December 1984]: 5).

[4] Built by the Great Western Railway Company in April 1838, the
236-foot-long *Great Western* was the first steamship in the transatlantic passenger trade, averaging fifteen and a half days to cross the
Atlantic. The 41.5-mile-long Croton aqueduct was opened on July
4, 1842, when the first water from the new dam on the Croton River
arrived at the distributing terminal at Fifth Avenue and Forty-Sec-
ond Street. The National Academy of Design, founded on January
19, 1826, showed only original work by living artists; its 1843 annual
exhibition opened on April 27 at its galleries on the upper floor of

the New York Society Library building at Broadway and Leonard Street. T could have seen a landscape by Asher Durand, portraits by Cephas Thompson and William Page, and "Return of Columbus" by Emanuel Leutze.

⁵ Prudence Ward gave T a microscope for his trip to Staten Island.

⁶ "Miss Errington" is either Harriet N. Errington (1815?-1896) or Georgiana Errington (1822?-1881), both of them daughters of Harriet Errington (1770?-1859). In 1843 the sisters were living in the Southfield area of Staten Island. The Errington school became a socially elite institution in Clifton, Staten Island.

⁷ Concord had recently seen a large influx of Irish workingmen, who helped build the Boston-Fitchburg railroad.

⁸ Lewis Tappan (1788-1873) established the Mercantile Agency in New York City, the first commercial credit-rating company in the United States, in 1841. His son, William Aspinwall Tappan, and Giles Waldo worked at the company's office. Lewis Tappan was a prominent abolitionist and a founder of the American Anti-Slavery Society. In 1840 he and his brother Arthur split with William Lloyd Garrison, another founding member, and formed the new American and Foreign Anti-Slavery Society.

⁹ Louisa Dunbar (1785-1866) lived with the Thoreaus; Jane (1784-1864) and Maria Thoreau (1794-1881) were frequent visitors.

*Copy-text:*  ALS (NN-BGC, Henry David Thoreau Collection, 1837-1917, Series III)

*Published:*  FL 1894, 84-87; FL 1906, 71-73; Cor 1958, 105-106

*Editor's Note*
    steam-boat] *PE*; steam- / boat *in MS*

*Author's Alterations*
    Concord] concord
    Stapleton,] *followed by cancelled* still
    Southfield] *interlined above cancelled* Castleton
    a] another
    my] *interlined above cancelled* her
    Father] father

## To Ralph Waldo Emerson
*May 23, 1843*

Castleton, Staten Island, May 23.[d]

My Dear Friend,

I was just going to write to you when I received your letter. I was waiting till I had got away from Concord. I should have sent you something for the Dial before, but I have been sick ever since I came here–rather unaccountably, what with a cold, bronchitis, acclimation &c–still unaccountably. I send you some verses from my journal which will help make a packet. I have not time to correct them–[a]if this goes by Rockwood Hoar.[1] If I can finish an account of a winter's walk in Concord in the midst of a Staten Island summer–not so wise as true I trust–I will send it to you soon.[2]

I have had no "later experiences" yet. you must not count much upon what I can do or learn in New York. I feel a good way off here–and it is not to be visited, but seen and dwelt in. I have been there but once, and have been confined to the house since. Every thing there disappoints me but the crowd–rather I was disappointed with the rest before I came. I have no eyes for their churches and what else they find to brag of. Though I know but little about Boston, yet what attracts me in a quiet way seems much meaner and more pretending than there–Libraries–Pictures–and faces in the street– You dont know where any respectability inhabits–[a] It is in the crowd in Chatham street. The crowd is something new and to be attended to.– It is worth a thousand Trinity Churches and Exchanges while it is looking at them–and will run over them and trample them under foot one day. There are two things I hear, and am aware that I live in the neighborhood of–The roar of the sea–and the hum of the city.

I have just come from the beach (to find your letter) and I like it much. Everything there is on a grand and generous scale–sea-weed, water, and sand; and even the dead fishes, horses and hogs[a] have a rank luxuriant[e] odor. Great shad nets spread to dry, crabs and horse-shoes crawling over the sand– Clumsy boats, only for service, dancing like sea-fowl on the surf, and ships afar off going about their business.

Waldo and Tappan carried me to their English ale-house the first Saturday[a], and Waldo spent two hours here the next day. But Tappan I have only seen. I like his looks and the sound of his silence. They are confined every day but Sunday, and then Tappan is obliged to observe the demeanor of a church goer to prevent open war with his father.[3]

I am glad that Channing has got settled, and that too before the inroad of the Irish. I have read his poems two or three times over, and partially through and under, with new and increased interest and appreciation. Tell him I saw a man buy a copy at Little and Brown's.[4] He may have been a virtuoso[5]–but we will give him the credit.

What with Alcott & Lane & Hawthorne too you look strong enough to take New York by storm. Will you tell L. if he asks, that I have been able to do nothing about the books yet.[6]

Believe that I have something better to write you than this. It would be unkind to thank you for particular deeds

Yr friend

Henry D Thoreau

*Correspondent:* See p. 53.

[1] Ebenezer Rockwood Hoar (1816-1895), son of Samuel and Sarah Sherman Hoar of Concord, graduated from Harvard University in 1835 and from the Harvard Law School in 1839. In 1840 he married Caroline Downes Brooks (1820-1892), daughter of Nathan and Caroline Downes Brooks. Like his father, Hoar was a prominent lawyer and public official. He opposed slavery and helped found the Free-Soil Party in 1848. Later in life he served as a judge, as Grant's attorney general, and as a member of Congress.

[2] T's essay "A Winter Walk" appeared in the October *Dial* (pp. 211-226; see *Excursions* 2007, pp. 55-77). See also p. 165, note 1.

3 Though he admired Rev. William Ellery Channing (1780-1842), the American leader of liberal Unitarian Christianity, Lewis Tappan became a staunch evangelical.

4 Little and Brown published Ellery Channing's *Poems* that summer, with the financial support of Samuel Gray Ward.

5 "One who has a special interest in, or taste for, the fine arts; a student or collector of antiquities, natural curiosities or rarities, etc.; a connoisseur; freq., one who carries on such pursuits in a dilettante or trifling manner" (*OED*).

6 In need of money after his investment in the Fruitlands experiment, Charles Lane sent with T to New York City some of the books from the collection he had brought from England, with a request to deposit them for sale at the publisher Wiley and Putnam's shop. The bookseller sold them all by early 1846. See pp. 141-142, note 1, and pp. 277-278.

*Copy-text:* ALS (CSmH, HM 22230)

*Published: Life* 1890, 75; "Emerson-Thoreau Correspondence," *AM* 69 (May 1892): 586-587; *FL* 1894, 92-94; *Life* 1896, 60-61; *FL* 1906, 78-80; *Magazine of History* 1915, 118; *Cor* 1958, 107-108

*Editor's Notes*
This letter is addressed "R. Waldo Emerson / Concord / Mass." and endorsed "H D Thoreau / May 1843". PE supplies the year "1843" following the endorsement.

luxuriant] *PE; possibly* luxurious *in MS*

*Author's Alterations*
them–] ~.
inhabits–] ~.
hogs] dogs
Saturday] saturday

## To Helen Louisa Thoreau

*May 23, 1843*

Castleton Staten Island May 23ᵈ 43.

Dear Helen,

In place of something fresher I send you the following verses from my journal, written some time ago.[1]

    Brother where dost thou dwell?
    What sun shines for thee now?

Dost thou indeed farewell?
   As we wished here below.

What season didst thou find?
   'Twas winter here.
Are not the fates more kind
   Than they appear?

Is thy brow clear again
   As in thy youthful years?
And was that ugly pain
   The summit of thy fears?

Yet thou wast cheery still,
   They could not quench thy fire,
Thou dids't abide their will,
   And then retire.

Where chiefly shall I look
   To feel thy presence near?
Along the neighboring brook
   May I thy voice still hear?

Dost thou still haunt the brink
   Of yonder river's tide?[a]
And may I ever think
   That thou art by my side?

What bird wilt thou employ
   To bring me word of thee?
For it would give them joy,
   'Twould give them liberty,
To serve their former lord
   With wing and minstrelsy.

A sadder strain has mixed with their song,
   They've slowlier built their nests,

Since thou art gone
    Their lively labor rests.

Where is the finch–the thrush,
    I used to hear?
Ah! they could well abide
    The dying year.

Now they no more return,
    I hear them not;
They have remained to mourn,
    Or else forgot
{*MS cut and torn*}

*Correspondent:*  See p. 26.

    [1] No version of this poem survives in T's extant Journal.

*Copy-text:*  AL (VtMiM, Thoreau/1)

*Published:*  *FL* 1894, 87-88; *T: Home* 1902, 51, 52; *FL* 1906, 74-75; *Cor* 1958, 108-110

*Editor's Note*
    This letter is addressed "Miss. Helen L. Thoreau / Concord / {*MS cut and torn*}". The closing and signature were cut and torn from the manuscript; the verso of the missing portion contained part of the address.

*Author's Alteration*
    tide?] ~,

*From Giles Waldo*
*June 2, 1843*

                                June 2/43
    I cannot see you to-day, as Mr. T$^{\text{n}}$. has gone to England.[1]
As soon as possible I will be at the Island,–but do not wait
for me.–  If you can come up, you will find me at the office, or Franklin House, Fulton Ferry, Brooklyn.
                                Yours
                                Giles Waldo.

H. D. Thoreau

*Correspondent:* Giles Waldo (1814-1849), son of Ebenezer and Eunice Devotion Waldo of Scotland, Connecticut, had taught school in Washington, D.C., before moving to Brooklyn. He was employed by Lewis Tappan. Encouraged by Emerson to become a writer, Waldo left Tappan's firm and spent part of the winter of 1843-1844 with Lewis Tappan's son William Tappan in a cabin in rural New York, reading and writing. After this failed venture, Waldo left New York and eventually became vice consul at Lahaina on the Sandwich Islands, now Hawaii.

[1] Lewis Tappan had suddenly decided to go to London for the meeting of the British and Foreign Anti-Slavery Society. He had sailed the previous day.

*Copy-text:* ALS (Sewall)

*Editor's Note*
This letter is endorsed "Giles Waldo."


## To Ralph Waldo Emerson
*June 8, 1843*

Staten Island, June 8th 43

Dear Friend,

I have been to see Henry James[1] and like him very much. It was a great pleasure to meet him. It makes humanity seem more erect and respectable. I never was more kindly and faithfully catechised. It made me respect myself more to be thought worthy of such sincere questions. He is a man, and takes his own way, or stands still in his own place. I know of no one so patient and determined to have the good of you. It is almost friendship, such plain and human dealing. I think he will not write or speak inspiringly–but he is a refreshing forward looking, and forward moving man, and has naturalized and humanized New York for me. He actually reproaches you by his respect for your poor words. I had three hours solid talk with him, and he asks me to make free use of his house. He wants an expression of your[a] faith, or to be sure that it is faith, and confesses that his own treads fast upon the heels of his understanding. He exclaimed at some careless answer of

mine "Well, you Transcendentalists are wonderfully consistent. I must get hold of this somehow."

He likes Carlyle's book,[2] but says that it leaves him in an
excited and unprofitable state, and that Carlyle is so ready
to obey his humor, that he makes the least vestige of truth
the foundation of any superstructure–not keeping faith
with his better genius nor truest readers.

I met Wright on the stairs of the Society Library and
Channing and Brisbane[3] on the steps. The former (Channing[a] is a concave man, and you see by his attitude, and
the lines of his face that he is retreating from himself and
from yourself, with sad doubts. It is like a fair mask swaying from the drooping boughs of some tree whose stem
is not seen. He would break with a conchoidal fracture.
You feel as if you would like to see him when he has made
up his[a] mind to run all the risks. To be sure he doubts
because he has a great hope to be disappointed, but he
makes the possible disappointment of too much consequence. Brisbane, with whom I did not converse, did not
impress me favorably. He looks like a man who has lived
in a cellar, far gone in consumption. I barely saw him, but
he did not look as if he could let Fourier go in any case
and throw up his hat. But I need'nt have come to N.Y. to
write this.[a]

I have seen Tappan for two or three hours, and like
both him and Waldo, but I always see those of whom I
have heard well with a slight disappointment. They are
so much better than the great herd, and yet the heavens
are not shivered into diamonds[a] over their heads. Persons
and things flit so rapidly through my brain now a days that
I can hardly remember them. They seem to be lying in the
stream, stemming the tide, ready to go to sea, as steam-
boats when they leave the dock go off in the opposite direction first until they are headed right, and then begins
the steady revolution of the paddle wheels but they are
not quite cheerily headed anywhither yet, nor singing

amid the shrouds as they bound over the billows. There is a certain youthfulness[a] and generosity about them, very attractive, and Tappans more reserved and solitary thought commands respect.

After some ado I discovered the residence of Mrs Black, but there was palmed off upon me in her stead, a Mrs Grey, quite an inferior color, who told me at last that she was not Mrs Black, but her mother,[4] but was just as glad to see me as Mrs Black would have been—and so forsooth would answer just as well. Mrs Black had gone with Palmer to New Jersey and would return on the morrow

I dont like the city better the more I see it, but worse. I am ashamed of my eyes that behold it. It is a thousand times meaner than I could have imagined. It will be something to hate that's the advantage it will be to me, and even the best people in it are a part of it, and talk coolly about it. The pigs in the streets are the most respectable portion of the population. When will the world learn that a million men are of no importance compared with one man—

But I must wait for a shower of shillings, or at least a slight dew or mizzling of sixpences, before I explore NY. very far.

The sea-beach is the best thing I have seen. It is very solitary and remote, and you only remember New York occasionally. The distances too along the shore, and inland in sight of it, are unaccountably great and startling. The sea seems very near from the hills, but it proves a long way over the plain, and yet you may be wet with the spray before you can believe that you are there. The far seems near, and the near far. Many rods from the beach I step aside for the atlantic, and I see men drag up their boats on to the sand, with oxen, stepping about amid the surf, as if it were possible they might draw up Sandy Hook.

I do not feel myself especially serviceable to the good people with I live, except as inflictions are sanctified to the righteous. And so too must I serve the boy. I can look

to the Latin and mathematics sharply, and for the rest[a] behave myself. But I cannot be in his neighborhood thereafter as his Educator of course, but as the hawks fly over my
own head. I am not attracted toward him but as to youth
generally. He shall frequent me however as much as he
can, and I'll be I.

Bradbury told[a] me when I passed through B. that he
was coming to NY. the following Saturday, and would
then settle with me; but he has not made his appearance
yet.[5] Will you the next time you go to B. present that order
for me which I left with you?

If I say less about W & T now it is perhaps because I may
have more to say by and by.

Remember me to your Mother, and Mrs. Emerson, who
I hope is quite well. I shall be very glad to hear from her,
as[a] well as from you. I have very hastily written out something for the Dial, and send it only because you are expecting something– Though something better. It seems
idle and Howittish,[6] but it may be of more worth in Concord where it belongs. In great haste

Farewell Henry D. Thoreau.

*Correspondent:* See p. 53.

[1] Henry James Sr.

[2] In the spring of 1843 Carlyle's *Past and Present* was published
in England by Chapman and Hall. On April 29, Emerson acknowledged receipt from Carlyle of a manuscript copy and arranged for
its publication by Little and Brown in an attempt to thwart the pirates, who often published cheap editions of English books priced
at less than a dollar. Little and Brown's edition, published in May,
gained four or five weeks on pirates in Boston, New York, and Chicago, and Carlyle realized a profit of almost one hundred dollars
as a result of Emerson's effort. James was becoming increasingly
interested in Carlyle, whose *Sartor Resartus* had made a great impression on him.

[3] Henry Gardiner Wright, William Henry Channing, and Albert
Brisbane.

[4] Rebecca Ashton Gray (b. 1781), mother of Rebecca Gray Black.

[5] Waymond Bradbury; see p. 148, note 5.

[6] T refers to "A Winter Walk"; see p. 165, note 1. William How-

itt (1792-1879) had published popular books on nature and rural seclusion, including *The Book of the Seasons; or, The Calendar of Nature.*

*Copy-text:* ALS (SE-LIBR, RAR 137 Da)

*Published:* "Emerson-Thoreau Correspondence," *AM* 69 (May 1892): 587-588; *FL* 1894, 95-99; *T: Home* 1902, 96; *FL* 1906, 80-84; *Americana: American Historical Magazine* 7 (May 1912): 527; *Magazine of History* 21 (July-December 1915): 119; Thomas F. Madigan, *Word Shadows of the Great* (New York: Frederick A. Stokes, 1930), 188-189; *Cor* 1958, 110-112

*Editor's Notes*
This letter is addressed "R. Waldo Emerson / Concord / Mass." and endorsed "H D Thoreau / June, 1843".
The copy-text is tipped into volume 7 of Manuscript Edition number 247.

*Author's Alterations*
your] a
(Channing] *inserted*
made up his] *interlined with a caret*
But ... this.] *added*
diamonds] *interlined above cancelled* splinters
youthfulness] youth
rest] *followed by cancelled* sharply
told] and
as] and

## To John Thoreau Sr. and Cynthia Dunbar Thoreau
*June 8, 1843*

Castleton, Staten Island, June 8th
1843

Dear Parents,

I have got quite well now, and like the lay of the land and the look of the sea very much– Only the country is so fair that it seems rather too much as if it were made to be looked at. I have been to N.Y. four or five times, and have run about the island a good deal. Geo. Ward when I last saw him, which was at his house in Brooklyn, was

studying the Daguerreotype process, preparing to set up
in that line. The boats run now almost every hour, from
8 AM. to 7 Pm. back and forth, so that I can get to the
city much more easily than before. I have seen there one
Henry James, a lame-man,[1] of whom I had heard before,
whom I like very much, and he asks me to make free use
of his house, which is situated in a pleasant part of the
city, adjoining the University. I have met several people
whom I knew before, and among the rest Mr Wright,[2] who
was on his way to Niagara.

I feel already about as well acquainted with New York
as with Boston, that is about as little, perhaps. It is large
enough now and they intend it shall be larger still. 15th
Street–where some of my new acquaintances live, is two
or three miles from the Battery[a] where the boat touches,
clear brick and stone and no give to the foot; and they
have layed out, though not built, up to the 149th Street
above. I had rather see a brick for a specimen for my part
such as they exhibited in old times.[3] You see it is quite
a day's training to make a few calls in different parts of
the city (to say[a] nothing of 12 miles by water and three by
land, ie. not brick or Stone) especially if it does not rain
shillings which might interest omnibuses in your behalf. Some Omnibuses are marked "Broadway–Fourth
Street[a]"–and they go no further–otherrs "8th Street" and so
on, and so of the other principal streets. This letter will be
circumstantial enough for Helen.

This is in all respects a very pleasant residence–much
more rural than you would expect of the vicinity of New
York. There are woods all around. We breakfast at half
past six–lunch if we will at twelve–and dine or sup at five.
Thus is the day partitioned off. From 9 to 2 or thereabouts
I am the schoolmaster–and at other times as much the
pupil as I can be–  Mr and Mrs Emerson and family are
not indeed of my kith or kin in any sense–but they are irreproachable and kind.

I have met no one yet *on the Island* whose acquaintance

I shall actually cultivate–or hoe around–unless it be our
neighbor Capt Smith–an old fisherman, who catches the
fish called moss-bonkers[4]–(so it sounds) and invites me
to come to the beach when he spends the week and see
him and his fish.

Farms are for sale all around here–  And so I suppose
men are for purchase.

North of us live Peter Wandell–Mr Mell–and Mr. Dis-
usway (dont mind the[a] spelling) as far as the Clove road;[5]
And south John Britton–Van Pelt, and Capt Smith, as far
as the Finger-board[e] road. Behind is the hill, some 250
feet high–on the side of which we live, and in front the
forest and the sea–the latter at the distance of a mile and
a half.

Tell Helen that Miss Errington is provided with assistance. This were as good a place as any to establish a
school, if one could wait a little. Families come down here
to board in the summer–and three or four have been[a] already established this season.

As for money matters I have not set my traps yet, but
I am getting the bait ready.[6] Pray how does the garden
thrive and what improvements in the pencil line?

I miss you all very much. Write soon and send a Concord paper to yr affectionate son

Henry D. Thoreau

*Correspondents:* John Thoreau Sr. (1787-1859), son of John and Jane
Burns Thoreau of Boston, married Cynthia Dunbar (1787-1872),
daughter of Asa and Mary Jones Dunbar. The Thoreaus settled in
Concord after their marriage in 1812; they moved to Chelmsford in
1818 and opened a grocery store there. The family moved to Boston
in 1821 and back to Concord in 1823. John, a quiet, well-respected
man, was a pencil maker; his work was good but seldom lucrative.

[1] In the summer of 1824, Henry James Sr., turning thirteen, badly
burned his leg while attempting to put out a fire caused by a tow
ball soaked in turpentine. His burn resulted in the amputation of
part of his right leg.

[2] Henry Gardiner Wright.

[3] Perhaps a reference to a passage in the second of Jonathan Swift's "Drapier Letters" (August 4, 1724): "I have heard of a Man who had a Mind to Sell his House, and therefore carried a Piece of *Brick* in his Pocket, which he shewed as a *Pattern* to encourage *Purchasers*" (*Fraud Detected; or, The Hibernian Patriot*, p. 44).

[4] The menhaden (*Brevoortia tyrannus*), a "fish of the herring family ... common on the east coasts of the United States" (*OED*, s.v. "mossbunker"). Menhaden were used on Staten Island as manure for crops, especially buckwheat, which was planted at the season when the fish were most plentiful. Farmers paid seventy-five cents per thousand for the menhaden. See *Transactions of the New-York State Agricultural Society* for the year 1842, pp. 208-209.

[5] Peter Wandel (1765?-1857), son of John and Letitia Swan Wandel, married Sarah Van Clief (1774-1857), daughter of Daniel and Martha Marshall Van Clief, in 1789. William Emerson bought his estate from the Wandels and Cornelius van Buskirk in August 1836. Gabriel Poillon Disosway (1799-1868), son of Israel and Ann Doty Disosway, graduated from Columbia University in 1819. He was a dry goods merchant with philanthropic and literary interests. In 1828 he married Diana Tabb Riddick (1810-1883), daughter of Mills and Mary Taylor Riddick of Virginia. The Clove is a deep valley that angles from the northeast shore of Staten Island to the Richmond Road, making a natural roadway. It formed part of the southeastern boundary of William Emerson's estate.

[6] T intended to pursue a publishing career in New York City.

*Copy-text:* ALS (NHi, Misc. Mss. Thoreau, Henry D.)

*Published:* FL 1894, 100-102; FL 1906, 84-86; Cor 1958, 113-114

*Editor's Notes*
    This letter is addressed "Mr. John Thoreau / Concord / Mass".
    Finger-board] PE; Finger- / board *in MS*

*Author's Alterations*
    Battery] battery
    city ⟨to say⟩] city–espe. to
    Street] street
    the] *inserted*
    been] *followed by cancelled* a

## From Charles Lane
*June 9, 1843*

Dear Friend,–The receipt of two acceptable numbers of the "Pathfinder"[1] reminds me that I am not altogether forgotten by one who, if not in the busy world, is at least much nearer to it externally than I am. Busy indeed we all are, since our removal here; but so recluse is our position, that with the world at large we have scarcely any connection. You may possibly have heard that, after all our efforts during the spring had failed to place us in connection with the earth, and Mr. Alcott's journey to Oriskany and Vermont[2] had turned out a blank,–one afternoon in the latter part of May, Providence sent to us the legal owner of a slice of the planet in this township (Harvard), with whom we have been enabled to conclude for the concession of his rights.[3] It is very remotely placed, nearly three miles beyond the village, without a road, surrounded by a beautiful green landscape of fields and woods, with the distance filled up by some of the loftiest mountains in the State. The views are, indeed, most poetic and inspiring. You have no doubt seen the neighborhood; but from these very fields, where you may at once be at home and out, there is enough to love and revel in for sympathetic souls like yours. On the estate are about fourteen acres of wood, part of it extremely pleasant as a retreat, a very sylvan realization, which only wants a Thoreau's mind to elevate it to classic beauty.

I have some imagination that you are not so happy and so well housed in your present position as you would be here amongst us; although at present there is much hard manual labor,–so much that, as you perceive, my usual handwriting[e] is very greatly suspended. We have only two associates[4] in addition to our own families; our house accommodations are poor and scanty; but the greatest want is of good female aid. Far too much labor devolves on Mrs. Alcott.[5] If you should light on any such assistance[v], it would be charitable to give it a direction this way. We may, perhaps, be rather particular about the quality; but the conditions will pretty well determine the acceptability of the parties without a direct adjudication on our part. For though to me our mode of life is luxurious in the highest degree, yet generally it seems to be thought that the setting aside of all impure diet, dirty habits, idle thoughts, and selfish feelings, is a course of self-denial, scarcely to be encountered or even thought of in such an alluring world as this in which we dwell.

Besides the busy occupations of each succeeding day, we form, in this ample theatre of hope, many forthcoming scenes. The nearer little copse is designed as the site of the cottages[v]. Fountains can be made to descend from their granite sources on the hill-slope to every apartment if required. Gardens are to displace the warm grazing glades on the south, and numerous human beings, instead of cattle, shall here enjoy existence. The farther wood offers to the naturalist and the poet an exhaustless haunt; and a short cleaning of the brook would connect our boat with the Nashua. Such are the designs which Mr. Alcott and I have just sketched, as, resting from planting, we walked round this reserve.

In your intercourse with the dwellers in the great city, have you alighted on Mr. Edward Palmer, who studies with Dr. Beach, the Herbalist?[6] He will, I think, from his previous nature-love, and his affirmations to Mr. Alcott, be animated on learning of this actual wooing and winning of Nature's regards. We should be most happy to see him with us. Having become so far actual, from the real, we might fairly enter into the typical, if he could help us in any way to types of the true metal. We have not passed away from home, to see or hear of the world's doings, but the report has reached us of Mr. W. H. Channing's fellowship with the Phalansterians, and of his eloquent speeches in their behalf.[7] Their progress will be much aided by his accession. To both these worthy men be pleased to suggest our humanest sentiments. While they stand amongst men, it is well to find them acting out the truest possible at the moment.

Just before we heard of this place, Mr. Alcott had projected a settlement at the Cliffs on the Concord River, cutting down wood and building a cottage; but so many more facilities were presented here that we quitted the old classic town for one which is to be not less renowned. As far as I could judge, our absence promised little pleasure to our old Concord friends; but at signs of progress I presume they rejoiced with, dear friend,

Yours faithfully,<br>Charles Lane.

*Correspondent:* Charles Lane (1800-1870), an English journalist and reformer, edited and managed the *London Mercantile Price Current* in the 1830s. During this time he met James Pierrepont Greaves, an English educational reformer who had founded a school in Surrey named "Alcott House." Lane later lived at the school and edited a health magazine aimed at promoting spiritual renewal. Lane and Alcott began a correspondence in 1839 that led to Alcott's visit to England in May 1842. In October of that year, Lane and his son came to the United States with Alcott. The two formed a short-lived reform community known as Fruitlands near the town of Harvard, Massachusetts, in 1843. After the failure of the experiment in January 1844, Lane lived briefly with the Shakers in Harvard before moving to New York City. He left the United States in 1846 and later resumed his career as a journalist in England. Though he espoused celibacy while in the United States, Lane had a son by an early marriage, and he married Hannah Bond in 1870.

[1] The *Pathfinder* was a weekly journal devoted to politics, literature, and the arts; Parke Godwin published it in New York City from February 25 to June 3 of 1843.

[2] Alcott took two weeks to visit his mother and siblings in Oriskany Falls, New York, and to spend time with his friend Benjamin Wilkins Dyer (1808-1877), an ardent abolitionist and temperance reformer, in Braintree, Vermont. Alcott had tried to interest his brother Junius in the reform community he was planning with Lane. He and Dyer had met in August 1840, when they attended a reform convention in Groton, Massachusetts.

[3] Maverick Wyman (1788-1868), son of Daniel and Lucy Wyman

of Bedford, Massachusetts, owned the property outside the town of Harvard; see p. 165, note 4.

⁴ One of the assistants was Samuel Larned (1824-1853), son of John Smith and Lucinda Martin Larned of Providence, Rhode Island. Before going to Fruitlands, Larned spent some time at Brook Farm. He later became a Unitarian minister in Mobile, Alabama, and married Julia H. Sanford (b. 1820?) in 1850. The other assistant's identity is uncertain. He has been variously identified by Alcott's biographers as Wood Abram, Abraham Wood, and Abraham Everett. Abigail Alcott in her diary lists "Wood Abraham" as one of a group of people visiting on July 18, 1843. In other places she mentions "Abraham" without indicating whether Abraham is a Christian or family name. She never refers to anyone with the name "Everett." Lane refers in a letter to a man named "Abraham" who was from Vermont, and Bronson Alcott names "Abraham Everett" as a member of the community in June 1843. The man in question may be Abram Everett (1803-1845), son of Joshua and Ruth Wood Everett.

⁵ Lane himself and his son William (b. 1832) were part of the burden Abigail Alcott bore. In her diary entry for January 7, 1844, she wrote: "The care of Mr Lane and William has been at times exceedingly arduous. My children have been too much bereft of their Mother and she has murmured at a lot which should deprive her of their society–" (MH-H, MS Am 1130.14 [1]).

⁶ Lane in September described Palmer as "a man of extreme gentleness but pretty firm" (Joel Myerson, "William Harry Harland's 'Bronson Alcott's English Friends,'" *Resources for American Literary Study* 8 [spring 1978]: 53). Wooster Beach (1794-1868), a physician and a reformer, opposed bloodletting and the use of mercury as a curative. He wrote an influential textbook, *The American Practice of Medicine*, 3 vols. (New York: Betts and Anstice, 1833).

⁷ On May 25, William Henry Channing spoke at National Hall in Manhattan at a meeting designed "to take preliminary steps toward the establishment of the North American Phalanx," a Fourierist reform community created in 1843 near Red Bank, New Jersey, by Albert Brisbane, with the help of Channing and Horace Greeley, among others. The community, which lasted until 1854, was based upon the "divine principles of Social Unity, Brotherhood and Harmony" ("Doctrine of Association," *New-York Daily Tribune*, May 27).

*Copy-text:* *HDT* 1882, 137-140

*Published:* *HDT* 1882, 137-140; *Alcott: His Life and Philosophy* 1893, 377-378; *T: Home* 1902, 111-112; *Cor* 1958, 115-116

*Editor's Notes*

PE supplies the date "June 9, 1843" based on information in *HDT* 1882. In *Alcott: His Life and Philosophy* 1893, Sanborn and Harris date the letter June 7 (p. 377).

handwriting] *PE*; hand- / writing *in copy-text*

*Substantive Variants*

The text of this letter is based on a published source, *HDT* 1882; potentially authoritative substantive readings in *Alcott: His Life and Philosophy* 1893 are reported below.

assistance] *in copy-text;* assistant *in Alcott: His Life and Philosophy 1893*

cottages] *in copy-text;* little cottages *in Alcott: His Life and Philosophy 1893*

## From Ralph Waldo Emerson

*June 10 and 15, 1843*

Concord, 10 June 1843

Dear Henry,

It is high time that you had some token from us in acknowledgment of the parcel of kind & tuneful things you sent us, as well as of your permanent rights in us all. The cold weather saddened our gardens & our landscape here almost until now but todays sunshine is obliterating the memory of such things. I have just been visiting my petty plantation and find that all your grafts live excepting a single scion and all my new trees, including twenty pines to fill up interstices in my "Curtain," are well alive. The town is full of Irish & the woods of engineers with theodolite & red flag singing out their feet & inches to each other from station to station. Near Mr Alcott's the road is already begun.– From Mr A. & Mr Lane at Harvard we have yet heard nothing. They went away in good spirits having sent "Wood Abram" & Larned[1] & Wm Lane before them with horse & plough a few days in advance of them to begin the spring work. Mr Lane paid me a long visit in which he was more than I had ever known him gentle & open, and it was impossible not to sympathize with & honour projects that so often seem without feet or hands.[2] They have near a hundred acres of land, which they do not want, & no house, which they want first of all. But they account this an advantage, as it gives them the occasion they so much desire of building after their own idea. In the event of their attracting to their company a carpenter or two, which is not impossible, it would be a great pleasure to see their building which could hardly fail to be new & beautiful. They have 15 acres of woodland with good timber. Ellery Channing is excellent company and we walk in all directions[3] He remembers[e] you with great faith & hope thinks you ought not to see Concord again these ten years, that you ought to grind up fifty Concords in your mill & much other opinion & counsel he holds in store on this topic. Hawthorne walked with me yesterday P. m. and not until after our return did I read his "Celestial Railroad" which has a serene strength[a] which one cannot afford not to praise,–in this low life.[4]

Our Dial thrives well enough in these weeks. I print W. E. C.'s "Letters" or the first ones, but he does not care to have them named as his for a while.[5] They are very agreeable reading, & their wisdom lightened by a vivacity very rare in the D.– Ward too has sent me some sheets on architecture,[6] whose good sense is eminent. I have a valuable manuscript–a sea voyage, from a new hand, which is all clear good sense, and I may make some of Mr Lane's graver sheets give way for this honest story, otherwise I shall print it in October.[7] I have transferred the publishing of the Dial to Jas. Munroe & Co.[8,e] Do not, I entreat you, let me be in ignorance of any thing good which you know of my fine friends Waldo & Tappan Tappan writes me never a word. I had a letter from H. James, promising to see you, & you must not fail to visit him. I must soon write to him, though my debts of this nature are perhaps too many. To him I much prefer to talk than to write. Let me know well how you prosper & what you meditate. And all good abide with you!

R. W. E.

15 June–  Whilst my letter has lain on the table waiting
for a traveller, your letter & parcel has safely arrived. I may
not have place now for the Winter's Walk in the July Dial[9]
which is just making up its last sheets & somehow I must
end it to-morrow–when I go to Boston. I shall then keep
it for October, subject however to your order if you find
a better disposition for it.–  I will carry the order to the
faithless booksellers. Thanks for all these tidings of my
friends at N.Y. & at the Island. & love to the last. I have
letters from Lane at "Fruitlands" & from Miss Fuller at Niagara. Miss F. found it sadly cold & rainy[a] at the Falls.[10]

*Correspondent:*  See p. 53.

[1] Charles Lane's two assistants at Fruitlands; see p. 190, note 4.

[2] Cameron (*Companion* 1964, p. 35) suggests an allusion to Luther, whom Emerson quoted in his 1835 lecture on Milton: "It is,
as Luther said of one of Melancthon's writings, 'alive, hath hands
and feet,–and not like Erasmus's sentences, which were made, not
grown'" (Emerson, *Early Lectures*, 3 vols., ed. Stephen E. Whicher
and Robert E. Spiller [Cambridge, Mass.: Harvard University Press,
1959-1972], 1:147).

[3] Emerson described one such walk in a journal entry dated May
20: "Walked with Ellery. In the landscape felt the magic of colour;
the world is all opal & those ethereal tints the mountains wear have
the finest effects of magic on us" (*JMN*, 8:405).

[4] Emerson recorded his conversation with Hawthorne in his
journal entry for June 10: "Hawthorne & I talked of the number of
superior young men we have seen. H. said, that he had seen several
from whom he had expected much, but they had not distinguished
themselves; and he had inferred that he must not expect a popular
success from such; he had in nowise lost his confidence in their
power" (*JMN*, 8:423). "The Celestial Railroad," a sharp satire on
Transcendentalism, appeared in the *United States Magazine, and
Democratic Review* 12 (May 1843): 515-523.

[5] The July 1843 number of the *Dial* published the first installment
of "The Youth of the Poet and the Painter" (pp. 48-58), Ellery Channing's autobiographical story written in the form of a series of letters between Edward Ashford and others. Three more installments
of such letters would appear in the October 1843 (pp. 174-186),
January 1844 (pp. 273-284), and April 1844 (pp. 427-454) numbers,
which were the last three numbers of the magazine.

⁶ Samuel Gray Ward (1817-1907), son of Thomas Wren and Lydia Gray Ward of Boston, graduated from Harvard in 1836 and married Anna Hazard Barker (1813-1900), daughter of Jacob and Eliza Hazard Barker, in 1840. He toyed with the idea of pursuing a career as a painter but instead followed his father in the Baring Brothers Bank. He and Ellery Channing were close friends from their boyhood days at the Round Hill School in Northampton, Massachusetts. His "Notes on Art and Architecture" appeared in the July *Dial* (pp. 107-115).

⁷ Benjamin Peter Hunt's "Voyage to Jamaica" appeared in two parts in the July (pp. 116-133) and October (pp. 227-244) numbers of the *Dial*. Hunt (1808-1877), son of Joshua and Olive Chamberlain Hunt, had been Emerson's pupil in 1825, and the editor's enthusiasm for his former student's piece was unabashed: "It delights me by its directness & veracity, by its plain strength and its insight, and by its capital art of compression & of omission which in all writing seems so much" (*Letters of RWE* 1939, 3:199). Despite this praise, Emerson thoroughly edited the manuscript by compressing it and creating a narrative line. To make room for Hunt's piece in the July number, Emerson broke Charles Lane's "Social Tendencies" into two parts and published them in the July (pp. 65-86) and October (pp. 188-204) numbers. Margaret Fuller thought that this was a mistake: "It was pity to break Mr Lane's piece. He needs to fall his whole length to show his weight" (*Letters of Margaret Fuller*, 3:136-137).

⁸ Weeks, Jordan, and Company published the first five numbers of the *Dial* before the publishing house went out of business in September 1841. William H. S. Jordan, former partner in the failed concern, published the next number, and Elizabeth Peabody then became the publisher for the following six numbers. James Munroe published the final four numbers.

⁹ T's essay "A Winter Walk" appeared in the October number (pp. 211-226; see *Excursions* 2007, pp. 55-77).

¹⁰ "We have had bad weather here, bitterly cold," wrote Fuller. "The place is what I expected: it is too great and beautiful to agitate or surprise: it satisfies: it does not excite thought, but fully occupies" (*Letters of Margaret Fuller*, 3:128).


*Copy-text:* ALS (NN-BGC, Henry David Thoreau Collection, 1837-1917, Series IV)

*Published:* *HDT* 1882, 135-136, 136-137; "E-T" May 1892, 589-590; *Alcott* 1893, 353; *FL* 1894, 111n, 143; *FL* 1906, 94n, 120; *Americana* 1912,

527; Clara Endicott Sears, comp., *Bronson Alcott's Fruitlands* (Boston: Houghton Mifflin, 1915), 20; *Cor* 1958, 117-118; *Letters of RWE* 1990-1995, 7:545-547; *The Selected Letters of Ralph Waldo Emerson*, ed. Joel Myerson (New York: Columbia University Press, 1998), 289-291

*Editor's Notes*
   This letter is addressed "Henry D. Thoreau / Care of Wm Emerson Esq / 64 Wall Street / New York."
   remembers] *PE*; re / members *in MS*
   Co.] *PE*; *possibly* Co.– *in MS*

*Author's Alterations*
   strength] *interlined with a caret*
   rainy] *preceded by cancelled* wet


## To Lidian Jackson Emerson

*June 20, 1843*

Staten Island
June 20th 1843

My very dear Friend,

   I have only read a page of your letter, and have come out to the top of the hill at sunset, where I can see the ocean to prepare to read the rest. It is fitter that it should hear it than the walls of my chamber. The very crickets here seem to chirp around me as they did not before. I feel as if it were a great daring to go on and read the rest, and then to live accordingly–   There are more than thirty vessels in sight going to sea–   I am almost afraid to look at your letter. I see that it will make[a] my life very steep, but it may lead to fairer prospects than this.

   You seem to me to speak out of a very clear and high heaven, where any one may be who stands so high. Your voice seems not a voice, but comes as much from the blue heavens, as from the paper.

   My dear friend it was very noble in you to write me so trustful an answer. It will do as well for another world as for this. Such a voice is for no particular time nor person,

but it makes him who may hear it stand for all that is lofty
and true[e] in humanity. The thought of you will constantly
elevate my life, it will be something always above the horizon to behold, as when I look up at the evening star. I
think I know your thoughts without seeing you, and as
well here as in Concord. You are not at all strange to me.

I could hardly believe after the lapse of one night that
I had[a] such a noble letter still at hand to read–that it was
not some fine dream. I looked at midnight to be sure that
it was real. I feel that I am unworthy to know you, and yet
they will not permit it wrongfully.

I, perhaps, am more willing to deceive by appearances
than you say you are; it[a] would not be worth the while to
tell how willing–but I have the power perhaps too much
to forget my meanness as soon as seen, and not be in-
cited by permanent sorrow. My actual life is unspeakably
mean, compared with what I know and see that it might
be–   Yet the ground from which I see and say this is some
part of it. It ranges from heaven to earth and is all things
in an hour. The experience of every past moment but
belies the faith of each present. We never conceive the
greatness of our fates. Are not these faint flashes of light,
which sometimes obscure the sun, their certain dawn?

My friend, I have read your letter as if I was not reading it. After each pause I could defer the rest forever. The
thought of you will be a new motive for every right action.
You are another human being whom I know, and might
not our topic be as broad as the universe. What have we to
do with petty rumbling news? We have our own great affairs. Sometimes in Concord I found my actions dictated
as it were by your influence, and though it lead almost to
trivial Hindoo observances, yet it was good and elevating
{MS torn}

To hear that you have sad hours is not sad to me. I rather
rejoice at the richness of your experience. Only think
of some sadness away in Pekin–unseen and unknown

there– What a mine it is. Would it not weigh down the Celestial[a] empire, with all its gay Chinese? Our sadness is not sad, but our cheap joys. Let us be sad about all we see and are, for so we demand and pray for better. It is the constant prayer–and whole Christian religion. I could hope that you would get well soon, and have a healthy body for this world, but I know this cannot be–and the Fates, after all, are the accomplishers of our hopes– Yet I do hope that you may find it a worthy struggle, and life seem grand still through the clouds.

What wealth is it to have such friends that we cannot think of them without elevation. And we can think of them any time time, and any where, and it costs nothing but the lofty disposition. I cannot tell you the joy your letter gives me–which will not quite cease till the latest time. Let me accompany your finest thought.

I send my love to my other friend and brother, whose nobleness I slowly recognise.

Henry

*Correspondent:* See p. 168.

*Copy-text:* ALS (Bruce Museum [Gift of Agnes Bell Clark])

*Published:* *LVP* 1865, 23-26; *Life* 1890, 73-74; *FL* 1894, 103-106; *T: Home* 1902, 232; *FL* 1906, 87-89; *Cor* 1958, 119-120

*Editor's Notes*
This letter is addressed "Mrs. Lidian Emerson / Concord / Mass." and postmarked "{*illegible*}EW-YOR{*illegible*} JUN 25".
true] *PE; possibly ~, in MS*

*Author's Alterations*
make] may
had] *interlined with a caret*
it] It
Celestial] celestial

## To Cynthia Dunbar Thoreau
*July 7, 1843*

Staten Island July 7th

Dear Mother,

I was very glad to get your letter and papers. Tell Father that circumstantial letters make very substantial reading, at any rate. I like to know even how the sun shines and garden grows with you.

I did not get my money in Boston and probably shall not at all.–[1] Tell Sophia that I have pressed some blossoms of the tulip tree for her. They look somewhat like white lilies. The magnolia too is in blossom here. Pray have you the Seventeen year locust[2] in Concord? The air here is filled with their din. They come out of the ground at first in an imperfect state, and crawling up the shrubs and plants, the perfect insect burst out through the back. They are doing great damage to the fruit and forest trees. The latter are covered with dead twigs which in the distance look like the blossoms of the chestnut. They bore every twig of last year's growth in order to deposit their eggs in it[a]. In a few weeks the eggs will be hatched, and the worms fall to the ground and enter it–and in 1860 make their appearance again. I conversed about their coming this season before they arrived. They do no injury to the leaves, but beside boring the twigs–suck their sap for sustenance. Their din is heard by those who sail along the shore–from the distant woods. Phar-r-r-aoh–Pha-r-r-aoh. They are departing now. Dogs, cats and chickens subsist mainly upon them in some places.

I have not been to N.Y. for more than three weeks.– I have had an interesting letter from Mr Lane,[3] describing their new prospects.– My pupil and I are getting on apace, He[a] is remarkably well advanced in Latin and is well advancing.

Your letter has just arrived. I was not aware that it was so long since I wrote home; I only knew that I had sent five[a] or six letters to the town. It is very refreshing to hear from you–though it is not all good news–  But I trust that Stearns Wheeler is not dead–[4]  I should be slow to believe it. He was made to work very well in this world.–  There need be no tragedy in his death.

The demon which is said to haunt the Jones family–hovering over their eye lids with wings steeped in juice of poppies–has commenced another campaign against me. I am "clear Jones" in this respect at least.[5] But he finds little encouragement in my atmosphere I assure you–for I do not once fairly lose myself–except in those hours of truce allotted to rest by immemorial custom. However, this skirmishing interferes sadly with my literary projects–and I am apt to think it a good day's work if I maintain a soldier's eye till night-fall[e]. Very well it does not matter much in what wars we serve–whether in the Highlands or the Lowlands–  Everywhere we get soldier's pay still.

Give my love to Aunt Louisa–whose benignant face I sometimes see right in the wall–as naturally and necessarily shining on my path as some star–of unaccountably greater age and higher orbit than myself. Let it be inquired by her of George Minott–as from me–for she sees him–If he has seen any pigeons yet–and tell him there are plenty of Jack-snipes[6,e] here.–  As for William P.[7] the "worthy young man"–as I live, my eyes have not fallen on him yet. I have not had the influenza–though here are its head-quarters–unless my first week's cold was it. Tell Helen I shall write to her soon. I have heard Lucretia Motte–[8]  This is badly written–but the worse the writing the sooner you get it this time–from

Yr Affectionate Son<br>H. D. T.

*Correspondent:*  See p. 161.

[1] T refers to the publication of "A Walk to Wachusett" in the *Boston Miscellany of Literature and Fashion*; see p. 148, note 5.

[2] Thaddeus William Harris gives a detailed description of the life cycle of the "seventeen-year Cicada," which he identifies as "*Cicada septendecim* of Linnaeus" in *A Report on the Insects of Massachusetts, Injurious to Vegetation*, p. 170. T reviewed this volume in "Natural History of Massachusetts," *Dial* 3 (July 1842): 19-40 (see *Excursions* 2007, pp. 3-28).

[3] Charles Lane.

[4] Wheeler had died in Leipzig on June 13; his obituary appeared in the July 11 *Boston Courier*.

[5] Narcolepsy is the "demon" that T refers to, a condition that ran in the Jones family, his maternal ancestors. Besides T, his uncle Charles Dunbar was also afflicted: in *Walden*, T describes his uncle as a man "who goes to sleep shaving himself, and is obliged to sprout potatoes in a cellar Sundays, in order to keep awake and keep the Sabbath" (*Walden* 1971, p. 259).

[6] In *The Birds of Long Island*, which Thoreau owned, Jacob P. Giraud Jr. notes that the pectoral sandpiper is called the "Jack Snipe" in Pennsylvania. He also comments that he has "occasionally seen it [on Long Island] during the month of July; but in such instances it has been alone," presumably having "loitered behind the migratory band" (p. 235).

[7] William MacKay Prichard (1814-1897), son of Moses and Jane Hallett Prichard, was a Concord native. He graduated from Harvard in 1833, studied law, and became William Emerson's law partner in New York City.

[8] Helen Lucretia Coffin Mott (1793-1880) was a radical abolitionist and a feminist. A member of the Society of Friends, she was first a minister and then a prominent speaker. In his July 21 letter to his sister Helen, T mentions that he had heard Mott "at the Quaker church in Hester St."; see p. 211 for T's detailed account of the Sunday service. Mott was closely associated with William Lloyd Garrison and was often publicly threatened for her ideas. She attended the American Anti-Slavery Society meetings in New York City held from May 9 to May 11; it is not clear whether T heard her at that time. In 1848 Mott joined with Elizabeth Cady Stanton to organize the Seneca Falls convention on women's rights.

*Copy-text:*  ALS (CSmH, HM 7004)

*Published: LVP* 1865, 31-33; *FL* 1894, 106-109; *FL* 1906, 89-92; *Cor* 1958, 121-122

*Editor's Notes*
    This letter is addressed "Mrs. Cynthia Thoreau / Concord / Mass." and postmarked "NEW-YORK JUL 7".

PE supplies the year "1843" from the contents of the letter.
night-fall] *PE*; night- / fall *in MS*
Jack-snipes] *PE*; Jack- / snipes *in MS*

*Author's Alterations*
  it] *interlined above cancelled* them
  He] he
  five] *preceded by cancelled* three


*To Ralph Waldo and Lidian Jackson Emerson*
*July 8, 1843*

                      Staten Island July 8th -43

Dear Friends,

    I was very glad to hear your voices from so far. I do not believe[a] there are eight hundred human beings on the globe– It is all a fable; And I cannot but think that you speak with a slight outrage and disrespect of Concord, when you talk of fifty of them. There are not so many. Yet think not that I have left all behind–for already I begin to track my way over the earth, and find the cope of heaven extending beyond its horizon–forsooth like the roofs of these Dutch houses.– Yet will my thoughts revert to those dear hills, and that *river* which so fills up the word to its brim, worthy to be named with Mincius and Alpheus[1]–still drinking its meadows while I am far away. How can it run heedless to the sea, as if I were there to countenance it– Geo. Minott too looms up considerably–and many another old familiar face– These things all look sober and respectable– They are better than the environs of New York, I assure you.

    I am pleased to think of Channing as an inhabitant of the grey town. Seven cities contended for Homer dead.[2] Tell him to remain at least long enough to establish Concord's right and interest in him. I was beginning to know the man. In imagination I see you pilgrims taking your way by the red lodge[3] and the cabin of the brave farmer man,[4] so youthful and hale, to the still cheerful woods–

And Hawthorne too I remember as one with whom I sauntered in old heroic times along the banks of the Scamander, amid the ruins of chariots and heroes.[5] Tell him not to desert even after the tenth year.[6] Others may say "Are[a] there not the cities of Asia"?–but what are they? Staying at home is the heavenly way.[7]

And Elizabeth Hoar–my brave townswoman[e]–to be sung of poets–if I may speak of her[a] whom I do not know.

Tell Mrs Brown that I do not forget her going her way under the stars through this chilly world–I did *not* think of the wind–and that I went a little way with her. Tell her not to despair–Concord's little arch does not span all our fate–nor is what transpires under it–law for the universe–

And least of all are forgotten those walks in the woods in ancient days–too sacred to be idly remembered– when their aisles were pervaded as by a fragrant atmosphere– They still seem youthful and cheery to my imagination as Sherwood and Barnsdale[8]–and of far purer fame.– Those afternoons when we wandered o'er Olympus–and those hills from which the sun was seen to set while still our day held on its way–

> "At last he rose, and twitched his mantle[a] blue;
> To-morrow to fresh woods and pastures new"[9]

I remember these things at midnight at rare intervals–

> But know, my friends, that I a good deal hate you all in my most private thought– –as the substratum of the little love I bear you. Though ye are a rare band and do not make half use enough of oneanother[e].[10]

I think this is a noble number of the Dial. It perspires thought and feeling. I can speak of it now a little like a foreigner. Be assured that it is not written in vain–it is not for me. I hear its prose and its verse–they provoke and inspire me, and[e] they have my sympathy. I hear the sober and earnest, the sad and cheery voices of my friends– and to me it is like a long letter of encouragement and reproof– And no doubt so it is to many another in the land. So dont give up the ship–[11] Methinks the verse is hardly enough better than the prose– I give my vote for the Notes from the Journal of a Scholar[12]–and wonder you dont print them faster– I want too to read the rest of the Poet[a] and the Painter[a].[13] Miss Fuller's is a noble piece. rich extempore writing–talking with pen in hand–[14] It is too good not to be better even. In writing conversation should be folded many times thick. It is the height of art that on the first perusal plain common sense should appear–on the second serene truth–and on the third beauty– And having these warrants for its depth and reality, we may then enjoy the beauty forever more.– The sea piece[15] is of the best that is going–if not of the best that is stay-ing– You have spoken a good word for Carlyle.–[16] As for the "Winter-Walk" I shall be glad to have it printed in the D. if you think it good enough, and will criticize it–other-wise send it to me and I will dispose of it. I have not been to N.Y. for a month and so have not seen W. & T.[17] James[18] has been at Albany meanwhile. You will know that I only describe my personal adventures with people–but I hope soon to see more of them and *judge* them too. I am sorry to hear that Mrs. E. is no better–[19] But let her know that the Fates[a] pay a compliment to those whom they make sick–and they have not to ask what have I done Remem-ber me to your mother, and remember me yourself as you are remembered by

                                                    H. D. T.

    I had a friendly and cheery letter from Lane[20] a month ago.

*Correspondent:* See p. 53 and p. 168.

    [1] The Mincius is a river in northen Italy that flows from Lake Garda to the river Po. The Alpheus is a river in Peloponnese, Greece, that flows from Arcadia to the Ionian Sea.
    [2] T refers to a well-known Greek epigram that alludes to the un-certainty of Homer's birthplace. In *The Age of Fable; or, Beauties of Mythology*, enl. and rev. ed., ed. E. E. Hale (Boston: S. W. Tilton,

1882), Thomas Bulfinch gives two versions of the epigram. One version reads: "Seven wealthy towns contend for Homer dead, / Through which the living Homer begged his bread." The cities were "Smyrna, Scio, Rhodes, Colophon, Salamis, Argos, and Athens" (p. 377).

³ The Channings' house; see p. 155, note 1.

⁴ T probably refers to Edmund Hosmer (1798-1881), son of John and Mary Vassall Prescott Hosmer of Concord, and a farmer given to books and thought. A friend of both Emerson and T, Hosmer helped T raise his house at Walden Pond and was often his visitor there.

⁵ Because the Concord River was closely associated with the Battle of Concord, T's transformation of the river into the Scamander of Troy links the Trojan War with the American Revolutionary War.

⁶ As prophesied, it took the Greeks ten years to subdue Troy. Although many of Troy's inhabitants fled the destroyed city, others stayed behind to rebuild.

⁷ When asked by a group of pilgrims "what he thought of *going out?* meaning, to assist *Ali*," Abu Musa answered: "Sitting still at Home *is the Heavenly Way.* The going out, *is the Way of the World*" (Simon Ockley, *The History of the Saracens*, 2:34). Abu al-Hasan al-Ash'ari (Abu Musa) (873-935?) was an Arab theologian and a disciple of Abu Ali al-Jubba'i, head of a sect in Basra. T copied the lines from Ockley in a Journal entry for December 27, 1840 (*Journal 1* 1981, p. 210).

⁸ Both forests are associated with Robin Hood. In a Journal entry dated December 23, 1841, T wrote the following: "A forest is in all mythologies a sacred place– As the oaks among the druids–and the grove of Egeria–and even in more familiar and common life, a celebrated wood is spoken of with respect–as 'Barnsdale wood' and 'Sherwood'–. Pan himself lives in the wood. Had Robin Hood no Sherwood to resort it would be difficult to invest his story with the charms it has got–"(*Journal 1* 1981, p. 347). T had read Joseph Ritson's *Robin Hood: A Collection of All the Ancient Poems, Songs, and Ballads.*

⁹ T quotes the closing lines of "Lycidas" (Milton, vol. 5, p. 50).

¹⁰ Describing friendship using the language of enmity was not uncommon among the Transcendentalists. For instance, on October 29, 1838, Emerson wrote in his journal: "J. Very charmed us all by telling us he hated us all" (*JMN*, 7:124). T uses similar language to express the relationship of love and hatred in Transcendental friendship in *A Week on the Concord and Merrimack Rivers*, in both prose and poetry (see *A Week* 1980, pp. 282, 287):

True Friendship can afford true knowledge. It does not depend on darkness and ignorance. A want of discernment
cannot be an ingredient in it. If I can see my Friend's virtues
more distinctly than another's, his faults too are made more
conspicuous by contrast. We have not so good a right to hate
any as our Friend.

and

Let such pure hate still underprop
Our love, that we may be
Each other's conscience,
And have our sympathy
Mainly from thence.

[11] The famous command of the dying Captain James Lawrence
(1781-1813) as his ship *Chesapeake* fought the British *Shannon* in
the War of 1812.

[12] Charles Chauncy Emerson, "Notes from the Journal of a
Scholar. No. II.", *Dial* 4 (July 1843): 88-92. Emerson's topics were the
writing of journals, nature, truth, and self and society.

[13] Ellery Channing, "The Youth of the Poet and the Painter," *Dial*
4 (July 1843): 48-58; see p. 193, note 5.

[14] Fuller's piece, "The Great Lawsuit. Man *versus* Men. Woman
*versus* Women.", opened the July number of the *Dial* (pp. 1-47). Emerson, in a letter to Fuller, called it "a piece of life"; in the same letter
Emerson also quoted T's compliment, beginning, "H. D. Thoreau,
who will never like anything, writes, . . ." (*Letters of RWE* 1939, 3:183).

[15] Benjamin P. Hunt's "Voyage to Jamaica"; see p. 194, note 7.

[16] Emerson negotiated the American publication of Carlyle's *Past
and Present*, which came out in May, and he reviewed the book in
the July *Dial*. Of Carlyle, he wrote: "Here is Carlyle's new poem,
his Iliad of English woes, to follow his poem on France, entitled
the History of the French Revolution. In its first aspect it is a political tract, and since Burke, since Milton, we have had nothing to
compare with it." The review clearly aimed at boosting sales, but
Emerson nonetheless described Carlyle's genius in its full com-
plexity: although "[in] this work, as in his former labors, Mr. Carlyle
reminds us of a sick giant" and "the habitual exaggeration of the
tone wearies whilst it stimulates," Carlyle "in his strange half mad
way, has entered the Field of the Cloth of Gold, and shown a vigor
and wealth of resource, which has no rival in the tourney play of
these times" (pp. 96, 99, 101).

[17] Giles Waldo and William Tappan.

[18] Henry James Sr.

[19] On June 19 Emerson wrote his brother William that "Lidian re-

mains still quite a wreck of dyspepsia & debility and it is high time for her to get a great deal better" (*Letters of RWE* 1939, 3:181).

    [20] Charles Lane.

*Copy-text:* ALS (NN-BGC, Henry David Thoreau Collection, 1837-1917, Series III)

*Published:* "E-T" May 1892, 590-591; *FL* 1894, 109-113; *T: Home* 1902, 244; *FL* 1906, 92-95; *Americana* 1912, 527; *Magazine of History* 1915, 119; *T as Remembered* 1917, 99-100; *Cor* 1958, 123-125

*Editor's Notes*
    This letter is addressed "R. Waldo Emerson / Concord / Mass.", postmarked "NEW-YORK JUL 8", and endorsed "H D Thoreau / July, 1843".
    townswoman] PE; towns- / woman *in MS*
    oneanother] *PE*; one- / another *in MS*
    and] *PE*; a{*text obscured by sealing wax*}

*Author's Alterations*
    believe] beleive
    Are] are
    her] one
    mantle] mantel
    Poet] poet
    Painter] painter
    Fates] fates

## *To James Munroe and Company*

*July 14, 1843*

paper which was sent for the Dial

*Correspondent:* James Munroe (1808-1861), who had published Emerson's *Nature* and *Essays*, founded his Boston and Cambridge publishing house in the early 1830s. He published the last four numbers of the *Dial*, starting with the July 1843 number. In 1849 Munroe published T's first book, *A Week on the Concord and Merrimack Rivers.*

*Copy-text: The Stephen H. Wakeman Collection of Books of Nineteenth Century American Writers* (New York: American Art Association, 1924), item 984

*Editor's Notes*
    PE supplies the date "July 14, 1843" based on information in the Wakeman sale catalog.

In the Wakeman sale this letter was offered with T's annotated copy of the *Dial*. The description in the sale catalog includes the following:

> Autograph Letter Signed by Thoreau. 1p. 4to, Concord, 14 July 1843, to the Publishers of "The Dial,".

## From Ralph Waldo Emerson
*July 20, 1843*

Concord 20 July 1843

Dear Henry,

Giles Waldo shall not go back[1] without a line to you if only to pay part of my debt in that kind long due. I am sorry to say that when I called on Bradbury & Soden nearly a month ago, their partner in their absence informed me that they could not pay you at present any part of their debt on account of the B. Miscellany. After much talking, all the promise he could offer, was, "that[e] within a year it would probably be paid," a probability which certainly looks very slender.[2] The very worst thing he said was the proposition[e] that you should take your payment in the form of B. Miscellanies! I shall not fail to refresh their memory at intervals. We were all very glad to have such cordial greetings from you as in your last letter on the Dial's & on all personal accounts. Hawthorn & Channing are both in good health & spirits & the last always a good companion[e] for me, who am hard to suit, I suppose. Giles Waldo has established himself with me by his good sense. I fancy from your notices that he is more than you have seen. I think that neither he nor W. A. T.[3] will be exhausted in one interview. My wife is at Plymouth to recruit her wasted strength but left word with me to acknowledge & heartily thank you for your last letter to her. Edith & Ellen are in high health, and as pussy has this afternoon nearly killed a young oriole, Edie tells all comers with great energy her one story, "Birdy–sick." Mrs Brown who just left the house desires kindest remembrances to you whom "she misses", & whom "she thinks of." In this fine weather we look very bright & green in yard & garden though this sun without showers will perchance spoil our potatoes– Our clover grew well on your patch between the dikes & Reuben Brown[4] adjudged that Cyrus Warren[5] should pay 14.00 this year for my grass. Last year he paid 8. All your grafts of this year have lived & done well. The apple trees & plums speak of you in every wind. You will have read & heard the sad news to the little village of Lincoln of Stearns Wheeler's death. Such an overthrow to the hopes of his parents made me think more of them than of the loss[a] the community[e] will suffer in his kindness diligence & ingenuous mind. The papers have contained ample notices of his life & death.– I saw Charles Newcomb the other day at Brook Farm,[6] & he expressed his great gratification in your translations & said that he had been minded to write you & ask of you to translate in like manner–Pindar. I advised him by all means to do so. But he seemed to think he had discharged his conscience. But it was a very good request. It would be a fine thing to be done since Pindar has no adequate translation no English equal to his fame.[7] Do look at the book with that in your mind, while Charles is mending his pen. I will soon send you word respecting the Winter Walk. Farewell.

R. W. Emerson.

*Correspondent:* See p. 53.

*Correspondent:* See p. 53.

[1] Waldo visited Emerson from July 15 to July 22. Emerson wrote Lidian on July 17: "He brings me a fine gentle spirit, great intelligence, & always interests me if in no other way by the beautiful friendship which subsists between him & Tappan" (*Letters of RWE* 1939, 3:185).

[2] T apparently never received payment for "A Walk to Wachusett."

[3] William Aspinwall Tappan.

[4] Reuben Brown (1781-1854), son of Reuben and Polly Brown of Concord, was known as a horticulturist and a charitable man of good temper, whose speech had "a spice of oddity" (*Memoirs of the Social Circle* 1888, pp. 168-171). Deacon of the First Parish from 1827 until his death, Brown was also a member of the Concord militia and twice represented the town in the legislature.

⁵ Cyrus Warren (1790-1866) came to Concord in 1811 as a shoe-maker. In 1819 he married Nancy Bacon (1793-1871), daughter of Thompson and Martha Hosmer Bacon of Bedford, Massachusetts. Warren later retired from his trade to be a farmer and was known both for his well-kept land (which bordered Emerson's) and for his penchant for planting trees throughout the town. Though close with a dollar, Warren was well liked in Concord. He succeeded Deacon Brown at the First Parish.

⁶ Charles King Newcomb (1820-1894), son of Henry Stearns and Rhoda Mardenbrough Newcomb of Providence, Rhode Island, was yet another young man whom Emerson thought destined for liter-ary distinction. His only publication in the *Dial* was "The Two Do-lons....The First Dolon" in July 1842 (pp. 112-123); he planned but did not complete a sequel. Newcomb spent some time at Brook Farm, but developed no talent for writing. Of this meeting, Emer-son wrote in his journal: "Charles N. I saw, & was relieved to meet again on something of the old footing, after hearing of so much ill-ness & sensitiveness" (*JMN*, 8:428).

⁷ T did work on his translations of Pindar in late summer and fall of 1843, either because of Emerson's prompting or as a continua-tion of a previous interest. He would publish some of the finished translations in two separate issues of the *Dial*, the January 1844 number ("Pindar," pp. 379-390) and the April 1844 number ("Frag-ments of Pindar," pp. 513-514). Drafts of almost five hundred lines survive in manuscript. T's source was Pindar, *Werke*, a bilingual edition in Greek and German. See *Translations* 1986, pp. 111-127, 129-131, 170-173.

*Copy-text:*  ALS (NNC-RB, Manuscript Collections)

*Published:* HDT 1882, 220-221; "Emerson-Thoreau Correspon-dence," *AM* 69 (May 1892): 591-592; *FL* 1894, 122n, 123; *FL* 1906, 102n-103n, 103; *Cor* 1958, 126-127; *Letters of RWE* 1990-1995, 7:551-552

*Editor's Notes*
   This letter is addressed "Henry D. Thoreau / Staten Island / Giles Waldo".
   The word "begun" is interlined in pencil above and following "that". It does not appear in *HDT* 1882, "Emerson-Thoreau Corre-spondence," *FL* 1894, or *FL* 1906. It may be a printer's note.
   proposition] *PE*; propo / sition *in MS*
   companion] *PE*; com / panion *in MS*
   community] *PE*; communi / ty *in MS*

*Author's Alteration*
   loss] *preceded by cancelled* regret

*To Helen Louisa Thoreau*
*July 21, 1843*

Staten Island July 21$^{st}$ 43

Dear Helen,

I am not in such haste to write home when I remember that I make my readers pay the postage– But I believe I have not taxed you before.– I have pretty much explored this island–inland and along the shore–finding my health inclined me to the peripatetic philosophy– I have visited Telegraph Stations–Sailor's Snug Harbors–Seaman's Retreats–Old Elm Trees, where the Hugonots landed–Brittons Mills–and all the villages on the island.[1] Last Sunday I walked over to Lake Island Farm–8 or 9 miles from here–where Moses Prichard lived, and found the present occupant, one Mr Davenport formerly from Mass.–with 3 or four men to help him–raising sweet potatoes and tomatoes by the acre. It seemed a cool and pleasant retreat, but a hungry soil. As I was coming away I took my toll out of the soil in the shape of arrow-heads–which may after all be the surest crop–certainly not affected by drought.[2]

I am well enough situated here to observe one aspect of the modern world at least–I mean the migratory–the western movement. Sixteen hundred imigrants arrived at quarrantine ground on the fourth of July, and more or less every day since I have been here. I see them occasionally washing their persons and clothes, or men women and children gathered on an isolated quay near the shore, stretching their limbs and taking the air, the children running races and swinging–on this artificial piece of the land of liberty–while their vessels are undergoing purification. They are detained but a day or two, and then go up to the city, for the most part without having *landed* here.

In the city I have seen since I wrote last–W H Channing–at whose house in 15$^{th}$ St. I spent a few pleasant hours, discussing the all absorbing question–What to do for the race. (He is sadly in earnest– –[a]About[a] going up the river to rusticate for six weeks–And issues a new periodical called The Present[3] in September.)– Also Horace Greeley Editor of the Tribune[4]–who is cheerfully in earnest.–at his office of all work–a hearty New Hampshire boy as one would wish to meet. And says "now be neighborly"–and believes only or mainly, first, in the Sylvania Association somewhere in Pennsylvania[5]–and secondly and most of all, in a new association to go into operation soon in New Jersey, with which he is connected.–[6] Edward Palmer came down to see me Sunday before last– As for Waldo and Tappan we have strangely dodged one another and have not met[a] for some weeks.

I believe I have not told you anything about Lucretia Motte. It was a good while ago that I heard her at the Quaker church in Hester St.[7] She is a preacher, and it was advertised that she would be present on that day. I liked all the proceedings very well–their plainly greater harmony and sincerity than elsewhere. They do nothing in a hurry. Every one that walks up the aisle in his square coat and expansive hat–has a history, and comes from a house to a house. The women come in one after another in their Quaker bonnets and handkerchiefs, looking all like sisters and so many chic-a-dees– At[a] length, after a long silence, waiting for the spirit, Mrs Motte rose, took off her bonnet, and began to utter very deliberately what the spirit suggested. Her self-possession was something to say if all else failed–but it did not. Her subject was the abuse of the Bible–and thence she straightway digressed to Slavery and the degradation of woman. It was a good speech–transcendentalism in its mildest form. She sat down at length and after a long[e] and decorous silence in which some seemed to be really digesting her words, the elders shook hands, and the meeting dispersed. On the whole, I liked their ways, and the plainness of their meeting-house– It looked as if it was indeed made for service. I think that Stearns Wheeler has left a gap in the

community not easy to be filled. Though he did not ex-
hibit the highest qualities of the scholar, he possessed
in a remarkable degree[a] many of the essential and rarer[e]
ones–and his patient industry and energy–his reverent
love of letters–and his proverbial accuracy–will cause
him to be associated in my memory even with many ven-
erable names of former days–  It was not wholly unfit that
so pure a lover of books should have ended his pilgrimage at the great book-mart of the world. I think of him as
healthy and brave, and am confident that if he had lived
he would have proved useful in more ways than I can
describe–  He would have been authority on all matters
of fact–and a sort of connecting link between men and
scholars of different walks and tastes. The literary enterprises he was planning for himself and friends[8] remind
me of an older and more studious time–  So much then
remains for us to do who survive.

Tell mother that there is no Ann Jones[9] in the Directory.
Love[a] to all–  Tell all my friends in Concord that I do not
send my love[e] to them but retain it still.

y affectionate Brother

H. D. T.

*Correspondent:* See p. 26.

[1] T's sightseeing included the semaphore station on Telegraph
Hill, which communicated with Sandy Hook and the Highlands.
The Sailors' Snug Harbor, a two hundred-acre site on the north
shore of Staten Island, was founded in 1801 and opened in 1833 as
a home for retired or disabled sailors. The Seamen's Retreat and
Hospital Fund, created in 1831, built a sailors' hospital. The giant
elm tree at the foot of New Dorp Lane had been a landmark for two
hundred years before it was undermined by the encroaching water.
A group of Huguenots from the Palatinate in Holland created the
first permanent European settlement in 1661 at what came to be
called Oude Dorp on Staten Island. In about 1825, Abraham Britton
(1787-1866) dammed the creek in the Clove to build a mill.

[2] T refers to "Lakes Island," which lies east of Burnt Island near
the mouth of Fresh Kill. The area was known as a source of Indian
relics. Moses Barnard Prichard (1818-1878), son of Moses and Jane

Hallett Prichard of Concord, Massachusetts, became a civil engineer.

[3] William Henry Channing created the *Present* to further his interest in social reform. He published poetry by Ellery Channing and essays by Margaret Fuller and Charles Lane, but the most notable writing in the magazine was by and about French socialists. The *Present* lasted only seven issues, published in 1843 and 1844.

[4] Horace Greeley (1811-1872) established the *New-York Daily Tribune* in April 1841; he later became T's champion and literary agent.

[5] Sylvania was the first community formed as a Fourierist phalanx. With Greeley as treasurer, it began in the spring of 1843 in Lackawaxen Township, Pennsylvania, on the Delaware River, fifteen miles from Port Jervis. Founded on twenty-three hundred acres of poor soil, the experiment lasted barely two years and cost Greeley his five-thousand-dollar investment.

[6] T refers to the North American Phalanx; see p. 190, note 7.

[7] No record of the Hester Street meeting survives.

[8] At the time of his death, Wheeler was translating Fredriech Kortüm's *Römische Geschichte* (Heidelberg: J. C. B. Mohr, 1843) for Jared Sparks, who planned to use the translation at Harvard. Wheeler had earlier produced an edition of *Herodotus, from the Text of Schweighaeuser*, 2 vols. (Boston: James Munroe and Company, 1843). He helped Emerson with the first edition of Carlyle's *Sartor Resartus* (1836) and with the first American edition of Carlyle's *Critical and Miscellaneous Essays* (1838-1839), and he prepared the first American edition of Carlyle's *German Romance*, 2 vols. (Boston: James Munroe and Company, 1841). Wheeler also edited Thomas Babington Macaulay's *Critical and Miscellaneous Essays*, 5 vols. (Boston: Weeks, Jordan, 1840) and arranged for the first American publication of Alfred Tennyson's *Poems* (1842).

[9] Probably one of T's Jones relatives.

*Copy-text:*  ALS (CSmH, HM 7005)

*Published:*  *LVP* 1865, 33-37; *HDT* 1882, 216; *Life* 1890, 72, 75, 78; *FL* 1894, 113-117; *Life* 1896, 60; *T: Home* 1902, 245; *FL* 1906, 95-98; *Cor* 1958, 127-129

*Editor's Notes*
    This letter is addressed "Mrs. Cynthia Thoreau / Concord / Mass." and postmarked "NEW-YO{*illegible*} JUL 21".
    a long] *PE*; along *in MS*
    rarer] *PE*; *possibly* saner *in MS*
    my love] *PE*; my l{*text obscured by sealing wax*}ve

*Author's Alterations*
 earnest- -] *second dash added in margin*
 About] about
 met] meet
 At] at
 in a remarkable degree] *interlined with a caret*
 Love] Tell


## From John Louis O'Sullivan
*July 28, 1843*

New York. July 28. 1843.

My dear Sir,

I am very sorry that with so much in it that I like very much there are others in the paper you have favored me with which have decided me against its insertion. I trust, however, soon to hear from you again,–especially should I like some of those extracts from your Journal, reporting some of your private interviews with nature, with which I have before been so much pleased.[1] That book of Etzler's I had for some time had my mind upon to review. If you have got it, I should be very much obliged to you for a sight of it, and if you would not object I think it very likely that some addition & modification made with your concurrence would put your review of it into the shape to suit my peculiar notion on the subject.[2] Articles of this nature are not in general published in the D. R. on the responsibility of the individual name of the author; but under the general impersonality of the collective "we"–(the name of the author being usually indicated in pencil on the Index in the copies sent to the editors of newspapers). This system renders a certain pervading homogeneity necessary, inviting often the necessity of this process of editorial revision, or rather communication.

Very Respectfully Yours,

J. L. O'Sullivan

I am at present staying out of town. When I return to the City, if you are still in these latitudes, I shall hope to be af-

forded the pleasure of renewing the acquaintance begun
under the auspices of our common friend Hawthorne.

*Correspondent:* John Louis O'Sullivan (1813-1895), son of John
William Thomas and Mary Rowly O'Sullivan, graduated from Co-
lumbia University in 1831 and from the Columbia Law School in
1834. In 1846 he married Susan Kearny Rodgers, daughter of Dr.
John Kearny Rodgers. O'Sullivan and S. D. Langtree founded the
*United States Magazine, and Democratic Review* in 1837 and published literary work as well as political commentary devoted to the
Democratic Party. O'Sullivan sold the magazine in 1846, supported
Narciso Lopez's filibustering expeditions in Cuba (1849-1851), and
was named minister to Portugal in 1854. During the Civil War he
lived abroad and wrote sympathetically about the Southern cause.

[1] O'Sullivan probably refers to "Natural History of Massachusetts," published in the July 1842 *Dial* (pp. 19-40; see *Excursions*
2007, pp. 3-28), or to "A Walk to Wachusett," published in the January 1843 *Boston Miscellany of Literature and Fashion* (pp. 31-36; see
*Excursions* 2007, pp. 29-46). T responded that he would search his
Journal for suitable notes on nature, and he offered to send a translation of a Greek drama (see p. 216). In the end, "The Landlord,"
rather than a nature essay, appeared in the October 1843 issue of
the *United States Magazine, and Democratic Review* (pp. 427-430;
see *Excursions* 2007, pp. 47-54).

[2] O'Sullivan had rejected T's "Paradise (To Be) Regained," an
essay-review of J. A. Etzler's *The Paradise within the Reach of All
Men*. T subsequently revised the essay, and O'Sullivan published
it in the November 1843 issue of the *United States Magazine, and
Democratic Review* (pp. 451-463; see *Reform Papers* 1973, pp. 19-47).

*Copy-text:* ALS (NN-BGC, Henry David Thoreau Collection, 1837-
1917, Series IV)

*Published:* *Cor* 1958, 130

*Editor's Note*
     This letter is addressed "Mr. Thoreau. / care of Wm. Emerson
Esq. / 64 Wall St. / New York.", postmarked "CITY DESPATCH JUL
29 4 oclock", and endorsed "J. L. O'Sullivan".

*To John Louis O'Sullivan*
*August 1, 1843*

Staten Island Aug.[a] 1st

Dear Sir,

I have not got Mr. Etzlers book nor can I tell where it is to be found    the copy which I used[a] in the spring was send from England to Mr R W[a] Emerson by Mr Alcott   But you must not think too serously of it–[e,a]   I believe my extracts[a] are rather too favorable, beside being improved[a] by the[a] liberties I have taken[e,a]. I dont wonder that you find much to object to in the remarks I sent you[a]   If I remember them[a] they content[a] me[a] perhaps as little as they do yourself[a]   Yet for the general tenor of them[a] I suppose[a] I should not[a] alter it[a].

If I should[a] find any[a] notes on nature in my Journal which I think will suit you I will send them[a]–

I am at present Reading Greek Poetry–   Would a translation–(in the manner of Prometheus Bound in the Dial which you may have seen) of some old drama[a],–be suited to your Review–?[1]

Please[a] send the Mss,[a] to[e] Wall st[2] as soon as convenient.[e] I expect to remain in this vicinity for some time[a] and shall be glad to meet you in New York[a]–[a]

*Correspondent:*  See p. 215.

[1] T published no translations in the *United States Magazine, and Democratic Review.* For his translations of Aeschylus, see p. 142, note 4.

[2] T asks that his review of Etzler's book be returned to him at William Emerson's Wall Street office.

*Copy-text:*  AL draft (CSmH, HM 13193, 13)

*Published:*  *CS* 15 (spring 1980): 19-21

*Editor's Notes*
The draft and alterations are in pencil. PE supplies the year "1843" from the contents of the letter. The document also contains a draft of part of T's translation of *The Seven against Thebes*: T notes

in his August 7, 1843, letter to Emerson that he has finished translating that work.

it-] *PE*; ~- - *in MS*
taken] *PE*; taken with *in MS*
to] *PE*; T *in MS*
convenient.] *PE*; ~? *in MS*

*Author's Alterations*

Aug.] July
used] saw
R W] *interlined above*
But ... it-] *interlined with a caret*
extracts] *cancelled* but new phenomena *interlined above*
improved] *cancelled* in form *interlined with a caret*
the] various
taken] *followed by uncancelled* with *and cancelled* original *and cancelled* them *interlined below cancelled* original
sent you] made upon
If ... them] *interlined above*
content] contented
me] myself
little ... yourself] little-
general tenor of them] sentiment contained in them
suppose] *interlined above* do not know that *enclosed in parentheses*
not] *interlined with a caret*
it] them
should] *interlined with a caret*
any] *followed by cancelled* thing in my
them] *followed by cancelled* to you
some old drama] some some other poem
Please] Will you
Mss,] Etzler
some time] sometime
New York] the City
I am ... York-] I am ... Review-? *marked for transposition with* Please ... York-

*To Cynthia Dunbar Thoreau*
*August 6, 1843*

Staten-Island Aug 6th 1843.
Dear Mother,

As Mr William Emerson is going to Concord on Teusday I must not omit[a] sending a line by him–though I wish
I had something more weighty for so direct a post.

I believe I directed my last letter to you by mistake, but
it must have appeared that it was addressed to Helen–  At
any rate this is to you without mistake. I am chiefly indebted to your letters for what I have learned of Concord
and family news, and am[a] very glad when I get one. I
should have liked to be in Walden woods with you, but not
with the railroad. I think of you all very often and wonder
if you are still separated from me only by so many miles
of earth, or so many miles of memory. This life we live is a
strange dream, and I dont believe at all any account men
give of it. Methinks I should be content to sit at the back-
door in Concord, under the poplar tree, henceforth forever. Not that I am homesick at all, for places are strangely
indifferent to me, but Concord is still a Cynosure to my
eyes, and I find it hard to attach it, even in imagination, to
the rest of the globe, and tell where the seam is.

I fancy that this Sunday eve you are poring over some
select book, almost transcendental perchance, ore else
"Burgh's Dignity," or Massillon, or the Christian Examiner.–[1] Father has just taken one more look at the garden, and is now absorbed in Chaptelle,[2] or reading the
newspaper quite abstractedly, only looking up occasionally over his spectacles to see how the rest are engaged,
and not to miss any newer news that may not be in the
paper.–  Helen has slipped in for the fourth time to learn
the very latest item–  Sophia, I suppose is at Bangor[3]–but
Aunt Louisa without doubt is just flitting away to some
good meeting–to save the credit of you all.

It is still a cardinal virtue with me to keep awake. I find

it impossible to write or read except at rare intervals, but am generally speaking tougher than formerly. I could make a pedestrian tour round the world, and sometimes think it would perhaps be better to do at once the things I *can*, rather than be trying to do what at present I cannot do well. However, I shall awake sooner or later.[4]

I have been translating some Greek, & reading English poetry–and a month ago sent a paper to the Democratic Review, which, at length, they were sorry they could not accept–but they could not adopt the sentiments. However, they were very polite, and earnest that I should send them something else, or reform that.

I go moping about the fields and woods here as I did in Concord, and, it seems, am thought to be a surveyor–an eastern man inquiring narrowly into the condition and value of land &c here, preparatory to an extensive speculation. One neighbor observed to me in a mysterious and half inquisitive way that he supposed I must be pretty well acquainted with the state of things–that I kept pretty close–he didn't see any surveying instruments, but perhaps I had them in my pocket.

I have received Helen's note, but have not heard of Frisbie Hoar[5] yet. She is a faint-hearted writer who could not take the responsibility of blotting one sheet alone. However I like very well the blottings I get. Tell her I have not seen Mrs Child nor Mrs. Sedgwick.[6]

> Love to All from
> Yr Affect[e] Son
> Henry D. Thoreau.

*Correspondent:* See p. 161.

*Correspondent:* See p. 161.

[1] T refers to two books and a magazine: James Burgh's *The Dignity of Human Nature*, Jean Baptiste Massillon's *Sermons*, and the *Christian Examiner and General Review*, then edited by William Ware. T had, in 1835, borrowed a 1767 edition of *The Dignity of Human Nature* from the Harvard College Library; whether he owned any edition of the book is not clear. He owned a copy of *Sermons*, but which edition it was is not known.

[2] Jean-Antoine-Claude Chaptal, comte de Chanteloup, wrote several books on the industrial and agricultural uses of chemistry; among them, *Chemistry Applied to Arts and Manufactures*, 4 vols. (London: Richard Phillips, 1807), would most likely interest T's father.

[3] Sophia was probably visiting the Thoreau relatives; see p. 312, note 8.

[4] T alludes to narcolepsy, a condition that ran in his family; see p. 200, note 5.

[5] George Frisbie Hoar (1826-1904), the second son of Samuel and Sarah Sherman Hoar, graduated from Harvard University in 1846 and from the Harvard Law School in 1849. Hoar married Mary Louisa Spurr (1831-1859), daughter of Samuel Danforth and Mary Lamb Spurr, in 1853. In 1862 he married Ruth Ann Miller (1830-1903), daughter of Henry Wilder and Nancy Merrick Miller. Following his father and brother in the profession, Hoar had a distinguished career in public service. A stalwart Republican, he later served in the Massachusetts legislature, represented Concord in Washington, D.C., and was elected to the U.S. Senate.

[6] Helen had probably asked T to meet two popular novelists: Lydia Child and Catharine Maria Sedgwick. Lydia Maria Francis (1802-1880), daughter of David Convers and Susannah Rand Francis and a reformer and ardent abolitionist, published her first novel in 1824. In 1828 she married the enthusiastic but improvident reformer David Child (1794-1874), son of Zachariah and Lydia Bigelow Child. In 1841 the Childs moved to New York City, where Lydia edited the *National Anti-Slavery Standard*; she resigned in May 1843 after the Garrisonians found her to be too mild. T had read three of her novels: *Hobomok: A Tale of Early Times, The Rebels; or, Boston before the Revolution*, and *Philothea: A Romance*. Sedgwick (1789-1867), daughter of Theodore and Pamela Dwight Sedgwick of Stockbridge, Massachusetts, published *A New-England Tale; or, Sketches of New-England Character and Manners* (New-York: E. Bliss and E. White) in 1822, followed by *Redwood: A Tale*, 2 vols. (New-York: E. Bliss and E. White, 1824) and *Hope Leslie; or, Early Times in the Massachusetts*, 2 vols. (New-York: White, Gallaher, and White, 1827). She frequently spent half her year in New York City.

*Copy-text:* ALS (ViU, Clifton Waller Barrett Library, Henry David Thoreau Collection [#6345])

*Published:* *LVP* 1865, 37-39; *Life* 1890, 76; *FL* 1894, 117-120; *T: Home* 1902, 60; *FL* 1906, 98-100; *Cor* 1958, 131-132

*Editor's Note*
This letter is addressed "Mrs. Cynthia Thoreau / Concord / Mass. / By W. Emerson Esq."

*Author's Alterations*
omit] miss
am] *inserted*


## To Ralph Waldo Emerson
*August 7, 1843*

1843.
Staten-Island Aug 7th

My Dear Friend,

I fear I have nothing to send you worthy of so good an opportunity. Of New-York I still know but little, though out of so many thousands there are no doubt many units whom it would be worth my while to know. James talks of going to Germany soon with his wife–to learn the language.[1] He says he must know it–can never learn it here– there he may absorb it–and is very anxious to learn beforehand where he had best locate himself, to enjoy the advantage of the highest culture, learn the language in its purity, and not exceed his limited means. I referred him to Longfellow–[2]  Perhaps[a] you can help him.

I have had a pleasant talk with Channing–and Greeley too it was refreshing to meet. They were both much pleased with your criticism on Carlyle,[3] but thought that you had overlooked what chiefly concerned them in the book–its practical aim and merits.

I have also spent some pleasant hours with W & T[4] at their counting room–or rather intelligence Office.

I must still reckon myself with the innumerable army of invalids–indoubtedly in a fair field they would rout the well–though I am tougher than formerly. Methinks I could paint the Sleepy God more truly than the poets have done, from more intimate experience–  Indeed I have not kept my eyes very steadily open to the things of this world of late, and hence have little to report concerning them. However I trust the awakening will come before the last trump–and then perhaps I may remember some of my dreams.

I study the aspects of commerce at its narrows here, where it passes in review before me, and this seems to be beginning at the right end to understand this Babylon.– I have made a very rude translation of the–Seven Against Thebes–and Pindar too I have looked at, and wish he was better worth translating–[5]   I believe even the best things are not equal to their fame. Perhaps it would be better to translate fame itself–or is not that what the poets themselves do? However I have not done with Pindar yet   I sent a long article on Etzler's book to the Dem. Rev. six weeks ago, which at length they have determined not to accept as they could not subscribe to all the opinions, but asked for other matter–purely literary I suppose. O'Sullivan wrote me that articles of this kind have to be referred to the circle who it seems are represented by this journal–and said something about "collective we" and "homogeneity"–

Pray dont think of Bradbury and Soden any more–[6]

"For good deed done through praiere
Is sold and bought too dear I wis–
To herte that of great valor is–"[7]

I see that they have given up their shop here[8]

Say to Mrs. Emerson that I am glad to remember how she too dwells there in Concord, and shall send her anon some of the thoughts that belong to her. As for Edith–I seem to see a star in the east over where the young child is.–[9]   Remember me to Mrs. Brown

yr friend
Henry D. Thoreau

*Correspondent:* See p. 53.

[1] Henry James Sr. and his family sailed on the *Great Western* on October 19. According to Alfred Habegger, James had wanted to settle in Concord, but Emerson, perhaps fearing the New Yorker's emotional intensity, deftly deflected his overture (*The Father: A Life of Henry James, Sr.* [New York: Farrar, Straus, and Giroux, 1994], pp. 206, 532).

[2] Henry Wadsworth Longfellow (1807-1882) was then the Smith Professor of French and Spanish Languages and Literatures at Harvard. Longfellow, whom James later called the "dear dismal old poet," was not a likely source of help (Habegger, *The Father*, p. 453).

[3] Emerson's review of *Past and Present* in the July *Dial* (pp. 96-102).

[4] Giles Waldo and William Tappan.

[5] For T's translations of Aeschylus and Pindar, see p. 142, note 4, and p. 209, note 7.

[6] T refers to the publication of "A Walk to Wachusett" in the *Boston Miscellany of Literature and Fashion*; see p. 148, note 5.

[7] Chaucer, "Romaunt of the Rose." T probably read the poem in Alexander Chalmers, ed., *The Works of the English Poets, from Chaucer to Cowper*, 1:209.

[8] Bradbury and Soden had a branch office at 127 Nassau Street in Manhattan.

[9] Matt. 2:9: "When they had heard the king, they departed; and, lo, the star, which they saw in the east, went before them, till it came and stood over where the young child was."

*Copy-text:* ALS (NN-BGC, Henry David Thoreau Collection, 1837-1917, Series III)

*Published:* LVP 1865, 26-28; HDT 1882, 216-217; FL 1894, 120-122; FL 1906, 101-103; Americana 1912, 527; Magazine of History 21 (July-December 1915): 119; Cor 1958, 133-134

*Editor's Note*
This letter is addressed "R. Waldo Emerson / Concord / Mass."

*Author's Alteration*
Perhaps] perhaps

*To Cynthia Dunbar Thoreau*
*August 29, 1843*

Tuesday Aug 29th –43

Dear Mother,

Mr Emerson has just given me a short warning that he is about to send to Concord, which I will endeavor to improve.– I am a good deal more wakeful than I was, and growing stout in other respects–so that I may yet accomplish something in the literary way–indeed I should have done so before now but for the slowness and poverty of[e] the Reviews[a] themselves. I have tried sundry methods of earning money in the city of late but without success, have rambled into every booksellers or publishers' house and discussed their affairs with them. Some propose to me to do what an honest man cannot–  Among others I conversed with the Harpers–to see if they might not find me useful to them–but they say that they are making fifty thousand dollars annually, and their motto is to let well alone.[1] I find that I talk with these poor men as if I were over head and ears in business–and a few thousands were no consideration with me–  I almost reproach myself for bothering them thus to no purpose–but it is very valuable experience–and the best introduction I could have.

We have had a tremendous rain here–last Monday night and Tuesday morning–  I was in the city at Giles Waldo's– and the streets at daybreak were absolutely impassible for the water–  Yet the accounts of the storm which you may have seen are exaggerated,[2] as indeed are all such things to my imagination.

On sunday I heard Mr Bellows preach here on the island–but the fine prospect over the bay and narrows from where I sat preached louder than he[3]–though he did far better than the average, if I remember aright.

I should have liked to see Dan. Webster walking about Concord, I suppose the town shook every step he took–[4] But I trust there were some sturdy Concordians who were not tumbled down by the jar, but represented still the upright town. Where was Geo. Minott? he would not have gone far to see him. Uncle Charles should have been there–he might as well have been catching cat naps in Concord as anywhere. And then what a whettor up of his memory this event would have been![5] You'd have had all the classmates again in alphabetical order reversed– and Seth Hunt & Bob Smith–and he was a student of my fathers–and where's Put[a] now? and I wonder, you, if Henry's been to see Geo. Jones[6] yet– A little account with Stow–Balcolm–Bigelow–poor miserable to-a-d (sound asleep) I vow you–what noise was that?– Saving grace– and few there be–[7] That's clear as preaching– Easter Brooks–morally[e] depraved– How charming is divine philosophy[e]–[8] Some wise and some otherwise[e]–[9] Heigh ho! (Sound asleep again)

Webster's a smart fellow–bears his age well–how old should you think he was–you does he look as if he were ten years younger than I?

I met, or rather was overtaken by Fuller, who tended for Mr How, the other day in Broadway–[10] He dislikes New York very much.– The Mercantile Library–ie its librarian–presented me with a stranger's ticket for a month– and I was glad to read the reviews there[11]–and Carlyle's late article.–[12]  In haste

from Yr affectionate son
Henry D. Thoreau

I have bought some pantaloons–and stockings show no holes yet  Thin[a] Pantaloons cost $2.25 ready made.

*Correspondent:* See p. 161.

[1] In 1843 Harper and Brothers was the largest American publishing house. Founded in 1817 by James and John Harper, the firm prospered primarily by reprinting British authors, though they had published Poe's *The Narrative of Arthur Gordon Pym* (1838) and Richard Henry Dana's *Two Years before the Mast* (1840).

[2] One such account reads: "It is not too much to say that so great

a quantity [of rain] never fell in this city in any previous twelve hours during the memory of the present generation. An immense amount of damage was done by the overflowing of side-walks, flooding of cellars and basements, washing in of yards, side-walks, &c" ("The Great Storm," *New-York Daily Tribune*, August 23, 1843).

³ Henry Whitney Bellows (1814-1882) graduated from Harvard University in 1832 and from the Harvard Divinity School in 1837. He was ordained at the First Congregational Church in New York City and remained there until his death. Bellows was a popular preacher but a man too much of the world to suit T.

⁴ Daniel Webster was in Concord as an attorney for William Wyman, who was being tried for embezzlement; see pp. 230-231, note 7. Webster (1782-1852) graduated from Dartmouth in 1801, studied law, and became a Federalist. He served in both the U.S. House (1813-1817) and the U.S. Senate (1827-1841, 1845-1850) and distinguished himself as an orator. He held the post of Secretary of State under William Henry Harrison and John Tyler (1841-1842) and again under Millard Fillmore (1850-1852). Webster, a Whig, was on the Massachusetts presidential ticket in 1836 and contended for the nomination in 1848 and 1852. His support for the Compromise of 1850, which enacted the Fugitive Slave Law, infuriated opponents of slavery, including Emerson.

⁵ Charles Jones Dunbar (1780-1856), son of Asa and Mary Jones Dunbar, was born in Princeton, Massachusetts. An eccentric man prone to narcolepsy, Uncle Charles was a favorite relative of T's and often spent months in the Thoreau household. Webster had courted Charles's sister Louisa Dunbar when she taught in Boscawen, New Hampshire, during the 1805-1806 school year; he visited her whenever he was in Concord.

⁶ Probably George Washington Jones (1799-1890), son of Aaron and Betsy Bush Jones and second cousin of Cynthia Dunbar Thoreau. In 1839 Jones married Caroline Partridge (1815-1893), daughter of Ezekiel and Anna Morey Partridge.

⁷ See Matt. 7:14: "Because, strait *is* the gate, and narrow *is* the way, which leadeth unto life, and few there be that find it."

⁸ *Comus*, line 476 (Milton, vol. 5, p. 324).

⁹ This English proverb dates from before 1659.

¹⁰ Probably Hiram Fuller (1814-1880), son of Thomas and Sally Sturtevant Fuller of Halifax, Massachusetts. Fuller studied at Andover and taught in Plymouth. In 1836 he became head of the Greene-Street School in Providence, Rhode Island, where Margaret Fuller (no relation) was one of his teachers. He married Emily Delaplaine (1825-1883), daughter of John and Julia Clason Delaplaine of New

York City, in 1844. At the time of T's letter, Fuller was probably working in New York City for the *New Mirror, of Literature, Amusement,
and Instruction*, a magazine. In 1844 he became one of the three
editors for the *Evening Mirror*, a daily newspaper that grew out of
the *New Mirror*, and he became the owner of the newspaper in
1846. Fuller later went to England and published a newspaper that
supported the Southern cause. Phineas How (1797-1852), son of Joseph and Lydia How of Methuen, Massachusetts, went to Concord
in 1821 and established a store there. In 1822 he married Cynthia
Currier (1802-1883), daughter of Jonathan and Hannah Clark Currier. He was an avid Whig with few interests other than his business
and politics.

   [11] Henry Swasey McKean (1810-1857) was the librarian of the
Mercantile Library Association in New York City. The library subscribed to eighty-five periodicals and newspapers at this time.
McKean, son of Rev. Joseph McKean and Amy Swasey McKean,
graduated from Harvard in 1828 and was a tutor there during T's
first two years. See p. 238 for T's further description of the library
privileges that McKean had granted him.

   [12] Carlyle, "Dr. Francia," *Foreign Quarterly Review* 31 (July 1843):
299-325.

*Copy-text:* ALS (NNPM, MA 920)

*Published: Boston Advertiser* (August 3, 1882); *Boston Traveller*
(August 3, 1882); *HDT* 1882, 92-93; "Thoreau's Manuscripts" 1883,
125; *FL* 1894, 124-127; *T: Home* 1902, 96; *FL* 1906, 104-106; *Cor* 1958,
134-136; *Concord Harvest* 1970, 67; *Response to Transcendental Concord* 1974, 235, 236; *ARLR* 1988, 54, 55

*Editor's Notes*
   This letter is addressed "Mrs. Cynthia Thoreau / Concord /
Mass." and postmarked "NEW-YORK AUG 29".
   of] *PE*; oft *in MS*
   morally] *PE*; mora{*MS torn*}
   philosophy] *PE*; p{*MS torn*}losophy
   otherwise] *PE*; other / wise *in MS*

*Author's Alterations*
   Reviews] reviews
   Put] put
   Thin] *added in margin*

*From Ralph Waldo Emerson*
*September 8, 1843*

Concord Sept 8 1843

Dear Henry

We were all surprised to hear one day lately from
G. Waldo that you were forsaking the deep quiet of the
Clove[1] for the limbo of the false booksellers,[2] & were soon
relieved by hearing that you were safe again in the Cottage at S.I.[v] I could heartily wish that this country wh.[v]
seems all opportunity, did actually offer more distinct &
just rewards of labor to that unhappy class of men who
have more reason & conscience than strength of back
& of arm, but the experience of a few cases that I have
lately seen looks I confess more like crowded England
& indigent Germany, than like rich & roomy nature. But
the few cases are deceptive, & tho'[v] Homer should starve
in the highway, Homer will know & proclaim that boun-
teous Nature has bread for all her boys.[3] Tomorrow our
arms will be stronger, tomorrow the wall before wh.[v] we
sat, will open of itself & show the new way. Ellery Channing works & writes as usual at his cottage to which Capt.[v]
Moore[4] has added a neat slat fence & gate. His wife as yet
has no more than five scholars,[5] but will have more presently. Hawthorn has returned from a visit to the seashore
in good spirits. Elizabeth Hoar is still absent since Evarts'
marriage.[6] You will have heard of our 'Wyman trial' & the
stir it made in the village[7]  But the Cliff & Walden, which
know something of the railroad, know[v] nothing of that:
not a leaf nodded, not a pebble fell: why should I speak
of it to you  Now the humanity of the Town suffers with
the poor Irish who receives but 60 or even 50 cents for
working from dark till dark, with a strain & a following up
that reminds one of negro driving. Peter Hutchinson[8] told
me he had never seen men perform so much; he should
never think it hard again if an employer should keep him
at work till after sundown[e]. But what can be done for their

relief as long as new applicants for the same labor are coming in every day. These of course reduce the wages to the sum that will suffice a bachelor to live, & must drive out the men with families. The work goes on very fast  The mole which crosses the land of Jonas Potter & Mr Stow from Ephraim Wheeler's highland to the depot, is 18 ft.[v] high & goes on two rods every day. A few days ago a new contract was completed from the terminus of the old contract to Fitchburg–the whole to built before Oct.[v] 1844.[9] So that you see our fate is sealed. I have not yet advertised my house for sale, nor engaged my passage for[v] Berkshire: have even suffered George Bradford to plan a residence with me next spring: & at this very day am[a] talking with Mr Britton of building a cottage in my triangle for Mrs Brown;[10] but I can easily forsee that some inconveniences may arise from the road when open, that shall drive me from my rest. I mean to send the Winter's Walk to the printer tomorrow for the Dial. I had some hesitation about it, notwithstanding its faithful observation & its fine sketches of the pickerel-fisher & of the woodchopper[e], on account of *mannerism*, an old charge of mine–as if by attention one could get the trick of the rhetoric, e.g.[v] to call a cold place sultry, a solitude public, a wilderness *domestic* (a favourite word) & in the woods to insult over cities, whilst the woods again are dignified by comparing them to cities armies &c[11]  By pretty free omissions however I have removed my principal objections. I ought to say that Ellery Channing admired the piece loudly & long & only stipulated for the omission of Douglas & one copy of verses on the Smoke.–[12]  For the rest we go on with the Youth of the Poet & Painter:[13] & with extracts from the Jamaica voyage.[14] And Lane has sent me a Day with the Shakers:[15] poetry have I very little. Have you no Greek translations ready for me. I beg you to tell my brother W[m] that[v] the Review of Channing's poems in the Democratic Review[16] has been interpolated with sentences & extracts to make it long by the Editor & I acknowledge as far as I remember little beyond the 1ˢᵗ page.ᵛ And now that I have departed so far from my indolence as to write this long letterᵛ I have yet to add to mine the affectionate greetings of my wife & my mother

Yourᵛ

R W Emerson

Henry D Thoreau
Staten Islandᵛ

*Correspondent:* See p. 53.

¹ A natural roadway in Castleton, Staten Island; see p. 186, note 5.

² In his August 19 letter to Emerson, Giles Waldo wrote, "Thoreau is making efforts to secure himself an opportunity to go a-peddling for some bookseller here–but he probably has told you all about it" (Waldo to Emerson, MH-H, MS Am 1280 [3331]). T was selling magazine subscriptions; see pp. 233-234.

³ Perhaps another allusion to the well-known Greek epigram, "Seven wealthy towns contend for Homer dead, / Through which the living Homer begged his bread"; see pp. 203-204, note 2.

⁴ Abel Moore.

⁵ Ellen Fuller (1820-1856), Margaret's sister, married Ellery Channing in Cincinnati on September 24, 1841. In the summer of 1843 she began schooling neighbors' children in the Channing home. The Channings' marriage was troubled, thanks to Ellery's mercurial temperament, and the couple separated for almost two years between 1853 and 1855.

⁶ William Maxwell Evarts (1818-1901), son of Jeremiah and Mehitabel Sherman Evarts and Elizabeth Hoar's cousin, married Helen Minerva Wardner (1820-1903), daughter of Allen and Minerva Bingham Wardner, on August 30. Evarts graduated from Yale in 1837 and became a lawyer in New York City. He had a distinguished career as a lawyer and public figure and later served as the U.S. attorney general and as the secretary of state.

⁷ On August 7, William Wyman and Thomas Brown Jr. of Charlestown, Massachusetts, went on trial for embezzling more than four hundred twenty thousand dollars from the Phoenix Bank in Charlestown. Daniel Webster and Rufus Choate were among the defendants' lawyers. On August 17 the jury acquitted Brown and reported itself hung on Wyman. Emerson was taken with the event: he entertained Webster and other lawyers at his home on August

15 and extolled Webster's performance in journal passages spanning several days. "He appeared," wrote Emerson, "among these
best lawyers of the Suffolk bar, like a schoolmaster among his boys"
(*JMN*, 8:357).

⁸ Peter Hutchinson (1799?-1882) was a free black laborer and
farmer in Concord; he was married to Nancy Dager (1805?-1857).

⁹ Jonas Potter (1784-1868), son of Jonas and Sarah Jones Potter,
was a Concord farmer. In 1812 he married Sarah Melvin (1790?-
1851), daughter of Jacob and Sarah Dexter Melvin. Mr. Stow is probably Cyrus Stow. Ephraim Wheeler (1773-1848), son of Ephraim
and Sarah Heywood Wheeler of Concord, was a successful farmer,
a "laborious, saving man, who took but small part in any other than
his own affairs" (*Memoirs of the Social Circle* 1888, p. 68). In 1799 he
married Sarah Parkman (1777-1856), daughter of William and Lydia
Proctor Parkman. The Fitchburg railroad was completed in stages:
the first section, from Boston to Waltham, opened in December
1843; the second, to Concord, in June 1844; the third, to Shirley, in
December 1844, and the fourth and final section, to Fitchburg, on
March 5, 1845.

¹⁰ Joel Britton (1801-1858), son of John and Jerusha Britton of
Easton, Massachusetts, was "a woodman who got out sleepers for
the R.R. and cut all the chestnut wood far and near" (John Shepard
Keyes and Adams Tolman, "Houses, & Owners or Occupants in
Concord, 1885," TS, n.d., p. 362 [MCo-SC, John Shepard Keyes Papers, 1837-1908, Series II, Box 1, Folder 2]). Britton had offered to
build the house for nothing if Emerson would let him use it as a
rental for a year. Emerson calculated that the materials would cost
seven hundred dollars and that, even if Lucy Brown did not want it,
he could keep it rented. Apparently Emerson changed his mind, for
the house he subsequently built and Lucy Brown occupied was not
on the "heater piece" (the New England expression for a triangu-
lar-shaped lot) across from his house, which he purchased in 1838,
but on a different parcel he bought in 1845.

¹¹ On the manuscript T's comment that the ice and crystals
"shame the galleries of Florence and Rome" is marked for deletion,
and the phrase does not appear in the essay as published in the
October 1843 *Dial* (pp. 211-226). This is an example of the "*mannerism*" Emerson disliked, and he is almost certainly responsible for
the deletion (see *Excursions* 2007, pp. 62, 428-430, 443).

¹² The passages from Gawain Douglas's "Description of Wynter"
to which Channing objected are marked for deletion in the manuscript and do not appear in the essay as published in the *Dial* (see
*Excursions* 2007, pp. 73-77, 429-430, 449-451). The identity of the

poem Channing disliked is not known; he seems to be referring to another poem about smoke than T's "The sluggish smoke curls up from some deep dell", which appears in the *Dial* version. About two-thirds of the manuscript survives; the omitted poem may have been in the missing third. For more information, see *Excursions* 2007, pp. 430, 444-446.

[13] Ellery Channing, "The Youth of the Poet and the Painter," *Dial* 4 (October 1843): 174-186; see also p. 193, note 5.

[14] Benjamin P. Hunt, "Voyage to Jamaica," *Dial* 4 (October 1843): 227-244; see also p. 194, note 7.

[15] Charles Lane, "A Day with the Shakers," *Dial* 4 (October 1843): 165-173.

[16] "Mr. Channing's Poems," *United States Magazine, and Democratic Review* 13 (September 1843): 309-314. Emerson began the article by stating that Channing "need not owe any advantage to the eminent name he wears, but is ready to add, to the distinction which already encircles it, the fame of poetry" (p. 309).

*Copy-text:* Facsimile of MSC by James Elliot Cabot (NNC-RB, Eleanor M. Tilton Papers, VI.7, Box 35)

*Published: HDT* 1882, 92; "Emerson-Thoreau Correspondence," *AM* 69 (May 1892): 592-593; *FL* 1894, 124; *FL* 1906, 104; *Cor* 1958, 136-138; *Letters of RWE* 1990-1995, 7:557-560

*Editor's Notes*
 sundown] *PE*; sun / down *in MS*
 woodchopper] *PE*; woodchopper woodchopper *in MS; the first instance is a catchword at the bottom of page 2.*

*Substantive Variants*
 The text of this letter is based on a copy of the manuscript made by James Elliot Cabot, dated "1896"; potentially authoritative substantive readings in *HDT* 1882 and "Emerson-Thoreau Correspondence," both of which could have been based on the recipient's copy, are reported below.
 S.I.] *in copy-text;* Staten Island *in "Emerson-Thoreau Correspondence"*
 wh.] *in copy-text;* which *in "Emerson-Thoreau Correspondence"*
 tho'] *in copy-text;* though *in "Emerson-Thoreau Correspondence"*
 wh.] *in copy-text;* which *in "Emerson-Thoreau Correspondence"*
 Capt.] *in copy-text;* Captain *in "Emerson-Thoreau Correspondence"*
 know] *in copy-text;* knew *in HDT 1882 and "Emerson-Thoreau Correspondence"*

ft.] *in copy-text;* feet *in "Emerson-Thoreau Correspondence"*

Oct.] *in copy-text;* October *in "Emerson-Thoreau Correspondence"*

for] *in copy-text;* to *in "Emerson-Thoreau Correspondence"*

e.g.] *in copy-text;* for example *in "Emerson-Thoreau Correspondence"*

W^m that] *in copy-text;* William that *in "Emerson-Thoreau Correspondence"*

1^st page.] *in copy-text;* first page. *in "Emerson-Thoreau Correspondence"*

long letter] *in copy-text;* letter *in "Emerson-Thoreau Correspondence"*

Your] *in copy-text;* Yours *in "Emerson-Thoreau Correspondence"*

Henry D Thoreau / Staten Island] *in copy-text; lacking in "Emerson-Thoreau Correspondence"*

*Alteration*

A change appearing in the manuscript copy is reported below; it could be either a faithful representation of the original manuscript or an error made and corrected by the copyist.

am] *followed by cancelled* planning


## To Ralph Waldo Emerson
*September 14, 1843*

Staten-Island Sep. 14^th

Dear Friend,

Miss Fuller will tell you the news from these parts,[1] so I will only devote these few moments to what she does not know as well.

I was absent only one day and night from the Island, the family expecting me back immediately. I was to earn a certain sum before winter, and thought it worth the while to try various experiments. I carried the Agriculturist about the city,[2] and up as far as Manhattanville,[3] and called at the Croton Reservoir, where indeed they did not want any Agriculturists, but paid well enough in their way. Literature comes to a poor market here, and even the little that I write is more than will sell. I have tried the Dem. Review–The New Mirror & Brother[a] Jonathan. The last two as well as the New-World, are overwhelmed with contributions, which cost nothing, and are worth no more. The Knickerbocker is too poor, and only the Ladies Companion pays.[4] O'Sullivan is printing the Manuscript I sent him some time ago,[5,a] having objected only to my want of sympathy with the Communities.–

I doubt if you have made more corrections in my manuscript[6] than I should have done ere this, though they may be better, but I am glad that you have taken any pains with it.– I have not prepared any translations for the Dial, supposing there would be no room–though it is the only place for them.

I have been seeing men during these days, and trying experiments upon trees; have inserted 3 or 4 hundred buds– Quite a Buddhist, one might say– Books I have access to through your brother and Mr Mackean[7]–and have read a good deal–Quarle's "Divine Poems" as well as Emblems are quite a discovery.[8]

I am sorry that Mrs. Emerson is so sick.[9] Remember me to her and to your mother. I like to think of you living on the banks of the mill-brook[e], in the midst of the garden with all its weeds, for what are botanical distinctions at this distance?

Your friend

Henry D. Thoreau

*Correspondent:* See p. 53.

[1] Fuller had been on a trip to Niagara, Chicago, and Wisconsin. She returned by way of Buffalo, down the Hudson River to New York City, where she saw T. Upon her return to New England, she spent two days with Emerson in Concord.

[2] The *American Agriculturist*, edited by Anthony Benezet Allen and his brother Richard Lamb Allen, had begun publication in April 1842. A monthly published in New York City, it became the most influential agricultural periodical in the nation. T apparently was selling subscriptions, which cost a dollar a year.

[3] Manhattanville was a village of almost five hundred residents near the present intersection of 125th Street and Broadway. At that time it was "open land and country residences" (*The Encyclopedia*

*of New York*, ed. Kenneth T. Jackson [New Haven, Conn.: Yale University Press, 1995], p. 724).

⁴ The *New Mirror, of Literature, Amusement, and Instruction*, a reincarnation of the original *New-York Mirror: A Weekly Journal, Devoted to Literature and the Fine Arts*, ran from April 1843 to September 1844. Edited by George Pope Morris and Nathaniel Parker Willis, it was, like its predecessor, known for its handsome steel engravings and eclectic mix of social and literary items. *Brother Jonathan: A Weekly Compend of Belles Lettres and the Fine Arts, Standard Literature, and General Intelligence*, a paper inclined toward sensational and serial fiction, was founded by Park Benjamin and Rufus Wilmot Griswold in July 1839. After resigning the paper to its publishers, Benjamin and Griswold started the *New World: A Weekly Family Journal of Popular Literature, Science, Art and News*, whose "pages were sometimes more than four feet long and eleven columns wide" (Frank Luther Mott, *A History of American Magazines*, 5 vols. [Cambridge, Mass.: Harvard University Press, 1938-1968], 1:359). The *New World* ran from June 1840 to May 1845; as did *Brother Jonathan*, it depended for material on pirating English fiction even before book publishers could produce pirated editions. The *Knickerbocker; or, New-York Monthly Magazine* was the most prominent of the New York City literary magazines, thanks to the editorship of Lewis Gaylord Clark. The magazine ran from January 1833 to October 1865 and published prominent writers from Irving to Whittier and Oliver Wendell Holmes. Clark, however, excluded the work of the Transcendentalists, whose ideas he disliked. William W. Snowden founded and edited the *Ladies' Companion, and Literary Expositor*, a monthly magazine devoted to literature and the fine arts, which ran from May 1834 to October 1844.

⁵ "Paradise (To Be) Regained," T's review of J. A. Etzler's *The Paradise within the Reach of All Men*, appeared in the November 1843 issue of the *United States Magazine, and Democratic Review* (pp. 451-463; see *Reform Papers* 1973, pp. 19-47).

⁶ T refers to "A Winter Walk," which Emerson revised and published in the October 1843 *Dial* (pp. 211-226; see *Excursions* 2007, pp. 55-77).

⁷ Henry Swasey McKean.

⁸ T read several of Francis Quarles's works, including *Divine Poems* (1630) and *Emblemes* (1635); he owned an 1825 edition of the latter, titled *Emblems, Divine and Moral*. No record exists of which edition of each work T read at the Mercantile Library.

⁹ In the September 8 letter to his brother William, Emerson wrote: "Lidian, I am sorry to say, is suffering again after getting to

the top of her condition by base fever turns." Lidian had also been ill in the late summer (*Letters of RWE* 1939, 3:205).

*Copy-text:* ALS (MBU, Richards Collection)

*Published:* "E-T" May 1892, 593-594; *FL* 1894, 127-129; *T: Home* 1902, 96; *FL* 1906, 107-108; *Americana* 1912, 527; *Magazine of History* 21 (July-December 1915): 120; *Cor* 1958, 138-139

*Editor's Notes*
　　This letter is addressed "R. Waldo Emerson / Concord / Mass." and endorsed "H. D. Thoreau / Sept. 1843". PE supplies the year "1843" following the endorsement.
　　mill-brook] *PE*; mill- / brook *in MS*

*Author's Alterations*
　　Brother] Bother
　　ago,] ~.

## From Margaret Fuller
*September 25, 1843*

Dear Henry,

　　You are not, I know, deeply interested in the chapter of little etiquettes, yet I think out of kindness you will be willing to read a text therein & act conformably in my behalf– As I read the text on the subject of Visits[a] or Visitations[a], our hosts martyr themselves every way for us, their guests, while we are with them, in time, temper, & purse, but we are expected to get to them and get away from them as we can.

　　Thus I ought to have paid for the carriage which came to take me away, though I went in another. But I did not see the man when I got down to the landing.– I do not know what is the due, but E. Hoar told me the enclosed was enough, will you pay it for me wherever it belongs & pardon the carelessness that gives you this trouble?

　　Immediately after my return I passed two days at Concord, a visit all too short, yet pleasant. The cottages of the Irish laborers look pretty just now but their railroad looks foreign to Concord.

Mr Emerson has written a fine poem, you will see it in the Dial.[1] Ellery will not go to the West, at least not this year. He regrets your absence, you, he says, are the man to be with in the woods.

I remember my visit to Staten Island with great pleasure, & find your histories and the grand pictures you showed me are very full in my mind. I have not yet dreamt of the fort, but I intend to some leisure night. With best regards to Mr & Mrs Emerson, whose hospitality I hold in grateful remembrance,

Yours

S. M. Fuller.

25th Sept[r]/43

*Correspondent:*  See pp. 70-71.

  [1] Emerson, "Ode to Beauty," *Dial* 4 (October 1843): 257-259.

*Copy-text:*  ALS (ICarbS, VFM 865)

*Published:*  *Cor* 1958, 140; *NEQ* 33 (1960): 372-373; *Companion* 1964, 182-183; *Letters of Margaret Fuller*, 3:148-149

*Editor's Note*
This letter is addressed "Mr Henry Thoreau / Care W. Emerson Esq / 61 Wall St / N. York." and endorsed "S. M. Fuller".

*Author's Alterations*
Visits] visits
Visitations] visitations

## To Cynthia Dunbar Thoreau
*October 1, 1843*

–Staten Island Oct 1st

–43

Dear Mother,

I hold together remarkably well as yet, speaking of my outward linen and woolen man, no holes more than I brought away, and no stitches needed yet. It is marvellous. I think the Fates must be on my side, for there is

less than a plank between me and–Time, to say the least.
As for Eldorado that is far off yet. My bait will not tempt
the rats; they are too well fed. The Democratic Review is
poor, and can only afford half or quarter pay–which it *will*
do–and they say there is a Ldy's Companion that pays–
but I could not write anything companionable. However,
speculate as we will, it is quite gratuitous, for life never
the less, and never the more, goes steadily on, well or ill
fed and clothed, somehow, and "honor bright" withal. It
is very gratifying to live[a] in the prospect of great successes
always, and for that purpose, we[a] must leave a sufficient
foreground to see them through. All the painters prefer
distant prospects for the greater breadth of view, and delicacy of tint.–   But this is no news, and describes no new
condition. Meanwhile I am somnambulic at least–stirring
in my sleep–indeed, quite awake. I read a good deal and
am pretty well known in the libraries of New York. Am in
with the Librarian, one Dr Forbes, of the Society Library[1]–
who has lately been to Cambridge to learn liberality, and
has come back to let me take out some un-take-out-able
books, which I was threatening to read on the spot. And
Mr Mackean,[2] of the Mercantile Library, is a true gentleman–[a]a former tutor of mine–and offers me every privilege there. I have from him a perpetual stranger's ticket,
and a citizen's rights besides–all which privileges I pay
handsomely for by improving

A canoe-race "came off" on the Hudson the other day,
between Chippeways and New Yorkers which must have
been as moving a sight as the buffalo hunt which I wit-
nessed. But canoes and buffaloes are all lost, as is[a] everything here, in the mob. It is only the people have come
to see oneanother. Let them advertise that there will be
a gathering at Hoboken–having bargained with the ferry
boats, and there will be, and they need not throw in the
buffaloes.[3]

I have crossed the bay 20 or 30 times and have seen a

great many immigrants going up to the city for the first
time–Norwegians who carry their old fashioned farming
tools to the west with them, and will buy nothing here
for fear of being cheated.–English operatives, known by
their pale faces and stained hands, who will recover their
birth-rights in a little cheap sun and wind,–English travellers on their way to the Astor House,[4] to whom I have
done the honors of the city.–Whole families of imigrants
cooking their dinner upon the pavements, all sun-burnt–
so that you are in doubt where the foreigner's face of flesh
begins–their tidy clothes laid on, and then tied to[a] their
swathed bodies which move about like a bandaged finger–Caps set on the head, as if woven of the hair, which
is still growing at the roots each and all busily cooking,
stooping from time to time over the pot, and having
something to drop into it, that so they may be entitled to
take something out, forsooth. They look like respectable
but straightened people, who may turn out to be counts
when they get to Wisconsin[5]–and will have this experience to relate to their children.

Seeing so many people from day to day one comes to
have less respect for flesh and bones, and think they must
be more loosely {*MS torn*} of less firm fibre, than the few
he had known.[e] It must have a very bad influence upon
children to see so many human beings at once–mere
herds of men.

I came across Henry Bigelow a week ago, sitting in front
of a Hotel in Broadway, very much is if he were under his
father's own stoop.[6] He is seeking to be admitted into the
bar in New York, but as yet, had not succeeded   I directed
him to Fuller's store, which he had not found, and invited
him to come and see[a] me, if he came to the island. Tell
Mrs & Miss ward that I have not forgotten them, and was
glad to hear from George, with whom I spent last night,
that they had returned to C.–[7] Tell Mrs Brown that it
gives me as much pleasure to know that she thinks of me

and my writing as if I had been the author of the piece in question; but I did not even read the papers I sent. The Mirror[8] is really the most readable journal here. I see that they have printed a short piece which I wrote to sell in the Dem Review, and still keep the review of Paradise that I may include in it a notice of another book by the same author,[9] which they have found, and are going to send me– I dont know when I shall come home– I like to keep that feast in store– Tell Helen that I do not see any advertisement for her–and I am looking for myself  If I could find a sure opening, I might be tempted to try with her for a year till I had payed my debts; but for such I am sure it is not well to go out of N. Eng. Teachers are but poorly recompensed even here.– Tell her and Sophia (if she is not gone) to write to me– Father will know that this letter is to him as well as to you–  I send him a paper which usually contains the news–if not all that is stirring–all that has stirred–and even draws a little on the future. I wish he would send me by and by the paper which contains the results of the Cattleshow[10]  You must get Helen's eyes to read this–though she is a scoffer at honest penmanship

yr affectionate son Henry D. Thoreau

*Correspondent:* See p. 161.

[1] Philip Jones Forbes (1807-1877), son of John and Martha Skidmore Forbes, married Elizabeth Anastasia Carroll (1813-1902) in 1845. He succeeded his father as librarian of the New York Society Library in 1824 and served until the library requested his resignation in May 1855 following a dispute over financial matters. He later became a bookseller in New York City.

[2] Henry Swasey McKean.

[3] P. T. Barnum had brought a band of Indians from Iowa to New York City to live in and perform at Barnum's American Museum. He had also purchased fifteen buffalo calves in Massachusetts and had brought them to New Jersey. He then began a newspaper campaign announcing the capture of a wild herd in New Mexico that was being brought to New York City. After raising public interest in the "wild" herd, he anonymously announced a "Grand Buffalo Hunt" to be held at Hoboken, New Jersey, on August 31,

when the audience would be treated to a spectacle of lassoing the beasts ("The Grand Buffalo Hunt," *New-York Daily Tribune*, August 30, 1843). The event was free, but Barnum had quietly chartered every ferry from Manhattan to Hoboken. A crowd of twenty-four thousand people took the ferries, and many more came from other parts of New Jersey. What they saw was a huddle of scared buffalo that finally panicked and ran among the crowd, which took it all in good humor. The event, instantly called a grand "humbug," amused the public and grossed Barnum thirty-five hundred dollars (P. T. Barnum, *Struggles and Triumphs; or, Forty Years' Recollections* [Buffalo, N.Y.: Warren, Johnson, 1872], p. 149). In addition to the buffalo hunt, Barnum had put the Indians in races against boat clubs: the *New-York Daily Tribune* for September 27 reported a race at Hoboken between a team of Indians and a "club race boat 'Thomas Jefferson'" and mentioned a recent race against a Philadelphia club ("Sport at Hoboken").

[4] The Astor House, located on Broadway, was the first luxury hotel in Manhattan. Built by John Jacob Astor, the five-story hotel opened in 1836.

[5] Margaret Fuller may have told T of the Hungarian count who had "a large tract of land in Wisconsin" and who moved there "with all his tenantry several hundred persons they say" (*Letters of Margaret Fuller*, 3:130).

[6] Henry Heartwell Bigelow (1822-1854), son of Heartwell and Lovinia Jones Bigelow of Concord, married Mary Ann Seaver (b. 1824?), daughter of Leonard and Sophia Morgan Seaver, and the couple moved to Illinois. The elder Bigelow owned a tavern in Concord.

[7] T refers to Prudence Bird Ward and her children, Prudence and George.

[8] The *New Mirror, of Literature, Amusement, and Instruction*; see p. 235, note 4.

[9] T's essay "The Landlord" appeared in the October 1843 issue of the *United States Magazine, and Democratic Review* (pp. 427-430; see *Excursions* 2007, pp. 47-54), and his review of J. A. Etzler's *The Paradise within the Reach of All Men* in the November issue (pp. 451-463; see *Reform Papers* 1973, pp. 19-47). The review does not, however, mention "another book" by Etzler; what T refers to in the letter is probably Etzler's *The New World; or, Mechanical System*, a sequel to *The Paradise within the Reach of All Men*.

[10] The *Concord Freeman* for October 6 described the annual Middlesex Cattle Show, which had opened on October 4 ("Middlesex County Cattle Show," October 6, 1843); it published a full report of the event in the issue for October 13 ("Middlesex Agricultural So-

ciety," October 13, 1843). T would have been interested in the announcements of the prizes awarded to farms, reclaimed meadows, and apple, peach, and pear orchards.

*Copy-text:* ALS (CSmH, HM 7006)

*Published: Boston Advertiser* (August 3, 1882); *Boston Traveller* (August 3, 1882); "Thoreau's Manuscripts" 1883, 125-126; *FL* 1894, 129-133; *T: Home* 1902, 96; *FL* 1906, 108-111; *Cor* 1958, 141-143; *Concord Harvest* 1970, 67-68; *Response to Transcendental Concord* 1974, 235, 236; *ARLR* 1988, 54, 55

*Editor's Notes*
    This letter is addressed "Mrs. Cynthia Thoreau / Concord / Mass" and postmarked "NEW-YORK OCT 2".
    known.] *PE*; know{*MS torn*}.

*Author's Alterations*
    live] life
    we] *preceded by cancelled* and for
    gentleman–] ~,
    is] if
    to] take
    see] ~,

## To Lidian Jackson Emerson
*October 16, 1843*

Staten Island Oct 16<sup>th</sup>

My Dear Friend,

    I promised you some thoughts long ago, but it would be hard to tell whether these are the ones. I suppose that the great questions of Fate, Freewill, Foreknowledge absolute,[1] which used to be discussed in Concord are still unsettled. And here comes Channing with his Present to vex the world again–a rather galvanic movement, I think. However, I like the man all the better, though his schemes the less. I am sorry for his confessions. Faith never makes a confession.[2]

    Have you had the annual berrying party, or sat on the Cliffs a whole day this summer? I suppose the flowers have fared quite as well since I was not there to scoff at them, and the hens without doubt keep up their reputation.

I have been reading lately what of Quarles' poetry I could get. He was a contemporary of Herbert, and a kindred spirit.[3] I think you would like him. It is rare to find one who was so much of a poet and so little of an artist. He wrote long poems, almost epics for length, about Jonah, Esther, Job, Samson & Solomon, interspersed with meditations after a quite original plan–Shepherds Oracles, Comedies, Romances, Fancies and Meditations–the Quintessence of Meditation–and Enchiridions of Meditation all divine–and what he calls his Morning Muse; besides prose works as curious as the rest. He was an unwearied Christian and a reformer of some old school withal. Hopelessly quaint, as if he lived all alone and knew nobody but his wife–who appears to have reverenced him. He never doubts his genius–it is only he and his God in all the world. He uses language sometimes as greatly as Shakspeare, and though there is not much straight grain in him, there is plenty of tough crooked timber. In an age when Herbert is revived, Quarles surely ought not to be forgotten.

I will copy a few such sentences as I should read to you if there. Mrs Brown too may find some nutriment in them.

Mrs Emerson must have been sicker than I was aware of, to be confined so long, for[a] they will not say that she is convalescent yet–though the Dr pronounces her lungs unaffected.[4]

How does the Saxon Edith[5] do? Can you tell yet to which school of philosophy she belongs–whether she will be a fair saint of some christian order, or a follower of Plato and the heathen? Bid Ellen a good night or a good morning from me, and see if she will remember where it comes from   And remember me to Mrs Brown and your mother[e] and Elizabeth Hoar.

Yr friend<br>
Henry.

*Correspondent:* See p. 168.

[1] T alludes to the fallen angels in Milton, vol. 2, *Paradise Lost*, 2.558-561, who

> reason'd high
> Of providence, foreknowledge, will, and fate,
> Fix'd fate, free will, foreknowledge absolute,
> And found no end, in wandering mazes lost.

[2] William Henry Channing had just published the first issue of the *Present*, for which he wrote a long, five-part "Confession of Faith" that discussed subjects ranging from the nature of "The Divine Being" to "The United States a Member of Christendom" (September 1843): 6-10.

[3] Francis Quarles (1592-1644) is best known for *Emblemes*, a collection of poems; he also published prose religious manuals. T mentions reading Quarles's poetry in his September 14 letter to Emerson (see p. 234). George Herbert (1593-1633), a clergyman and poet, is best known for *The Temple: Sacred Poems and Private Ejaculations*, a collection of 164 poems. T quotes both Quarles and Herbert in *A Week on the Concord and Merrimack Rivers*.

[4] Susan Haven Emerson became ill in late September, near the end of Margaret Fuller's visit to New York City.

[5] Emerson's daughter Edith.

*Copy-text:* ALS (NN-BGC, Henry David Thoreau Collection, 1837-1917, Series III)

*Published: LVP* 1865, 29-30; *Life* 1890, 74; *FL* 1894, 133-135; *FL* 1906, 112-113; *Magazine of History* 1915, 120; *Cor* 1958, 143-144

*Editor's Notes*
> This letter is addressed "Mrs. Lidian Emerson / Concord / Mass."
> PE supplies the year "1843" from the contents of the letter.
> mother] *PE*; *possibly* Mother *in MS*

*Author's Alteration*
> for] *interlined above cancelled* though

## To Ralph Waldo Emerson

*October 17, 1843*

Staten Island Oct 17th

My Dear Friend,

I went with my pupil to the Fair of the American Institute,[1] and so lost a visit from Tappan whom I met returning from the Island. I should have liked to hear more news from his lips, though he had left me a letter, and the Dial which is a sort of circular letter itself– I find Channing's letters[2] full of life and enjoy their wit highly. Lane writes straight and solid like a guide-board, but I find that I put off the Social Tendencies to a future day[3]–which may never come– He is always Shaker fare, quite as luxurious as his principles will allow. I feel as if I were ready to be appointed a committee on poetry, I have got my eyes so whetted and proved of late, like the Knife-sharpener[e] I saw at the Fair[a] certified to have been in constant use in a gentleman's family for more than two years. Yes,[a] I ride along the ranks of the English poets casting terrible glances, and some I blot out, and some I spare.[4]

Mackean has imported within the year several new editions and collections of old poetry, which I have the reading of but there is a good deal of chaff to a little meal, hardly worth bolting. I have just opened Bacon's Advancement of Learning[5] for the first time, which I read with great delight. It is more like what Scott's novels were than anything[e].

I see that I was very blind to send you my manuscript in such a state,[6] but I have a good second sight (?)[a] at least. I could still shake it in the wind to some advantage, if it would hold together. There are some sad mistakes in the printing.– It is a little unfortunate that the Ethnical scripture[7] should hold out so well, though it does really hold out. The Bible ought not to be very large. Is it not singular that while the religious world is gradually picking to pieces its old testaments, here are some coming slowly after on the sea-shore picking up the durable relics of perhaps older books and putting them together again?

Your letter to contributors is excellent and hits the nail on the head. It will taste sour to their palates at first no doubt, but it will bear a sweet fruit at last.[8]

I like the poetry, especially the Autumn verses.[9] They ring true. Though I am quite weather beaten with poetry having weathered so many epics of late. The Sweep Ho[10] sounds well this way. But I have a good deal of fault to find with your ode to Beauty. The tune is altogether unworthy of the thoughts. You slope too quickly to the rhyme, as if that trick had better be performed as soon as possible–or as if you stood over the line with a hatchet and chopped off the verses as they came out–some short and some long. But give us a long reel and we'll cut it up to suit ourselves. It sounds like parody. "Thee knew I of old" "Remediless thirst" are some of those stereotyped lines[a].[11] I am frequently reminded I believe of Jane Taylors Philosopher's scales, and how the world

"Flew out with a bounce"

which–"jerked the philosopher out of his cell."[12] or else of "From[a] the climes of the sun all war-worn and weary".[13] I had rather have the thoughts come ushered with a flourish of oaths and curses. Yet I love your poetry as I do little else that is near and recent–especially when you get fairly round the end of the line, and are not thrown back upon the rocks.–  To read the lecture on the Comic,[14] is as good as to be in our town meeting or Lyceum once more[a].

I am glad that the concord farmers have plowed well this year, it promises that something will be done these summers. But I am suspicious of that Brittonner who advertises so many cords of *good*[a] oak chestnut and maple wood for sale–[15]  *Good*! aye, good for what? And there shall not be left a stone upon a stone.[16] But no matter let them hack away–  The sturdy Irish arms that do the work are of more worth than oak or maple. Methinks I could look with equanimity upon a long street of Irish cabins and pigs and children revelling in the genial Concord dirt, and I should still find my Walden wood[a] and Fair Haven in their tanned and happy faces.–  I write this in the corn field–it being washing day–with the inkstand[e] Elizabeth Hoar gave me–though it is not redolent of corn-stacks–I fear.

Let me not be[e] forgotten by Channing & Hawthorne–nor our grey-suited neighbor[17] under the hill–

Yr friend H. D. Thoreau

*Correspondent:* See p. 53.

[1] The annual fair of the American Institute of the City of New York opened on October 11 at Niblo's Garden and ran until October 27. Advertisements claimed that forty-five thousand people attended during three days of its last week. Patrons viewed mechanical inventions, agricultural implements, and horticultural exhibits. The American Institute had been founded in 1829 "for the purpose of encouraging and promoting Domestic Industry in this State and the United States, in Agriculture, Commerce, Manufactures, and the Arts" (*Merchants' Magazine and Commercial Review* 3 [1840]: 418).

[2] Ellery Channing, "The Youth of the Poet and the Painter," *Dial* 4 (October 1843): 174-186; see p. 193, note 5.

[3] T apparently had read Charles Lane's essay "A Day with the Shakers" (*Dial* 4 [October 1843]: 165-173) but had not yet read the second part of "Social Tendencies" (pp. 188-204); the first part of the essay was published in the July number (pp. 65-86).

[4] In the fall of 1841 T began, with Emerson's encouragement and financial aid, to work on a literary project probably intended to be an anthology of English poetry with historical and critical commentary. He copied twenty pages of poetry from Emerson's commonplace book into one of his own and spent two weeks in November and December of that year at Harvard reading, copying, and annotating old English poets. T resumed the work in August 1843, when he gained access to libraries in New York City, among them the Mercantile Library, where McKean was the librarian. As Robert Sattelmeyer notes, T's Journal for the Staten Island period includes quotations from or estimations of Marlowe, Spenser, Francis Quarles, William Drummond of Hawthornden, Thomas Carew, George Peele, Samuel Daniel, Lovelace, and Donne ("Thoreau's Projected Work on the English Poets," *SAR* 1980, p. 248). It is not known which specific volumes T read at the Mercantile and New York Society libraries, and, whatever his original conception, T stopped working on the project when he returned to Concord in December 1843.

[5] The Mercantile Library owned an 1825 edition of Francis Bacon's *Of the Proficience and Advancement of Learning*, which was first published in 1605.

[6] T refers to "A Winter Walk," which Emerson revised and published in the October *Dial* (pp. 211-226; see *Excursions* 2007, pp. 55-77). See also p. 229.

[7] In the *Dial*, under "Ethnical Scriptures," Emerson had regularly

included excerpts from the scriptures and sacred books of several religions. For the October number, T apparently helped Emerson make the selections from David Collie's translation of *The Chinese Classical Work Commonly Called the Four Books*, which includes excerpts from Mencius, Confucius, and others ("Chinese Four Books," *Dial* 4 [October 1843]: 205-210; see *Early Essays* 1975, pp. 147-153).

[8] Emerson's letter, a response to several letters to the editor of the *Dial*, covers such topics as railroads, communities, the discontent of the young, and educated men; it also includes an account, translated from the *Deutsche Schnellpost* (see p. 254, note 7), of Bettina von Arnim's latest work. T may refer to Emerson's expression of impatience with bored young men: "Apathies and total want of work and reflection on the imaginative character of American life, &c &c., are like seasickness, which never will obtain any sympathy, if there is a woodpile in the yard, or an unweeded patch in the garden" (*Dial* 4 [October 1843]: 267).

[9] Ellery Channing, "Autumn," *Dial* 4 (October 1843): 186-187.

[10] Ellen Sturgis Hooper, "Sweep Ho!", *Dial* 4 (October 1843): 245.

[11] T refers to Emerson, "Ode to Beauty," *Dial* 4 (October 1843): 257-259. The lines to which T objects are the following: "Say when in lapsed ages / Thee knew I of old" and "Love drinks at thy banquet / Remediless thirst; / Thou intimate stranger! / Thou latest and first!" (p. 257).

[12] Jane Taylor (1783-1824), a writer of children's verse, is best known for "Twinkle, Twinkle, Little Star." Her poem "The Philosopher's Scales" was published in a number of editions of two collections of her work, *The Contributions of Q. Q. to a Periodical Work* and *The Writings of Jane Taylor*. In an 1832 Boston edition of the latter work, the last two lines of the poem read: "While the scale with the soul in, so mightily fell, / That it jerked the philosopher out of his cell." The opening stanza of the poem contains the line "The flow of murmuring waters, day by day," and the sixth stanza contains the line "And down, down, the farthing's worth came with a bounce" (3:117-120).

[13] T quotes the opening line in William Gillespie's poem "The Highlander," which appears in an 1836 Boston edition of a textbook that he owned (*The American First Class Book; or, Exercises in Reading and Recitation*, ed. John Pierpont, p. 230). The poem is also included in a number of other nineteenth-century textbooks. For example, an 1838 textbook published in London, *Selections from Modern Authors: For the Use of the Higher Classes in Schools, and for Young Persons Generally*, contains both "The Philosopher's

Scales" and "The Highlander," but it is not known whether T had read that book.

[14] Emerson's lecture "Comedy" was part of his "Human Life" series. He first read it in Boston on January 30, 1839, and then repeated it in Concord on May 1, when T most likely heard it. The October *Dial* essay "The Comic" (pp. 247-256) is a version of this lecture.

[15] In the *Concord Freeman* of October 13, Joel Britton had advertised "from 700 to 1000 cords of Oak, Chesnut, Pine and Maple Wood, separated and corded" to be sold from a lot in Lincoln ("Wood for Sale," October 13, 1843).

[16] T alludes to Jesus's prophecy of the future destruction of the Temple in Jerusalem, recorded in all three synoptic Gospels: "See ye not all these things? verily I say unto you, There shall not be left here one stone upon another, that shall not be thrown down" (Matt. 24:2; cf. Mark 13:2 and Luke 19:44).

[17] Edmund Hosmer.

*Copy-text:* ALS (NN-BGC, Henry David Thoreau Collection, 1837-1917, Series III)

*Published:* "Emerson-Thoreau Correspondence," *AM* 69 (May 1892): 594-595; *FL* 1894, 135-139; *FL* 1906, 113-117; *Magazine of History* 21 (July-December 1915): 120; *Cor* 1958, 145-146

*Editor's Notes*
This letter is addressed "R. Waldo Emerson / Concord / Mass." and endorsed "H. D Thoreau. / Oct. 1843". PE supplies the year "1843" following the endorsement.
    Knife-sharpener] *PE*; Knife- / sharpener *in MS*
    anything] *PE*; amything *in MS*
    inkstand] *PE*; ink- / stand *in MS*
    be] *PE*; {*text obscured by sealing wax*}e

*Author's Alterations*
    Fair] fair
    Yes,] ~–
    (?)] *inserted*
    lines] *interlined above cancelled* verses
    "From] *preceded by cancelled* the
    more] most
    *good*] *interlined with a caret*
    wood] *interlined with a caret*

*To Helen Louisa Thoreau*
*October 18, 1843*

Staten Island Oct 18th 43

Dear Helen,

What do you mean by saying that "*we* have written eight times by private opportunity"? Is'nt it the more the better?– And am I not glad of it? But people have a habit of not letting me know it when they go to Concord from New York. I endeavored to get you "The[a] Present," when I was last in the City, but they were all sold–and now another is out, which I will send if I get it   I did not send the Dem. Rev. because I had no copy, and my piece was not worth fifty cents.–[1]   You think that Channing words would apply to me too,[a] as living more in the natural than the moral world, but I think that you mean the world of men and women rather, and reformers generally. My objection to Channing and all that fraternity is that they need and deserve sympathy themselves, rather than are able to render it to others. They want faith, and mistake their private ail for an infected atmosphere; but let any one of them recover hope for a moment, and right his *particular* grievance, and he will no longer train in that company.[2] To speak or do any thing that shall concern mankind, one must speak and act as if well, or from that grain of health which he has left–   This Present book indeed is blue, but the hue of its thoughts is yellow.–   I say these things with the less hesitation because I have the jaundice myself, but I also know what it is to be well. But do not think that one can escape from mankind, who is one of them, and is so constantly dealing with them.

I could not undertake to form a nucleus of an institution for the development of infant minds, where none already existed–   It would be too cruel,–And then as if looking all this while one way with benevolence, to walk off another about ones own affairs suddenly[a]!–   Something of this kind is an unavoidable objection to that.

I am very sorry to hear such bad news about Aunt Maria, but I think that the worst is always the least to be apprehended–for nature is averse to it as well as we. I trust to hear that she is quite well soon   I send love to her and to Aunt Jane.

Mrs Emerson is not decidedly better yet, though she is not extremely sick. For three months I have not known whether to think of Sophia as in Bangor or Concord, and now you say that she is going directly. Tell her to write to me, and establish her whereabouts, and also to get well directly–  And see that she has something worthy to do when she gets down there, for that's the best remedy for disease.

{*four-fifths page missing*}

judge that the prospect was as good as anywhere in the west–and yet *I* think it very uncertain, though perhaps not for anything that I know in particular[e]–unless that she got

{*four-fifths page missing*}

Tell Father and Mother I hope to see them before long–

yr affectionate brother

H. D. Thoreau.

*Correspondent:* See p. 26.

[1] T had published "The Landlord" in the October 1843 issue of the *United States Magazine, and Democratic Review* (pp. 427-430; see *Excursions* 2007, pp. 47-54).

[2] T may refer to William Henry Channing's "Confession of Faith," published in the first issue of the *Present.* Channing's claim, for instance, "[t]hat our duties will not be done, our ideal will not be fulfilled, till we solve the problem of united interests" (September [1843]: 9), would have had scant appeal for T.

*Copy-text:* ALS (CSmH, HM 7007)

*Published: LVP* 1865, 39-41; *FL* 1894, 140-142; *FL* 1906, 117-119; *Cor* 1958, 147-148

*Editor's Note*

in particular] *PE*; i{*MS cut*} p{*MS cut*}ti{*MS cut*}lar

*Author's Alterations*
    The] the
    too,] *inserted*
    suddenly] *interlined with a caret*


## From Ralph Waldo Emerson
*October 25, 1843*

                                Concord, Oct 25, 1843–
Dear Henry,

I have your letter this evening by the advent of Mrs
Fuller to Ellery C.s[1] and am heartily glad of the robust
greeting. Ellery brought it me & as it was opened won-
dered whether he had not some right to expect a letter.
So I read him what belonged to him. He is usually in good
spirits & always in good wit, forms stricter ties with George
Minott, and is always merry with the dulness of a world
which will not support him.[2] I am sorry you will dodge my
hunters T. & W.[3] W. T. is a very satisfactory[e] person, only
I could be very willing he should read a little more.  he
speaks seldom but easily & strongly, & moves like a deer.
H James[4] too has gone to England–  I am the more sorry
because you liked him so well. In Concord no events. We
have had the new Hazlitt's Montaigne which contained
the "Journey into Italy"–new to me, & the narrative of the
death of the renowned friend Etienne de la Boétie. Then
I have had Saadi's *Gulistan* Ross's translation; and Marot;
& Roman de la Rose; and Robert of Gloucester's rhymed
Chronicle.[5] Where are my translations of Pindar for the
Dial?[6] Fail not to send me something good & strong. They
send us the "Rivista Ligure," a respectable magazine from
Genoa; "la Democratie Pacifique," a bright daily paper
from Paris; the Deutsche Schnellpost,–German New York
paper; and Phalanx from London;[7] the New Englander[e]
from New Haven, which angrily affirms that the Dial is
not as good as the Bible.[8] By all these signs we infer that
we make some figure in the literary world, though we are

not yet encouraged by a swollen subscription list. Lidian says she will write you a note herself. If, as we have heard, you will come home to Thanksgiving, you must bring something that will serve for Lyceum lecture[9]–the craving thankless town!

Yours affectionately
Waldo Emerson–

Henry Thoreau

*Correspondent:* See p. 53.

[1] Margarett Crane Fuller (1789-1859) was Ellery Channing's mother-in-law.

[2] Emerson habitually recorded Ellery Channing's witticisms in his journal; entries from this period contain these two comments by Channing: "Wordsworth writes like a man who takes snuff" and "Writers never do any thing: they are passive observers. Some of them seem to do, but they do not; H[enry] will never be a writer he is as active as a shoemaker" (*JMN*, 9:41; 9:45).

[3] William Tappan and Giles Waldo had been deer hunting in Hamilton County, New York; each shot a deer.

[4] Henry James Sr.

[5] Emerson had borrowed these books from the Harvard library on October 4. William Hazlitt (1811-1893), son of the famous essayist, produced editions of a number of French authors, including *The Complete Works of Michael de Montaigne* (1842). "A Diary of the Journey of Michael de Montaigne into Italy," translated by Hazlitt, appears in this edition (pp. 523-629); the account of Étienne de la Boétie's life appears in a letter from Montaigne to his father (pp. 630-635). *The Gulistan, or Flower-Garden, of Shaikh Sadī of Shiraz*, translated from Persian by James Ross, was published in London in 1823 (Emerson wrote an introduction for a later edition of the work, published by Ticknor and Fields in 1865). The volume by the poet Clément Marot (1496-1544) that Emerson borrowed is possibly the first volume of either *Œuvres complètes de Clément Marot* (1824) or *Œuvres de Clément Marot* (1731). Emerson also borrowed volume 1 of Dominique Martin Méon's edition of *Le Roman de la Rose* (1814) and both volumes of *Robert of Gloucester's Chronicle* (1724).

[6] T's translations, "Pindar" and "Fragments of Pindar," appeared in the January 1844 (pp. 379-390) and April 1844 (pp. 513-514) numbers of the *Dial* respectively (see *Translations* 1986, pp. 111-127, 129-131).

⁷ Emerson had received issues of these foreign journals in exchange for issues of the *Dial*. *Rivista Ligure* was published in Genoa from 1843 to 1846 by the Società di Letture e Conversazioni Scientifiche. *La Démocratie Pacifique*, Victor Considérant's Fourierist paper, ran from 1843 to 1851. The semiweekly *Deutsche Schnellpost*, then edited by Wilhelm von Eichthal, was published in New York City from 1843 to 1851. The *London Phalanx* was published from April 3, 1841, to May 1843.

⁸ The *New Englander* was founded in January 1843 by Edward Royall Tyler (1800-1848), an 1825 Yale graduate and a Congregational minister, and continued until 1892; its supporters, mostly Yale graduates, included Horace Bushnell. The October 1843 issue published "A Plain Discussion with a Transcendentalist" (pp. 502-516), in which "Mr. A.," a Transcendentalist, and "Mr. B.," an opponent, debate. After Mr. A. avers that "The Dial is a clear indication that there is still faith, genius and inspiration among us," Mr. B. retorts: "To place the Dial and the Bible, as it respects their inspiration, on the same footing, is certainly intelligible, and in all other respects is truly transcendental. Pardon me, Mr A., but I must ask you if you are serious in this?" (pp. 513-514).

⁹ T went home for Thanksgiving and lectured at the Concord Lyceum on November 29; his lecture was on "Ancient Poets." He included portions of the lecture in the January 1844 *Dial* essay "Homer. Ossian. Chaucer." (pp. 290-305; see *Early Essays* 1975, pp. 154-173) and later included passages from the essay in *A Week on the Concord and Merrimack Rivers*.

*Copy-text:* ALS (NN-BGC, Henry David Thoreau Collection, 1837-1917, Series IV)

*Published:* "Emerson-Thoreau Correspondence," *AM* 69 (May 1892): 595-596; *Cor* 1958, 148-149; *Letters of RWE* 1990-1995, 7:572-574

*Editor's Notes*
This letter is addressed "Henry D. Thoreau. / Castleton. / Staten Island. / N.Y."
    satisfactory] *PE*; satisfac / tory *in MS*
    Englander] *PE*; Eng / lander *in MS*

## To Henry Swasey McKean
*Before November 7, 1843*

{*MS torn*}be kind
{*MS torn*}me take
{*MS torn*}hapman's Trans-
{*MS torn*} of the Greek Pastoral
{*MS torn*}ts"[1] & "Ossian's
Genuine Remains"?[2]

Yrs resp[ly]
Henry D. Thoreau.

*Correspondent:* Henry Swasey McKean (1810-1857), librarian of the Mercantile Library Association in New York City, was the son of Rev. Joseph McKean and Amy Swasey McKean. The elder McKean was the Boylston Professor of Rhetoric at Harvard until his death in 1818. Henry McKean graduated from Harvard in 1828 and was a tutor there during T's first two years. With Charles Stearns Wheeler, McKean helped Emerson produce the first two volumes of a four-volume edition of Carlyle's *Critical and Miscellaneous Essays* (Boston: James Munroe, 1838-1839). McKean later pursued a career as a civil engineer in Boston. In 1851 he married Anna Hunstable Hosmer (1827-1903), daughter of Ephraim and Sarah Hunstable Hosmer.

[1] M. J. Chapman, trans., *The Greek Pastoral Poets: Theocritus, Bion, and Moschus.*

[2] T refers to *The Genuine Remains of Ossian, Literally Translated.* As were many others of his generation, T was enthusiastic about the poetry that James MacPherson (1736-1796) attributed to Ossian. He wrote in his Journal on November 7, 1843: "In the oldest poems only the most simple and enduring features of humanity are seen, such essential parts of a man–as stonehenge exhibits of a temple" (*Journal 1* 1981, p. 485). Meditations on Ossian and other poets that T recorded on several pages of his Journal in November formed the basis of his lecture "Ancient Poets," which he delivered at the Concord Lyceum on November 29. He included portions of the lecture in the January 1844 *Dial* essay "Homer. Ossian. Chaucer." (pp. 290-305; see *Early Essays* 1975, pp. 154-173) and later included passages from the essay in *A Week on the Concord and Merrimack Rivers. The Genuine Remains of Ossian* was later exposed as a hoax: MacPherson had freely translated and rewritten selections of traditional Gaelic verse and published the volume as a literal translation of the work of an ancient poet named Ossian.

*Copy-text:* ALS (VtMiM, Thoreau/2)

*Published: Cor* 1958, 150; *Transcendentalists and Minerva* 1958, 2:371-372

*Editor's Notes*
   This letter is addressed "Mr Mackean / {*MS torn*}".

   The copy-text, written in pencil, is probably the recipient's copy; perhaps McKean returned T's note with the books T asked to borrow. The document also contains a long list that T made of sixteenth- and seventeenth-century English poets and dramatists; this list may be part of the literary project that he began in the fall of 1841 and resumed in August 1843 (see p. 247, note 4).

   PE supplies the date "Before November 7, 1843" based on the fact that T first quotes Ossian in his Journal on that date. From May to December 1843 T lived on Staten Island with the William Emerson family.


## From Ralph Waldo Emerson
*November 23, 1843*

                                                  Thursday P. m.

Dear Henry,

   I am not today quite so robust as I expected to be & so have to beg that you will come down & drink tea with Mr Brownson & charge yourself with carrying him to the Lyceum & introducing him to the curators.[1] I hope you can oblige me so far.

                                                  Yours,
                                                  R. W. E.

*Correspondent:* See p. 53.

   [1] Emerson was one of the curators of the Concord Lyceum for this season. Orestes Brownson lectured on "Demogogism" on November 23.

*Copy-text:* ALS (CSmH, HM 7321)

*Published:* "Emerson-Thoreau Correspondence," *AM* 69 (June 1892): 736; *Cor* 1958, 150; *Letters of RWE* 1990-1995, 7:577

*Editor's Notes*
   This letter is addressed "Henry D. Thoreau."

   PE supplies the date "November 23, 1843," the only Thursday on which Brownson spoke before the Concord Lyceum.

## From Sophia Peabody Hawthorne
*December 3, 1843*

Mr Thoreau,

Will you be kind enough to take to New York the letter
to Mr O'Sullivan, & if it be convenient for you, to carry my
letter to Boston?[1] If you cannot call at West St, it is just as
well to put it into the Boston Post Office–

S A. Hawthorne.

Dec. 3[d] 1843

*Correspondent:* Sophia Amelia Peabody (1809-1871), daughter of
Nathaniel and Elizabeth Palmer Peabody of Salem, Massachusetts,
married Nathaniel Hawthorne in 1842. The couple then took up
residence at the Old Manse in Concord. Sophia was educated by
her elder sister Elizabeth and was encouraged by her family to develop her skills in drawing and oil painting.

[1] T went back to Staten Island after Thanksgiving but stayed there
for only a short period of time; he was back in Concord by December 17. Nathaniel Hawthorne's letter to O'Sullivan is not extant.
Sophia's letter was to her mother, who was staying with Sophia's
sister Elizabeth in Boston. It contains domestic news and an inquiry about her other sister Mary Peabody Mann (1807-1887), wife
of Horace Mann.

*Copy-text:* ALS (NNPM, MA 920)

*Published: Cor* 1958, 151

*Editor's Note*
This letter is addressed "Henry D Thoreau." and endorsed "Mrs.
S. A. Hawthorne".

## From Charles Lane
*December 3, 1843*

Boston Dec[r] 3/43

Dear friend

As well as my wounded hands permit I have scribbled
something for friend Hecker[1] which if agreeable may be
the opportunity for entering into closer relations with
him; a course I think likely to be mutually encouraging,

as well as beneficial to all men. But let it reach him in the manner most conformable to your own feelings.

That from all perils of a false position you may shortly be relieved[2] and landed in the position where you feel "at home" is the sincere wish of yours most friendly

Charles Lane

Henry Thoreau

*Correspondent:* See p. 189.

[1] Isaac Thomas Hecker (1819-1888), an enthusiastic and deeply religious young man, stayed with the Thoreaus from April 24 to June 17 in 1844. He began a correspondence with T in July, but their friendship was short lived.

[2] Lane probably refers to T's position as tutor in the home of William Emerson.

*Copy-text:* ALS (MHvFM)

*Published:* *FL* 1894, 146-147; *FL* 1906, 123; *Cor* 1958, 152

*Editor's Note*
This letter is addressed "Mr Hy. Thoreau / Earl House / Coach Office." and endorsed "Charles Lane".

## From Isaac Thomas Hecker
*July 31, 1844*

Henry Thoreau

It was not altogether the circumstance of our immediate physical nearness, tho this may been the consequence of a higher affinity, that inclined us to commune[e] with each other. This I am fully sensible since our seperation. Oftentimes we observe ourselves to be passive or co-operative agents of profounder principles than we at the time ever dream of.

I have been stimulated to write to you at this present moment on account of a certain project which I have formed, in which your influence has no[a] slight share I imagine in forming. It is to work our passage to Europe, and to walk, work, and beg, if needs be, as far when there as we are inclined to do. We wish to see how it looks. And to court difficulties; for we feel an unknown depth of un-tried virgin strength which we know of no better way at the present time to call into activity and so dispose of. We desire to go without purse or staff[1] depending upon the all embracing love of God, Humanity, and the spark of courage imprisoned in us. Have we the will we have the strong arms, hand & hands, to work with, and sound feet to stand upon, and walk with. The heavens shall be our vaulted roof, and the green Earth beneath our bed, and for all other furniture purposes. These are free and may be so used. What can hinder us from going but our bod-ies, and shall they do it. We can as well deposit them there as here. Let us take a walk over the fairest portion of the[e] planet Earth and make it ours by seeing them. Let us see what the genius and stupidity of our honored fore fathers have heaped up. We wish to kneel at their shrines and embrace their spirits and kiss the ground which they have hallowed with their presence. We shall prove the dollar is not almighty and the impossible moonshine. The wide world is before us[a] beckoning us to come    let us accept and embrace it. Reality shall be our antagonist and our lives if sold not at a good bargain for a[a] certainty.

How does the idea strike you? I prefer at least to go this way before going farther in the woods. The past let us take with us. We reverence, we love it, but forget not that our eyes are in our face set to the beautiful unimagined future. Let us be Janus faced with a beard and beardless face.[2] Will you accept this invitation? Let me know what your impressions are. As soon as it is your pleasure.

Remember me to your kind family. Tomorrow I take the first step towards becoming a *visible* member of the Roman Catholic Church.[3]

If you and your good family do not become greater sinners I shall claim[a] you all as good Catholics, for she claims "All baptised infants, all innocent children of every

religious denomination; and all grown up Christians[a] who
have preserved their baptismal innocence[4] though they
make no outward profession of the Catholic faith, are yet
claimed as her children by the Roman Catholic Church.

Yours<br>Very Truly<br>Isaac Hecker

N.Y. Thursday July 31./44

*Correspondent:* Isaac Thomas Hecker (1819-1888), son of German
immigrants John and Caroline Friend Hecker, began his career as
a baker, but his friendship with Orestes Brownson turned his interests toward books, ideas, and political activism. Hecker lived
at Brook Farm from January until July 11, 1843, and then stayed at
Fruitlands until July 25, when he returned to New York City. He
came to Concord in April 1844 to study classical languages with
George Bradford and boarded with the Thoreaus from April 24
to June 17. Hecker became a Roman Catholic in August 1844 and
joined the Redemptorist order in 1845. He then traveled to Europe
(after unsuccessfully urging T to accompany him), was ordained in
London in 1849, and served as a missionary priest in New York City
from 1851 to 1857. In 1858 Hecker founded the Paulist order.

[1] When Jesus gave his disciples their missionary charge, he
"commanded them that they should take nothing for *their* journey,
save a staff only; no scrip, no bread, no money in *their* purse: But *be*
shod with sandals; and not put on two coats" (Mark 6:8-9). Should
T assent to his proposal, Hecker would be assured that it had been
God's will that he go to Concord: "if H.T. consent to go therefore it
was we were sent to Concord.... 'God works by mysterious ways'"
(*Diary of Isaac T. Hecker* 1988, p. 233).

[2] The ancient deity Janus, who presided "over all gates and av-
enues," is often represented with two faces looking in opposite
directions "because he was acquainted with the past and the future; or, according to others, because he was taken for the sun who
opens the day at his rising, and shuts it at his setting" (*Classical
Dictionary* 1806).

[3] Hecker recorded his baptism by Bishop McCloskey in his diary
(*Diary of Isaac T. Hecker* 1988, p. 233).

[4] Baptismal innocence refers to the Roman Catholic doctrine of
the "state of one after receiving Baptism when there is no attach-
ment to sin and the soul enjoys sanctifying grace" (*The Maryknoll*

*Catholic Dictionary*, comp. and ed. Albert J. Nevins [New York: Dimension Books, 1965], p. 295).

*Copy-text:* ALS (CSmH, HM 20110)

*Published:* "Correspondence between Thoreau and Hecker" 1902, 371-372; *Correspondence between Thoreau and Hecker* Worcester 1902, 5-7; "Correspondence between Thoreau and Hecker" 1902-1903, 60-62; *FL* 1906, 405; *Cor* 1958, 154-155; *ATQ* 14 (1972): 67

*Editor's Notes*
    This letter is addressed "Henry W Thoreau. / Concord. / Massachusetts.", postmarked "NEW-YORK AUG 1", and endorsed "Hecker".
    commune] *PE*; *possibly* commence *in MS*
    the] *PE*; *possibly* this *in MS*

*Author's Alterations*
    no] not
    us] *inserted*
    a] *inserted*
    claim] claims
    Christians] Christs

## To Isaac Thomas Hecker
*August 14, 1844*

Concord Aug. 14$^{th}$ 44

Friend Hecker,

    I am glad to hear your voice from that populous city, and the more so for the tenor of its discourse. I have but just returned from a pedestrian excursion, some what similar to that you propose, *parvis componere magna*,[1] to the Catskill mountains, over the principal mountains of this state, subsisting mainly on bread and berries, and slumbering on the mountain tops–[2] As usually happens, I now feel a slight sense of dissipation. Still I am strongly tempted by your proposal, and experience a decided schism between my outward and inward tendencies. Your method of travelling especially–to *live* along the road–citizens of the world, without haste or petty plans–I have often proposed this to my dreams, and still do–   But the fact is, I cannot so decidedly postpone exploring the *Farther Indies*, which are to be reached you know by other routs and other methods of travel. I mean that I constantly return from every external enterprise with disgust to fresh faith in a kind of Brahminical Artesian, Inner Temple[a], life.[3] All my experience, as yours probably, proves only this reality.

Channing wonders how I can resist your invitation, I, a single man–unfettered–and so do I. Why–there are Roncesvalles, the cape de Finisterre, and the three kings of Cologne;[4] Rome, Athens, & the rest–to be visited in serene untemporal hours–and all history to revive in one's memory as he went by the way with splendors to bright for this world–  I know how it is. But is not here too Roncesvalles with greater lustre? Unfortunately it may prove dull and desultory weather enough here but better trivial days with faith than[a] the fairest ones lighted by sun-shine alone. Perchance my wanderjahre[5] has not arrived. But you cannot wait for that. I hope you will find a companion who will enter as heartily into your schemes as I should have done

I remember you, as it were, with the whole Catholic church at your skirts–  And the other day for a moment I think I understood your relation to that body, but the thought was gone again in a twinkling, as when a dry leaf falls from its stem over our heads, but is instantly lost in the rustling mass at our feet–

I am really sorry that the Genius will not let me go with you, but I trust that it will conduct to other adventures, and so if nothing prevents we will compare notes at last[6]

> Yrs &c
>
> Henry D. Thoreau.

*Correspondent:* See p. 260.

[1] See Virgil, *Eclogues*, 1:23-24: "Sic canibus catulos similes, sic matribus hædos / Nôram: sic parvis componere magna solebam." ("Thus I knew puppies were like dogs, and kids like their dams; thus I used to compare great things with small." [Loeb])

² T had gone on foot to Saddleback Mountain (now Mount Grey-lock), in western Massachusetts, where he spent the night. Ellery Channing joined him at Pittsfield, and the two went to the Hudson River. They took a boat down river to the Catskills, where they climbed the mountains. T returned to Concord on August 1.

³ T refers to the Hindu priestly class, free-flowing, pure, deep water wells, and the Jewish Temple.

⁴ The pass at Roncesvalles in the Pyrenees is where Roland, legendary nephew of Charlemagne and subject of *La Chanson de Roland*, died; Cape Finisterre is the westernmost point of Spain; the Gothic cathedral at Cologne contains bones reputed to be those of the Magi who visited the infant Jesus as related in Matt. 2:1-12.

⁵ Wandering year, with perhaps a reference to Goethe's *Wilhelm Meisters Wanderjahre*.

⁶ The day after he received this letter, Hecker, who had just sent his August 15 letter to T, still hoped that T would change his mind: "I think it is yet possible that he may make up his mind to go" (*Diary of Isaac T. Hecker* 1988, p. 246).

*Copy-text:* ALS (CSmH, HM 20109)

*Published:* "Correspondence between Thoreau and Hecker" 1902, 372-373; *Correspondence between Thoreau and Hecker* Worcester 1902, 7-8; "Correspondence between Thoreau and Hecker" 1902-1903, 62-63; *FL* 1906, 405-407; *Cor* 1958, 155-156; *ATQ* 14 (1972): 68

*Editor's Note*
This letter is addressed "Isaac Hecker / New-York / N.Y."

*Author's Alterations*
Temple] temple
than] that


## From Isaac Thomas Hecker

*August 15, 1844*

I know not but that I shall receive an answer to the letter I sent you a fortnight ago before you will receive this one, however as the idea of making an indefinite pedestrian tour on the other side of the Antlantic has in all possible ways increased in my imagination and given me a desire to add a few more words on the project I will do so in the hope of stimulating you to a decision. How the thought

has struck you I know not, its impractibility or impossibility in the judjment of others would not I feel assured deter
you in any way from the undertaking, it would rather be
a stimulas to the purpose I think in you as it is in me. Tis
impossible; Sir, therefore we do it. The conceivable is possible, it is in harmony with the inconceivable we should
act. Our true life is in the can-not, to do what we can do is
to do nothing, is death. Silence is much more respectable
than repetition. The idea of making such a tour I have
opened to one or two who I thought might throw some
light on the subject. I asked the opinion of the Catholic
Bishop[1] who has travelled considerable in Europe but I
find that in every man there are certain things within him[a]
which are beyond the ken & counsel of others. The age is
so effeminate that it is too timid to give heroic counsel. It
neither will enter the kingdom of heaven or have others to
do so.[2] I feel, and beleive you feel so too, that to doubt the
ability to realize such a thought is only[a] worthy of a smile
& pity. We feel ourself mean in conceiving such a feasable
thing and would keep it silent. This is not sufficient self
abandonment for our being, scarce[e] enough to affect it.
To die is easy, scarce worth a thought, but to be and live
is an inconceivable greatness. It would be folly to sit still
and starve from mere emptiness, but to leave behind the
easement in battling for some hidden idea is an[a] attitude
beyond conception a monument more durable than the
chisel can sculpture. I imagine us walking among the past
and present greatness of our ancestors. (for tho present
in fact the present of the old world to us is ancient) doing
reverence to their remaining glory. If tho I am inclined
to bow[a] more lowly to the spiritual hero than the exhibition of great physcal strength still not all of that primi-
tive heroic blood of our forefathers has been lost before
it reached our veins. We feel it exult some times as tho
it were cased in steel and the huge broad axe of Cour de
Lion[3] seems glittering before us and we awake in another
world as in a dream. I know of no other person but you

that would be inclined to go[a] on such an excursion. The idea and yourself were almost instantaneous. If needs be for a few dollars we can get acrost the ocean. The ocean! if but to cross this being like being it were not unprofitable. The Bishop thought it might be done with certain amount of funds to depend on. If this makes it practible for others to us it will be but sport. It is useless for me to speak this to you for if there are reasons for your not going they are others than these.

You will inform me how you[a] are inclined as soon as practible. Halfe inclined I sometimes feel to go[a] alone if I cannot get your company.[4] I do not know now what could have directed my steps to Concord other than this. May it prove so. It is only the fear of death–makes us reason of impossibilities. We[a] shall possess all if we but abandon ourselves.

NY. Aug 15–/44                         Yours sincerely
To Henry Thoreau.                              Isaac–


Correspondent: See p. 260.

[1] Probably John McCloskey (1810-1885), Hecker's spiritual advisor. McCloskey was appointed bishop coadjutor of the Diocese of New York in March 1844 and became the first American cardinal in 1875.

[2] Matt. 23:13: "But woe unto you, scribes and Pharisees, hypocrites! for ye shut up the kingdom of heaven against men: for ye neither go in *yourselves*, neither suffer ye them that are entering to go in."

[3] Richard I (1157-1199), Coeur de Lion, was king of England from 1189 to 1199.

[4] Hecker did go to Europe alone, but to study, not to go on a walking tour.

*Copy-text:* ALS (CSmH, HM 20108)

*Published:* "Correspondence between Thoreau and Hecker" 1902, 373-374; *Correspondence between Thoreau and Hecker* Worcester 1902, 8-9; "Correspondence between Thoreau and Hecker" 1902-1903, 63-64; *Cor* 1958, 157-158; *ATQ* 14 (1972): 68

*Editor's Notes*
   This letter is addressed "Henry D Thoreau / Concord / Massachusetts.", postmarked "NEW-YORK AUG 16", and endorsed "Hecker".
   scarce] *PE*; scare *in MS*

*Author's Alterations*
   him] *interlined with a caret*
   only] *interlined with a caret*
   an] and
   bow] *interlined with a caret*
   go] *inserted*
   you] your
   go] *inserted*
   We] *preceded by cancelled* Heavens

## To Isaac Thomas Hecker

*After August 15, 1844*

I improve the occasion of my mothers[e] sending to acknowledge the receipt of your stirring letter. You have probably received mine by this time. I thank you for not anticipating any vulgar objections on my part– *Far* travel, very *far* travel, or travail, comes near to the worth of staying at home–[1]  Who knows whence his education is to come! Perhaps I may[e] drag my anchor at length, or rather, when the *winds* which blow *over* the deep fill my sails, may stand away for distant ports–for now I seem to have a firm *ground* anchorage, though the harbor is low-shored[e] enough, and the traffic with the natives inconsiderable–   I may be away to Singapoor by the next tide.

I like well the ring of your last maxim–"It is only the fear of death makes us reason of impossibilities"–  And but for fear death itself is an impossibility.

Believe me I can hardly let it end so. If you do not go soon let me hear from you again.

Yrs in great haste
Henry D. Thoreau

*Correspondent:* See p. 260.

¹ T alludes to lines from Simon Ockley's *The History of the Saracens*; see p. 204, note 7.

*Copy-text:* ALS (CSmH, HM 20107)

*Published:* "Correspondence between Thoreau and Hecker" 1902, 374; *Correspondence between Thoreau and Hecker* Worcester 1902, 10; "Correspondence between Thoreau and Hecker" 1902-1903, 65; *FL* 1906, 407-408; *Cor* 1958, 158-159; *ATQ* 14 (1972): 68

*Editor's Notes*
This letter is addressed "Isaac Hecker / New York."

PE supplies the date "After August 15, 1844" from the contents of the letter: T acknowledges Hecker's letter of August 15 and suggests that Hecker has probably received his letter of August 14. On page 2 of the manuscript Hecker later wrote: "The proposition made to Thoreau was to take nothing with us, work our passage acrost the Atlantic, and so through England France, Germany and Italy. I. T. H."

mothers] *PE*; *possibly* Mothers *in MS*
may] *PE*; my *in MS*
low-shored] *PE*; low- / shored *in MS*

## To James Munroe and Company
*October 14, 1844*

Concord Oct 14ᵗʰ

James Munroe & Co,

Please to send me a dozen copies of Mr. Emerson's Address¹ by the bearerᵉ–

Yrs respectˡʸ
Henry D. Thoreau.

*Correspondent:* See p. 206.

¹ On September 9 Munroe published Emerson's speech to the Concord Women's Anti-Slavery Society as *An Address Delivered in the Court-House in Concord, Massachusetts, on 1st August, 1844, on the Anniversary of the Emancipation of the Negroes in the British West Indies.*

*Copy-text:* ALS (MB, Ch.B.6.16)

*Published:* *Cor* 1958, 159

*Editor's Notes*
    This letter is addressed "James Munroe & Co." and endorsed "H. D. Thoreau / Concord. Oct. 9. 1844".
    PE supplies the year "1844" following the endorsement.
    bearer] *obscured in MS by* Done *written in a different hand*

## From Ellery Channing
*March 5, 1845*

New York March 5, 45

My dear Thoreau
    the hand-writing of your letter is so miserable, that I am not sure I have made it out. If I have it seems to me you are the same old sixpence you used to be, rather rusty, but a genuine piece.

    I see nothing for you in this earth but that field which I once christened "Briars";¹ go out upon that, build yourself a hut, & there begin the grand process of devouring yourself alive. I see no alternative, no other hope for you. Eat yourself up; you will eat nobody else, nor anything else.

    Concord is just as good a place as any other; there are indeed, more people in the streets of that village, than in the streets of this. This is a singularly muddy town; muddy, solitary, & silent.²

    They tell us, *it* is March; *it* has been all March in this place, since I came. It is much warmer now, than it was last November, foggy, rainy, stupefactive weather indeed.

    In your line, I have not done a great deal since I arrived here; I do not mean the Pencil line, but the Staten Island line, having been there once, to walk on a beach by the Telegraph,³ but did not visit the scene of your dominical duties. Staten Island is very distant from No. 30 Ann St.

    I saw polite William Emerson in November last, but have not caught any glimpse of him since then.⁴ I am as usual suffering the various alternations from agony to despair, from hope to fear, from pain to pleasure. Such wretched one-sided productions as you, know nothing of the universal man; you may think yourself well off.

That baker,–Hecker, who used to live on two crackers a day I have not seen, nor Black, nor Vathek, nor Danedaz, nor Rynders, or any of Emerson's old cronies, excepting James, a little fat, rosy Swedenborgian amateur, with the look of a broker, & the brains & heart of a Pascal.–[5]  W$^m$ Channing[6] I see nothing of him; he is the dupe of good feelings,[7] & I have all-too-many of these now.

I have seen something of your friends, Waldo, and Tappan,[8] & have also seen our good man "McKean", the keeper of that stupid place the "Mercantile Library". I have been able to find there no book which I should like to read.

Respecting the country about this city, there is a walk at Brooklyn rather pleasing, to ascend upon the high ground, & look at the distant Ocean. This, is a very agreeable sight. I have been four miles up the island in addition, where I saw, the bay; it looked very well, and appeared to be in good spirits.

I should be pleased to hear from Kamkatscha occasionally; my last advices from the Polar Bear are getting stale. In addition to this, I find that my Corresponding members at Van Dieman's land, have wandered into limbo.[9] I acknowledge that I have not lately corresponded very much with that section.

I hear occassionally from the World; everything seems to be promising in that quarter, business is flourishing, & the people are in good spirits. I feel convinced that the Earth has less claims to our regard, than formerly; these mild winters deserve a severe censure. But I am well aware that the Earth will talk about the necessity of routine, taxes, &c. On the whole, it is best not to complain without necessity.

Mumbo Jumbo[10] is recovering from his attack of sore

eyes, & will soon be out, in a pair of canvas trousers, scarlet jackets, & cocked hat. I understand he intends to de-
molish all the remaining species of Fetishism[a] at a meal;
I think it is probable it will vomit him. I am sorry to say,
that Roly-Poly has received intelligence of the death of his
only daughter, Maria; this will be a terrible wound to his
paternal heart.

I saw Teufelsdrock a few days since; he is wretchedly
poor, has an attack of the colic, & expects to get better immediately. He said a few words to me, about you. Says he,
that fellow Thoreau might be something, if he would only
take a Journey through the "Everlasting No", thence for the
North Pole. By God", said the old Clothes-bag "warming
up", I should like to take that fellow out into the Everlasting No, & explode him like a bomb-shell; he would make
a loud report. He needs the Blumine flower business; that
would be his salvation. He is too dry, too confused, too
chalky, too concrete. I want to get him into my fingers. It
would be fun to see him pick himself up". I "camped" the
old fellow in a majestic style.[11]

Does that execrable compound of Sawdust & Stagna-
tion, Alcott still prose about nothing, & that nutmeg-
grater of a Hosmer[12] yet shriek about nothing,–does anybody still think of coming to Concord to live, I mean new
people? If they do, let them beware of you philosophers.

Ever yrs my dear Thoreau
WEC

*Correspondent:* See pp. 154-155.

[1] Channing's name for Emerson's land at Walden, where later
that month T began cutting wood to build his house.

[2] Channing had gone to New York City in November 1844 to work
on Horace Greeley's *New-York Daily Tribune*, where Margaret
Fuller was to join him in December. Even less suited to city life than
T, Channing lasted only a few months there; in mid-March 1845 he
returned to Concord and bought a farm.

[3] Channing refers to the semaphore station on Telegraph Hill. T
mentions visiting it in his July 21, 1843, letter to his sister Helen; see
p. 210.

[4] Channing had not yet visited William Emerson's residence, the site of T's tutoring duties, on Staten Island. Waldo Emerson had asked his brother to invite Channing for a visit and William obliged. Channing, who could be pointedly antisocial, never went.

[5] Black may be Rebecca Gray Black. Vathek is probably John Wilhelm Vethake (1798-1876), son of Frederick Albertus and Maria Johanna Jansen Vethake. Vethake graduated from the Columbia Medical School in 1823. He married Sarah Brush (b. 1803?) in 1824 in Chillicothe, Ohio, where he practiced medicine before joining the faculty of Dickinson College in 1826. In 1827 he helped found the medical school of Washington College in Baltimore. Vethake, a Swedenborgian and one of the original "Loco-Foco" Democrats, knew Isaac Hecker, Charles Lane, Bronson Alcott, William Henry Channing, and Margaret Fuller. In two March 1843 numbers of Parke Godwin's *Pathfinder* (March 11, pp. 35-36; March 18, pp. 51-52), Vethake published "Femality" under the name "Vathek," a play on his own name and the title of a novel by William Beckford. The only two Rynders listed in the 1845 city directory were Isaiah Rynders (1804-1885), a U.S. marshal and Tammany politician who at one time led a mob against Garrison, and Theodore Rynders (1825?-1861), a bookbinder who became a policeman and a deputy marshal. Why Channing would mention either is not clear. James is Henry James Sr., and Blaise Pascal (1623-1662) was a French mathematician and philosopher best known for his posthumous *Pensées*.

[6] Ellery had visited his cousin William Henry Channing's church early in December 1844 but "was not vivified" ("Letters of William Ellery Channing the Younger" 1989, p. 211).

[7] Perhaps a modification of a question William Hazlitt poses in "On the Pleasure of Hating": "the dupe of friendship, and the fool of love; have I not reason to hate and to despise myself?" (*The Plain Speaker: Opinions on Books, Men, and Things*, 1:327).

[8] Though he never became close to Giles Waldo, Channing came to admire William Tappan. A few days after this letter he wrote Emerson: "With Tappan I have formed adamantine bonds, never to be broken" ("Letters of William Ellery Channing the Younger" 1990, p. 165).

[9] Kamkatscha is probably Channing's name for Concord; "Polar Bear" likely refers to Emerson, and Van Diemen's Land, an earlier name of Tasmania, to the Fruitlands community, which had broken up in January 1844.

[10] Very likely Channing's name for Greeley.

[11] Channing alludes to Carlyle's *Sartor Resartus*: Teufelsdröckh is the name of the hero; "Everlasting No," "North Pole," "Clothes-

bag," and "Blumine" are all found in the book. To whom Channing refers, however, is unknown.

¹² Edmund Hosmer.

*Copy-text:* ALS (VtMiM, Channing W E/2)

*Published:* *HDT* 1882, 209-210, 210-211, 218; *Life* 1890, 81-82; *FL* 1894, 144-145; *Life* 1896, 64; *FL* 1906, 121-122; *Cor* 1958, 161-163; "Letters of William Ellery Channing the Younger" 1990, 162-164

*Editor's Note*
This letter is addressed "Henry Thoreau / Concord. / <u>Mass.</u>", postmarked "BOSTON MASS MAR 5", and endorsed "W E. Channing".

*Author's Alteration*
Fetishism] Fetishes

## From Daniel Waldo Stevens
*May 24, 1845*

Charlestown May 24th, 1845.

Dear Sir,

Permit me to ask a favor from you, although a stranger. It is this; I wish to have permission to reprint your translation of Prometheus Bound.¹ It appeared, as you will recollect, in the January number of the Dial, in 1843. It would be useless for me to pass any encomium on the merits of your translation since it corresponds in literal lines to the original, which needs no comment. Whether you conclude to confer the favor or not, I wish you would have the kindness to write to me as soon as convenient, for I wish to know soon.

Yours truly,
D. W. Stevens

D. H. Thoreau Esq.²

*Correspondent:* Daniel Waldo Stevens (1820-1891), son of Isaac and Catharine Felton Stevens of Marlborough, Massachusetts, graduated from Harvard University in 1846 and from the Harvard Divinity School in 1848. In 1846 he married Caroline Partridge (1819-1849), daughter of Henry and Anna Partridge. Stevens was ordained in Mansfield in 1850.

[1] T's translation of *The Prometheus Bound* (see p. 142, note 4), according to Ellery Channing, was used by Harvard students as a surreptitious aid for their Greek recitations (*Thoreau: The Poet-Naturalist* [Boston: Roberts Brothers, 1873], p. 40). There is no record that T responded to Stevens's request; Stevens may have used T's translation without permission or Channing may have based his claim on this letter.

[2] Stevens's use of "D. H. Thoreau," the original form of T's name that he abandoned soon after graduating from Harvard, suggests that he probably got T's name and address from the college records.

*Copy-text:* ALS (Dawson)

*Editor's Note*
This letter is addressed "David H. Thoreau Esq. / Concord / Mass.", postmarked "CHARLESTOWN MS. MAY 25", and endorsed "D. W. Stevens".

## To Benjamin Marston Watson
*August 5, 1845*

One box is full of red huckleberries,[1] warranted not to change their hue, or lose their virtues in any climate, though I will not speak for the condition of this box when opened.
The other contains half a dozen cherries (Sand-Cherries, Bigelow?)[2]  The last grew within a rod of my lodge.
I plucked them all today
The third box–which should contain the seeds of the Carpinus Americana[3]–hopwood[4,e]–False Elm[5] &c waits for their seeds to ripen

Yrs

Henry D Thoreau

Aug 5th 1845

*Correspondent:* Benjamin Marston Watson (1820-1896), son of Benjamin M. and Lucretia Burr Sturges Watson of Plymouth, Massachusetts, had probably known T at Harvard. After his graduation in 1839, Watson returned to Plymouth and became a horticulturist and naturalist. In 1845 Watson built his home "Hillside" and established the Old Colony Nurseries on eighty acres near Plymouth. His extensive interests included trees, wild flowers, and the large-scale production of fruits and vegetables for the Boston market (he had, at one time, more than three thousand peach trees). The plants and seeds T sent him were probably intended to help him with these projects. In February 1846 Watson married Mary Howland Russell (1820-1906), whom the Thoreau brothers were interested in for a time.

¹ A "pale-fruited form of Black Huckleberry (namely *Gaylussacia baccata* forma *leucocarpa*)" that is rarely found in Concord ("Two Thoreau Letters" 1983, pp. 1-2).

² In *Florula Bostoniensis: A Collection of Plants of Boston and Its Vicinity*, a volume that T owned, Jacob Bigelow describes the sand cherry (*Prunus depressa*) as a "small, trailing shrub, spreading its branches close to the ground" (p. 193). Ray Angelo describes the sand cherry (*Prunus susquehanae*) as "an uncommon shrub in Concord found in dry, sandy, open situations" ("Two Thoreau Letters" 1983, p. 2); he explains that the *Prunus susquehanae* is not distinguished from the *Prunus depressa* in the botanical manuals T used ("Botanical Index to the Journal of Henry David Thoreau," *Thoreau Quarterly* 15 [1983; repr., Layton, Utah: Peregrine Smith, 1984], p. 197n261; this resource is available in electronic form at http://www.ray-a.com/ThoreauBotIdx).

³ A "small tree of moist, rich woods," now known "as *Carpinus caroliniana*, or commonly as Ironwood or American Hornbeam," uncommon in Concord ("Two Thoreau Letters" 1983, p. 2).

⁴ The hop-hornbeam (*Ostrya virginiana*), "whose fruit looks like hops" ("Two Thoreau Letters" 1983, p. 2).

⁵ "False Elm" is "another name for American Hackberry (*Celtis occidentalis*)," the "rarest of the species Thoreau lists" ("Two Thoreau Letters" 1983, p. 2).

*Copy-text:* ALS (MH-G, Walter Deane [1848-1930] Papers, Autograph Collection)

*Published:* "Two Thoreau Letters" 1983, 1

*Editor's Notes*
This letter is addressed "Marston Watson" and endorsed "Thoreau-'45".
hopwood] *PE*; hop- / wood *in MS*

## To James Munroe and Company

*September 17, 1845*

Concord Sep. 17th 45

Dear Sir,

The Ladies[a] have concluded to pay you your dues, and take the remaining adddresses at once.[1] Your bill has been mislaid and they may be mistaken in the amount. I noticed what seemed to me one error in the false correction (in the bill) of what was apparently the original & correct charge,–adding your 4 cents per copy to the 52 which Mr Emerson took. These of course were no more than the author usually takes, and properly speaking, were not left on sale. If they are not mistaken

whole amount =  16.96
False charge    =   2.08
               14.88

Will you adjust this, and forward the remaining copies by express.[2]

Yrs respec[ly]
Henry D Thoreau
agent for the Society

P.s. They are willing you should keep 25 copies on the original terms

*Correspondent:* See p. 206.

[1] The Concord Women's Anti-Slavery Society apparently asked T to purchase on its behalf the remaining copies of Emerson's *Emancipation* address; see p. 267, note 1.

[2] A note pencilled below the address by the recipient indicates that Munroe and Company complied with both of T's requests. The note asks the owner of the express service Munroe used to bring back a receipt from T for the adjustment and the requested copies of Emerson's address: "Will Mr. Adams please bring a receipt for this money $14.88, & the Books sent for". Augustus Adams ran an express service between Boston and Concord.

*Copy-text:* ALS (PHC, Charles Roberts Autograph Letters Collection, Collection 130: American Prose Writers)

*Editor's Note*
This letter is addressed "James Munroe & Co. / Washington St. / Boston," and endorsed "H D Thoreau / Concord Sept 17/45".

*Author's Alteration*
Ladies] ladies

## From Ralph Waldo Emerson
*October 8, 1845*

Dear Henry

Can you not without injurious delay to the shingling[1] give a quarter or a half hour tomorrow morning[e] to the direction of the Carpenter who builds Mrs Brown's fence? Cutler[2] has sent another man, & will not be here to repeat what you told him so that the new man wants new orders. I suppose he will be on the ground at 7, or a little after & Lidian shall keep your breakfast warm.

But do not come to the spoiling of your day.

R. W. E.

Wednesday
p. m. 5 o'clock

*Correspondent:* See p. 53.

    [1] T was at this time shingling his house at Walden.
    [2] Isaac Cutler (1800-1877), son of Nathaniel and Anna Childs Cutler of Lexington, Massachusetts, was a carpenter in Concord. He married Lydia Braman (1805-1890), daughter of William and Lydia Harvey Braman of Norton, in 1825. Cutler later moved to Cambridge and became a prosperous lumber dealer.

*Copy-text:* ALS (MH-H, MS Am 1189)

*Published:* *ESQ* 22 (1961): 96; *Companion* 1964, 183-184; *Letters of RWE* 1990-1995, 8:57

*Editor's Notes*
This letter is addressed "H. D. Thoreau".
PE supplies the date "October 8, 1845" based on Tilton, who conjectures this date from an entry in Emerson's account book for 1845-1849, which records on October 10, 1845, "a payment to Tho-

reau of $5.00 'for building fence'" (*Letters of RWE* 1990-1995, 8:57).
In 1845, October 8 fell on a Wednesday.

morning] *PE*; morn / ing *in MS*


## From Ralph Waldo Emerson
*Fall 1845*

Dear Sir,

Mrs Brown wishes very much to see you at her house
tomorrow (Saturday) Evening to meet Mr Alcott. If you
have any leisure for the useful arts, L. E.[1] is very desirous[e]
of your aid. Do not come at any risk of the Fine.

R. W. E.

*Correspondent:* See p. 53.

[1] Lidian Emerson.

*Copy-text:* ALS (NN-BGC, Henry David Thoreau Collection, 1837-
1917, Series IV)

*Published: Letters of RWE* 1939, 2:183; *Cor* 1958, 33; *Companion*
1964, 226

*Editor's Notes*
This letter is addressed "H. D. Thoreau."

PE supplies the date "Fall 1845" from the contents of the letter.
On the basis of nonauthorial manuscript evidence, Rusk conjectures February 15, 1839, as the date of the letter (*Letters of RWE* 1939,
2:183). However, Emerson's reference to Mrs. Brown's house, into
which she moved in September 1845, and his allusion to T's practice of the "fine" arts strongly suggest fall 1845.

desirous] *PE*; de / sirous *in MS*


## From Charles Lane
*February 17, 1846*

New York
February 17/46

Dear Friend

The books you were so kind as to deposite about two
years and a half ago with Mess[rs] Wiley and Putnam have all

been sold,[1] but as they were left in your name it is needful in strict business that you should send an order to them to pay to me the amount due. I will therefore thank you to enclose me such an order at your earliest convenience in a letter addressed to your admiring friend

> Charles Lane
> Post Office
> New York City.

*Correspondent:* See p. 189.

[1] In May 1843, Lane sent with T to New York City some of the books from a collection he had brought from England, with a request to deposit them for sale at the publisher Wiley and Putnam's shop; see p. 175.

*Copy-text:* Facsimile of ALS (Bicknell)

*Published:* *FL* 1894, 147; *FL* 1906, 123; *Cor* 1958, 168

*Editor's Note*
This letter is addressed "Henry D. Thoreau / Sylvan / favored / by A. B. A." and endorsed "C. Lane". "A. B. A." is Amos Bronson Alcott.


## From Charles Lane
*March 30, 1846*

> Boonton N.J.
> March 30/46

D[r] friend

If the human nature participates of the elemental I am no longer in danger of becoming sub urban, or super urban, that is to say too urbane. I am now more likely to be converted into a petrifaction for slabs of rock and foaming waters never so abounded in my neighborhood. A very Peter I shall become: on this rock *He* has built *his church*.[1] You would find much joy in these eminences and in the views therefrom.

My pen has been necessarily unproductive in the continued motion of the sphere in which I have lately[a] been moved.[2] You I suppose have not passed the winter to the world's unprofit.

You never have seen, as I have, the book with a preface of 450 pages and a text of sixty. My letter is like unto it.

I have only to add that your letter of the 26th Feb^y did its work, and that I submit to you cordial thanks for the same

yours truly

Chas Lane

I hope to hear occasionally of your doings & those of your compeers in your classic "ploughings and diggings."

*Correspondent:* See p. 189.

[1] Matt. 16:18: "And I say also unto thee, That thou art Peter, and upon this rock I will build my church; and the gates of hell shall not prevail against it."

[2] From October 1842 to August 1845, Lane had espoused communal living, first at Fruitlands, then at the Shaker community at Harvard, Massachusetts. In the spring of 1846 he lived in Boonton, New Jersey, where abolition was warmly supported. Lane probably wrote essays for the reforming local newspaper, the *New Jersey Freeman*, but he did not lead an active public life.

*Copy-text:* ALS (ViU, Clifton Waller Barrett Library, Henry David Thoreau Collection [#6345])

*Published:* FL 1894, 147-148; *FL* 1906, 123-124; *Cor* 1958, 168-169

*Editor's Note*
This letter is addressed "To / Henry D. Thoreau. / Concord Woods" and endorsed "C. Lane".

*Author's Alteration*
lately] *interlined with a caret*


## From Horace Greeley
*August 16, 1846*

New York, Aug. 16, 1846.

My dear Thoreau,

Believe me when I say that I *mean* to do the errand you have asked of me, and that soon. But I am not sanguine of success, and have hardly a hope that it will be immediate if ever. I hardly know a work that could publish your article all at once, and "To be continued" are words[a] shunned like a pestilence. But I know you have written a good thing about Carlyle–too solidly good, I fear, to be profitable to yourself or attractive to publishers.[1] Didst thou ever, O my friend! ponder on the significance and cogency of the assurance, "Ye cannot serve God and Mamon,"[2] as applicable to Literature–applicable, indeed, to all things whatsoever. God grant us grace to endeavor to serve Him rather than Mammon–that ought to suffice us. In my poor judgment, if any thing is calculated to make a scoundrel[e] of an honest man, writing to sell is that very particular thing.

Yours, heartily,<br>
Horace Greeley.

Remind Ralph Waldo Emerson and wife of my existence and grateful remembrance.

*Correspondent:* Horace Greeley (1811-1872), son of Zaccheus and Mary Woodburn Greeley of Amherst, New Hampshire, married Mary Young (or Youngs) Cheney (1811-1872), daughter of Silas and Polly Young (or Youngs) Cheney, in 1836. He established the *New-York Daily Tribune* in April 1841 as a Whig paper. By the middle of the decade it had become the best paper in the country. In 1844 he hired Margaret Fuller to be his book editor and later published the letters she wrote from Europe. An indefatigable reformer, Greeley admired Fourier, hated slavery, and opposed the Mexican War. As T's champion and literary agent, Greeley gave him advice, sent his work to editors and publishers, and faithfully reviewed and complimented his writing.

[1] T had delivered a lecture on Carlyle at the Concord Lyceum on February 4, 1846. He sent an essay based on the lecture to Greeley, who sent it to Rufus Wilmot Griswold on August 25 to publish in *Graham's Magazine*, calling it "a brilliant as well as vigorous essay" by "one of the only two men in America capable of giving it." The essay, Greeley wrote, "gives a daguerreotype of Carlyle and Carlylism which no man living but Emerson could excel" (Greeley to Griswold, MB, Gris. Mss. 434). When the article did not appear in *Graham's*, Greeley demanded of Griswold, "Why didn't Graham publish my friend Thoreau's article on Carlisle? He has nothing in

the January that would be read with greater interest" (Greeley to Griswold, December 16, 1846, MB, Gris. Mss. 436). Greeley's impatience was rewarded when T's essay appeared in two parts in the March (pp. 145-152) and April 1847 (pp. 238-245) issues of *Graham's* as "Thomas Carlyle and His Works" (see *Early Essays* 1975, pp. 219-267).

² The well-known injunction found in Matt. 6:24 and Luke 16:13.

*Copy-text:* ALS (RPB, Albert Edgar Lownes Collection on Henry David Thoreau, 1837-1965, Ms. 80.1, Series 1, Box 1, Folder 5)

*Published:* *HDT* 1882, 219; *Cor* 1958, 169-170

*Editor's Notes*
This letter is addressed "Henry D. Thoreau, / Concord, / Massachusetts.", postmarked "NEW-YORK 5 CtS 17 AUG", and endorsed "H. Greeley".
scoundrel] *PE*; scoun / drel *in MS*

*Author's Alteration*
words] *interlined with a caret*


## From Horace Greeley
*September 30, 1846*

I learned to-day, through Mr. Griswold, former editor of "Graham's Magazine," that your lecture is accepted, to appear in that magazine.¹ Of course it is to be paid for at the usual rate, as I expressly so stated when I inclosed it to Graham. He has not written me a word on the subject, which induces me to think he may have written you. Please write me if you would have me speak further on the subject. The pay, however, is sure, though the amount may not be large, and I think you may wait until the article appears, before making further stipulations on the subject.

*Correspondent:* See p. 280.

¹ "Thomas Carlyle and His Works" appeared in *Graham's Magazine* in March 1847 (pp. 145-152) and April 1847 (pp. 238-245); see *Early Essays* 1975, pp. 219-267. Griswold had been the magazine's assistant editor from May 1842 to October 1843. George Rex Gra-

ham (1813-1894) of Philadelphia created the magazine in 1840 and made it one of the best of its time and one of the very few that paid its contributors. He pioneered the use of engraved plates made especially for the magazine, and he supported and appealed to women writers and readers. His writers included Lydia Sigourney, Catherine Sedgwick, Longfellow, and, most prominently, Poe, who preceded Griswold as editor.

*Copy-text: HDT* 1882, 219-220

*Published: HDT* 1882, 219-220; *Cor* 1958, 170

*Editor's Notes*
    PE supplies the date "September 30, 1846" based on information in *HDT* 1882.
    Greeley suggests that Graham might have written to T; Sanborn's footnote in *HDT* 1882 states "No such letter appears."

## From Ralph Waldo Emerson
*Late September 1846*

Will Mr Thoreau please to bear in mind that when there is good mortar in readiness, Mr Dean[1] must be summoned to fit the air-tight stove to the chimney in the school-room; unless Mr T. can do it with convenience[a] himself.

*Correspondent:* See p. 53.

    [1] As Tilton suggests, Dean is probably James Dean, a Concord mason (*Letters of RWE* 1990-1995, 8:91-92n67).

*Copy-text:* AL (NN-BGC, Henry David Thoreau Collection, 1837-1917, Series IV)

*Published:* "Emerson-Thoreau Correspondence," *AM* 69 (June 1892): 742; *Cor* 1958, 195; *Letters of RWE* 1990-1995, 8:91-92

*Editor's Notes*
    This letter is addressed "H. D. Thoreau".
    PE supplies the date "Late September 1846" based on two of Emerson's letters to Lidian, dated September 11 and 15 respectively, as well as information from Emerson's account book. In his letters Emerson mentions making "a chamber over the schoolroom in

the barn" and indicates that "Thoreau is to build" the barn room (*Letters of RWE* 1939, 3:347, 348). In Emerson's account book for 1845-1849, "an 1846 entry under the date September 30" records a payment in advance "to Thoreau of $15" (*Letters of RWE* 1990-1995, 8:91-92n67).

*Author's Alteration*
  convenience] ease

## From Horace Greeley
*October 26, 1846*

New York, Oct. 26ª, 1846

My Friend Thoreau,

  I know you think it odd that you have not heard farther, and perhaps blame my negligence or engrossing cares, but if so without good reason.

  I have to-day received a letter from Griswold in Phila-delphia, who says:

  "The article by Thoreau on Carlyle is in type and will be paid for 'liberally.'"

  'Liberally' is quoted as an expression of Graham's. I know well the difference between a publisher's and an author's idea of what *is* 'liberally,' but I give you the best I can get, as the result of three letters to Phila. on this subject.

  Success to you, my friend! Remind Mr and Mrs. Em-erson of my existence, and my lively remembrance of their various kindnesses. Yours, very busy in our Political contest,[1]

Horace Greeley.

*Correspondent:* See p. 280.

[1] Greeley, who founded the *New-York Daily Tribune* as a Whig organ, busily championed the candidacy of John Young and Ham-ilton Fish, the Whig candidates for governor and lieutenant gov-ernor, respectively, in 1846. The ballot that year was crowded with important state issues, including proposals to revise the state con-stitution, reform the judiciary, and grant suffrage to blacks, all of

which the *Tribune* favored. The election was held on November 4: Young was elected but Fish lost; the constitution was reformed (though it lost in New York City), but voters defeated black suffrage by a large margin.

*Copy-text:* Facsimile of ALS (Bicknell)

*Published:* HDT 1882, 221-222; *Cor* 1958, 171

*Editor's Note*
   This letter is addressed "H. D. Thoreau, Esq / care of R. W. Emerson, / Concord, Massachusetts", postmarked "N{*illegible*}K 5 CtS 27 OCT", and endorsed "H. Greeley".

*Author's Alteration*
   26] 16


## From Horatio Robinson Storer
*January 17, 1847*

                              Boston Jan. 17th. 1847.
Dear Sir,
   Understanding from my Father[a], Dr Storer,[1] that you took a deep interest in the study of Ichthyology, and presuming that the other branches of the Animal Kingdom are not devoid of attraction to you, I have taken the liberty to ask a favor of you. I have for several years paid considerable attention to Oology and have made quite a respectable collection of bird's eggs, and I should be much obliged for your cooperation in assisting me to augment it; from the situation of your residence you probably have many advantages during the building season of procuring specimens. If I can be of any assistance to you in your researches in[a] Natural History, although I have but little time, being a student at Old Harvard, pray command me,
                              yr's resp'ctfully
                              Horatio R. Storer
                              14 Winter St.

*Correspondent:* Horatio Robinson Storer (1830-1922), son of David Humphrys and Abby Jane Brewer Storer, was a member of the

Harvard class of 1850. He studied with Louis Agassiz and with Asa Gray, and he went on a Labrador expedition to collect data that would serve as the basis of a published work on the fishes of Nova Scotia and Labrador. He later became a doctor. One of the first gynecologists in the United States, he worked to decriminalize abortions and furthered the use of chloroform in obstetrics. Storer was married three times. In 1853 he married Emily Elvira Gilmore (1833-1872), daughter of Addison and Emily Patten Gilmore; in 1872 he married Emily's sister Augusta Charlotte Gilmore (1841-1874); in 1876 he married Frances S. Mackenzie (d. 1910).

[1] David Humphrys Storer (1804-1891), son of Woodbury and Margaret Boyd Storer, graduated from Bowdoin College in 1822 and from the Harvard Medical School in 1825. In 1829 he married Abby Jane Brewer (1810-1885), daughter of Thomas and Abigail Stone Brewer. Specializing in obstetrics, Storer helped to found the Tremont Street Medical School in Boston and joined the Harvard Medical School after it was reorganized in 1854. A distinguished naturalist, Storer published reports on the fish of Massachusetts (see pp. 294-295, note 1).

*Copy-text:* ALS (Dawson)

*Editor's Note*
This letter is addressed "Henry D. Thoreau, Esq. / Concord, / Mass.", postmarked "BOSTON {*illegible*} JAN 25", and endorsed "H. Storer".

*Author's Alterations*
Father] father
in] *interlined above cancelled* on

## From Horace Greeley
*February 5, 1847*

New York, Feb. 5th, 1847.[a]

My Dear Thoreau:
Although your letter only came to hand to-day, I attended to its subject yesterday, when I was in Philadelphia on my way home from Washington. Your article is this moment in type, and will appear about the 20th inst. as *the leading article* in Graham's Mag. for next month. Now don't object to this, nor be unreasonably sensitive at

the delay.[1] It is immensely more important to you that the article should appear thus (that is, if you have any literary aspirations,) than it is that you should make a few dollars by issuing it in some other way. As to lecturing, you have been at perfect liberty to deliver it as a lecture a hundred times if you had chosen–the more the better. It is really a good thing, and I will see that Graham pays you fairly for it. But its appearance there is worth far more to you than money.

I know there has been too much delay, and have done my best to obviate it. But I could not. A Magazine that pays, and which it is desirable to be known as a contributor to, is always crowded with articles, and has to postpone some for others of even less merit. I[a] do thus myself with good things that I am not required to pay for.

Thoreau, do not think hard[a] of Graham. Do not try to stop the publication of your article. It is best as it is. But just set down and write a like article about Emerson, which I will give you $25 for if you cannot do better with it; then one about Hawthorne at your leisure, &c. &c. I will pay you the money for each of these articles on delivery, publish them when and how I please, leaving to you the copyright expressly. In a year or two, if you take care not to write faster than you think, you will have the material of a volume worth publishing, and then we will see what can be done.

There is a text somewhere in St. Paul–my Scriptural reading is getting rusty–which says 'Look not back to the things which are behind, but rather to those which are before,'[2] &c. Commending this to your thoughtful appreciation, I am,

Yours, &c.<br>Horace Greeley.

Regards to Mr[a]. and Mrs. Emerson.

*Correspondent:* See p. 280.

[1] T was unhappy with Griswold's delay in publishing "Thomas

Carlyle and His Works" and about the decision to publish it in two installments (see pp. 279-280).

² Phil. 3:13-14: "but *this* one thing *I do*, forgetting those things which are behind, and reaching forth unto those things which are before, I press toward the mark for the prize of the high calling of God in Christ Jesus."

*Copy-text:*  ALS (VtMiM, Greeley/1)

*Published:  HDT* 1882, 222-224; *Cor* 1958, 173-174

*Editor's Note*
   This letter is addressed "Henry D. Thoreau, Esq. / care of R. W. Emersons / Esq. / Concord, / Massachusetts.", postmarked "U.S. EXPRESS MAIL N.Y. N. YORK FEB 5", and endorsed "H. Greeley".

*Author's Alterations*
   Feb. 5ᵗʰ, 1847.] *interlined above cancelled* Jan
   I] ~,
   hard] *preceded by cancelled* of
   Mr] Mrs


## To Horatio Robinson Storer
*February 15, 1847*

Concord Feb. 15ᵗʰ 1847

Dear Sir,

   I have not forgotten your note which I received some-time since. Though I live in the woods I am not so attentive an observer of birds as I was once, but am satisfied if I get an occasional sight of or sound from them. My pursuits at present are such that I am not very likely to meet with any specimens which you will not have obtained. Moreover, I confess to a little squeamishness on the score of robbing their nests, though I could easily go to the length of ab-stracting an egg or two gently, now and then, and if the advancement of science obviously demanded it might be carried even to the extreme of deliberate murder.

   I have no doubt that you will observe a greater num-ber of species in or near the College Yard than I can here. I have noticed that in an open country, where there are but few trees, there are more attractions for many species of birds than in a wooded one. They not only find food there in greater abundance, but protection against birds of prey; and even if they are no more numerous than elsewhere, the few trees are necessarily more crowded with nests. Many of my classmates were quite successful in collecting birds nests and eggs, and they did not have to go far from the college-yard to find them– I remember a pigeon woodpecker's nest in the[a] grove on the east side of the yard, which annually yielded a number of eggs to collectors, while the bird steadily supplied the loss like a hen, until my chum demolished the whole with a hatchet. I found another in the next field chipped nearly two feet into a solid stump. And in one of the fields near the yard I used to visit daily in the winter the dwelling of an ermine-weasel in a hollow apple tree. But of course one must be a greater traveller than this if he would make anything like a complete collection.

There are many whipporwills & owls about my house, and perhaps with a little pains one might find their nests. I hope you have more nimble and inquisitive eyes to serve you than mine now are– However, if I should chance to stumble on any rarer nest I will not forget your request. If you come to Concord again, as I understand you sometimes do, I shall be[e] glad to see you at my hut–

Trusting that you will feather your own nest[1] comfortably without stripping those of the birds quite bare– I am

Yrs &c

Henry D. Thoreau.

*Correspondent:* See pp. 284-285.

[1] The proverb "feather one's nest" was current by the sixteenth century.

*Copy-text:* ALS (VtMiM, Thoreau/3)

*Published: Saturday Review of Literature* 21 (November 11, 1939): 9; *NEQ* 13 (1940): 30-31; Reginald Lansing Cook, *The Concord Saunterer: Including a Discussion of the Nature Mysticism of Thoreau*

(Middlebury, Vt.: Middlebury College Press, 1940), 62-63; *Cor* 1958, 175-176

*Editor's Notes*
    This letter is addressed "Horatio B. Storer / 14 Winter Street / Boston", postmarked "CONCORD MASS FEB 16", and endorsed "Henry D. Thoreau / Concord / Mass. / Feb 15^th 1847. / <u>Oology</u>".
    be] *PE*; b{*MS torn*}

*Author's Alteration*
    the] *interlined with a caret*


## From Henry Williams Jr.
*March 1, 1847*

                                        *Boston, March 1, 1847.*
*Dear Sir,*
    The following inquiries are made agreeably to a vote passed at the Last Annual Meeting of the Class, with a view to obtain authentic information concerning each one of its members, and to enable the Secretary to record facts now easily obtainable, but which, from year to year, it will be more and more difficult to collect.
    You are respectfully requested to answer the questions proposed, as fully as may be convenient and agreeable to you, and to add such other facts concerning your life, before or after entering College, as you are willing to communicate. The answers are to be recorded in the Class Book for future reference.
    *Please to address* Henry Williams, Jr., *Boston; post paid.*
                        *Very Respectfully and Truly Yours,*
                        Henry Williams, Jr., *Class Secretary.*
                            ————^e

    1. When and where were you born?
    2. Where were you fitted for College, and by whom?
    3. If married, when, where, and to whom?
    4. What is your profession? If learned, with whom studied? If mercantile, where and with whom begun?

5. What are your present employment and residence?

6. Mention any general facts of importance before or since graduating.

*Correspondent:* Henry Williams Jr. (1816-1901), son of Henry and Harriet Dickinson Williams, was the Harvard class of 1837 secretary. He studied medicine but abandoned the profession to become a schoolmaster in Boston. In 1840 he married Julia West Williams (1818-1874), daughter of Ralph and Pamelia Ware Williams.

*Copy-text:*  Printed document (MH-Ar, HUD 237.505)

*Published:*  *ESQ* 7 (1957): 5; *Cor* 1958, 176-177

*Editor's Notes*
   T's copy of the form letter is not extant, but his September 30 response to Williams indicates that he had received it. The copy-text is the form letter returned by T's classmate John Weiss; Weiss's responses have been omitted.
   All of the document except "Henry Williams, Jr.," is printed.
   ———] *PE*; *double line in copy-text*

## From James Elliot Cabot
*May 3, 1847*

I carried them[1] immediately to Mr. Agassiz,[2] who was highly delighted with them,[e] and began immediately to spread them out and arrange them for his draughtsman. Some of the species he had seen before, but never in so fresh condition. Others, as the breams and the pout, he had seen only in spirits, and the little turtle[v] he knew only from the books. I am sure you would have felt fully repaid for your trouble, if you could have seen the eager satisfaction with which he surveyed each fin and scale. He said the small mud-turtle was really a very rare species, quite distinct from the snapping-turtle. The breams and pout seemed to please the Professor very much. He would gladly come up to Concord to make a spearing excursion, as you suggested, but is drawn off by numerous and pressing engagements. Of the perch Agassiz remarked that it was almost identical with that of Europe, but distinguishable, on close examination, by the tubercles on the sub-operculum.... More of the painted tortoises would be acceptable. The snapping turtles are very interesting to him as forming a transition from the turtles proper to the alligator and crocodile.... We have received three boxes from you since the first.

*Correspondent:* James Elliot Cabot (1821-1903), son of Samuel and Elizabeth Perkins Cabot, graduated from Harvard University in 1840 and from the Harvard Law School in 1845. He became an architect after a two-year stint as a lawyer. In 1857 he married Elizabeth Dwight (1830-1901), daughter of Edmund and Mary Eliot Dwight. Cabot helped Emerson arrange and publish his late works, and he published a two-volume *Memoir of Ralph Waldo Emerson* in 1887. At the time of this letter, Cabot was an assistant to Jean Louis Rodolphe Agassiz, professor of zoology and geology at Harvard's Lawrence Scientific School.

[1] T had sent several specimens of Concord fauna to Cabot, who delivered them to Agassiz. In a letter dated "Saturday 1 May 1847" and mailed from Cambridge to Brookline, Agassiz wrote Cabot about T's specimens (MH-H, MS Am 1719 [2]):

> I have been highly pleased to find that the small mud Turtle was really the Sternothorus odoratus, as I suspected, a Very rare species quite distinct from the Snapping Turtle, and should be much obliged if it was possible for you to secure some more specimens for me. The suckers were all of one and the same species, the Catostomus tuberculatus; the female has the tubercles.
>
> As I am very anxious to send some Snapping Turtles home with my first boxes I would thank your friend very much if he could have some taken for me.–

Sanborn quotes Agassiz's letter to Cabot in *FL* 1894 and indicates that it was written on the same day as Cabot's letter to T, which Sanborn in *HDT* 1882 dates "May 3, 1847." Agassiz's letter, however, is correctly dated: May 1 was a Saturday in 1847.

[2] Jean Louis Rodolphe Agassiz (1807-1873), born in Switzerland, was an internationally known zoologist and geologist. He had a distinguished career at the University of Neuchâtel from 1832 to 1846, where he made his reputation with his self-published *Histoire naturelle des poissons d'eau douce de l'Europe centrale* (Neuchâtel:

d'O. Petitpierre, 1839-1845) and *Études sur les glaciers* (Neuchâtel: Jent et Gassmann, 1840). Agassiz opposed the theories of Charles Darwin, and he was the first to publicize the idea that the earth had once experienced an ice age. He immigrated to the United States in 1846 and taught at Harvard from 1847 to 1873.

*Copy-text:* PE lines 290.20-21 (I carried ... with them,), *HDT* 1882, 243-244; PE lines 290.21-22 (and began ... draughtsman.), *FL* 1894, 155; PE lines 290.23-34 (Some of ... engagements.), *HDT* 1882, 244; PE lines 290.34-291.7 (Of the perch ... first.), *FL* 1894, 156

*Published:* HDT 1882, 243-244; FL 1894, 155-156, 156; FL 1906, 130, 131; Cor 1958, 177-178

*Editor's Notes*
The copy-text is a composite of two published sources, *HDT* 1882 and *FL* 1894. PE supplies the date "May 3, 1847" based on information in *HDT* 1882. The ellipsis points are in *FL* 1894, the copy-text for the portion in which they appear.
    them,] *PE;* them. *in copy-text (HDT 1882)*

*Substantive Variant*
The two published sources, *HDT* 1882 and *FL* 1894, overlap from 290.20 to 290.21 (was highly delighted) and from 290.23 to 290.28 (Some ... scale.). *HDT* 1882 is the copy-text for these lines; a potentially authoritative substantive reading in *FL* 1894 and *FL* 1906 is reported below.
    turtle] *in copy-text (HDT 1882);* tortoise *in FL 1894 and FL 1906*

## To James Elliot Cabot
*May 8, 1847*

Concord May 8th

-47

Dear Sir
    I believe that I have not yet acknowledged the receipt of your notes and a 5 dollar bill. I am very glad that the fishes afforded M. Agassis so much pleasure. I could easily have obtained more specimens of[a] the *Sternothaerus odoratus.* They are quite numerous here. I will send more of them ere long.

Snapping turtles are perhaps as frequently met with in our muddy river as anywhere, but they are not always to be had when wanted. It is now rather late in the season for them. As No one makes a business of seeking them, and they[a] are valued for soups, science may be forestalled by appetite in this market, and it will be necessary to bid pretty high to induce persons to obtain or preserve them. I think that from 75 cts to a dollar apiece would secure all that are[a] in any case[a] to be had, and will set this price upon their heads, if the treasury of science is full enough to warrant it.

You will excuse me for taking toll in the shape of some it may be impertinent and unscientific inquiries.

There are found in the waters of Concord, so far as I know, the following kinds of fishes.

Pickerel–  Beside the common fishermen distinguish the Brook or Grass Pickerel[a]–[e]which bites differently–and has a shorter snout–  Those caught in Walden pond by my house are easily distinguished from those caught in the river, being much heavier in proportion to their size, stouter–firmer fleshed, and lighter colored. The little pickerel which I sent last jumped into the boat in its fright.

Pouts. Those in the pond are of different appearance from those I have sent.

Breams–  Some more green others more brown.

Suckers–  The *Horned*[a] which I sent first–& the black. I am not sure whether the *Common or Boston* sucker is found here. Are the three which I sent last which were speared[a] in the river–identical with the 3 *black suckers* taken by hand in a brook, which I sent before? I have never examined them minutely.[a]

Perch–  The river perch of which I sent 5 specimens in the box–are darker colored than those found in the pond. There are myriads of small ones in the latter place and but few large ones. I have counted 10 transverse bands on some of the smaller.

Lampreys– very scarce since the dams at Lowell & Billerica were built.

Shiners– *Leuciscus Crysoleucas*–silver & golden– What
is the difference?

Roach or Chivin– *Leuciscus pulchellus–Argenteus*–or
what not– The *white* and the *red*–the former described
by Storer[1]–but the latter which deserves distinct notice,
not described to my knowledge.– Are the Minnows
(called here dace) of which I sent 3 live specimens I believe, one larger & 2 smaller, the young of this species?

Trout of different appearance in different brooks in this
neighborhood.

Eels–[a]

Red-finned Minnows, of which I sent you a dozen alive– I
have never recognized these in any book.

> Have they any scientific name? If convenient will you
> let Dr. Storer see these?[a]

Brook Minnows,

There is also a kind of Dace or fresh water smelt in the
pond–which is perhaps distinct from any of the above.

What of the above does M. Agassis particularly wish
to see– Does He want more specimens of kinds which I
have already sent? There are also minks muskrats–frogs–
lizards–tortoises, snakes caddice worms, leeches, mus-
cles, &c &c or rather *here* they are[a]

The funds which you sent are nearly exhausted. Most
fishes can now be taken with the hook–and it will cost but
little trouble or money to obtain them. The snapping turtles will be the main expense. I should think that 5 dollars
more at least might be profitably expended here

Yrs &c

Henry D. Thoreau

*Correspondent:* See p. 291.

[1] D. Humphreys Storer and William B. O. Peabody, *Reports on the
Fishes, Reptiles and Birds of Massachusetts*, pp. 55-57. T owned a

copy of this volume and discussed it in "Natural History of Massachusetts," *Dial* 3 (July 1842): 19-40 (see *Excursions* 2007, pp. 3-28).

*Copy-text:* ALS (MCR-S, Cabot Family. Papers, 1786-1945, A-99, Folder 95)

*Published:* *FL* 1894, 150-153; *FL* 1906, 126-128; *Cor* 1958, 179-180

*Editor's Notes*
    This letter is addressed "J Elliot Cabot / 27 New Granite Buildings / Court Square / Boston", postmarked "CONCORD MAS. MAY 8", and endorsed "H. D. Thoreau".
    Pickerel–]*PE*; –Pickerel *in MS*

*Author's Alterations*
    of] *inserted*
    they] as
    are] *inserted*
    case] *followed by cancelled* are
    Pickerel] *interlined with a caret*
    Horned] *horned*
    speared] *interlined above cancelled* caught
    I have ... minutely.] *added*
    Eels–] *added*
    If ... these?] *added*
    or ... are] *added*


*From Isaac Thomas Hecker*
*May 15, 1847*

                                        May 15. 1847. Wittem.
Dear Friend.
    My interest in your greatest welfare compels me to write you a few lines, perhaps they may aid you in your progress. I have found my centre and of course my place in the Roman Catholic Church. This gives me the peace and liberty which have long been the object of my persuit. I have come to this result not as one who is ignorant or worse who has an erroneous idea of the C. Church would suppose, by being false to my nature, no, but by being true, true to my highest aspirations and ideal. My ideal is

real, or rather the ideal of humanity is the R. C. Church. I can readily conceive that those who know not what the Church is, will smile at this statement. But I repeat it. The Catholic Church is the ideal of every individual of the race, the universal ideal of humanity. It is for her communion the hearts of men sigh, it is for her perfection their souls aspire, she is the inspiration of humanity. Let those my friend smile who wish. Your singularities so called in your uncatholic community, and not only yours, are to a catholic so many proofs of this assertion. They are the evidences of the secret workings of that life which will and eventually must, so that you remain true, bring you into the unity of the one, holy, catholic Church. Be true O my friend! for all my hopes of ever meeting you[a] depend upon my confidence in your[a] fidelity, heroic fidelity. Be true the catholic Church is one and universal, take what road you will you will arrive into the bosom of her who is destined to receive the human race entire. Be true, for your ideal is real, divine, and means more than you are now aware of.

The soul once in actual communion with the Church a new life is commenced. It enters upon a higher, sublimer supernatural career. The beatific instinct of the soul fed with a supernatural food, invigorated with an uniterrupted divine excitement,–"grace",–gradually elevates the soul towards its ultimate end. It passess through violent combats and victories from sphere to sphere. After having passed countless struggles and made frequent conquests sustained only by this supernatural force, its forces and fidelity having been tried and purified, it reaches the end of its creation, the perfect union with, and immediate vision of God. This is the highest end for which the soul of Man can aspire. This is the destiny of each individual and of humanity. And this is the work of the C. Church. For she alone directs and furnishes her children with the means of obtaining this sublime end of their creation. This is but a simple statement of the Church in her rapport with the individual soul from the religious or mystic point of view. Her rapport with humanity, with society is equally triumphant and divine. Wherever her influence penetrates Man acts from a higher inspiration. She is the life of art, of poesy, of social happiness, of political freedom. True heroism is only found in her bosom. This is evident from its nature and prooven too by fact. A hero is one who possesses virtue in a heroic degree, invariable, constant even unto death. But this surpasses the natural forces of Man. Hence a Hero necessarily supposes the aid of a force supernatural, divine. A heroic act[a] is possible but an act does not make a Hero. But the Church, the Catholic Church is the sole organ of this force divine. Hence out of her communion heroism is impossible. For the fact. No sect seperated from the R. C. Church can show one example which will bear this test. Let them produce one example of a constant invariable heroic life in all the virtues if they can. They cannot. But this is the test of a Hero, a Saint in the language of the Church. It is such she has never ceased, and[a] never will cease to produce. This prooves her divine origin and sanctity and their cant and falsehood. It is a sad fact that Carlyle and many others, tho they recognize this[a] truth in the middle ages, when speaking of the present, make use of the same cant that all the flunkies have employed against the Church from Martin Luther to Joe Smith.[1] A little more disinterested research and study will it is to be hoped lead them to see what they are now ignorant of. The fact is my friend the protestant world lays under great ignorance, and is sadly deluded concerning the C. Church. The future lies hid in her bosom. O happy is he who sees it and becomes its voice.

Tho now my friend within cloistered walks in my cell I am infinitely freer than I was when breathing the air on Concord cliffs. After having passed one years Novitiate I was admitted to take the "vows". Let me tell thee my friend it is no small affair to be scholar in that school where Jesus the God-Man is Master. From the Novitiate I came to[a] the College where I now am. The community of this house is composed of upwards a hundred members.[2] The order is prohibited from begging and from holding benefices, thus it is thrown upon & supported by providence, the voluntary spontaneous[a] charity of the faithful. When I remember the dreams of fruitlands and see how far below[a] their boldest aspirations fall from what has existed for centuries in the C. Church and now exists, I am led to smile, but I esteem truly these men as far as they went. Would to God that they knew what they were striving after and had the manliness to act up to their aspirations. Tho the primary object of the order of which I am a member is the same as all other religious orders[a] {*MS torn*} render its members saints,–its distinctive characteristic is devotion[e] to the cause of the poor "the souls the most abandoned".[3] Its life is half contemplative & half active. Its founder St. Alphonse of Ligouri of Naples who lived in the latter part of the 18teenth century. If these men who say that the Church is dead would look a little below the surface of things they would see that the life of the middle ages which they laud so high is not dead, but only retarded by the enemies of the Church for a few centuries past, and which is now ready to burst upon the world in all its glory. We don't want the Middle Ages, but we want its inspiration. It is here my friend, it is here. Mon Dieu could you see & feel it once!

Your true & sincere Friend<br>I. Hecker

My address is. Chez les R. {*MS torn*} Redemptoristes. Wittem. Province de Limbourg[e] Hollande.

*Correspondent:* See p. 260.

[1] Joseph Smith (1805-1844) founded the Church of Jesus Christ of Latter-Day Saints in 1830.

² After spending a year at the Redemptorist novitiate in St. Trond, Belgium, Hecker went to the "house of studies" in Wittem, Holland, and became a Redemptorist, a member of the Congregation of the Most Holy Redeemer, a Roman Catholic missionary order dedicated to establishing missions and schools. The Redemptorist order was founded in 1732 by Alfonso Maria de' Liguori (1696-1787), a Neapolitan nobleman who was ordained in 1726 and became a bishop in 1762, and who was known as a reformer and moral theologian. The order began work in the United States in 1839 and was particularly effective among German immigrants.

³ Hecker refers to Liguori's vision of Redemptorists as missionaries to the most "abandoned" souls.

*Copy-text:* ALS (DStPC, Hecker Collection, Box 22, Folder 6)

*Editor's Notes*
    This letter is addressed "Henry Thorough / Concord. / <u>Massachusetts</u>."
    devotion] *PE*; d{*MS torn*}tion
    Limbourg] *PE*; Limbou{*MS torn*}

*Author's Alterations*
    you] *interlined with a caret*
    your] *preceded by cancelled* in
    act] *interlined with a caret*
    and] *preceded by cancelled* to
    this] the
    I came to] *interlined with a caret*
    spontaneous] *interlined with a caret*
    below] *preceded by cancelled* the
    orders] *followed by cancelled* Saint

## From James Elliot Cabot
*May 27, 1847*

Mr. Agassiz^v was very much^v surprised and pleased at the extent of the collections you sent during his absence in New York^e; the little fox he has established in comfortable quarters in his backyard^e, where he is doing well. Among the fishes you sent^v there is one, and^e probably two, new species. The fresh-water smelt he does not know. He is very anxious to see the pickerel with the long snout, which he suspects may be the *Esox estor*, or Maskalongé; he has seen this at Albany.... As to the minks, etc., I know they would all be very acceptable to him. When I asked him about these, and more specimens of what you have sent, he said, "I dare not make any request, for I do not know how much trouble I may be giving to Mr. Thoreau; but my method of examination requires many more specimens than most naturalists would care for."

*Correspondent:* See p. 291.

*Copy-text:* PE lines 299.31-36 (Mr. Agassiz ... new species.), *HDT* 1882, 244; PE lines 299.36-300.7 (The fresh-water ... care for."), *FL* 1894, 156-157

*Published:* *HDT* 1882, 244; *FL* 1894, 156-157; *FL* 1906, 131; *Cor* 1958, 181

*Editor's Notes*
   The copy-text is a composite of two published sources, *HDT* 1882 and *FL* 1894. PE supplies the date "May 27, 1847" based on information in *HDT* 1882 and *FL* 1894. The ellipsis points are in *FL* 1894, the copy-text for the portion in which they appear.
   in New York] *FL 1894; lacking in copy-text (HDT 1882)*
   backyard] *PE*; back- / yard *in copy-text (HDT 1882)*
   and] *FL 1894; lacking in copy-text (HDT 1882)*

*Substantive Variants*
   The two published sources, *HDT* 1882 and *FL* 1894, overlap from 299.31 to 299.32 (Agassiz ... absence) and from 299.34 to 299.36 (Among ... species). *HDT* 1882 is the copy-text for these lines; potentially authoritative substantive readings in *FL* 1894 and *FL* 1906 are reported below.
   Mr. Agassiz] *in copy-text (HDT 1882);* Agassiz *in FL 1894 and FL 1906*
   very much] *in copy-text (HDT 1882);* much *in FL 1894 and FL 1906*
   fishes you sent] *in copy-text (HDT 1882);* fishes *in FL 1894 and FL 1906*

## To Evert Augustus Duyckinck
*May 28, 1847*

Concord May 28th –47
Dear Sir,
   I should not have delayed sending you my manuscript so long,[1] if I had not known that delay would be no

inconvenience to you, and an[a] advantage to the reader. I will remind you, to save time, that I wish to be informed for what term the book is to be the property of the publishers,[a] and on what terms I can have 30 copies cheaply bound in boards without immediate expense.– If you take it–It[a] will be a great convenience to me to get through with the printing as soon as possible, as I wish to take a journey of considerable length[2] and should not be willing that any other than myself should correct the proofs.

If you will inform me, as soon as may be, whether you want the manuscript, and what are the most favorable terms on which you will print & publish it, you will greatly oblige

Yr's &c

Henry D. Thoreau.

*Correspondent:* Evert Augustus Duyckinck (1816-1878), son of Evert and Harriet June Duyckinck, graduated from Columbia University in 1835 and married Margaret Wolfe Panton (1820?-1890), daughter of Henry and Margaret Wolfe Panton, in 1840. Duyckinck, whose father was a New York publisher, studied law and became editor of a succession of literary magazines. The center of a movement he styled "Young America," Duyckinck edited Wiley and Putnam's Library of Choice Reading and championed Hawthorne and Melville as literary nationalists. He and his brother George Long Duyckinck published and edited the influential *Literary World* from October 1848 until the periodical went out of existence in 1853.

[1] For some time T's Concord friends had recommended him to Duyckinck, who had considerable influence with Wiley and Putnam. In his March 12, 1847, letter to Duyckinck, Emerson gave a forceful recommendation of T's account of his river excursion with John: "This book has many merits. It will be as attractive to *lovers of nature*, in every sense.... It will be attractive to scholars for its excellent literature, & to all thoughtful persons for its originality & profoundness.... It is really a book of the results of the studies of years" (*Letters of RWE* 1939, 3:384). Replying on March 15, Duyckinck told Emerson that he would like to read the manuscript (*Letters of RWE* 1939, 3:384n54). T continued revising and adding to the manuscript of *A Week on the Concord and Merrimack Rivers* for several weeks before submitting it to Duyckinck with this letter. He was evidently unaware of the consequences of his delay: by May

1847 Duyckinck had fallen into disfavor with Wiley and Putnam. For more information, see *A Week* 1980, pp. 458-462.

² Emerson had recommended T to his brother-in-law, Charles T. Jackson, who was to undertake a geological survey of the United States mineral lands in Michigan. Nothing came of the proposal, though T clearly was willing to go.

*Copy-text:* ALS (NN, Manuscripts and Archives Division, Duyckinck Family Papers, Literary Correspondence of Evert A. and George L. Duyckinck, Box 16)

*Published:* *Cor* 1958, 181-182

*Editor's Note*
This letter is addressed "Evert A. Duyckinck Esq / Care of Wiley & Putnam / 161 Broadway / New-York."

*Author's Alterations*
an] and
publishers,] ~~
It] if

## To James Elliot Cabot
*June 1, 1847*

Concord June 1ˢᵗ –47

Dear Sir,

I send you 15 pouts–17 perch–13 shiners–1 larger land tortoise, and 5 muddy tortoises all from the pond by my house also 7 perch–5 shiners–8 breams 4ᵃ dace? 2 muddy tortoises–5 painted do. and 3 land do.¹–all from the river–1 black snake alive & one deer-mouse? caught last night in my cellar. The tortoises were all put in alive–the fishes were alive yesterday i.e. Monday, and some this morn-ing.– Observe the difference between those from the pond which is pure water & those from the river–

I will send the light-colored trout & the pickerel with the longer snout–which is our large one when I meet with them. I have set a price upon the heads of snap-ping turtles–though it is late in the season to get them. If I wrote red-finned eel, it was a slip of the pen, I meant red finned-minnow. This is their name here, though smaller specimens have but a slight-reddish tinge at the base of the pectorals.

Will you at your leisure answer these queries. Do you mean to say that the 12 banded minnows which I sent are undescribed, or only one–? What are the scientific names of those minnows which have any?– Are the 4 dace I send today identical with one of the former–and what are they called?

Is there such a fish as the black Sucker described[a]–distinct from the common?

Yrs in great haste<br>Henry D. Thoreau.

*Correspondent:* See p. 291.

[1] By "do" T means "ditto," i.e., painted tortoises and land tortoises.

*Copy-text:* ALS (MCR-S, Cabot Family. Papers, 1786-1945, A-99, Folder 95)

*Published:* *FL* 1894, 153-154; *FL* 1906, 128-129; *Cor* 1958, 182-183

*Editor's Notes*
This letter is addressed "J Elliot Cabot / 27 New Granite Buildings / Court Square / Boston" and endorsed "H. D. Thoreau".

The document also contains pencilled notes in an unknown hand relating to Cabot's June 1, 1847, response to the questions T asks in this letter.

*Author's Alterations*
4] *preceded by cancelled* 5
described] *interlined with a caret*


## From James Elliot Cabot
*June 1, 1847*

Agassiz is delighted to find one, and he thinks two, more new species; one is a Pomotis,–the bream without the red spot in the operculum, and with a red belly and fins. The other is the shallower and lighter colored shiner. The four dace you sent last are *Leuciscus argenteus*. They are different from that you sent before under this name, but which was a new species. Of the four kinds of minnow, two are new. There is a black sucker (*Catastomus nigricans*), but there has been no specimen among those you have sent, and A. has never seen a specimen. He seemed to know your mouse, and called it the white-bellied mouse. It was the first specimen he had seen. I am in hopes to bring or send him to Concord, to look after new *Leucisci*, etc.

*Correspondent:* See p. 291.

*Copy-text: FL* 1894, 157

*Published: FL* 1894, 157; *FL* 1906, 131-132; *Cor* 1958, 183

*Editor's Note*
    PE supplies the date "June 1, 1847" based on information in *FL* 1894.

## To Evert Augustus Duyckinck
*June 14, 1847*

Concord Jun 14th 1847

Dear Sir,

    Will you please inform Mr Wiley that I have concluded to wait a fortnight for his answer.[1] As I should like to make some corrections in the MSS in the meanwhile, I will thank you if you will send it to me by Harnden's express to Boston and by Adams' to Concord,[2] and I will return it in ten days.

Yrs &c
Henry D. Thoreau

*Correspondent:* See p. 301.

[1] T had sent a version of *A Week on the Concord and Merrimack Rivers* to Duyckinck on May 28; see pp. 300-301.
[2] Augustus Adams ran a local express from Concord to the City Tavern in Boston.

*Copy-text:* ALS (CU-I, Special Collections and Archives, MS-S001)

*Published:* Adrian H. Joline, *Rambles in Autograph Land* (New York: G. P. Putnam's Sons, 1913), 293; *Cor* 1958, 173

## To Evert Augustus Duyckinck
*July 3, 1847*

Concord July 3ᵈ 1847.

Dear Sir,

I sent you my MSS.[1] this (Saturday) morning by Augustus Adams' and Harnden's expresses, and now write this, for greater security, that you may inform me if it does not arrive duly. If Mr. Putnam[2] is not likely to return for a considerable time yet, will you please inform

Yrs &c
Henry D. Thoreau.

*Correspondent:* See p. 301.

[1] T resubmitted the manuscript of *A Week on the Concord and Merrimack Rivers* after originally submitting it in May and getting it back from Duyckinck in June to make corrections. See pp. 300-301, 304.

[2] George Putnam of Wiley and Putnam.

*Copy-text:* ALS (NN, Manuscripts and Archives Division, Duyckinck Family Papers, Literary Correspondence of Evert A. and George L. Duyckinck, Box 16)

*Published:* *Cor* 1958, 184

*Editor's Note*

The copy-text is mounted on a heavier sheet; the present editor was able to inspect only page 1.

## To Evert Augustus Duyckinck
*July 27, 1847*

Concord July 27ᵗʰ 1847

Dear Sir

It is a little more than three weeks since I returned my MSS, sending a letter by mail at the same time for security, so I suppose that you have received it. If Mess^rs Wiley & Putnam are not prepared to give their answer now, will you please to inform me what further delay, if any, is *unavoidable*, that I may determine whether I had not better carry it elsewhere–for time is of great consequence to me.[1]

Yrs respectfully<br>Henry D Thoreau.

*Correspondent:*  See p. 301.

[1] No reply from Duyckinck survives, but Emerson wrote William Henry Furness on August 6 that, despite Duyckinck's "favorable opinion" of it, Wiley and Putnam "declined publishing" *A Week on the Concord and Merrimack Rivers*. In the same letter Emerson asked whether Abraham Hart or the firm of Kay and Brother would be interested in T's manuscript (*Letters of RWE* 1990-1995, 8:122).

*Copy-text:*  ALS (MHvFM)

*Published:*  *Cor* 1958, 184

*Editor's Note*
This letter is addressed "Evert A. Duyckinck Esq. / Care of Wiley & Putnam / 161 Broadway / New York." and postmarked "CONCORD {*illegible*}".

## To James Munroe and Company
*August 28, 1847*

Concord Aug 28^th 1847

Dear Sir,
Mr Emerson has showed me your note to him, and says that he thinks you^a must have misunderstood him.[1] If you will inform me how large an edition you contemplated, and what will be the whole or outside of the expense–(The book is about the size of one vol. of Emerson's essays)–I will consider whether I will pay one half the same–(or whatever of my part one^a half the profits has failed to pay)–*at the end of six months after the day of publication*, if that is agreeable to you. This arrangement to affect onely one edition. The MSS is quite ready and is now in New York.

Please answer this as soon as convenient.

> Yrs &c
>
> Henry D. Thoreau

PS. I should have said above–that I decline your proposition as it now stands.[2]

*Correspondent:* See p. 206.

[1] Munroe's note to Emerson is not extant, but it was apparently about the terms under which Munroe would agree to publish *A Week on the Concord and Merrimack Rivers*. T's November 14 letter to Emerson indicates that Munroe was one of four publishers who "declined printing it with the least risk to themselves" (see p. 316). See also *A Week* 1980, pp. 461-470.

[2] Emerson mistakenly thought that T and Munroe would come to terms, and he wrote Fuller the next day that "Thoreaus book is not yet published. though now on the point of concluding the contract" (*Letters of RWE* 1939, 3:413).

*Copy-text:* ALS (PHi, Ferdinand J. Dreer Collection, American Prose Writers)

*Published:* *American Literature* 25 (1954): 497; *Cor* 1958, 185

*Editor's Note*
This letter is addressed "James Munroe & Co. / Boston / Mass.", postmarked "CONCORD MAS. AUG 28", and endorsed "H. D. Thoreau / Aug 28/47".

*Author's Alterations*
you] A
one] to

*To Henry Williams Jr.*
*September 30, 1847*

> Concord Sept 30th 1847

Dear Sir,

I confess that I have very little class spirit, and have almost forgotten that I ever spent four years at Cambridge. That must have been in a former state of existence. It is difficult to realize that the old routine is still kept up. However, I will undertake at last to answer your questions as well as I can in spite of a poor memory and a defect of information.

1$^{st}$ then, I was born, they say, on the 12$^{th}$ of July 1817, on what is called the Virginia Road, in the east part of Concord.

2$^{nd}$ I was fitted, or rather made unfit, for College, at Concord Academy & elsewhere, mainly by myself, with the countenance of Phineas Allen, Preceptor.

3$^{d}$ I am$^a$ not married.

4$^{th}$ I dont know whether mine is a profession, or a trade, or what not. It is not yet learned, and in every instance has been practised before being studied. The mercantile part of it was begun *here* by myself alone.

–It is not one but legion.[1] I will give you some of the monster's heads. I am a Schoolmaster$^e$–a Private Tutor, a Surveyor–a Gardener, a Farmer–$^a$a Painter, I mean a House Painter, a Carpenter, a Mason, a Day-laborer$^e$, a Pencil-Maker, a Glass-paper$^a$ Maker, a Writer$^a$, and sometimes a Poetaster. If you will act the part of Iolas, and apply a hot iron to any of these heads,[2] I shall be greatly obliged to you.

5$^{th}$ My present employment is to answer such orders as may be expected from so general an advertisement as the above–that is, if I see fit, which is not always the case, for I have found out a way to live without what is commonly called employment or industry attractive or otherwise. Indeed my steadiest employment, if such it can be called, is to keep myself at the top of my condition, and ready for whatever may turn up in heaven or on earth. For the last two or three years I have lived in Concord woods alone, something more than a mile from any neighbor, in a house built entirely by myself.

6$^{th}$ I cannot think of a single general fact of any importance before or since graduating

Yrs &c

Henry D Thoreau

PS. I beg that the Class will not consider me an object of charity, and if any of them are in want of pecuniary assistance, and will make known their case to me, I will engage to give them some advice of more worth than money.

*Correspondent:* See p. 290.

[1] When Jesus asks him what his name is, the man with an unclean spirit in the country of the Gadarenes answers, "My name *is* Legion: for we are many" (Mark 5:9); see also Luke 8:30.

[2] Hercules's friend Iolaus helped him slay the nine-headed Lernæan Hydra: when Hercules cut off a head, Iolaus applied a burning iron to cauterize the wound, thus preventing the re-growth of two heads in the place of the severed one.

*Copy-text:* ALS (MH-Ar, HUD 237.505)

*Published: Memorials of the Class of 1837* (Boston: George H. Ellis, 1887), 38, 41-42; *Life* 1896, 88-89; *Pertaining to T* 1901, 163-164, 168-169; *T: Home* 1902, 324-325; *Cor* 1958, 185-186

*Editor's Notes*
This letter is addressed "Henry Williams Jr. / Boston / Mass.", postmarked "CONCORD M{*illegible*}. SEP{*illegible*}", and endorsed "Thoreau / Sep 30th 1847".
    Schoolmaster] *PE*; School- / master *in MS*
    Day-laborer] *PE*; Day- / laborer *in MS*

*Author's Alterations*
    am] was
    –] *added in margin*
    Glass-paper] glass-paper
    Writer] writer

## To Sophia Elizabeth Thoreau
*October 24, 1847*

Concord Oct 24th –47

Dear Sophia

I thank you for those letters about Ktadn and hope you will save and send me the rest and[a] anything else you may meet with relating to the Maine woods. That Dr Young is both young and green too at travelling in the woods.[1] However I hope he got "yarbs"[2] enough to satisfy him.– I went to Boston the 5th of this month to see Mr Emerson off to Europe. He sailed in the Washington Irving packet ship, the same in which Mr Hedge went before him.[3] Up to this trip, the first mate aboard this ship, was as I hear, one Stephens, a Concord boy–son of Stephens the carpenter who used to live[a] above Mr. Dennis'–[4] Mr E's state-room was like a carpeted dark closet, about six feet square, with a large key-hole for a window. The window was about as big as a saucer and the glass 2 inches thick.– not to mention another sky-light[e] over head in the deck, of the size of an oblong doughnut and about as opaque; of course it would be in vain to look up if any contemplative promenader had his foot upon it. Such will be his lodgings for two or three weeks–and instead of a walk in Walden woods, he will take a promenade on deck, where the few trees you know are stript of their bark. The steam tug carried the ship to sea against a head wind, without a rag of sail being raised.

I dont remember whether you have heard of the new telescope at Cambridge[5] or not. They think it is the best one in the world–and have already seen more than Lord Ross or Herschel.[6] I went to see Perez Blood's some time ago with Mr E.[7] He had not gone to bed, but was sitting in the woodshed in the dark alone, in his astronomical chair, which is all legs and rungs, with a seat which can be inserted at any height, we saw Saturn's ring, and the mountains in the moon, and the shadows in their craters, and the sunlight on the spurs of the Mts in the dark portion. &c &c  When I asked him the power of his glass, he said it was 85. But what is the power of the Cambridge glass? 2000!!! The last is about 23 feet long.

I think you may have a grand time this winter pursuing some study–keeping a Journal, or the like–while the snow lies deep without   Winter[a] is the time for study, you know, and the colder it is the more studious we are.

Give my respects to the whole Penobscot tribe,[8] and tell

them that I trust we are good brothers still, and endeavor to keep the chain of friendship bright–though I do dig up a hatchet now & then.

–I trust you will not stir from your comfortable winters quarters–Miss Bruin–or even put your head out of your hollow tree, till the sun has melted the snow in the Spring, and "the green buds, they are a swellin."[9]

from your
Brother Henry.

*Correspondent:* See p. 172.

[1] Aaron Young (1819-1898) was known for having explored Mount Katahdin in Maine; an account of his travel, "Dr. Young's Botanical Expedition to Mount Katahdin," was published in the *Bangor Daily Whig and Courier* from September 7 to September 11, 1847. Sophia, who was visiting the Thoreaus' Bangor relatives, had sent T some of the five-part essay. Young attended Bowdoin College in Brunswick, Maine, and Jefferson Medical College in Philadelphia, but he graduated from neither. He established himself as an apothecary in Bangor and pursued his love of botany through an appointment as the state botanist that lasted from 1847 to 1849. He published *A Flora of Maine* (Bangor, Maine: S. S. Smith) in 1848.

[2] A common pronunciation of "herbs".

[3] Emerson sailed for England from Boston on October 5 and arrived on October 22; Hedge had sailed on June 5. The two did not meet on the continent, as Emerson had expected they would. Emerson sailed from England on July 15, 1848, and arrived in Boston on July 27. T lived in Emerson's house during his absence.

[4] Probably Samuel Dennis.

[5] In May 1846, three years after the appearance of the Great Comet of 1843, Harvard ordered a refracting telescope with a fifteen-inch lens from Merz and Mahler of Munich. It was at the time the most powerful telescope in the United States. On June 23, 1847, Harvard astronomers viewed the Andromeda Nebula and determined that it was not a nebula but was composed of separate stars. On September 19 they discovered the eighth moon of Saturn.

[6] William Parsons, third Earl of Rosse (1800-1867), began building telescopes in 1827 and eventually designed and built a reflecting telescope with a six-foot mirror mounted at the end of a tube fifty-eight feet long. He began making observations in February 1845. John Frederick William Herschel (1792-1871) was the foremost

astronomer of his era. Son of the eminent astronomer Friedrich Wilhelm Herschel (1738-1822), Herschel continued his father's observations of nebulae and double stars and led an expedition to study the southern sky from Capetown.

[7] Perez Blood (1785-1856), son of Thaddeus and Hannah Blood, had a farm near the Carlisle town line. An amateur astronomer, Blood had "used his small inheritance of money from his father to buy a telescope and celestial globe" (*JMN*, 10:315). T visited Blood again in 1851 and observed in his Journal: "I was amused to see what sort of respect this man with a telescope had obtained from his neighbors–something akin to that which savages award to civilized men–though in this case the interval between the parties was very slight." Blood, "with his scull cap on his short figure–his north European figure", made T think of the sixteenth-century Danish astronomer Tycho Brahe. T concluded then that he himself was "still contented to see the stars with [his] naked eye" (*Journal 3: 1848-1851*, ed. Robert Sattelmeyer, Mark R. Patterson, and William Rossi [Princeton, N.J.: Princeton University Press, 1990], p. 289). In March 1854, however, T bought himself a spyglass-type telescope which he had long wanted and of which he was "prepared to make a perfect use" (*Journal 8: 1854*, ed. Sandra Harbert Petrulionis [Princeton, N.J.: Princeton University Press, 2002], pp. 41, 61).

[8] The Thoreau relatives in Bangor included T's cousins Rebecca Jane Billings, married to George Augustus Thatcher, and Mary Ann Billings, married to Charles Lowell, and their families; see p. 45, note 5, and p. 385.

[9] T alludes to the following stanza from the ballad "Barbara Allen's Cruelty" (Thomas Percy, ed., *Reliques of Ancient English Poetry*, 3:125):

> All in the merrye month of may,
>> When greene buds they were swellin,
> Yong Jemmye Grove on his death-bed lay,
>> For love of Barbara Allen.

*Copy-text:* ALS (NjP, Robert H. Taylor Collection of English and American Literature, 1280s-1950, Series III, Box 19, Folder 34)

*Published:* *HDT* 1882, 281; *Life* 1890, 138; "Emerson-Thoreau Correspondence," *AM* 69 (June 1892): 736-737; *FL* 1894, 158-160; *FL* 1906, 132-134; *Cor* 1958, 187-188

*Editor's Note*
  sky-light] *PE*; sky- / light *in MS*

*Author's Alterations*
   the rest and] *interlined with a caret*
   live] love
   Winter] winter

## To Ralph Waldo Emerson
*November 14, 1847*

Concord Nov 14ᵗʰ 1847.

Dear Friend,

I am but a poor *neighbor* to you here–a very poor companion am I–  I understand that very well–but that need
not prevent my *writing* to you now. I have almost never
written letters in my life, yet I think I can write as good
ones as I frequently see, so I shall not hesitate to write this
such as it may be, knowing that you will welcome anything that reminds you of Concord.

I have banked up the young trees against the winter
and the mice, and I will look out in my careless way to
see when a pale is loose, or a nail drops out of its place.
The broad gaps at least I will occupy. I heartily wish that
I could be of good service to this household–but I who
have used only these ten digits so long to solve the problem of a living–how can I? This world is a cow that is hard
to milk–  Life does not come so easy–and ah! how thinly
it is watered ere we get it–  But the young bunting calf–he
will get at it. There is no way so direct. This is to earn one's
living by the sweat of his brow. It is a little like joining a
community–this life–to such a hermit as I am–and as I
dont keep the accounts I dont know whether this experiment will succeed or fail finally. At any rate, it is good for
society–& I do not regret my transient–nor my permanent
share in it.¹

Lidian and I make very good housekeepers–she is a
very dear sister to me–  Ellen & Edith & Eddy² & Aunty
Brown³ keep up the tragedy & comedy & tragi-comedy of
life as usual. The two former have not forgotten their old

acquaintance–even Edith carries a young memory in her head, I find. Eddie can teach us all how to pronounce. If you should discover any new and rare breed of wooden or pewter horses I have no doubt he will know how to appreciate it. He occasionally surveys mankind from my shoulders as widely & wisely as ever Johnson did.[4] I respect him not a little, though it is I that lift him up there so unceremoniously– And sometimes I have to set him down again in a hurry, according to his "mere will & good pleasure."[5] He very seriously asked me the other day–"Mr Thoreau–will you be my father?" I am occasionally Mr Rough-and-Tumble with him–that I may not miss *him*, and lest he should miss you too much– So you must come back soon, or you will be superseded.

Alcott has heard that I laughed & so set the people a laughing at his arbor, though I never laughed louder than when on the ridge pole.[6] But now I have not laughed for a long time, it is so serious. He is very grave to look at. But not knowing all this I strove innocently enough the other day to engage his attention to my mathematics. "Did you ever study geometry?"– "The relation of straight lines to curves–the transition from the finite to the infinite?"– "Fine things about it in Newton & Leibnitz."– But he would hear none of it.– Men of taste preferred the natural curve– Ah! he is a crooked stick himself. He is getting on now so many *knots* an hour– There is one knot at present occupying the *point* of highest elevation–the present highest point–and as many knots as are *not* handsome, I presume, are thrown down & cast into the pines.[7] Pray show him this if you meet him anywhere in London, for I cannot make him hear much plainer words here. He forgets that I am neither old, nor young, nor anything in particular, and behaves as if I had still some of the animal heat in me. As for the building I feel a little oppressed when I come near it, it has so great a disposition to be beautiful. It is certainly a wonderful structure on the whole, and the fame of the architect will endure as long- -as it shall stand. I should not show you this side alone if I did not suspect that Lidian had done ample justice to the other.

Mr Hosmer has been working at a tannery in Stow for a fortnight, though he has just now come home sick- It seems that he was a tanner in his youth-& So he has made up his mind a little at last. This comes of reading the New Testament[a]. Was'nt one of the apostles a tanner?[8] Mrs Hosmer remains here, and John looks stout enough to fill his own shoes and his father's too.[9]

Mr. Blood and his company have at length seen the stars through the great telescope, and he told me that he thought it was worth the while. Mr Peirce[10,a] made them wait till the crowd had dispersed (it was a Saturday evening) & then was quite polite. He conversed with him & showed him the Micrometer &c- He said that Mr B's glass was large enough for all ordinary astronomical work. Mr Frost & Dr Bartlett[11] seemed disappointed that there was no greater difference between the Cambridge glass and the Concord one. They used only a power of four hundred. Mr B tells me that he is too old to study the Calculus or higher mathematics

They think that they have discovered traces of another satellite to Neptune- They have been obliged to exclude the public altogether at last-the very dust which they raised "which is filled with minute crystals &c &c" as professors declare, having to be wiped off the glasses, would ere long wear them away. It is true enough. Cambridge college is really beginning to wake up and redeem its character & overtake the age. I see by the new catalogue that they are about establishing a Scientific school in connexion with the University-at which any one above eighteen, on paying one hundred dollars annually-(Mr Lawrence's 50000 will probably diminish this sum) may be instructed in the highest branches of Science[12]-in

Astronomy theoretical and practical, with the use of the instruments–so the great Yankee Astronomer may be born without delay–in Mechanics and Engineering to the last degree–  Agassiz will ere long commence his lectures in the zoological department–a[a] Chemistry Class has already been formed, and is under the direction of Prof. Horsford–[13]  A new and adequate building for these purposes is already being erected. They have been foolish enough to put at the end of all this earnest the old joke of a diploma. Let every sheep keep but his own skin, I say.[14]

I have had a tragic correspondence, for the most part all on one side, with Miss Ford.[15] She did really wish to–I hesitate to write–marry me–that is the way they spell it. Of course I did not write a deliberate answer–how could I deliberate upon it? I sent back as distinct a *No*, as I have learned to pronounce after considerable practice, and I trust that this No has succeeded. Indeed I wished that it might burst like hollow shot after it had struck and buried itself, and make itself felt there. *There was no other way.* I really had anticipated no such foe as this in my career.

I suppose you will like to hear of my book–though I have nothing worth writing about it–indeed for the last month or two I have forgotten it–but shall certainly remember it again. Wiley & Putnam–Munroe[16]–The Harpers–& Crosby & Nichols–have all declined printing it with the least risk to themselves–but Wiley & Putnam will print it in their series–and any any of them anywhere at *my* risk. If I liked the book well enough I should not delay, but for the present I am indifferent. I believe this is after all the course you advised–to let it lie.

I do not know what to say of myself. I sit before my green desk in the chamber at the head of the stairs–and attend to my thinking–sometimes more sometimes less distinct. I am not unwilling to think great thoughts if there are any in the wind, but what they are I am not sure. They suffice to keep me awake while the day lasts, at any rate. Perhaps they will redeem some portion of the night ere long.

–I can imagine you astonishing–bewildering–con-
founding and sometimes delighting John Bull with your
Yankee notions–and that he begins to take a pride in the
relationship at last–introduced to all the stars of England
in succession after the lectures,[17] until you pine to thrust
your head once more into a genuine & unquestionable
nebula–if there be any left. I trust a common man will be
the most uncommon to you before you return to these
parts. I have thought there was some advantage even in
death, by which we "minghle with the herd of common
men."[18]

Hugh still has his eyes on the Walden agellum, and
orchards are waving there in the windy future for him.[19]
That's-the-where-I'll-go-next thinks he–[a]but no important steps are yet taken. He[e] reminds me occasionally of
this open secret of his with which the very reason seems
to labor, and affirms sincerely that as to his wants, wood,
stone, or timber–I know better than he. That is a clincher
which I shall have to consider how to avoid to some
extent, but I fear that it is a wrought nail and will not
break. Unfortunately the day after Cattle-show[e]–the
day after small beer, he was among the missing, but
not long this time. The Ethiopian cannot change his skin,
nor the leopard his spots[20]–nor indeed Hugh his[a] Hugh.

As I walked over Conantum the other afternoon I saw
a fair column of smoke rising from the woods directly
over my house that was, as I judged, and already began
to conjecture if my deed of sale would not be made in-
valid by this. But it turned out to be John Richardson's
young wood[21] on the SE of your field–  It was burnt nearly
all over & up to the rails and the road. It was set on fire
no doubt by the same Lucifer that lighted Brooks' lot before.[22] So you see that your small lot is comparatively safe
for this season, the back fires having been already set for
you.

They have been choosing between John Keyes & Sam
Staples if the world wants to know it[a] as representatives of

this town–and Staples is chosen.[23] The candidates for Governor[a]–think of my writing this to you–were Gov. Briggs
& Gen Cushing–& Briggs is elected, though the Democrats have gained.[24] Aint I a brave boy to know so much
of politics for the nonce? but I should'nt have known it if
Coombs[25] had'nt told me. They have had a Peace[a] meeting
here–  I should'nt think of telling you of it if I did'nt know
that anything would do for the English market, and some
men–Dea Brown at the head–have signed a long pledge
swearing that they will "treat all mankind as brothers"
henceforth. I think I shall wait and see how they treat me
first. I think that nature meant kindly when she made our
brothers few. However, my voice is still for peace.

So Good-bye and a truce to all joking–My Dear Friend–
from H. D. T.

*Correspondent:*  See p. 53.

[1] A play on the title of Theodore Parker's 1841 sermon published
as *A Discourse on the Transient and Permanent in Christianity*.

[2] Edward Waldo Emerson (1844-1930), the Emersons' second
son.

[3] Lucy Brown.

[4] T alludes to the opening lines in "The Vanity of Human Wishes"
(*The Works of Samuel Johnson*, 1:207):

> Let Observation, with extensive view,
> Survey mankind from China to Peru;
> Remark each anxious toil, each eager strife,
> And watch the busy scenes of crowded life;

[5] Cameron (*Companion* 1964, p. 44) suggests a possible echo of
Phil. 2:13: "For it is God which worketh in you both to will and to do
of *his* good pleasure."

[6] The ridge pole is the horizontal beam at the ridge of the roof.
Emerson, T, and Alcott went to Walden on June 14, 1847, to cut
hemlocks for a summerhouse that the latter two were to build for
Emerson. Alcott was clearly taken with the project, which he called
"Sylvan." He "set the nine upright joists, to form the corners for the
nine Muses to this poet's bower." His "sweeping brackets" recalled
some design features of Egyptian architecture, and he found himself "pursuing [his] charming occupation to bed and all through
the night long, in happy dreams" (*Journals of Bronson Alcott* 1938,

pp. 196-197). Emerson, unimpressed, wrote Lidian in August: "Mr Alcott & Henry are laboring at the summer house, which, in spite of their joint activity, has not yet fallen. A few more spikes driven would to all appearance shatter the supporters. I think to call it Tumbledown-Hall" (*Letters of RWE* 1939, 3:411). Doubtless, Alcott saw the general public bemusement that the building evoked: "It impresses all as something very curious, and belongs to a department of handicraft with which they are but vaguely familiar" (*Journals of Bronson Alcott* 1938, p. 197).

⁷ Cameron (*Companion* 1964, p. 44) suggests a parody of Matt. 7:19: "Every tree that bringeth not forth good fruit is hewn down, and cast into the fire."

⁸ Simon the tanner lived in Joppa (Acts 9:43); he was not one of the apostles.

⁹ Edmund Hosmer married Sally Peirce (1795-1890), daughter of James and Sarah Davis Peirce, on October 14, 1823. The couple's first child was John Hosmer (1824-1882), who married Lucy Jane Buttrick (1827-1908), daughter of Stedman and Mary Hunt Buttrick, on February 8, 1853.

¹⁰ Benjamin Peirce (1809-1880) graduated from Harvard in 1829, taught at the Round Hill School in Northampton, Massachusetts, and became a professor of mathematics and astronomy at Harvard in 1833. He joined the U.S. Coast Survey in 1852 and became its superintendent in 1867, a post he held until 1874.

¹¹ Barzillai Frost and Dr. Josiah Bartlett.

¹² Harvard founded its Lawrence Scientific School in February 1847, thanks to an endowment of fifty thousand dollars given by Abbott Lawrence (1792-1855), principal partner in one of the wealthiest manufacturing and mercantile firms in Boston. Son of Samuel and Susanna Parker Lawrence of Groton, Massachusetts, Lawrence was instrumental in expanding textile manufacturing in the state and in founding a textile manufacturing town close to Lowell, named Lawrence in his honor. Active in Whig politics, Lawrence served two terms in the U.S. House of Representatives (1835-1837, 1839-1840) and was the American minister to Great Britain from 1849 to 1852. The Lawrence Scientific School's faculty, some of whom were also on the college faculty, included Eben Horsford, Louis Agassiz, and Henry Lawrence Eustis. The entering class graduated four members in 1851, one of whom later became the president of MIT. The Lawrence School closed in 1906.

¹³ Eben Norton Horsford (1818-1893) graduated from Rensselaer Polytechnic Institute in 1838, taught for a while, and studied in Germany. He was appointed to Harvard and the Lawrence School in

1847, where he taught for sixteen years. He later became an industrial chemist.

[14] Although T received and kept his undergraduate diploma, Emerson's statement in his eulogy of T that "[n]o college ever offered him a diploma" probably helped to create the apocryphal story that he declined it (Joel Myerson, "Emerson's 'Thoreau': A New Edition from Manuscript," *SAR* 1979, p. 47).

[15] Sophia Foord (1802-1885), daughter of James and Hannah Blake Foord of Milton, Massachusetts, had come to Concord to live in Alcott's home as part of his "consociate family." After that idea failed, Emerson engaged her in the spring of 1846 to teach his children, as well as those of the Alcotts, the Channings, and others in the schoolroom he built in his barn. Foord lived in the Emerson home until her departure in the spring of 1847.

[16] James Munroe and Company.

[17] In a three-week period beginning November 2, Emerson gave three lectures in Manchester and six in Liverpool. On December 2, the day he received this letter from T, Emerson wrote Lidian: "my reception here is rather dubious & by no means so favorable as Henry pleases to fancy. I am preached against every Sunday by the Church of England, & by the Church of Swedenborg, and the Athenaeum & the Examiner newspaper denounced in the newspapers for letting in such a wolf into the English fold" (*Letters of RWE* 1939, 3:444).

[18] T alludes to the first stanza of a song in *Cupid and Death* (*The Dramatic Works and Poems of James Shirley*, 6:355):

> Victorious men of earth, no more
>> Proclaim how wide your empires are;
> Though you bind in every shore,
>> And your triumphs reach as far,
>>> As night or day,
> Yet you, proud monarchs, must obey,
> And mingle with forgotten ashes, when
> Death calls ye to the crowd of common men.

[19] After T left his Walden house in September 1847, Emerson bought it from T and resold it to his gardener, Hugh Whelan, who moved it to the site of T's bean field, intending to convert it into a cottage for his family. In Latin, "agellum" ("agellus" in the nominative case) means "a small plot of land."

[20] Jer. 13:23: "Can the Ethiopian change his skin, or the leopard his spots?"

[21] T describes the land owned by John Hancock Richardson (1803-1850), son of John and Hannah Bemis Richardson of Concord. Richardson graduated from Harvard in 1825 and became a

lawyer. In 1831 he married Lydia Ann Thaxter (1810-1847), daughter of Levi and Lydia Bond Thaxter of Watertown, Massachusetts. In 1849 Richardson married Mary Caroline Patten (1819-1860), daughter of Joel and Mary Richardson Patten of Temple, New Hampshire. He was elected to the Massachusetts House of the General Court but died before he could serve.

[22] Probably a lot of Nathan Brooks's that had been set afire by a passing train (the "Lucifer").

[23] Of the 272 ballots cast, Sam Staples won 155, John Shepard Keyes 103, Samuel Barrett 8, John Stacy 4, and Elijah Wood 1.

[24] George Nixon Briggs (1796-1861), who began his political career as a Democrat but became a Clay Whig, served in the U.S. Congress from 1831 to 1843, when he was elected governor of Massachusetts; he was reelected to seven one-year terms as governor and served until 1851. A conscience Whig, Briggs opposed the Mexican War, the annexation of Texas, and the extension of slavery. Caleb Cushing (1800-1879), the Democratic nominee, graduated from Harvard in 1817 and became a lawyer. He served in the U.S. Congress as a Whig from 1835 to 1843 but then broke with his party and sided with John Tyler. Cushing was elected to the Massachusetts General Court in 1846, but he resigned in early 1847 to raise a regiment in support of the Mexican War. In April he was promoted to brigadier general, but the war ended before he saw action. The contest for the governorship centered on the war.

[25] Eseck Coombs (1818-1848), son of Eseck and Priscilla Parks Coombs of Lincoln, Massachusetts, was "a tall, beardless, mean, thievish, nondescript trapper and hunter" (*Remembrances of Concord and the Thoreaus: Letters of Horace Hosmer to Dr. S. A. Jones*, ed. George Hendrick [Urbana: University of Illinois Press, 1977], p. 113). His death record describes him as "Intemperate" and reports that he was "Found dead in the woods" (Massachusetts Vital Records 33:22).

*Copy-text:* ALS (NjP, Robert H. Taylor Collection of English and American Literature, 1280s-1950, Series III, Box 19, Folder 32)

*Published:* "E-T" June 1892, 737-740; *Alcott* 1893, 433-434; *FL* 1894, 161-169; *T: Home* 1902, 145, 233; *FL* 1906, 135-141; *Friendly Craft* 1908, 26-29; *Magazine of History* 1915, 121; *Life of HDT* 1917, 300; *T as Remembered* 1917, 102; *Cor* 1958, 188-192

*Editor's Notes*
    This letter is addressed "R. W. Emerson / Care of Baring & Brothers / London / England" and endorsed "H D Thoreau / 1847".
    He] *PE*; H{*MS blotted*}

Cattle-show] *PE*; Cattle- / show *in MS*

*Author's Alterations*
    New Testament] new testament
    Peirce] Pierce
    a] A
    he–] ~,
    his] ~~
    if … it] *interlined with a caret*
    Governor] governor
    Peace] peace


## To Abel Adams
*November 15, 1847*

                                    Concord Nov 15th –47
Dear Sir,
    Mrs Emerson requests me to forward this circular[1] to
you. Mr E. had anticipated it, and, as she thinks, said that
you would take care of it. She is sure that he will take new
shares.
    She desires to be kindly remembered to your family,
and would have written herself, if not prevented by a
slight indisposition–
    We have not yet heard from Mr E.

                                    Yrs respectfully
                                    H. D. Thoreau


                Office of the Fitchburg Rail-Road Company,
                        Boston, November 10, 1847.
    You are hereby notified that the Directors of the Fitch-
burg Rail-Road Company have, this day, created New
Stock, and every Stockholder holding Old Stock at the
close of the twentieth day of November, current, is entitled to subscribe for the New Stock, in the proportion of
One New Share for every Four Shares of Old Stock, which
may be held by said Stockholder, provided notice is given
to the Treasurer, in writing, on or before the first day of

December next, after which time, all Shares and fractional parts of Shares not subscribed for, will be forfeited to the Company.

The First Assessment of Twenty-five Dollars on each of the New Shares created by said Directors of the Fitchburg Rail-road Company, has been laid, payable on the sixth day of December next.

And the Second Assessment of Twenty-five Dollars per share, has been laid, payable, on the Sixth day of January next, to the Treasurer of the Fitchburg Rail-Road Company; Office, No. 15, Merchants Exchange, State Street, Boston.

J. P. Welch, Treasurer.

————ᵉ

To the Treasurer of the Fitchburg Rail-Road Company:

*I hereby subscribe for*    *Shares in the New Stock, created November* 10, 1847, *to which I am entitled as holder of*    *Shares of the Old Stock in said Company.*

————ᵉ

*Correspondent:* Abel Adams (1792-1867), son of Levi and Lydia Farrar Adams, was the principal partner of the banking firm Barnard, Adams, and Company. A member of Boston's Second Church when Emerson was its minister, Adams became Emerson's chief financial advisor and a close friend. In 1817 he married Abby Larkin (1798-1883), daughter of Isaac and Ruth Ingalls Larkin.

   ' T wrote on the verso of the form letter distributed by the Fitchburg Railroad Company to its stockholders. Before he left for England, Emerson had granted Adams his power of attorney.

*Copy-text:* ALS on printed document (MHi, Washburn Autograph Collection)

*Published:* *Cor* 1958, 193

*Editor's Notes*

   T's letter is handwritten; Welch's letter is printed. See "To Abel Adams, November 15, 1847," following p. 406.

   ————] *PE; wavy line in copy-text*

   ————] *PE; wavy line in copy-text*

## From Ralph Waldo Emerson

*December 2, 1847*

Manchester, 2 Dec. 1847.

Dear Henry,

   Very welcome in the parcel was your letter, very precious your thoughts & tidings. It is one of the best things
connected with my coming hither that you could &
would keep the homestead, that fireplace shines all the
brighter,–and has a certain permanent glimmer there-
for. Thanks, evermore thanks for the kindness[e] which
I well discern to the *youths* of the house, to my darling
little horseman of pewter, leather, wooden, rocking &
what other breeds, destined, I hope, to ride Pegasus
yet, and I hope not destined to be thrown,[1] to Edith who
long ago drew from you verses which I carefully preserve[e],[2] & to Ellen who by speech & now by letter I find old
enough to be companionable, & to choose & reward her
own friends in her own fashions. She sends me a poem
today, which I have read three times!–  I believe, I must
keep back all my communication on English topics until
I get to London which is England. Everything centralizes,
in this magnificent machine which England is. Manufacturer for the world she is become or becoming one
complete tool or engine in herself.–  Yesterday the *time*
all over the kingdom was reduced to Greenwich time. At
Liverpool, where I was, the clocks were put forward 12
minutes. This had become quite necessary on account of
the railroads which bind the whole country into swiftest
connexion, and require so much accurate interlocking,
intersection, & simultaneous arrival, that the difference
of time produced confusion.[3] Every man in England carries a little book in his pocket called "Bradshaws Guide",
which contains time tables of every arrival & departure
at every station on all the railroads of the kingdom.[4] It is
published anew on the first day of every month & costs
sixpence. The proceeding effects of Electric telegraph
will give a new importance to such arrangements.–  But

lest I should not say what is needful, I will postpone England once for all,–and say that I am not of opinion that
your book should be delayed a month. I should print it
at once[e], nor do I think that you would incur any risk in
doing so that you cannot well afford. It is very certain to
have readers & debtors here as well as there. The Dial is
absurdly well known here. We at home, I think, are always
a little ashamed of it,–*I* am,–and yet here it is spoken of
with the utmost gravity, & I do not laugh.–  Carlyle writes
me that he is reading Domesday Book.–[5]  You tell me in
your letter one odious circumstance, which we will dismiss from remembrance henceforward. Charles Lane
entreated me, in London, to ask you to forward his Dials
to him, which must be done, if[a] you consent, thus. Three
bound vols are among his books in my library  The 4th Vol
is in unbound numbers at J Munroe & Co's[6] shop received
there in a parcel to my address a day or two before I sailed
& which I forgot to carry to Concord  It must be claimed
without delay  It is certainly there–was opened by me,
& left. And they can enclose all 4 vols. to Chapman[7] for
me.–  Well I am glad the Pleasaunce at Walden suffered
no more but it is a great loss as it is which years will not
repair.–  I see that I have baulked you by the promise of
a letter which ends in as good as none  But I write with
counted minutes & a miscellany of things before me.

Yours affectionately,

R. W. E.

*Correspondent:* See p. 53.

[1] Pegasus was a winged horse that sprang from Medusa's blood
after Perseus slew her. He was the horse of the muses and thus associated with poetry. The hero Bellerophon was thrown from Pegasus when he attempted to ride to Olympus.

[2] Emerson copied the poem T addressed to Edith into his note-
book (MH-H, MS Am 1280H [137], p. 95):

*To Edith.*

Thou little bud of being, Edith named,
With whom I've made acquaintance on this earth,
Who knowest me without impediment,

As flowers know the winds that stir their leaves,
And rid'st upon my shoulders as the sphere,
Turning on me thy sage reserved eye,
Behind whose broad & charitable gaze
Floats the still true & universal soul
With the pure azure of the general day,
Not yet a peopled & a vulgar town,
Rather a pure untarnished country ground;
For thou art whole, not yet begun to die,
While men look on me with their shrivelled rays
Streaming through some small chink of the broad sky;
Pure youthful soul, thou hast begun to be,
To cumulate thy sin & piety.

[3] On December 1, 1847, the Railway Clearing House mandate to use Greenwich time at all stations in Great Britain went into effect. The Post Office and several railways had previously adopted "London time," which varied by twenty-three seconds from Greenwich time.

[4] In 1839 George Bradshaw (1801-1853), a mapmaker, published a volume of railroad timetables that was supplemented each month by an updated schedule. In 1841 he developed a paper-bound monthly timetable, *Bradshaw's Monthly Railway Guide* (London: Bradshaw, 1841-1842).

[5] On November 30, Carlyle told Emerson that he was "busy with William Conqueror's *Domesday Book* and with the commentaries of various blockheads on it" (*The Correspondence of Emerson and Carlyle*, ed. Joseph Slater [New York: Columbia University Press, 1964], p. 435).

[6] James Munroe and Company.

[7] John Chapman (1821-1894) began his career as a watchmaker; he later studied medicine and eventually became a publisher in London in 1844. Among other American and English authors, he published Emerson, James Martineau, and Herbert Spencer. He was the first to bring Mary Ann Evans (George Eliot) to the public's attention, publishing in 1846 her translation of David Friedrich Strauss's *Life of Jesus, Critically Examined*, the earliest English version of the work. In 1851 Chapman purchased the *Westminster Review* and Evans edited it behind the scenes for two years.

*Copy-text:* ALS (NN-BGC, Henry David Thoreau Collection, 1837-1917, Series IV)

*Published:* "Emerson-Thoreau Correspondence," *AM* 69 (June 1892): 741-742; *FL* 1894, 149, 170, 187n; *FL* 1906, 125, 142, 156n; *Cor* 1958, 194-195; *Letters of RWE* 1990-1995, 8:135-137; *The Selected Let-*

*ters of Ralph Waldo Emerson*, ed. Joel Myerson (New York: Columbia University Press, 1998), 332-333

*Editor's Notes*
This letter is addressed "P Hibernia S / Henry D. Thoreau / Concord / Mass." and postmarked "PAID AT LIVERPOOL DEC 4 1847" and "BOSTON MS. SHIP DEC 25".
    kindness] *PE*; kind / ness *in MS*
    preserve] *PE*; pre / serve *in MS*
    once] *PE*; {*MS torn*}ce

*Author's Alteration*
    if] in

## To Ralph Waldo Emerson

*December 15, 1847*

Concord Dec 15th 1847

Dear Friend,

You are not so far off but the affairs of *this* world still attach to you.[1] Perhaps it will be so when we are dead. Then[a] look out.–  Joshua R. Holman,[2] of Harvard,[e,a] who says he lived a month with Lane at Fruitland's wishes to *hire* said Lane's farm for one or more years, and will pay $125 rent, taking out of the same what is necessary for repairs–as, for a new bank-wall to the barn cellar, which he says is indispensable. Palmer is gone, Mrs Palmer is going.[3] This is all that is known, or that is worth knowing.

    Yes or No

    What to do?

Hugh's plot begins to thicken.[4] He stands thus. 80 dollars on one side–Walden field & house on the other. How to bring these together so as to make a garden & a palace.

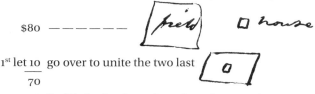

$80  — — — — — —  [field]  ☐ house

1st let 10  go over to unite the two last  [ o ]
    ——
    70

    6  for Wetherbee's[5] rocks to found your palace on.
    ——
    64

        64  so far indeed we have already got.
         4  to bring the rocks to the field.
        ――
        60

save 20  by all means to manure the field, and you have
 left 40  to complete the palace–build cellar–& dig well.

Build the cellar yourself–& let *well* alone–&
now how does it stand? $40 to complete the
palace, somewhat like this–for when one asks

–What do you want? Twice as much room more, is the
reply. Parlor kitchen & bedroom–these make the palace.– Well, Hugh, what will you do? Here are forty dollars to buy a new house 12 feet by 25 and add it to the
old.– Well, Mr Thoreau, as I tell you, I know no more
than a child about it. It shall be just as you say.– Then
build it yourself–get it roofed & get in. Commence at one
end & leave it half done, and let time finish what money's
begun.

So you see we have forty dollars for a nest egg–sitting
on which, Hugh & I, alternately & simultaneously, there
may in course of time be hatched a house, that will long[a]
stand, and perchance even lay fresh eggs one day for its
owner, that is, if when he returns he gives the young chick
20 dollars or more in addition by way of "swichin"–to give
it a start in the world.

Observe this– I got your check changed into thirty
dollars the other day, & immediately[e] paid[a] away sixteen
for Hugh. To-day Mr Cheney[6] says that they in Boston
refuse to answer it–not having funds enough to warrant
it– There must be some mistake &c– We shall pay back
the thirty dollars & await your orders.[7]

The Mass. Quart. Review came out on the 1st of Dec.,[8]
but it does not seem to be making a sensation–at least not
hereabouts. I know of none in Concord who takes, or has
seen, it yet.

We wish to get by all possible means some notion of
your success or[a] failure in England–more than your two
letters have furnished– Can't you send a fair sample

both of Young & of Old England's criticism, if there is any printed?⁹ Alcott & Channing¹⁰ are equally greedy with myself.

Henry Thoreauᵉ

*Correspondent:* See p. 53.

¹ Cameron (*Companion* 1964, p. 46) suggests a possible allusion to 2 Tim. 2:4: "No man that warreth entangleth himself with the affairs of *this* life; that he may please him who hath chosen him to be a soldier."

² Joshua Reed Holman (1817-1886), son of Porter and Persis Reed Holman of Sterling, Massachusetts, was a peddler; he married Nancy Palmer (1820?-1893), daughter of Joseph and Nancy Tenny Palmer, in 1838.

³ Joseph Palmer (1789-1873), son of Thomas and Margaret Palmer of Leominster, Massachusetts, married a widow, Nancy Thompson Tenny (1784?-1859), in 1818. He was notorious in the 1830s for his long beard and served a year in jail after refusing to pay a fine for defending himself against a group of men who assaulted him and tried to shave the offending beard. Palmer was the only experienced farmer who lived at Fruitlands during the experiment. In August 1846 he bought the farm from Charles Lane for seventeen hundred dollars, with Emerson acting as trustee. Lane and Palmer planned to combine this property with others in Leominster to form another consociation, but Lane subsequently returned to England. Palmer lived at Fruitlands for the rest of his life and opened the farm to outcasts of many kinds. In his December 31 letter to Lidian, Emerson asked her to remind T that Palmer, not Lane, owned Fruitlands (*Letters of RWE* 1939, 3:462). Palmer did not finish making his payments to Lane until 1852.

⁴ See p. 320, note 19.

⁵ Solomon Wetherbee (b. 1784), son of Abraham and Joanna Sawtell Wetherbee of Cheshire, New Hampshire, married Sarah Wetherbee (1786-1850), daughter of Thomas and Mary Gates Wetherbee, in 1807.

⁶ John Milton Cheney (1797-1869), son of Hezekiah and Sally Swan Cheney of Phillipston, Massachusetts, was Emerson's classmate in Harvard's class of 1821. His family had moved to Concord in 1803, but Cheney was raised in Lincoln after his mother's death. He taught school, studied law, and became the cashier of the Concord Bank in 1832. In 1833 he married Louisa P. Hosmer (1809-1885), daughter of Rufus and Amelia Paine Hosmer.

⁷ In his December 31 reply to Lidian, the normally even-tempered Emerson wrote: "Foul fall the faithless 'Atlantic Bank'ers that

would protest cheque of mine!" He had already remitted money to the bank twice and enclosed a new order to replace the rejected one that T refers to (*Letters of RWE* 1939, 3:461).

[8] T met with Emerson, Parker, and nine others on April 14, 1847, to discuss the creation of a successor to the *Dial*, which had ended in 1844. Thanks mostly to Parker's enthusiasm and energy, the *Massachusetts Quarterly Review* began publication soon afterwards, with a first issue in December 1847. Unlike Emerson, Parker was cool toward T's writing, and nothing by T ever appeared in the journal. Emerson disapproved of the principles of the journal and contributed but four short notices.

[9] The Young England party, which included John Manners, George Augustus F. P. S. Smythe, and, most prominently, Benjamin Disraeli, was formed by a group of conservative writers and politicians who repudiated middle-class values and turned instead to the aristocracy, church, and monarchy as the sources of reform for England's social problems. Disraeli embodied their romanticized ideas in his novels *Coningsby* and *Sybil*.

[10] Ellery Channing.

*Copy-text:* ALS (ViU, Clifton Waller Barrett Library, Henry David Thoreau Collection [#6345])

*Published:* "Emerson-Thoreau Correspondence," *AM* 69 (June 1892): 740-741; *FL* 1894, 170-173; *FL* 1906, 142-144; *Magazine of History* 21 (July-December 1915): 121; *Cor* 1958, 196-197

*Editor's Notes*
    This letter is endorsed "H. D. Thoreau / Dec. 1847".
    Holman, of Harvard,] *PE*; Holman of Harvard,, *in MS*
    immediately] *PE*; immedia{*MS blotted*}ly
    Henry Thoreau] *followed in MS by postscript by Lidian Emerson to Ralph Waldo Emerson:*

        CTJ[1] takes the Quarterly (new one) and will lend it to us. Are you not going to send your wife some news of your good or ill success by the newspapers?

    [1] Charles Thomas Jackson, Lidian Emerson's brother.

*Author's Alterations*
    Then] then
    of Harvard,] *interlined with a caret*
    long] *interlined with a caret*
    paid] pay
    or] of

## To James Munroe and Company

*December 27, 1847*

Concord Dec 27<sup>th</sup> 1847

Gentlemen,

In a letter from R. W. Emerson, which I received this morning, he requests me to send him Charles Lane's Dials. Three bound vols accompany this letter to you– "The fourth", to quote his own words, "is in unbound numbers at J Munroe & Co's[1] shop, received there in a parcel to my address a day or two before I sailed, and which I forgot to carry to Concord– It is certainly there, was opened by me, & left".– And he wishes me to ask you to "enclose all four vols. to Chapman" for him (Emerson).

If all is right, will you please say so to the express-man– or at any rate give me an opportunity to look for the fourth vol, if it is missing.

I may as well inform you that I do not intend to print *my book* anywhere immediately.

Yrs
Respectfully
Henry Thoreau

*Correspondent:* See p. 206.

[1] James Munroe and Company.

*Copy-text:* ALS (MB, Ch.B.6.15)

*Published:* *Cor* 1958, 198

*Editor's Note*
This letter is addressed "James Munroe & Co. / Washington St / Boston." and endorsed "Henry Thoreau / Dec 27<sup>th</sup>/47".

## To Ralph Waldo Emerson

*December 29, 1847*

Concord Dec 29<sup>th</sup> 1847.

My Dear Friend,

I thank you for your letter– I was very glad to get it– And I am glad again to write to you. However slow the steamer, no time intervenes between the writing and the reading of thoughts, but they come fresh to the most distant port.– I am here still, & very glad to be here– and shall not trouble you with my complaints because I do not fill my place better. I have had many good hours in the chamber at the head of the stairs–a solid time, it seems to me. Next week I am going to give an account to the Lyceum of my expedition to Maine.[1] Theodore Parker lectures tonight–[2] We have had Whipple[a] on Genius–too mighty a subject for him–with his antithetical[a] defini-tions–new-vamped[e]–what it[a] *is*, & what it is *not*–[3] But altogether what it is *not*. Cuffing it this way, & cuffing it that, as if it were an India rubber ball. Really, it is a subject which should[a] expand–&[a] accumulate[a] itself before the speaker's eyes, as he goes on,–like the snow balls which boys roll in the streets–& when he stops[a], it should be so large that he cannot start it–but must leave it there–[a] – Hudson too has been here with a dark shadow in the core of him, and his desperate wit so much indebted to the surface of him–wringing out his words and snapping them off like a dish-cloth–very remarkable but not mem-orable.[4] Singular that these two best lectures should have so much "wave" in their timber–their solid parts too be made and kept solid by shrinkage and contraction of the whole–with consequent checks & fissures– Ellen and I have a good understanding– I appreciate her genuine-ness– Edith tells me after her fashion–"By & by, I shall grow up to be a woman, and then I shall remember how you exercised me."– Eddie has been to Boston to Christ-mass–but can remember nothing but the coaches–all Ken-dall's coaches[5]– –there is no variety of that vehicle that he is not familiar with.– He *did* try once to tell us something else, but after thinking and stuttering a long time–said–"I dont know what the word is"–the *one* word, forsooth that would have disposed of all that Boston phenomenon. If you did not know him better than I–I could tell you more.

He is a good companion for me–& I am glad that we are all natives of Concord– It is *Young Concord*–Look out–World.– Mr Alcott seems to have sat down for the winter. He has got Plato and other books to read.[6] He[a] is as large featured–and hospitable to travelling thoughts & thinkers as ever–but with the same creaking & sneaking Connecticut philosophy as ever, mingled with what is better. If he would only stand up straight and toe the line!–though he were to put off several degrees of largeness–and put on a considerable degree of littleness.– After all, I think we must call him particularly *your* man.– I have pleasant walks and talks with Channing.–[7] James Clark[8]–the swedenborgian that was–is at the Poor House[a]–insane with too large views, so that he cannot support himself– I see him working with Fred[a] and the rest. Better than be there not insane. It is strange that they will make an ado when a man's body is buried–and not when he thus really & tragically dies–or seems to die. Away with your funeral processions,–into the ball-room with them– I hear the bell toll hourly over there.

Lidian & I have a standing[a] quarrel as to what is a suitable state of preparedness for a travelling Professor's[a] visits[9]–or for whomsoever else–but further than this we are not at war. We?[a] have made up a dinner–we have made up a bed–we have made up a party–& our own minds & mouths three several times for your Professor, and he came not– Three several turkies have died the death–which I myself carved, just as if he had been here[a]–and the company too convened and demeaned themselves[a] accordingly– Everything was done up in good style, I assure you–with only the part of the Professor omitted.[10] To have seen the preparations–though Lidian says it was nothing extraordinary–I should certainly have said he was a coming–but he did not. He must have found out some shorter way. to Turkey–some overland rout–I think.– By[a] the way, he was complimented at the conclusion of his course in Boston by the Mayor[a] moving the appointment of a committee to draw up resolutions expressive of &c &c which was done.[11]

I have made a few verses lately– Here are some–though perhaps not the best–at any rate they are the shortest on that universal theme–your's as well as mine, & several other people's

> The good how can we trust?
> Only the wise are just.
> The good we use,
> The wise we cannot choose.
> These there are none above;
> The good they know & love,
> But are not known again
> By those of lesser ken.–
> They do not charm us with their eyes,
> But they transfix with their advice.
> No partial sympathy they feel,
> With private woe or private weal,
> But with the universe joy & sigh,
> Whose knowledge is their sympathy.[12]

I am sorry to send such a medley as this to you.

Good night

Henry Thoreau

I have forwarded Lane's[13] Dials to Monroe,[14] with the proper instructions, and he tells the express man that all is right.

---

*Correspondent:* See p. 53.

[1] T gave his lecture "An Excursion to Ktaadn," an account of his 1846 trip to Maine, on January 3, 1848. In his journal entry for the same day, Alcott wrote: "Mrs A. accompanied me to the Lyceum where we heard a lecture from *Thoreau* on a jaunt of his to *Kotarden*, the highest mountain in Maine.– The lecture gave a very lively picture of the so wild scenery and of his adventures in ascending the rivers to reach the summit of Kotarden.–" (MH-H, MS Am 1130.12 [17], p. 7).

[2] Alcott records in his journal entry for December 29: "Evening I heard a lecture at the Lyceum on Genius of Americans by Parker" (MH-H, MS Am 1130.12 [16], p. 706).

[3] Edwin Percy Whipple (1819-1886), son of Matthew and Lydia Gardiner Whipple, grew up in Salem, Massachusetts, and became a banker, but he later turned to lecturing and writing. In 1847 he married Charlotte Billings Hastings (1821-1907), daughter of Cyrus and Eliza Bullard Hastings. Whipple was a regular on the lyceum circuit. He repeated the lecture on genius in Boston the following February and published it in *Lectures on Subjects Connected with Literature and Life* (Boston: Ticknor, Reed and Fields, 1850). In this lecture, Whipple attempts a broad and "true" definition of genius: genius "reasons, but it is not reasoning; it judges, but it is not judgment; it imagines, but it is not imagination; it feels deeply and fiercely, but it is not passion" (pp. 158-159).

[4] Henry Norman Hudson (1814-1886) graduated from Middlebury College in 1840, taught for a time, and then began to lecture professionally on Shakespeare. He published his very successful performances as *Lectures on Shakespeare* (New York: Baker and Scribner, 1848). In 1852 he married Emily Sarah Bright (1826-1891), daughter of Henry and Abigail Fisk Bright. Hudson later became an Episcopal minister but resumed his work as a Shakespearean scholar and popularizer after the Civil War. The date and topic of his lecture at the Concord Lyceum are not known.

[5] Eddie probably remembered the Concord stage driver Obadiah Kendall (1783-1849), son of Reuben and Betsey Kendall of Cheshire, New Hampshire.

[6] Alcott spent the summer and fall of 1847 landscaping and tending his garden while the family was sinking ever deeper into poverty. His journal entry for December 22, 1847, contains a list of "Proposed Reading for this Season–1848," in which he named *Schleiermacher's Introductions to the Dialogues of Plato* as one of his books. At the end of his journal entry for December 26, Alcott outlined the chapters of Schleiermacher's book (MH-H, MS Am 1130.12 [16], pp. 699, 702-703).

[7] Ellery Channing.

[8] James Clark (1815-1851), son of John Brooks and Lydia Flint Clark, bought T's house at Walden from Hugh Whelan in 1849 and, with the help of his brother, Daniel, moved it to the Carlisle Road. See p. 320, note 19.

[9] The traveling professor is John Pringle Nichol (1804-1859), Regius Professor of Practical Astronomy at the University of Glasgow, who was lecturing in Boston at this time. Emerson's 1841 reading

of Nichol's *Views of the Architecture of the Heavens* (Edinburgh: W. Tait, 1837) prompted him to write several extended journal passages on the size of the universe and on human perception. Nichol had solicited Emerson's help in arranging lecture venues, but, despite his admiration for Nichol's work, Emerson could offer little more than general suggestions. When the two met in Liverpool in November 1847, Emerson gave him letters of introduction to Parker and Longfellow.

[10] Elizabeth Hoar described one of the dinners for the absent Nichol in her November 29 letter to Emerson: "Lidian summoned me to dine with Dr. Nicholl to-day at 3 oclock but come he did not, though Ellery and Henry awaited him in black coats, like gentlemen of the old school–so we had a gay dinner without him, a weight being removed of course from all minds" ("Elizabeth of Concord: Selected Letters of Elizabeth Sherman Hoar [1814-1878] to the Emersons, Family, and the Emerson Circle [Part Three]," ed. Elizabeth Maxfield-Miller, *SAR* 1986, p. 149). Emerson speculated that Nichol had instead mistakenly gone to Concord, New Hampshire, "than which no vexation could be more complete" (*Letters of RWE* 1939, 3:455). In January Hoar wrote Emerson again about these dinners: "Lidian gives us little dinner parties ever week or two, for Dr. Nicholl, & we go & enjoy them, & the Dr. Don't come" ("Elizabeth of Concord," *SAR* 1986, p. 155).

[11] Nichol delivered six lectures on "Mechanism and Physical Constitution of Our Solar System" in Boston between December 6 and December 23. Following the conclusion of his course, "the Mayor suggested the appointment of a Committee to draw up a set of resolutions expressive of the sense in which the audience held the importance of the views promulgated by the lectures, and the esteem in which they held the scientific character of the Professor. The step was carried into effect, and a set of resolutions reported and unanimously adopted" ("Compliment to Prof Nichol," *Boston Daily Evening Transcript*, December 24, 1847).

[12] T included this poem in *A Week on the Concord and Merrimack Rivers* (*A Week* 1980, p. 281).

[13] Charles Lane.

[14] James Munroe.

*Copy-text:* ALS (NN-BGC, Henry David Thoreau Collection, 1837-1917, Series III)

*Published:* "Emerson-Thoreau Correspondence," *AM* 69 (June 1892): 742-744; *FL* 1894, 173-177; *T: Home* 1902, 233; *FL* 1906, 144-148; *Magazine of History* 1915, 121; *Cor* 1958, 199-201

*Editor's Notes*

    This letter is addressed "R. W. Emerson / care of <u>Alexander Ire-land</u> Esq. / <u>Manchester</u> Examiner Office / England. / via New York / & Steamer Hibernia" and endorsed "H. D. Thoreau / Jan 1848".

    new-vamped] *PE*; new- / vamped *in MS*

*Author's Alterations*

    Whipple] whipple
    antithetical] *preceded by cancelled* two-columned
    it] is
    should] *followed by cancelled* dilate &
    &] *interlined with a caret*
    accumulate] accumulating
    stops] *interlined above cancelled* leaves off
    there–] *followed by cancelled* perchance, to thaw in the sun & feed the Pierian springs.
    He] His
    House] house
    Fred] *interlined above cancelled* Breed
    standing] standard
    Professor's] professor's
    We?] ? *inserted*
    here] there
    themselves] *interlined with a caret*
    –By] – *added in margin*
    Mayor] mayor


*To Ralph Waldo Emerson*

*January 12, 1848*

                              Concord Jan 12th 1848.
It is hard to believe that England is so near as from your letters it appears–and that this identical piece of paper has lately come all the way from there hither–begrimmed with the English dust, which made you hesitate to use it[1]– –from England which is only historically firm-land to me–to America which I have put my spade into, and about which there is no doubt.

    I thought that you needed to be informed of Hugh's progress.[2] He has moved his house, as I told you, & dug his cellar, and purchased stone of Sol Wetherbee[3] for the last–though he has not hauled it–All which has cost $16.00 which I have paid.–  He has also, as next in order, run away from Concord without a penny in his pocket– "crying" by the way–having had another long difference with strong beer–& a first one, I suppose, with his wife– who seems to have complained that he sought other soci- ety–the one difference leading to the other, perhaps, but I don't know which was the leader. He writes back to his wife from Sterling near Worcester, where he is chopping wood wood his distantly kind reproaches to her–which I read straight through to her (not to his bottle, which he has with him and, no doubt, addresses orally)  He says that he will go on to the South in the Spring, and will never return to Concord. Perhaps he will not. Life is not tragic enough for him.–and he must try to cook up a more highly seasoned dish for himself. Towns which keep a barroom & a gun-house & a reading room–should also keep a steep precipice where-off impatient soldier may jump.

The sun went down *to me* bright & steady enough in the west–but it never came up in the east–  Night intervenes. He departed, as when a man dies suddenly–& perhaps wisely if he has[e] to go–without settling his affairs.

They knew that that was a thin soil, and not well calcu- lated for pears. Nature is sore & sensitive on the score of nurseries–you may cut down orchards & grown forests at your pleasure.

Sand watered with strong beer–though stirred with industry–will not produce grapes. He dug his cellar for the new part too near the old house–Irish like–though I warned him & it has caved and let one end of the house down. Such is the state of his domestic affairs I laugh with the Parcae[4] only.

He had got the upland and the orchard & a part of the meadow plowed by Warren[5]–at an expense of 8 dollars still unpaid, which of course is no affair of yours.

I think that if an honest, small familied man who has no affinity for moisture in him–but who has an affinity for Sand–can be found–it would be safe to rent him the Shanty, *as it is*, & the land–or you[a] can very easily & simply let Nature[a] keep them still without great loss.– It may be so managed, perhaps, as to be a home for somebody–who shall in return serve you as fencing stuff–& to fix and locate your lot,–as we plant a tree in sand or on the edge of a stream.–without expense to you in the meanwhile & without disturbing its possible future values.

I read a part of the story of my excursion to Ktadn to quite a large audience of men & boys the other night–whom it interested.[6] It contains many facts & some poetry I have also written what will do for a lecture on Friendship.[7]

I think that the article on you in Blackwood[8] is a good deal to get from the Reviewers–[a] The first purely literary notice as I remember– The writer is far enough off in every sense to speak with a certain authority– It is a better judgment of posterity than the public had.– It is singular how sure he is to be mystified by any uncommon sense– But it was generous to put Plato in the list of mystics– His confessions on this subject suggest several thoughts which I have not room to express here– The old word *Seer*, I wonder what the reviewer thinks that means–whether that *he* was a man who could *see more than himself*.

I was struck by Ellen's asking me yesterday, while I was talking with Mrs.[a] Brown–If I did not use *colored* words. She said that she could tell the color of a great many–words, and amused the children at school by so doing.

Eddie climbed up the sofa the other day *of his own accord* and kissed the picture of his father, 'Right[a] on his shirt, I did'

I had a good talk with Alcott this afternoon[e]– He is certainly the youngest man of his age we have seen–just on the threshold of life–but when I looked at his grey hairs his conversation sounded pathetic–but I looked again, and they reminded me of the gray dawn. He is getting better acquainted with Channing[9]–though he sees that if they were to live in the same house they would soon sit with their backs to each other. You must excuse me if I do not write with sufficient directness to yourself–who are a far-off traveller. It is a little like shooting on the wing–I confess.

Farewell<br>Henry Thoreau

*Correspondent:* See p. 53.

[1] Emerson began his letter of December 15 to Lidian, "I must write on this soiled paper as the only print I have been able to procure of Lord Middleton's beautiful house which I spent some time in gazing at last Saturday" (*Letters of RWE* 1939, 3:449).

[2] See p. 320, note 19.

[3] Solomon Wetherbee.

[4] The three Fates (Parcae), Clotho, Lachesis, and Atropos, were "the arbiters of the life and death of mankind, and whatever good or evil befals us" (*Classical Dictionary* 1806).

[5] Probably Cyrus Warren.

[6] "An Excursion to Ktaadn"; see p. 334, note 1.

[7] T had for several years been thinking and writing about friendship. The new work he refers to was probably a revision of what he had drafted for the manuscript of *A Week on the Concord and Merrimack Rivers*. He never lectured on the subject.

[8] William Henry Smith, "Emerson," *Blackwood's Edinburgh Magazine* 62 (December 1847): 643-657. In comparing Emerson with Montaigne and Sir Thomas Brown, Smith observes: "This class of writers may be described as one whose members, though not deficient in the love of *truth*, are still more conspicuous for their love of *thought*. They crave intellectual excitement; they have a genuine, inexhaustible ardour of reflection" (p. 647).

[9] Ellery Channing.

*Copy-text:* ALS (ViU, Clifton Waller Barrett Library, Henry David Thoreau Collection [#6345])

*Published:* "Emerson-Thoreau Correspondence," *AM* 69 (June 1892): 744-745; *FL* 1894, 177-181; *T: Home* 1902, 136, 237; *FL* 1906, 148-

151; *Magazine of History* 1915, 122; Carroll A. Wilson, *Thirteen Author Collections of the Nineteenth Century* ... (New York: Charles Scribner's Sons, 1950), 1:333-334; *Cor* 1958, 203-205

*Editor's Notes*
   This letter is endorsed "H D Thoreau / Jan. 1848".
   has] *PE*; *possibly* was *in MS*
   afternoon] *PE*; after- / noon *in MS*

*Author's Alterations*
   you] *interlined with a caret*
   Nature] nature
   Reviewers-] ~..
   Mrs.] mrs.
   Right] right

## From Ralph Waldo Emerson
*January 28, 1848*

> 2 Fenny Street; Higher Broughton;
> Manchester; 28 January 1848

Dear Henry,

   One roll of letters has gone today to Concord & to New York, and perhaps I shall still have time to get this into the leathern bag, before it is carted to the wharf. I have to thank you for your letter which was a true refreshment. Let who or what pass, there stands the dear Henry,–if indeed any body had a right to call him so,–erect, serene, & undeceivable[e]. So let it ever be! I should quite subside into idolatry of some of my friends, if I were not every now & then apprised that the world is wiser than any one of its boys, & penetrates us with its sense, to the disparagement of the subtleties of private gentlemen. Last night, as I believe I have already told Lidian, I heard the best man in England make perhaps his best speech. Cobden,[1] who is the cor cordis,[2] the object of honor & belief to risen & rising England. a man of great discretion, who never overstates, nor states prematurely, nor has a particle of unnecessary genius or hope to mislead him, no waste

strength, but calm, sure of his fact, simple & nervous in
stating it, as a boy in laying down the rules of the game
of football which have been violated–above all educated
by his dogma of Free Trade, led on by it to new lights &
correlative liberalities, as our abolitionists have been by
their principle to so many Reforms. Then this man has
made no mistake    he has dedicated himself to his work
of convincing this kingdom of the impolicy of Corn laws,
lectured in every town where they would hear him, & at
last carried his point against immense odds, & yet has
never accepted any compromise or stipulation from the
Government. He might have been in the ministry. He will
never go there, except with absolute empire for his principle, which cannot yet be conceded. He had neglected
& abandoned his prosperous calico-printing to his part-
ners. And the triumphant[e] League have subscribed between 60 & 80 000 pounds, as the Cobden Fund; whereby
he is made independent.–[3]  It was quite beautiful, even
sublime, last night, to notice the moral radiations which
this Free Trade dogma seemed to throw out, all-unlooked-for, to the great Audience, who instantly & delightedly adopted them. Such contrasts of sentiment to
the vulgar hatred & fear of France & jealousy of America,
that pervades the newspapers. Cobden himself looked
thoughtful & surprised, as if he saw a new Future. Old Col.
Peyronnet Thompson, the Father of Free Trade, whose
catechism on the Corn Laws set all these Brights & Cob-
dens first on cracking this nut,[4] was present, & spoke in
a very vigorous rasp-like tone. Gibson,[5] a member of the
Brit.[a] Government, a great Suffolk Squire, & a convert to
these opinions, made a very satisfactory speech and our
old Abolition Friend, George Thompson,[6] brought up the
rear; though he, whom I now heard for the first time, is
merely a piece of rhetoric & not a man of facts & figures
& English solidity, like the rest. The Audience play no in-
active part, but the most acute & sympathizing; and the

agreeable result was the demonstration[e] of the arithmeti-
cal as well as the moral optimism of peace & generosity.
Forgive, forgive this most impertinent scribble.

Your friend,

R. W. E.

I surely did not mean to put you off with a Report when I
begun. But–

*Correspondent:* See p. 53.

[1] Richard Cobden (1804-1865) was joined by William Moles-
worth, John Arthur Roebuck, and Joseph Hume in establishing
the Anti-Corn Law League in 1838. The league sought to repeal the
restrictions put on the importation of foreign corn (wheat). A self-
taught man, Cobden made a fortune as a manufacturer of fabrics
in Manchester and then entered Parliament, where he became
known as one of the most effective public speakers of his generation. Emerson heard his speech to the Free Trade Association
meeting in Manchester.

[2] Heart of hearts.

[3] Although the fund was large, almost all of it went to settle the
losses Cobden had incurred during his services for the Anti-Corn
Law League.

[4] Thomas Perronet Thompson (1783-1869) pursued successful
careers in the military (he rose to the rank of general), in writing,
and in politics. An early follower of Jeremy Bentham, Thompson
was part of the circle that founded the *Westminster Review*, which
he later owned. His often-reprinted *A Catechism on the Corn Laws*
was influential in the ensuing anti-corn law reform. Thompson
also wrote and spoke in favor of Catholic emancipation, against the
House of Lords, and for currency reforms. He served three terms
in Parliament, beginning in 1835. John Bright (1811-1889), a manufacturer, entered public life as an opponent of the church and the
monarchy and as a defender of free trade in opposition to land-
owners. In 1835 he joined Cobden in the free-trade, anti-corn law
agitation. Also an impressive speaker, Bright entered the House of
Commons in 1843 and championed many reform efforts. He and
Cobden were prominent supporters of the Union during the American Civil War.

[5] Thomas Milner-Gibson (1806-1884) graduated from Cambridge
in 1830 and was elected to Parliament in 1837 as a Tory. He later
changed his political views and became an ardent free-trade advo-

cate. Prime Minister John Russell made him vice president of the Board of Trade in his government and then a privy councillor.

[6] George Thompson (1804-1878) was a member of the Anti-Corn Law League and a member of Parliament at the time. Known as an abolitionist, Thompson visited the United States in 1834-1835, lectured often, agitated for the abolition of slavery, and thus found himself the center of a heated controversy. Margaret Fuller described his voice as one "of uncommon compass and beauty" (*Letters of Margaret Fuller*, 1:218).

*Copy-text:* ALS (NN-BGC, Henry David Thoreau Collection, 1837-1917, Series IV)

*Published:* "Emerson-Thoreau Correspondence," *AM* 69 (June 1892): 745-746; *Cor* 1958, 205-206; *Letters of RWE* 1990-1995, 8:144-146

*Editor's Notes*
This letter is addressed "Henry D. Thoreau / Concord. / Massachusetts. / By steamer / from Liverpool" and postmarked "MANCHESTER JA 28 1848" and "JA 29".
    undeceivable] *PE*; undeceiv / able *in MS*
    triumphant] *PE*; tri / umphant *in MS*
    demonstration] *PE*; dem / onstration *in MS*

*Author's Alteration*
    Brit.] *added in margin*


## To Ralph Waldo Emerson
*February 23, 1848*

Concord Feb 23[d] 1848

Dear Waldo,

For I think I have heard that that is your name–[1] My letter which was put last into the leathern bag arrived first– Whatever I may *call* you, I know you better than I know your name, and what becomes of the fittest name– if in any sense you are here with him who *calls*, and not there simply to be called.

I believe I never thanked you for your lectures–one and all–which I have heard formerly read here in Concord–  I *know* I never have–there was some excellent reason each time why I did not–but it will never be too late. I have had that advantage at least, over you in my education.

Lidian is too unwell to write to you and so I must tell you what I can about the children and herself. I am afraid she has not told you how unwell she is, or today perhaps we may say–has been. She has been confined to her chamber four or five weeks, and three or four weeks, at least to her bed–with the jaundice, accompanied with *constant* nausea, which makes life intolerable to her. This added to her general ill health has made her *very sick*. She is as yellow as saffron– The Doctor,[2] who comes once a day does not let her read (nor can she now) nor *hear* much reading. She has written her letters to you till recently sitting up in bed–but he said that he would not come again if she did so. She has Abby and Almira[3] to take care of her, & Mrs Brown to read to her, and I also occasionally have something to read or to say. The Doctor says she must not expect to "take any comfort of her life" for a week or two yet. She wishes me to say that she has written 2 long and full letters to you about the household economies &c which she hopes have not been delayed.

The children are quite well and full of spirits–and are going through a regular course of picture seeing, with commentary by me–every evening–for Eddy's behoof. All the annuals and "diadems" are in requisition,[4] and Eddy is forward to exclaim when the hour arrives–"Now for the dem dems"! I overheard this dialogue when Frank[5] came down to breakfast the other morning.– Eddy–Why Frank, I am *astonished* that you should leave your boots in the dining-room.– Frank. I guess you mean *surprised*, dont you?– Eddy–No–Boots!– "If Waldo were here", said he the other night at bed-time, "we'd be four going up stairs".

Would he like to tell Papa anything? "No–not anything" but finally "Yes"–he would–that one of the white horses in his new barouche is broken. Ellen and Edith will perhaps speak for themselves as I hear something about letters to be written by them.

Mr Alcott seems to be reading well[a] this winter Plato–Montaigne–Ben Jonson–Beaumont & Fletcher–Sir Thomas Browne &c &c–[6] "I believe I have read them all now–or nearly all"–those English authors He is rallying for another foray with his pen, in his latter years, not discouraged by the past–into that crowd of unexpressed ideas of his–that undisciplined Parthian army[7]–which as soon as a Roman soldier would face retreats on all hands–occasionally firing behind–easily routed–not easily subdued–hovering on the skirts of society. Another summer shall not be devoted to the raising of vegetables (Arbors?)[8] which rot in the cellar for want of consumers– but perchance to the arrangement of the material–the brain-crop which the winter has furnished  I have good talks with him.[a]

His respect for Carlyle has been steadily increasing for some time. He has read him with new sympathy and appreciation.[9]

I see Channing often. He also goes often to Alcott's, and confesses that he has made a discovery in him–and give vent to his admiration or his confusion in characteristic exaggerations–but between this extreme & that you may get a fair report–& draw[a] an inference if you can. Sometimes *he will* ride a broom stick still–though there is nothing to keep him or it up–but a certain centrifugal force of whim which is soon spent–and there lies your stick–not worth picking up to sweep an oven with now. His accustomed path is strewn with them  But then again & perhaps for the most part he sits on the cliffs amid the lichens, or flits past on noiseless pinion like the Barred Owl in the day time–as wise & unobserved.

He brought me a poem the other day–for me–on "Walden Hermitage"[10] not remarkable–

Lectures begin to multiply in my desk– I have one on Friendship which is new[11]–and the materials of some others. I read one last week to the Lyceum on the Rights & Duties of the Individual in relation to Government.–much to Mr. Alcott's satisfaction.–[12] Joel Britton has failed and gone into Chancery–but the woods continue to fall before the axes of other men– Neighbor Coombs[13] was lately found dead in the woods near Goose Pond–with his half empty jug–after he had been missing a week.– Hugh by the last accounts was still in Worcester County.– Mr Hosmer who is himself again, and living in Concord–has just hauled the rest of your wood–amounting to about 10 1/2 cords.– The newspapers[e] say that they have printed a pirated edition of your Essays in England.[14] Is it as bad as they say–an undisguised unmitigated piracy?

I thought that the printed scrap would entertain Carlyle–notwithstanding its history. If this generation will see out of its hind head[e], why then you may turn your back on its forehead. Will you forward it to him from me.?[15] This stands written in your Day Book. "Sept. 3[d] Rec[d] of Boston Savings Bank–on account of Charles Lane his deposit with interest  131.33  16th Rec[d] of Joseph Palmer on account of Charles Lane three hundred twenty three 36/100 dollars being the balance of a note on demand for four hundred dollars with interest.  323.36"[16]

If you have any directions to give about the trees you must not forget that spring will soon be upon us.

Farewell–from<br>your friend Henry Thoreau

*Correspondent:* See p. 53.

[1] T addresses Emerson as "Waldo" for the only time in their extant correspondence; see p. 354 for Emerson's acknowledgment.

[2] Josiah Bartlett.

[3] Abby and Almira Stevens worked for the Emersons. Abby married Louis Munner (Monnier?) the following August.

[4] T was reading "annuals," yearly gift books, to the children. Em-

erson had published poems in the 1846 and 1847 issues of *The Dia-dem for [year]: A Present for All Seasons* (Philadelphia: Carey and Hart), each of which included ten engravings.

⁵ Francis Charles Browne (1829-1900) was the son of Charles and Lucy Cotton Brown (he added an "e" to the end of his family name). He graduated from Harvard in 1851 and became a farmer and naturalist. In 1854 he married Elizabeth Wheeler Goodwin (1835-1900), daughter of John Marston and Emeline Philleo Goodwin of Boston. A shy, reserved man, Browne had poor eyesight, but he was an avid collector of bird skins, shells, and coins.

⁶ "Montaigne's book," wrote Alcott in his journal, "is the only one, almost, which I wish were longer." Of the dramatists, he commented: "It is refreshing to read these phrases of theirs. They admit us into an intimacy so entire with the thoughts and manners and speech of their day" (*Journals of Bronson Alcott* 1938, pp. 202-203).

⁷ The Parthians, an Indo-European dynasty that spread from Bactria to Babylonia, met the Romans in battle on several occasions; their strategy of appearing to flee only to turn and fire lethal volleys of arrows is the origin of the expression "Parthian shot."

⁸ As he did each year the family lived at Hillside, Alcott spent the summer of 1847 developing his elaborate gardens and orchards. In late spring 1846 he had built himself an "arbour" on the ridge, which prompted Emerson to ask him to build one on his property, with T's help (see pp. 318-319, note 6).

⁹ Alcott, who had met and quarreled with Carlyle in London in 1842 (see *Journals of Bronson Alcott* 1938, pp. 161-162), continued to read his work with enthusiasm, as he had done from the start. A month before this letter, Alcott wrote in his journal, "Carlyle has a broader and solider dramatic range than any living modern writer. What movement! What storm!" His "energy is almost demonic, and even under his calmest and stillest sentences there seems to slumber a hell of fires that shall break forth and scorch and consume you as you read" (*Journals of Bronson Alcott* 1938, pp. 199-200).

¹⁰ Ellery Channing published this poem in *Thoreau: The Poet-Naturalist* (Boston: Roberts Brothers, 1873), pp. 196-199.

¹¹ See p. 340, note 7.

¹² Alcott's journal entries for January 26 and February 13 indicate that T lectured twice on the topic of the individual and the state. These lectures were probably the basis for the essay "Resistance to Civil Government," which T published in 1849 (see p. 147), and which was published in 1866 as "Civil Disobedience." In the January 26 entry, Alcott called T's lecture, delivered that evening, "an admirable statement of the rights of the individual to self-govern-

ment" and described the audience as "attentive." He found much to compliment in this lecture: "His allusions to the Mexican War, to Mr. Hoar's expulsion from Carolina, his own imprisonment in Concord Jail for refusal to pay his tax, Mr. Hoar's payment of mine when taken to prison for a similar refusal, were all pertinent, well considered, and reasoned. I took great pleasure in this deed of Thoreau's" (*Journals of Bronson Alcott* 1938, p. 201). In his February 13 journal entry, Alcott wrote: "Passed an hour or two with Thoreau at Emerson's conversing on the State upon which he is now writing and preparing a Lecture for the Concord Lyceum" (MH-H, MS Am 1130.12 [17], p. 120). These two journal entries suggest that the second lecture must have been somewhat different from the first. Based on the dates of Alcott's second journal entry (Sunday, February 13) and of this letter (Wednesday, February 23), Bradley P. Dean and Ronald Wesley Hoag conjecture that T delivered his second lecture on Wednesday, February 16, as the Concord Lyceum usually met on Wednesday evenings ("Thoreau's Lectures before *Walden*: An Annotated Calendar," *SAR* 1995, pp. 154-155).

[13] Eseck Coombs.

[14] The *Boston Daily Evening Transcript* for January 8 noted the publication in London of a pirated edition of Emerson's *Essays, Lectures and Orations* (William S. Orr, 1848).

[15] This enclosure is not extant.

[16] Emerson apparently had asked T to confirm the amount of Lane's money that he had accumulated. When Lane sold the Fruitlands property to Joseph Palmer in August 1846, Emerson agreed to act as Lane's trustee. In that capacity he wrote Palmer on August 7, 1847, to request a payment of $323.36 by September 14, for he wanted to give the money to Lane when he was in England. Emerson received money for Lane on September 3 from the Boston Savings Bank, and on September 16 he recorded the payment from Palmer in his account book. In his October 27 letter to Lidian, Emerson reported that he had paid Lane "£92 17 s 9 pence–(of which payment let this record be kept until I get it into my Journal at home)" (*Letters of RWE* 1939, 3:425).

*Copy-text:* ALS (NN-BGC, Henry David Thoreau Collection, 1837-1917, Series III)

*Published:* "Emerson-Thoreau Correspondence," *AM* 69 (June 1892): 746-748; *Alcott* 1893, 444-445; *FL* 1894, 181-186; *T: Home* 1902, 149; *FL* 1906, 151-155; *Magazine of History* 21 (July-December 1915): 122; *Cor* 1958, 207-209

*Editor's Notes*

This letter is addressed "R. Waldo Emerson / care of Alexander Ireland Esq. / Examiner Office / Manchester / England / By Hibernia / from New York / Feb 26<sup>th</sup>" and endorsed "H. D. Thoreau / March, 1848."

  newspapers] *PE*; news- / papers *in MS*
  hind head] *PE*; *possibly* hindhead *in MS*

*Author's Alterations*
  well] *added in margin*
  I ... him.] *interlined below*
  draw] drag

## To James Elliot Cabot
*March 8, 1848*

Concord March 8<sup>th</sup> –48

Dear Sir,

Mr Emerson's address is as yet–"R. W. Emerson, care<sup>e</sup> of Alexander Ireland Esq.–Examiner Office, Manchester, England."[1] We had a letter from him on Monday dated at Manchester 10<sup>th</sup> Feb, and he was then preparing to go to Edinburg the next day–where he was to lecture.[2] He thought that he should get through his northern journeying by the 25<sup>th</sup> of Feb. & go to London to spend March & April[a], and, if he did not go to Paris, May–& then come home.[3] He has been eminently successful, though the papers this side of the water have been so silent about his adventures.

My book fortunately did not find a publisher ready to undertake it[4]–and you can imagine the effect of delay on an author's estimate of his own work. However, I like it well enough to mend it, and shall look to it again directly when I have despatched some other things.

I have been writing lectures for our Lyceum this winter, mainly for my own pleasure & advantage. I esteem it a rare happiness to be able to *write* anything, but there, if I ever get there, my concern for it is apt to end. Time &

Co. are after all the only quite honest & trustworthy publishers that we know. I can sympathize perhaps with the barberry bush whose business it is solely to *ripen* its fruit–though that may not be to sweeten it–& to protect it with thorns, so[a] that it holds on all winter even, unless some hungry crows come to pluck it.

But I see that I must get a few dollars together presently in order to manure my roots–  Is your journal[5] able to pay anything–provided it likes an article well enough? I do not promise one–  At any rate, I mean always to spend only words enough to purchase silence with–and I have found that this which is so valuable–though many writers do not prize it–does not cost much after all

I have not obtained any more of the mice which I told you were so numerous in my cellar, as my house was removed[6] immediately after I saw you, and I have been living in the village since. I captured one snapping turtle, but suffered it to go again–as Mr Agassiz was in New York. However, if I should happen to meet with anything rare I will forward it to you. I thank you for your kind offers–and will avail myself of them so far as to ask if you[a] you can anwhere borrow for me for a short time the[a] copy of the Revue des Deux Mondes containing a notice of Mr Emerson[7]  I should like well to see it, & to read it to Mrs E. & others. If this work is not easy to be obtained[e] do not by any means trouble yourself about it

Yrs truly<br>Henry Thoreau

*Correspondent:* See p. 291.

[1] Alexander Ireland (1810-1894), whom Emerson had met in Edinburgh in 1833, moved to Manchester in 1843 and became the publisher of the *Manchester Examiner*, a paper supporting liberal interests, including the Anti-Corn Law League. Ireland, whom Carlyle called a "solid, dark, broad, rather heavy man; full of energy, and broad sagacity and practicality," was interested in literature and later published a biography of Emerson (*The Correspondence of Emerson and Carlyle*, ed. Joseph Slater [New York: Columbia

University Press, 1964], p. 419). Ireland invited Emerson to lecture to Mechanics' Institutes in English industrial cities, and he offered to make all the business arrangements. Emerson arrived in Liverpool on October 22, 1847. From November 1847 to February 1848 he lectured frequently in the northern part of England and in Scotland. Between June 6 and June 17, 1848, he delivered a six-lecture course in London and then lectured three more times between June 23 and June 30.

[2] T is slightly in error here, for on February 10 Emerson wrote Lidian from Gateshead upon Tyne, rather than from Manchester. Having missed his train to Edinburgh the following day, he arrived barely in time to deliver his lecture "Natural Aristocracy" (*Letters of RWE* 1939, 4:15, 4:18). Though Emerson was well received, he thought the Scots "[g]reat talkers, very fond of argument, but aimless & insane." They "are plainer drest, plainer mannered, than the English, not so clean; & many of them look drunk when they are sober" (*JMN*, 10:218).

[3] Emerson arrived in London on March 2, went to Paris on May 6, returned to London on June 3, and left Liverpool for Boston on July 15.

[4] T refers to *A Week on the Concord and Merrimack Rivers*; see pp. 301-302, note 1, and p. 306, note 1.

[5] The *Massachusetts Quarterly Review*, for which Cabot was the corresponding secretary and business manager.

[6] See p. 320, note 19.

[7] Emile Montégut, "Un penseur et poète Américain: Ralph Waldo Emerson," *Revue des Deux Mondes* 19 (1847): 462-493.

*Copy-text:* ALS (MCR-S, Cabot Family. Papers, 1786-1945, A-99, Folder 96)

*Published:* "E-T" June 1892, 748; *FL* 1894, 186-188; *T: Home* 1902, 146; *FL* 1906, 155-157; *Cor* 1958, 210-211

*Editor's Notes*
This letter is addressed "J. Elliot Cabot Esq. / New Granite Buildings / Court Square / Boston", postmarked "CONCORD Ms. 8 MAR", and endorsed "H. Thoreau. March. 1848."
    care] *PE; possibly* Care *in MS*
    obtained] *PE;* obtain{*MS torn*}

*Author's Alterations*
    April] april
    so] even
    you] *followed by cancelled* know where
    the] a

## To Ralph Waldo Emerson
*Before March 24, 1848*

Dear Friend[e]

Lidian[e] says I must write a sentence about the children. Eddie[e] says he cannot sing "not till mother is agoing to be well". We shall hear his voice very soon in that case I trust. Ellen is already thinking what will be done when you come home, but then she thinks it will be some loss that I shall go away. Edith says that I shall come and see them, and always at tea time so that I can play with her   Ellen thinks she likes father best because he jumps her sometimes

This is the latest news from yours &c

Henry.

P.s. I have received three newspapers from you duly which I have not acknowledged. There is an anti-sabbath convention held in Boston today to which Alcott has gone.[1]

*Correspondent:* See p. 53.

[1] Alcott had taken a lively part in the 1841 Anti-Sabbath Convention, but there is no record of his part in the 1848 meeting called by Garrison, Parker, and a number of their abolitionist friends. The Anti-Sabbath Convention met in Boston on March 23 and March 24 "to confer together, and to decide upon such measures for the dissemination of light and knowledge, on this subject, as may be deemed expedient." The reformers objected to the mandatory observance of the Sabbath as a day of rest on the first day of every week: "We claim for ourselves and for all mankind, the right to worship God according to the dictates of our own consciences. This right, inherent and inalienable, is cloven down in the United States" (*Proceedings of the Anti-Sabbath Convention, Held in the Melodeon, March 23d and 24th* [Boston, 1848], pp. 6, 7-8).

*Copy-text:* ALS (ViU, Clifton Waller Barrett Library, Henry David Thoreau Collection [#6345])

*Published:* "Emerson-Thoreau Correspondence," *AM* 69 (June 1892): 749; *FL* 1894, 189; *FL* 1906, 157-158; *Cor* 1958, 211

*Editor's Notes*
This letter is addressed "R. Waldo Emerson / Care of Alexan-

der Ireland Esq. / Examiner Office, / <u>Manchester</u> / <u>England</u> / via New York / & Steamer / 'Cambria' / March 25th"; postmarked "BOSTON Mass. MAR 24", "AMERICA LIVERPOOL AP 8 1848", and "MANCHEST{*illegible*} AP 9 1848"; and endorsed "H D Thoreau".

The leaf was folded and secured with sealing wax in six places, probably in order to enclose items Lidian Emerson sent to her husband (see "To Ralph Waldo Emerson, Before March 24, 1848," following p. 406). These may have included her letter of March 15 and 18 or her letter of March 24 (in both of these letters, Lidian refers to sending other material along with the letter). See *Letters of Lidian Jackson Emerson* 1987, pp. 141-146. Although "March 23, 1848" is written in pencil in another hand on page 1 of the manuscript, PE supplies the date "Before March 24, 1848" based on the Boston postmark.

   Dear Friend] *PE*; Dea{*MS torn*} Fri{*MS torn*}
   Lidian] *PE*; Lid{*MS torn*}
   Eddie] *PE*; {*MS torn*}die


## From Ralph Waldo Emerson
*March 25, 1848*

                                        London, 25 March, 1848.
Dear Henry,
   Your letter was very welcome and its introduction[1] heartily accepted. In this city & nation of pomps, where pomps too are solid, I fall back on my friends with wonderful refreshment. It is pity, however[a], that you should not see this England, with its indiscribable material superiorities of every kind; the just confidence which immense successes of all sorts have generated in the Englishman that he can do everything, and which his manners, though he is bashful & reserved, betray; the abridgment of all expression, which dense population & the roar of nations enforces; the solidity of science & merit which in any high place you are sure to find (the Church, & some effects of primogeniture excepted)[2]–but I cannot tell my story now. I admire the English I think never more than when I meet Americans–as, for example, at Mr Bancroft's American soiree,[3] which he holds every Sunday night.–  Great is the self respect of Mr Bull. He is very shortsighted & without his eye-glass cannot see as far

as your eyes, to know how you like him, so that he quite neglects that point. The Americans see very well, too well, and the travelling portion are very light troops. But I must not vent my ill humour on my poor compatriots–they are welcome to their revenge & I am quite sure have no reason to spare me if they too are at this hour writing letters to their gossips. I have not gone[a] to Oxford yet, though I still correspond with my friend there, Mr Clough.[4] I meet many young men here, who come to me simply as one of their School of thought, but not often in this class any giants. A Mr Morell who has written a History[a] of Philosophy,[5] and Wilkinson[6] who is a Socialist now & gone to France, I have seen with respect. I[a] went last Sunday for the first time to see Lane at Ham & dined with him. He was full of friendliness & hospitality has a school of 16 children, one lady as matron, then Oldham,–that is all the household.[7] They looked just comfortable. Mr Galpin,[8] tell the Shakers,[9] has *married*. I spent the most of that day in visiting Hampton Court & Richmond & went also into Popes Grotto at Twickenham & saw Horace Walpoles Villa of Strawberry Hill.[10]

> Ever Your friend,
> Waldo E.

*Correspondent:* See p. 53.

[1] Emerson refers to T's uncharacteristically familiar salutation, "Dear Waldo," in his February 23 letter.

[2] Emerson sharply criticized the Church of England in *English Traits*: "when the hierarchy is afraid of science and education, afraid of piety, afraid of tradition, and afraid of theology, there is nothing left but to quit a church which is no longer one" (*The Collected Works of Ralph Waldo Emerson*, vol. 5, *English Traits*, ed. Philip Nicoloff, Robert E. Burkholder, and Douglas Emory Wilson [Cambridge, Mass.: Harvard University Press, 1994], p. 130). A few days after this letter to T, Emerson wrote in his journal: "Col Thompson's theory of Primogeniture, is, that it is to make one son strong enough to force the public to support all the rest" (*JMN*, 10:254).

[3] George Bancroft (1800-1891), a prominent Democrat, was the American minister to Great Britain from 1846 to 1849. On March 14,

1848, Emerson dined with Thomas Babington Macaulay, Christian Karl Josias von Bunsen (the Prussian ambassador to Great Britain), Richard Monckton Milnes, and others at the Bancrofts' home. Bancroft had served as secretary of the navy; he wrote a ten-volume *History of the United States* (Boston: Little, Brown, 1834-1875).

[4] Emerson went to Oxford on March 30 for a short visit. Arthur Hugh Clough (1819-1861), a poet, held a fellowship at Oriel College, Oxford, from 1842 to 1848. He and Emerson were together in Paris later in the spring. In October 1852 Clough came to the United States, visited Emerson, and settled in Cambridge, Massachusetts, until July 1853.

[5] John Daniel Morell (1816-1891), a Nonconformist minister, published *An Historical and Critical View of the Speculative Philosophy of Europe in the Nineteenth Century*. In his journal, Emerson included Morell in a list of "men of literary & social note" who, "dull & mediocre," owed their fame to "a sort of beaver activity & not by any superiority of talent to the masses among which their names resounded" (*JMN*, 10:300).

[6] James John Garth Wilkinson (1812-1899), a homeopathic doctor and a Swedenborgian, was close to Henry James Sr. and to Carlyle. In his journal, Emerson called Wilkinson "the scholar, the catholic cosmic intellect, Bacon's own son, the Lord Chief Justice on the muses' Bench" (*JMN*, 10:146).

[7] In 1838, James Pierrepont Greaves founded an experimental school at Ham Common, Surrey, near London. Named "Alcott House" and founded on the educational principles of Alcott and of the Swiss educational reformer Johann Pestalozzi, the school drew together a band of reformers that included Charles Lane and William Oldham (1790-1879), a failed hat manufacturer. After Greaves died in 1842, Oldham continued as the school's business manager. When Lane returned to England, he taught again at Alcott House until Oldham closed it in 1848 or 1849. Thereafter, Lane resumed his work as editor of the *London Mercantile Price Current*.

[8] Tilton speculates that this is William Galpin, an associate of Robert Owen (*Letters of RWE* 1990-1995, 8:165n93).

[9] The United Society of Believers in Christ's Second Appearing, known as the Shakers, was founded by "Mother" Ann Lee (1736-1784), who settled her group in Watervliet, New York, in 1776. Ann Lee organized a community in Harvard, Massachusetts, as early as 1781; by 1791 she and her followers had built a meeting house and were constructing a Shaker village.

[10] Emerson had visited several sites in the London borough of Richmond upon Thames. Hampton Court, near Richmond in Sur-

rey, dates from the sixteenth century, when Henry VIII appropriated it from Cardinal Wolsey. On his property in Twickenham, Alexander Pope built a tunnel to connect his villa with his extensive garden. In the middle of the tunnel he constructed a grotto, which he decorated elaborately. Horace Walpole had his home at Strawberry Hill, also in Twickenham, transformed into a gothic castle in an elaborate construction project that lasted from 1747 to 1792. The building was the model for his popular novel *The Castle of Otranto: A Story*, trans. William Marshal (Dublin: J. Hoey et al., 1765).

*Copy-text:* ALS (NN-BGC, Henry David Thoreau Collection, 1837-1917, Series IV)

*Published:* "Emerson-Thoreau Correspondence," *AM* 69 (June 1892): 749; *FL* 1894, 148-149; *FL* 1906, 124-125; *Cor* 1958, 212; *Letters of RWE* 1990-1995, 8:164-165

*Author's Alterations*
  however] that
  gone] been
  History] history
  I] *preceded by cancelled* But

       .

## From Harrison Gray Otis Blake
*Before March 27, 1848*

It[1] has revived in me a haunting impression of you, which I carried away from some spoken words of yours. . . . When I was last in Concord, you spoke of retiring farther from our civilization. I asked you if you would feel no longings for the society of your friends. Your reply was in substance, "No, I am nothing." That reply was memorable to me. It indicated a depth of resources, a completeness of renunciation, a poise and repose in the universe, which to me is almost inconceivable; which in you seemed domesticated, and to which I look up with veneration. I would know of that soul which can say "I am nothing." I would be roused by its words to a truer and purer life. Upon me seems to be dawning with new significance the idea that God is here; that we have but to bow before Him in profound submission at every moment, and He will fill our souls with his presence. In this opening of the soul to God, all duties seem to centre; what else have we to do? ... If I understand rightly the significance of your life, this is it: You would sunder yourself from society, from the spell of institutions, customs, conventionalities, that you may lead a fresh, simple life with God. Instead of breathing a new life into the old forms, you would have a new life without and within. There is something sublime to me in this attitude,–far as I may be from it myself.... Speak to me in this hour as you are prompted.... I honor you because you abstain from action, and open your soul that you may *be* somewhat. Amid a world of noisy, shallow actors it is noble to stand aside and say, "I will simply *be.*" Could I plant myself at once upon the truth, reducing my wants to their minimum, ... I should at once be brought nearer to nature, nearer to my fellow-men,–and life would be infinitely richer. But, alas! I shiver on the brink.

*Correspondent:* Harrison Gray Otis Blake (1816-1898), son of Francis and Eliza Chandler Blake of Worcester, Massachusetts, graduated from Harvard University in 1835 and from the Harvard Divinity School in 1838. Though he preached occasionally in 1838 and 1839, Blake never became a minister. In 1839 he opened a school for boys in Charlestown; after leaving that school, he taught sporadically until 1857. Blake was married twice: to Sarah Chandler Ward (1817-1846), daughter of Samuel and Sarah Chandler Ward, in 1840, and to Nancy Pope Howe Conant (1828-1872), daughter of Jacob and Betsy Pope Conant, in 1852. More than a friend, Blake was a disciple who received T's most elaborate and philosophical letters. After T's death, Blake edited four volumes of extracts from T's Journal from the manuscripts Sophia Thoreau bequeathed him.

[1] Sanborn identifies the subject of the letter's first sentence as T's "Aulus Persius Flaccus," an essay that appeared in the July 1840 *Dial* (pp. 117-121; see *Early Essays* 1975, pp. 122-127).

*Copy-text:* FL 1894, 190-191

*Published:* FL 1894, 190-191; FL 1906, 158-159; *Cor* 1958, 213; *Spiritual Seeker* 2004, 33-34

*Editor's Note*

PE supplies the date "Before March 27, 1848" from the contents of T's reply to Blake, which was dated "March 27, 1848."

## To Harrison Gray Otis Blake

*March 27, 1848*

Concord, March 27, 1848.

I am glad to hear that any words of mine, though spoken so long ago that I can hardly claim identity with their author, have reached you. It gives me pleasure, because I have therefore reason to suppose that I have uttered what concerns men, and that it is not in vain that man speaks to man. This is the value of literature. Yet those days are so distant, in every sense, that I have had to look at that page again, to learn what was the tenor of my thoughts then. I should value that article, however, if only because it was the occasion of your letter.

I do believe that the outward and the inward life correspond; that if any should succeed to live a higher life, others would not know of it; that difference and distance are one. To set about living a true life is to go a journey to a distant country, gradually to find ourselves surrounded by new scenes and men; and as long as the old are around me, I know that I am not in any true sense living a new or a better life. The outward is only the outside of that which is within. Men are not concealed under habits, but are revealed by them; they are their true clothes. I care not how curious a reason they may give for their abiding by them. Circumstances are not rigid and unyielding, but our habits are rigid. We are apt to speak vaguely sometimes, as if a divine life were to be grafted on to or built over this present as a suitable foundation. This might do if we could so build over our old life as to exclude from it all the warmth of our affection, and addle it, as the thrush builds over the cuckoo's egg, and lays her own atop, and hatches that only;[1] but the fact is, we–so there is$^v$ the partition–hatch them both, and the cuckoo's always by a day first, and that young bird crowds the young thrushes out of the nest. No. Destroy the cuckoo's egg, or build a new nest.

Change is change. No new life occupies the old bodies;–they decay. *It* is born, and grows, and flourishes. Men very pathetically inform the old, accept and wear it. Why put up with the almshouse when you may go to Heaven? It is embalming,–no more. Let alone your ointments and your linen swathes, and go into an infant's body. You see in the catacombs of Egypt the result of that experiment,– that is the end of it.

I do believe in simplicity. It is astonishing as well as sad, how many trivial affairs even the wisest man thinks he must attend to in a day; how singular an affair he thinks he must omit. When the mathematician would solve a difficult problem, he first frees the equation of all encumbrances, and reduces it to its simplest terms. So simplify the problem of life, distinguish the necessary and the real. Probe the earth to see where your main roots run. I would stand upon facts. Why not see,–use our eyes? Do men know nothing? I know many men who, in common things, are not to be deceived; who trust no moonshine; who count their money correctly, and know how to invest it; who are said to be prudent and knowing, who yet will stand at a desk the greater part of their lives, as cashiers in banks, and glimmer and rust and finally go out there. If they *know* anything, what under the sun do they do that for? Do they know what *bread* is? or what it is for? Do they know what life is? If they *knew* something, the places which know them now would know them no more forever.

This, our respectable daily life, in$^v$ which the man of common sense, the Englishman of the world, stands so squarely, and on which our institutions are founded, is in fact the veriest illusion, and will vanish like the baseless fabric of a vision;[2] but that faint glimmer of reality which sometimes illuminates the darkness of daylight for all men, reveals something more solid and enduring than adamant, which is in fact the corner-stone of the world.

Men cannot conceive of a state of things so fair that it cannot be realized. Can any man honestly consult his experience and say that it is so? Have we any facts to appeal to when we say that our dreams are premature? Did you ever hear of a man who had striven all his life faithfully and singly toward an object and in no measure obtained it? If a man constantly aspires, is he not elevated? Did ever a man try heroism, magnanimity, truth, sincerity, and find that there was no advantage in them? that it was a vain endeavor? Of course we do not expect that our paradise will be a garden. We know not what we ask.[3] To look at literature;–how many fine thoughts has every man had! how few fine thoughts are expressed! Yet we never have a fantasy so subtle and ethereal, but that *talent merely*, with more resolution and faithful persistency, after a thousand failures, might fix and engrave it in distinct and enduring words, and we should see that our dreams are the solidest facts that we know. But I speak not of dreams.

What can be expressed in words can be expressed in life.

My actual life is a fact in view of which I have no occasion to congratulate myself, but for my faith and aspiration I have respect. It is from these that I speak.– Every man's position[e] is in fact too simple to be described. I have sworn no oath. I have no designs on society–or nature–or God. I am simply what I am, or I begin to be that. I *live* in the *present*. I only remember the past–and anticipate the future. I love to live. I love reform better than its modes. There is no history of how bad became better. I believe something, and there is nothing else but that. I know that I am–I know that another[e] is who knows more than I who takes[e] {*MS torn*} interest[e] in me, whose creature and yet[e]

{*MS torn*} kindred[e], in one sense, am I. I know that the enterprise is worthy– I know that things work well. I have heard no bad news.

As for positions–as for combinations and details–What are they? In clear weather when we look into the heavens, what do we see, but the sky and the sun?

If you would convince a man that he does wrong–do right. But do not care to convince him.– Men will believe what they see– Let them see. Pursue, keep up with, circle round and round your life as a dog does his master's chaise. Do what you love. Know[a] your own bone; gnaw at it, bury it, unearth it, and gnaw it still. Do not be too moral. You may cheat yourself out of much life so. Aim above morality. Be not *simply* good–be good for something.– All fables indeed have their morals, but the innocent enjoy the story.

Let nothing come between you and the light.[4] Respect men as brothers only When[a] you travel to the celestial city carry no letter of introduction. When you knock ask to see God–none of the servants. In what concerns you much[e] do not think that you have companions–know that you are alone in the world.

Thus I write at random. I need to see you, and I trust I shall, to correct my mistakes. Perhaps you have some oracles for me

Henry Thoreau.

*Correspondent:* See p. 358.

[1] The British–but not the American–cuckoo lays its eggs in another bird's nest.

[2] T alludes to Prospero's speech to Ferdinand and Miranda after Prospero dissolved the group of spirits he had created (Shakespeare, vol. 1, *The Tempest*, 4.1.151-156):

> And, like the baseless fabric of this vision,
> The cloud-capp'd towers, the gorgeous palaces,
> The solemn temples, the great globe itself,
> Yea, all which it inherit, shall dissolve;
> And, like this insubstantial pageant faded,
> Leave not a rack behind:

³ T alludes to Mark 10:38: "Ye know not what ye ask: can ye drink of the cup that I drink of?"

⁴ T alludes to the meeting of Alexander and Diogenes as related in *Plutarch's Lives of the Most Select and Illustrious Characters of Antiquity*: when Alexander asked Diogenes if there was anything he could "serve him in", Diogenes replied, "Only stand a little out of my sunshine" (p. 304).

*Copy-text:* PE lines 359.6-361.24 (Concord ... in life.), *LVP* 1865, 41-45; PE lines 361.25-362.11 (My actual ... bone; gnaw), AL (NN-BGC, Henry David Thoreau Collection, 1837-1917, Series III); PE line 362.12 (at), ALS (MH-G, Walter Deane [1848-1930] Papers, Autograph Collection); PE line 362.12 (it, bury ... gnaw it), AL (NN-BGC, Henry David Thoreau Collection, 1837-1917, Series III); PE line 362.12 (still. Do not be too), ALS (MH-G, Walter Deane [1848-1930] Papers, Autograph Collection); PE lines 362.13-25 (moral. You ... for me), AL (NN-BGC, Henry David Thoreau Collection, 1837-1917, Series III); PE line 362.26 (Henry Thoreau.), ALS (MH-G, Walter Deane [1848-1930] Papers, Autograph Collection)

*Published:* *LVP* 1865, 41-46; *FL* 1894, 192-197; *T: Home* 1902, 209; *FL* 1906, 160-164; *Cor* 1958, 214-217; *Spiritual Seeker* 2004, 35-39

*Editor's Notes*
This letter is addressed "H. G. O. Blake / Worcester / Mass."

The copy-text is a composite of a published source, *LVP* 1865, and two manuscript sources, one at NN-BGC, the other at MH-G. The manuscript was originally a folio, only one leaf of which survives. Blake cut the signature out of the surviving leaf, which is at NN-BGC. Beneath the address on that leaf are a pencilled drawing of a face, several doodles, and Blake's note in ink:

> The signature of this letter 'Henry Thoreau' I have cut out to-day on the application of Mrs. Edward Hoar of Concord, for Mr. Dean, a botanist, I understand. H. G. O. Blake. July 26, 1886. On the reverse side of the paper was a part of 'at it', the word 'still.' & 'Do not be too'

The portion that Blake cut out is now at MH-G; on the verso he wrote:

> Frm. letter dated March 27, 1848, in vol. of. 'Letters.'

For images of the parts of the manuscript, see "To Harrison Gray Otis Blake, March 27, 1848," following p. 406.

position] *PE*; posi{*MS blotted*}n
another] *PE*; {*MS torn*}ther
takes] *PE*; tak{*text obscured by sealing wax*}

interest] *PE*; {*MS torn*}nterest
yet] *PE*; ye{*text obscured by sealing wax*}
kindred] *PE*; {*MS torn*}ndred
much] *PE*; muc{*MS cut*}

*Substantive Variants*
    A portion of the text of this letter is based on a published source, *LVP* 1865; potentially authoritative substantive readings in *FL* 1906 are reported below.

    so there is] *in copy-text (LVP 1865);* so thin is *in FL 1906*
    in] *in copy-text (LVP 1865);* on *in FL 1906*

*Author's Alterations*
    Know] know
,   When] when


## From Horace Greeley

*April 3, 1848*

New-York, April 3, 1848.

My Friend Thoreau:

    I have but this moment received yours of 31st ult.[1] and was greatly relieved by[a] the breaking of your long silence. Yet it saddens and surprises me to know that your article was not paid for by Graham; and, since my honor is involved in the matter, I will see that you *are* paid, and that at no distant day.[2] I shall not forget the matter, and hope you will not feel annoyed at my interference in the premises. I choose to speak about it, and don't believe Graham will choose to differ with me. Don't fear for my time; I expect to visit Philadelphia on my own business next week, and will have time to look into the matter.

    As to "Katahdin and the Maine Woods," I will take it and send you the money if I cannot dispose of it more to your advantage within the week ensuing.[3] I hope I can.

Yours,
Horace Greeley.

*Correspondent:* See p. 280.

    [1] That is, March 31; the letter is not extant.
    [2] T's article "Thomas Carlyle and His Works" was accepted by

*Graham's Magazine* in September 1846 and published in the March 1847 (pp. 145-152) and April 1847 (pp. 238-245) issues (see *Early Essays* 1975, pp. 219-267). T did not receive any payment until May 1848. See Greeley's letters of September 30 and October 26, 1846, and May 17, 1848, for details (pp. 281, 283, 372-373).

³ T's "Ktaadn, and the Maine Woods" appeared in the *Union Magazine of Literature and Art* in five parts between July and November 1848 (see p. 388, note 1). The essay formed the first part of *The Maine Woods* (see *The Maine Woods*, ed. Joseph J. Moldenhauer [Princeton, N.J.: Princeton University Press, 1972], pp. 3-83).

*Copy-text:*  ALS (NNPM, MA 920)

*Published:*  *HDT* 1882, 224; *FL* 1894, 204; *FL* 1906, 169-170; *Cor* 1958, 217

*Editor's Note*
   This letter is addressed "Henry D. Thoreau, / Concord, / Mass.", postmarked "NEW-YORK 5 CtS 4 APR", and endorsed "H. Greeley". In writing the address, Greeley first wrote "Mr" and then altered "Mr" to "Henry".

*Author's Alteration*
   by] to


## From Horace Greeley
*April 17, 1848*

                                          New York, April 17, 1848.
My Friend Thoreau,

   I have been hurried about a thousand things, including a Charter Election,¹ and have not yet settled your business with Graham. I went to Philadelphia last Wednesday, and called twice at Graham's office with-out finding him; and though I *did* see him in the evening, it was at a crowded dinner party where I had no chance to speak with him on business. But I have taken that matter in hand, and I will see that you are paid,–within a week, I hope, but at any rate soon.

   I enclose you $25 for your article on Maine Scenery,² as promised. I know it is worth more, though I have not yet found time to read it; but I have tried once[a] to sell it without success. It is rather long for my[a] columns and too fine[a] for the million; but I consider it a cheap bargain, and shall print it myself if I do not dispose of it to better advantage. You will not of course consider yourself under any sort of obligation to me, for my offer was in the way of business and I have got more than the worth of my money. Send me a line acknowledging the receipt of the money, and say if all is right between us. I am a little ashamed of Graham's tardiness, but I shall correct it, and I would have done so long ago if I had known he had neglected you. I shall make it come round soon.

If you will write me two or three articles in the course of the summer, I think I can dispose of them for your benefit. But write not more than half as long as your article just sent me, for that is tooo[e] long for the Magazines. If that were in two it would be far more valuable.

What about your book?[3] Is any thing going on about it now? Why did not Emerson try it in England? I think the Howitts could get it favorably before the British public.[4] If you can suggest any way wherein I can put it forward, do not hesitate, but command me.

Yours,<br>Horace Greeley.

$25 enclosed

    $5. Appleton Boston

    5. Bridgeport, Conn

    5 Globe, Providence[e]

    5 Brattleboro, Vt.

    5[a] F & CU. Burlington Vt.[5]

*Correspondent:* See p. 280.

[1] New York City's annual Charter Election chose members of the municipal government. In 1848 the incumbent Whigs, whom Greeley supported, were voted out of power, losing the mayor's office as well as their majority on the common council.

[2] The enclosed twenty-five dollars was Greeley's advance pay-

ment for "Ktaadn, and the Maine Woods." On May 17, Greeley sent
T fifty dollars of the seventy-five he got from Graham for "Thomas
Carlyle and His Works," repaying himself the twenty-five dollars
he sent with this letter and promising to pay T a larger amount for
the Ktaadn essay after he succeeded in placing it (see pp. 372-373).
After T assured him that twenty-five dollars would be satisfactory,
Greeley again sent him that amount (pp. 376, 382-383); on May 21
T reported to Emerson that "Greeley has sent me $100 dollars and
wants more manuscript" (p. 380). In October 1848 Greeley sold
the Ktaadn essay for seventy-five dollars; he then sent T another
twenty-five dollars and kept the remaining fifty dollars, twenty-five
to repay himself and twenty-five to cover his expenses (see pp. 387-
388).

[3] *A Week on the Concord and Merrimack Rivers* did not appear
until May 26 the following year.

[4] Both William Howitt (1792-1879) and his wife Mary Botham
Howitt (1799-1888) were writers and editors. William Howitt's *Book
of the Seasons* (London: Henry Colburn and Richard Bentley, 1831)
was well known, and T quoted from it in his college essays and
in his Journal. Mary Howitt wrote popular tales for children and
translated the Swedish novels of Fredrika Bremer. The Howitts coedited a weekly periodical, *Howitt's Journal*, that ran from January
1847 to June 1848.

[5] Greeley sent T bank notes issued by each of these five banks.

*Copy-text:* ALS (CtY-BR, Yale Collection of American Literature,
ZA Letter File)

*Published: HDT* 1882, 226, 227; *New York Times*, March 14, 1909, p.
8; *Cor* 1958, 218-219

*Editor's Notes*
This letter is addressed "Henry D. Thoreau, Esq. / Concord, /
Middlesex Co. Massachusetts.", postmarked "NEW-YORK APL 19",
and endorsed "H. Greeley".
    tooo] *PE*; *posssibly* two *in MS*
    Providence] *PE*; Providene *in MS*

*Author's Alterations*
    once] one
    my] me
    fine] find
    5] $

*To Harrison Gray Otis Blake*
*May 2, 1848*

Concord, May 2, 1848.

"We must have our bread." But what is our bread? Is it baker's bread? Methinks it should be very *home-made* bread. What is our meat? Is it butcher's meat? What is that which we *must* have? Is that bread which we are now earning sweet? Is it not bread which has been suffered to sour, and then been sweetened with an alkali, which has undergone the vinous, acetous, and sometimes the pu-trid fermentation, and then been whitened with vitriol? Is this the bread which we must have? Man must earn his bread by the sweat of his brow,[1] truly, but also by the sweat of his brain within his brow. The body can feed the body only. I have tasted but little bread in my life. It has been mere grub and provender for the most part. Of bread that nourished the brain and the heart, scarcely any. There is absolutely none even on the tables[v] of the rich.

There is not one kind of food for all men. You must and you will feed those faculties which you exercise. The la-borer whose body is weary does not require the same food with the scholar whose brain is weary. Men should not labor foolishly like brutes, but the brain and the body should always, or as much as possible, work and rest to-gether, and then the work will be of such a kind that when the body is hungry the brain will be hungry also, and the same food will suffice for both; otherwise the food which repairs the waste energy of the over-wrought body will oppress the sedentary brain, and the degenerate scholar will come to esteem all food vulgar, and all getting a living drudgery.

How shall we earn our bread is a grave question; yet it is a sweet and inviting question. Let us not shirk it, as is usually done. It is the most important and practical ques-tion which is put to man. Let us not answer it hastily. Let us not be content to get our bread in some gross, careless, and hasty manner. Some men go a-hunting, some a-fishing, some a-gaming, some to war; but none have so pleasant a time as they who in earnest seek to earn their bread. It is true actually as it is true really; it is true materially as it is true spiritually, that they who seek honestly and sincerely, with all their hearts and lives and strength, to earn their bread, do earn it, and it is sure to be very sweet to them. A very little bread,–a very few crumbs are enough, if it be of the right quality, for it is infinitely nutritious. Let each man, then, earn at least a crumb of bread for his body before he dies, and know the taste of it,–that it is identical with the bread of life,[2] and that they both go down at one swallow.

Our bread need not ever be sour or hard to digest. What Nature is to the mind she is also to the body. As she feeds my imagination, she will feed my body; for what she says she means, and is ready to do. She is not simply beautiful to the poet's eye. Not only the rainbow and sunset are beautiful, but to be fed and clothed, sheltered and warmed aright, are equally beautiful and inspiring. There is not necessarily any gross and ugly fact which may not be eradicated from the life of man. We should endeavor practically in our lives to correct all the defects which our imagination detects. The heavens are as deep as our aspirations are high. So high as a tree aspires to grow, so high it will find an atmosphere suited to it. Every man should stand for a force which is perfectly irresistible. How can any man be weak who dares *to be* at all? Even the tenderest plants force their way up through the hardest earth, and the crevices of rocks; but a man no material power can resist. What a wedge, what a beetle, what a catapult, is an *earnest* man! What can resist him?

It is a momentous fact that a man may be *good*, or he may be *bad*; his life may be *true*, or it may be *false*; it may be either a shame or a glory to him. The good man builds himself up; the bad man destroys himself.

But whatever we do we must do confidently (if we are timid, let us, then, act timidly), not expecting more light, but having light enough. If we confidently expect more, then let us wait for it. But what is this which we have? Have we not already waited? Is this the beginning of time? Is there a man who does not see clearly beyond, though only a hair's breadth beyond where he at any time stands?

If one hesitates in his path, let him not proceed. Let him respect his doubts, for doubts, too, may have some divinity in them. That we have but little faith is not sad, but that we have but little faithfulness. By faithfulness faith is earned. When, in the progress of a life, a man swerves, though only by an angle infinitely small, from his proper and allotted path (and this is never done quite unconsciously even at first; in fact, that was his broad and scarlet sin,[3]–ah, he knew of it more than he can tell), then the drama of his life turns to tragedy, and makes haste to its fifth act. When once we thus fall behind ourselves, there is no accounting for the obstacles which rise up in our path, and no one is so wise as to advise, and no one so powerful as to aid us while we abide on that ground. Such are cursed with *duties*, and the *neglect of their duties*. For such the decalogue was made, and other far more voluminous and terrible codes.

These departures,–who have not made them?–for they are as faint as the parallax of a fixed star, and at the commencement we say they are nothing,–that is, they originate in a kind of sleep and forgetfulness of the soul when it is naught. A man cannot be too circumspect in order to keep in the straight road, and be sure that he sees all that he may at any time see, that so he may distinguish his true path.

You ask if there is no doctrine of sorrow in my philosophy. Of acute sorrow I suppose that I know comparatively little. My saddest and most genuine sorrows are apt to be but transient regrets. The place of sorrow is supplied, perchance, by a certain hard and proportionably[v] barren indifference. I am of kin to the sod, and partake largely of its dull patience,–in winter expecting the sun of spring.

In my cheapest moments I am apt to think that it is not my business to be "seeking the spirit," but as much its business to be seeking me.

I know very well what Goethe meant when he said that he never had a chagrin, but he made a poem out of it.[4] I have altogether too much patience of this kind. I am too easily contented with a slight and almost animal happiness. My happiness is a good deal like that of the woodchucks[e].

Methinks I am never quite committed, never wholly the creature of my moods, being[v] always to some extent their critic. My only integral experience is in my vision. I see, perchance, with more integrity than I feel.

But I need not tell you what manner of man I am,–my virtues or my vices. You can guess if it is worth the while; and I do not discriminate them well.

I do not write this time at[v] my hut in the woods. I am at present living with Mrs. Emerson, whose house is an old home of mine, for company during Mr. E.'s absence.

You will perceive that I am as often talking to myself, perhaps, as speaking to you.

Henry Thoreau

*Correspondent:* See p. 358.

[1] See Gen. 3:19: "In the sweat of thy face shalt thou eat bread." See also p. 375 and *Walden*: "It is not necessary that a man should earn his living by the sweat of his brow, unless he sweats easier than I do" (*Walden* 1971, p. 71).

[2] John 6:35: "And Jesus said unto them, I am the bread of life."

[3] The phrase "scarlet sin" probably derives from Isa. 1:18: "though your sins be as scarlet, they shall be white as snow."

[4] T possibly refers to the following sentence in Goethe's autobiography: "And thus began that bent of mind from which I could not deviate my whole life through; namely, that of turning into an image, into a poem, every thing that delighted or troubled me, or

otherwise occupied my attention" (*The Auto-Biography of Goethe*, vol. 1, pt. 2, p. 66).

*Copy-text: LVP* 1865, 47-52

*Published: LVP* 1865, 47-52; *FL* 1894, 197-203; *FL* 1906, 164-168; *Cor* 1958, 219-222; *Spiritual Seeker* 2004, 40-44

*Editor's Note*
    woodchucks] *PE*; wood- / chucks *in copy-text*

*Substantive Variants*
    The text of this letter is based on a published source, *LVP* 1865; potentially authoritative substantive readings in *FL* 1906 are reported below.
    none even on the tables] *in copy-text;* none on the tables even *in FL 1906*
    proportionably] *in copy-text;* proportionately *in FL 1906*
    moods, being] *in copy-text;* moods, but *in FL 1906*
    this time at] *in copy-text;* this at *in FL 1906*

## From Horace Greeley
*May 17, 1848*

New-York, May 17, 1848.

Dear Friend Thoreau,

I trust you have not thought me neglectful or dilatory with regard to your business. On the contrary, I have done my very best throughout, and it is only to-day that I have been able to lay my hand on the money due you from Graham. I have been to see him in Philadelphia, but[a] did not catch him in his business-office, then I have been here to meet him and been referred to his brother,[1] &c. I finally found the two Nos. of his work in which your article was published (not easy, I assure you, for he has them not, nor his brother, and I hunted them up and bought one of them at a very out-of-the-way place,) and with these I made[a] out a regular bill for the contribution, drew a draft on G. R. G.[2] for the amount, gave it to his brother here for collection, and today received the money. Now you see how to get pay for yourself another time. I have pioneered the way, and you can[a] follow it easily yourself. There has been no intentional injustice on Graham's part, but he is overwhelmed with business, has too many irons in the fire, drinks some, and we did not go at him the right way. Had you drawn a draft on him at first, and given it to the Concord Bank to send on for collection, you would have received[a] your money long since.

Enough of this. I have made Graham pay you $75, but I only send you $50, because, having got so much for Carlyle, I am ashamed to take your Maine Woods for $25. On the contrary, I shall now stand even with you in money, but in debt to you for whatever I may obtain for the Maine article. I have expectations of procuring it a place in a new Magazine of high character,[3] that will pay. I don't expect to get so much for it as for Carlyle, but I hope to get $50.

Thoreau, if you will only write one or two articles when in the spirit about *half the length* of this, I can sell it readily and advantageously. The length of your papers is the only impediment to their appreciation by the magazines. Give me one or two shorter, and I will try to coin them speedily.

If you are satisfied to take the $25 for your Maine Woods, say so, and I will send on the money, but I don't want to seem a Jew buying your articles at half price to speculate you. If you choose to let it go that way, it shall be so; but I would sooner do my best for you, and send you the money.

Yours,
Horace Greeley.

*Correspondent:* See p. 280.

[1] George Rex Graham's brother William H. Graham was also a publisher. He moved from Philadelphia to New York City in 1844 and rented office space from Greeley in the *Tribune* building.

[2] George Rex Graham.

[3] Greeley refers to the *Nineteenth Century: A Quarterly Miscellany*, which had begun publication in January 1848 in Philadelphia under the editorship of Charles Chauncey Burr (1815?-1883), son

of Martin and Abigail Baxter Burr of Mercer, Maine. Dedicated to
Douglas Jerrold, an English satirist and critic and a popular contributor to *Punch*, the first issue opened with an engraving of Greeley and included essays by Burr, Greeley, William Henry Furness,
and John Neal. On May 19 Greeley wrote Burr, "I shall secure an
article from Thoreau of Concord. Though not in the Reforming
vein, it is full of Poetry and Nature. Shall I send it before, or bring
it with me when I come to Philadelphia on the 5th of June?" (Horace Greeley to C. Chauncey Burr, May 19, 1848, NHi, James Wright
Brown Collection, Greeley, Horace). Burr later became a notorious supporter of the South during the Civil War; he relentlessly attacked Lincoln and strongly opposed the nomination of Greeley as
the Republican candidate for president in 1872.

*Copy-text:* ALS (ViU, Clifton Waller Barrett Library, Horace Greeley Collection [#7669])

*Published:* HDT 1882, 224-225, 226, 228; *FL* 1894, 204; *FL* 1906, 170;
*Cor* 1958, 222-223

*Editor's Note*
    This letter is addressed "Henry D. Thoreau, Esq. / Concord, /
Mass." and endorsed "H. Greeley."

*Author's Alterations*
    but] bud
    made] *followed by cancelled* a
    can] *followed by cancelled* get
    received] gone


## To Horace Greeley
*May 19, 1848*

                                        Concord May 19th 1848.
My Friend Greeley,
    I received from you fifty dollars to-day.–
    For the last five years I have supported myself solely
by the labor of my hands–  I have not received one cent
from any other source, and this has cost me so little time,
say a month in the spring and another in the autumn,
doing the coarsest work of all kinds, that I have probably enjoyed more leisure for literary pursuits than any

contemporary. For more than two years past I have lived alone in the woods, in a good plastered and shingled house entirely of my own building, earning only what I wanted, and sticking to my proper work. The fact is man need not live by the sweat of his brow–unless he sweats easier than I do[1]–he needs so little. For two years and two months all my expenses have amounted to but 27 cents a week, and I have fared gloriously in all respects. If a man must have money, and he needs but the smallest amount, the true and independent way to earn it is by day-labor with his hands at a dollar a day–  I have tried many ways and can speak from experience.–  Scholars are apt to think themselves privileged to complain as if their lot was a peculiarly hard one. How much have we heard about the attainment of knowledge under difficulties of poets starving in garrets–depending on the patronage[a] of the wealthy–and finally dying mad. It is time that men sang another song–  There is no reason why the scholar who professes to be a little wiser than the mass of men, should not do his work in the ditch occasionally, and by means of his superior wisdom make much less suffice for him–  A wise man will not be unfortunate. How then would you know but he was a fool?

This money therefore comes as a free and even[e] unexpected gift to me–

My Friend Greeley, I know not how to thank you for your kindness–to thank you is not the way–  I can only assure you that I see and appreciate it–  To think that while I have been sitting comparatively idle here, you have been so active in my behalf!

You have done well for me. I only wish it had been in a better cause–  Yet the value of good deeds is not affected by the unworthiness of their object. Yes–that was the right way, but who would ever have thought of it? I think it might not have occurred even to some what of a business man. I am not one in the common sense at all–that is I am not acquainted with the forms– I might have way-laid him perhaps. I perceive that your way has this advantage too, that he who draws the draft determines the amount which[a] it is drawn for. You prized it well, that was the exact amount.

If more convenient the Maine article might be printed in the form of letters; you have only to leave off at the end of a day, and put the date before the next one. I shall certainly be satisfied to receive $25.00 for it–that was all I expected *if* you *took* it–but I do not by any means consider you bound[a] to pay me that–the article not being what you asked for, and being sent after so long a delay. You shall therefore, if you take it, send me 25 dollars now, or[a] when you have disposed of it, whichever is most convenient– that is, after deducting the necessary expenses which I perceive you must have incurred. This is all I ask for it.

The carrier it is commonly who makes the money– I am concerned to see that you as carrier make nothing at all–but are in danger of losing a good deal of your time as well as some of your money.

So I get off–or rather so I am compelled to go off muttering my ineffectual[a] thanks– But believe me, my Friend, the gratification which your letter affords me is not wholly selfish.

Trusting that my Good Genius will continue to protect me on this accession of wealth, I remain

Yours

Henry Thoreau

P.S. My book is swelling again under my hands, but as soon as I have leisure I shall see to those shorter articles. So look out.

*Correspondent:* See p. 280.

[1] Gen. 3:19; see p. 371, note 1.

*Copy-text:* ALS (MB, Gris. Mss. 1080)

*Published: New-York Daily Tribune* (May 25, 1848), 2; *FL* 1894, 205-207; *Passages from the Correspondence and Other Papers of Rufus W. Griswold* (Cambridge, Mass.: W. M. Griswold, 1898), 233-235; *FL* 1906, 170-172; *Cor* 1958, 223-225; *Companion* 1964, 175; *ARLR* 1993, 80

*Editor's Notes*
This letter is addressed "Horace Greeley, Esq. / Tribune Office / New-York / N.Y." and postmarked "CONCORD MS 19 MAY".
even] *PE*; *possibly* ever *in MS*

*Author's Alterations*
patronage] patrons
which] *preceded by cancelled* for
bound] bond
or] *followed by cancelled* you shall send me 25 dollars
ineffectual] *preceded by cancelled* thanks.


## To Ralph Waldo Emerson
*May 21 and 22, 1848*

Concord May 21ˢᵗ 1848

Dear Friend

Mrs Emerson is in Boston whither she went with Eddy yesterdayᵃ saturday, and I do not know that my news will be worth sending alone. Perhaps she will come home in season to send with me from Concord  The Steam mill was burnt last night & it was a fine sight lighting up the rivers and meadows– The owners who bought it the other day for seven thousand dollars, though it was insured for 6 I hear sinceᵃ, will be gainers rather than losers–but some individuals who hired of them have lost–my Fatherᵃ probably more than any–from four to five hundred dollars, not being insured.¹ Some think that it was set on fire. I have no doubt that the wise fates *did* set it on fire, and I quite agree with them that that disgrace to Concord enterprise & skill needed to be burnt away. It was a real purification as far as it went, and evidence of it was borne to every man's door. I picked up cinders *in your yard* this morning 6 inches long–though there was no wind.

Your trees are doing very well; but one died in the winter–the Watson pear, a native, which apparently grew more than any other last year, and hence it died. I am a constant[a] foe to the caterpillars

Mr Alcott recommenced work on the Arbor yesterday, or rather commenced repairs–[2]  But[a] enough of this.

Mr Warren[3] tells me that he is on the point of buying the hill field for you, perhaps for a hundred dollars, and he remembers that you would allow him and Stow[4] the privelege of a *way* to their fields–  I should beware how I suffered him to transact this business with such an implied privilege for his compensation. It would certainly greatly reduce the value of the field to you.

Your island wood was severely burnt[5]–but Reuben Brown says that it may stand till winter without harm before it is cut. He suffered his own to stand last year.

There are applications for the Walden field and house which await your attention when you come home.

The proposition for a new journal is likely to fall among inflammable materials here–& excite another short and ineffectual blaze. As for me, I cannot yet join the *journalists* any more than the Fourierites–for I can not adopt their principles–  One reason is because I do not know what they are.[6]

Men talk as if you couldn't get good things printed, but I *think* as if you could'nt get them written. That at least is the whole difficulty with me.

I am more interested in the private journal than the public one, and it would be better news to me to hear that there were two or three valuable papers lying written in England & America–that might be printed sometime–than that there were 30,000 dollars[a] to defray expenses–& forty thousand men standing *ready to write* merely, but no certainty of anything valuable being written. The blacksmiths[e] met together looking grim and voted to have a thunderbolt, if they could only get some one to launch it, but all the while there was not one man among them who could *make* anything better than a horse-shoe nail.

Who has any desire to split himself any further up by straddling the Atlantic? We are extremities enough already. There is danger of one's straddling so far that he can never recover[a] an upright position. There are certain men in Old[a] & New England who aspire to the renown of the Colossus of Rhodes, and to have ships sail under them.[7]

Those who build castles in the air generally have one foot in the moon.[8]

What after all is the value of a journal, the best that we know–but a short essay once in 2 or 3 years which you can read–separated by impassable swamps of ink & paper–   It is the combination that makes the swamp, but not the firm oasis.

A journal 2 or 3 times as good as the best English one even would not be worth the while–   It would not interest you nor[a] me.

To be sure there is no telling what an individual may do, but it is easy to tell what half a dozen men may *not* do unless they are to a certain extent united as one. How was it with the Mass. Quart. Rev? Several men undertook to make a small book for mankind to read–& advertised then what they were about some months before hand– and after considerable delay they brought it out–& I read it, or what I could of it, and certainly if one man had written it all a wise publisher would not have advised to print it. It should have been suppressed for nobody was starving for *that*. It probably is not so good a book as the Boston Almanack[9]–or that little book of[a] about the same size which Mr Spaulding has just put out called his Practical[a] Thoughts–for Mr Spaulding's contains more of autobiography at least. In this case there is nothing to come to

the rescue of. Is it the publisher?–or the reputations of
the editors? The journal itself has no character. Shall we
make a rush to save a piece of paper which is falling to the
ground? It is as good as anybody seriously designed that
it should be or meant to make it.–  But I am ashamed to
write such things as these.

  I am glad to hear that you are writing so much–  Lectu-
ring[a] is of little consequence. Dont forget to inquire after
Persian and Hindoo books in London or Paris. Ellen &
Edith are as well as flies. I have had earnest letters from H.
G. O. Blake. Greeley has sent me $100 dollars[10] and wants
more manuscript.

  But this–and all this letter are nothing to the purpose.

H. Thoreau.

  P.S.  22nd  Mrs E. has come home tonight and openened
your letter   I am glad to find that you are expecting a line
from me, since I have a better excuse for sending this hard
scrawl. I trust however that the most prosaic Concord
news acquires a certain value by the time it reaches London, as Concord cranberries have done. But dont think
that these berries have soured by the way, as did the first
receives–  They are naturally harsh and sour. Yet I think
that I could listen kindly and without selfishness to men's
projected enterprises if they were not too easy.–if they
were struggles not unto death but even unto life.[11] I read
in a Texas paper sent to you that there was a farm for sale
in that country "suitable for a man of small force"  You
had better make a minute of this for the benefit of some
of your literary acquaintances.

*Correspondent:*  See p. 53.

  [1] The Concord Steam Mill Company was owned by Abel Moore,
Sherman Barrett, and others who had bought stock in the company. In March 1848 Moore and Barrett leased the mill to Alfred
Fisher. The fire totally destroyed the mill: one estimate was that
"the whole mass of [the] machinery is about the same as entirely
ruined, with the exception of the Boilers which are much injured

by fire" (Otis Tufts to Abel Moore, June 22, 1848, MCo-SC, Nathan Brooks Family Papers, Series V, Box 44, Folder 3). Caleb Wheeler, citing a contemporaneous newspaper report that describes the property as a "sawmill, grist mill and lead pencil manufactury," speculates that the Thoreau family may have "rented part of this mill to manufacture the wooden part of the pencils" (*Cor* 1958, p. 228).

2 Work on Emerson's summerhouse continued through the fall of 1847 and resumed in the spring of 1848; see pp. 318-319, note 6.

3 Cyrus Warren.

4 Cyrus Stow.

5 On April 10 a passing locomotive set fire to Emerson's wood-lot, burning slightly "less than two acres" that were "bounded on one side by the railroad, & on all other sides by a wet meadow." On August 31 Emerson wrote to the Fitchburg Railroad Company from Concord; he requested, and later received, fifty dollars in compensation (*Letters of RWE* 1939, 4:110).

6 Talk of new journals was frequent during spring 1848. Emerson wrote to Lidian that John Chapman proposed "to establish a journal common to Old & New England" (*Letters of RWE* 1939, 4:56), a plan that prompted T's comments in this letter. Alcott also mentioned Chapman's idea in a letter to Charles Lane: "Ellery Channing wrote from my room lately a proposition to edit a better [journal] for Chapman, and we set down as contributors Emerson, Thoreau, Channing, Newcomb, Alcott, on our side" (*The Letters of A. Bronson Alcott*, ed. Richard L. Herrnstadt [Ames: Iowa State University Press, 1969], p. 141). Furthermore, Alcott noted in his journal that Henry James Sr. "intends to print a journal devoted to the views of Fourier and Swedenborg" (*Journals of Bronson Alcott* 1938, p. 205).

7 One of the seven wonders of the world, the Colossus of Rhodes was a bronze statue 110 feet high, believed to have stood in front of the harbor entrance on the Mediterranean island of Rhodes, with legs spanning the entrance so that ships passed beneath. T appropriates the image from Emerson, who wrote of Chapman's plan for a new journal in a letter to Lidian: "Let the Mass. Q. give place to this, & we should have two legs, & bestride the sea" (*Letters of RWE* 1939, 4:56).

8 T writes in *Walden*, "If you have built castles in the air, your work need not be lost; that is where they should be. Now put the foundations under them" (*Walden* 1971, p. 324).

9 *The Boston Almanac for the Year* ... was published from 1836 to 1871.

[10] See Editor's Note, pp. 383-384.

[11] In his June 8 reply, Emerson asked Lidian to thank T for his letter: "He is always *absolutely* right, and *particularly* perverse" (*Letters of RWE* 1939, 4:81).

*Copy-text:* ALS (MH-H, MS Am 1280 [3212])

*Published: Letters of RWE* 1939, 4:81-83; *Cor* 1958, 225-228

*Editor's Notes*
This letter is addressed "R. Waldo Emerson / Care of <u>Baring & Brothers</u> / <u>London</u> / <u>England</u> / By 'Cambria' / from New York."
  blacksmiths] *PE*; black- / smiths *in MS*

*Author's Alterations*
  yesterday] *interlined with a caret above cancelled* on
  6 I hear since] *interlined above cancelled* eight
  Father] father
  constant] *interlined with a caret*
  But] but
  dollars] doll–
  recover] *followed by cancelled* and
  Old] old
  nor] no
  of] *interlined above*
  Practical] practical
  Lecturing] lecturing

## From Horace Greeley
*May 25, 1848*

N. York, May 25[ath], '48,

Dear Thoreau,

Yours received. I send you the $25 for your 'Maine Woods', as you positively say that will be enough; but I shall feel like a Jew when I sell the article for more, and pocket the money. However, we'll see about that. Meantime, write me something shorter when the spirit moves (never write a line otherwise, for the hack-writer is slavish beast, *I* know) and I will sell it for you soon, and *won't* make any thing out of it. I want one shorter article from your pen, that will be quoted, as these long articles cannot be, and let the public know something of your way of thinking and seeing. It will do good.

Don't scold at my publishing a part of your last private letter in this morning's paper.[1] It will do great good, and I think you will not be recognized by more than half a dozen persons, who know the whole truth already. I was very careful not to allow any locality to be named, nor any specific allusions except to your house, which only the few can know any thing about. I am so importuned by young loafers who want to be hired in some intellectual capacity so as to 'develop their minds'–that is, get a broadcloth living without doing any vulgar labor–that I could not refrain from using against them the magnificent weapon you so unconsciously furnished me. I mean never to do so again.

Yours,<br>Horace Greeley.

P.S. What do you think of following out your thought in an essay on 'The Literary Life?'[a] You need not make a personal allusion, but I know you can write an article worth reading in that theme when you are in the vein.

H. G.<br>Enclosed <u>$25</u>

*Correspondent:* See p. 280.

[1] Greeley's article "A Lesson for Young Poets" includes a slightly revised version of the entire second paragraph of the letter T wrote him on May 19.

*Copy-text:* ALS (ViU, Clifton Waller Barrett Library, Horace Greeley Collection [#7669])

*Published:* *HDT* 1882, 228; *Cor* 1958, 228-229

*Editor's Notes*

This letter is endorsed "H. Greeley".

Greeley may have misdated this letter by a few days. In his May 21 and 22, 1848, letter to Emerson, T writes, "Greeley has sent me $100 dollars and wants more manuscript" (p. 380). Before T re-

ceived the $25 enclosed in this letter, Greeley's payment to him
amounted to $75.

*Author's Alterations*
  25] 23
  Life?'] ~'?


## To George Augustus Thatcher
*August 24, 1848*

Concord Aug. 24,[th] 1848.

Dear Cousin,

If it is not too late I will thank you for your letter and
your sympathy. I send you with this the Third Part[a], as
they have chosen to call it, of that everlasting mountain
story.[1] I presume that the other two have reached you.
They had bargained, as I thought to send me many copies
for distribution, but I have received none. It should have
been printed all together in some large newspaper–and
then it would have gone down as one dose by its very
gravity. I was sorry to hear that you came so near Concord
without coming here. It always does us good to see you.
Mr Emerson came home on the Europa 3 or 4 weeks ago,
in good health and spirits.[2] I think that he has seen English men, such as are worth seeing, more thoroughly than
any traveller. He has made them better acquainted with
one another and with Americans[a]. He had access to circles which are inaccessible to most travellers, but which
are none the better for that. He has seen the elephant–or
perhaps I should say the British lion now, and was made
a lion of himself.[3] He found Carlyle the most interesting
man–as I expected he would–Stonehenge the most interesting piece of antiquity–and the London Times Newspaper the best book which England is printing now a days.[4]

Travelling is so cheap at present that I am tempted to
make you a visit–but then, as usual, I have so much idle
business that cannot be postponed–if any will believe it!

The probable failure of the melon crop this season is

*melon*-choly–but fortunately *our* potatoes do not rot yet

I feel somewhat encouraged at the political prospects of the country–not because the new party have chosen such a leader, but because they are perhaps worthy of a better one. The N. E. delegation seems to have managed affairs in a bungling manner– If they had gone prepared they might have had their own man–[5] But who is he? It is time to be done selecting available men; for what are they not available who do thus?

–Father desires to be remembered to you & to Mrs Thatcher–and to the last named does also.

Yours sincerely

Henry Thoreau

*Correspondent:* George Augustus Thatcher (1806-1885), son of Samuel and Sarah Brown Thatcher, was a businessman in Bangor, Maine. In 1832 he married T's cousin Rebecca Jane Billings (1813-1883), daughter of Caleb and Nancy Thoreau Billings. Thatcher was active in the antislavery cause, and he accompanied T on his 1846 and 1853 trips to Maine.

[1] "Ktaadn, and the Maine Woods"; see p. 365, note 3.

[2] Emerson arrived in Boston on July 27 after an eleven-and-a-half-day crossing.

[3] "To see the elephant" is an American slang phrase for seeing all there is to see, parallel to the British usage "to see the lion" (to see celebrated or curious things).

[4] Emerson's response to Carlyle was complicated. He still deemed Carlyle a major intellectual power but found him "a very unhappy man, profoundly solitary, displeased & hindered by all men & things about him" (*Letters of RWE* 1939, 3:424). "His seal," wrote Emerson in his journal, "holds a griffin with the word, *Humilitate*" (*JMN*, 10:551). Carlyle and Emerson visited Stonehenge, to which Emerson devoted a full chapter in *English Traits*, as he did for the London *Times* (*The Collected Works of Ralph Waldo Emerson*, ed. Philip Nicoloff, Robert E. Burkholder, and Douglas Emory Wilson [Cambridge, Mass.: Harvard University Press, 1994], chaps. 15 and 16).

[5] On August 9, 1848, a convention of three political groups–the Barnburner Democrats, the Liberty Party, and the New England Conscience Whigs–met to form the Free-Soil Party. The Free-Soil Party nominated Martin Van Buren for president and Charles Fran-

cis Adams for vice president to oppose Lewis Cass, the national Democrat, and Zachary Taylor, the Whig candidate. Although the New England contingent distrusted Van Buren, they could not counter the highly organized Barnburners.

*Copy-text:* ALS (VtMiM, Thoreau/4)

*Published:* Reginald Lansing Cook, *The Concord Saunterer: Including a Discussion of the Nature Mysticism of Thoreau* (Middlebury, Vt.: Middlebury College Press, 1940), 64-65; *Cor* 1958, 229-230

*Editor's Note*
This letter is addressed "Geo. A. Thatcher / Bangor / Me." and endorsed "Henry Thoreau / August 1848".

*Author's Alterations*
Third Part] third part
Americans] americans

## From Nathaniel Hawthorne
*October 21, 1848*

Salem, October 21st. 1848.

My dear Sir,

The Managers of the Salem Lyceum, some time ago, voted that you should be requested to deliver a Lecture before that Institution, during the approaching season.[1] I know not whether M^r Chever,[2] the late Corresponding^e Secretary, communicated the vote to you; at all events, no answer has been received; and, as Mr Chever's successor in office, I am instructed to repeat the invitation. Permit me to add my own earnest wishes that you will accept it– and also, laying aside my official dignity, to express my wife's desire and my own that you will be our guest, if you do come.

In case of your compliance, the Managers would be glad to know at what time it will best suit you to deliver the Lecture.

Very truly Yours,
Nath^l Hawthorne,
Cor. Sec^y
Salem Lyceum.

P.S. I live at at No 14, Mall-street–where I shall be very happy to see you. The stated fee for Lecturers is $20.

*Correspondent:* Nathaniel Hawthorne (1804-1864), son of Nathaniel and Elizabeth Clark Manning Hathorne, graduated from Bowdoin College in Brunswick, Maine, in 1825 and returned to his native Salem, Massachusetts, to become a writer. On July 9, 1842, Hawthorne married Sophia Peabody (1809-1871), daughter of Nathaniel and Elizabeth Palmer Peabody of Salem; that afternoon, the couple took up residence at the Old Manse in Concord. In 1845 they returned to Salem and lived there until 1850. Though he would become T's friend, Hawthorne was candid in his estimation of T: in his October 21, 1842, letter to Epes Sargent, who was starting *Sargent's New Monthly Magazine*, Hawthorne described T as "a wild, irregular, Indian-like sort of fellow" who was "somewhat tinctured with Transcendentalism" but who had "stuff in him to make a reputation of" (*Letters of Nathaniel Hawthorne*, 15:656).

[1] T addressed the Salem Lyceum on November 22; his topic was "Student Life in New England, Its Economy." Much of the lecture would later be published in the opening chapter of *Walden*.

[2] George Francis Chever (1819-1871), son of James and Lydia Dean Chever, graduated from Harvard in 1840 and became a lawyer and an amateur nature writer in his native Salem.

*Copy-text:* ALS (NN-BGC, Henry David Thoreau Collection, 1837-1917, Series IV)

*Published:* *HDT* 1882, 275-276; *Cor* 1958, 230-231; *Letters of Nathaniel Hawthorne*, 16:243; *Selected Letters of Nathaniel Hawthorne*, ed. Joel Myerson (Columbus: Ohio State University Press, 2002), 128-129

*Editor's Notes*
This letter is addressed "Henry D. Thoreau, / Concord, / Massachusetts.", postmarked "SALEM Mass. OCT 22", and endorsed "N. Hawthorne".

Corresponding] *PE*; *possibly* corresponding *in MS*

## From Horace Greeley

*October 28, 1848*

I break a silence of some duration to inform you that I hope on Monday to receive payment for your glorious account of "Ktaadn and the Maine Woods," which I bought of you at a Jew's bargain, and sold to the "Union Magazine."[1] I am to get $75 for it, and, as I don't choose to *exploiter* you at such a rate, I shall insist on inclosing you $25 more in this letter, which will still leave me $25 to pay various charges and labors I have incurred in selling your articles and getting paid for them,–the latter by[v] far the more[v] difficult portion[v] of the business. {*text lacking?*} You must write to the magazines in order to let the public know who and what you are. Ten years hence will do for publishing books,

*Correspondent:* See p. 280.

[1] T's "Ktaadn, and the Maine Woods" appeared in volume 3 of the *Union Magazine of Literature and Art* in five parts between July and November 1848 (pp. 29-33, 73-79, 132-137, 177-182, 216-220; see *The Maine Woods*, ed. Joseph J. Moldenhauer [Princeton, N.J.: Princeton University Press, 1972], pp. 3-83). The *Union Magazine*, founded in New York City in 1847 and edited by Caroline Kirkland and John Hart, also published material by Poe, Longfellow, and Lowell. In September 1848, John Sartain (1808-1897), an English engraver who had been associated with *Graham's Magazine*, bought the *Union Magazine* with the help of William Sloanaker, moved it to Philadelphia in January 1849, and changed its name to *Sartain's Union Magazine of Literature and Art.*

*Copy-text:* PE lines 387.36-388.7 (I break ... business.), *HDT* 1882, 227; PE lines 388.8-10 (You must ... books,), *Catalogue–Part I of the Valuable Autograph Collection of the Late Miss Mary B. Hathaway ... together with the Collection of the Late Frederick P. Richardson* (Boston: C. F. Libbie, 1911), item 1177

*Published:* *HDT* 1882, 227; *Life of HDT* 1917, 370; *Cor* 1958, 231-232

*Editor's Notes*
The copy-text is a composite of two published sources, *HDT* 1882 and the Hathaway-Richardson sale catalog. PE supplies the date "October 28, 1848" based on information in *HDT* 1882.
The description in the Hathaway-Richardson sale catalog includes the following:
    Horace Greeley, a. l. s. 3 pages 4°, to Thoreau, N. Y., 1848.
    "I hope on Monday to receive payment for your glorious account of Ktaadn and the Maine Woods, which I bought of you

at a Jew's bargain and sold to the Union Magazine. I am to get
$75 for it. * * * You must write to the magazines in order to let
the public know who and what you are. Ten years hence will
do for publishing books," etc.

HDT 1882 supplies text following "for it" that the Hathaway-Richardson catalog omits. PE uses "{*text lacking?*}" to acknowledge the
possibility that HDT 1882 omits text between "business." and "You".

*Substantive Variants*
   For the portion of the text of this letter that is based on *HDT* 1882,
potentially authoritative readings in *Life of HDT* 1917 are reported
below.
   latter by] *in copy-text (HDT 1882);* latter being by *in Life of HDT*
*1917*
   more] *in copy-text (HDT 1882);* most *in Life of HDT 1917*
   portion] *in copy-text (HDT 1882);* part *in Life of HDT 1917*


## From Horace Greeley
*November 19, 1848*

New York, Nov. 19, 1848.
Friend Thoreau,

   Yours of the 17th received. Say we are even on money
counts, and let the matter drop. I have tried to serve you,
and have been fully paid for my own disbursements and
trouble in the premises. So we will move on.

   I think you will do well to send me some passages from
one or both of your new works,[1] to dispose of to the Magazines. This will be the best kind of advertisement whether
for a publisher or for readers. You may write with an an-
gel's pen, yet your writings have no mercantile, money
value till you are known and talked of as an author. Mr.
Emerson would have been twice as much known and
read if he had written for the Magazines a little, just to let
common people know of his existence. I believe a chapter
from one of your books printed in Graham or The Union
will add many to the readers of the volume when issued.
Here is the reason why British books sell so much better
among us than American–because they are thoroughly[a]

advertised through the British Reviews, Magazines and
journals which circulate or are copied among us.– However, do as you please. If you choose to send me one of
your MSS. I will get it published, but I cannot promise
you any considerable recompense; and, indeed, if Monroe[2] will do it, that will be better. Your writings are in advance of the general mind here–  Boston is nearer their
standard.

I never saw the verses you speak of. Won't you send
them again? I have been buried up in politics for the last
six weeks.

Kind regards to Emerson. It is doubtful about my seeing
you this season.

Yours,
Horace Greeley.

*Correspondent:*  See p. 280.

[1] T was at this time working on the manuscripts of both *A Week
on the Concord and Merrimack Rivers* and *Walden*.
[2] James Munroe.

*Copy-text:*  ALS (VtMiM, Greeley/2)

*Published:*  HDT 1882, 229-230; *Cor* 1958, 232-233

*Editor's Note*
This letter is endorsed "H. Greeley".

*Author's Alteration*
thoroughly] *preceded by cancelled* read


## From Nathaniel Hawthorne
*November 20, 1848*

Boston. Nov[r] 20th. 1848
My dear Thoreau,

I did not sooner write you, because there were pre-
engagements for the two or three first lectures; so that I
could not arrange matters to have you come during the
present month. But, as it happens, the expected lecturers

have failed us; and we now depend on you to come this very next Wednesday.[a] I shall announce you in the paper of tomorrow; so you *must* come. I regret that I could not give you longer notice.

We shall expect you on Wednesday, at No. 14 Mall. street.

> Yours truly,
> Nath[l] Hawthorne.

If it be utterly impossible for you come, pray write me a line so that I may get it Wednesday morning. But, by all means, come.

This secretaryship is an intolerable bore. I have travelled thirty miles, this wet day, on no other business.[1]

*Correspondent:*  See p. 387.

[1] Sophia Hawthorne wrote to her mother that Hawthorne was to go to West Newton, Massachusetts, on November 20 to see Horace Mann about lecturing in Salem (*Letters of Nathaniel Hawthorne*, 16:247n2).

*Copy-text:*  ALS (NNPM, MA 920)

*Published:*  *HDT* 1882, 276; *Cor* 1958, 233-234; *Letters of Nathaniel Hawthorne*, 16:247

*Editor's Note*
This letter is addressed "Henry Thoreau, Esq. / Concord, / Massachusetts.", postmarked "BOSTON 5 cts 21 NOV", and endorsed "N. Hawthorne".

*Author's Alteration*
Wednesday.] ~,

## To George Augustus Thatcher
*December 26, 1848*

I hear that the Gloucester paper has me in print again, and the Republican–whatever they may say is not to the purpose only as it serves as an advertisement of me.[1] There are very few whose opinion I value.

*Correspondent:* See p. 385.

¹ T's lecture on "Economy" before the Gloucester Lyceum on December 20 was reviewed in local newspapers: both the *Gloucester News* and the *Gloucester Telegraph* of December 23 commented on the lecture, but no mention has been found in the *Springfield Republican.*

*Copy-text: Library of the Late Adrian H. Joline of New York City, Part V: American Autographs Including a Complete Set of the Signers of the Declaration of Independence* (New York: The Anderson Auction Company, 1915), item 536

*Published: Cor* 1958, 234

*Editor's Notes*

PE supplies the date "December 26, 1848" based on information in the Joline sale catalog.

The description in the Joline sale catalog includes the following:
A. L. S., 2 pp. 4to. Concord, December 26, 1848. Inlaid.

*To George A. Thatcher, his cousin, reading in part: "I hear that the Gloucester paper has me in print again, and the Republican–whatever they may say is not to the purpose only as it serves as an advertisement of me. There are very few whose opinion I value."

# EDITORIAL APPENDIX

# Notes on Illustrations

From Elizabeth Sherman Hoar, May 2, 1843,
pp. 158-159                                    following page 406

The recipient's copy of Elizabeth Hoar's letter to Thoreau is
not extant; the text on pp. 158-159 is based on a version edited
by Franklin Benjamin Sanborn and published as a footnote
in "The Emerson-Thoreau Correspondence" in the *Atlantic
Monthly* for May 1892. In keeping with the policy for letters
based on published sources, the introductory sentence by Sanborn ("This inkstand . . . copied.") has been omitted and the
signature has been normalized from capital and display capital
letters to capital and lower-case letters (see the Textual Introduction, p. 469).

To Abel Adams, November 15, 1847,
pp. 322-323

At Lidian Emerson's request, Thoreau wrote to Abel Adams,
Waldo Emerson's financial advisor, forwarding a notice of a
stock offering from the Fitchburg Railroad Company. Thoreau
inscribed his note on the back of the company's form letter. At
this time Emerson was lecturing in England and Thoreau was
part of the Emerson household. Reproduction courtesy of the
Massachusetts Historical Society.

To Ralph Waldo Emerson, December 15, 1847,
pp. 327-330

Thoreau's calculations and drawings graphically convey Hugh
Whelan's arduous process of determining how to spend his
$80 to get what he wants–"Twice as much room more" includ-
ing "Parlor kitchen & bedroom". In a November 14, 1847, letter
to Emerson, Thoreau made it clear that Whelan depended on
his guidance in making decisions: "He . . . affirms sincerely that
as to his wants, wood, stone, or timber–I know better than he"
(p. 317). Reproduction courtesy of the Clifton Waller Barrett Library, The Albert H. Small Special Collections Library, University of Virginia Library.

## To Ralph Waldo Emerson, Before March 24, 1848, pp. 353-354

Having written a note to Emerson on one side of this leaf, Thoreau addressed the other side and then folded the leaf to enclose material from Lidian to Waldo. Thoreau's use of sealing wax in six places to secure the packet indicates that the enclosures were substantial. The wax can be seen through paper tape that has been used to repair the leaf where it was torn when Emerson opened the packet. Reproduction courtesy of the Clifton Waller Barrett Library, The Albert H. Small Special Collections Library, University of Virginia Library.

## To Harrison Gray Otis Blake, March 27, 1848, pp. 359-364

Most of Thoreau's letter to Blake is based on the version published in *Letters to Various Persons*, but the last part of the letter survives in manuscript, as a single leaf. As he did with several of Thoreau's letters to him, Blake cut out Thoreau's signature to give away as a memento. Blake notes on the manuscript that he gave the cut-out portion to "Mrs. Edward Hoar of Concord, for Mr. Dean, a botanist". The signature is in Walter Deane's papers at Harvard's Gray Herbarium; the rest of the leaf is in the Berg Collection at the New York Public Library. In the illustration, the two parts of the leaf are brought together. Reproductions courtesy of the Henry W. and Albert A. Berg Collection of English and American Literature, The New York Public Library, Astor, Lenox and Tilden Foundations; and the Archives of the Gray Herbarium, Harvard University. Digital reconstruction of the manuscript leaf by Tom Moon, Digitization Unit Head, Davidson Library, University of California, Santa Barbara.

## From Horace Greeley, October 28, 1848, pp. 387-389

The recipient's copy of Horace Greeley's letter to Thoreau is not extant; the text on pp. 387-388 is a composite of the two published sources shown here. In 1882, Sanborn published a paragraph from the letter in *Henry D. Thoreau* (image on left). The letter was offered at auction in 1911; the auction catalog, *Catalogue–Part I of the Valuable Autograph Collection of the*

*Late Miss Mary B. Hathaway . . . together with the Collection of the Late Frederick P. Richardson* (Boston: C. F. Libbie, 1911), includes part of the paragraph Sanborn used and two sentences that apparently followed that paragraph in the manuscript (image on right, entry 1177). For discussions of the editorial treatment of composites and of the treatment of design features and contextual material in published sources, see the Textual Introduction, p. 463 and pp. 469-470.

# Acknowledgments

For permission to publish manuscript material, the editor is indebted to Abernethy Library, Middlebury College, Middlebury, VT; Archives of the Gray Herbarium, Harvard University, Cambridge, MA; Berg Collection of English and American Literature, The New York Public Library, Astor, Lenox and Tilden Foundations, New York, NY; Bruce Museum, Greenwich, CT; Clifton Waller Barrett Library, The Albert H. Small Special Collections Library, University of Virginia Library, University of Virginia, Charlottesville, VA; Fruitlands Museum, Harvard, MA; Harry Ransom Humanities Research Center, The University of Texas at Austin, Austin, TX; Harvard University Archives, Harvard University, Cambridge, MA; Haverford College Library, Haverford College, Haverford, PA; The Historical Society of Pennsylvania, Philadelphia, PA; Houghton Library, Harvard University, Cambridge, MA; The Huntington Library, San Marino, CA; John Hay Library, Brown University Library, Brown University, Providence, RI; Kungliga Biblioteket, National Library of Sweden, Stockholm, Sweden; Lilly Library, Indiana University, Bloomington, IN; Manuscripts and Archives Division, The New York Public Library, Astor, Lenox and Tilden Foundations, New York, NY; Manuscripts Division of the Department of Rare Books and Special Collections, Princeton University Library, Princeton University, Princeton, NJ; Massachusetts Historical Society, Boston, MA; The Morgan Library & Museum, New York, NY; The New-York Historical Society, New York, NY; Paulist Fathers Archives, Office of Paulist History and Archives, St. Paul's College, Washington, DC; Perkins School for the Blind, Watertown, MA; Rare Book and Manuscript Library, Columbia University, New York, NY; Rare Books Department, Boston Public Library, Trustees of the Boston Public Library, Boston, MA; Schlesinger Library, Radcliffe Institute, Harvard University, Cambridge, MA; Special Collections, Boston University Library, Boston University, Boston, MA; Special Collections, Morris Library, Southern Illinois University Carbondale, Carbondale, IL; Special Collections and Archives, UC Irvine Libraries, University of California, Irvine, Irvine, CA; Thoreau Society Archives, Thoreau Institute at Walden Woods, Lincoln, MA; University Archives, University of Notre Dame, Notre Dame, IN; University of Illinois Library at Urbana-Champaign, University of Illinois, Urbana-Champaign, IL; Walden Woods Project, Thoreau Institute at Walden Woods, Lincoln, MA; William Munroe Special Collections, Concord Free Public Library, Concord, MA.

The editor is grateful to Kent Bicknell, James Dawson, Chris Hobby, Russell W. Hobby, Charlotte A. Morrier, David Sewall, and the children of Dr. John William Lowder for permission to publish manuscript material.

The following individuals have generously contributed their expertise, time, and good will in the creation of this volume: Jack Belsom, Kent Bicknell, Ronald A. Bosco, Mark N. Brown, Maureen Brunsdale, Leslie Cabezas, Mary Ann T. Campbell, Lisa Careau, Jeffrey S. Cramer, Bradley P. Dean, Lisa DeCesare, Carlotta DeFillo, Kathryn C. Dolan, Sarah Dunlap, Denise Eggers, Jennifer Eimers, Sara Englum, Brandon Fastman, Michael J. Frederick, Geneva Frost, Ian Geiger, Marguerite M. Geis, Tom Gibbons CSP, Jayne Gordon, Nicholas Graham, Robert D. Habich, Susan Hamson, Steven Hartman, Sarah Hartwell, Tiffany Hayes, Ruth C. Hoffman, Harley P. Holden, Jeannette Howland, Margaret Hrabe, Joan W. Kaufman, Susan Kayorie, Selby Kiffer, Heather King, Allan Kulikoff, David Kuzma, Meghan Kyle, Doris Lamont, William Landis, Dana Lippett, Fr. John E. Lynch CSP, Catherine L. Mason, Philip Milito, Minka Misangyi, Joseph J. Moldenhauer, Tom Moon, Leslie Morris, Robert Morstein-Marx, Wesley T. Mott, Klaus Musmann, Joel Myerson, Natalie Nelson, Gudrun Oettinger, Beverly Palmer, Maurice Jacquelin Pecquet, Diana Franzusoff Peterson, Mark Piel, Dianne Piper-Rybak, Ben Primer, Robert D. Purrington, Devon L. Pyle-Vowles, Karen Reiber, Kathleen Reilly, Sandra Richey, Gene K. Rinkel, Katharine A. Salzmann, Mary Lamb Shelden, Margaret M. Sherry, Andrew Sidle, Megan Sniffin-Marinoff, John D. Stinson, Saundra Taylor, Meghan Tierney, Kevin Van Anglen, Gustaaf Van Cromphout, Michael A. Volmar, Reta Warman, Neil Watkins, Sarah Weber, Robert W. Wilder, Leslie Perrin Wilson, Heather Wolfe, Deborah Zak, Kai Zhang, Roberta Zonghi.

The editor would like to thank the National Endowment for the Humanities for a research fellowship and the University of Redlands for a sabbatical leave and other research support.

# Editorial Contributions

PRELIMINARY TRANSCRIPTIONS of the manuscripts on which *Correspondence 1* is based were prepared by students and staff members at the Textual Center, Princeton University. Thomas Blanding, Mary Dobbie, Kristin Fossum, Walter Harding, Lorna Carey Mack, Randy Nelson, and Elizabeth Witherell read transcripts against original manuscripts. The final review of transcripts against manuscripts was done by Robert N. and M. Catharine Hudspeth. Mr. Hudspeth also confirmed the establishment of the texts and apparatus, with the assistance of Thoreau Edition staff members. Mr. Hudspeth wrote the Historical Introduction; Ms. Witherell wrote the Textual Introduction; Mr. Hudspeth and Ms. Witherell wrote the General Introduction. Mr. Hudspeth and Thomas Roche prepared copy for the index. Mr. Hudspeth drafted the annotations; Lihong Xie and Mr. Roche reviewed them. Ms. Witherell and Ms. Xie reviewed copy throughout work on the volume.

# General Introduction

THOREAU'S ACTIVITY as a letter-writer spans almost three decades, from an 1834 request to have his Harvard dormitory room "painted and whitewashed" to an April 2, 1862, letter to his publisher, Ticknor and Fields, dictated to his sister Sophia and sent with the manuscript of "Wild Apples." The first letters that he received, in 1836 and 1837, came from Harvard classmates; the last came from Ticknor and Fields, and from readers and friends who knew he was dying. Almost six hundred and fifty letters survive from the intervening twenty-eight years; letters by Thoreau outnumber those to him by a small margin.

In most of his correspondence, Thoreau was engaged in transacting the business associated with lecturing, publishing, surveying, and, after his father's death in February 1859, the sale of plumbago; in pursuing his interests in science and history; in responding to fans and filling requests for his books; and in exchanging news with family members and friends. Many of these letters served quotidian purposes, and many he received were welcome, as indicated in a letter he wrote to his mother from Staten Island on July 7, 1843:

> I was very glad to get your letter and papers. Tell Father that circumstantial letters make very substantial reading, at any rate. I like to know even how the sun shines and garden grows with you. (*Cor 1* 2013, p. 198)

But the highest use of correspondence was served by another kind of letter, the long, musing, philosophical kind he often wrote to his Worcester friend Harrison Gray Otis Blake. He acknowledged the difference at the end of an April 17, 1857, letter to Blake that is mostly taken up with news and arrangements: "Consider this a business letter, which you know *counts* nothing in the game we play" (*Cor* 1958, p. 477).

For Thoreau, the association of letters with the world of business was not limited to the content of correspondence: he saw the postal system itself as an instrument of commerce. The American postal system was established by the U.S. government partly to facilitate the dissemination of newspapers and circulars, important vehicles of business, and in many towns the post office operated in a place of business. During Thoreau's lifetime, the Concord post office moved several times as the position of postmaster changed hands, from one store to another and for a short time to an inn. These locations were all on or near the Milldam, the commercial heart of the village.[1] There was no home delivery in Concord, and picking up the mail, which arrived twice a day,[2] was an unavoidably social event.

Several important changes took place in the postal system during the time Thoreau sent and received letters, and his correspondence reflects those changes. Before 1845, postage was charged on the basis of the number of sheets of paper being sent and the distance the letter was to travel; the cost of a letter could approach $1.00, a day's wages for a laborer (*Spreading the News* 1995, p. 159). To reduce the number of sheets and thus the cost, correspondents sometimes resorted to cross-writing: this involved turning a completed page ninety degrees and writing across the existing contents of the letter. Thoreau used the technique himself to keep his October 8, 1841, letter to Isaiah Thornton Williams in Buffalo within the confines of two sheets. To eliminate postage altogether, "[t]ravellers everywhere took letters for their friends and acquaintances" (*Reminiscences* 1993, p. 132). There

---

[1] Ruth Robinson Wheeler, "Concord Postmasters" (typescript, [1966]), Concord Pamphlet Collection, Concord Free Public Library (C.Pam. 77, Item 8).

[2] *Reminiscences* 1993, p. 132. In a Journal entry of December 10, 1856, Thoreau mentions being at the post office at 7:15 in the morning and again at sunset (*Journal* 1906, 9:174, 177).

is evidence that Thoreau and his correspondents some-
times followed this practice. For example, the address on
Charles Lane's February 17, 1846, letter to Thoreau, "Henry
D. Thoreau / Sylvan / favored / by A. B. A.", indicates that
Bronson Alcott hand delivered it (*Cor 1* 2013, p. 278).

The Postal Act of 1845 simplified the basis on which
postage was calculated, and in 1851 the rate was fixed at
$0.03 per half ounce. The ultimate effect of these postal
reforms was the transformation of the postal system from
an agent of political and cultural unification in a new
nation to a means of communication much more commonly used by people at all social and economic levels.
Thoreau's correspondence reflects this increased use:
after 1854 requests in letters for responses by return mail
became more frequent.

Before the passage of the Postal Act of 1845, the use of
an envelope to enclose a letter added the cost of an extra
sheet of paper that contained only the address. To avoid
that cost, correspondents often simply folded the sheet or
sheets on which a letter was written into a small rectangle. One folded edge was tucked under another in such a
way as to hold the small packet together; a drop of sealing
wax could be used to reinforce the closure.[3] Sometimes
the writer continued the letter in the margins of the outside page, but the central part of that page contained only
the address (see "To Harrison Gray Otis Blake, March 27,
1848," following p. 406); postmarks and notes of postage
paid were added at the post office. After 1845, commer-
cially made envelopes began to be more widely used; the
first surviving envelope of this kind in Thoreau's correspondence that can be reliably dated is from 1854.[4]

[3] The process of folding and sealing is described in detail in Eliza
Ware Rotch Farrar's book of instructions in the practical aspects of letter-writing, *The Youth's Letter-Writer; or, The Epistolary Art Made Plain
and Easy to Beginners, through the Example of Henry Moreton* (New
York: H. and S. Raynor, 1836), pp. 48-52.

[4] Relatively few envelopes associated with letters Thoreau sent or received have been preserved, but the proportion of letters with integral

Until 1855 it was possible to send a letter without pre-paying; the recipient paid when picking up the letter (*Spreading the News* 1995, pp. 160-161). This circumstance made writers more conscious of the value of what they had to communicate, and more attentive to the etiquette involved in the decision to prepay or not. A comment in a July 21, 1843, letter Thoreau sent his sister Helen from Staten Island suggests that he did not always prepay: "I am not in such haste to write home when I remember that I make my readers pay the postage" (*Cor 1* 2013, p. 210). Markings associated with postage payment on almost one hundred of the letters that survive in manuscript support the conclusion that Thoreau followed both practices, but there are not enough examples to reveal any consistency about situations in which he prepaid and those in which he did not. The markings do provide evidence that by 1848 both Thoreau and those who wrote to him usually prepaid the postage for the letters they sent.[5]

Beginning in 1856 letter-writers were required to prepay by using postage stamps or pre-stamped envelopes. Stamps, which had been introduced in 1847, came into common use after 1851; they were also used as currency. The first of several mentions of using stamps as a substitute for cash occurs in a January 18, 1856, letter from Tho-

---

address leaves to those that lack any address, and so were likely to have been sent in envelopes, begins to reverse in 1851. From 1834 through 1851, about 84% of the surviving manuscript letters have integral address leaves; about 16% have no address. From 1852 through 1862, about 15% have integral address leaves and about 85% either have no address leaves or are associated with envelopes.

[5] In an e-mail message dated March 13, 2012, R. Neil Coker of the American Philatelic Research Library explained that "a manuscript or handstamped postal marking of 'Paid' . . . meant that the sender paid the postage. . . . If the writer sent the folded letter without paying, it normally received a handwritten number for the amount due." Half of the letters that provided evidence for this examination were sent from 1836 through 1847: in this group 37% were prepaid and 63% were paid for by recipients. The other half were sent from 1848 through 1855: in this group 92% were prepaid and only 8% were paid for by recipients.

reau to Calvin Harlowe Greene: "The price [of *A Week on the Concord and Merrimack Rivers*] is $1.25 If you care enough for it to send me that sum by mail, (stamps will do for change) I will forward you the copy by the same conveyance" (*Cor* 1958, p. 406).

Another kind of expense, to which Thoreau may have attended even more carefully than to monetary cost, was the time and effort required to keep up a correspondence. He measured the cost of writing letters and of maintaining the relationships they represented according to the formula he articulated in *Walden*: "the cost of a thing is the amount of what I will call life which is required to be exchanged for it, immediately or in the long run" (*Walden* 1971, p. 31). In a letter of October 14, 1860, Daniel Ricketson, with whom Thoreau had been corresponding for six years and with whom he had exchanged visits, wrote to ask whether Thoreau's silence of "some nine or ten months," after an invitation to visit Ricketson in New Bedford, meant that their friendship was at an end (*Cor* 1958, p. 593). Thoreau's need to protect his time and freedom is revealed in his November 4 response:

> You know that I never promised to correspond with you, & so, when I do, I do more than I promised.
>
> Such are my pursuits and habits that I rarely go abroad, and it is quite a habit with me to decline invitations to do so. Not that I could not enjoy such visits, if I were not otherwise occupied. I have enjoyed very much my visits to you and my rides in your neighborhood, and am sorry that I cannot enjoy such things oftener; but life is short, and there are other things also to be done. I admit that you are more social than I am, and far more attentive to "the common courtesies of life" but this is partly for the reason that you have fewer or less exacting private pursuits. . . .
>
> I am very busy, after my fashion, little as there is to show for it, and feel as if I could not spend many days nor dollars in travelling, for the shortest visit must have a fair margin to it, and the days thus affect the weeks, you know. (*Cor* 1958, pp. 599-600)

Having thus explained himself, Thoreau continued to correspond with Ricketson until the end of his life.[6]

---

[6] Three letters from Thoreau to Ricketson and eleven from Ricketson

reminded, I believe, of Jane Taylor's Philosopher's Scales, and how the world

"Flew out with a bounce,"

which

"Yerked the philosopher out of his cell;"

or else of

"From the climes of the sun all war-worn and weary."

I had rather have the thought come ushered with a flourish of oaths and curses. Yet I love your poetry as I do little else that is near and recent, especially when you get fairly round the end of the line, and are not thrown back upon the rocks. To read the lecture on The Comic is as good as to be in our town meeting or Lyceum once more.

I am glad that the Concord farmers ploughed well this year; it promises that something will be done these summers. But I am suspicious of that *Brittonner*, who advertises so many cords of *good* oak, chestnut, and maple wood for sale. *Good!* ay, good for what? And there shall not be left a stone upon a stone. But no matter, — let them hack away. The sturdy Irish arms that do the work are of more worth than oak or maple. Methinks I could look with equanimity upon a long street of Irish cabins, and pigs and children reveling in the genial Concord dirt; and I should still find my Walden wood and Fair Haven in their tanned and happy faces.

I write this in the cornfield — it being washing-day — with the inkstand Elizabeth Hoar gave me; [1] though it is not

[1] This inkstand was presented by Miss Hoar, with a note dated "Boston, May 2, 1843," which deserves to be copied.

DEAR HENRY, — The rain prevented me from seeing you the night before I came away, to leave with you a parting assurance of good will and good hope. We have become better acquainted within the two past years than in our whole life as schoolmates and neighbors before; and I am unwilling to let you go away without telling you that I, among your other friends, shall miss you much, and follow you with remembrance and all best wishes and con-

redolent of cornstalks, I fear. Let me not be forgotten by Channing and Hawthorne, nor our grey - suited neighbor under the hill [Edmund Hosmer].

Your friend,    H. D. THOREAU.

This letter and that of Emerson preceding it (No. XIII.) will be best explained by a reference to the Dial for October, 1843. The Ethnical Scriptures were selections from the Brahminical books, from Confucius, etc., such as we have since seen in great abundance. The Autumn verses are by Channing; Sweep Ho! by Ellen Sturgis, afterwards Mrs. Hooper; the Youth of the Poet and Painter also by Channing. The Letter to Contributors, which is headed simply A Letter, is by Emerson, and has been much overlooked by his later readers; his Ode to Beauty is very well known, and does not deserve the slashing censure of Thoreau, though, as it now stands, it is better than first printed. Instead of

"Love drinks at thy banquet
*Remediless* thirst,"

we now have the perfect phrase,

"Love drinks at thy *fountain*
*False waters of thirst.*"

The Comic is also Emerson's. There is a poem, The Sail, by William Tappan, so often named in these letters, and a sonnet by Charles A. Dana, now of the New York Sun.

XVI. EMERSON TO THOREAU.

CONCORD, *October* 25, 1843.

DEAR HENRY, — I have your letter

fidence. Will you take this little inkstand and try if it will carry ink safely from Concord to Staten Island? and the pen, which, if you can write with steel, may be made sometimes the interpreter of friendly thoughts to those whom you leave beyond the reach of your voice, — or record the inspirations of Nature, who, I doubt not, will be as faithful to you who trust her in the sea-girt Staten Island as in Concord woods and meadows. Good - by, and εὖ πράττειν, which, a wise man says, is the only salutation fit for the wise.

Truly your friend,    E. HOAR.

From Elizabeth Sherman Hoar, May 2, 1843, pp. 158-159

Concord Nov 15th 47

Dear Sir,

Mrs Emerson request
me to forward this circular to you
Mr E. had anticipated it, and, as she
thinks, said that you would take
care of it. She is sure that he will
take new stand.

She desires to be kindly remembered to
your family, and would have written
herself, if not prevented by a slight
indisposition.

We have not yet heard from
Mr. E.

Yours respectfully,
H. D. Thoreau

To Mr. Abel Adams
Boston

To Abel Adams, November 15, 1847 (recto), pp. 322-323

OFFICE OF THE FITCHBURG RAIL-ROAD COMPANY,
Boston, November 10, 1847.

You are hereby notified that the Directors of the FITCHBURG RAIL-ROAD COMPANY have, this day, created New Stock, and every Stockholder holding Old Stock at the close of the twentieth day of November, current, is entitled to subscribe for the New Stock, in the proportion of One New Share for every Four Shares of Old Stock, which may be held by said Stockholder, provided notice is given to the Treasurer, in writing, on or before the first day of December next, after which time, all Shares and fractional parts of Shares not subscribed for, will be forfeited to the Company.

The First Assessment of Twenty-five Dollars on each of the New Shares created by said Directors of the Fitchburg Rail-road Company, has been laid, payable on the sixth day of December next.

And the Second Assessment of Twenty-five Dollars per share, has been laid, payable, on the Sixth day of January next, to the Treasurer of the Fitchburg Rail-Road Company; Office, No. 15, Merchants Exchange, State Street, Boston.

J. P. WELCH, TREASURER.

---

TO THE TREASURER OF THE FITCHBURG RAIL-ROAD COMPANY:

*I hereby subscribe for*     *Shares in the New Stock, created November 10, 1847,*
*to which I am entitled as holder of*     *Shares of the Old Stock in said Company.*

To Abel Adams, November 15, 1847 (verso), pp. 322-323

Concord Dec 15' 1847

Dear Friend,

You are not so far off
but the affairs of this world still attack
you. Perhaps it will be so when we
are dead. Then look out. — Joshua R.
Holman, of Harvard, who says he lived a month with Lane
at Fruitlands, wishes to hire said Lane's
farm for one or more years, and will pay
$125. rent, taking out of the same what
is necessary for repairs — as, for a new
bank-wall to the barn cellar, which he
says is indispensable. Palmer is gone,
Mrs Palmer is going. This is all
that is known, or that is worth knowing.
                        Yea or no —
              What to do?

        Hugh's plot begins to thicken. Bestard
then. 10 dollars on one side — Holden
field & house on the other. How to bring
these together so as to make a garden or a
palace.
$ 80  ———————————————— field  □ house
·let 10    go over to unite the two last        ☐
   70
    6    for wotherbee's rock & found your palace on.
   64

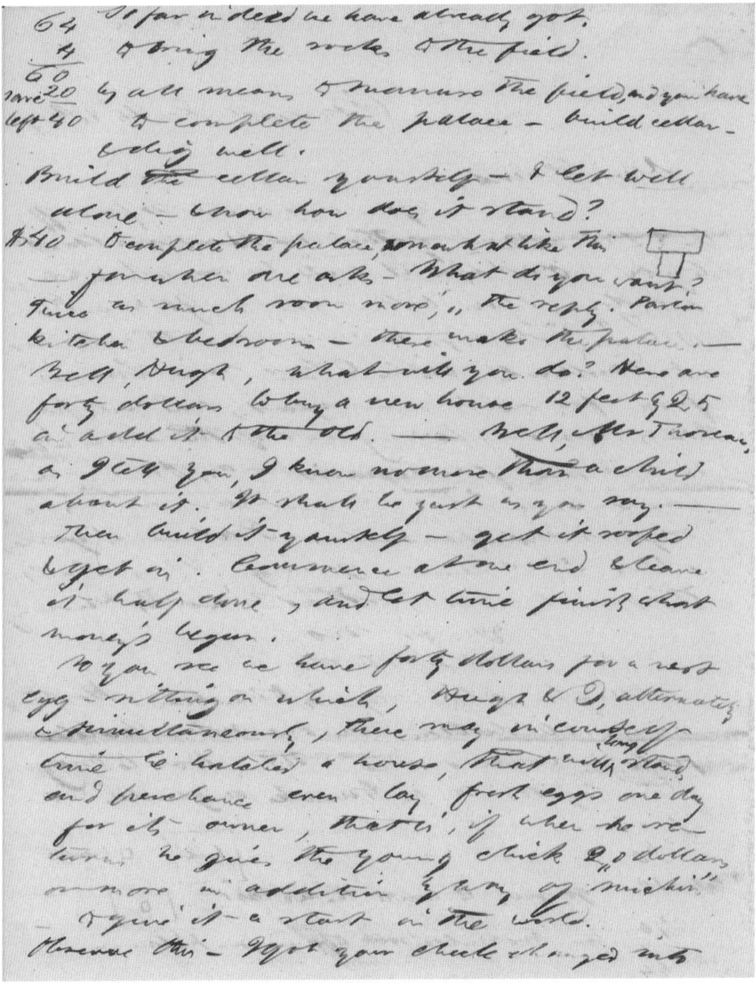

64 So far indeed we have already got.
4 To bring the rocks to the field.
60
save 20 by all means to manure the field, and you have
left 40 to complete the palace — build cellar
& dig well.
Build the cellar yourself — & let well
alone — Now how does it stand?
$40 To complete the palace, somewhat like this
— for which are asks — What do you want?
Twice as much room more, is the reply. Parlor
kitchen & bedroom — these make the palace. —
Well, Hugh, what will you do? Here are
forty dollars to buy a new house 12 feet by 25
and add it to the old. — Well, Mr Thoreau,
as I tell you, I know no more than a child
about it. It shall be just as you say. —
Then build it yourself — get it roofed
& get in. Commence at one end & leave
it half done, and let time finish what
money's begun.
So you see we have forty dollars for a nest
egg — sitting on which, Hugh & I, alternately
& simultaneously, there may in course of
time be hatched a house, that will long stand,
and perchance even lay fresh eggs one day
for its owner, that is, if when he returns he gives the young chick 20 dollars
or more in addition by way of "nichin"
to give it a start in the world.
Observe this — I got your check changed into

To Ralph Waldo Emerson, December 15, 1847 (verso), pp. 327-330

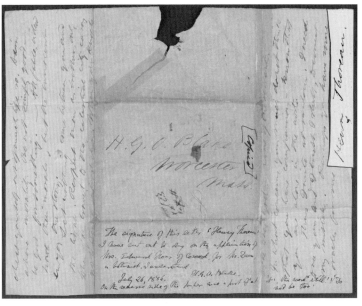

To Harrison Gray Otis Blake, March 27, 1848, pp. 359-364

From Horace Greeley, October 28, 1848, pp. 387-389

## HORACE IN THE RÔLE OF MÆCENAS. 227

On the 28th of October, 1848, he writes:

"I break a silence of some duration to inform you that I hope on Monday to receive payment for your glorious account of 'Ktaadn and the Maine Woods,' which I bought of you at a Jew's bargain, and sold to the 'Union Magazine.' I am to get $75 for it, and, as I don't choose to *exploiter* you at such a rate, I shall insist on inclosing you $25 more in this letter, which will still leave me $25 to pay various charges and labors I have incurred in selling your articles and getting paid for them, — the latter by far the more difficult portion of the business."

In the letter of April 17, 1848, Mr. Greeley had further said:—

"If you will write me two or three articles in the course of the summer, I think I can dispose of them for your benefit. But write not more than half as long as your article just sent me, for that is too long for the magazines. If that were in two, it would be far more valuable. What about your book (the 'Week')? Is anything going on about it now? Why did not Emerson try it in England? I think the Howitts could get it favorably before the British public. If you can suggest any way wherein I can put it forward, do not hesitate, but command me."

---

1174  THOMSON, Charles, Secy. to Continental Congress, two d. s., 1780 and 1785, the first a war resolve, the second an ordinance establishing the mint at Phila. (2)

1175  [THOREAU.] Horace Greeley, a. l. s. 1 page 4° to Thoreau, N. Y., 1846. Fine letter referring to Emerson.

"I hardly know a man that would publish your article all at once and 'to be continued' are words shunned like a pestilence. But I know you have written in good taste about Carlyle—too solidly good I fear, to be profitable to yourself," etc.

1176  [THOREAU.] Horace Greeley, a. l. s. 2 pages 4°, to Thoreau, N. Y., 1847.

"Your article * * * will appear as the leading article in Graham's Mag. for next month. Now don't object to this * * * but just sit down and write a like article about Emerson * * * then one about Hawthorne at your leisure, &c. I will pay you the money for each of these articles on delivery," etc.

1177  [THOREAU.] Horace Greeley, a. l. s. 3 pages 4°, to Thoreau, N. Y., 1848.

"I hope on Monday to receive payment for your glorious account of Ktaadn and the Maine Woods, which I bought of you at a Jew's b— and sold to the Union Magazine. I am to get $75 for it. * * * You must write to the magazines in order to let the public know who and what you are. Ten years hence will do for publishing books," etc.—

1178  THOREAU, Henry D., a. l. s. 6 pages 4°, Concord, Sept. 26, 1855. To his friend the editor, H. G. O. Blake.

* * "I do not see how strength is to be got into my legs again. * * I was glad to hear the other day that Higginson and Brown were gone to Kansas; it must be so much better to go to than a Woman's Rights or Abolition Convention," etc.

1179  THOREAU, Henry D., a. l. s. (initials) 9 pages 4°, Concord, Dec. 6, 1856. To his friend Blake.

"That Walt Whitman, of whom I wrote to you, is the most interesting fact to me at present. I have just read his 2nd Edition (which he gave me) and it has done me more good than any reading for a long time. Perhaps I remember the poem An American and the Sun Down Poem," etc.

1180  THOREAU, Henry D., a. l. s. (initials) 8 pages 4°, Concord, Jan. 1, 1859. To Blake.

"I have lately got back to that glorious society called Solitude, where we meet our friends continually. Yet some of my acquaintance would fain hustle me into the almshouse for the sale of society, as if I were pining for that diet, when I seem to myself a most befriended man. * * * However they do not believe a word I say. They have got a club, the handle of which is on the Parker House of Boston, and with this they beat me from time to time.

The dogs are all agreed that I am suffering for want of society. * * * First I did not know that I was suffering at all, secondly as an Irishman might say, I had thought it was indigestion of the society I got. It is indispensable that I should take a dose of Lowell & Agassiz & Woodman. * * *

My last essay is called Autumnal Tins," etc.

Thoreau's view of the post office and of the materials it conveyed remained complex throughout his life. In a January 3, 1853, Journal entry, he makes the post office stand for society and government: "I have a room all to my self; it is Nature   It is a place beyond the jurisdiction of human governments. . . . There are two worlds–the post office & Nature–  I know them both" (*Journal 5* 1997, p. 422). And in *Walden*, he expresses his disdain for the superficiality he believes the post office encouraged:

> For my part, I could easily do without the post-office. I think that there are very few important communications made through it. To speak critically, I never received more than one or two letters in my life–I wrote this some years ago–that were worth the postage. (*Walden* 1971, p. 94)

But Thoreau also understood that letters made possible and strengthened relationships that he valued. The connections to family and friends afforded by letters were deeply important to him. Traveling in Minnesota in June 1861, he begins a long letter to Franklin Benjamin Sanborn by describing his pleasure at picking up mail in Red Wing:

> I was very glad to find awaiting me, on my arrival here on Sunday afternoon, a letter from you. I have performed this journey in a very dead and alive manner, but nothing has come so near waking me up as the receipt of letters from Concord. I read yours, and one from my sister, (and Horace Mann, his four) near the top of a remarkable isolated bluff here. (*Cor* 1958, p. 618)

Eventually the post office became part of what Thoreau cherished about his life in Concord. In a November 1, 1858, Journal passage in which he describes his pleasure at recognizing the November events that have "come round again," the post office plays a significant role:

---

to Thoreau survive from early spring 1861 through spring 1862. Ricketson's last letter is dated May 4, 1862, two days before Thoreau's death. In a May 13 letter of condolence to Sophia, Ricketson asks whether that letter had arrived in time for Thoreau to read it. A week later, Sophia assures him that she had read it to her brother: "He enjoyed your letters, and felt disappointed not to see you again" (*Ricketson and Friends* 1902, p. 143).

> I leaned over a rail in the twilight on the Walden Road–waiting for the evening mail–to be distributed–when such thoughts visited me– I seemed to recognize this November evening as a familiar thing come round again–& yet I could hardly tell whether I had ever known it or only divined it. . . . The long RR causeway–through the meadows west of me–the still twilight in which hardly a cricket was heard (?)–the dark bank of clouds in the horizon–the villagers crowding to the P. O.–& the hastening home to supper by candle light–had I not seen all this before–! What new sweet am I to extract from it? . . . And yet there is no more tempting novelty–than this new November– No going to Europe or another world–is to be named with it  Give me the old familiar walk P. O. & all–with this ever new self–with this infinite expectation & faith–which does not know when it is beaten.[7]

After Thoreau's death on May 6, 1862, his correspondents started sending his letters back to Concord, a customary way of offering comfort to bereaved family members. These letters added to the material that Thoreau left behind, which his sister Sophia was handling. In Thoreau's last months he had taken care to plan the dispersal of his library, directing that specific volumes should go to Emerson and to Alcott, but he had not told Sophia what to do with his manuscripts, which included his Journal, his commonplace books, his literary and scientific writings, and these letters he had written as well as those he had received.[8]

No documentary evidence exists of Thoreau's attitude toward the publication of his own correspondence, but he did value the letters of others, including family letters of his great uncle, Cotton Mather's letter about the Great

[7] Thoreau's MS Volume 27, pp. 289-291 (MA 1302:33 at the Morgan Library & Museum, New York); for a full transcript, see http://thoreau.library.ucsb.edu/writings_journals_pdfs/J14f1-f3.pdf.

[8] On May 26, 1862, Sophia wrote Daniel Ricketson: "Henry left a vast amount of manuscript. He made disposition of some of his effects, and he often spoke of yourself, Mr. Blake and Brown, but I regret that he did not decide what should be given to these friends" (*Ricketson and Friends* 1902, p. 148).

Snow of 1717, and the letters of the Jesuits who explored New France, as more direct and revealing than other forms of writing. He read the letters of John Donne, Sir Thomas Browne, Abigail Adams, and Daniel Webster, among others, and made no recorded objection to these private expressions being made public.

In December 1863, James T. Fields, with whom Thoreau corresponded in his last months to arrange the publication of a number of essays, began to plan an edition of letters that would complement the volume of *Excursions* he had issued the previous March. Fields published *The Maine Woods* in May 1864 and *Cape Cod* in March 1865. *Letters to Various Persons*, a selection of Thoreau's letters, appeared in July 1865 in the context of an expanded corpus of Thoreau's writings.

The path by which *Letters to Various Persons* reached the public was not straightforward. In February 1863, Benjamin B. Wiley of Chicago sent his Thoreau letters to Emerson, suggesting that Emerson had begun to gather material for an edition of letters, or possibly for use in a biography. By September 1863 Emerson was openly discussing with Alcott the possibility of an edition that would center on the letters Thoreau had written to H. G. O. Blake. In his journal for September 11, 1863, Alcott writes, "See Emerson and talk about Thoreau's letters to Blake, which we agree Blake should edit. There are some forty or more, and, as Thoreau wrote always with consideration on his own themes, these must all be good for printing. A few might be added to the collection, written by him to Emerson, [Thomas] Cholmondeley, Ricketson, and perhaps other persons" (*Journals of Alcott* 1938, p. 357).

Blake came to Concord in December 1863, probably to discuss the matter with Sophia and with Emerson, Sophia's advisor at this time. Blake, however, declined to take on the responsibility. On December 15 Sophia writes to Ricketson that Blake "shrinks from undertaking such a book as Mr. Fields desires to make of the letters–thinks he lacks literary skill." Sophia continues, "I trust, however, that he will simply edit the letters if nothing more," suggesting that Fields may have had in mind a more ambitious "life and letters" memorial volume of the sort that Emerson and others had edited in 1852 after Margaret Fuller's death (*Ricketson and Friends* 1902, p. 159).

Sometime during 1864 the letters project generated the first of several instances of hard feelings. Sophia probably, and Emerson certainly, continued to press Blake to edit a volume of the letters. Blake finally refused, and Emerson apparently wrote a stern, even harsh, reply. Almost twenty years later, Blake wrote James Elliot Cabot, who was then gathering Emerson's letters, that he was sending all of Emerson's letters to him, save one that he "thinks he destroyed" because in it Emerson had rebuked him for his unwillingness to edit or help others edit Thoreau's letters. Blake revealed to Cabot that he had asked for "some compensation for the work" in case he undertook it (*Letters of RWE* 1990-1995, 9:166).

It was now generally agreed in the circle of Thoreau's close friends that his letters should be published, but Blake's refusal left Sophia without an editor. Alcott and Ellery Channing were both writers, but neither had the temperament or talent for editing. The task fell to Emerson: as with the *Memoirs of Margaret Fuller Ossoli*, he accepted the call to duty though he had not sought the responsibility. He was a reluctant editor and memorialist: he had found while helping with the Fuller collection that this kind of work hurt his own creativity, draining his energy and attention, both of which increasingly diminished as he grew older.

In July 1864, probably in preparation for editing the letters, Emerson began a new notebook, "HT" (Henry Thoreau). It contains references to and quotations from Thoreau's Journal, a list of the titles of eleven of Thoreau's poems, several questions about and quotations from

Thoreau's letters, and some anecdotes about Cynthia Thoreau.[9]

In retrospect, Emerson's editorship seems inevitable. He had served as a mentor and a friend, in what was probably Thoreau's most significant relationship outside the family circle. He had read extensively in Thoreau's Journal soon after his friend died. He had already influenced the public's knowledge of Thoreau's life by writing an obituary and a eulogy that he expanded into a long essay in the *Atlantic Monthly*, at the end of which he included a selection of pithy quotations from the Journal. In each of his assessments of Thoreau, Emerson had described his friend as a Stoic, a term that for Emerson denoted a manner of perceiving and living that he thought exemplary. Emerson deemed Thoreau the best contemporary example of Stoic virtue, but Sophia was of a different opinion. She was convinced neither that Stoicism was especially valuable nor that her brother fit the description of a Stoic. "Henry never impressed me as the Stoic which Mr. E. represents him. I think Henry was a person of much more faith than Mr. Emerson," she wrote Ricketson in February 1863 (*Ricketson and Friends* 1902, p. 155). Both Emerson and Sophia recognized that an edition of Thoreau's letters would have an important effect on readers' understanding of Thoreau's life and work. Each knew that letters gave concrete definition to a personality, and that the image thus created would take on a life of its own. A clash of viewpoints between the two, apparent when Emerson began his work, eventually escalated into a test of wills.

Emerson had gathered letters from the Thoreau family and from Blake and a few others, adding them to his own collection, which included letters to his wife Lidian and her sister Lucy Jackson Brown. He began his work on *Letters to Various Persons* in July 1864 and in February 1865

---

[9] A transcript of "HT" appears in *JMN,* 15:483-492.

the proofs arrived in Concord. The volume contained sixty-five letters Thoreau had written to fourteen individuals, along with nine poems that Emerson considered worthy of publication. Emerson included more letters to Blake–twenty-nine–than to any other correspondent. Those letters and twelve written to Ricketson made up two-thirds of *Letters to Various Persons*. Emerson used only six letters to family members, three to Thoreau's sister Helen, two to his mother, Cynthia, and one to his sister Sophia. He chose six written to Lucy Jackson Brown[10] and three to Lidian; two each to Richard Fuller and B. B. Wiley; one each to Bronson Alcott, F. B. Sanborn, Myron Benton, and Parker Pillsbury; and one that Thoreau had written to him.

In *Letters to Various Persons,* Emerson presented an image of Thoreau that was consistent with the Stoic ethic he had attributed to his friend in 1862. He apparently did not consult Sophia, but by chance she had the opportunity to express her disagreement with this image and in the end to revise it. She told the story in a July 17, 1865, letter to Ricketson. Emerson was away from home when proofs arrived in February, so they were sent to Sophia to correct. "I was disappointed to find that some passages betraying natural affection had been omitted," she wrote. She first consulted Lidian, who reminded her that Waldo "was a Greek, and that he treated his own writings in the same manner." Sophia, however, was not deterred, and she decided to make some changes herself. She restored some of the omitted expressions such as "Shake a day-day to Edith, and say 'good-night' to Ellen for me" at the end of a letter to Lidian. Without this tender closing, she wrote, "the world might never have known that he loved the babies" (*Ricketson and Friends* 1902, p. 166). Not surprisingly, Sophia "did not see any of the proofs

[10] One of these was a draft; see *LVP* 1865, pp. 15-18, and *Cor 1* 2013, pp. 121n2-122n2.

after Mr. Emerson's return." She wrote Ricketson about Emerson's displeasure: "He told me that he had *bragged* that the coming volume would be a most perfect piece of stoicism, and he feared that I had marred his classic statue" (*Ricketson and Friends* 1902, p. 166). In July 1865 the "marred statue" appeared, the fourth posthumous book by Henry Thoreau, the first based on manuscripts not intended for publication, and one of the first books of letters by an American author.

Emerson's selection of the contents for *Letters to Various Persons* was influenced by several circumstances. First and most obviously, he was limited to the letters to which he had access. These included letters Thoreau wrote to him and to members of his family, letters in the possession of the Thoreau family–those to his mother and father, and to John, Helen, and Sophia–and letters other correspondents had given him. He had many, if not all, of the letters Thoreau wrote to Blake and Ricketson, but he did not have the ones to Cholmondeley and probably not those to Horace Greeley, nor the ones to Thoreau's college classmates. Whether he had Thoreau's letters to his New England friends such as Benjamin Marston Watson and Thomas Wentworth Higginson is not clear; neither is it clear whether he had Thoreau's "business" letters–those regarding his lecture engagements, the family pencil business, and his dealings with his publishers. Emerson published none of these.

In the letters he chose to include, Emerson naturally emphasized the characteristics of Thoreau he most valued: his Stoicism, his Idealism, his life as a seeker. He wanted the world to know the Thoreau who meditated on life, spent time in the woods, and wrote two exemplary books, rather than the competent young man whom he invited into his home and who became his handyman, gardener, and surrogate brother. So Emerson used very few of the letters Thoreau wrote to him and his family, concentrating instead on the long, philosophical letters to Blake and Ricketson. The Blake letters exemplify Thoreau's best efforts; their length, intensity, breadth, and imaginative speculation are unmatched by any of the others he wrote. The letters to Ricketson, though more reserved and less frequent, share many of the qualities of the Blake letters. These are the letters that "counted" for Thoreau and his correspondents: in them Thoreau is truest to his Transcendentalist principles, focusing on the ideal and the universal rather than the circumstantial.

In letters to his own family members Henry was playful, punning, and imaginative; in those to Emerson himself he often wrote at length about the Emerson household. The good humor and occasional high spirits displayed in these letters would have softened the Stoicism and diluted the Transcendentalist rigor that Emerson sought to highlight. Emerson may also have felt that it was inappropriate to expose Thoreau's most personal characteristics–as well as the intimate details of his own household–to public view.[11] He was obviously satisfied with his selection: when he finished, he declared that *Letters to Various Persons* was "thus far the most important of [Thoreau's] printed books, though the least in size" (*Letters of RWE* 1990-1995, 9:186).

*Letters to Various Persons* was conceived in the depths of the Civil War. The times were oppressive to Emerson, who burst out in his journal: "Goethe said, that we are in hell: and I find this Civil War abominably in my way" (*JMN*, 15:274). His journal during the time he was work-

---

[11] An example of this reticence appears in Emerson's account in "HT" of Lidian's reluctance to share Thoreau's letters to her with Thoreau's family after his death:

When Henry was at Staten Island, he wrote two or three letters to my wife. She spoke of them to his family, who eagerly wished to see them. She consented, but said, "She was almost ashamed to show them, because Henry had exalted her by very undeserved praise." (*JMN*, 15:490)

ing on Thoreau's letters consistently reveals a man who is tense and depressed, one who feels that his world is intolerable. In April 1863, Emerson reminded himself that Stoicism was always attractive, but then he made it specific to his time: "And yet it must be confessed that the new world lies in chaos & expectation until now; that this mad war has made us all mad, that there was no minority to stand fast for eternal truth" (*JMN*, 15:337). Thoreau was the man who had made just such resistance; the strength of his commitment to principle was heartening in a time of bloodshed and deprivation. Emerson created and persisted in keeping alive this Thoreau, who embodied the tenacity and self-control he himself desperately needed in the midst of a society at war.

Finally, although Emerson could be passionate about ideas, his emotional reserve was even greater than Thoreau's own: he simply could not expose the deep level of enthusiasm he clearly felt for his friend. None of his public representations of Thoreau–not the obituary, nor the *Atlantic Monthly* essay, nor *Letters to Various Persons*– reveals the keen appreciation he had of Thoreau. In the privacy of his own journal, however, Emerson marveled:

> In reading Henry Thoreau's Journal, I am very sensible of the vigor of his constitution. That oaken strength which I noted whenever he walked or worked or surveyed wood lots, the same unhesitating hand with which a field-laborer accosts a piece of work which I should shun as a waste of strength, Henry shows in his literary task. He has muscle, & ventures on & performs feats which I am forced to decline. In reading him, I find the same thought[,] the same spirit that is in me, but he takes a step beyond, & illustrates by excellent images that which I should have conveyed in a sleepy generality. 'Tis as if I went into a gymnasium, & saw youths leap, climb, & swing with a force unapproachable,–though their feats are only continuations of my initial grapplings & jumps. (*JMN*, 15:352-353)

Complete or partial manuscript sources are extant for fifty-eight of the sixty-five letters in *Letters to Various Per-*

*sons*. In an "Editor's Notice" following the title page, Emerson wrote:

> It may interest the reader of this book to know that nearly all these letters have been printed directly from the original autographs furnished by the persons to whom they were addressed. A few have been carefully copied, but without alteration, from the worn and torn originals. In some letters, passages have been omitted on account of private or personal references. Otherwise, the letters have been printed as they stood, with very few verbal corrections.

A comparison of what appears in print with the surviving manuscript sources reveals that Emerson is indeed surprisingly faithful to the manuscripts and, given the contemporary norm for such work, makes relatively few editorial intrusions. Following the customary practice of his time, Emerson consistently repunctuates the letters, regularizes the datelines, and standardizes upper- and lower-case letters. He expands ampersands and sometimes omits Thoreau's underscores. He frequently disguises the names of the recipients (and some of the people mentioned in the letters) by using initials followed by dashes.

Emerson does omit sentences and phrases in 40% of the letters included in the volume for which manuscripts survive. Some of the excisions, such as the omission of three paragraphs in which Thoreau describes Channing's personality to Ricketson, remove "personal references."[12] Others, such as omitting Thoreau's comment that Franklin Peirce was in town to visit Hawthorne, may fall into the category Emerson deemed private. In twenty-eight of the letters, Emerson changes a word to clarify a passage or to make it more euphonious to his own ear: for example, he prints "great" for "just" when it is used to describe "grief," "rarest success" for "rarest means," and "glad" for "ready."

[12] Emerson copied the excised paragraphs into "HT" without comment (*JMN*, 15:486).

A few changes are mistaken readings. Emerson reads "Tarkile" for "Tarkiln," the name of the railroad stop nearest Ricketson's estate, despite a question to himself in "HT" about how the word is spelled.[13] He reads "would" for "should" and "work" for "mark" once each, errors that are easy to make given Thoreau's difficult handwriting.

When Emerson published *Letters to Various Persons*, all of the principals, except for Thoreau's sister Helen, his brother, and his father, were still alive. Emerson omitted references to himself, to Lidian's health, to the owner of a resort hotel whom Thoreau describes acerbically, to Edmund Hosmer's frugality, and to Ellery Channing's troubled marriage. Thoreau's description of Channing, mentioned above, which is personal, frank, and accurate, is the longest single omission.

Though Thoreau had only a modest audience in the mid-1860s, *Letters to Various Persons* received more than passing attention by reviewers. Between the first notice in the *New-York Tribune* on July 20, 1865, and the last in the San Francisco *Bulletin* on November 13, 1865, almost forty comments appeared in print. The letters seem to have confirmed already-formed opinions of Thoreau held by the reviewers: those who were sympathetic to him found much to admire, while those who thought him overrated scoffed. Such words as "eccentric" or "quaint" recur, as do slighting remarks about his religious "pantheism." The *Tribune* reviewer, probably George Ripley, observed that the volume, being of "an almost purely intellectual cast," emphasized Thoreau's "hermit" nature. Two days later, a reviewer for the *Boston Transcript* admired the letters for their "wit, satire, feeling." In the *Boston Review* it was observed that "[l]etter-writing was not Thoreau's forte"; in the *Yale Literary Magazine*, his descriptive style was praised as "probably, the best in our literature"

[13] "What is the orthography of Tarkiln (?) Hill, New Bedford? Taskila (?)" (*JMN*, 15:485).

(*HDT Bibliography* 1992, pp. 110-120, numbers 640, 641, 673, 690).

The review published in the New York *Independent* quoted passages from several letters to support the reviewer's thesis that "[n]othing so reveals the inner life as letters, if written, as they are not always, without regard to a future public. . . . These of Thoreau are among the truest, so far as sincerity and frankness go." As if to confirm Sophia's opinion, the reviewer found the letters "not so much gossipy as literary." However, though they "talk but little of the delightful nothings of daily life . . . [k]indly sentiments as son, and brother, and friend, joined with good sense, give a plain every-dayishness to many of the letters."[14]

Of all the reviews, James Russell Lowell's, published in the October 1865 issue of the *North American Review* and reprinted more than any other, has generated the most comment and continues to receive attention today. Although nominally about *Letters to Various Persons*, Lowell's piece is actually a report of his negative response to Thoreau's character and career based on his reading of the six published volumes of Thoreau's writings. It is an acerbic attack that begins with an unsympathetic critique of the origins and major figures of Transcendentalism. Lowell does not turn to Thoreau until the fifth page of the review, and while his description of the personal and intellectual qualities in Thoreau that irritate him is quite detailed, he provides very little evidence from the books themselves to support his impressions. Lowell denounces Thoreau's failures as thinker, observer, and writer. He concludes that Thoreau had "little active imagination" and that "his critical power, from want of continuity of mind, [was] very limited and inadequate".

---

[14] "Thoreau's Letters," reproduced in *Literary Comment in American Renaissance Newspapers*, ed. Kenneth Walter Cameron (Hartford, Conn.: Transcendental Books, 1977), pp. 46-47.

"It is curious," Lowell remarks, "considering what Thoreau afterwards became, that he was not by nature an observer." In Lowell's opinion, Thoreau "had no humor" and held a "very shallow view that affirms trees and rocks to be healthy, and cannot see that men in communities are just as true to the laws of their organization and destiny." Lowell's concluding praise–"there are sentences of his as perfect as anything in the language, and thoughts as clearly crystallized"–did little to mitigate his attack.[15] Lowell's authority as a successful and widely read poet, a Harvard professor, and a former editor of the *Atlantic Monthly* ensured that his assessment of Thoreau would be taken seriously.

Lowell's influence notwithstanding, sales of *Letters to Various Persons* were steady, though not large. Ticknor and Fields records show that from 1881 to 1893 the book sold 1,547 copies, an average of 119 per year.

There is no extant record of the letters Emerson collected for *Letters to Various Persons*: neither the total number of letters nor the names of correspondents are known. However, it is likely that after the volume was published, Emerson gave Sophia the manuscripts he had gathered (he may have retained the letters Lidian wrote to Thoreau; these have never surfaced). When Sophia moved to Bangor, Maine, in April 1873, she left three containers of papers and books with Bronson Alcott. In 1874, unhappy with Alcott's stewardship of the material, Sophia had the containers moved to the Concord Free Public Library; at that time she gave the library about fifty of her brother's books. Two years later Sophia died, leaving all but Thoreau's surveys and his surveying field notes to Blake. On December 20, 1876, Emerson arranged for the Adams Express Company to deliver to Blake two

---

[15] James Russell Lowell, "Critical Notices: Thoreau, *Letters to Various Persons*," *North American Review* 209 (October 1865): 597-608; passages quoted are on pp. 602, 604, 605, and 607.

trunks of manuscripts that weighed all together about 225 pounds.[16]

While Alcott was in possession of Thoreau's papers, he found among them "several letters which should be published in a second edition of the *Letters*" (*Journals of Alcott* 1938, p. 432). There is no evidence that either Emerson or Alcott seriously entertained the idea of publishing a second edition of *Letters to Various Persons*, but apparently Sanborn had been planning a new, more extensive collection of letters since the publication of Emerson's volume.[17] An accomplished individual with unshakeable confidence in himself, Sanborn was in the right place at the right time to acquire and disseminate information about some of the major figures of nineteenth-century American letters. He had met Emerson, Alcott, Hawthorne, and Thoreau, and he was eager to represent them to the public by writing their biographies and editing their works.

Sanborn and Thoreau became acquainted in 1855 through an exchange of letters. Sanborn was then a senior at Harvard and editor of the *Harvard Magazine*, which had published a review of *Walden*. Thoreau stopped at Sanborn's room to leave a copy of *A Week on the Concord and Merrimack Rivers* for the author of the *Walden* review, but Sanborn was out. On January 30, 1855, he wrote to Thoreau, asking if he could visit Thoreau in Concord some time. Later in 1855 Sanborn moved to Concord at Emerson's invitation, to keep school; for several years he rented a room in the house Ellery Channing owned, which was across Main Street from the Thoreau family's

---

[16] *Letters of RWE* 1939, 6:298-299.

[17] In the introduction to the first edition of *Familiar Letters*, Sanborn states that Sophia's dissatisfaction with "Emerson's rule of selection among the letters," which she expressed to Sanborn, "determined [him], should occasion offer, to give the world some day a fuller and more familiar view of our friend" (*FL* 1894, p. viii).

Yellow House.[18] Except for a period from 1872 to 1874 when he was editor of the *Springfield Republican*, Sanborn lived in Concord until his death in 1917.

Emerson had known Thoreau almost as intimately as Thoreau's own family had, but Sanborn and Thoreau had not been close friends. However, Sanborn had access to those who had known Thoreau well and to a great deal of original material, and from 1882 until 1917 he published or made available to others to publish almost two hundred letters by and to Thoreau.

Just before Emerson's death in April 1882, Sanborn published *Henry D. Thoreau* in Houghton Mifflin's American Men of Letters series (*Life of HDT* 1917, p. x). This volume made available for the first time a sizable body of letters to Thoreau, most notably two letters from Margaret Fuller and twenty-four from Horace Greeley. Altogether, complete or excerpted texts of forty-two letters to Thoreau and thirteen from him were included; forty-five of these had not been published previously.

As Sanborn collected material for a new edition of the letters, several others who had been inspired by Thoreau's ideas were working to make the Concord author known to a wider circle. Sanborn had already been contacted by one of these men, Henry S. Salt, an Englishman who was writing about Thoreau. Sanborn probably provided Salt with the texts of seven letters from Thoreau that were published for the first time in Salt's 1890 biography *Life of Henry David Thoreau* (Salt included forty-three letters in all, all but three of them from Thoreau). In the spring of 1890, Samuel A. Jones, an Ann Arbor, Michigan, homeopathic physician, sent copies of his first essay on Thoreau to Salt, Daniel Ricketson, and H. G. O. Blake.[19] Salt had

---

[18] Channing in turn boarded with Sanborn and his family in their house on the Sudbury River for the last ten years of his life, 1891 to 1901.

[19] According to the introduction to the 1993 edition of Salt's unpublished 1908 biography, *Life of Henry David Thoreau* (ed. George Hen-

already begun corresponding with Ricketson, Blake, Edward Waldo Emerson, and several others with firsthand knowledge of Thoreau. Jones made a connection with Alfred Winslow Hosmer, a native Concordian who had photographed some of Thoreau's favorite locations in and around Concord. Jones, Salt, and Hosmer maintained a correspondence focused on Thoreau for over a decade. The material they collected and published and the contacts they made were fundamental in establishing Thoreau's modern reputation.[20]

Writing in spring 1890, Jones asked Blake to edit a volume that would include both Blake's and Thoreau's letters, an idea that Blake firmly rejected: "Judging by my feelings generally when I read old letters of my own, it wd. be a somewhat mortifying occupation to read them even, still more to edit them."[21] At about the same time, Jones apparently suggested to Salt that he undertake an edition of correspondence to replace *Letters to Various Persons*, but the Englishman replied on April 12, 1890, that he knew that Sanborn was planning just such a volume and that he "could hardly offer to step in between [Sanborn] and his proposal." Jones, who disliked Sanborn and later came to detest him, probably reiterated his proposal, for Salt wrote Jones on June 30: "As to the *Letters*, you will, I am sure, understand my position. Mr. Sanborn has been exceedingly courteous and kind to me in helping me with

drick, Willene Hendrick, and Fritz Oehlschlaeger [Urbana: University of Illinois Press]), Sanborn and Jones were the two Thoreauvians who gave Salt the most help when he was writing the 1890 edition (pp. xvii-xviii).

[20] See *T's Modern Reputation* 1979, "Introduction," pp. 1-54.

[21] H. G. O. Blake to S. A. Jones, March 10, 1890; quoted in *T's Modern Reputation* 1979, p. 67. Given Blake's reticence, he probably destroyed his letters to Thoreau before his death in 1898, for no trace of them exists beyond the portion of the one initiating their correspondence, to which Thoreau replied on March 27, 1848 (*Cor 1* 2013, pp. 357-358, 359-362). Sanborn published this portion of Blake's letter in 1894 in *Familiar Letters* (pp. 190-191); the manuscript is no longer extant.

the *Life*, and I would not on any account do anything which could be construed into a slight on him ."[22]

Four years passed before Sanborn's *Familiar Letters of Henry David Thoreau* was published. During that period, the *Atlantic Monthly* published three articles by Sanborn in which he illuminated Thoreau's relationships with Emerson ("The Emerson-Thoreau Correspondence," in two installments) and with the Englishman Thomas Cholmondeley ("Thoreau and His English Friend Thomas Cholmondeley").[23] In *Letters to Various Persons*, Emerson had printed three letters Thoreau wrote to Lidian and only one Thoreau wrote to him; "The Emerson-Thoreau Correspondence" includes seventeen letters from Thoreau to Emerson and one to both Lidian and himself, and seventeen to Thoreau from Emerson (sixteen complete and one an excerpt), as well as two to Sophia Thoreau, one to James Cabot, and one from Elizabeth Hoar to Thoreau. In introducing the first installment of "The Emerson-Thoreau Correspondence" Sanborn wrote,

> These letters have been in my hands for ten years past, and there seems to be no reason now why they should not be given to the public. They will, I think, open a new view of Thoreau's character to those readers–perhaps the majority–who fancy him a reserved, stoical, and unsympathetic person.[24]

"Thoreau and His English Friend Thomas Cholmondeley" includes six letters from Cholmondeley and one from Thoreau. Sanborn used excerpts from several of Thoreau's letters to Ricketson and Blake and two letters

---

[22] Henry Salt to S. A. Jones, April 12, 1890, and Henry Salt to S. A. Jones, June 30, 1890; quoted in *T's Modern Reputation* 1979, pp. 71 and 75.

[23] "The Emerson-Thoreau Correspondence," ed. Franklin Benjamin Sanborn, *Atlantic Monthly* 69 (May 1892): 577-596; (June 1892): 736-753, and "Thoreau and His English Friend Thomas Cholmondeley," ed. Franklin Benjamin Sanborn, *Atlantic Monthly* 72 (December 1893): 741-756.

[24] "The Emerson-Thoreau Correspondence," *Atlantic Monthly* 69 (May 1892): 577.

from the British publisher and bookseller John Chapman to provide contemporary details about Cholmondeley's travels and his gift to Thoreau of twenty-two titles, some in several volumes, covering Eastern religion, literature, and history. In these three articles Sanborn made available forty-one previously unpublished letters. In 1893, Sanborn and William T. Harris published *A. Bronson Alcott: His Life and Philosophy* in two volumes (Boston: Roberts Brothers, 1893), which include three previously unpublished letters, one from Alcott and two to Benjamin Marston Watson, and excerpts from seven that had appeared before.

In July 1893 Sanborn visited Salt in England and, according to Salt, talked "of publishing another volume of Thoreau letters shortly."[25] On January 25, 1894, Houghton Mifflin issued a contract "to electrotype & publish at their own risk, a volume of the Familiar Letters of Henry D. Thoreau, Edited by Frank B. Sanborn, and to pay Mr. Sanborn a royalty of ten per cent. on the retail price of all copies sold" (Houghton Mifflin Company Records, D. [101], p. 107). In a March letter to Jones, Salt wrote: "I hear from Sanborn that his edition of the *letters* is now printing, but may perhaps not appear till the autumn."[26]

Throughout the spring of 1894 Houghton Mifflin urged Sanborn to work more speedily, but he fell behind, especially with the index. His delay frustrated the publishers: anxious to get the volume out to subscribers who were "early birds for leaving the cities," they advertised the book for a May 26 publication, and their "success . . . in that respect depends largely upon prompt action now" (Houghton Mifflin Company Records, F. [197], p. 594). The large-paper edition of *Familiar Letters* was published on

[25] Henry Salt to S. A. Jones, July 16, 1893; quoted in *T's Modern Reputation* 1979, p. 177.

[26] Henry Salt to S. A. Jones, March 15, 1894; quoted in *T's Modern Reputation* 1979, p. 190.

June 15, but the trade edition did not appear until September 1 (*Thoreau Bibliography* 1982, p. 86).

The 1894 edition of *Familiar Letters* includes a total of 160 letters or excerpts from letters, 136 from Thoreau and twenty-four to him. Forty-five letters appeared for the first time, including fifteen from Thoreau to Blake, nine to family members, and four to Ricketson. Sanborn also included every letter that had appeared in *Letters to Various Persons*[27] and many that he and Salt had published in 1890, 1892, and 1893. By including Thoreau's letters to his parents and siblings and those to Emerson, as well as letters to Blake and Ricketson that had not been made available before, Sanborn offered evidence to complicate the Stoic persona that Emerson had presented in 1865. While Emerson had concealed the identities of some recipients by using initials and dashes, Sanborn identified all of the correspondents. *Letters to Various Persons* contains only a perfunctory preface and allows the letters to speak for themselves, but *Familiar Letters* is a more traditional "life and letters" work, which connects sets of letters with a biographical narrative, mixing autobiography and biography.

In *Familiar Letters*, as in *Letters to Various Persons*, the datelines, salutations, closings, and signatures are regularized. Comparison with surviving manuscripts shows that dashes become commas and periods, commas are added, upper- and lower-case letters are standardized, and spelling is normalized. Quotation marks are added around book titles, Thoreau's underlining is sometimes omitted, and paragraphing is often altered. These kinds of modifications are well within the normal practice of the time; in fact, some may have been made by house editors. Sanborn restores some material that Emerson omitted from *Letters to Various Persons* to spare the feelings of

[27] Including a draft to Lucy Jackson Brown; see *FL* 1894, pp. 53-56, and *Cor 1* 2013, pp. 121n2-122n2.

those yet living in 1865, but Sanborn's practice is inconsistent: in many instances he substitutes his own words for Emerson's emendations rather than restoring Thoreau's language, and he makes substantive emendations of his own in passages Emerson did not change.

In the 1882 biography, Sanborn used the letters to illustrate and reinforce his story: for more than half of the letters he printed only excerpts and he made multiple substantive emendations to letters so that they served his purposes better. Compared to the biography, many more of the letters in *Familiar Letters* are printed in full, but Sanborn manipulates some of the originals in ways that change them radically. For example, he prints two 1852 letters to Higginson as one letter, though the manuscripts clearly show them as independent letters with their own addresses, dates, and salutations. He prints one 1856 letter to Ricketson as two letters with different dates.[28] Introducing Thoreau's May 19, 1848, letter to Greeley, Sanborn signals his intervention by characterizing his text as "substantially" the same as Thoreau's. Then he prints a version he has reworked from start to finish; hardly a phrase remains as Thoreau wrote it.[29]

This inconsistency was characteristic of Sanborn's treatment of quotations in all of his editions of Thoreau's correspondence. Francis H. Allen, the editor of Houghton Mif-

[28] The 1852 letters are dated April 2 and April 3; both are brief and deal with a lecture Thoreau was to read. Sanborn simply appends the contents of the second letter at the end of the first, without a break (*FL* 1894, pp. 227-228). The 1856 letter is dated March 5: it includes three paragraphs in which Thoreau gives a frank description of Channing's personality. Emerson omitted those paragraphs from the letter in *LVP* 1865, and Sanborn prints Emerson's version with the date of March 5 (*FL* 1894, pp. 322-324). He follows that with the omitted paragraphs, formatted as a separate letter and dated March 27 (*FL* 1894, pp. 324-325). In the 1906 edition of *Familiar Letters*, however, he restores the omitted paragraphs and prints the entire letter as Thoreau wrote and dated it (*FL* 1906, pp. 273-276).

[29] See Walter Harding, "Franklin B. Sanborn and Thoreau's Letters," *Boston Public Library Quarterly* 3 (October 1951): 288-293.

flin's twenty-volume 1906 edition of Thoreau's writings, had worked with Sanborn on his 1917 biography of Thoreau. Allen knew that Sanborn "had followed his custom of using great freedom in the treatment of quoted matter" and asked him to add a statement to his preface about the differences between some of his quotations and their previously printed versions.[30] Sanborn agreed, but he died the day the proofs were sent to him and it was left to Allen to compose the following carefully worded explanation:

> Mr. Sanborn was not a slavish quoter, and in dealing with Thoreau's Journals and those other of his writings which Thoreau himself had not prepared for publication, he used the privilege of an editor who is thoroughly familiar with his author's subjects and habits of thought to rearrange paragraphs, to omit here, to make slight interpolations there, and otherwise to treat the rough and unpolished sentences of the Journals, letters, etc., much as it may be supposed the author himself would have treated them had he prepared them for the press. If, therefore, the reader finds occasional discrepancies between the extracts from Thoreau's Journals as here given and the forms in which the same passages appear in the scrupulously exact transcription contained in the published *Journal*, he is not to set them down to carelessness, but is rather to thank Mr. Sanborn for making these passages more orderly and more readable. (*Life of HDT* 1917, pp. xiv-xv)

The reception of *Familiar Letters* was almost uniformly positive. In general the reviewers took Sanborn's lead and commented on the more relaxed nature of the book. A reviewer in *Outlook* went so far as to say that the letters

---

[30] *Thoreau's Editors: History and Reminiscence* (n. p.: Thoreau Society, 1950), p. 15. Later in the same piece, Allen neatly sums up the response many readers have had to Sanborn's position in Thoreau studies: "However much one might be irritated by Sanborn's attitude of ownership of all that pertained to Thoreau, one had to admit that he occupied a unique position as the only one of Thoreau's biographers who had had an actual personal acquaintance with him, and who was at the same time an active and energetic seeker for information about his life and writings, also that he had a keen mind as well as a gift of expression" (p. 26).

reveal Thoreau "in a character which is entirely different from the personality expressed in his books." In his letters Thoreau "is social, friendly, human, and takes a large interest in life" (*HDT Bibliography* 1992, p. 324, number 1824). Several other reviewers noted that Thoreau's fame was steadily growing, and that the letters would add to the continuing interest in his work. Earlier criticism of Thoreau's pantheism had disappeared by this time, and his departures from Christian orthodoxy, most strongly felt in the 1860s, now went unremarked.

Sales of *Letters to Various Persons* continued to be respectable after the publication of Sanborn's 1882 biography of Thoreau: Houghton Mifflin records show that an average of 121 copies per year were sold between 1882 and 1893. In 1894, however, Emerson's edition of the letters sold only nine copies, while *Familiar Letters* sold 1,215 in both large paper and trade formats (Houghton Mifflin Company Records, C. [32]). After almost three decades, Emerson's edition had been superseded.

During the next eight years, fourteen new letters were published in five different sources. These include Jones's *Some Unpublished Letters of Henry D. and Sophia E. Thoreau: A Chapter in the History of a Still-Born Book* (Jamaica, New York: Marion Press, 1899), which presents six letters from Thoreau to Calvin H. Greene, a Rochester, Michigan, reader whom Jones had located (pp. 27-28, 31-32, 34-36, 37, 42-43, 46-47), and one from the English author James A. Froude discovered by Hosmer (pp. 11-13). In the September 1902 issue of the *Atlantic Monthly*, Elias Harlow Russell, who had inherited the Thoreau manuscripts from Blake after Blake's death in 1898, published "A Bit of Unpublished Correspondence between Henry Thoreau and Isaac Hecker," which includes four new letters, two by Thoreau and two by Hecker (pp. 371-374).[31]

---

[31] In addition to these, Sanborn published one new letter from Thoreau to Emerson in "Thoreau's Poems of Nature," *Scribner's Magazine* 17 (March 1895), pp. 352-353; Henry Brownson included a new letter

The next publication of a significant group of new letters occurred in 1902 when, four years after Daniel Ricketson died, his daughter Anna and son Walton published
*Daniel Ricketson and His Friends* (Boston: Houghton,
Mifflin and Company). Material about and by Thoreau
makes up about half of this memorial volume. It includes Ricketson's brief essay describing Thoreau as he
knew him, a reproduction of a pencilled sketch Ricketson
made of Thoreau in his traveling outfit, and passages from
Thoreau's Journal about several of Thoreau's trips to New
Bedford and one of Ricketson's to Concord. Most impor-
tantly, the volume contains fifty-eight letters between the
two–thirty-three from Ricketson and twenty-five from
Thoreau. Thirty-eight of these, mostly from Ricketson
to Thoreau, had not been published before. For the first
time, a significant correspondence between Thoreau and
a friend came into print, allowing readers to witness their
interaction over a period of time. Ricketson had understood the value of Thoreau's letters: he wrote to Salt in
1889 that "[i]t would be through [Thoreau's] private correspondence to his intimate friends that he would be best
known" (*Ricketson and Friends* 1902, p. 247).

The Ricketsons handled the letters, all but three of which
survive in manuscript or as facsimiles of manuscript, in
much the same way as Emerson and Sanborn had before
them. They freely repunctuate and reformat but are more
careful with the substantives, emending few words. Accidentals in the eighteen letters previously published in
*Familiar Letters* closely follow their counterparts in that
volume; those letters could have been printed from Sanborn's versions rather than from manuscripts.

Between 1902 and 1917, the year in which Sanborn's

from Thoreau to his father Orestes, in *Orestes A. Brownson's Early Life:
From 1803 to 1844* (Detroit, Mich.: H. F. Brownson, 1898), pp. 204-206;
and in *Thoreau: His Home, Friends and Books* (New York: Thomas Y.
Crowell, 1902), pp. 248-250, Annie Russell Marble published for the first
time Ricketson's second to last letter to Thoreau, which she may have
obtained from E. H. Russell.

final biography of Thoreau and Edward Emerson's *Henry Thoreau as Remembered by a Young Friend* were published, eighteen more new letters or excerpts appeared in eleven sources, one or two or three to a source. Four of these sources were the work of Sanborn. Of the other seven, one was the 1906 edition of Thoreau's Journal–in an August 8, 1857, entry he quoted part of a letter from Marston Watson, in which Watson had enclosed six live glow-worms (four escaped before Thoreau received the package; see *Journal* 1906, 10:3). Another was Edward Emerson's memoir, in which he published a letter full of Concord news that Thoreau had written to Edward's sister Ellen when she was eleven and visiting her uncle's family on Staten Island (*T as Remembered* 1917, pp. 131-134).[32]

The second, expanded edition of *Familiar Letters*, published as volume 6 in the 1906 *Writings of Henry David Thoreau*, was the largest collection yet published: it includes 181 letters or excerpts from letters.[33] There are no previously unpublished letters, but to the texts in the 1894 edition Sanborn added twenty-one letters that had ap-

[32] Sanborn published two new letters in *The First and Last Journeys of Thoreau*, 2 vols. (Boston: Bibliophile Society, 1905), 2:10-11, 44; three in "A Concord Note-Book," *Critic* 48 (April 1906), pp. 344, 345, 346; one in "Early Letter of Thoreau during an Absence from College," *Fifth Year Book* (Boston: Bibliophile Society, 1906), pp. 55-56; and part of one in *Recollections of Seventy Years*, 2 vols. (Boston: R. G. Badger, 1909), 2:399. Sources other than the 1906 Journal and Edward Emerson's memoir are Bliss Perry, *Park-Street Papers* (Boston: Houghton Mifflin Company, 1908), pp. 216-217, for two new letters; the *Vermont Botanical Club Bulletin*, no. 3 (1908), pp. 37-38, for excerpts from three; a brief article in the March 14, 1909, edition of the *New York Times* covering the sale of four of Greeley's letters to Thoreau by Charles F. Libbie and Company, for an excerpt from one; Adrian H. Joline, *Rambles in Autograph Land* (New York: G. P. Putnam's Sons, 1913), p. 293, for one; and *Two Thoreau Letters* ([Mesa, Ariz.: Printed by E. B. Hill, 1916]), for two. (Hill may have received the texts of these two from Samuel Arthur Jones, his friend and physician.)

[33] Including a draft to Lucy Jackson Brown; see *FL* 1906, pp. 46-48, and *Cor 1* 2013, pp. 121n2-122n2.

peared in print after 1894.[34] Again one finds inconsistencies in Sanborn's handling of the material. For the most part, he reprints the letters from the 1894 edition with little change. Some of his occasional emendations in the accidentals restore readings in the manuscript versions; some depart even further from the originals.

The year 1917 marked the appearance of the last publications by those who had known Thoreau. Sanborn died in February and in May his final biography, *The Life of Henry David Thoreau*, was published by Houghton Mifflin; in July the same publisher brought out Edward Emerson's *Henry Thoreau as Remembered by a Young Friend*. For the next forty years, the work of Emerson, Sanborn, and the Ricketson siblings remained the most accessible sources of primary material for readers and scholars interested in Thoreau's life and ideas as expressed in his letters, and the biographical scholarship done in the first half of the twentieth century rested in part on that work.

By the 1950s, Thoreau's manuscripts had become valuable commodities, collected by individuals and by libraries, where they were available to researchers. In gathering manuscripts for the first complete, scholarly edition of the letters, Walter Harding and Carl Bode searched institutional collections, contacted private collectors, and located distant relatives of Thoreau and descendants of those who had known him. In 1958 New York University Press published *The Correspondence of Henry David Thoreau*. This edition has three important strengths: first, it expands the number of letters to 498, an increase of 218 over the number published by the end of 1917; second, Harding and Bode based their texts on manuscript sources whenever they were available; and third, the

---

[34] These twenty-one letters are made up of three of the four letters from the Hecker correspondence that Russell had published in 1902, all six of Thoreau's letters to Greene that Jones had published in 1899, and twelve letters from the Ricketson correspondence that Anna and Walton Ricketson had published in 1902.

editors faithfully reproduce the words, punctuation, and paragraphing of the texts as they appear in the sources. As the volume's title indicates, Harding and Bode present the extant body of letters written by and to Thoreau. They print all the letters to Blake and the entire extant corpus of the correspondence with Ricketson. They also introduce new correspondents, as diverse as Isaiah Williams, an earnest young man who had been inspired by a visit to Concord to investigate Transcendentalism; Mary Moody Emerson, Waldo Emerson's aunt, whom Thoreau thought a genius; James Redpath, the abolitionist editor and journalist who had supported John Brown; and the last publisher Thoreau negotiated with, Ticknor and Fields.

The importance of the 1958 edition cannot be overstated. For the first time readers had access to documents representing the entire range of Thoreau's life, from his college days to his final weeks. He is seen at the center of his family, as part of a circle of friends, as a businessman and as a surveyor. He wrote and received letters that demonstrate his interests in botany and ornithology, in entomology and ethnology, and in local history, as well as in abolition, social responsibility, and ethical living. Many of the people he knew, both the famous and the ordinary, are present, and the running colloquy between Thoreau and his correspondents reveals not only Thoreau's influence on his contemporaries but also theirs on him.

So far, 151 more letters to and from Thoreau have surfaced since the publication of Harding and Bode's volume. These letters are included, along with 493 of those that are in the 1958 edition,[35] in the Princeton Edition of

[35] Five of the letters in *Cor* 1958 have been excluded from the Princeton Edition: a January 25, 1843, draft from Thoreau to Lucy Jackson Brown (*Cor* 1958, pp. 79-80); Thoreau's March 12, 1845, letter to the *Liberator*, which was written for publication (*Cor* 1958, pp. 163-166); a reference to a letter Thoreau says he wrote on March 6, 1854, for an Irishman to his wife in Ireland (*Cor* 1958, p. 324); a January 4, 1856, letter from John F. Trow, now assumed to have been addressed to Thoreau's father (*Cor* 1958, p. 406); and a passage from Thoreau's Harvard Class Book

*The Correspondence of Henry D. Thoreau. Correspondence* is the only work in the Princeton Edition that includes the writing of individuals other than Thoreau; letters to Thoreau are treated in the same way as the letters he wrote. This edition also adds several kinds of information that has not been available in any of the earlier editions. Documentary features of the letters that survive in manuscript are reported, including authorial alterations, addresses, postmarks, and endorsements. Editorial judgments about dating and interpretations of words are recorded. Quotations from dealers' catalogs are supplied when they contain information about letters that is otherwise unavailable. A brief biography of each correspondent, annotations that identify people, places, and the sources of quotations and allusions, and an analyzed index provide better understanding of and access to the contents of the letters. A historical introduction contextualizes the letters in each of the three volumes.

The Princeton Edition includes every extant letter Thoreau wrote and received, but it is clear that the correspondence is not complete. Some letters have disappeared without a trace; the existence of 143 letters that have not been located is confirmed by information in surviving letters as well as in sources such as dealers' catalogs and Thoreau's Journal entries. Of those 143, fifty-six were written by Thoreau and eighty-seven to him. From the point of view of biographical information, one of the most interesting of these would have been the exchange with Sophia Foord, of whom Thoreau wrote to Emerson,

> I have had a tragic correspondence, for the most part all on one side, with Miss Ford. She did really wish to–I hesitate to write–marry me–that is the way they spell it. Of course I did not write a deliberate answer–how could I deliberate upon it? I sent back as distinct a *No*, as I have learned to pronounce after considerable practice, and I trust that this No has succeeded.

entry that has been judged not to be part of a letter to Henry Williams Jr., the secretary of the class of 1837 (*Cor* 1958, p. 654).

Indeed I wished that it might burst like hollow shot after it had struck and buried itself, and make itself felt there. *There was no other way.* I really had anticipated no such foe as this in my career. (*Cor 1* 2013, p. 316)

Correspondence with Ellen Sewall, to whom both Thoreau and his brother John proposed in 1840, would provide direct insight into a relationship known only through the accounts of others and cryptic references in Thoreau's Journal. None of the letters Thoreau is known to have received from family members, including his parents, siblings, and his Bangor cousin George Thatcher, is now extant. Thoreau's letters to his family show him at his most relaxed and comfortable; the letters they sent to him would deepen and enrich that picture. Nor do letters written by Lidian Emerson, to whom Thoreau wrote, "[y]ou must know that you represent to me woman" (*Cor 1* 2013, p. 166), or by her sister, Lucy Jackson Brown, to whom Thoreau expressed himself easily, survive.

Of the twenty-four or more letters that Blake wrote to Thoreau, only a portion of one survives; Blake probably destroyed these himself while all of the manuscripts were in his possession. Blake's letters would shed light on his friendship with Thoreau, and might help to explain how he elicited Thoreau's best letters.

Much of Thoreau's side of the correspondence with Horace Greeley, his self-appointed agent, is lacking. Sanborn, whose speculations are not always founded on evidence, writes in the 1894 edition of *Familiar Letters* that "[t]he letters of Greeley in this entertaining series are all preserved; but Greeley seems to have given Thoreau's away for autographs" (p. 208). These letters, as well as the portions of the correspondence with Ticknor and Fields that are no longer extant, would fill in many details of Thoreau's transactions as an author operating in the literary marketplace.

In November 1860 Thoreau wrote to Ricketson, "Some

are accustomed to write many letters, others very few. I am one of the last" (*Cor* 1958, p. 600). Because the body of Thoreau's correspondence is so limited, any new letter is a significant addition, and manuscripts of letters do continue to be discovered. Since Harding and Bode's edition came out in 1958, manuscripts have surfaced for 151 letters for which Harding and Bode were obliged to use published sources as copy-texts, in addition to the 151 new letters mentioned above.

The letters Thoreau wrote and received provide rare, direct access to a network of relationships he participated in throughout his life. In his Journal, he converses with himself, but his letters are his conversations with friends, relatives, acquaintances, fans, employers, and foes, and they reveal aspects of his personality not seen in any of his other writing. Letters serve to connect the people between whom they travel; that connection is extended to the readers of *The Correspondence of Henry D. Thoreau*.

*Short Titles*

*Cor* 1958
>*The Correspondence of Henry David Thoreau*, ed. Walter Harding and Carl Bode (New York: New York University Press, 1958)

*Cor 1* 2013
>*The Correspondence of Henry D. Thoreau*, ed. Robert N. Hudspeth, vol. 1, *1834-1848* (Princeton, N.J.: Princeton University Press, 2013)

*FL* 1894
>*Familiar Letters of Henry David Thoreau*, ed. Franklin Benjamin Sanborn (Cambridge, Mass.: Riverside Press, 1894)

*FL* 1906
>*The Writings of Henry David Thoreau: Familiar Letters*, enl. ed., ed. Franklin Benjamin Sanborn (Boston: Houghton Mifflin and Company, 1906)

*HDT Bibliography* 1992
>Gary Scharnhorst, *Henry David Thoreau: An Annotated Bibliography of Comment and Criticism before 1900* (New York: Garland, 1992)

Houghton Mifflin Company Records

    Houghton Library, Harvard University. Houghton Mifflin Company Records. Series: MS Am 2030. I. Records of the publisher Houghton Mifflin Company and its predecessors.

        C. Records relating to sales and earnings, including books sales (1880-1923), book earnings (1880-1920), book journals (1881-1898), book showings (1881-1920), records relating to the Ticknor and Company purchase (1889-1910), and special sales (1897-1902).

            (32) Record of book sales. 1891 - 1907

        D. Records relating to manuscripts received (1880-1941), contracts (1891-1968), and royalties (1864-1915).

            (101) Contract record. 16 Jan 1891 - 20 Apr 1899

        F. Pressed letter books, including letters from Henry Oscar Houghton (1879-1885), George H. Mifflin (1894-1909), the editorial department (1890-1909), and the treasurer (1908-1916).

            (197) Editorial department, pressed letter book. 8: 19 Jan 1894 - 16 Aug 1894

*JMN*

    Ralph Waldo Emerson, *The Journals and Miscellaneous Notebooks of Ralph Waldo Emerson*, ed. William H. Gilman et al., 16 vols. (Cambridge, Mass.: Belknap Press of Harvard University Press, 1960-1982)

*Journal* 1906

    Henry D. Thoreau, *The Journal of Henry David Thoreau*, ed. Bradford Torrey and Francis H. Allen, 14 vols. (Boston: Houghton Mifflin and Company, 1906)

*Journal 5* 1997

    Henry D. Thoreau, *Journal 5: 1852-1853*, ed. Patrick F. O'Connell (Princeton, N.J.: Princeton University Press, 1997)

*Journals of Alcott* 1938

    Amos Bronson Alcott, *The Journals of Bronson Alcott*, ed. Odell Shepard (Boston: Little, Brown and Company, 1938)

*LVP* 1865

    Henry D. Thoreau, *Letters to Various Persons*, ed. Ralph Waldo Emerson (Boston: Ticknor and Fields, 1865)

*Letters of RWE* 1939

    Ralph Waldo Emerson, *The Letters of Ralph Waldo Emerson*, ed. Ralph L. Rusk, 6 vols. (New York: Columbia University Press, 1939)

*Letters of RWE* 1990-1995

    Ralph Waldo Emerson, *The Letters of Ralph Waldo Emerson*,

ed. Eleanor M. Tilton, 4 vols. (New York: Columbia University Press, 1990-1995)

*Life of HDT* 1917

Franklin Benjamin Sanborn, *The Life of Henry David Thoreau* (Boston: Houghton Mifflin and Company, 1917)

*Reminiscences* 1993

Edward Jarvis, *Traditions and Reminiscences of Concord, Massachusetts: 1779-1878*, ed. Sarah Chapin (Amherst: University of Massachusetts Press, 1993)

*Ricketson and Friends* 1902

*Daniel Ricketson and His Friends: Letters Poems Sketches Etc.*, ed. Anna and Walton Ricketson (Boston: Houghton, Mifflin and Company, 1902)

*Spreading the News* 1995

Richard R. John, *Spreading the News: The American Postal System from Franklin to Morse* (Cambridge, Mass.: Harvard University Press, 1995)

*T as Remembered* 1917

Edward W. Emerson, *Henry Thoreau as Remembered by a Young Friend* (Boston: Houghton Mifflin Company, 1917)

*T's Modern Reputation* 1979

*Toward the Making of Thoreau's Modern Reputation: Selected Correspondence of S. A. Jones, A. W. Hosmer, H. S. Salt, H. G. O. Blake, and D. Ricketson*, ed. Fritz Oehlschlaeger and George Hendrick (Urbana: University of Illinois Press, 1979)

*Thoreau Bibliography* 1982

Raymond R. Borst, *Henry David Thoreau: A Descriptive Bibliography* (Pittsburgh, Pa.: University of Pittsburgh Press, 1982)

*Walden* 1971

Henry D. Thoreau, *Walden*, ed. J. Lyndon Shanley (Princeton, N.J.: Princeton University Press, 1971)

*Note on Web Resources*

Information that is too detailed or speculative to include in the volumes of *Correspondence* is available at the Thoreau Edition website, http://thoreau.library.ucsb.edu/resources_additions.html.

# Historical Introduction

THE FIRST VOLUME of *The Correspondence of Henry D. Thoreau* comprises 163 letters and takes Thoreau from 1834, during his first year at Harvard, through December 1848, when he was on the threshold of publishing his first book. Thoreau graduated from Harvard in 1837; during the period covered by this volume he pursued a career as a writer while supporting himself in various ways. In 1847 he responded to a questionnaire from the class secretary with this wry catalog of the jobs he had held: "I am a Schoolmaster–a Private Tutor, a Surveyor–a Gardener, a Farmer–a Painter, I mean a House Painter, a Carpenter, a Mason, a Day-laborer, a Pencil-Maker, a Glass-paper Maker, a Writer, and sometimes a Poetaster" (p. 308).

The primary outlet for Thoreau's writing during this period was the Transcendentalist periodical the *Dial* (1840-1844), edited first by Margaret Fuller and then by Ralph Waldo Emerson. Thoreau published fifteen poems and six essays in the *Dial*, as well as three selections of poetry and one play, *The Prometheus Bound*, translated from the Greek. He did place a few essays in other periodicals. In 1843, he published "A Walk to Wachusett" in the *Boston Miscellany*, and "The Landlord" and a book review in the *United States Magazine, and Democratic Review*. In 1847, "Thomas Carlyle and His Works" appeared in *Graham's Magazine*; in 1848 the *Union Magazine of Literature and Art* serialized his most extended and accomplished piece to date, "Ktaadn, and the Maine Woods." Throughout this time, he was keeping a Journal–his observations and reflections from fall 1837 until the end of 1848 fill sixteen manuscript volumes–and he also maintained several reading lists and commonplace books of extracts. In addition, during the time he lived at Walden Pond, from July 1845 until September 1847, he completed the first draft of his first book, *A Week on the Concord and Merrimack Rivers*, and began his second, *Walden*.

Thoreau lived with his family for almost seven of the twelve-and-a-half years covered by this volume. In addition to the two years, two months, and two days that he spent at Walden, he lived in the Waldo Emerson household from spring 1841 until spring 1843 and again for ten months in 1847-1848. In the only extended period away from Concord after his college years in Cambridge, Thoreau lived on Staten Island with William Emerson and his family, employed as a tutor to one of the Emerson children, from May until December 1843. In 1846, while he was living at Walden, he traveled to the Maine woods to climb Mount Katahdin; he took no other extended trips during this period.

The letters in this volume provide a perspective on Thoreau's path from college student to serious author as reflected in relationships with family members, friends, and business acquaintances that produced correspondence. Thoreau's letters to and from his college friends, few of which survive, were written mostly between 1836 and 1838. Five of these are either signed or addressed using the name with which Thoreau was christened, David Henry; after 1838, he was Henry David to virtually all of his correspondents. In letters written in 1836, Thoreau received news about what his classmates had been doing during his absence from Harvard in the spring of 1836, and he made plans to room with Henry Vose during his senior year. In letters written after graduation in summer 1837, Thoreau and his friends discussed teaching positions. Thoreau and Vose were employed almost immediately; as of September 7, James Richardson was still looking. A severe economic depression gripped the country, and when Thoreau quit his job at the Center School in Concord after two weeks, he was unable to find another until he started his own school in 1838. In fall 1837

and into 1838 he communicated with classmates, poten-
tial employers, and even Josiah Quincy, the president of
Harvard, in his search for a position.

For at least three years following graduation, Thoreau
kept up some ties with his friends, but his connections
to Harvard were to these individuals, not to the class as
a whole or to the institution. In the letter noted above,
Richardson chastised Thoreau for disappearing on the
evening of commencement. That absence was typical:
though he responded to the class secretary's 1847 questionnaire about class members' lives and activities "before or after entering College" (p. 289 and pp. 307-309),
Thoreau never attended any of the yearly gatherings. He
wrote to or heard from Richardson and Vose on business
matters in 1842 and 1843, but surviving letters reveal only
one close friendship with a classmate–that with Charles
Stearns Wheeler.

A native of nearby Lincoln, Wheeler had attended the
Concord Academy with Thoreau. He was a promising,
scholarly young man with a deep interest in Carlyle and
other contemporary thinkers. He had anticipated Thoreau's stay at Walden Pond by building a shanty at Flint's
Pond where he sometimes spent college vacations; Thoreau spent six weeks with him there, probably in the summer of 1837. After graduation, Wheeler stayed at Harvard
as a tutor. At Thoreau's request, Wheeler checked out and
returned library books for him; as a curator of the Concord Lyceum, Thoreau invited Wheeler to lecture. In 1842
Wheeler left to study in Germany, where he died in June
1843. While he was abroad, he wrote to Emerson and to
other members of the class of 1837, but if he and Thoreau
corresponded the letters have been lost. Wheeler's death
was a blow to Thoreau; his description of the loss in his
July 21, 1843, letter to his sister Helen suggests that he saw
something of himself in Wheeler, and that their friendship
might have flourished had Wheeler lived (pp. 211-212).

A substantial number of letters Thoreau wrote to family members during the early years of his correspondence survive: with warmth, playfulness, and wit, he wrote from Concord to his siblings, who were often teaching in other Massachusetts towns, and from Staten Island during the eight months he lived there in 1843. In a fall 1837 letter to his brother John, Thoreau assumed the persona of a fellow Indian chieftain (pp. 27-29). In March 1838, he gave his brother a lively, moment-by-moment account of how the family received and reacted to a box John had sent them (pp. 36-37). In an October 1838 letter to Helen, Thoreau made recommendations on selecting texts for her classes (pp. 48-49); in January 1840 he wrote her a letter in Latin in which he described a snowstorm and offered opinions on reading and writing (pp. 58-61). These and the letters from Staten Island provide glimpses of Thoreau within the family, of his emotional connections with his brother and sisters, and they suggest how much he must have lost when John died in 1842, and then when Helen died seven years later in 1849. Unfortunately, there are no extant letters to Thoreau from family members. (There is no evidence that the family destroyed papers, but few manuscripts of any kind by anyone other than Henry survive.) The letters to John, Helen, Sophia, and his parents allow us to judge their importance to Thoreau, but it is much harder to assess his role in their lives.

Also lost is whatever correspondence there might have been between Thoreau and Ellen Sewall, a young woman to whom both he and John proposed in 1840. Reminiscences of others who knew the young people, along with one letter from Ellen to Prudence Ward, provide the only evidence of this important and fraught relationship, to which Thoreau alludes only obliquely in a few Journal passages from summer 1839 and summer 1840.

Correspondence between Thoreau and Sewall might have displayed a more intense version of the romantic idealism found in Thoreau's surviving letters to Lidian Emerson's sister, Lucy Jackson Brown. She married Charles Brown, a merchant in Boston, in 1820; he abandoned the family in 1835 after his business failed. Lucy Brown stayed for long periods with the Emersons and later lived next to them. In 1837 Thoreau wrote what is perhaps his best known poem, "Sic Vita," for her. When she returned for a time to her home in Plymouth, Thoreau sent her imaginative and heartfelt letters that suggest a close friendship in which he felt both stimulated and comfortable. On October 5, 1841, he wrote, "You know there is a high table-land which not even the east wind reaches. Now can't we walk and chat upon its plane still, as if there were no lower latitudes? Surely our two destinies are topics interesting and grand enough for any occasion" (p. 87). Thoreau's language creates an intimacy, yet the relationship remained safely on the upper "table-land," an image he also used in the August 6, 1841, Journal entry in connection with the elevation he felt when reading Hindu religious scripture (*Journal 1* 1981, p. 316).

During the same period, Thoreau renewed a friendship with Isaiah Thornton Williams, who had become acquainted with Henry and John as well as Emerson while teaching school in Concord. Williams wrote Thoreau in September 1841 to ask for guidance. At the time Williams was assiduously pursuing a course of reading, and for several months the two exchanged letters full of book talk and literary allusion. Williams, a law student in Buffalo, New York, was trying to decide upon a vocation at a time when Thoreau was confronting the same problem himself. The twenty-four-year-old Thoreau had failed to establish himself as a teacher, and his literary aspirations were not yet fully formed. As he worked out these personal questions, he also began to think about his relation with a larger society whose values he found troubling. In his October 8 reply, Thoreau offered a doctrine of self-culture whose power depends on the inner divinity of the individual: "Let us trust that we have a good conscience. The steady light whose ray every man knows will be enough for all weathers" (p. 89). Williams wrote again in late November, but Thoreau did not respond until after John's death and his own subsequent illness. Grief and a sharp recognition of life's seriousness mark their correspondence in 1842. To Williams, Thoreau asserted the individual's partnership with God in determining the course of his life: "If God shapes my ends–he shapes me also–and his means are always equal to his ends. His work does not lack this completeness, that the creature consents. *I* am my destiny" (p. 108). Williams was a ready audience at a time when Thoreau felt a need to define his life, to articulate and affirm his faith in the divinity that he believed inheres in each individual.

Williams's response in June shows that he was not completely convinced by Thoreau's carefully worked-out faith. He strove to "live this life well" but felt "a presentiment that [he would] fail in part–if not totally fail to do so," and he expressed an almost obsessive need to know whether Emerson found consolation for Waldo's death in Transcendentalism: "If there is consolation from his philosophy in trials like those–it will do much toward settling my belief–  I wish to know minutely on this point–." Struggling with little success to abide by Thoreau's ethic of self-reliance, Williams chose instead to plunge into "the reforms of the day," making Temperance speeches, going to Sabbath School to instruct the children, taking any opportunity he saw to help others (pp. 111-113). Thoreau waited until October to reply, if reply he did, for no recipient's copy has survived–only a partial draft of an answer. He responded directly to Williams's "presentiment": "perhaps even our own failure does not concern us. Something will succeed–  Let us sympathise then with success–not with failure. Give me but the sight to see success, and no matter into what sloughs my feet lead. . . . Is not adversity always respectable? It should be a field worthy of us" (pp. 114-115). No response from Williams survives. Perhaps he found no solace in Thoreau's challenging faith; perhaps Thoreau did not send the letter and thus brought this phase of the correspondence to an end. In any event, the next surviving letter comes almost fifteen years later: on February 17, 1857, Williams writes to Thoreau, in part, "I came home from Cleveland and found yours of the 7th inst" (*Cor* 1958, p. 466). Their 1841-1842 exchange, though brief, was significant because it moved Thoreau to work out ideas about fate, God, the soul, and human endeavor–topics that he would take up again in epistolary form in 1848, when his correspondence with Harrison Gray Otis Blake began.

During the years represented in the first volume of *Correspondence*, Thoreau's relationship with the Emersons was almost as important as that with his own family; Thoreau's friendship with Waldo Emerson was certainly his most significant one during this period. The two had extensive exchanges of letters on two occasions, first in 1843 and later in 1847. In early 1843, Emerson undertook a lecture tour involving several East Coast cities; Thoreau, who lived in the Emerson household from April 26, 1841, to May 6, 1843, wrote and received letters as a member of the family. Emerson had assumed the editorship of the *Dial* in March 1842, and he depended on Thoreau's help during his absence. He inquired about the progress of the next number of the *Dial* and asked Thoreau to make decisions about the contents. In his February 12, 1843, letter, Emerson wrote of Charles Lane: "If (as he is a ready man) he offers us anything at once, I beg you to read it, & if you see & say decidedly that it is good for us you need not send it to me: but if it is of such quality that you can less surely pronounce, You must send it to me" (p. 139). In reply, Thoreau described what Lane had sent and promised to "give it a faithful reading directly" (p. 141). The letters show that Emerson gave Thoreau a good deal of latitude and that Thoreau acted as Emerson's agent in gathering, evaluating, and arranging the writings from contributors.

In his letters, Thoreau included entertaining anecdotes about their mutual acquaintances and the Emerson household, and Emerson's responses show that he savored these descriptions. In his January 24 letter Thoreau gave Emerson the following report of his two daughters: Edith "says 'papa' less and less abstractedly every day, looking in my face–which may sound like a Ranz-des Vaches to yourself" and Ellen "declares every morning that 'Papa *may* come home to-night'–and by and by it will have changed to such positive street news as that 'Papa came home *lakst* night.'" Of Lidian he wrote: "I have made slight acquaintance also with one Mrs Lidian Emerson, who almost persuades me to be a Christian, but I fear I as often relapse into Heathenism." John Louis O'Sullivan, publisher of the *United States Magazine, and Democratic Review*, "was here three days," Thoreau reported; "We had nothing to say to one another, and therefore we said a great deal" (pp. 123-124).

Emerson returned to Concord with an offer from his brother William, a lawyer who lived on Staten Island, for Thoreau to tutor William Emerson Jr. and live at the family home. Thoreau left Concord on May 6 and lived with William Emerson and his family until Thanksgiving; after spending the holiday at home, he went back for a couple of weeks and returned to Concord for good in mid-December. Thoreau's stay on Staten Island gave him reasons to write and receive letters–to hear from his family, to get news from Concord, and to report his experiences on Staten Island and in Manhattan. Almost all of the letters he wrote to and received from Concord during this time were family letters, including the letters to and from the

Emerson household, where he was considered a family member.

An easy intimacy characterizes most of these letters between Thoreau and the Emersons. Thoreau's absence from Concord brought full, descriptive letters from Emerson, who reported local events, discussed the ever-consuming *Dial* matters, and gave advice. The letter of July 20, for example, contains information about his attempt to collect money a publisher owed Thoreau, an account of Edith's reaction to a bird mauled by the family cat, news of Wheeler's death, and encouragement for Thoreau to translate Pindar (pp. 207-208).

In return, Thoreau gave Emerson sharp, detailed descriptions of Staten Island and Manhattan. He told Emerson on May 23 that everything on the beach of Staten Island "is on a grand and generous scale–sea-weed, water, and sand; and even the dead fishes, horses, and hogs have a rank luxuriant odor" (pp. 174-175). He wrote again on June 8 and described the beach as "very solitary and remote" and the distances "along the shore, and inland in sight of it" as "unaccountably great and startling" (p. 181). By comparison, Thoreau's feelings about Manhattan were at best ambivalent. He found the city mean and pretentious: "Every thing there disappoints me but the crowd. . . . I have no eyes for their churches and what else they find to brag of" (p. 174). The more he saw of Manhattan, the less he liked it: "I am ashamed of my eyes that behold it. . . . The pigs in the street are the most respectable portion of the population" (p. 181). Yet in the city he met, through Emerson's letters of introduction, Henry James Sr., who "naturalized and humanized New York" for him (p. 179), Giles Waldo, William Tappan, William Henry Channing, and Horace Greeley. To both Waldo and Lidian, Thoreau sent detailed accounts of his visits and sharp, accurate observations of his new acquaintances. Henry James Sr. "actually reproaches you by his respect for your

poor words." Waldo and Tappan had "a certain youthfulness and generosity about them," but Thoreau nonetheless felt "a slight disappointment" because "they are not
quite cheerily headed anywhither yet" (pp. 179, 181, 180).
Despite his reservations about Channing, a forthright reformer who had just begun a new periodical "to vex the
world," Thoreau liked "the man all the better, though his
schemes the less" (p. 242). With Greeley, "a hearty New
Hampshire boy" who "says 'now be neighborly'" (p. 211),
Thoreau formed a lasting and important friendship.

Thoreau wrote similarly detailed letters about his new
environs to his family. He described his explorations of
Manhattan from the Battery up to the northern reaches
of Manhattanville. He saw some of P. T. Barnum's spectacles, observed the immigrants passing through on
their way West, and found the city's libraries a welcome
antidote to its noise, dirt, and crowds. Thanks to William
Emerson, Thoreau had access to the New York Society Library, whose librarian allowed him to "take out some un-
take-out-able books" (p. 238). Charles McKean, a former
tutor of Thoreau's at Harvard, granted him privileges at
the Mercantile Library Association. These libraries gave
Thoreau the chance to read current European and American periodicals. He read Bacon's *Advancement of Learning* for the first time and continued the extensive reading
of English poetry that he had begun earlier.

Thoreau's letters to his family indicate as clearly as
those to the Emersons that he preferred Staten Island to
the city. Though it was not Middlesex County, the island
had its rural interests. There Thoreau saw the seventeen-
year locust hatching, compared the blossoming trees with
those at home, and, as always, found arrowheads. He was
abroad on the island so much that at one point he was
mistaken for a surveyor. Despite his efforts, though, Thoreau never "subsided" into liking the place, as he hoped
he might when he wrote his first letter to his mother: "I

must not know any thing about my condition and relations here till what is not permanent is worn off. I have not yet subsided. Give me time enough and I may like it. All my inner man heretofore has been a Concord impression, and here come these Sandy Hook and Coney Island breakers to meet and modify the former, but it will be long before I can make nature look as innocently grand and inspiring as in Concord" (p. 161).

Thoreau was too busy to pay focused attention to the natural world, which might have grounded him more firmly. Although his tutorial duties were light, he was reading and writing with the aim of getting published, and he spent time in the city canvassing publishers, even selling subscriptions to magazines. He was initially unwell and later experienced symptoms of narcolepsy, which several members of his mother's family also displayed: "The demon which is said to haunt the Jones family–hovering over their eye lids with wings steeped in juice of poppies–has commenced another campaign against me" (p. 199). Thoreau missed his life at home, and memories of Concord surface poignantly in his letters, particularly in the August 6 letter to his mother. There he envisioned her, his father, and Helen in a detailed Concord landscape, one he would have gladly shared: "Methinks I should be content to sit at the back-door in Concord, under the poplar tree, henceforth forever." He went on, however, a bit defensively, "Not that I am homesick at all, for places are strangely indifferent to me" (p. 218). He had written to his parents on June 8, "Mr and Mrs Emerson and family are not indeed of my kith or kin in any sense–but they are irreproachable and kind" (p. 184); later in the fall he described in his Journal the "hollow glazed life as on a painted floor which some couples lead. . . . Such a life only as is in the shell on the mantel piece–" (*Journal 1* 1981, p. 478). If this were Thoreau's view of William Emerson and his wife after having shared their home for several months, he must have been quite uncomfortable during his time there.

The most intriguing letter of the Staten Island period is the one Thoreau wrote to Lidian on June 20, 1843. In the two years Thoreau lived with the Emersons as handyman, gardener, and companion for Lidian and the children when Waldo was away on extended lecture tours, he and Lidian came to know each other well. A month after his move to Staten Island, Thoreau wrote to her, "The thought of you will constantly elevate my life, it will be something always above the horizon to behold, as when I look up at the evening star. I think I know your thoughts without seeing you, and as well here as in Concord. You are not at all strange to me." Some have assumed that Thoreau intended this to be a love letter, and perhaps he did. However, he concluded with a message to Waldo, "I send my love to my other friend and brother, whose nobleness I slowly recognise", an unlikely ending to an intentional love letter (pp. 196-197). In addition, in a February 12, 1843, letter to Waldo, Thoreau had expressed a similarly lyrical and idealistic picture of the mutual trust found in a true friendship: "The kindness I have longest remembered has been of this sort,–the sort unsaid; so far behind the speaker's lips that almost it already lay in my heart. It did not have far to go to be communicated" (pp. 137-138). Finally, nothing in the surviving record suggests that the Emersons took exception to the fondness Thoreau displayed toward Lidian. Several of Thoreau's letters from Staten Island express a similar keenness of emotion, and his distance from family and friends and from the familiar scenes of Concord probably contributed to the intensity of his feelings.

The rich cycle of letters between Staten Island and Concord, combined with other letters occasioned by Thoreau's resettlement and his search for professional connections, amount to an unusually large correspondence for 1843: altogether fifty-one letters survive, thirty-two by Thoreau and nineteen to him. (By contrast, a total of fifty letters survive for the seven years from 1836 through 1842.) In the three years after 1843, the number of letters drops sharply; only five letters survive from 1844, six from 1845, and six from 1846. This period includes the twenty-six-month sojourn at Walden Pond, but Thoreau apparently reserved his descriptions of his life there for the lectures he gave and the book he ultimately published: neither he nor his correspondents does more than allude to his circumstances at the pond. On March 5, 1845, several months before Thoreau moved to Walden, Ellery Channing wrote to him about Emerson's land at Walden: "I see nothing for you in this earth but that field which I once christened 'Briars'; go out upon that, build yourself a hut, & there begin the grand process of devouring yourself alive" (p. 268). On August 5, 1845, Thoreau sent Benjamin Marston Watson three boxes of plant specimens, including "half a dozen cherries (Sand-Cherries, Bigelow?)" that "grew within a rod of [his] lodge" (p. 273). In a February 15, 1847, response to Horatio Robinson Storer, who had requested that Thoreau send birds' eggs for his collection, Thoreau mentioned living in the woods and concluded with an invitation: "If you come to Concord again, as I understand you sometimes do, I shall be glad to see you at my hut–" (p. 288).

Thoreau's correspondence fell off when he lived at the pond as a natural consequence of the other writing he had to do. He wrote poetry; he lectured and wrote an essay about Carlyle; he traveled to Katahdin in the Maine woods and completed the first draft of an essay about the trip; he gave a lecture about his life at Walden that became part of the draft of his most famous book; and he finished the first draft of *A Week on the Concord and Merrimack Rivers*, the book he had gone to the pond to write. He engaged in a calculated withdrawal from daily distractions, and he cultivated a form of solitude that would not be threatened by the nearness of his family and the Emersons. Moreover, Thoreau had no correspondents at a distance who could draw him out: he had put his college friends behind him; his brother John and Stearns Wheeler were dead; the rest of his family and the Emersons were nearby in Concord. His most engaged letters are those of spring 1847 to James Elliot Cabot, to whom Thoreau sent specimens he had collected for Louis Agassiz, professor of zoology and geology at Harvard. Thoreau and Horace Greeley, Thoreau's most influential friend in Manhattan as well as his literary agent, corresponded about the publication of "Thomas Carlyle and His Works," which Greeley placed in *Graham's Magazine* for March and April 1847, but only Greeley's letters to Thoreau survive.

The one friendship that Thoreau did form at this time, with Isaac Hecker, a young baker, echoes his earlier friendship with Isaiah Williams. In 1844 Thoreau and Hecker briefly corresponded. Hecker, the son of German immigrants, visited Brook Farm and spent some time in Concord, where, like Williams before him, he boarded with the Thoreaus. A religious enthusiast on the verge of conversion to Catholicism, Hecker took warmly to Thoreau, who apparently found him congenial. After his return to Manhattan in 1844, Hecker urged his friend to join him on a walking pilgrimage through Europe–"to walk, work, and beg, if needs be, as far when there as we are inclined to do." Hecker made a passionate plea: "We wish to see how it looks. And to court difficulties; for we feel an unknown depth of untried virgin strength which we know of no better way at the present time to call into activity and so dispose of" (pp. 258-259). Thoreau, a man with no interest in foreign travel, deflected Hecker's proposal: "Your method of travelling especially–to *live* along the road–citizens of the world, without haste or petty plans–I have often proposed this to my dreams, and still do– But the fact is, I cannot so decidedly postpone exploring the *Farther Indies*, which are to be reached you know by other routs and other methods of travel." Thoreau concluded his letter with an apology and an invitation to reconnect in the future: "I am really sorry that the Genius will not let me go with you, but I trust that it will conduct to other adventures, and so if nothing prevents we will compare notes at last" (pp. 261-262). In 1847, Hecker, who had become a priest, wrote a passionate defense of the Church and appealed to Thoreau to join, a proposal that must have been even less attractive than a trip to Europe (pp. 295-298). Thoreau respected Hecker's idealism, but he had no use for old forms, for doctrine, or for ritual.

After Thoreau left Walden in September 1847, he again lived in Emerson's home; this time Waldo was away on an extended lecture tour in Great Britain. As in 1843, the two corresponded at length. This period, during which Thoreau addressed Emerson as Waldo for the first and only time in their correspondence (p. 344), is in many ways the apex of their friendship, at least as reflected in their letters. Two writers, one established and one emerging, wrote as near-brothers, mixing family news and literary talk. As in the letters from early 1843, when Emerson was away lecturing, Thoreau charted the routine events of life around him, knowing that his correspondent across the ocean would crave detail. In his first letter to Emerson, for example, Thoreau gave news of the children and of the townspeople; described the comic results of Alcott's labor to build an "arbor" for Emerson; reported his continuing efforts to publish *A Week*, the improbable offer of marriage he received from Sophia Foord, and the news that Emerson's woodlot survived a fire nearby; and concluded with the results of local elections (pp. 313-318). It is a concise, witty, shrewd, and engaging slice of life in Concord.

Thoreau is at his best in describing their mutual friends. Of Alcott he wrote, "He is rallying for another foray with his pen, in his latter years, not discouraged by the past–into that crowd of unexpressed ideas of his–that undisciplined Parthian army." Reporting Channing's assessment of Alcott, he remarked that Channing "give[s] vent to his admiration or his confusion in characteristic exaggerations–but between this extreme & that you may get a fair report" and that he sometimes "*will* ride a broom stick still" (p. 346). Thoreau knew that what had amused him would also amuse Emerson.

Emerson, with no domestic detail to report, gave instead an account of Great Britain after the end of the Corn Law controversy. He heard Richard Cobden, "the best man in England," making "perhaps his best speech," and he admired the "moral radiations which this Free Trade dogma seemed to throw out, all-unlooked-for, to the great Audience, who instantly & delightedly adopted them" (pp. 341-342). He commented, "Great is the self respect of Mr Bull. He is very shortsighted & without his eye-glass cannot see as far as your eyes, to know how you like him, so that he quite neglects that point" (pp. 354-355). This is Emerson as the traveling intellectual, a role he rarely plays in his letters to Thoreau. Despite their common interests in writers and ideas, their substantial body of correspondence during these ten months touches infrequently on philosophical or political topics. Neither makes a single reference to the revolutions of 1848 in Europe, and Thoreau says nothing about the formation of the Free-Soil Party and the ensuing national election. Emerson introduced Victorian England into his friend's life; Thoreau stuck to Concord, which apparently satisfied Emerson, who had other sources for political news.

The two writers influenced each other through their letters, though Thoreau was conscious of Emerson's greater force. He had written during his first winter at Walden that Emerson's "personal influence upon young persons" was "greater than any man's" (*Journal 2: 1842-1848*, ed. Robert Sattelmeyer [Princeton, N.J.: Princeton University Press, 1984], p. 224). In his 1847 and 1848 letters, Thoreau expresses himself to Emerson as an equal; he displays more confidence in himself and more security in the relationship than in his letters of 1843. In a letter of May 21, 1848, he cautioned Emerson about granting an easement through a piece of property Emerson was interested in buying: "Mr Warren tells me that he is on the point of buying the hill field for you, perhaps for a hundred dollars, and he remembers that you would allow him and Stow the privelege of a *way* to their fields– I should beware how I suffered him to transact this business with such an implied privilege for his compensation. It would certainly greatly reduce the value of the field to you." In the same letter, he expressed skepticism about Emerson's enthusiasm for starting a new transatlantic journal, observing dryly: "The proposition for a new journal is likely to fall among inflammable materials here–& excite another short and ineffectual blaze" (referring no doubt to Channing and Alcott). "As for me," he stated, "I cannot yet join the *journalists* any more than the Fourierites. . . . What after all is the value of a journal, the best that we know–but a short essay once in 2 or 3 years which you can read–separated by impassable swamps of ink & paper– It is the combination that makes the swamp, but not the firm oasis" (pp. 378-379).

After Emerson's return from Great Britain, he and Thoreau corresponded only about routine matters or on occasions when Thoreau fulfilled specific roles, as when he journeyed to Fire Island in 1850 at Emerson's behest to superintend the aftermath of Margaret Fuller's death. When Thoreau was moved by that experience to write out his thoughts, he addressed them to H. G. O. Blake, not to Emerson, a change that speaks for itself.

All the young people whom Emerson befriended had to come to terms with his commanding presence. Margaret Fuller, Caroline Sturgis, or Charles Newcomb could have written what Thoreau wrote in his Journal in the winter of 1845-1846: "Emerson has special talents unequalled– The divine in man has had no more easy methodically distinct expression" (*Journal 2: 1842-1848*, ed. Robert Sattelmeyer [Princeton, N.J.: Princeton University Press, 1984], p. 224). The problem for all of them was how to live independently of this presence, how to do something other than merely echo or paraphrase Emerson. For Thoreau, the only one of them living in Concord, the solution was an emotional withdrawal that was commensurate with his progress in establishing his literary career. This withdrawal was probably accelerated when Emerson declined to review *A Week* for the *Massachusetts Quarterly Review*, and when he offered Thoreau critical comments only after the publication of the book, rather than during the long process of writing and revising. Thoreau described the situation in a well-known Journal entry from after September 11, 1849: "I had a friend, I wrote a book, I asked my friend's criticism, I never got but praise for what was good in it–my friend became estranged from me and then I got blame for all that was bad,–& so I got at last the criticism which I wanted" (*Journal 3: 1848-1851*, ed. Robert Sattelmeyer, Mark R. Patterson, and William Rossi [Princeton, N.J.: Princeton University Press, 1990], p. 26). While there was never an open break, Thoreau withdrew to a position from which he could be a companion to Emerson without being close to him.

In early 1848 Thoreau began a correspondence with H. G. O. Blake, a Worcester minister-turned-teacher whom he probably met when the two were at Harvard. This correspondence became the centerpiece of Thoreau's letter-writing: to no one else did he write such long, intellectually ambitious essays. Blake, a year older than Thoreau, perfectly fulfilled the role of a friend as Thoreau described it in his Journal for December 29, 1840: "An echo makes me enunciate distinctly– So the sympathy of a friend gives plainness and point to my speech. This is the advantage of letter writing" (*Journal 1* 1981, p. 211). Even when Thoreau felt such a sympathy in his relationship with Emerson, their correspondence usually focused on quotidian business rather than on the philosophical and spiritual realms he often explored in his letters to Blake. Two of forty-nine surviving letters from Thoreau to Blake appear in the first volume of *Correspondence*; Blake's side of the correspondence, except for part of one letter, is no longer extant, though aspects of it can be inferred from Thoreau's responses.

Blake initiated the correspondence by writing to tell Thoreau that he had read his essay on Persius, published in the July 1840 *Dial*. That essay reminded Blake of a comment Thoreau had made when Blake had seen him in Concord, which had provoked an epiphany: "Upon me seems to be dawning with new significance the idea that God is here; that we have but to bow before Him in profound submission at every moment, and He will fill our souls with his presence. In this opening of the soul to God, all duties seem to centre; what else have we to do? . . . If I understand rightly the significance of your life, this is it: You would sunder yourself from society, from the spell of institutions, customs, conventionalities, that you may lead a fresh, simple life with God. Instead of breathing a new life into the old forms, you would have a new life without and within" (pp. 357-358). Gratified that an essay written years before still had the power to move, Thoreau replied on March 27, "It gives me pleasure, because I have therefore reason to suppose that I have uttered what concerns men, and that it is not in vain that man speaks to man." He went on to discuss change, simplicity in life, reform, and self-trust, in language that occasionally foreshadows *Walden*: "So simplify the problem of life, distinguish the necessary and the real. Probe the earth to see where your main roots run. I would stand upon facts." In this letter, as in others, Thoreau exhorted Blake to follow his highest impulses: "Let nothing come between you and the light. Respect men as brothers only  When you travel to the celestial city carry no letter of introduction. When you knock ask to see God–none of the servants. In what concerns you much do not think that you have companions–know that you are alone in the world" (pp. 359, 360, 362). In his second letter to Blake, Thoreau acknowledged that he was writing as much to himself as to Blake, a situation he refers to again in letters that will appear in later volumes of *Correspondence*: "You will perceive that I am as often talking to myself, perhaps, as speaking to you" (p. 371).

The first volume of *Correspondence*, ending in December 1848, about five months before the publication of *A Week*, contains an important record of Thoreau's progress toward a literary career. The letters describe his 1843 trips to Manhattan, where he talked to editors about their journals and about his work, only to find that they paid poorly or not at all and that his writing was probably not what they wanted. They record his discussion with Emerson about Bradbury and Soden's failure to pay him for "A Walk to Wachusett," which they had published in the *Boston Miscellany*. They show Margaret Fuller rejecting his essay "The Service" for the *Dial*, and they report his meeting with John Louis O'Sullivan, the New York publisher who came to Concord to lecture and asked Thoreau to write a review for the *United States Magazine, and Democratic Review*.

The letters also reveal Thoreau's relationship with Horace Greeley, his New York literary agent–a better one the young man could hardly have found. Greeley shrewdly advised Thoreau on how to develop his magazine writing (advice Thoreau mostly ignored) and negotiated with editors on Thoreau's behalf. He arranged for the publication of both "Thomas Carlyle and His Works," in *Graham's American Monthly Magazine* in 1847, and "Ktaadn, and the Maine Woods," in John Sartain's *Union Magazine of Literature and Art* in 1848, and in addition published a paragraph from one of Thoreau's letters in his *New-York Daily Tribune* on May 25, 1848. When George R. Graham failed to pay Thoreau for the Carlyle essay, Greeley became Thoreau's collection agent and eventually succeeded in getting the money, which came to Thoreau "as a free and even unexpected gift" after a period of five years of supporting himself "solely by the labor of [his] hands" (pp. 375, 374).

Finally, letters to James Munroe and Evert Duyckinck, John Wiley's editor in New York, document Thoreau's effort to market his manuscript of *A Week*. Thoreau thought the book ready to publish in mid-1847, but neither Wiley and Putnam nor James Munroe was willing to take it on terms that Thoreau thought profitable. Thoreau met with no better luck in his first attempt to publish his book than he had in his frustrating exploration of the magazine market in 1843.

The slow start to his writing career compelled Thoreau to try the lyceum circuit outside of Concord. Starting in early 1843, Thoreau developed the habit of presenting before the Concord Lyceum material he was working on for publication; on three occasions he had lectured out of town, twice on March 10, 1844, at Amory Hall in Boston and once, on January 19, 1847, in Lincoln. On November 22, 1848, at the Salem Lyceum, he gave a lecture based on material he later published in the "Economy" chapter of *Walden*; his friend Nathaniel Hawthorne had moved from Concord back to Salem and, as the corresponding secretary of the lyceum there, helped to make the arrangements. This lecture was very well received and it gave Thoreau's lecturing career a boost: a month later he spoke on the same topic in Gloucester, and over the next five months he gave seven more lectures in various New England towns on subjects drawn from his life at Walden. Welcome as it may have been financially, however, Thoreau's success as a lecturer put him at the mercy of his auditors, which he counted as a cost. In the final document in *Correspondence 1*, a surviving fragment of a letter to his cousin George Thatcher, he expressed characteristic ambivalence about receiving the attention of the public: "I hear that the Gloucester paper has me in print again, and the Republican–whatever they may say is not to the purpose only as it serves as an advertisement of me. There are very few whose opinion I value" (p. 391).

# Textual Introduction

*Correspondence 1* contains 163 letters written from 1834 through 1848. Thoreau wrote ninety-six of them to thirty-four recipients; sixty-seven were sent to him by twenty-six correspondents. None of these letters was originally written for publication.[1] They are conservatively emended and are printed in a modified form of clear text.[2]

THE LETTER TEXTS

Of the 163 letters in this volume, 139 are based on surviving manuscript or printed recipients' copies[3] or on facsimiles of manuscript recipients' copies.[4] In addition, two letters are based on drafts,[5] two are based on composites

---

[1] Thoreau's March 12, 1845, letter to the *Liberator*, published in the March 28 issue, is not included in this volume because Thoreau wrote it for publication. For the text, see *Reform Papers*, ed. Wendell Glick (Princeton, N.J.: Princeton University Press, 1973), pp. 59-62.

[2] Superscripted characters indicate documentation following each letter, and descriptions of features of the source document that affect the text appear within the letter, set in italic type and enclosed in braces. Examples of such descriptions include {*four-fifths page missing*}, {*MS torn*}, {*text obscured by sealing wax*}, and {*text lacking*}.

[3] Thoreau's copy of the March 1, 1847, printed form letter from Henry Williams Jr., the secretary of Thoreau's Harvard class, is no longer extant; the text is based on a copy received by John Weiss, one of Thoreau's classmates. See pp. 289-290.

[4] For letters based on facsimiles of recipients' copies, see pp. 35-36, 46-47, 51-52, 63-64, 65, 78-79, 134-136, 277-278, and 283-284. Most of these facsimiles were obtained by Walter Harding, the founder of the Thoreau Edition and coeditor with Carl Bode of *The Correspondence of Henry David Thoreau* (New York: New York University Press, 1958), from individuals or dealers who owned the manuscripts at the time but who are no longer the owners. Advertisements were placed in print publications and on websites in an attempt to locate the current owners of these manuscripts, both to obtain permission to publish and to be able to read transcripts against the original manuscripts. In two cases, the owner was located but access to the original was not provided. In these two cases as well as the others listed above, the copy-text note reads "Facsimile of ALS."

[5] It is not certain that Thoreau completed and sent these letters, but circumstances strongly suggest that he did. The first of these is

of surviving manuscript portions and published sources,[6] sixteen are based wholly on published sources, and four are based on manuscript copies made by someone other than the author of the letter.

For all letters and portions of letters based on authorial manuscripts or facsimiles of authorial manuscripts, *Correspondence 1* presents the final surviving form of the author's original composition.[7] All authorial alterations, whether in ink or in pencil, are incorporated, and they are reported in apparatus following each letter.

Postscripts by authors of letters are treated as parts of those letters; postscripts and other material written for and by others are included in editor's notes. Enclosures that the author of a letter intended for its recipient are printed with that letter when they are extant; when they are no longer extant, these enclosures are noted in annotations. Enclosures for others in letters to or from Thoreau are noted in annotations or editor's notes, as appropriate. Endorsements (the name of the author of a letter written on the manuscript, usually by the recipient of the letter)

---

Thoreau's October 10, 1842, draft of a response to Isaiah Thornton Williams's June 23, 1842, letter to him (pp. 114-115). Thoreau's letter closes a series of exchanges in 1841 and 1842, but a surviving portion of a February 17, 1857, letter from Williams to Thoreau, in which Williams refers to a recent letter from Thoreau (see *Cor* 1958, p. 466), provides evidence that the two maintained a relationship. The draft is included on this basis.

The second is Thoreau's August 1, 1843, draft of a letter to John Louis O'Sullivan, the editor of the *United States Magazine, and Democratic Review* (pp. 216-217). In this draft Thoreau asks for the return of the manuscript of his review of J. A. Etzler's book, *The Paradise within the Reach of All Men.* That Thoreau received the manuscript, revised it, and sent it back to O'Sullivan is indicated by the article's publication in the November 1843 issue of O'Sullivan's periodical.

[6] See pp. 30-34 and 359-364.

[7] Four of the letters that are based on facsimiles in this volume (pp. 35-36, 134-136, 277-278, 283-284) were originally published by Franklin Benjamin Sanborn, who almost certainly had access to recipients' copies. The facsimiles have been chosen as the copy-texts, however, because comparison of them with Sanborn's versions reveals a number of misreadings and manipulations of punctuation and format in the latter.

are reported in editor's notes. Additions to the manuscripts by persons other than the author in the course of
later uses of the document are generally neither included
nor reported. Examples of such additions are Ralph
Waldo Emerson's editorial marks on the manuscripts of
letters that were published in *Letters to Various Persons*
(Boston: Ticknor and Fields, 1865), dealers' notations,
and marks by libraries signifying ownership. However,
when the recipient of a letter from Thoreau cut out Thoreau's signature to give away, his note supplying what had
been written on the portion he cut out is included in the
editor's notes for that letter (see p. 363). Thoreau's uses of
letters as scrap paper are not reported except when such
uses provide evidence for authentication or dating.

Unusual positioning of text in letters is generally not
noted. Examples include cross writing, text added at the
top of a page or at ninety degrees to the body of the letter,
and writing around blank spaces left for the sealing wax
so the text was not damaged when the letter was opened.

Drawings are photographically reproduced. Their
placement in the printed text represents as faithfully as
possible their relationship to the words of the manuscript.

Sixteen letters or portions of letters are extant only in
published form; four more survive only as copies made
by someone other than the author. Both formats are
less authoritative than manuscript recipients' copies or
drafts: it is impossible to know how faithful these medi-
ated texts are to the unavailable originals. Most of the
letters or portions of letters based on published sources
are drawn from editions by Emerson and Franklin Benjamin Sanborn; a few come from dealers' catalogs.[8] These

[8] For texts based on Emerson's *Letters to Various Persons*, see pp. 76-
78, 87-88, and 368-372. For texts based on books and articles edited by
Sanborn, see pp. 136-138, 143-146, 158-159, 187-191, 281-282, 303-304, and
357-359. For texts based solely on dealers' catalogs, see pp. 157-158, 206-
207, and 391-392. For a fuller discussion of the nineteenth- and early
twentieth-century editions of Thoreau's letters, see the General Introduction, pp. 408-431.

sources regularize or apply house styling to punctuation and elements such as datelines, salutations, and closings. Most of these regularizations are accepted in this edition; no attempt is made to supply conjectural authorial punctuation or manuscript format.

Of the sixteen letters based on published sources, three are composites of two published sources (see pp. 290-292, 299-300, and 387-389). In all three cases, each source contains some unique material, and some parts of the letter appear in both sources. The sources are equally authoritative. For the parts that overlap, the earlier version has been chosen as the copy-text, and additions in the later version are accepted as emendations.

Emerson and Sanborn approached the letters with different interests and motives, and each made substantive revisions that suited the purpose of the edition he was preparing. For example, both omitted material from some letters, and Sanborn occasionally conflated letters. In order to collect information about the reliability of the various published sources, collations against surviving manuscripts and collations among versions of letters appearing in more than one published source were performed. The collations of published versions against manuscript sources reveal that Emerson took fewer liberties with the originals than Sanborn. The collations of one published version against another show differences in both editorial sensibilities and house styling between the two. For example, Emerson regularly redacts names of correspondents while Sanborn gives them in full.

Although dealers' catalogs typically quote only a portion of a letter, they often provide details about the manuscript that would not have been available otherwise, such as number of pages, format of the leaves, and the contents of addresses and postmarks. In *Correspondence 1*, such details are included in editor's notes when they appear in catalog descriptions (see pp. 51-52, 65, 157-158, 206-207, 387-389, and 391-392).

Accepting the fact that each published text is unfaithful to the original in its own way, this edition uses the earliest published version of a letter as the copy-text. Substantive variants in later published versions are reported because of the possibility that the recipient's copy was available to the editor and is the source of variants.

Four letters in this volume are based on manuscript copies or facsimiles of manuscript copies. One copyist is unknown (pp. 12-16); the others are Ralph Waldo Emerson (pp. 25-26), Elizabeth Hoar (pp. 106-110), and James Elliot Cabot (pp. 228-233). Each copy reflects the orthographic habits of the person who made it. For example, the unknown copyist seems to have tried to maintain Thoreau's lineation and to have indicated it by the way he or she positioned the ends of lines. Hoar placed open double quotation marks in the left margin of each line of poetry in the copy she made. Cabot used a catchword at the bottom of the second page of the manuscript. These idiosyncrasies are noted in the apparatus following each letter. Alterations in manuscript copies, which could be either faithful representations of the original or errors made and corrected by the copyist, are reported in the apparatus following each letter. Cabot's copy, of Emerson's September 8, 1843, letter, is the only one for which later published versions have been deemed to be potentially authoritative; substantive variants in those later versions are reported in apparatus following that letter.

It is assumed that most, if not all, of the letters had addresses when they were sent, including those that were hand delivered (see the General Introduction, pp. 403-406, for a discussion of nineteenth-century mail delivery methods). The published collections that supply copy-texts for some of the letters in *Correspondence 1* do not provide addresses, but catalog descriptions usually include address information.

Addresses survive for 121 letters in this edition that are based on manuscripts or facsimiles of manuscripts; in one additional case a catalog description provides the full address. All of these addresses are integral to the letter document; none is written on a separate leaf. Manuscripts were folded to show the address and enclose the contents of the letter. A folding technique seen in many of the manuscripts produced a small rectangle that was closed by tucking one flap under another. It was common to add a drop of sealing wax to secure the flaps.[9]

The contents of available addresses, postmarks, and endorsements are reported in editor's notes; their positions on the documents are not described.

Six compound words hyphenated at the end of the line in this edition are hyphenated within the line in the source text. These are listed below to allow accurate transcription of the text for the purposes of quotation and reprinting.

27.20-21 arrow-heads
31.6-7 frost-bitten
104.18-19 blue-birds
175.6-7 ale-house
218.18-19 back-door
369.1-2 a-fishing

## EMENDATION POLICY AND PRACTICE

The texts in *Correspondence 1* are conservatively emended. The letters based on manuscripts contain anomalies inevitable in handwritten documents not intended for publication. Errors and inconsistencies in spelling, grammar, capitalization, punctuation, and word division; incorrect or missing diacritical marks in foreign words; abbreviations of common words; and occasional *lacunae* in words are all permitted to stand if they do not seriously affect the sense of a passage.

In most cases, emendation is based on editorial judgment informed by knowledge of Thoreau's usual prac-

[9] See "To Ralph Waldo Emerson, Before March 24, 1848," following p. 406, for an unusual example of the use of sealing wax.

tice in particular and the usual practice of nineteenth-century American writers in general. The following situations in letters based on manuscripts call for emendation.

> Miswritings and misspellings that, if permitted to stand, would confuse the sense of a passage. For example, an incorrect spelling is emended if the context does not clarify the word's exact meaning or if the misspelling affects pronunciation.

> Possible readings. A writer's handwriting sometimes suggests two or more possible readings that make sense in the context, usually because certain letters (e.g., *r/s*, *j/y*, *n/r*, *s/z*, *o/e*, *u/w*) are difficult to distinguish or because the punctuation is ambiguous.

> Blotted words, letters, or punctuation marks. In all cases, the original manuscript was studied in an effort to decipher the blotted element. Undeciphered elements are reported in editor's notes (position] *PE*; posi{*MS blotted*}n).

> Damage to the manuscript. Damage that has destroyed a large part of a letter is reported in the text in braces, using such rubrics as {*MS torn*}, {*MS cut*}, and {*four-fifths page missing*}. When smaller areas of damage, such as those caused by breaking a letter's seal or by sealing wax adhering to a manuscript, destroy or obscure only part of a word, and the word can be conjectured from context, it is emended and reported in editor's notes (have] *PE*; h{*MS torn*}e).[10]

> Unhyphenated end-of-line syllables that are not part of a compound word. When a writer neglects to hyphenate such end-of-line syllables, the space is closed up.

Three of the letters based on published sources are emended to revise or remove elements introduced by the editor. In Thoreau's February 20, 1843, letter to Emerson,

---

[10] Sometimes the part of the letter text that tore away when the letter was opened remains stuck to the wax, and in a few cases the characters that were written on the scrap of paper adhering to the wax can be read through the back of the scrap. When the characters are difficult to decipher, a digital image of the scrap can be electronically reversed to make it possible to read them. If the characters on the scrap can be read, no emendation is necessary. Similarly, if sealing wax obscures characters on one page of a leaf but they can be read through the back of the leaf, no emendation is necessary.

Sanborn in "The Emerson-Thoreau Correspondence" (*Atlantic Monthly* 69 [May 1892]: 577-596) adds "[F. H.]" before "Hedge" and "[Theodore]" before "Parker". These editorial additions are emended out (see pp. 143, 145). James Elliot Cabot's May 3 and May 27, 1847, letters to Thoreau are both composites of excerpts from two of Sanborn's published sources, *Henry D. Thoreau* (Boston: Houghton, Mifflin, 1882) and *Familiar Letters of Henry David Thoreau* (Cambridge, Mass.: Riverside Press, 1894). Sanborn omits parts of the original text in both letters. There is some overlap in what appears in each source, but parts of the excerpts are unique to each. In order to create coherent composite texts, a period is emended to a comma in the first letter; a phrase and a word lacking in the source are emended into the second letter (see pp. 290, 292, 299, 300).

Compound words hyphenated at the ends of lines occur in both manuscript and published sources. When an end-of-line hyphen in the copy-text divides a compound word (*bread-* / *trough*), the word must be resolved and emended to one of two forms: closed (*breadtrough*) or hyphenated (*bread-trough*), based on a writer's habitual practice or contemporaneous standards. This edition identifies as a compound any word containing two or more words of standard English: *workshops*, *spear-head*, *earth-worm*. Words formed with prefixes and suffixes, such as *unguarded* and *forward*, and words inadvertently resembling compounds, such as *seasons* and *handsome*, are excluded.

To resolve the forms of hyphenated end-line compounds in Thoreau's letters, they are checked against a list of compound words collected from Thoreau's manuscripts and from first editions of his works published during his lifetime. In letters by other writers whose usual practices are not known, contemporaneous dictionaries have been consulted. In *Correspondence 1*, all compounds hyphenated at the ends of lines in the sources have been resolved to the forms that appear as keywords in the editor's notes.

The following features of handwriting and spacing in the manuscripts are silently standardized or omitted.

Imperfectly formed handwriting in short words of frequent occurrence (*of, to, so, in*); in suffixes; in certain letters formed with loop or flourish strokes (*a, e, m, n, r, s, w*); and in "run-on" letters formed with linked strokes (*th, to, is, ey, ry*). (If a possible ambiguity results from imperfectly formed handwriting, the form rejected by the editor is reported in the editor's notes as a possible reading.)

Irregular spacing of dashes, hyphens, quotation marks, apostrophes, and other punctuation marks. For example, when a writer's placement of quotation marks and apostrophes slants far right (*word. "* or *word '*s), this edition standardizes the spacing by closing up the gap. However, a writer's irregular positioning of text and punctuation (*word"*. or *whats'*) is respected unless an ambiguity exists. Dashes, which Thoreau and his contemporaries use in several different ways, have been standardized as follows:

Dashes used as internal punctuation (comma, semicolon, colon, or parenthesis). These are printed as a closed one-en dash: *word–word*.

Dashes used as end punctuation (period, question mark, or exclamation mark). These are printed as a half-closed one-en dash: *word–  Word*.

Unusual features of handwriting that elude exact reproduction in typography. When pen strokes inadvertently connect separate words (*thatboy*) or break within a word (*numb ers*), for example, the presentation of these words is standardized (*that boy, numbers*). Brackets deemed to be design features and flourishes under signatures and in addresses and endorsements are omitted.

Underlining. Words and characters in letter texts that are underlined in sources are represented by italic type in this edition whereas double underlining in sources is retained (see p. 383). Underlining and double underlining are represented as such in addresses and endorsements, which are reported in editor's notes (see pp. 8, 42, 299). When abbreviations are both underlined and superscripted, the underlining is not represented: it functions only as a convention confirming abbreviation, not as an indication of emphasis.

Elements in the manuscripts that are not meaningful. Uncancelled false starts, and blots, flourishes, and stray marks that cannot be construed as letters or marks of punctuation are omitted without report.

Elements in the manuscripts that relate to later uses of the manuscripts or uses by others. With the exception of postscripts by others, endorsements, and in a few cases Thoreau's notes, all of which are reported in editor's notes, later uses of the manuscripts or uses by persons other than the author are silently omitted.

Irregular positioning of text on manuscript pages. Within a letter, variable margins and paragraph indentations are standardized; a paragraph that begins at the left margin but is preceded by a sentence that ends short of the right margin is indented. The position of material written vertically or horizontally in blank spaces at the top of a letter, in the margins, or around the address is generally not reported.

In letters based on printed documents, such as Henry Williams Jr.'s March 1, 1847, form letter to members of the Harvard Class of 1837 (pp. 289-290), typographic elements are simplified. Words in all capitals and words in display capitals are presented as capital and lower case. Italic text is presented as such, but differences in italic fonts are neither noted nor represented.

In letters based on published sources, design features involving all capitals and display capitals and features added to adapt Thoreau's text to the published context, such as indentation and open and closed quotation marks, are normalized to the usual presentation in handwritten letters. Text surrounding excerpts from Thoreau's letters in published sources is silently omitted. Salutations and extracts from letters that appear as part of a narrative within the source text begin flush left in this edition.

In letters based on catalog descriptions, italicized text is presented in roman type, open and closed quotation marks are removed, and extracts from letters that appear as part of a narrative within the source text are set flush left in this edition.

## DOCUMENTATION

The presentation of text and documentation in the Princeton Edition of *Correspondence 1* differs from that in the volumes of Journal and writings in the series. Rather than collecting apparatus, keyed to page and line numbers in the text, at the end of the volume, *Correspondence 1* marks annotated text and apparatus keywords within each letter with superscript characters that link to annotations, editor's notes, and lists of alterations and substantive variants immediately following that letter. Annotations are numbered. The following characters are used to indicate apparatus entries: superscript "e" (*word*[e]) for an editor's note; superscript "a" (*word*[a]) for an alteration; and superscript "v" (*word*[v]) for a substantive variant.

Some or all of the following categories of documentation follow each letter, arranged in the order given below.

### Correspondent

This section provides significant and pertinent biographical information about the correspondent. Only the first letter to or from a given correspondent receives a full biographical note; the note for all subsequent letters to or from that correspondent consists of a cross-reference to the full note.

### Annotations

These explanatory notes provide several kinds of information: sources of direct quotations and identifiable allusions; completion of references to authors and books; translations of passages and phrases in foreign languages; identification of obscure or archaic terms; contexts for topical references; significant biographical facts that pertain to the letters; description of prominent local places and landscape features; and identification of persons, places, and events. Contextual punctuation appears outside of quotation marks when ambiguity would result from using the standard form. Quotations, references, and people the editor has been unable to identify are not noted.

For works that Thoreau quotes or refers to, the edition he used is cited whenever possible. Where his edition is unknown, either his probable source (for example, an edition Emerson owned) or one that could have been available to him is cited. For works other writers quote or refer to, either the edition Thoreau read or an appropriate contemporaneous edition is cited. Full citations for abbreviated titles cited or referred to by the author of a letter can be found in the Bibliography, pp. 485-493. Full citations for abbreviated titles cited in support of an explanation can be found in the list of short titles, pp. 479-483.

*Copy-Text*

This section identifies and locates the copy-text.[11] For manuscript sources, the state of the original is described, using the following rubrics: "AL" for an unsigned manuscript letter; "ALS" for a signed manuscript letter; "AL draft" for an unsigned draft of a manuscript letter; "Facsimile" for an image of a manuscript letter; and "MSC" for a copy of a manuscript letter made by someone other than the author. When the copyist has been identified, he or she is named. Library locations are abbreviated using the current Library of Congress MARC codes; see the list of library symbols, pp. 476-478, for expanded versions of the names of libraries and collections. Manuscripts in

---

[11] Physical descriptions of manuscripts and printed documents are available at the Thoreau Edition website, http://thoreau.library.ucsb.edu/resources_additions.html.

private collections are identified appropriately. When the location of a manuscript is not known, that is indicated in the copy-text line.

For printed documents, abbreviated library locations are supplied.

For published sources, either full citations or abbreviated titles are given, followed by page numbers and, when necessary, other pertinent bibliographic information; see the list of short titles, pp. 479-483, for complete citations.

Five letters in this volume are composites, each of which has been constructed by combining partial versions from different sources (see pp. 30-34, 290-292, 299-300, 359-364, and 387-389). For these letters, the copy-text note supplies page and line numbers for the portion of the letter deriving from each source, manuscript or published.

*Published*

Previous publications of the letter, complete or partial, are noted here in order of date of publication. Through 1917, the year of Sanborn's death, appearances in both collections of letters and biographies are reported; after 1917, only appearances in publications focused on letters are cited. Full citations for abbreviated titles can be found in the list of short titles on pp. 479-483. Publications in dealers' catalogs are not included.

*Editor's Notes*

Editor's notes provide information about the copy-text and document editorial decisions. They report the contents of addresses, postmarks, and endorsements. In cases in which the manuscript is undated or incompletely dated, these notes explain the basis for supplying part or all of the date for the letter. They describe significant physical features of the copy-text and provide the contents of postscripts added for or by individuals other than the letters' authors. They also report emendations of the copy-text, including possible readings and the resolution of compound words hyphenated at end-line in the manuscripts. Emendations are indicated by a superscript "e" in the body of the letter. In the editor's notes, the emended reading appears to the left of the bracket, and the original reading appears to the right, with editorial descriptions italicized. "*PE*" following the bracket indicates readings based on editorial judgment.

*Alterations*

This section provides a sequential list of all substantive changes, in ink and pencil, to letters based on manuscripts, whether recipients' copies or copies of originals made by others. Alterations are indicated in the body of the letter by a superscript "a". In the list of alterations, the revised reading appears to the left of the bracket; the original reading or editorial description, set in italic type, appears to the right. A wavy dash (~) to the right of the bracket replaces the word to the left in cases where only punctuation is altered. The form of reporting usually describes the result of a change rather than the process by which it was made. For example, the report "of] us" indicates that the writer first wrote "us" and then altered it to "of", but it does not explain whether he or she cancelled, erased, or wrote over "us". In most of the letters included in this volume, the alterations are few and minor. Alterations in Thoreau's two draft letters, however, are more extensive and some are more complex; these are reported descriptively (see pp. 114-115 and 216-217).

Alterations that change the appearance of words but do not affect meaning are not reported in the apparatus. These include:

Corrections of meaningless misspellings, such as "peope" altered to "people".

Corrections of false starts, such as a cancelled "cl" preceding "core". In this instance, where the cancelled letters never became a word, the writer may have corrected a misspelling or considered another word. Yet the possibility of a substantive change is only hypothetical, since neither the alteration nor the context can suggest a word.

Corrections of handwriting in which words or letters are reformed, repeated, or retraced for greater clarity.

Corrections of handwriting where the original letters are now impossible to read, such as "pond" written over a completely erased word or the "d" of "pond" written over an illegible letter. If an erased word is still legible, the change is reported as an alteration.

### Substantive Variants

When the copy-text is a published source or a copy made by someone other than the author of the letter, substantive variants in versions published later are reported if the later versions could also plausibly have been based on the now-missing manuscript.

#### DESIGN AND PRODUCTION

Each letter is preceded by an editorially supplied headnote giving the full name(s) of Thoreau's correspondent(s) and the date of the letter. Following the headnote, the positions of the usual formal elements of a letter are standardized: the location and date as well as the closing and signature are set flush right; the salutation is set flush left. Paragraph indentation follows copy. The indentation of quoted material is standardized. A running head at the top of each page corresponds to the date of the letter on that page.

The text of *Correspondence 1* is based on transcripts of published sources and of photocopies of surviving manuscripts and printed documents.[12] Most of the initial tran-

[12] Photocopies of manuscripts that Walter Harding and Carl Bode used when they coedited *The Correspondence of Henry David Thoreau* are now in the Thoreau Edition files. This resource has been kept up to date by adding images of newly discovered manuscripts as well as new-format images of known manuscripts.

scripts and preliminary apparatus were prepared between 1972 and 1982 by graduate and undergraduate assistants at the Textual Center of the Thoreau Edition at Princeton University. The transcript of each letter has been read at least four times against a photocopy of the manuscript or published source. For letters based on extant manuscripts, a number of transcripts were read against original manuscripts by Textual Center staff members; these readings were carried out primarily between 1975 and 1995. In addition, all but one transcript[13] have been read against original manuscripts by the volume editor, Robert N. Hudspeth, assisted by M. Catharine Hudspeth. The editor drafted the final version of most of the apparatus, and Thoreau Edition staff members reviewed and revised it. At each stage in the composition of the book–galley proofs, page proofs, revised pages, and digital bluelines–printed copy has received multiple readings both against the preceding stage and for internal consistency.

[13] The exception is Thoreau's June 8, 1843, letter to Ralph Waldo Emerson (pp. 179-182).

# Library Symbols

## *California*

| | |
|---|---|
| CSmH | The Huntington Library, San Marino |
| CU-I | University of California, Irvine, UC Irvine Libraries, Special Collections and Archives, Irvine |

## *Connecticut*

| | |
|---|---|
| Bruce Museum | Bruce Museum, Greenwich |
| CtY-BR | Yale University, Beinecke Rare Book and Manuscript Library, New Haven |

## *District of Columbia*

| | |
|---|---|
| DFo | Folger Shakespeare Library, Washington |
| DStPC | St. Paul's College, Office of Paulist History and Archives, Paulist Fathers Archives, Washington |

## *Illinois*

| | |
|---|---|
| ICarbS | Southern Illinois University Carbondale, Morris Library, Special Collections, Carbondale |
| IU | University of Illinois, University of Illinois Library at Urbana-Champaign, Urbana-Champaign |

## *Indiana*

| | |
|---|---|
| InNd | University of Notre Dame, University Archives, Notre Dame |
| InU-Li | Indiana University, Lilly Library, Bloomington |

## *Massachusetts*

| | |
|---|---|
| MaLiTIW | Thoreau Institute at Walden Woods, Lincoln |
| MB | Boston Public Library, Rare Books Department, Boston |
| MBU | Boston University, Boston University Library, Special Collections, Boston |
| MCo-SC | Concord Free Public Library, William Munroe Special Collections, Concord |
| MCR-S | Harvard University, Radcliffe Institute, Schlesinger Library, Cambridge |

| MH-Ar | Harvard University, Harvard University Archives, Cambridge |
| MH-G | Harvard University, Archives of the Gray Herbarium, Cambridge |
| MH-H | Harvard University, Houghton Library, Cambridge |
| MHi | Massachusetts Historical Society, Boston |
| MHvFM | Fruitlands Museum, Harvard |
| MWatP | Perkins School for the Blind, Watertown |

*New Jersey*

| NjP | Princeton University Library, Manuscripts Division of the Department of Rare Books and Special Collections, Princeton University, Princeton |

*New York*

| NHi | The New-York Historical Society, New York |
| NN | New York Public Library, Manuscripts and Archives Division, New York |
| NN-BGC | New York Public Library, Berg Collection of English and American Literature, New York |
| NNC-RB | Columbia University, Rare Book and Manuscript Library, New York |
| NNPM | The Morgan Library & Museum, New York |

*Pennsylvania*

| PHC | Haverford College, Haverford College Library, Haverford |
| PHi | The Historical Society of Pennsylvania, Philadelphia |

*Rhode Island*

| RPB | Brown University, Brown University Library, John Hay Library, Providence |

*Texas*

| TxAuHRH | The University of Texas at Austin, Harry Ransom Humanities Research Center, Austin |

*Vermont*

| VtMiM | Middlebury College, Abernethy Library, Middlebury |

*Virginia*

ViU      University of Virginia, University of Virginia Library, The Albert H. Small Special Collections Library, Charlottesville

*Sweden*

SE-LIBR      National Library of Sweden, Kungliga Biblioteket, Stockholm

# Short Titles

*Alcott: His Life and Philosophy* 1893 / *Alcott* 1893

Franklin Benjamin Sanborn and William T. Harris, *A. Bronson Alcott: His Life and Philosophy*, 2 vols. (Boston: Roberts Brothers, 1893)

*AM*

*Atlantic Monthly*

*Americana* 1912

*Americana: American Historical Magazine* 7 (May 1912)

*ARLR*

*American Renaissance Literary Report: An Annual*, ed. Kenneth Walter Cameron (Hartford, Conn.: Transcendental Books)

*ATQ*

*American Transcendental Quarterly*

*A Week* 1980

Henry D. Thoreau, *A Week on the Concord and Merrimack Rivers*, ed. Carl F. Hovde, William L. Howarth, and Elizabeth Hall Witherell (Princeton, N.J.: Princeton University Press, 1980)

*Classical Dictionary* 1806

John Lempriere, *A Classical Dictionary; Containing a Copious Account of All the Proper Names Mentioned in Ancient Authors*, 6th ed., cor. (London: T. Cadell, 1806)

*Collected Poems* 1964

Henry D. Thoreau, *Collected Poems of Henry Thoreau*, enl. ed., ed. Carl Bode (Baltimore: Johns Hopkins University Press, 1964)

*Companion* 1964

Kenneth Walter Cameron, *Companion to Thoreau's Correspondence with Annotations, New Letters and an Index of Principal Words, Phrases and Topics* (Hartford, Conn.: Transcendental Books, 1964)

*Concord Harvest* 1970

*Concord Harvest: Publications of the Concord School of Philosophy and Literature with Notes on Its Successors and Other Resources for Research in Emerson, Thoreau, Alcott and the Later Transcendentalists*, ed. Kenneth Walter Cameron, 2 vols. (Hartford, Conn.: Transcendental Books, 1970)

*Cor* 1958

*The Correspondence of Henry David Thoreau*, ed. Walter

Harding and Carl Bode (New York: New York University Press, 1958)

"Correspondence between Thoreau and Hecker" 1902

"A Bit of Unpublished Correspondence between Henry Thoreau and Isaac Hecker," ed. E. Harlow Russell, *Atlantic Monthly* 90 (September 1902): 370-376

"Correspondence between Thoreau and Hecker" 1902-1903

"A Bit of Unpublished Correspondence between Henry D. Thoreau and Isaac T. Hecker," ed. E. Harlow Russell, in *Proceedings of the American Antiquarian Society*, n.s. 15 (April 1902-April 1903): 58-69

*Correspondence between Thoreau and Hecker* Worcester 1902

*A Bit of Unpublished Correspondence between Henry D. Thoreau and Isaac T. Hecker*, ed. E. Harlow Russell (Worcester, Mass.: Press of Charles Hamilton, 1902)

*CS*

*Concord Saunterer*

*Dial*

*The Dial: A Magazine for Literature, Philosophy, and Religion*, 1840-1844

*Diary of Isaac T. Hecker* 1988

*Isaac T. Hecker: The Diary*, ed. John Farina (New York: Paulist Press, 1988)

*Early Essays* 1975

Henry D. Thoreau, *Early Essays and Miscellanies*, ed. Joseph J. Moldenhauer and Edwin Moser, with Alexander C. Kern (Princeton, N.J.: Princeton University Press, 1975)

"Emerson-Thoreau Correspondence" / "E-T"

"The Emerson-Thoreau Correspondence," ed. Franklin Benjamin Sanborn, *Atlantic Monthly* 69 (May 1892): 577-596; (June 1892): 736-753

*ESQ*

*The Emerson Society Quarterly*

*Excursions* 2007

Henry D. Thoreau, *Excursions*, ed. Joseph J. Moldenhauer (Princeton, N.J.: Princeton University Press, 2007)

*FL* 1894

*Familiar Letters of Henry David Thoreau*, ed. Franklin Benjamin Sanborn (Cambridge, Mass.: Riverside Press, 1894)

*FL* 1906

*The Writings of Henry David Thoreau: Familiar Letters*, enl. ed., ed. Franklin Benjamin Sanborn (Boston: Houghton Mifflin and Company, 1906)

*Friendly Craft* 1908
> *The Friendly Craft: A Collection of American Letters*, ed. Elizabeth Deering Hanscom (New York: Macmillan, 1908)

*HDT* 1882
> Franklin Benjamin Sanborn, *Henry D. Thoreau* (Boston: Houghton, Mifflin, 1882)

*JMN*
> *Journals and Miscellaneous Notebooks of Ralph Waldo Emerson*, ed. William H. Gilman et al., 16 vols. (Cambridge, Mass.: Belknap Press of Harvard University Press, 1960-1982)

*Journal 1* 1981
> Henry D. Thoreau, *Journal 1: 1837-1844*, ed. Elizabeth Hall Witherell, William L. Howarth, Robert Sattelmeyer, and Thomas Blanding (Princeton, N.J.: Princeton University Press, 1981)

*Journals of Bronson Alcott* 1938
> *The Journals of Bronson Alcott*, ed. Odell Shepard (Boston: Little, Brown and Company, 1938)

*Letters of Lidian Jackson Emerson* 1987
> *The Selected Letters of Lidian Jackson Emerson*, ed. Delores Bird Carpenter (Columbia: University of Missouri Press, 1987)

*Letters of Margaret Fuller*
> *The Letters of Margaret Fuller*, 6 vols., ed. Robert N. Hudspeth (Ithaca, N.Y.: Cornell University Press, 1983-1994)

*Letters of Nathaniel Hawthorne*
> *The Letters, 1813-1843*, ed. Thomas Woodson, L. Neal Smith, and Norman Holmes Pearson. Vol. 15 of *The Centenary Edition of the Works of Nathaniel Hawthorne*, ed. William Charvat et al. (Columbus: Ohio State University Press, 1984)
>
> *The Letters, 1843-1853*, ed. Thomas Woodson, L. Neal Smith, and Norman Holmes Pearson. Vol. 16 of *The Centenary Edition of the Works of Nathaniel Hawthorne*, ed. William Charvat et al. (Columbus: Ohio State University Press, 1985)

*Letters of RWE* 1939
> *The Letters of Ralph Waldo Emerson*, ed. Ralph L. Rusk, 6 vols. (New York: Columbia University Press, 1939)

*Letters of RWE* 1990-1995
> *The Letters of Ralph Waldo Emerson*, ed. Eleanor M. Tilton, 4 vols. (New York: Columbia University Press, 1990-1995)

"Letters of William Ellery Channing the Younger"
> "The Selected Letters of William Ellery Channing the

Younger (Part One)," ed. Francis B. Dedmond, in *Studies in the American Renaissance*, ed. Joel Myerson (Charlottesville: University Press of Virginia, 1989), 115-218

"The Selected Letters of William Ellery Channing the Younger (Part Two)," ed. Francis B. Dedmond, in *Studies in the American Renaissance*, ed. Joel Myerson (Charlottesville: University Press of Virginia, 1990), 159-241

*Life* 1890

Henry S. Salt, *Life of Henry David Thoreau* (London: Richard Bentley, 1890)

*Life* 1896

Henry S. Salt, *Life of Henry David Thoreau* (London: Richard Bentley, 1896)

*Life of HDT* 1917

Franklin Benjamin Sanborn, *The Life of Henry David Thoreau* (Boston: Houghton Mifflin, 1917)

Loeb

Translation from the Loeb Classical Library

*LVP* 1865

*Letters to Various Persons*, ed. Ralph Waldo Emerson (Boston: Ticknor and Fields, 1865)

*Magazine of History* / *Magazine of History* 1915

*Magazine of History with Notes and Queries* 21 (July-December 1915)

*Memoirs of the Social Circle* 1888

*Memoirs of Members of the Social Circle in Concord, Second Series, from 1795 to 1840* (Cambridge, Mass.: privately printed, Riverside Press, 1888)

*NEQ*

*New England Quarterly*

*OED*

*Oxford English Dictionary* (1970)

*Orestes A. Brownson's Early Life* 1898

Henry F. Brownson, *Orestes A. Brownson's Early Life: From 1803 to 1844* (Detroit, Mich.: H. F. Brownson, 1898)

*Pertaining to T* 1901

*Pertaining to Thoreau*, ed. Samuel Arthur Jones (Folcroft, Pa.: Folcroft Press, 1901)

*Recollections* 1909

Franklin Benjamin Sanborn, *Recollections of Seventy Years*, vol. 2 (Boston: Richard G. Badger, 1909)

*Reform Papers* 1973

Henry D. Thoreau, *Reform Papers*, ed. Wendell Glick (Princeton, N.J.: Princeton University Press, 1973)

*Response to Transcendental Concord* 1974

> *Response to Transcendental Concord: The Last Decades of the Era of Emerson, Thoreau, and the Concord School as Recorded in Newspapers*, ed. Kenneth Walter Cameron (Hartford, Conn.: Transcendental Books, 1974)

*SAR*

> *Studies in the American Renaissance*, ed. Joel Myerson (Boston: Twayne Publishers, 1977-1982; Charlottesville: University Press of Virginia, 1983-1996)

*Spiritual Seeker* 2004

> *Letters to a Spiritual Seeker*, ed. Bradley P. Dean (New York: W. W. Norton, 2004)

*T: Home* 1902

> Annie Russell Marble, *Thoreau: His Home, Friends and Books* (New York: Crowell, 1902)

*T as Remembered* 1917

> Edward Waldo Emerson, *Henry Thoreau as Remembered by a Young Friend* (Boston: Houghton Mifflin, 1917)

"Thoreau's Manuscripts" 1883

> Franklin Benjamin Sanborn, "Reading from Thoreau's Manuscripts," in *Concord Lectures on Philosophy*, collected and arranged by Raymond L. Bridgman (Cambridge, Mass.: Moses King, 1883), 124-126

*Transcendentalists and Minerva* 1958

> *The Transcendentalists and Minerva: Cultural Backgrounds of the American Renaissance with Fresh Discoveries in the Intellectual Climate of Emerson, Alcott, and Thoreau*, ed. Kenneth Walter Cameron, 3 vols. (Hartford, Conn.: Transcendental Books, 1958)

*Translations* 1986

> Henry D. Thoreau, *Translations*, ed. K. P. Van Anglen (Princeton, N.J.: Princeton University Press, 1986)

*TSB*

> *Thoreau Society Bulletin*

"Two Thoreau Letters" 1983

> Ray Angelo, "Two Thoreau Letters at Harvard," *Thoreau Society Bulletin* 162 (winter 1983): 1-2

*Walden* 1971

> Henry D. Thoreau, *Walden*, ed. J. Lyndon Shanley (Princeton, N.J.: Princeton University Press, 1971)

# Bibliography

Abercrombie, John. *Inquiries concerning the Intellectual Powers, and the Investigation of Truth*. Harper's Stereotype ed., from the 2nd Edinburgh ed. New-York: J. and J. Harper, 1832.

Adam, Alexander. *Adam's Latin Grammar: With Numerous Additions and Improvements, Designed to Aid the More Advanced Student by Fuller Elucidations of the Latin Classics*. Edited by Charles Dexter Cleveland. Philadelphia: William Marshall, 1836.

———. *Adam's Latin Grammar, with Some Improvements, and the Following Additions: Rules for the Right Pronunciation of the Latin Language; a Metrical Key to the Odes of Horace; a List of Latin Authors.* . . . Edited by Benjamin A. Gould. Boston: Hilliard, Gray, Little, and Wilkins; and Richardson and Lord, 1829.

Aeschylus. *Tragoediae: Ad exemplar Glasguense accurate expressae*. Edited by [G. H. Schaefer]. Leipzig: Tauchnitz, 1819.

Alcott, Amos Bronson. *Conversations with Children on the Gospels*. 2 vols. Boston: James Munroe and Company, 1836-1837.

———. *The Doctrine and Discipline of Human Culture*. Boston: James Munroe and Company, 1836.

Bacon, Francis. *Essays Moral, Economical, and Political*. Boston: Joseph Greenleaf, 1807.

———. *The Two Books of Francis, Lord Verulam. Of the Proficience and Advancement of Learning, Divine and Human*. London: William Pickering, 1825.

Barbour, John. *The Bruce; or, The History of Robert I. King of Scotland.* . . . 3 vols. London: G. Nicol, 1790.

Beaumont, Francis. *The Works of Mr. Francis Beaumont, and Mr. John Fletcher*. 10 vols. London: J. and R. Tonson and S. Draper, 1750.

Bellenden, John. "Allegorie of Vertue and Delyte." In *Chronicle of Scottish Poetry; from the Thirteenth Century, to the Union of the Crowns.* . . . Edited by James Sibbald. 4 vols. Edinburgh: J. Sibbald, 1802.

Bigelow, Jacob. *Elements of Technology, Taken Chiefly from a Course of Lectures Delivered at Cambridge, on the Application of the Sciences to the Useful Arts*. Boston: Hilliard, Gray, Little, and Wilkins, 1829.

———. *Florula Bostoniensis: A Collection of Plants of Boston and Its Vicinity, with Their Generic and Specific Characters, Principal Synonyms, Descriptions, Places of Growth, and Time of Flowering, and Occasional Remarks*. 2nd ed., enl. Boston: Cummings, Hilliard, 1824.

Blackstone, William. *Commentaries on the Laws of England: In Four Books; with an Analysis of the Work*. 19th ed. 4 vols. London: S. Sweet, A. Maxwell, and Stevens and Sons, 1836.

Brisbane, Albert. "Means of Effecting a Final Reconciliation between Religion and Science." *Dial* 3 (July 1842): 90-96.

Brown, Thomas. *Lectures on the Philosophy of the Human Mind*. Corr. ed. 2 vols. Hallowell, Maine: Glazier, Masters, 1833.

[Brownson, Orestes]. "Introductory Remarks." *Boston Quarterly Review* 1 (January 1838): 1-8.

Burgh, James. *The Dignity of Human Nature; or, A Brief Account of the Certain and Established Means for Attaining the True End of Our Existence*. . . . 2 vols. London: J. Johnson and J. Payne, 1767.

Byron, George Gordon Byron, Baron. *The Works of Lord Byron, in Verse and Prose, including His Letters, Journals, Etc., with a Sketch of His Life*. New York: George Dearborn, 1835.

Campbell, Thomas. *The Poetical Works of Thomas Campbell: Including Theodric, and Many Other Pieces Not Contained in Any Former Edition*. Philadelphia: J. Crissy, and J. Grigg, 1826.

Carlyle, Thomas. *Critical and Miscellaneous Essays*. 4 vols. Boston: James Munroe and Company, 1838-1839.

———. "Dr. Francia." *Foreign Quarterly Review* 31 (July 1843): 299-325.

———. *On Heroes, Hero-Worship, and the Heroic in History*. . . . London: James Fraser, 1841.

———. *Past and Present*. Boston: Charles C. Little and James Brown, 1843.

[———]. *Sartor Resartus*. . . . Boston: James Munroe and Company, 1836.

*Carminum poetarum novem, lyricæ poeseωs principum, fragmenta*. . . . and Pindar. *Pindari Olympia, Pythia, Nemea, Isthmia. Græce & Latine*. . . . 2 vols. in 1. [Heidelberg]: Jerome Commelin, 1598.

Carové, Friedrich Wilhelm. *Story without an End*. Translated by Sarah Austin. Boston: Joseph H. Francis, 1836.

Chalkhill, John. *Thealma and Clearchus: A Pastoral Romance*. Rev. and corr. ed. Chiswick: C. Whittingham, 1820.

Chalmers, Alexander, ed. *The Works of the English Poets, from Chaucer to Cowper; including the Series Edited, with Prefaces, Biographical and Critical, by Dr. Samuel Johnson*. . . . 21 vols. London: J. Johnson et al., 1810.

Channing, William Ellery. "Autumn." *Dial* 4 (October 1843): 186-187.

———. *Poems*. Boston: Charles C. Little and James Brown, 1843.

———. "The Youth of the Poet and the Painter." Pts. 1-4. *Dial* 4 (July 1843): 48-58; (October 1843): 174-187; (January 1844): 273-284; (April 1844): 427-454.

Channing, William Henry. "A Confession of Faith." *Present* 1 (September 1843): 6-10.

Chapman, M. J., trans. *The Greek Pastoral Poets: Theocritus, Bion, and Moschus*. London: James Fraser, 1836.

Chateaubriand, [François-René, vicomte de]. *Œuvres complètes*. 28 vols. Paris: Ladvocat, 1826-1831.

[Child, Lydia]. *Hobomok: A Tale of Early Times*. Boston: Cummings, Hilliard, 1824.

Child, [Lydia]. *Philothea: A Romance*. Boston: Otis, Broaders, 1836.

[———]. *The Rebels; or, Boston before the Revolution*. Boston: Cummings, Hilliard, and Company, 1825.

Cleveland, Charles Dexter. *First Lessons in Latin; upon a New Plan; Combining Abstract Rules, with a Progressive Series of Practical Exercises*. Boston: Benjamin Perkins, 1829.

Collie, David, trans. *The Chinese Classical Work Commonly Called the Four Books; Translated, and Illustrated with Notes*. Malacca: Mission Press, 1828.

Croly, George. *The Poetical Works of the Rev. George Croly*. 2 vols. London: Henry Colburn and Richard Bentley, 1830.

[Emerson, Charles Chauncy]. "Notes from the Journal of a Scholar. No. II." *Dial* 4 (July 1843): 88-92.

Emerson, Ralph Waldo. *An Address Delivered in the Court-House in Concord, Massachusetts, on 1st August, 1844, on the Anniversary of the Emancipation of the Negroes in the British West Indies*. Boston: James Munroe and Company, 1844.

[———], ed. "Chinese Four Books." *Dial* 4 (October 1843): 205-210.

[———]. "The Comic." *Dial* 4 (October 1843): 247-256.

———. *Essays*. Boston: James Munroe and Company, 1841.

[———]. "A Letter." *Dial* 4 (October 1843): 262-270.

———. *The Method of Nature: An Oration, Delivered before the Society of the Adelphi, in Waterville College, in Maine, August 11, 1841*. Boston: Samuel G. Simpkins, 1841.

[———]. "Mr. Channing's Poems." *United States Magazine, and Democratic Review* 13 (September 1843): 309-314.

[———]. *Nature*. Boston: James Munroe and Company, 1836.

[———]. "Ode to Beauty." *Dial* 4 (October 1843): 257-259.

[———]. Review of *Past and Present*, by Thomas Carlyle. *Dial* 4 (July 1843): 96-102.

Etzler, J. A. *The New World; or, Mechanical System, to Perform the Labours of Man and Beast by Inanimate Powers, That Cost Nothing, for Producing and Preparing the Substances of Life*. Philadelphia: C. F. Stollmeyer, 1841.

———. *The Paradise within the Reach of All Men, without Labor, by Powers of Nature and Machinery: An Address to All Intelligent Men. . . .* 2nd English ed. London: J. Cleave, 1842.

[Fuller, Margaret]. "The Great Lawsuit. Man *versus* Men. Woman *versus* Women." *Dial* 4 (July 1843): 1-47.

Gillespie, William. "The Highlander." In *The American First Class Book; or, Exercises in Reading and Recitation: Selected Principally from Modern Authors of Great Britain and America; and Designed for the Use of the Highest Class in Public and Private Schools*. 25th ed. Edited by John Pierpont. Boston: Charles Bowen, 1836.

Giraud, Jacob P., Jr. *The Birds of Long Island*. New-York: Wiley and Putnam, 1844.

Goethe, Johann Wolfgang von. *The Auto-Biography of Goethe: Truth and Poetry; From My Life*. Edited by Parke Godwin. 2 vols. New York: Wiley and Putnam, 1846-1847.

———. *Wilhelm Meisters Wanderjahre; oder, die Entsagenden*. Stuttgart und Tübingen: Cotta, 1821.

[Greaves, James Pierrepont]. *Spiritual Culture; or, Thoughts for the Consideration of Parents and Teachers*. Boston: Joseph Dowe, 1841.

[Greene, William Batchelder]. "First Principles." *Dial* 2 (January 1842): 273-285.

Guillaume, de Lorris, and Jean, de Meun. *Le Roman de la Rose*. Edited by Dominique Martin Méon. 4 vols. Paris: P. Didot l'Aîné, 1814.

[Harris, Thaddeus William]. *A Report on the Insects of Massachusetts, Injurious to Vegetation*. Cambridge, Mass.: Folsom, Wells, and Thurston, 1841.

Hawthorne, Nathaniel. "The Celestial Railroad." *United States Magazine, and Democratic Review* 12 (May 1843): 515-523.

Hazlitt, William, ed. *The Complete Works of Michael de Montaigne; Comprising; the Essays (Translated by Cotton); the Letters; the Journey into Germany and Italy; Now First Translated; a Life, by the Editor; Notes from All the Commentators; the Critical Opinions of Eminent Authors on Montaigne*. . . . London: John Templeman, 1842.

[———]. *The Plain Speaker: Opinions on Books, Men, and Things*. 2 vols. London: Henry Colburn, 1826.

Hemans, Felicia. *The Poetical Works of Mrs. Felicia Hemans; Complete in One Volume*. Philadelphia: Grigg and Elliot, 1836.

Herbert, George. *The Temple: Sacred Poems and Private Ejaculations*. Cambridge: Thom. Buck and Roger Daniel, 1633.

Homer. *The Iliad of Homer*. Translated by Alexander Pope. 2 vols. Baltimore: Philip H. Nicklin, Fielding Lucas, Jun., and Samuel Jefferis; New-York: M. and W. Ward, 1812.

———. *The Odyssey of Homer*. Translated by Alexander Pope. 2 vols. Georgetown, D.C.: Richards and Mallory, 1813-1814.

[Hooper, Ellen Sturgis]. "Sweep Ho!" *Dial* 4 (October 1843): 245.

Horace. *Opera omnia ex editione J. C. Zeunii.* . . . 4 vols. London: A. J. Valpy, 1825.

Howitt, William. *The Book of the Seasons; or, The Calendar of Nature.* Philadelphia: Carey and Lea, 1831.

[Hunt, Benjamin Peter]. "Voyage to Jamaica." Pts. 1 and 2. *Dial* 4 (July 1843): 116-133; (October 1843): 227-244.

Irving, Washington. [Geoffrey Crayon, pseud.] *Tales of a Traveller.* 4 vols. Philadelphia: H. C. Carey and I. Lea, 1824.

Johnson, Samuel. *The Works of Samuel Johnson, LL.D.* . . . 12 vols. London: J. Johnson et al., 1806.

Jones, William. *The Works of Sir William Jones.* . . . 6 vols. London: G. G. and J. Robinson, and R. H. Evans, 1799.

[Lamb, Charles]. *Elia: Essays Which Have Appeared under That Signature in the London Magazine.* 2nd ser. Philadelphia: Carey, Lea and Carey, 1828.

[Lane, Charles]. "A. Bronson Alcott's Works." *Dial* 3 (April 1843): 417-454.

[————]. "Catalogue of Books." *Dial* 3 (April 1843): 545-548.

[————]. "A Day with the Shakers." *Dial* 4 (October 1843): 165-173.

[————]. Review of *The Life and Times of Girolamo Savonarola*, by John A. Heraud. *Dial* 3 (April 1843): 536-540.

[————]. "Social Tendencies." Pts. 1 and 2. *Dial* 4 (July 1843): 65-86; (October 1843): 188-204.

[————]. "State Slavery–Imprisonment of A. Bronson Alcott–Dawn of Liberty." *Liberator*, January 27, 1843.

Lieber, Francis, ed. *Encyclopaedia Americana: A Popular Dictionary of Arts, Sciences, Literature, History, Politics and Biography, Brought Down to the Present Time; Including a Copious Collection of Original Articles in American Biography; on the Basis of the Seventh Edition of the German Conversations-Lexicon.* 13 vols. Philadelphia: Carey, Lea and Carey; Carey and Lea; Carey, Lea, and Blanchard, 1829-1833.

Locke, John. *An Essay concerning Human Understanding.* . . . 2 vols. Boston: Cummings and Hilliard and J. T. Buckingham, 1813.

Lodge, Thomas. *Glaucus and Silla, with Other Lyrical and Pastoral Poems.* Chiswick: C. Whittingham, 1819.

Lyell, Charles. *Principles of Geology: Being an Inquiry How Far the Former Changes of the Earth's Surface Are Referable to Causes Now in Operation.* 5th ed. 4 vols. London: John Murray, 1837.

[Macpherson, James]. *The Genuine Remains of Ossian, Literally Translated; with a Preliminary Dissertation.* Edited by Patrick MacGregor. London: Smith, Elder, 1841.

[Manu]. *Institutes of Hindu Law; or, The Ordinances of Menu, according to the Gloss of Cullúca, Comprising the Indian System of Duties Religious and Civil: Verbally Translated from the Original Sanscrit.* Translated by [Sir William Jones]. Calcutta, 1794.

Marot, Clément. *Œuvres complètes de Clément Marot.* 3 vols. Paris: Rapilly, 1824.

———. *Œuvres de Clément Marot.* 6 vols. The Hague: P. Gosse and J. Neaulme, 1731.

Massillon, Jean B. *Sermons by J. B. Massillon, Bishop of Clermont.* . . . Translated by William Dickson. 2 vols. Edinburgh: J. Ogle; Robert Morison and Son et al., 1797.

Milton, John. *The Poetical Works of John Milton.* . . . 6 vols. London: J. Johnson et al., 1801.

Montagu, Elizabeth. *The Letters of Mrs. Elizabeth Montagu, with Some of the Letters of Her Correspondents.* Edited by Matthew Montagu. 3 vols. Boston: Wells and Lilly, 1825.

Montégut, Émile. "Ralph Waldo Emerson: Un penseur et poète Américain." *Revue des Deux Mondes* 19 (July-August 1847): 462-493.

Montgomery, James. *The West Indies, and Other Poems.* Boston: Munroe and Francis, 1810.

Morell, J. D. *An Historical and Critical View of the Speculative Philosophy of Europe in the Nineteenth Century.* 2 vols. London: William Pickering, 1846.

Murray, Hugh, James Wilson, R. K. Greville, [Robert] Jameson, Whitelaw Ainslie, William Rhind, [William] Wallace, and Clarence Dalrymple. *Historical and Descriptive Account of British India, from the Most Remote Period to the Present Time.* . . . 3 vols. New-York: J. and J. Harper, 1832.

Ockley, Simon. *The History of the Saracens.* . . . 2nd ed. 2 vols. London: R. Knaplock et al.; Bernard Lintot, 1718.

Parker, Theodore. *A Discourse on the Transient and Permanent in Christianity; Preached at the Ordination of Mr. Charles C. Shackford, in the Hawes Place Church in Boston, May 19, 1841.* 2nd ed. Boston: Printed for the author, 1841.

[———]. "Hollis Street Council." *Dial* 3 (October 1842): 201-221.

[Peabody, Elizabeth Palmer]. "Fourierism." *Dial* 4 (April 1844): 473-483.

[———]. "A Glimpse of Christ's Idea of Society." *Dial* 2 (October 1841): 214-228.

[———]. *Method of Spiritual Culture: Being an Explanatory Preface to the Second Edition of "Record of a School."* Boston: James Munroe, 1836.

[———]. "Plan of the West Roxbury Community." *Dial* 2 (January 1842): 361-372.

[———]. *Record of a School: Exemplifying the General Principles of Spiritual Culture.* Boston: James Munroe and Company, 1835.

Pellico, Silvio. *My Prisons, Memoirs of Silvio Pellico of Saluzzo*. 2 vols. Cambridge, Mass.: Charles Folsom, 1836.

Percy, Thomas, ed. *Reliques of Ancient English Poetry: Consisting of Old Heroic Ballads, Songs, and Other Pieces of Our Earlier Poets*. . . . 3 vols. London: J. Dodsley, 1765.

Pindar. *Pindarus Werke*. Edited by Friedrich Thiersch. 2 vols. Leipzig: Gerhard Fleischer, 1820.

"A Plain Discussion with a Transcendentalist." *New Englander* 4 (October 1843): 502-516.

Plutarch. *Plutarch's Lives of the Most Select and Illustrious Characters of Antiquity*. Translated by John Langhorne, William Langhorne, and others. Compiled by William Mavor. New-York: W. C. Borradaile, 1832.

Pope, Alexander. *The Poetical Works of Alexander Pope, Esq*. 2 vols. Baltimore: Neal, Wills, and Cole, 1814.

Quarles, Francis. *Divine Poems*. . . . London: John Marriott, 1630.

———. *Emblemes*. London: G. M., 1635.

———. *Emblems, Divine and Moral*. Chiswick: C. and C. Whittingham, 1825.

Raleigh, Walter. *The Works of Sir Walter Ralegh, Kt. Now First Collected: To Which Are Prefixed the Lives of the Author, by Oldys and Birch*. 8 vols. Oxford: University Press, 1829.

[Ripley, George]. Review of *A Letter to Those Who Think*, by Edward Palmer. *Dial* 1 (October 1840): 251-256.

[Ritson, Joseph], ed. *Robin Hood: A Collection of All the Ancient Poems, Songs, and Ballads, Now Extant, Relative to That Celebrated English Outlaw*. . . . 2 vols. London: T. Egerton and J. Johnson, 1795.

Robert of Gloucester. *Robert of Gloucester's Chronicle*. . . . 2 vols. Oxford: Printed at the Theater, 1724.

Rollin, [Charles]. *The Ancient History of the Egyptians, Carthaginians, Assyrians, Babylonians, Medes and Persians, Macedonians, and Grecians*. 12th ed. 8 vols. Boston: Etheridge and Bliss; Hastings, Etheridge, and Bliss; Charles Williams, 1807-1811.

———. *The Ancient History of the Egyptians, Carthaginians, Assyrians, Babylonians, Medes and Persians, Macedonians and Grecians*. 4 vols. New-York: George Long, 1837.

Ross, James, trans. *The Gulistan, or Flower-Garden, of Shaikh Sadī of Shiraz*. . . . London: J. M. Richardson, 1823.

Shakespeare, William. *The Dramatic Works of William Shakspeare, Accurately Printed from the Text of the Corrected Copy Left by the Late George Stevens, Esq., with a Glossary, and Notes*. 2 vols. Hartford, Conn.: Andrus and Judd, 1833.

Shirley, James. *The Dramatic Works and Poems of James Shirley, Now First Collected; with Notes by the Late William Gifford, Esq.*

*and Additional Notes, and Some Account of Shirley and His Writings, by the Rev. Alexander Dyce.* 6 vols. London: John Murray, 1833.

[Smith, William Henry]. "Emerson." *Blackwood's Edinburgh Magazine* 62 (December 1847): 643-657.

Stewart, Dugald. *Elements of the Philosophy of the Human Mind.* 2 vols. Cambridge, Mass.: James Munroe and Company, 1833.

[Storer, D. Humphreys, and William B. O. Peabody]. *Reports on the Fishes, Reptiles and Birds of Massachusetts.* Boston: Dutton and Wentworth, 1839.

Storer, Thomas. *The Life and Death of Thomas Wolsey, Cardinall: Divided into Three Parts, His Aspiring, Triumph, and Death.* London, 1599; reprinted in *Heliconia: Comprising a Selection of English Poetry of the Elizabethan Age; Written or Published between 1575 and 1604.* Edited by Thomas Park. Vol. 2. London: Longman, Hurst, Rees, Orme, and Brown, 1815.

[Swift, Jonathan]. *Fraud Detected; or, The Hibernian Patriot, Containing All the Drapier's Letters to the People of Ireland. . . .* Dublin: George Faulkner, 1725.

Taylor, Jane. *The Writings of Jane Taylor.* 5 vols. Boston: Perkins and Marvin, 1832.

Tennyson, Alfred. *Poems.* 2 vols. Boston: William D. Ticknor, 1842.

[Thompson, Thomas Perronet]. *A Catechism on the Corn Laws; with a List of Fallacies and the Answers.* London: James Ridgway, 1827.

[Thoreau, Henry D.], trans. "Anacreon." *Dial* 3 (April 1843): 484-490.

[———]. "Aulus Persius Flaccus." *Dial* 1 (July 1840): 117-121.

[———], trans. "Fragments of Pindar." *Dial* 4 (April 1844): 513-514.

[———]. "Friendship." *Dial* 2 (October 1841): 204-205.

———. "Homer. Ossian. Chaucer." *Dial* 4 (January 1844): 290-305.

———. "Ktaadn, and the Maine Woods." Pts. 1-5. *Union Magazine of Literature and Art* 3 (July 1848): 29-33; (August 1848): 73-79; (September 1848): 132-137; (October 1848): 177-182; (November 1848): 216-220.

———. "The Landlord." *United States Magazine, and Democratic Review* 13 (October 1843): 427-430.

[———], ed. "The Laws of Menu." *Dial* 3 (January 1843): 331-340.

[———]. "Natural History of Massachusetts." *Dial* 3 (July 1842): 19-40.

[———]. "Paradise (To Be) Regained." *United States Magazine, and Democratic Review* 13 (November 1843): 451-463.

Thoreau, [Henry D.], trans. "Pindar." *Dial* 4 (January 1844): 379-390.

[———], trans. "The Prometheus Bound." *Dial* 3 (January 1843): 363-386.

———. "Resistance to Civil Government." *Aesthetic Papers* (1849): 189-211.

[———]. "Sic Vita." *Dial* 2 (July 1841): 81-82.

[———]. "Stanzas." *Dial* 1 (January 1841): 314.

[———]. "Sympathy." *Dial* 1 (July 1840): 71-72.

———. "Thomas Carlyle and His Works." Pts. 1 and 2. *Graham's American Monthly Magazine of Literature and Art* 30 (March 1847): 145-152; (April 1847): 238-245.

[———]. "A Walk to Wachusett." *Boston Miscellany of Literature and Fashion* 3 (January 1843): 31-36.

[———]. "A Winter Walk." *Dial* 4 (October 1843): 211-226.

Turner, Sharon. *The History of the Anglo-Saxons.* 2nd ed., corr. and enl. 2 vols. London: Longman, Hurst, Rees, and Orme, 1807.

Virgil. *P. Vergilii Maronis Opera.* . . . Philadelphia: M. Carey and Son, 1817.

[Ward, Samuel Gray]. "Notes on Art and Architecture." *Dial* 4 (July 1843): 107-115.

[Wheeler, Charles Stearns]. "Letters from Germany." *Pioneer: A Literary and Critical Magazine* 1 (March 1843): 143-144.

[———]. "Literary Intelligence." *Dial* 3 (January 1843): 388-397; (April 1843): 541-544.

Williams, Roger. "A Key into the Language of America." *Collections of the Massachusetts Historical Society*, 1st ser., vol. 3 (1794; repr. 1810): 203-239.

# Index

Abercrombie, John (1780–1844), 49; *Inquiries concerning the Intellectual Powers, and the Investigation of Truth*, 50n7

Abram, Wood (Abraham Wood), and Fruitlands, 190n4, 191

Abu al-Hasan al-Ash'ari (Abu Musa; 873–935?), 204n7

Adam, Alexander, *Adam's Latin Grammar*, 48, 49n1, 49n2

Adams, Abby Larkin (1798–1883), 323

Adams, Abel (1792–1867), 323
—*Letter to,* 322–323

Adams, Augustus, 304n2

Adams Express, 304, 305

Admetus, 80, 81n6, 118, 120

Aeschylus (525–456 BCE), 141; *The Prometheus Bound*, 142n4, 216, 272, 273n1; *The Seven against Thebes*, 142n4, 216–217, 222

·Agassiz, Jean Louis Rodolphe (1807–1873), 291n2, 316, 351; *Études sur les glaciers*, 291n2; *Histoire naturelle des poissons d'eau douce de l'Europe centrale*, 291n2; letter to Cabot, James Elliot, quoted, 291n1; Thoreau sends specimens to, 290–291, 292–294, 299–300, 302–304

Alcott, Abigail May (1800–1877), 74n1, 187, 190n4; quoted, 190n5

Alcott, Amos Bronson (1799–1888), 74, 90, 91n4, 124, 175, 189n2, 191, 216, 270, 277, 329; and Boston Anti-Sabbath Convention, 353; on Carlyle, 346, 348n9; and Channing, Ellery, 340, 346; on "Civil Disobedience," 348n12; and Concord Lyceum, 124–125, 127n16, 127n17; debts of, 74n1; and the *Dial*, 141, 142n2, 143, 149; and Emerson, 74; —, builds summer house for, 314–315, 318n6, 378, 381n2; and England, 1842 trip to, 109, 110n7; and Fruitlands, 126n10, 165, 187–189, 191–192; and gardening, 188, 335n6, 348n8; goes to jail, 124–125, 127n14, 128n20, 348n12; and Lane, Charles, 126n10, 128n20, 141, 142n2, 187, 188, 189, 356n7, 381n6; —, "A. Bronson Alcott's Works," 141, 142n2, 143, 144n1; —, "State Slavery–Imprisonment of A. Bronson Alcott–Dawn of Liberty," 125, 128n20; on Montaigne, 348n6; and nature, 145–146; reading of, 333, 335n6, 346; Thoreau on, 314–315, 333, 339–340, 346; on Thoreau's lecture "An Excursion to Ktaadn," 334n1; on Thoreau's lecture on the rights of the individual to self-government, 348n12; and Wright, Henry Gardiner, 127n13
—*Works: Conversations with Children on the Gospels*, 141, 142n2; *The Doctrine and Discipline of Human Culture*, 83, 86n8, 90, 99, 100n10; journals of, quoted, 318n6, 334n1, 335n2, 348n6, 348n9, 348n12, 381n6

Alcott, William Andrus (1798–1859), 39n10

Alcott House, England, 355, 356n7

Allen, Amanda Cole (1823–1904), 25n6

Allen, Anna Minot Weld (1820–1907), 6n17

Allen, Clarissa Fiske (1801–1887), 18n5

Allen, Joseph Henry (1820–1898), 3, 6n17

Allen, Phineas (1801–1885), 16, 308; Thoreau on, 18n5

Allen, William (1815–1895), 23, 25n6

Alpheus (Alpheo), 201, 203n1

*American Agriculturalist*, 233, 234n2

American Institute of the City of New York, 244, 245, 247n1

Anacreon (572?–488? BCE), 142n3

Anti-Corn Law League, 342–343

Anti-Sabbath Convention (Boston), 353

Apollo, 80, 81n6, 120

Aristotle (384–322 BCE), 143, 144n2

Astor House, 239, 241n4

Bacon, Francis (1561–1626): "Of Boldnesse," quoted, 152n1; *Of the Proficience and Advancement of Learning*, 247n5; —, Thoreau on, 245

Bacon, John (1817–1881), 3, 6n13

Ball, Benjamin West (1823–1896), 164, 165n3; Emerson on, 165n3

Ball, Dora S. Hurd (1827–1902), 165n3

Ball, Nehemiah, 18n3, 33n2

Bancroft, George (1800–1891), 354, 355n3

"Barbara Allen's Cruelty" (ballad), 311, 312n9

Barbour, John (1316?–1395), *The Bruce; or, The History of Robert I. King of Scotland*, 110

Barclay, Rev. John (1734–1798), 132n7

Barnsdale Forest, England, 202, 204n8

Barnum, Phineas Taylor (1810–1891), 238, 240n3

Barrett, Mary Fuller (1805–1853), 120, 123n6

Barrett, Sherman, 380n1

Barrett, Samuel (1812–1872), 321n23

Barrett, Susan Hudson (1783–1855), 120, 123n6

Bartlett, Josiah (1797–1878), 73, 315, 345

Bartlett, Martha Tilden Bradford (1799–1860), 73n2

Bartlett, Robert (1817–1843), 74, 139, 140n4, 141, 152

Beach, Wooster (1794–1868), 188, 190n6; *The American Practice of Medicine*, 190n6

Beaumont, Francis (1584–1616), 346; *The Elder Brother*, quoted, 3, 5n12

Beck, Charles (1798–1866), 17, 19n8

Bellenden, John (fl. 1533–1587), "Allegorie of Vertue and Delyte," quoted, 104, 105–106

Bellows, Henry Whitney (1814–1882), 224, 226n3

Bellows, John Nelson (1805–1857), 46, 47n1

Bellows, Mary Nichols (1810–1887), 47n1

Bemis, Charles Vose (1816–1906), 22, 24n3

Bemis, Elizabeth Fanny Henry (1821–1888), 24n3

Bemis, George (1816–1878), 22, 24n3

Bemis, George F. (1809–1890), 24n5

Berean Institute, Emerson lectures at, 130, 132n7

biblical quotations and allusions: Acts 9:43, 315, 319n8; Acts 26:28, 124, 126n6; 1 Cor. 2:9, 31, 33n5; Eccles. 12:4, 97, 100n2; Gal. 6:9, 14, 15n11; Gen. 3:19, 368, 371n1, 375; Gen. 8:9, 82, 85n1; Gen. 25:29–34, 109; Isaiah 1:18, 370, 371n3; Isaiah 2:4, 124, 128n18; Jer. 13:23, 317, 320n20; John 6:35, 369, 371n2; 1 John 3:17, 51, 52n2; Luke 16:13, 280, 281n2; Mark 5:9, 308, 309n1; Mark 6:8–9, 259, 260n1; Mark 10:38, 361, 363n3; Matt. 2:9, 82, 85n2, 222, 223n9; Matt. 6:24, 280, 281n2; Matt. 6:26, 109, 110n5; Matt.

7:14, 225, 226n7; Matt. 7:19, 314, 319n7; Matt. 16:18, 278, 279n1; Matt. 23:13, 264, 265n2; Matt. 24:2, 246, 249n16; Phil. 2:13, 314, 318n5; Phil. 3:13–14, 286, 287n2; Ps. 137:2, 48, 50n3; Rev. 1:10–11, 116, 117n1; Rev. 22:5, 98, 100n4; 2 Tim. 2:4, 327, 329n1

Bigelow, Amelia Sargent Stanwood (1806–1893), 47

Bigelow, Andrew (1795–1877), 46–47
—Letter to, 46

Bigelow, Henry Heartwell (1822–1854), 239, 241n6

Bigelow, Henry Jacob (1818–1890), 3, 5n8

Bigelow, Jacob (1786–1879), 36n2; Elements of Technology, 35–36, 36n2; Florula Bostoniensis: A Collection of Plants of Boston and Its Vicinity, 273, 274n2

Bigelow, Mary Ann Seaver (b. 1824?), 241n6

Bigelow, Susan Sturgis (1825–1853), 5n8

Billings, Caleb Callender (1788–1833), 45n5

Billings, Nancy Thoreau (1789–1815), 45n5

bird eggs, 284, 287–288

Black, John (d. 1847), 169n5

Black, Rebecca Gray (1805–1853?), 167, 169n5, 181, 269, 271n5

black snake, 302

Blackstone, William (1723–1780), Commentaries on the Laws of England, 99, 100n9

black sucker, 293, 303, 304

Blake, Harrison Gray Otis (1816–1898), 358, 380; on ethical living, 357–358
—Letter from, 357–358
—Letters to, 359–362, 368–371

Blake, Nancy Pope Howe Conant (1828–1872), 358

Blake, Sarah Chandler Ward (1817–1846), 358

Blood, Perez (1785–1856), telescope of, 310, 312n7, 315

Bolton, Mass., 117, 118n2

Boston Almanac, 379, 381n9

Boston and Fitchburg railroad, 156, 157n4, 191, 218, 231n9, 322–323; fires caused by, 317, 321n22; —, on Emerson's property, 381n5; and Irish laborers, 173n7, 228, 236

Boston Miscellany of Literature and Fashion, 148n5; and "A Walk to Wachusett," 207, 222

Boston Quarterly Review, 32, 33; Brownson, Orestes Augustus, on, 33n8

Bowen, Francis (1811–1890), 2–3, 4n6

Bradbury, Waymond (1811–1875), 148n5, 182

Bradbury and Soden, 223n8; fails to pay Thoreau for "A Walk to Wachusett," 147, 148n5, 182, 193, 198, 207, 208n2, 222

Bradford, George Partridge (1807–1890), 74, 229, 260; Thoughts on Spiritual Subjects, Translated from the Writings of Fenelon, 143, 145n6

Bradshaw, George (1801–1853), 326n4

Bradshaw's Monthly Railway Guide, 324, 326n4

bream, 290, 293, 302, 303

Briggs, George Nixon (1796–1861), 318, 321n24

Brigham, Charles Henry (1820–1879), 37–38, 39n8

Bright, John (1811–1889), 342, 343n4

Brisbane, Albert (1809–1890): Emerson on, 129–130, 131n2; and Fourierism, 131n2, 180, 190n7; "Means of Effecting a Final Reconciliation between Religion and Science," 131n2; Thoreau on, 180

Britton, Abraham (1787–1866), 212n1

Britton, Joel (1801–1858), 229, 231n10, 246, 249n15, 347

Britton, John, 185

Broadway (Manhattan), 161

Brook Farm, 208, 260

Brookfield, Mass., 9–10, 11n4

Brooklyn, N.Y., 161, 269

Brooks, Mary Merrick (1801–1868), 47n3

Brooks, Nathan (1785–1863), 46, 47n3, 53n1, 317, 321n22

*Brother Jonathan: A Weekly Compend of Belles Lettres and the Fine Arts, Standard Literature, and General Intelligence*, 233–234, 235n4

Brown, Charles, 77

Brown, Lucy Jackson (1798–1868), 77, 167, 202, 207, 239–240, 243, 277, 313; and daughter Sophia's death, 119, 121n2, 122n3; and Emerson, Lidian, illness of, 345; house of, 229, 231n10, 276; marriage of, 77
   —*Letters to*, 76–77, 79–80, 87, 101–103, 119–120, 121n2

Brown, Reuben (1781–1854), 208, 318, 378

Brown, Sophia (1821?–1842), death of, 119, 121n2, 122n3

Brown, Thomas (1778–1820), 49; *Lectures on the Philosophy of the Human Mind*, 50n5

Brown, Thomas, Jr., trial of, 230n7

Browne, Elizabeth Wheeler Goodwin (1835–1900), 348n5

Browne [Brown], Francis Charles (1829–1900), 345, 348n5

Browne, Thomas (1605–1682), 346

Brownson, Orestes Augustus (1803–1876), 32–33, 256, 260; and *Boston Quarterly Review*, 33n8; "Demogogism," 256n1; "Government," 116
   —*Letter from*, 116
   —*Letter to*, 30–32

Brownson, Henry Francis (1835–1913), 33n9

Brownson, John Healy (1829–1857), 33n9

Brownson, Orestes A., Jr. (1828–1892), 33n9

Brownson, William Ignatius (1834–1864), 33n9

Brownson, Sally Healey (1804–1872), 32

Bryant, William Cullen (1794–1878), 164n1

Bulwer-Lytton, Edward George (1803–1873), 58, 60, 61n4

Burgh, James (1714–1775), *The Dignity of Human Nature*, 218, 219n1

Burr, Charles Chauncey (1815?–1883), 373n3

Byron, George Gordon, Lord (1788–1824), 3; *Childe Harold's Pilgrimage*, 93; —, quoted, 95n3, 98, 100n5; *Don Juan*, quoted, 107–108

Cabot, Elizabeth Dwight (1830–1901), 291

Cabot, James Elliot (1821–1903), 291, 352n5
   —*Letters from*, 290–291, 299–300, 303–304
   —*Letters to*, 292–294, 302–303, 350–351

Campbell, Thomas (1777–1844), "The Exile of Erin," 135n3

Cape Finisterre, Spain, 262, 263n4

Carlyle, Thomas (1795–1881), 347; Alcott on, 346, 348n9; *Critical and Miscellaneous Essays*, 52; "Dr. Francia," 225; and Emerson, 203, 205n16, 325, 326n5; Emerson on, 221, 223n3, 384, 385n4; Hecker, Isaac Thomas, on, 297; on Ireland, Alexander, 351n1; James, Henry, Sr., on, 180; *On Heroes, Hero-Worship, and the Heroic in History*, 83, 86n6; *Past and Present*, 180, 182n2, 203, 205n16; *Sartor Resartus*, 182n2, 270, 271n11; Thoreau's essay on, 279–280, 281, 283, 285–286

*Carminum poetarum novem,* 142n3

Carové, Friedrich Wilhelm (1789–1852), 78n1; *Story without an End,* 78

Carter, Robert (1819–1879), 150n5

Castleton (Staten Island), 171

Catholic Church. *See* Roman Catholic Church

Cecil, William (1520–1598), *Certaine Preceptes, or Directions, for the Well Ordering and Carriage of a Mans Life,* 166, 168n2

Chalkhill, John (fl. 1600), *Thealma and Clearchus: A Pastoral Romance,* 110

Channing, Ellen Fuller (1820–1856), 154, 228, 230n5

Channing, Ellery (1817–1901), 154–155, 228, 237, 252, 262, 273n1, 329, 333, 336n10, 381n6; and Alcott, 340, 346; on Concord, 268, 269; and the *Dial,* 192, 193n5, 203, 229, 232n13, 244–245, 247n2, 248n9; and Emerson, 164, 192, 193n3, 207, 269; Emerson on, 164, 207, 252, 253n2; on Greeley, Horace, 269–270; in Manhattan, 270n2; poetry of, 155, 175; —, reviewed by Emerson, 229–230, 232n16; and Red Lodge (Concord), 153–154, 155n1, 201; on Staten Island, 268; on Tappan, William, 271n8; on Thoreau, 229, 231n12, 268; Thoreau on, 175, 201, 244–245, 346; travels to Catskills with Thoreau, 261, 263n2
—*Works:* "Autumn," 245, 248n9; *Poems,* 176n4; *Thoreau: The Poet-Naturalist,* 348n10; "Walden Hermitage," 346, 348n10; "The Youth of the Poet and the Painter," 192, 203, 205n13, 229, 244–245
—*Letters from,* 153–154, 157, 268–270

Channing, Julia Allen (1813–1889), 131n3

Channing, William Ellery, the Younger. *See* Channing, Ellery (1817–1901)

Channing, William Henry (1810–1884), 129, 131n3, 221; Channing, Ellery, on, 269, 271n6; "Confession of Faith," 242, 244n2, 251n2; and Fourier, 129, 131n3, 190n7; and North American Phalanx, 188, 190n7; *The Present,* as editor of, 211, 213n3, 242, 244n2, 251n2; Thoreau on, 180, 210–211, 242, 250

Chapin, Edwin Hubbell (1814–1880), and Concord Lyceum, 149, 150n8

Chapman, John (1821–1894), 325, 326n7, 381n6

Chaptal [Chaptelle], Jean-Antoine-Claude, comte de Chanteloup (1756–1832), 218; *Chemistry Applied to Arts and Manufactures,* 220n2

Chateaubriand, François-René, vicomte de (1768–1848), *Voyages en Amérique et en Italie,* 10, 11n6

Chaucer, Geoffrey (1340?–1400): "Clerkes Tale," quoted, 166, 168n1; "Romaunt of the Rose," quoted, 222

Cheney, John Milton (1797–1869), 328, 329n6

Cheney, Louisa P. Hosmer (1809–1885), 329n6

Chever, George Francis (1819–1871), 386, 387n2

Child, David (1794–1874), 220n6

Child, Lydia Maria Francis (1802–1880), 219, 220n6

Choate, Rufus (1799–1859), 230n7

*Christian Examiner and General Review,* 218, 219n1

cicada (*Cicada septendecim*), 198, 200n2

*Cincinnati Gazette,* 154

Claiborne, William Charles Coles (1775–1817), 162n9

Clark, James (1815–1851), 333, 335n8

Clarke, Frances Lemist (b. 1817), 21n3

Clarke, Manlius Stimson (1816–1853), 20, 21n3, 55, 57

Cleveland, Charles Dexter, *First Lessons in Latin*, 48, 49n1

Clough, Arthur Hugh (1819–1861), 355, 356n4

Cobden, Richard (1804–1865), 341–342, 343n1, 343n3

Colossus of Rhodes, 379, 381n7

Colum Cille (Saint Columba; 521–597), 167, 168n3

Conantum, 317

Concord, 380; the Cliffs, 189, 242, 297; Channing, Ellery, on, 192, 268, 269; First Parish of, 69n2; —, Thoreau withdraws from, 72; Irish in, 171, 173n7, 191, 228–229, 236, 246; Middlesex cattle show of, 240, 241n10; music in, 68–69; Rice, Charles Wyatt, on, 10; Thoreau on, 79, 152, 161, 167, 170, 201–202, 218, 224–225; Williams, Isaiah Thornton, on, 97; *Yeoman's Gazette*, 23, 24n5

Concord Academy, 16, 17, 29, 73; Thoreau on, 18n5, 308

Concord Lyceum: and Alcott, Amos Bronson, 124–125, 127n16, 127n17; and Brownson, Orestes Augustus, 116, 256; and Chapin, Edwin Hubbell, 149, 150n8; and Dawes, Thomas, 55n1, 57; and Emerson, 63, 64n1, 249n14, 256; and Greenough, William Whitwell, 55, 56n3; and Haskins, David Greene, 65; and Hudson, Henry Norman, 332, 335n4; and Lane, Charles, 125; and Parker, Theodore, 125, 128n23, 135, 332, 335n2; and Spear, Charles M., 124–125, 127n17; and Thoreau, 51, 52n1, 55, 57, 63–64, 65, 125, 135, 136n5,

253, 254n9, 255n2, 256, 332, 334n1, 339, 347, 348n12, 350; and Wheeler, Charles Stearns, 51, 52n1, 55, 57, 63–64, 65; and Whipple, Edwin Percy, 332, 335n3

Concord River, 68, 69n5, 201, 204n5

Concord Steam Mill Company, 377–378, 380n1

Concord Women's Anti-Slavery Society, 26, 38n5, 267n1, 275n1

Concord woods, 308

Coney Island, 161

Congregation of St. Paul (Paulists), 260

Congregation of the Most Holy Redeemer (Redemptorists), 260, 298, 299n2

Considérant, Victor Prosper (1809–1893), 254n7

Coombs, Eseck (1818–1848), 318, 321n25, 347

Corn Laws. *See* Anti-Corn Law League

Crocker, Alvah (1801–1874), 157n4

Crocker families, 40

Croly, George (1780–1860), *Catiline: A Dramatic Poem*, quoted, 98, 100n8

Crosby and Nichols, 316

Croton Reservoir, 171, 172n4, 233

Cushing, Caleb (1800–1879), 318, 321n24

Cutler, Isaac (1800–1877), 276

Cutler, Lydia Braman (1805–1890), 276n2

dace, 294, 302, 303, 304

Dall, Caroline Healey (1822–1912), 21n3

Dall, Charles Henry Appleton (1816–1886), 20, 21n3, 57

Dana, Richard Henry (1815–1882), 20, 21n3, 55

Dana, Sarah Watson (1814–1907), 21n3

Davenport, Mr., 210

Davis, Betsey Gardner Waters (1784–1847), 41n5

Davis, Helen Russell (1825–1900), 157n2

Davis, Josiah (1773–1847), 40, 41n5

Davis, William (1818–1853), 156, 157n2

Davy, Humphry (1778–1829), 4n4

Dawes, Lydia Ames Sawin (1823–1892), 57n1

Dawes, Thomas (1818–1904), 55n1, 57

Dean, James, 282

*Democratic Review. See United States Magazine, and Democratic Review*

*Démocratie Pacifique, La*, 252, 254n7

Demosthenes (385?–322 BCE), 152

Dennett, William H., 150n2

Dennis, Cynthia Barrett (1791–1857), 23n1

Dennis, Hiram Barrett (1816–1846), 22, 24n3

Dennis, Samuel (1784–1864), 23n1, 310, 311n4

*Deutsche Schnellpost* (Manhattan), 252, 254n7

*Diadem*, 347n4

*Dial*, 141; and Alcott, Amos Bronson, 141, 142n2, 143, 149; and Brisbane, Albert, 131n2; and Channing, Ellery, 192, 193n5, 203, 229, 244–245, 248n9; editorial discussions, between Emerson and Thoreau, 138–139, 140–141, 143–144, 149, 192, 193, 202–203, 244–246; and Emerson, Charles Chauncy, 203, 205n12; Emerson's contributions to, 203, 205n16, 237, 245–246, 248n8, 248n11, 249n14; ethnical scriptures section of, 139n1, 245, 247n7; and Fuller, Sarah Margaret, 70–71, 81n8, 93–94, 95n1, 194n7, 203, 205n14, 237; and Greaves, James Pier-

repont, 141, 142n2; and Hooper, Ellen Sturgis, 245; and Hunt, Benjamin Peter, 192, 194n7, 203, 229, 232n14; and Lane, Charles, 138, 140–141, 142n2, 143–144, 145n6, 149, 150n6, 192, 194n7, 229, 232n15, 245, 247n3, 325, 331; and the *Massachusetts Quarterly Review*, as successor to, 330n8; and Newcomb, Charles King, 209n6; and Parker, Theodore, 128n23, 330n8; and Peabody, Elizabeth Palmer, 141, 142n2, 146–147, 149, 150n7, 194n8; publishers of, 192, 194n8, 206, 331; reputation of, 252–253, 325; Thoreau's contributions to, 71n1, 78n1, 79, 81n2, 91, 92n1, 93–94, 95n1, 110n6, 141, 164, 165n1, 174, 182, 193, 203, 209n7, 229, 234, 245, 247n6, 252, 253n6, 254n9, 272; and Ward, Samuel Gray, 192, 194n6; and Wheeler, Charles Stearns, 140n4, 149, 150n5; and Williams, Isaiah Thornton, 99

Diogenes (412?–323 BCE), 363n4

Disosway, Diana Tabb Riddick (1810–1883), 186n5

Disosway, Gabriel Poillon (1799–1868), 185, 186n5

Douglas, Gawain (1474?–1522), "Description of Wynter," 229, 231n12

Drake, Samuel Gardner (1798–1875), 11n3; Antiquarian Bookstore of, 9, 11n3; *Indian Biography*, 11n3

Dunbar, Charles Jones (1780–1856), 72, 226n5; narcolepsy of, 200n5, 225; Thoreau on, 225

Dunbar, Louisa (1785–1866), 173n9, 199, 218

Duyckinck, Evert Augustus (1816–1878), 301, 305n1, 306n1
  —*Letters to,* 300–301, 304, 305, 305–306

Duyckinck, Margaret Wolfe Panton (1820?–1890), 301

Dyer, Benjamin Wilkins (1808–1877), 189n2

education: Alcott House, 355, 356n7; Thoreau on, 48–49; Williams, Isaiah Thornton, on, 84, 98–99. *See also* Thoreau: teaching
eel, 294, 302
Eichthal, Wilhelm von, 254n7
Emerson, Charles Chauncy (1808–1836), 159; "Notes from the Journal of a Scholar," 203, 205n12
Emerson, Edith (1841–1929), 126n2, 133n12, 207; Thoreau on, 123, 134–135, 168, 222, 243, 313–314, 324, 332, 346, 353, 380; Thoreau's poem to, 324, 325n2
Emerson, Edward Waldo (1844–1930), 318n2, 335n5, 339, 345, 353, 377; Thoreau on, 313–314, 332–333, 345–346
Emerson, Ellen Tucker (1839–1909), 126n4, 207; on colors of words, 339; Emerson on, 324; Thoreau on, 123–124, 168, 243, 313, 332, 346, 353, 380
Emerson, John Haven (1840–1913), 168, 169n7
Emerson, Lydia (Lidian) Jackson (1802–1892), 121n2, 135, 168, 182, 222, 253, 277, 315, 336n10, 353, 371; and Emerson, Ralph Waldo, 18n3, 53, 130, 131; health of, 196–197, 203, 205n19, 207, 234, 235n9, 345; *Letters of Lidian Jackson Emerson*, quoted, 78n1, 126n6, 168; and nature, 145–146; postscripts from, to Ralph Waldo Emerson, 145–146, 330; and Thoreau, 124, 126n6, 145–146, 313, 333; Thoreau's declarations of friendship for, 125, 166–167, 195–197, 202

—*Letters to,* 166–168, 195–197, 201–203, 242–243
Emerson, Ralph Waldo (1803–1882), 16, 18n3, 38, 53, 90, 116–117, 128n22, 153n3, 156, 163, 286, 312n7, 322, 331, 347n4, 371, 389; on Americans, 355; and Carlyle, 205n16, 325, 326n5; —, edition of *Past and Present*, 182n2, 203, 205n16; on Carlyle, 203, 205n16, 221, 223n3, 385n4; and Channing, Ellery, 154, 155, 192, 193n3, 269, 271n9; on Channing, Ellery, 164, 175, 207, 252, 253n2; and Clough, Arthur Hugh, 356n4; and Concord Lyceum, 63, 64n1; and death of Waldo, 113; and the *Dial* (*see under Dial*); on England, 324–325, 341–343, 354–355; and Fourierism, 129–130, 131n2, 132n4; on friendship, 204n10; on Fruitlands, 191–192; —, sale of property of, 349n16; and Fuller, Sarah Margaret, 53n1, 54n6, 94; Greeley solicits essay on, 286; on Hawthorne, 192, 193n4; and lecturing, 130, 131, 132n7, 317, 320n17, 328–329, 344–345, 351n1, 352n2; *Letters of RWE*, quoted, 78n1, 126n7, 131n1, 131n2, 133n10, 153n3, 163n1, 194n7, 205n14, 205n19, 208n1, 235n9, 301n1, 306n1, 307n2, 318n6, 320n17, 329n7, 336n10, 340n1, 349n16, 381n15, 381n6, 381n7, 382n11, 385n4; and the *Massachusetts Quarterly Review*, 330n8; and Nichol, John Pringle, 335n8; postscripts to, from Lidian Emerson, 145–146, 330; on the Scots, 352n2; summer house of, built by Alcott and Thoreau, 314–315, 318n6, 378, 381n2; and Thoreau, as editor of, 229, 231n11, 234, 245, 247n6; on Thoreau, 163n1, 341, 382n11; and Thoreau's *A Week on the Concord and Merrimack*

*Rivers*, 301n1, 306, 307n2, 325, 366; travels to Europe (1847–1848), 310, 311n3, 350, 351n1, 352n3, 354–355, 356n4, 384, 385n2; and Walden, Thoreau's house at, 320n19, 327–328, 378

—*Essays:* "The Comic," 246, 249n14; *English Traits*, 355n2, 385n4; *Essays*, 83, 85n4; *Essays, Lectures and Orations* (pirated edition), 347, 349n14; "A Letter," 245, 248n8; *The Method of Nature: An Oration*, 90, 91n3, 99; "Mr. Channing's Poems," 229–230, 232n16; *Nature*, 83, 85n3; review of Carlyle, 223n3

—*Journal:* 39n11, 165n3, 169n4, 204n10, 209n6, 230n7, 253n2, 312n7, 352n2, 355n2, 356n5, 356n6, 385n4

—*Lectures: An Address Delivered in the Court-House in Concord, Massachusetts, on 1st August, 1844, on the Anniversary of the Emancipation of the Negroes in the British West Indies*, 267, 275; "Comedy," 246, 249n14; "Divinity School Address," 83, 86n7; "Domestic Life," 133n11; "Genius of the Anglo-Saxon Race," 133n9; "John Milton," quoted, 193n2; "Manners and Customs of New England," 133n9; "Natural Aristocracy," 352n2; "The Origins of New England Character," 132n7; "Politics," 133n11; "The Present Age," 63, 64n1; "Recent Literature and Spiritual Influences," 133n9; "Results and Tendencies," 133n9; "The Times," 106n2; "Trade," 132n7, 133n9

—*Poem:* "Ode to Beauty," 237, 245–246, 248n11

—*Letters from*, 52–53, 74, 75, 129–131, 138–139, 164–165, 191–193, 207–208, 228–230, 252–253, 256, 276, 277, 282, 324–325, 341–343, 354–355

—*Letters to*, 78, 104–106, 123–125, 134–135, 136–138, 140–141, 143–144, 149, 174–175, 179–182, 201–203, 221–222, 233–234, 244–246, 313–318, 327–329, 331–334, 337–340, 344–347, 353, 377–380

Emerson, Ruth Haskins (1768–1853), 168, 169n8

Emerson, Susan Haven (1807–1868), 132n8, 162n1, 184; illness of, 243, 244n4, 251

Emerson, Waldo (1836–1842), 103n3, 107, 345; death of, Isaiah Thornton Williams on, 113; death of, Thoreau on, 102, 107

Emerson, William (1769–1811), 169n8

Emerson, William (1801–1868), 132n8, 164, 184, 186n5, 200n7, 216n2, 218, 224, 229, 268, 271n4; and Emerson's lecturing, 130; hires Thoreau as tutor, 150n9, 152, 153n3, 258

Emerson, William (1835–1864), 132n8, 150n9, 152, 153n3, 181–182, 198, 244

*Encyclopaedia Americana*, 35, 36n1

Errington, Georgiana (1822?–1881), 171, 173n6, 185

Errington, Harriet N. (1815?–1896), 171, 173n6, 185

ethical living, 88–89, 108–109, 121n2, 196, 359–362, 368–371; Blake, Harrison Gray Otis, on, 357; and change, 360; and conscience, 89; and free will, 108; and freedom, 31; and grief, 108, 121n2; and habit, 359; and labor, 109, 368–369; and simplicity, 360; and sincerity, 152; and sorrow, 370–371; Williams, Isaiah Thornton, on, 111–112, 114

Ethnical Scriptures (in the *Dial*), 139n1, 245, 247n7

Etzler, J. A. (John Adolphus; 1791–1846?), 138, 141; *The New World; or, Mechanical System*, 240, 241n9; *The Paradise within the Reach of All Men*, 126n9, 214, 216, 240; —, reviewed by Thoreau, 138, 139n2, 215n2, 222, 240, 241n9

Evarts, Helen Minerva Wardner (1820–1903), 230n6

Evarts, William Maxwell (1818–1901), 228, 230n6

Everett, Abram (1803–1845), 190n4, 191

Fair Haven Hill, 75, 246

false elm (*Celtis occidentalis*), 273, 274n5

Farrar, Mr., 45

Fisher, Alfred, 380n1

Fitchburg Railroad Company. *See* Boston and Fitchburg railroad

Fletcher, John (1579–1625), 346; *The Elder Brother*, quoted, 3, 5n12

Follen, Charles (1796–1840), 55, 56n4

Follen, Eliza Lee Cabot (1787–1860), 56n4

Foord, Sophia (1802–1885), 320n15; proposes marriage to Thoreau, 316

Forbes, Elizabeth Anastasia Carroll (1813–1902), 240n1

Forbes, Philip Jones (1807–1877), 238, 240n1

Fourier, François Marie Charles (1772–1837), 131n2, 180; quoted, 132n4

Fourierism, 129–130, 180, 190n7, 378; and Emerson, 129–130, 131n2, 132n4; and James, Henry, Sr., 133n10. *See also* North American Phalanx; Sylvania Association

Fox, George (1624–1691), 109

freedom, Thoreau on, 31

Free Soil party, 385n5; Thoreau on, 385

friendship: and communication, 66–67, 137; and confidence, 137; Emerson on, 204n10; and enmity, 202, 204n10; Thoreau on, 79, 87, 204n10; Thoreau's planned lecture on, 339, 340n7, 347

friendships, Thoreau's: with Brown, Lucy Jackson, 76–77, 120, 167; with Emerson, Lidian, 121n2, 125, 166–167, 195–197, 202

Frost, Barzillai (1804–1858), 16, 18n4, 51, 315

Frost, Elmira Stone (1810–1891), 18n4

Fruitlands, 189, 191–192; and Alcott, Amos Bronson, 126n10, 165, 187–189; beginnings of, 126n10, 165; Channing, Ellery, on, 269; daily life at, 187–188; Emerson on, 191–192; and Hecker, Isaac Thomas, 260, 298; and Lane, Charles, 126n10, 165, 176n6, 187–189, 190n4, 191–192, 279n2, 327, 329n3, 347, 349n16; and Lane, William, 190n5, 191; and Larned, Samuel, 190n4, 191; and May, Samuel, 126n10, 165n4; sale of property of, to Joseph Palmer, 329n3, 347, 349n16

Fuller, Emily Delaplaine (1825–1883), 226n10

Fuller, Hiram (1814–1880), 225, 226n10, 239

Fuller, Margarett Crane (1789–1859), 252, 253n1

Fuller, Richard Frederick (1824–1869), 118, 120
—*Letters to*, 117–118, 151–152

Fuller, Sarah K. Batchelder (1829–1856), 118

Fuller, Sarah Margaret (1810–1850), 52, 53n1, 54n6, 70, 96n8, 193, 233, 234n1; critiques Thoreau's "With frontier strength

ye stand your ground," 81n8, 93–94, 95n1, 96n5; and the *Dial*, 70–71, 81n8, 93–94, 95n1, 194n7, 203, 205n14; "The Great Lawsuit. Man *versus* Men. Woman *versus* Women," 203, 205n14; *Letters of Margaret Fuller*, quoted, 194n7, 194n10, 241n5, 344n6; and Thoreau, 93–94, 236, 237; rejects Thoreau's "The Service," 70, 71n1
—*Letters from*, 70, 93–95, 236–237
Furness, William Henry (1802–1896), 306n1

Gallup, William (1805–1883), 53, 54n6
Galpin, William, 355, 356n8
Gillespie, William (1776–1825), "The Highlander," 248n13; quoted, 246
Giraud, Jacob P., Jr. (1811–1870), *The Birds of Long Island*, quoted, 200n6
Gloucester Lyceum, 392n1
*Gloucester News*, 392n1
*Gloucester Telegraph*, 392n1
Godwin, Parke (1816–1904), 163n1, 189n1
Goethe, Johann Wolfgang von (1749–1832), *The Auto-Biography of Goethe*, 371; —, quoted, 371n4
Goodwin, Amelia Mackay (1806?–1846), 53, 54n4, 54n6
Goodwin, Hersey Bradford (1805–1836), 54n4
Goose Pond, 347
Gourgas, Abigail P. Hastings (1817–1896), 54n5
Gourgas, Francis Richard (1811–1853), 53, 54n5, 54n6
Gove, Mary (1810–1884), 127n13
Graham, George Rex (1813–1894), 280n1, 281, 285–286, 364, 365, 366, 372–373
Graham, William H., 372, 373n1

*Graham's Magazine*, 389; Thoreau's "Thomas Carlyle and His Works" in, 280n1, 281, 283, 285–286, 364n2, 365, 372–373
Gray, Rebecca Ashton (b. 1781), 181, 182n4
*Great Western* (ship), 171, 172n4
Greaves, James Pierrepont (1777–1842), 127n13, 189; and Alcott House, 356n7; and books given to Charles Lane, 141n1; *Spiritual Culture; or, Thoughts for the Consideration of Parents and Teachers*, 141, 142n2
*The Greek Pastoral Poets: Theocritus, Bion, and Moschus*, 255
Greeley, Horace (1811–1872), 221, 269–270, 280, 380; on Emerson, 389; "A Lesson for Young Poets," 383; letter to Burr, Charles Chauncey, quoted, 373n3; on magazine writing, 280, 388, 389–390; and *New-York Daily Tribune*, 211, 213n4, 280, 283n1; and North American Phalanx, 190n7, 211; political activity of, 283, 365, 366n1, 390; solicits essays from Thoreau, 286, 373, 382–383; and Sylvania Association, 211, 213n5; on Thoreau, 280n1; Thoreau on, 211; Thoreau's gratitude to, 375–376; and Thoreau's "Ktaadn, and the Maine Woods," 365–366, 373, 376, 380, 382, 387–388; and Thoreau's "Thomas Carlyle and His Works," 279–280, 281, 283, 285–286; —, payment for, 286, 364, 365, 366n2, 372–373, 374–376; and Thoreau's *A Week on the Concord and Merrimack Rivers*, 366
—*Letters from*, 279–280, 281, 283, 285–286, 364, 365–366, 372–373, 382–383, 387–388, 389–390

Greeley, Horace (*cont.*)
—*Letter to,* 374–376
Greeley, Mary Young Cheney (1811–1872), 280
Greene, Nathaniel, *Tales and Sketches: Translated from Italian, French and German,* 146n2
Greene, William Batchelder (1819–1878), 145, 146n2
Greenough, Catherine Scolay Curtis (1820–1899), 56n3
Greenough, William Whitwell (1818–1899), 55; "The Life and Writings of Sir Philip Sidney," 56n3
grief: Thoreau on, 105, 107–108, 119–120, 121n2, 196–197; Thoreau's at John Thoreau's death, 101–102; Thoreau's at Waldo Emerson's death, 102
Griswold, Rufus Wilmot (1815–1857), 92; as editor of Thoreau, 92n1; *The Poets and Poetry of America,* 92; and Thoreau's "Thomas Carlyle and His Works," 280n1, 281, 283
—*Letter to,* 91–92
Grymes, Cayetana Susana Bosque y Fangui (1796–1881), 161, 162n9
Grymes, John Randolph (1786–1854), 162n9
Guillaume, de Lorris (fl. 1230), *Le Roman de la Rose,* 252, 253n5

Hale, Horatio Emmons (1817–1896), 9, 11n2
Hale, Margaret Pugh (1834–1910), 11n2
Hammer-Purgstall, Joseph von (1774–1856), 149; *Geschichte der Schönen Redekünste Persiens,* 150n3
Hampton Court, England, 355, 356n10
Harnden, William Frederick (1812–1845), 139n3
Harnden's Express, 139, 145, 304, 305

Harper and Brothers, 225n1; and *A Week on the Concord and Merrimack Rivers,* 316; Thoreau seeks employment from, 224
Harris, Thaddeus William (1795–1856), *A Report on the Insects of Massachusetts, Injurious to Vegetation,* 200n2
Hart, Abraham (1810–1885), 306n1
Harvard College, 1, 287–288; class of 1837, 9, 11n1, 20, 21n5, 289–290, 307–309; —, graduation of, 16, 17n1, 18n2; Davy Club in, 2, 4n4; the Delta at, 3, 6n14; disturbances at, 2–3, 7, 20, 21n5; and Guy Fawkes bonfires, 7, 8n1; Lawrence Scientific School of, 315–316, 319n12; telescope of, 310, 311n5, 315
Harvard College Library, 219n1
Haskins, David Greene (1818–1896), 35; and Concord Lyceum, 65
—*Letters to,* 34, 65
Haskins, Mary Cogswell Daveis (1820–1909), 35
Hawkins, Mr., letter to, mentioned, 34
Hawthorne, Nathaniel (1804–1864), 120, 122n5, 165, 175, 207, 215, 228, 257, 387; "The Celestial Railroad," 192, 193n4; Emerson on, 192, 193n4, 207; Greeley solicits essay on, 286; and O'Sullivan, John Louis, 124, 126n7; on Thoreau, 387; Thoreau on, 202
—*Letters from,* 386–387, 390–391
Hawthorne, Sophia Peabody (1809–1871), 120, 122n5, 257, 387
—*Letter from,* 257
Hayward, Charles (1817–1838), 34, 35n1
Hazlitt, William (1778–1830), "On the Pleasure of Hating," quoted, 271n7
Hazlitt, William (1811–1893), edition of *The Complete Works of Michael de Montaigne,* 252, 253n5

Hecker, Isaac Thomas (1819–1888), 257–258, 260, 269; and Fruitlands, 260, 298; and proposed trip to Europe with Thoreau, 258–259, 261–262, 263–266; on Roman Catholic Church, 259–260, 295–298; on Thoreau, 260n1, 263n6
—*Letters from,* 258–260, 263–265, 295–298
—*Letters to,* 261–262, 266

Hedge, Frederic Henry (1805–1890), 143, 144n5

Hemans, Felicia (1793–1835), "The Cambrian in America," quoted, 84, 86n10

Heraud, John Abraham (1799–1887), *The Life and Times of Girolamo Savonarola,* 149, 150n6

Herbert, George (1593–1633), 243; *The Temple: Sacred Poems and Private Ejaculations,* 244n3

Hercules, 309n2

Herodotus, 149, 150n4

Herschel, Friedrich Wilhelm (1738–1822), 311n6

Herschel, John Frederick William (1792–1871), 310, 311n6

Highlands of Navesink, N.J., 161, 162n7

Hildreth, Samuel Tenney (1817–1839), 3–4, 6n17, 20

Hoar, Caroline Downes Brooks (1820–1892), 175n1

Hoar, Ebenezer Rockwood (1816–1895), 174, 175n1

Hoar, Elizabeth Sherman (1814–1878), 124, 126n5, 131, 145, 159, 167–168, 202, 228, 236, 246; letter to Emerson, quoted, 336n10
—*Letter from,* 158–159

Hoar, George Frisbie (1826–1904), 219, 220n5

Hoar, Mary Louisa Spurr (1831–1859), 220n5

Hoar, Ruth Ann Miller (1830–1903), 220n5

Hoar, Samuel (1778–1856), 16, 18n6, 29, 46, 73, 156; expelled from South Carolina, 348n12; gets Alcott out of jail, 127n14, 348n12

Hoar, Sarah Sherman (1783–1866), 18n6

Holman, Joshua Reed (1817–1886), 327, 329n2

Holman, Nancy Palmer (1820?–1893), 329n2

Homer, 12, 14, 99, 201, 203n2, 228, 230n3, 238; *The Iliad,* quoted, 83, 86n9, 112, 114n1; *The Odyssey,* 13, 14n8

Hooper, Ellen Sturgis (1812–1848), "Sweep Ho!," 245, 248n10

hop-hornbeam (*Ostrya virginiana*), 273, 274n4

Horace (65–8 BCE), *Odes,* quoted, 58, 59–60

Horsford, Eben (1818–1893), 316, 319n13

Hosmer, Edmund (1798–1881), 204n4, 270, 315, 319n9, 347; Thoreau on, 201

Hosmer, John (1824–1882), 315, 319n9

Hosmer, Lucy Jane Buttrick (1827–1908), 319n9

Hosmer, Sally Peirce (1795–1890), 315, 319n9

How, Cynthia Currier (1802–1883), 226n10

How, Phineas (1797–1852), 225, 226n10

Howe, Julia Bowen Amory (1804–1841), 40, 41n6

Howe, Julia Ward (1819–1910), 73

Howe, Mark Antony DeWolf (1809–1895), 40, 41n6

Howe, Samuel Gridley (1801–1876), 73
—*Letter to,* 72–73

Howitt, Mary Botham (1799–1888), 366, 367n4

Howitt, William (1792–1879), 182, 366, 367n4; *The Book of the Seasons,* 182n6, 367n4

Hudson, Emily Sarah Bright (1826–1891), 335n4

Hudson, Henry Norman (1814–1886): *Lectures on Shakespeare*, 335n4; Thoreau on, 332

Hunt, Benjamin Peter (1808–1877), 194n7; "Voyage to Jamaica," 192, 194n7, 203, 229

Hunt, Seth, 225

Hutchinson, Nancy Dager (1805?–1857), 231n8

Hutchinson, Peter (1799?–1882), 228, 231n8

immigrants, 210, 238–239, 241n5

Indians, 9–10, 14, 210, 212n2; and Barnum, P. T., 240n3; Thoreau on, 27, 38n1

Iolas, 308, 309n2

Ireland, and Colum Cille, 168n3

Ireland, Alexander (1810–1894), 350, 351n1; Carlyle on, 351n1

ironwood (*Carpinus caroliniana*), 273, 274n3

Irving, Washington (1783–1859), "The Poor Devil Author," quoted, 160, 162n3

Jackson, Charles Thomas (1805–1880), 147, 148n3, 157n1, 302n2, 330

Jackson, Susan Bridge (1816–1899), 155–156, 157n1

James, Henry, Sr. (1811–1882), 130, 163, 182n2, 185n11, 203, 381n6; on Carlyle, 180; Channing, Ellery, on, 269; and Emerson, 130, 133n10, 192; Emerson on, 133n10; "Inward Reason of Christianity," 133n10; *Moralism and Christianity*, 163; Thoreau on, 179–180, 184; travels to Europe, 221, 223n1, 252
—*Letter from*, 163

James Munroe and Company, 206; and the *Dial*, 192, 194n8, 206, 325, 331; and Emerson's *An Address Delivered in the Court-House in Concord, Massachusetts, on 1st August, 1844, on the Anniversary of the Emancipation of the Negroes in the British West Indies*, 267, 275; and Thoreau's *A Week on the Concord and Merrimack Rivers*, 206, 306–307, 316, 331
—*Letters to*, 206, 267, 275, 306–307, 331

Jarvis, Almira Hunt (1804–1884), 39n6

Jarvis, Edward (1803–1884), 37, 39n6

Jefferson, Thomas (1743–1826), quoted, 167, 169n6

Jefts, Elbridge G. (1812–1856), 24n5

Johnson, Samuel (1709–1784), 314; "The Vanity of Human Wishes," quoted, 318n4

Jones, Ann, 212, 213n9

Jones, Caroline Partridge (1815–1893), 226n6

Jones, George Washington (1799–1890), 225, 226n6

Jones family, narcolepsy in, 199, 200n5, 225, 226n5

Jonson, Ben (1573?–1637), 346

Jordan, William H. S., 194n8

Katahdin [Ktaadn, Ktadn], Mount, 309, 311n1; Thoreau's essay "Ktaadn, and the Maine Woods," 364, 365n3, 365–366, 373, 376, 382, 384, 387–388; Thoreau's lecture "An Excursion to Ktaadn," 332, 334n1, 339

Kay and Brother, 306n1

Kendall, Obadiah (1783–1849), 332, 335n5

Keyes, Ann Stow Shepard (1792–1881), 47n2

Keyes, John (1787–1844), 46, 47n2, 317–318, 321n23

Kill van Kull (tidal strait), 161, 162n8

Kimball, Daniel (1778–1862), 17, 19n7

King, Jacob Gore (1819–1867), 3, 6n16

King, John (1816–1890), 3, 6n16
Knapp, Francis Bellows (1820–1896), 128n23
Knapp, Frederick Newman (1821–1889), 128n23
*Knickerbocker; or, New-York Monthly Magazine*, 234, 235n4

La Boétie, Étienne de (1530–1563), 252, 253n5
*Ladies' Companion, and Literary Expositor*, 234, 235n4, 238
Lamb, Charles (1775–1834), "Distant Correspondents," quoted, 13
lamprey, 294
Lane, Charles (1800–1870), 124, 127n17, 139, 145, 189, 198, 203, 381n6; and Alcott, Amos Bronson, 126n10, 128n20, 187, 188, 189; and Alcott House, 355, 356n7; books of, 175, 176n6, 277–278, 278n1; and the *Dial*, 138, 140–141, 142n2, 143–144, 149, 150n6, 192, 194n7, 229, 245, 247n3, 325, 331; and Fruitlands, 126n10, 165, 176n6, 187–189, 190n4, 190n5, 191–192, 279n2, 327, 329n3, 347, 349n16; and gardening, 188; and the Shakers, 245, 279n2; Thoreau edits, 143, 144n3, 144n4
—*Works:* "Catalogue of Books," 140, 141n1, 142n3, 143, 144n4; "A Day with the Shakers," 229, 232n15, 245, 247n3; review of "A. Bronson Alcott's Works," 141, 142n2, 143, 144n1, 144n3, 149; review of Bradford's *Thoughts on Spiritual Subjects, Translated from the Writings of Fenelon*, 143, 145n6; "Social Tendencies," 192, 194n7, 245, 247n3; "State Slavery–Imprisonment of A. Bronson Alcott–Dawn of Liberty," 125, 128n20
—*Letters from,* 187–189, 257–258, 277–278, 278–279

Lane, Hannah Bond, 189
Lane, William (b. 1832), and Fruitlands, 190n5, 191
Langtree, S. D., 215
langue d'oc, 134, 135n1
Lapham, Luther, 63n2
Lapham, Sophia Dunbar (1781–1868), 63
Larned, Julia H. Sanford (b. 1820?), 190n4
Larned, Samuel (1824–1853), and Fruitlands, 190n4, 191
Lawrence, Abbott (1792–1855), 315, 319n12
Lawrence, James (1781–1813), 205n11; quoted, 203
lecturing: and Emerson, 130, 131, 132n7, 317, 320n17, 328–329, 344–345, 351n1, 353n2; and Thoreau, 135, 136n5, 350; Thoreau on, 149, 380. *See also* Berean Institute; Concord Lyceum; Emerson: lectures; Salem Lyceum; Thoreau: lectures
Lee, Ann (1736–1784), 356n9
Leibnitz, Gottfried Wilhelm von (1646–1716), 314
letter-writing: Lamb, Charles, on, 13; Thoreau on, 13–14, 25–26, 104, 121n2, 134, 198, 313
*Lexington* (steamboat), 58, 60, 61n5
*Library of Health, and Teacher on the Human Constitution*, 38, 39n10
Ligouri, Alphonso Maria de' (1696–1787), 298, 299n2, 299n3
Lippitt, George Warren (1816–1891), 74
Lippitt, Matilda Florianna von Miller, 74n1
*Literary World*, 301
Little, Abby Wheaton (1820–1875), 50n4
Little, Charles Coffin (1799–1869), 50n4
Little, Sarah Ann Hilliard (1808–1848), 50n4
Little and Wilkins, 48, 50n4

Locke, John (1632–1704), 49; *An Essay concerning Human Understanding*, 50n5

Lodge, Thomas (1558–1625), *Glaucus and Silla, with Other Lyrical and Pastoral Poems*, 110

*London Mercantile Price Current*, 189, 356n7

*London Phalanx*, 252, 254n7

Longfellow, Henry Wadsworth (1807–1882), 221, 223n2

Longfellow, Samuel (1819–1892), 152, 153n5

Long Island, 161

Lowell, Caleb Callender (1836–1902), 45n5

Lowell, Charles (1807–1895), 45n5, 312n8

Lowell, Elizabeth (1835–1909), 45n5

Lowell, James Russell (1819–1891), 149; *Pioneer*, 150n5

Lowell, Mary Ann Billings (1810–1888), 45, 312n8

Luther, Martin (1483–1546), 191–192, 297; quoted, 193n2

lyceum. *See* Concord Lyceum; Salem Lyceum

Lyell, Charles (1797–1875), *Principles of Geology*, 144n2

MacKay, Tristram Bernard (1802–1884), 130, 131, 132n6

MacPherson, James (1736–1796), *The Genuine Remains of Ossian, Literally Translated*, 255

Magi (Kaspar, Melchior, and Balthazar), 262, 263n4

Manhattan: and immigrants, 238–239; Thoreau looks for work in, 224, 228, 230n2, 233–234, 238; Thoreau on, 160, 161, 170–171, 174, 181, 185, 221–222, 224, 238–239

Manhattanville, N.Y., 233, 234n3

Mann, Mary Peabody (1807–1887), 257n1

Manu, 90n1, 110n6; *Institutes of Hindu Law; or, The Ordinances of Menu*, quoted, 88–89, 109

Marot, Clément (1496–1544), 252, 253n5

Marston, Anna Randall (d. 1804), 40n1

Marston, John (1756–1846), 40

Mason, Lowell, *The Boston Handel and Haydn Society Collection of Church Music*, 40

*Massachusetts Quarterly Review*, 330n8, 352n5, 379–380; and Emerson, 328, 381n7; as successor to the *Dial*, 330n8; and Thoreau, 330n8, 351

Massillon, Jean Baptiste (1663–1742), 218; *Sermons*, 219n1

May, Samuel Joseph (1797–1871), and Fruitlands, 126n10, 165n4

McCloskey, John (1810–1885), 264, 265

McKean, Anna Hunstable Hosmer (1827–1903), 255

McKean, Henry Swasey (1810–1857), 225, 227n11, 234, 238, 245, 255, 269
—*Letter to*, 255

Mell, Mr., 185

menhaden (*Brevoortia tyrannus*), 185, 186n4

Mercantile Library Association, 227n11, 235n8, 255, 269; Emerson lectures at, 133n11; and Thoreau, 225, 238, 247n4

Mill Brook, 234

Milner-Gibson, Thomas (1806–1884), 342, 343n5

Milton, John (1608–1674), 3; *Comus*, quoted, 225; "Lycidas," quoted, 202; *Paradise Lost*, quoted, 3, 5n11, 98, 100n6, 100n7, 242, 243n1

Mincius (Mincio), 201, 203n1

mink, 300

minnow, 294, 302–303, 304

Minott, George (1783–1861), 124, 199, 201, 225, 252; Thoreau on, 126n11

Montagu, Elizabeth (1720–1800), *The Letters of Mrs. Elizabeth Montagu*, quoted, 20, 21n2

Montaigne, Michel Eyquem de (1533–1592), 252, 253n5, 346; Alcott on, 348n6

Montégut, John Baptiste Joseph Émile (1826–1895), "Un penseur et poète Américain: Ralph Waldo Emerson," 351, 352n7

Montgomery, James (1771–1854), "The West Indies," quoted, 97

Moore, Abel (1777–1848), 155n1, 228, 380n1

Morell, John Daniel (1816–1891), 355, 356n5

Morison, Horace (1810–1870), 55

Morison, Mary Elizabeth Lord (b. 1817), 55n2

moss-bonkers (menhaden; *Brevoortia tyrannus*), 185, 186n4

Mott, Helen Lucretia Coffin (1793–1880), 199, 200n8; Thoreau on, 211

mourning. *See* grief

mouse: deer, 302, 351; white-bellied, 304

Muenscher, Lydia Brown Monro (1802–1858), 40, 41n4

Muenscher, William (1796–1871), 40, 41n4

Munner (Monnier?), Louis, 347n3

Munroe, James (1808–1861), 149, 150n2, 390; and the *Dial*, 194n8, 206. *See also* James Munroe and Company

Murray, Hugh (1779–1846), *Historical and Descriptive Account of British India*, 88n1

Narrows (New York Bay), 161, 162n5

National Academy of Design, 171, 172n4

*National Anti-Slavery Standard*, 121n1

nature, 9, 84, 145–146; and communication, 138; and death, 102, 104–105, 107; Fuller, Sarah Margaret, on, 93–94; Lane, Charles, on, 187; on Staten Island, 161, 170, 198; Thoreau on, 77, 90, 102, 104–105, 118, 138, 141, 152, 161, 170, 198, 338, 369; Williams, Isaiah Thornton, on, 84

Nawshawtuck, 13, 28, 30n6

Nelson, Albert Hobart (1812–1858), 22, 24n2, 28–29, 30n8, 43, 44n3, 68

Nelson, Elizabeth B. Phinney (1815–1907), 24n2

Newark Bay, 161

Newcomb, Charles King (1820–1894), 208; Emerson on, 209n6

*New Englander*, 254n8; critiques the *Dial*, 252, 254n8

*New Mirror, of Literature, Amusement, and Instruction*, 226n10, 233–234, 235n4; Thoreau on, 240

Newton, Isaac (1642–1727), 314

*New World: A Weekly Family Journal of Popular Literature, Science, Art and News*, 233–234, 235n4

New York City charter election, 365, 366n1

*New-York Daily Tribune*, 121n1; and elections of 1846, 283n1; and Greeley, Horace, 211, 213n4, 280; quoted, 225n2, 240n3

New York Society Library, 240n1, 247n4; Emerson lectures at, 130, 133n9

Nichol, John Pringle (1804–1859), 333–334, 336n10; "Mechanism and Physical Constitution of Our Solar System," 336n11; *Views of the Architecture of the Heavens*, 335n9

*Nineteenth Century: A Quarterly Miscellany* (Philadelphia), 373

North American Phalanx, 188, 190n7, 211, 213n6

Ockley, Simon (1678–1720), *The History of the Saracens*, 266; —, quoted, 202, 204n7

Oldham, William (1790–1879), 355, 356n7

oology, 284, 287–288

Ossian, Thoreau on, 255n2

Ossoli, Giovanni Angelo (1821–1850), 71

O'Sullivan, John Louis (1813–1895), 126n7, 215, 257; and Emerson, 126n7, 126n8; and Hawthorne, 126n7; Thoreau on, 124; as Thoreau's publisher, 126n9, 214, 219, 222, 234; and *United States Magazine, and Democratic Review*, 126n7, 215, 219
—*Letter from,* 214–215
—*Letter to,* 216

O'Sullivan, Susan Kearny Rodgers, 215

Paestum, Italy, 135, 136n4

Pahlavi [Pehlvi], 134, 135n2

Palmer, Edward (1802–1886), 139, 181, 211; Emerson on, 140n5; Lane, Charles, on, 188, 190n6; *A Letter to Those Who Think*, 140n5

Palmer, Joseph (1789–1873), 327; and Fruitlands, sale of, 329n3, 347, 349n16

Palmer, Nancy Thompson Tenny (1784?–1859), 327, 329n3

Pandora, 37, 38n4

Parcae, 338, 340n4

Parker, Theodore (1810–1860), 128n23; at the Concord Lyceum, 125, 128n23, 135, 332, 335n2; and the *Dial*, 128n23, 330n8; *A Discourse on the Transient and Permanent in Christianity*, 83, 85n5, 318n1; "The Hollis Street Council," 128n23; and the *Massachusetts Quarterly Review*, 330n8

Parsons, William, third Earl of Rosse (1800–1867), 310, 311n6

Parthian army, 346, 348n7

Pascal, Blaise (1623–1662), 269; *Pensées*, 271n5

*Pathfinder*, 187, 189n1

Paulist order, 260

Peabody, Augustus Goddard (1818–1877), 4, 45
—*Letter from,* 1–4

Peabody, Elizabeth Palmer (1804–1894), 90, 91n4, 147, 164; *Aesthetic Papers*, 147; and the *Dial*, 141, 142n2, 146–147, 149, 150n7, 194n8; *Method of Spiritual Culture: Being an Explanatory Preface to the Second Edition of "Record of a School,"* 90; *Record of a School: Exemplifying the General Principles of Spiritual Culture*, 141, 142n2
—*Letter from,* 146–147

Peabody, Elizabeth S. Holway (1820–1895), 4

Pegasus, 324, 325n1

Peirce, Benjamin (1809–1880), 315, 319n10

Pellico, Silvio (1789–1854), *My Prisons*, 125, 128n21

pencil and lead manufacture, 147, 148n4, 185

perch, 290–291, 293, 302

Phillips, Grenville T. (1816–1863), 9, 11n2

pickerel, 293, 299–300, 302

Pindar (522?–443 BCE), 142n3, 208, 252; translated by Thoreau, 209n7, 222, 252, 253n6

Plato (427?–347 BCE), 333, 339, 346

Plutarch (46?–120), 362, 363n4

poetry, Thoreau on, 79–80, 81n3, 119, 141

Pope, Alexander (1688–1744): *An Essay on Man*, 59, 60; —, quoted, 62n8; *The Iliad* (trans.), 83, 86n9, 99, 100n11, 112, 114n1; *The Odyssey* (trans.), 99, 100n11

Porter, Mr., 139

Potter, Jonas (1784–1868), 229, 231n9

Potter, Sarah Melvin (1790?–1851), 231n9

pout, 290, 293, 302

*Present*, 211, 213n3, 242, 244n2, 250, 251n2

Prichard, Moses Barnard (1818–1878), 210, 212n2

Prichard, William MacKay (1814–1897), 199, 200n7

Prince, Frederick O. (1818–1899), 9, 11n2

Prince, Helen Susan Henry (1822–1885), 11n2

proverbs, 20, 21n4, 37, 38n3, 49, 50n6, 225, 226n9, 288, 384, 385n3

publishing, 91–92, 199, 216; and Duyckinck, Evert Augustus, 300–301, 304, 305–306; of "Ktaadn, and the Maine Woods," payment for, 364, 365–366, 373, 376, 382, 387–388; of "A Lesson for Young Poets," 383; in magazines, and Greeley, 280, 281, 283, 285–286, 364, 365–366, 373, 382–383, 387–388, 389–390; and Munroe, James, 306–307; and O'Sullivan, John Louis, 214, 216, 219; of "Thomas Carlyle and His Works," payment for, 364, 365, 366n2, 372–373, 374–376; Thoreau looks for work in Manhattan, 224, 228, 230n2, 233–234, 238; Thoreau on, 351, 378–380; and *United States Magazine, and Democratic Review*, 222, 238; of "A Walk to Wachusett," payment for, 147, 148n5, 182, 198, 207, 208n2, 222; of *A Week on the Concord and Merrimack Rivers*, 206, 300–301, 304, 305–307, 316, 325, 331, 350, 352n4, 366, 367n3. *See also* Bradbury and Soden; *Dial*; Greeley, Horace; James Munroe and Company; O'Sullivan,

John Louis; *United States Magazine, and Democratic Review*

Putnam, George Palmer (1814–1872), 305

Quarles, Francis (1592–1644): *Divine Poems*, 234, 235n8; *Emblemes*, 234, 235n8, 244n3; Thoreau on, 243

Quincy, Eliza Susan Morton (1773?–1850), 42

Quincy, Josiah (1772–1864), 3, 5n9, 16, 17, 21n5, 42, 73
—*Letter from,* 41–42

railroad. *See* Boston and Fitchburg railroad

Raleigh [Ralegh], Walter (1552?–1618): Thoreau's lecture on, 135, 136n5; *The Works of Sir Walter Ralegh, Kt,* 110

red huckleberry (*Gaylussacia baccata*), 273, 274n1

Red Lodge (Concord), 153–154, 155n1, 201

Redemptorists, 260, 297–298, 299n2

reform communities. *See* Brook Farm; Fourierism; Fruitlands; North American Phalanx; Sylvania Association

religion: and conscience, 88–89; and nature, 77; and sin, 108; Thoreau on, 77, 88–89, 102, 108, 245, 262; Thoreau withdraws from First Parish, 72; Williams, Isaiah Thornton, on, 83, 98, 112–113. *See also* biblical quotations and allusions; ethnical scriptures; Manu; Redemptorists; Roman Catholic Church; Shakers

*Revue des Deux Mondes*, 351, 352n7

Rice, Charles Wyatt (1817–1844), 10, 17n1
—*Letter from,* 9–10
—*Letter to,* 12–14

Rice, Mary A. Chambers, 10

Richard I (1157–1199), 264, 265n3

Richardson, Henrietta Harris (b. 1828?), 17

Richardson, James, Jr. (1817–1863), 1, 17, 152, 153n4
—*Letters from,* 16–17, 116–117

Richardson, James, Sr. (1771–1858), 19n9

Richardson, John Hancock (1803–1850), 317, 320n21

Richardson, Lydia Ann Thaxter (1810–1847), 320n21

Richardson, Mary Caroline Patten (1819–1860), 320n21

Richardson, Sarah Elizabeth Richards (1789–1820), 19n9

Ripley, Ezra (1751–1841), 32, 33n7

Ritson, Joseph (1752–1803), *Robin Hood: A Collection of All the Ancient Poems, Songs, and Ballads,* 204n8

*Rivista Ligure* (Genoa), 252, 254n7

roach, 294

Robert of Gloucester (fl. 1260–1300), *Robert of Gloucester's Chronicle,* 252, 253n5

Robin Hood, 204n8

Rollin, Charles (1661–1741), 59, 60; *The Ancient History of the Egyptians, Carthaginians, Assyrians, Babylonians, Medes and Persians, Macedonians, and Grecians,* 61n6

Roman Catholic Church, 262; and baptismal innocence, 260; and Hecker, Isaac Thomas, 259–260, 295–298

Roncesvalles, Spain, 262, 263n4

Russell, Charles Theodore (1815–1896), 10, 11n5

Russell, Sarah Elizabeth Ballister (1817–1897), 11n5

Rynders, Isaiah (1804–1885), 269, 271n5

Rynders, Theodore (1825?–1861), 269, 271n5

Saadi (1184?–1291), *The Gulistan, or Flower-Garden, of Shaikh Sadi of Shiraz,* 252, 253n5

Saddleback Mountain (Mount Greylock), 263n2

Saint Columba (Colum Cille), 167, 168n3

Salem Lyceum, 391n1; invites Thoreau to lecture, 386, 387n1, 390–391

sand cherry (*Prunus depressa*), 273, 274n2

Sandy Hook, N.J., 161, 162n6, 167, 181, 210, 212n1

Sartain, John (1808–1897), 388n1

*Sartain's Union Magazine of Literature and Art,* 388n1

Scamander River, 202, 204n5

Schleiermacher, Friedrich Ernst Daniel (1768–1834), *Schleiermacher's Introductions to the Dialogues of Plato,* 335n6

Sedgwick, Catharine Maria (1789–1867), 219, 220n6

seventeen-year locust (*Cicada septendecim*), 198, 200n2

Shakers, 355, 356n9; and Lane, Charles, 245; —, "A Day with the Shakers," 229, 232n15, 245, 247n3

Shakespeare, William (1564–1616), 3, 119, 243; *Hamlet,* 97; —, quoted, 100n3, 108, 113; *Macbeth,* 37; —, quoted, 38n3; *Romeo and Juliet,* quoted, 66, 67n1; *The Tempest,* 360–361; —, quoted, 22, 24n2, 362n2

Shattuck, Daniel (1790–1867), 53, 54n3

Shattuck, Sarah Edwards (1794–1859), 54n3

Sherwood Forest, England, 202, 204n8

shiner, 294, 302, 304

Shirley, James (1596–1666), *Cupid and Death,* quoted, 317, 320n18

smelt, 299

Smith, Captain, 185

Smith, Joseph (1805–1844), 297, 298n1
Smith, Robert, 225
Smith, William Henry (1808–1872), "Emerson," 339; —, quoted, 340n8
snake, black, 302
Society Library (Manhattan), 238, 240n1, 247n4; Emerson lectures at, 130, 133n9
Soden, Ferona A. Johnson, 148n5
Soden, Samuel S. (1819–1844), 148n5
Sparhawk, Oliver (1805–1835), 1
—Letter to, 1
Sparhawk, Sarah B. Coffin (1809?–1861), 1
sparrow: rush (field) sparrow (Fringilla juncorum), 45; song sparrow (Fringilla melodious), 45
Spaulding, Mr., 379
Spear, Charles M. (1801–1863), 124–125, 127n16, 127n17
Springfield Republican, 392n1
Stacy, John, 321n23
Staples, Lucinda Wesson (1818–1881), 127n15
Staples, Samuel (1813–1895), 124, 127n15, 317–318, 321n23
Staten Island, 257n1; Britton's Mill, 210, 212n1; the Clove, 185, 186n5, 212n1, 228; Channing, Ellery, on, 268; elm tree, 210, 212n1; and immigrants, 210; Lake Island Farm, 210, 212n2; New Brighton, 171; Port Richmond, 171; Quarantine, 171, 172n1; Richmond, 171; Sailors' Snug Harbor, 210, 212n1; Stapleton, 170–171; telegraph station on, 210, 212n1, 268, 270n3; Thoreau's stay on, 150n9, 153n3, 159–161, 167–168, 170–171, 174–175, 181–182, 184–185, 198, 210, 212n1, 219, 257n1
Stearns, Elijah Wyman (1813–1896), 45

Stephens, Mr., 310
Stevens, Abigail, 345, 347n3
Stevens, Almira, 345, 347n3
Stevens, Caroline Partridge (1819–1849), 272
Stevens, Daniel Waldo (1820–1891), 272, 273n1, 273n2
—Letter from, 272
Stewart, Dugald (1753–1828), 49; Elements of the Philosophy of the Human Mind, 50n5
Stonehenge, 384, 385n4
Storer, Abby Jane Brewer (1810–1885), 285n1
Storer, Augusta Charlotte Gilmore (1841–1874), 285
Storer, David Humphrys (1804–1891), 284, 285n1, 294; Reports on the Fishes, Reptiles and Birds of Massachusetts, 294n1
Storer, Emily Elvira Gilmore (1833–1872), 285
Storer, Frances S. Mackenzie (d. 1910), 285
Storer, Horatio Robinson (1830–1922), 284–285
—Letter from, 284
—Letter to, 287–288
Storer, Thomas (1571–1604), The Life and Death of Thomas Wolsey, Cardinall, quoted, 114, 115n1
Stow, Cyrus (1787–1876), 72, 229, 378
—Letter to, 72
Stow, Matilda Wyman (1803?–1878), 72
Strawberry Hill, England, 355, 356n10
sucker, 291n1, 293, 303, 304
Sudbury River, Thoreau sails on, 13
Swift, Jonathan (1667–1745), "Drapier Letters," 184; —, quoted, 186n3
Sylvania Association, 211, 213n5

Tahattawan [Tahatawan], 27, 29n3

Tappan, Caroline Sturgis (1819–
1888), 131n1

Tappan, Lewis (1788–1873),
171–172, 173n8, 176n3, 178,
179n1

Tappan, William Aspinwall (1819–
1905), 130, 131n1, 164, 171, 173n8,
182, 192, 203, 208n1, 211, 253n3;
and Channing, Ellery, 269,
271n8; and Emerson, 129, 131n1;
Emerson on, 207, 252; Thoreau
on, 175, 180–181, 221, 244; and
Waldo, Giles, 208n1

Taylor, Jane (1783–1824), "The
Philosopher's Scales," quoted,
246, 248n12

Thatcher, George Augustus
(1806–1885), 312n8, 385
—Letters to, 384–385, 391

Thatcher, Rebecca Jane Billings
(1813–1883), 312n8, 385

Thompson, George (1804–1878),
342, 344n6

Thompson, Thomas Perronet
(1783–1869), 342, 343n4, 355n2

Thoreau, Cynthia Dunbar (1787–
1872), 39n9, 53n1, 62, 63n3, 161,
185; postscript from, to Sophia
Thoreau, 62–63
—Letters to, 159–161, 183–185,
198–199, 218–219, 224–225,
237–240

Thoreau, Elizabeth (1784–1839),
45

Thoreau, Helen Louisa (1812–
1849), 26, 62n10, 124, 199, 218,
219; postscript from, to John
Thoreau Jr., 40; and teaching,
26, 45n1, 156, 171, 185, 240
—Letters to, 25–26, 48–49, 58–
61, 66–67, 176–178, 210–212,
250–251

Thoreau, Henry David (1817–
1862): and Agassiz, Jean Louis
Rodolphe, 290–291, 292–294,
299–300, 302–304, 316, 351; on
Alcott, 314–315; on aspiration,
361, 379; on bird eggs, 287–288;
and Brown, Lucy Jackson,

79, 87, 202; on change, 360;
on Channing, Ellery, 201; on
Channing, William Henry, 242,
250; on Concord, 79, 152, 161,
167, 170, 201–202, 218, 224–225;
and Concord Lyceum, 51,
52n1, 55, 57, 63–64, 65, 125, 135,
136n5, 253, 254n9, 255n2, 256,
332, 334n1, 339, 347, 348n12,
350; on conscience, 88–89; on
death, 101–102, 104–105, 107,
199; on destiny, 108–109; and
the Dial (see under Dial); on
diplomas, 316, 320n14; on duty,
370; and Emerson, builds summer house for, 314–315, 318n6,
381n2; Emerson on, 163n1, 341;
and Emerson's editing of, 229,
231n11, 234, 245, 247n6; on Emerson's poetry, 245–246, 248n11;
and Emersons, expresses
gratitude to, 125; on England,
337; on ethical living, 31, 88–89,
108–109, 114–115, 121n2, 151–152,
195–197, 359–362, 368–371; on
Free Soil party, 385; on free
will, 108–109; on freedom, 31;
on friendship, 66–67, 76–77,
79, 87, 120, 121n2, 125, 136–138,
166–167, 195–197, 202, 204n10,
339, 340n7, 347; and Fuller,
Sarah Margaret, 70, 71n1, 80,
81n8, 93–95, 96n5, 236; on grief,
101–102, 105, 107–108, 119–120,
121n2, 196–197; and Hawthorne,
202; Hawthorne on, 387; health
of, 103, 106–107, 170, 174, 199,
221; and Hecker, Isaac Thomas,
258–260, 261–262, 263–265, 266;
income of, 233, 374–376; —,
and Bradbury and Soden, 147,
148n5, 182, 193, 198, 207, 208n2,
222; —, and Graham, George
Rex, 286, 364, 365, 372–373; —,
and Greeley, Horace, 283, 285–
286, 365–366, 372–373, 374–376,
380, 382, 387–388, 389–390;
on Indians, 27, 38n1; on labor,
109, 144, 313, 368–371, 374–376;

and Lane, Charles, 143–144, 277–279; on lecturing, 135, 149, 350–351, 380; on letter-writing, 13–14, 25–26, 66–67, 104, 121n2, 134, 198, 313; in Manhattan, searches for publishing work, 224, 228, 230n2, 233–234, 238; on Manhattan, 160–161, 170–171, 174, 181, 184, 221–222, 224, 238–239; and the *Massachusetts Quarterly Review*, 330n8; on music, 118n3; and music box, 117, 118n1; narcolepsy of, 199, 200n5, 218–219, 221–222, 224, 238; on nature, 77, 88, 90, 102, 104–105, 118, 138, 141, 152, 161, 170, 198, 338, 369; on Ossian, 255n2; on poetry, 119, 141; on poetry writing, 79–80, 81n3; on the present, 361; and publishing (*see under* publishing); on Quaker service, 211; on reading, 59, 60–61, 119; reading of, 10, 11n6, 61n6, 204n8, 219n1, 220n6, 223n7, 234, 235n8, 380; ——, English poetry, for planned anthology, 243, 245, 247n4; receives marriage proposal, 316; on reform, 210, 242, 250, 318; on religion, 77, 88–89, 102, 108, 245, 262; on simplicity, 360; on sincerity, 76, 152; on sorrow, 370–371; and Staten Island, stay on, 150n9, 153n3, 159–161, 162n1, 167–168, 170–171, 174–175, 181–182, 184–185, 198, 210, 212n1, 219, 257n1; and teaching, 16, 18n3, 20, 29, 31–32, 33n2, 34, 37, 39n7, 41–42, 43, 44, 45n1, 46, 48–49, 72–73, 181–182, 198, 240; on time, 108, 143, 238, 350–351, 361; on trust, 137, 195–196; on truth, 89; as tutor on Staten Island, 150n9, 152, 153n3, 181–182, 184, 198, 244, 258; Walden house of, 270n1, 276n1, 317, 320n19, 327–328, 337–339; on walking, 117; on writing, 32, 88, 151, 203, 238, 350–351, 378–380

—*Books: The Maine Woods*, 365n3, 388n1; *Walden*, 200n5, 371n1, 381n8, 387n1, 390n1; *A Week on the Concord and Merrimack Rivers*, 69n5, 71, 78n1, 96n4, 96n9, 136n5, 204n10, 244n3, 254n9, 255n2, 301n1, 336n12, 340n7, 376, 390n1

—*Essays:* "Aulus Persius Flaccus," 71n1, 357, 358n1, 359; "Civil Disobedience," 348n12; "Homer. Ossian. Chaucer.," 254n9, 255n2; "Ktaadn, and the Maine Woods," 384, 385n1; "The Landlord," 126n9, 162n3, 215n1, 240, 241n9, 250, 251n1; "Natural History of Massachusetts," 200n2, 214, 215n1, 294n1; "Paradise (To Be) Regained," 126n9, 138, 141, 214, 216, 219, 222, 234, 240; "Resistance to Civil Government," 128n21, 147, 348n12; "The Service," 70, 71n1; "Thomas Carlyle and His Works," 279–280, 281, 283, 285–286; "A Walk to Wachusett," 78n1, 96n4, 118n2, 214, 215n1; "A Winter Walk," 165n1, 174, 175n2, 182, 193, 203, 208, 229, 231n11, 231n12, 234, 235n6, 245, 247n6

—*Ethnical Scriptures* (in the *Dial*): 90n1, 110n6, 139n1, 245, 247n7

—*Journal:* 38n1, 39n11, 69n5, 80n1, 81n9, 88n1, 90n1, 96n7, 103n2, 118n3, 126n11, 141, 142n3, 144n2, 204n7, 204n8, 214, 216, 247n4, 255n2, 312n7

—*Lectures:* "Ancient Poets," 254n9, 255n2; "The Commercial Spirit of Modern Times," 17n1; "Economy," 392n1; "An Excursion to Ktaadn," 332, 334n1, 339; on friendship,

Thoreau, Henry David (*cont.*)
339, 347; "The Life and Character of Sir Walter Raleigh,"
135, 136n5; on the rights and
duties of the individual in
relation to government, 347,
348n12; "Student Life in New
England, Its Economy," 386,
387n1, 390–391
—*Poems:* "The Bluebirds,"
39n11; "Brother where
dost thou dwell?," 176–178;
"Friendship," 71n1, 79,
81n2, 91, 92n1, 204n10; "The
good how can we trust?,"
334; "In days of yore, 'tis
said, the swimming alder,"
12–13; "Inspiration," 81n7;
"Sic Vita," 71n1, 91, 92n1;
"The sluggish smoke curls
up from some deep dell,"
229, 231n12; "Stanzas," 71n1;
"Sympathy," 71n1, 91–92; "To
Edith," 324, 325n2; "With
frontier strength ye stand
your ground," 78n1, 81n8,
93–94, 95n1, 95n2
—*Translations:* 138, 139n1, 141,
142n3, 142n4, 208, 209n7,
215n11, 216–217, 219, 222, 223n5,
229, 234, 252, 253n6, 272;
"Anacreon," 139n1, 142n3;
"Fragments of Pindar," 209n7,
252, 253n6; "Pindar," 209n7,
252, 253n6; *The Prometheus
Bound*, 142n4, 216, 272, 273n1;
*The Seven against Thebes*,
142n4, 216–217, 222
Thoreau, Jane (1784–1864),
173n9
Thoreau, John, Jr. (1814–1842), 22,
24n3, 29, 39n11, 66, 73n1; death
of, 101–102, 103n1, 106–107, 113;
postscript to, from Helen Thoreau, 40; and teaching, 24n3,
26n1, 29, 73n1
—*Letters to,* 27–29, 35–36, 36–
38, 44–45
Thoreau, John, Sr. (1787–1859),

29, 39n9, 53, 63n3, 161, 171, 185,
240, 377
—*Letter to,* 183–185
Thoreau, Maria (1794–1881),
173n9, 251
Thoreau, Sophia Elizabeth (1819–
1876), 45, 62n10, 172, 198, 218,
220n3, 240, 251; postscript to,
from Cynthia Dunbar
Thoreau, 62–63; and teaching,
156, 172
—*Letters to,* 58–61, 170–172,
309–311
time: Thoreau on, 108, 143, 238,
350–351, 361; Williams, Isaiah
Thornton, on, 97
*Times* (London), 384, 385n4
tortoises: land tortoise, 302; mud
tortoise, 302; painted tortoise,
302
trout, 294, 302
Turner, Sharon (1768–1847), *The
History of the Anglo-Saxons*,
quoted, 80, 81n9
turtles: snapping turtle, 291, 293,
294, 302, 351; *Sternothaerus
odoratus* (mud turtle), 290,
291n1, 292
Twickenham, England, 355,
356n10
Tyler, Edward Royall (1800–1848),
254n8

*Union Magazine of Literature
and Art*, 365n3, 388, 389
*United States Magazine, and
Democratic Review*, 126n7,
215; editorial policies of, 214;
and Emerson, 229–230; and
Thoreau, 124, 139n2, 214, 215n1,
216, 219, 222, 233, 238, 240,
241n9, 250

Valhalla, 120, 122n4
Van Pelt, Mr., 185
Vethake, John W. (1798–1876),
269, 271n5
Vethake, Sarah Brush (b. 1803?),
271n5

Virgil (Publius Vergilius Maro; 70–19 BCE): *Eclogues*, quoted, 59, 61, 62n9, 261, 262n1; *Georgics*, 12; —, quoted, 14n2

Vose, Henry (1817–1869), 8, 10, 17n1
  —*Letter from*, 22–23
  —*Letters to*, 7–8, 19–20, 43, 155–156

Vose, Martha Barrett Ripley (1817–1870), 8

Wachusett, Mount: Thoreau's essay "A Walk to Wachusett," 78n1, 96n4, 118n2, 214, 215n1; Thoreau's excursion to, 117, 118n2

Walden field, 378, 381n5

Walden Pond, 268, 293, 318n6; Thoreau's house at, 270n1, 276n1, 308, 317; —, bought and moved by Hugh Whelan, 327–328, 320n19, 337–339, 378

Walden woods, 218, 246, 308, 310, 317, 325

Waldo, Giles (1814–1849), 164, 165n2, 171, 173n8, 175, 179, 182, 192, 203, 211, 224, 228, 252, 253n3; and Channing, Ellery, 269, 271n8; and Emerson, 165n2; Emerson on, 207, 208n1; and Tappan, William Aspinwall, 208n1; on Thoreau, 172n3, 230n2; Thoreau on, 180–181
  —*Letter from*, 178

Wall Street, 161

Wandel, Peter (1765?–1857), 185, 186n5

Wandel, Sarah Van Clief (1774–1857), 186n5

Ward, Anna Hazard Barker (1813–1900), 194n6

Ward, George Washington (1802–1855), 171, 172n2, 183–184, 239

Ward, Prudence (1795–1874), 37, 38n5, 124, 171, 173n5, 239

Ward, Prudence Bird (1765–1844), 239

Ward, Samuel Gray (1817–1907), 194n6; "Notes on Art and Architecture," 192, 194n6

Ware, Henry, Jr. (1794–1843), 2, 4n3

Ware, Henry, Sr. (1764–1845), 2, 4n3

Warren, Cyrus (1790–1866), 208, 209n5, 338, 378

Warren, Nancy Bacon (1793–1871), 209n5

*Washington Irving* (ship), 310

Watson, Benjamin Marston (1820–1896), 103n5, 273–274
  —*Letter to*, 273

Watson, Mary Howland Russell (1820–1906), 103, 274

Webster, Daniel (1782–1852), 224, 226n4, 230n7

Webster, John White (1793–1850), 3, 5n10

Weeks, Jordan, and Company, 194n8

Weiss, John (1818–1879), 3, 6n15

Weiss, Sarah Fiske Jennison (1818–1909), 6n15

Wetherbee, Sarah Wetherbee (1786–1850), 329n5

Wetherbee, Solomon (b. 1784), 327, 329n5, 337

Wheeler, Caleb, 380n1

Wheeler, Charles Stearns (1816–1843), 3, 6n17, 7, 20, 51–52, 74, 110n1, 139, 141; and Concord Lyceum, 52n1, 55, 57, 63–64; death of, 199, 200n4, 208; and the *Dial*, 140n4, 149, 150n3, 105n5; literary career of, 213n8; Thoreau on, 199, 211–212
  —*Letters from*, 57, 64
  —*Letters to*, 51, 55, 63–64, 110

Wheeler, Ephraim (1773–1848), 229, 231n9

Wheeler, Sarah Parkman (1777–1856), 231n9

Whelan, Hugh, 167, 347; Emerson on, 169n4; and Thoreau's house at Walden, 317, 320n19, 327–328, 335n8, 337–338

Whipple, Charlotte Billings Hastings (1821–1907), 335n3

Whipple, Edwin Percy (1819–1886), 335n3; *Lectures on Subjects Connected with Literature and Life*, 335n3; Thoreau on, 332

White, E., Miss, 62, 63

White Pond (Concord), 28, 30n5

Whiting, Hannah Conant (1788–1859), 69n3

Whiting, William (1788–1862), 68, 69n3

Wiley, John (1808–1891), 304, 306

Wiley and Putnam, 277, 301n1, 306, 316

Wilkins, John Hubbard (1794–1861), 50n4

Wilkins, Thomasine Bond Minot (1778?–1864), 50n4

Wilkinson, James John Garth (1812–1899), 355, 356n6

William the Conqueror (ca. 1028–1087), *Domesday Book*, 325, 326n5

Williams, Ellen E. White (1826–1877), 85

Williams, Henry, Jr. (1816–1901), 2, 3, 4n5, 290
  —*Letter from*, 289–290
  —*Letter to*, 307–309

Williams, Isaiah Thornton (1819–1886), 85, 87; on education, 84, 98–99; on ethical living, 111–112, 114; on religion, 83, 98, 112–113; on time, 97; on Transcendentalism, 82–83
  —*Letters from*, 82–85, 97–100, 111–113
  —*Letters to*, 88–90, 106–109, 114–115

Williams, Julia West Williams (1818–1874), 290

Winkelried, Arnold von, 125, 128n19

Wood, Abram (Abraham), 190n4, 191

Wood, Elijah (1790–1861), 68, 69n1, 321n23

Wood, Elizabeth Farmer (1795–1843), 69n1

Wood, Lucy Barrett (1792–1869), 69n1

Wright, Henry Gardiner (1814–1846), 124, 139, 180, 184; Alcott on, 127n13

Wyman, Maverick (1788–1868), 165n4, 189n3

Wyman, William, trial of, 226n4, 228, 230n7

*Yeoman's Gazette* (Concord), 23, 24n5

Young, Aaron (1819–1898), 309; "Dr. Young's Botanical Expedition to Mount Katahdin," 311n1

Young England party, 329, 330n9